AWS CERTIFIED SOLUTIONS ARCHITECT ASSOCIATE

MASTER THE EXAM (SAA-C03): 10 PRACTICE TESTS, 650 RIGOROUS EXAM QUESTIONS, SOLID FOUNDATIONS, GAIN WEALTH OF INSIGHTS, EXPERT EXPLANATIONS AND ONE ULTIMATE GOAL

SECOND EDITION – 2024 RELEASE

D1731050

ANAND M
AMEENA PUBLICATIONS

DEDICATION

To the Visionaries in My Professional Odyssey

This book is dedicated to the mentors and leaders who guided me through triumph and adversity in my professional universe. Your guidance has illuminated the path to success and taught me to seize opportunities and surmount obstacles. Thank you for imparting the advice to those who taught me the value of strategic thinking and the significance of innovation to transform obstacles into stepping stones. Your visionary leadership has inspired my creativity and motivated me to forge new paths.

Thank you for sharing the best and worst of your experiences with me, kind and severe employers. As I present this book to the world, I am aware that you have been my inspiration. All of your roles as mentors, advisors, and even occasional adversaries have helped me become a better professional and storyteller.

This dedication is a tribute to your impact on my journey, a narrative woven with threads of gratitude, introspection, and profound gratitude for the lessons you've inscribed into my story.

With deep gratitude and enduring respect,
Anand M

FROM TECH TO LIFE SKILLS – MY EBOOKS COLLECTION

Dive into my rich collection of eBooks, curated meticulously across diverse and essential domains.

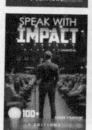

Pro Tips and Tricks Series: *Empower yourself with life-enhancing skills and professional essentials with our well-crafted guides.*

Hot IT Certifications and Tech Series: *Stay ahead in the tech game. Whether you're eyeing certifications in AWS, PMP, or prompt engineering, harnessing the power of ChatGPT with tools like Excel, PowerPoint, Word, and more!, we've got you covered!*

Essential Life Skills: *Embark on a journey within. From yoga to holistic well-being, Master the art of culinary, baking, and more delve deep and rediscover yourself.*

Stay Updated & Engaged
For an entire world of my knowledge, tips, and treasures, follow me on Amazon
https://www.amazon.com/author/anandm

Your Feedback Matters!
Your support, feedback, and ratings are the wind beneath my wings. It drives me to curate content that brings immense value to every aspect of life. Please take a moment to share your thoughts and rate the books. Together, let's keep the flame of knowledge burning bright!

★★★★★

Best Regards,

ANAND M

INTRODUCTION

Determined to conquer the **AWS Certified Solutions Architect Associate Exam** in 2024? Welcome to your comprehensive study companion. Dive into "**AWS Certified Solutions Architect Associate: Master the Exam, 10 Practice Tests, 650 Meticulously Crafted Questions, Expert Explanations, and One Ultimate Goal**" to not only grasp but genuinely master the intricate concepts and cutting-edge strategies you'll encounter on exam day.

In today's rapidly evolving cloud landscape, AWS certifications are more than advantageous—they're crucial. Achieving the AWS Certified Solutions Architect Associate status is not just an endorsement of your cloud capabilities; it signifies a deep proficiency in the world's leading cloud platform. Whether you're a seasoned cloud practitioner aiming for validation or a newcomer striving to carve a niche in cloud architecture, this book is your strategic ally, intertwined with real-world scenarios and practical insights.

Every question within this detailed guide is scrupulously curated, accompanied by thorough explanations that demystify complexities, ensuring your preparation is both broad and profound.

In a digital era where businesses and services are heavily reliant on cloud infrastructures, possessing the esteemed AWS Certified Solutions Architect Associate qualification enhances your standing in the cloud domain. Whether your goal is to excel as a Solutions Architect, Cloud Developer, or further your expertise in AWS solutions, this book lays the foundation for your ascent in the AWS cosmos.

For those embarking on this ambitious quest, here's a concise breakdown of the exam's key elements:

Duration: 130 minutes
Language options: Presented in English [and other languages if applicable]
Exam format: A blend of multiple-choice and scenario-based questions, conducted in an AWS-approved examination setting.
Pre-requisites: None
Experience (Recommended): A robust 2 years in the AWS environment, with a particular focus on designing scalable, cost-efficient, and fault-tolerant systems on AWS.

Set forth on your odyssey to AWS supremacy, with this book as your guiding beacon.

ADVANTAGES OF CERTIFICATION

Before embarking on the AWS Solutions Architect journey, it's imperative to grasp the tangible benefits that come with this certification. As you consider undertaking the AWS Certified Solutions Architect - Associate Exam, ponder upon these undeniable advantages:

Demand & Recognition: In today's digital transformation age, cloud technologies have emerged as a linchpin. AWS, being a market leader in cloud services, has escalated the demand for certified AWS Solutions Architects. Holding this prestigious certification places you in an elite group of cloud professionals, ensuring your skills don't go unnoticed.

Elevated Career Path: This certification isn't just a testament to your AWS expertise. It symbolizes your dedication, adaptability, and forward-thinking approach. A large cohort of cloud professionals affirm that such certifications have unlocked doors to challenges and opportunities previously perceived as unattainable.

Monetary Benefits: The correlation between certifications and salary enhancements isn't mere speculation. Numerous surveys and reports substantiate that AWS certified professionals often enjoy a competitive edge in terms of compensation, underscoring the certification's ROI.

Enhanced Visibility: Amidst the vast sea of IT professionals, the AWS Certified Solutions Architect badge acts as a shining beacon. It isn't just about landing a job—it's about securing the right position that aligns with your passion and long-term career goals.

Holistic Cloud Proficiency: Beyond just theoretical know-how, this certification ensures practitioners possess hands-on experience with AWS services. As a certified Solutions Architect, you won't just design scalable and reliable applications on AWS—you'll strategize, troubleshoot, and innovate, distinguishing yourself from the general pool of cloud enthusiasts.

Network Expansion: Being AWS certified invariably draws you into a global community of like-minded professionals. This provides avenues for collaboration, knowledge sharing, and even potential job opportunities, giving a substantial boost to your professional network.

In essence, the AWS Certified Solutions Architect - Associate certification is not just an emblem of your cloud competency—it's a compass directing your consistent growth in the dynamic realm of cloud computing.

CONTENTS

PRACTICE TEST 1 - QUESTIONS ONLY

QUESTION 1

A financial services company is planning to deploy a critical application on AWS which will handle sensitive customer data. The application architecture includes Amazon EC2 instances for web servers, Amazon RDS for database services, and Amazon S3 for storing backups and reports. Considering the sensitive nature of the data, the company wants to ensure that access is tightly controlled with Multi-Factor Authentication (MFA) for all IAM users and root accounts. What strategy should the company adopt to secure access controls?

A) Enable MFA for IAM users but not for the root account, as it might lead to access issues.
B) Enforce MFA for both IAM users and the root account, and implement IAM roles for EC2 instances accessing S3 buckets.
C) Only use IAM roles for EC2 instances and avoid MFA, as it complicates the login process.
D) Disable all IAM user accounts and solely rely on the root account with MFA enabled for administrative tasks.
E) Implement MFA only for IAM users accessing the RDS database, as it contains sensitive information.

QUESTION 2

A company plans to deploy a highly available application across multiple AWS Regions to enhance security and ensure disaster recovery. What architectural considerations should they make to align with AWS's best practices for global infrastructure security and resiliency?

A) Use Amazon CloudFront and AWS Shield for global distribution and DDoS protection.
B) Store data redundantly in multiple Availability Zones within a single Region.
C) Deploy the application on EC2 instances across multiple Regions, using Amazon Route 53 for region health checks.
D) Utilize AWS Wavelength Zones for application deployment to minimize latency.
E) Implement AWS Outposts across various Regions for a consistent hybrid experience.

QUESTION 3

A multinational online retailer is looking to enhance its security against increasingly sophisticated cyber threats. With a focus on threat management, they need to protect their AWS-hosted web applications from DDoS attacks, SQL injection, and other web vulnerabilities. Considering the need for both proactive and reactive defense mechanisms, which AWS services should they employ?

A) AWS Shield Advanced for DDoS protection, AWS WAF for filtering malicious web traffic, and Amazon Inspector for security assessments.

B) Amazon CloudFront for content delivery network security, Amazon Cognito for user authentication, and AWS IAM for access management.

C) AWS Lambda for executing custom security scripts, AWS Systems Manager for managing server configurations, and AWS CloudTrail for logging API activities.

D) Amazon GuardDuty for threat detection, AWS Config for configuration compliance, and Amazon

Macie for data security and privacy.

E) Amazon Route 53 for DNS security, AWS Fargate for serverless application security, and AWS KMS for encryption key management.

QUESTION 4

Your company is planning to migrate its on-premises database to AWS for better scalability and availability. As a solutions architect, you need to design a secure network architecture using Amazon VPC. The company's main requirement is to ensure that only authorized users can access the database, and all data transfers between the on-premises environment and AWS are encrypted. Additionally, the company wants to minimize latency for database queries. Which solution should you recommend?

A) Configure a VPN connection between the on-premises network and Amazon VPC, and use AWS Direct Connect for dedicated private network connectivity. Implement security groups to control access to the database instance, and configure SSL/TLS encryption for data in transit.

B) Use AWS Direct Connect for dedicated private network connectivity between the on-premises network and Amazon VPC. Implement network ACLs to control inbound and outbound traffic to the database subnet, and configure Amazon RDS with encryption at rest and in transit.

C) Set up a VPN connection between the on-premises network and Amazon VPC for encrypted communication. Utilize AWS PrivateLink to securely access the database without exposing it to the internet, and configure AWS KMS for encryption of data at rest and in transit.

D) Deploy AWS VPN CloudHub to establish secure communication between the on-premises network and Amazon VPC. Use AWS Transit Gateway to simplify network connectivity, and configure AWS Certificate Manager for SSL/TLS certificates to encrypt data in transit.

E) Configure AWS Site-to-Site VPN to connect the on-premises network with Amazon VPC. Implement security groups to restrict access to the database instance, and utilize AWS Key Management Service (KMS) for encryption of data at rest and in transit.

QUESTION 5

You are tasked with designing an IAM policy to grant access to a specific Amazon S3 bucket for a group of developers working on a new project. The policy should ensure that the developers have read and write access to objects in the bucket, but they should not be able to delete objects. Which IAM policy configuration meets this requirement?

A) Allow s3:GetObject, s3:PutObject, s3:GetObjectVersion for the specified bucket.
B) Allow s3:GetObject, s3:PutObject, s3:GetObjectVersion, s3:DeleteObject for the specified bucket.
C) Allow s3:GetObject, s3:PutObject, s3:GetObjectVersion, s3:DeleteObject, s3:ListBucket for the specified bucket.
D) Allow s3:GetObject, s3:PutObject, s3:GetObjectVersion, s3:ListBucket for the specified bucket.
E) Allow s3:GetObject, s3:PutObject, s3:GetObjectVersion, s3:DeleteObject, s3:ListBucket, except s3:DeleteObject for the specified bucket.

QUESTION 6

You are designing a serverless architecture for a highly sensitive application that requires stringent security measures. Which approach should you take to ensure secure authentication and authorization in this scenario?

A) Implement Amazon Cognito user pools for user authentication and authorization. Use Amazon API Gateway with IAM authorization for API access control.

B) Utilize AWS Identity and Access Management (IAM) roles for authentication and authorization. Use AWS Lambda authorizers with API Gateway for fine-grained access control.

C) Deploy custom authentication and authorization logic within AWS Lambda functions. Use Amazon S3 to store user credentials securely and authenticate users before accessing sensitive data.

D) Integrate third-party identity providers (IdPs) with Amazon Cognito for user authentication. Use AWS Lambda authorizers with API Gateway for role-based access control.

E) Set up API Gateway with OAuth 2.0 for user authentication and authorization. Use AWS Secrets Manager to securely store client secrets and keys for token validation.

QUESTION 7

A healthcare company is planning to use AWS to store and manage patient records. Compliance with HIPAA requires that all patient data be encrypted at rest and in transit. The solution architect must design a key management system that meets these requirements while ensuring the keys are managed securely and efficiently. Which setup should the architect recommend?

A) Use AWS KMS with customer-managed keys (CMKs) and enable automatic rotation.
B) Use instance store volumes with Amazon EC2 and manage encryption keys manually.
C) Store encryption keys in Amazon S3 and apply S3 server-side encryption.
D) Implement AWS CloudHSM to manage keys outside of AWS managed services.
E) Use AWS KMS with AWS managed keys (default) for encryption and manually rotate them annually.

QUESTION 8

A multinational corporation wants to enhance their security posture by leveraging AWS for real-time threat detection and compliance monitoring. They are particularly interested in identifying unauthorized API calls and suspicious login attempts. Which solution should they implement? Select Two.

A) Use AWS IAM Identity Center for monitoring and alerts.
B) Implement AWS CloudWatch for real-time threat detection.
C) Utilize Amazon GuardDuty for intelligent threat detection and alerts.
D) Deploy AWS WAF for real-time threat detection.
E) Set up AWS Security Hub for centralized security and compliance monitoring.

QUESTION 9

You are designing a secure architecture for a web application that handles sensitive user data. The application must protect against common web-based attacks, such as SQL injection and cross-site scripting (XSS). The company is also required to comply with strict regulatory standards for data protection. Which of the following strategies is most effective for integrating AWS services to achieve this security goal?

A) Implementing AWS WAF with rules to filter incoming web traffic, ensuring compliance with regulatory standards

B) Utilizing Amazon Cognito for user authentication and authorization, providing secure access control for sensitive data

C) Configuring Amazon API Gateway with rate limiting and authentication mechanisms, ensuring secure access to APIs handling user data

D) Enabling AWS Shield Advanced for DDoS protection, safeguarding against potential disruptions to the web application

E) Deploying AWS Key Management Service (KMS) for encrypting user data at rest, ensuring compliance with data protection regulations

QUESTION 10

A logistics company is migrating its package tracking system to AWS and requires a solution that ensures package status updates are processed in real-time while also providing the ability to handle sudden spikes in package tracking requests during promotional events. Which option should the company choose to implement this requirement?

A) Use Amazon SQS FIFO queue with exactly-once processing enabled.
B) Use Amazon SQS FIFO queue with message deduplication enabled.
C) Use Amazon SQS FIFO queue with a batch mode of 10 messages per operation.
D) Use Amazon SQS standard queue to process the messages.
E) Use Amazon SQS FIFO queue with default settings to process the messages.

QUESTION 11

An international news portal, experiencing high traffic volumes, seeks to fortify its architecture against sophisticated DDoS attacks while ensuring low latency for global readers. They aim to leverage AWS services for an integrated solution that includes a content distribution network, enhanced DDoS protection, and automated application scaling.

A) AWS Shield Standard, Amazon S3, and AWS Auto Scaling
B) Amazon CloudFront, AWS Shield Advanced, and AWS WAF
C) AWS Global Accelerator, Amazon Inspector, and Amazon CloudWatch
D) Amazon Route 53, AWS Network Firewall, and AWS Lambda
E) Amazon API Gateway, AWS Direct Connect, and AWS Fargate

QUESTION 12

A global online retail company wishes to simplify and secure access for developers to AWS services across multiple regions. They need to implement a centralized identity management system that integrates with their existing on-premises Microsoft Active Directory (AD) without replicating identities into AWS. The solution must support single sign-on (SSO) capabilities to allow developers to access AWS resources based on their existing group memberships in AD.

A) Configure AWS Directory Service AD Connector for direct AD integration.
B) Implement AWS IAM Identity Center (SSO) with SAML 2.0 federation to on-premises AD.
C) Utilize Amazon Cognito with federation to on-premises AD for developer authentication.
D) Deploy AWS Lambda functions to synchronize identities from on-premises AD to AWS IAM users.
E) Set up an AWS VPN tunnel to connect on-premises AD with AWS IAM roles for access control.

QUESTION 13

A large financial institution is developing a new API to allow customers to access their account information securely. The institution wants to ensure robust protection for the API and prevent unauthorized access. Which strategy should the institution consider for enhancing API security?

A) Integrating AWS WAF with Amazon API Gateway for advanced protection.
B) Implementing AWS IAM for user authentication.
C) Configuring AWS CloudFront with AWS Shield for DDoS protection.
D) Enabling AWS Lambda authorizers for API Gateway authentication.
E) Utilizing Amazon Inspector for continuous security monitoring.

QUESTION 14

A healthcare technology company is looking to automate compliance checks for HIPAA regulations across its AWS environment. The solution must provide detailed reports on compliance status, identify configurations that do not meet HIPAA requirements, and suggest remediations.

A) Utilize AWS Config and AWS Audit Manager for continuous compliance monitoring and reporting.

B) Implement AWS CloudTrail and Amazon Inspector for real-time security analysis and HIPAA compliance auditing.

C) Leverage Amazon Macie for PHI data discovery and classification, integrated with AWS Lambda for automated remediation of non-compliant configurations.

D) Deploy AWS Systems Manager to automate patch management and use AWS Trusted Advisor for best practices and compliance checks.

E) Configure Amazon GuardDuty for threat detection and AWS Security Hub for centralized compliance management, focusing on HIPAA benchmarks.

QUESTION 15

A streaming service company plans to archive its vast library of original content to Amazon S3 for long-term storage. The content needs to be uploaded in a cost-effective manner without sacrificing data integrity or security. The company's primary concern is minimizing storage costs while ensuring data durability. Which combination of AWS features should be utilized?

A) Use AWS Snowball for initial data transfer, then store data using Amazon S3 Glacier.

B) Implement Amazon S3 Intelligent-Tiering to automatically optimize storage costs.

C) Leverage Amazon DataSync for ongoing data uploads and Amazon S3 Standard-Infrequent Access for storage.

D) Opt for multipart uploads to Amazon S3, followed by lifecycle policies to transition to Amazon S3 Glacier Deep Archive.

E) Configure AWS Transfer for SFTP directly into Amazon S3 Glacier for secure uploads.

QUESTION 16

A multinational corporation is restructuring its AWS account architecture to improve security and compliance across its business units. Which approach would best facilitate this objective while ensuring segregation of duties? Select TWO.

A) Utilize AWS Organizations to centrally manage multiple AWS accounts and enforce service control policies.

B) Implement IAM roles with cross-account access for each business unit to share resources securely.

C) Configure AWS Resource Access Manager (RAM) to share resources across accounts without compromising security.

D) Utilize AWS Single Sign-On (SSO) to enable unified access to all AWS accounts with a single set of credentials.

E) Implement AWS Control Tower to automatically provision and configure a multi-account environment with pre-established security baselines.

QUESTION 17

For a multinational corporation looking to deploy a disaster recovery site in AWS, the key requirements are minimal data transfer latency, high data throughput, and secure connectivity between their primary site and AWS. They seek a cost-effective solution that can be rapidly implemented.

A) Establish an AWS Site-to-Site VPN for secure connectivity and Amazon CloudFront for reduced latency.
B) Set up AWS Direct Connect for high data throughput and AWS Transit Gateway for simplified network management.
C) Implement AWS Direct Connect along with Amazon S3 Transfer Acceleration for high-speed data transfer.
D) Use multiple AWS Direct Connect connections with AWS Global Accelerator to enhance network performance.
E) Configure AWS Direct Connect with AWS Backup for seamless data replication and disaster recovery.

QUESTION 18

A media company is transitioning its video processing and content management system to AWS to enhance performance and security. The migration requires high throughput for video processing, the ability to scale resources dynamically, and strict access controls to protect intellectual property.

A) Configure AWS Elastic Transcoder for video processing, Amazon CloudFront for content delivery, and AWS IAM for access control.

B) Employ AWS Snowmobile for large-scale video data transfer, AWS Elemental MediaConvert for video processing, and Amazon Cognito for user authentication.

C) Utilize AWS DataSync to transfer video files, AWS Lambda for serverless video processing, and AWS WAF for web application security.

D) Implement AWS Step Functions for orchestrating video processing workflows, Amazon S3 for scalable storage, and Amazon GuardDuty for threat detection.

E) Leverage Amazon Kinesis Video Streams for real-time video processing, AWS Auto Scaling for resource management, and AWS Shield for DDoS protection.

QUESTION 19

A software development company is deploying a serverless application on AWS and needs to manage configurations securely while ensuring efficient integration with AWS services. The company wants to minimize manual intervention in configuration updates and ensure robust access control mechanisms. Which of the following approaches would best suit the company's requirements?

A) Use AWS AppConfig to store application configurations and leverage AWS Lambda triggers for automatic updates. Implement IAM roles with fine-grained permissions to control access to AppConfig configurations.

B) Maintain configuration settings within environment variables directly in AWS Lambda functions. Implement AWS IAM policies to restrict access to Lambda environment variables based on function roles.

C) Store configuration files in plaintext format within an encrypted Amazon S3 bucket. Implement AWS Lambda functions to fetch and decrypt configuration files at runtime.

D) Utilize AWS Systems Manager Parameter Store to manage configurations centrally. Develop AWS Lambda functions to retrieve and apply configuration updates from Parameter Store as needed.

E) Implement a custom configuration management solution using AWS DynamoDB. Store configurations in DynamoDB tables encrypted with AWS KMS and use AWS Lambda to retrieve and apply updates dynamically.

QUESTION 20

A social media platform is facing challenges in managing maintenance tasks on specific Amazon EC2 instances within an Auto Scaling group. Each time maintenance patches are applied, the instances briefly show as out of service, leading to Auto Scaling provisioning replacements. What actions would you suggest as a solutions architect to mitigate this issue efficiently?

A) Suspend the Launch process type for the Auto Scaling group and apply the maintenance patch to the instance. Once the instance is ready, manually set the instance's health status back to healthy and activate the Launch process type again.

B) Suspend the ReplaceUnhealthy process type for the Auto Scaling group and apply the maintenance patch to the instance. Once the instance is ready, manually set the instance's health status back to healthy and activate the ReplaceUnhealthy process type again.

C) Stop the instance, apply the maintenance patch, and then start the instance.

D) Temporarily suspend the AddToLoadBalancer process type for the Auto Scaling group and apply the maintenance patch to the instance. Once the instance is ready, manually set the instance's health status back to healthy and activate the AddToLoadBalancer process type again.

E) Take a snapshot of the instance, create a new Amazon Machine Image (AMI), and then launch a new instance using this AMI. Apply the maintenance patch to this new instance and then add it back to the Auto Scaling Group by using the manual scaling policy. Terminate the earlier instance that had the maintenance issue.

QUESTION 21

A popular ride-sharing company is expanding its services to new cities globally and needs an architecture that can handle a surge in user registrations, ride requests, and driver assignments. The solution should automatically scale to accommodate increased demand while ensuring minimal downtime and optimal user experience.

A) Deploy Amazon EC2 instances with Auto Scaling for backend processing, Amazon S3 for storing user and ride data, Amazon CloudFront for content delivery, and Amazon Aurora for a scalable relational database.

B) Utilize AWS Lambda for serverless backend logic, Amazon API Gateway for managing ride APIs, Amazon ElastiCache for caching frequently accessed data, and AWS Global Accelerator for optimizing user connectivity.

C) Implement Amazon ECS for containerized microservices, Amazon RDS with Multi-AZ deployment for database resilience, AWS Direct Connect for dedicated network connectivity, and Amazon Route 53 for DNS management.

D) Configure AWS App Runner for easy deployment and scaling, Amazon DynamoDB with On-Demand Capacity for flexible database management, Amazon CloudFront for global content delivery, and AWS Auto Scaling for compute resources.

E) Leverage Amazon EKS for Kubernetes-based service orchestration, Amazon Redshift for analyzing large datasets, Amazon S3 Glacier for archival storage, and Amazon Route 53 for traffic routing and health checking.

QUESTION 22

A financial services company is building an event-driven architecture for processing transactions in real-time. They want to ensure that the system can handle large volumes of transactions securely and cost-effectively. What solution should they choose?

A) Utilize Amazon Kinesis Data Analytics for processing real-time transactions with SQL queries.
B) Implement Amazon MQ to decouple components and ensure reliable message delivery.
C) Use AWS Step Functions to orchestrate transaction processing workflows with Lambda functions.
D) Employ Amazon S3 as a data lake for storing transaction data and analyze it with Amazon Athena.
E) Utilize AWS Glue for ETL processing of transaction data before sending it to downstream systems.

QUESTION 23

A financial services company is planning to migrate its legacy monolithic application to AWS and wants to ensure fault tolerance and scalability while optimizing costs. The company requires a solution that minimizes expenses while maintaining high availability. Which AWS service would best support this requirement?

A) Utilize Amazon EC2 instances across multiple Availability Zones with AWS Auto Scaling for automated scaling based on traffic patterns to ensure high availability and cost efficiency

B) Implement Amazon S3 for static content storage with Amazon CloudFront for global content delivery to reduce latency and improve performance while minimizing costs

C) Deploy Amazon Aurora for relational database storage with Multi-AZ deployment for automated failover and cost-efficient scaling to maintain high availability with minimal expenses

D) Utilize AWS Lambda with Amazon DynamoDB for serverless application components and data storage to achieve high scalability with low operational costs

E) Implement Amazon ECS with AWS Fargate for containerized deployment and scaling of application components to optimize costs while ensuring fault tolerance and scalability

QUESTION 24

Your company is launching a new e-commerce platform that requires a highly scalable and secure architecture to handle peak traffic during sales events. Additionally, the platform needs to support global customers with low-latency access to product catalogs. Which AWS services should you recommend to build this platform?

A) Amazon EC2 for scalable compute capacity
B) Amazon CloudFront for content delivery with edge locations
C) Amazon Aurora for highly available relational database
D) Amazon SQS for decoupling application components
E) Amazon Route 53 for global DNS resolution

QUESTION 25

A gaming company has detected an unusual surge in unauthorized AWS API queries during off-peak hours, with no visible impact on system performance. The management seeks an automated solution to promptly alert relevant teams during such occurrences. Which solution would be most suitable in this scenario?

A) Implement AWS Config Rules to monitor API activity and define rules to detect unauthorized API calls. Configure AWS Config to trigger an AWS Lambda function upon rule evaluation to notify relevant stakeholders.

B) Create an Amazon CloudWatch metric filter to process AWS CloudTrail logs containing API call details. Establish an alarm based on this metric's rate to send an Amazon SNS notification to the required team.

C) Leverage AWS Trusted Advisor to publish metrics about check results to Amazon CloudWatch. Set up an alarm to track status changes for checks in the Service Limits category for the APIs, triggering notifications when service quotas are exceeded.

D) Use Amazon Athena SQL queries against AWS CloudTrail log files stored in Amazon S3 buckets. Generate reports using Amazon QuickSight for managerial dashboards.

E) Configure AWS CloudTrail to stream event data to Amazon Kinesis. Utilize Amazon Kinesis stream-level metrics in Amazon CloudWatch to trigger an AWS Lambda function that will initiate an error workflow.

QUESTION 26

A global e-commerce company is planning to migrate its monolithic application to a microservices architecture on AWS to improve scalability and resilience. As the solutions architect, you need to recommend a solution for inter-service communication that ensures low latency and high availability. Which option would best meet this requirement?

A) Utilize Amazon SQS to decouple microservices and facilitate asynchronous communication between them.

B) Implement AWS Step Functions to orchestrate the execution of microservices and handle inter-service communication.

C) Deploy Amazon API Gateway to manage and expose HTTP endpoints for microservices, enabling synchronous communication between them.

D) Configure AWS AppSync to provide a GraphQL API layer for microservices, allowing efficient data fetching and real-time updates.

E) Use Amazon EventBridge to build event-driven architectures and enable seamless communication between microservices via events.

QUESTION 27

A multinational e-commerce company is designing a serverless workflow for processing customer orders. The company wants to ensure that the workflow is resilient and can handle spikes in order volumes during sales events. Which of the following options best addresses the requirement for resilient workflow orchestration using AWS services?

A) Utilize AWS Step Functions for orchestrating workflow tasks
B) Implement Amazon SQS for message queuing to handle order processing
C) Deploy AWS Lambda for event-driven processing of order data
D) Leverage Amazon ECS for containerized execution of order processing tasks
E) Utilize Amazon EKS for managing order processing tasks in Kubernetes pods

QUESTION 28

A company is developing a new serverless workflow for processing user-submitted videos. The workflow includes transcoding videos, analyzing content for compliance, and storing both original and processed videos securely. Considering scalability, cost-efficiency, and security, which architecture should be used?

A) Use AWS Lambda for video processing, Amazon Rekognition for compliance analysis, store videos in Amazon S3, and secure access with Amazon Cognito.

B) Utilize Amazon EC2 instances for video processing, use Amazon Inspector for compliance analysis, store videos in Amazon EFS, and manage access with AWS IAM.

C) Deploy Amazon ECS for video processing, leverage Amazon GuardDuty for security analysis, store videos in Amazon Glacier, and secure access with AWS Directory Service.

D) Implement AWS Step Functions for orchestrating video processing workflows, use AWS Lambda for transcoding, Amazon Rekognition for compliance analysis, Amazon S3 for storage, and AWS IAM for access control.

E) Use AWS Fargate for containerized video processing, Amazon SNS for compliance notifications, store videos in Amazon S3 Glacier, and manage access with Amazon Cognito.

QUESTION 29

A global e-commerce platform is preparing for a major sales event where they expect a significant increase in traffic. They need a load balancing solution that can efficiently handle dynamic traffic patterns and distribute traffic to multiple instances across different Availability Zones (AZs). Which option aligns with best practices for this scenario?

A) Implement Amazon Route 53 with Latency routing policy for global traffic distribution
B) Deploy an Application Load Balancer (ALB) with Target Groups for dynamic traffic routing
C) Set up an Amazon Elastic Load Balancer (ELB) with Classic Load Balancer for legacy compatibility
D) Utilize Amazon CloudFront with Lambda@Edge for real-time traffic optimization
E) Configure Amazon Elastic Load Balancing (ELB) with Network Load Balancer (NLB) for network-level routing

QUESTION 30

A global tech conference organizer is live-streaming keynote sessions to attendees in different countries. Due to speaker agreements, they need to restrict access to attendees only in certain countries. How can they effectively enforce this restriction?

A) Use Amazon Route 53 based geolocation routing policy to restrict access to attendees located in the authorized countries

B) Implement Amazon Route 53 based weighted routing policy to balance traffic across regions based on predetermined weights

C) Utilize Amazon Route 53 based latency-based routing policy to direct attendees to the closest streaming server for optimal performance

D) Employ Amazon Route 53 based failover routing policy to reroute traffic to backup servers in case of server failures

E) Apply Amazon Route 53 based geoproximity routing policy to direct traffic based on the proximity of attendees to streaming servers

QUESTION 31

A multinational corporation seeks to consolidate their disparate data sources into a unified data lake on AWS. Their primary objectives are to improve data analytics, enhance customer understanding, and secure sensitive information in compliance with global data privacy laws. Which architecture and services would best meet their requirements for building a scalable, secure data lake with integrated analytics capabilities?

A) Utilize Amazon S3 for data storage, AWS Lake Formation for building and securing the data lake, Amazon Athena for querying data, and AWS Glue for data cataloging and preparation.

B) Deploy Amazon RDS for data storage, Amazon Redshift for data warehousing, AWS KMS for encryption, and Amazon QuickSight for analytics and visualization.

C) Implement Amazon EBS for block storage, Amazon EC2 for data processing, Amazon CloudFront for data distribution, and AWS WAF for security.

D) Use Amazon DynamoDB for NoSQL data storage, Amazon EMR for big data processing, Amazon Kinesis for real-time analytics, and Amazon Macie for data security and privacy.

E) Choose AWS Storage Gateway for on-premises integration, AWS Direct Connect for dedicated network connection, Amazon Redshift Spectrum for querying data across the data lake, and Amazon GuardDuty for threat detection.

QUESTION 32

A multinational e-commerce corporation is planning to migrate its database infrastructure to AWS to handle the increasing volume of transactions. They need a solution that offers high availability, scalability, and low latency. Which approach should the corporation take to ensure optimal performance and reliability?

A) Implement Amazon DynamoDB with on-demand scaling and global tables for seamless scalability and multi-region availability.

B) Utilize Amazon RDS with Aurora Serverless for cost optimization and automated scaling based on workload demand.

C) Deploy Amazon Aurora with multi-master replication and fast failover for real-time updates and continuous availability.

D) Migrate to Amazon Redshift for analytics and scalability while maintaining high availability with cross-region replication.

E) Configure Amazon DocumentDB with encryption at rest and fine-grained access control for regulatory compliance and data security.

QUESTION 33

A financial institution is planning to deploy a new application in AWS, which requires a resilient and secure network architecture. The application will be hosted in Amazon EC2 instances across multiple Availability Zones (AZs) for high availability. The institution also wants to connect its on-premises data center to AWS to ensure smooth data synchronization and hybrid cloud functionality. The architecture should provide robust network security measures to protect sensitive financial data. Based on these requirements, which of the following options should the Solutions Architect recommend?

A) Utilize Amazon VPC with public and private subnets, deploying EC2 instances in private subnets and using NAT Gateways for internet access. Establish a VPN connection between the on-premises data center and the VPC. Utilize Security Groups and NACLs for fine-grained access control.

B) Deploy all EC2 instances in public subnets within an Amazon VPC. Set up AWS Direct Connect for a dedicated network connection to the on-premises data center. Rely on Security Groups alone for network security.

C) Use an Amazon VPC with EC2 instances deployed in public subnets. Establish a Site-to-Site VPN connection and utilize AWS Network Firewall for centralized network security. Ignore NACLs as they are redundant with Security Groups.

D) Implement Amazon VPC with private subnets for EC2 instances, using AWS Direct Connect for hybrid cloud connectivity. Deploy AWS Network Firewall for network security, supplemented with Security Groups and NACLs for additional layers of security.

E) Set up a fully public VPC with no private subnets, ensuring all EC2 instances are internet-facing to simplify access. Use a Site-to-Site VPN connection for on-premises connectivity and rely on AWS Shield for network security.

QUESTION 34

A healthcare company is planning to deploy a critical patient data management application on AWS, ensuring high availability and data integrity. The application requires a relational database with automatic failover, scalable storage, and the ability to perform complex queries on stored data. Which deployment strategy meets these requirements?

A) Deploy the application using Amazon DynamoDB with global tables for storage.
B) Utilize Amazon Aurora Serverless with multi-AZ deployment for the database layer.
C) Implement the database layer on Amazon RDS for MySQL with a single-AZ deployment.
D) Use Amazon S3 with S3 Transfer Acceleration for storage, and Amazon Athena for querying.
E) Configure the application to use Amazon DocumentDB (with MongoDB compatibility) with replication across multiple regions.

QUESTION 35

A gaming company is developing a multiplayer game and needs to implement real-time communication features, such as in-game chat and live updates. They require a solution that can handle high concurrency and low-latency communication. Which setup should they configure using Amazon API Gateway to meet these requirements effectively?

A) Utilize RESTful APIs on Amazon API Gateway with Amazon RDS for real-time communication

B) Implement WebSocket APIs on Amazon API Gateway with Amazon DynamoDB for real-time communication

C) Create HTTP APIs on Amazon API Gateway and integrate with Amazon ElastiCache for real-time communication

D) Deploy GraphQL APIs on Amazon API Gateway with Amazon S3 for real-time communication

E) Configure RESTful APIs on Amazon API Gateway with Amazon Redshift for real-time communication

QUESTION 36

Your company is migrating its on-premises data warehouse to AWS. As part of the migration strategy, you need to ensure the new AWS-based data warehouse is highly scalable and reliable while optimizing costs. Which combination of AWS services and best practices should you incorporate into the architecture to meet these requirements effectively? Select TWO.

A) Deploy Amazon Redshift for data warehousing with Auto Scaling enabled.
B) Utilize Amazon S3 for data storage and leverage S3 Intelligent-Tiering to optimize costs.

C) Implement AWS Glue for ETL (Extract, Transform, Load) processes to prepare and load data into Redshift.

D) Utilize Amazon CloudWatch to monitor Redshift performance and trigger alarms for scaling actions.
E) Set up Amazon Athena for ad-hoc query analysis to avoid the need for additional infrastructure.

QUESTION 37

Your company has recently migrated its web application to AWS, and you are tasked with designing a comprehensive monitoring and logging solution to ensure operational insight and timely troubleshooting. The application consists of microservices deployed on Amazon ECS, with AWS Lambda functions handling background tasks. What approach should you take to implement effective monitoring and logging, considering the distributed nature of the architecture and the need for real-time visibility into system health? Select TWO.

A) Configure Amazon CloudWatch Logs agent on ECS instances to stream logs to CloudWatch Logs. Implement AWS X-Ray for tracing Lambda function invocations and API calls.

B) Utilize Amazon CloudWatch Container Insights to collect and analyze performance metrics from ECS clusters. Set up CloudTrail to capture API activity for Lambda functions and integrate with Amazon S3 for long-term storage.

C) Deploy AWS CloudTrail with multi-region logging enabled to track API calls across regions. Implement Amazon CloudWatch Alarms to monitor ECS CPU utilization and Lambda function errors.

D) Integrate AWS X-Ray with ECS and Lambda to trace requests across services and analyze performance bottlenecks. Use CloudWatch Events to trigger Lambda functions based on application-level events for proactive monitoring.

E) Implement Amazon CloudWatch Logs Insights to query and visualize log data from ECS containers and Lambda functions in real-time. Configure AWS Config to monitor resource configurations changes and send notifications via Amazon SNS.

QUESTION 38

You are designing an architecture for a web application that experiences highly variable traffic patterns throughout the day. The application consists of several microservices, each requiring different computational resources. Additionally, the architecture needs to be cost-effective without sacrificing performance. Which AWS compute services would you recommend to meet these requirements? Select THREE.

A) Utilize Amazon EC2 Auto Scaling to automatically adjust compute capacity based on traffic fluctuations.

B) Implement AWS Lambda for serverless execution of code in response to events, reducing costs for sporadic workloads.

C) Deploy AWS Fargate for serverless containers, allowing efficient resource utilization without managing underlying infrastructure.

D) Utilize Amazon ECS for containerized microservices, providing scalability and cost optimization through efficient resource allocation.

E) Implement AWS Batch for batch computing workloads, ensuring efficient resource provisioning and cost management.

QUESTION 39

A company needs to design a network architecture that ensures high availability, low latency, and secure hybrid connectivity for its global applications. Which solution would best meet these requirements?

A) Implement Amazon CloudFront with AWS Shield for DDoS protection and Amazon Route 53 for DNS routing.

B) Utilize Amazon VPC with public and private subnets, employing AWS Direct Connect for dedicated network connections, and AWS VPN for secure hybrid connectivity.

C) Configure Amazon CloudFront with AWS WAF for global content delivery and protection against web attacks.

D) Deploy Amazon Route 53 with AWS Global Accelerator for efficient DNS routing and global application acceleration.

E) Use AWS Transit Gateway for scalable and efficient network connectivity across multiple VPCs.

QUESTION 40

A logistics company wants to develop a package tracking system to provide real-time updates to its customers. They require a solution that can process tracking data from various sources and deliver timely notifications to customers without manual intervention. Which setup should they configure using AWS serverless components to meet these requirements effectively?

A) Utilize AWS Lambda with Amazon S3 for processing tracking data and Amazon RDS for storing notification data

B) Implement Amazon Kinesis Data Firehose with AWS Lambda for processing tracking data and Amazon ElastiCache for storing notification data

C) Ingest tracking data into Amazon Kinesis Data Streams, which triggers an AWS Lambda function for processing and stores notification data in Amazon DynamoDB

D) Ingest tracking data into Amazon SQS, which triggers an AWS Lambda function for processing and stores notification data in Amazon Redshift

E) Use Amazon API Gateway to ingest tracking data, which is processed by an application running on an Amazon EC2 instance, and store notification data in Amazon Elasticsearch Service

QUESTION 41

A multinational e-commerce company is expanding its operations globally and needs to ensure low-latency access to its website for customers in different regions. They want to design a solution that optimizes content delivery while maintaining high availability and security. Which AWS service should the company use to achieve these objectives?

A) Configure Amazon CloudFront with AWS Global Accelerator to optimize content delivery and ensure low-latency access globally.

B) Implement AWS Direct Connect to establish dedicated network connections between the company's data centers and AWS regions for low-latency access.

C) Utilize AWS Transit Gateway to create a scalable and secure hub for connecting VPCs and on-premises networks globally.

D) Deploy AWS PrivateLink to securely access AWS services without traversing the public internet.

E) Implement Amazon Route 53 with latency-based routing to direct user traffic to the nearest AWS edge location.

QUESTION 42

You are tasked with designing a high-performing architecture for a large e-commerce platform. The platform experiences high traffic volumes during peak hours, resulting in database performance bottlenecks. Which solution would best address this challenge?

A) Implement Amazon RDS with read replicas in multiple Availability Zones (AZs).
B) Deploy the database layer on Amazon EC2 instances using Amazon EBS volumes.
C) Utilize Amazon DynamoDB with provisioned capacity to handle peak traffic.
D) Configure Amazon Aurora Serverless for auto-scaling based on demand.
E) Use Amazon ElastiCache for caching frequently accessed data.

QUESTION 43

You are designing a high-performance data lake architecture for a large e-commerce company. The company needs to efficiently store and analyze massive amounts of customer transaction data in real-time. Which approach should you recommend to meet these requirements?

A) Implement AWS Lake Formation to build a secure data lake and manage data access.
B) Utilize Amazon S3 for cost-effective storage of transaction data at scale.
C) Implement data ingestion with AWS Glue to automate the process of loading data into the data lake.

D) Design for data query performance with Amazon Athena to enable fast and interactive querying of transaction data.

E) Ensure data lake security and compliance with AWS policies and practices.

QUESTION 44

Your company is designing a real-time data processing system to analyze customer behavior on an e-commerce website. The system needs to handle high volumes of data with low latency to provide personalized recommendations to users. Which architecture would be most suitable for this scenario?

A) Utilize Amazon Kinesis Data Firehose to ingest data from the website, then process it using AWS Lambda functions before storing it in Amazon DynamoDB for real-time access.

B) Implement Amazon Kinesis Data Streams to capture website events, process them with Apache Flink running on Amazon EC2 instances, and store results in Amazon Redshift for analysis.

C) Deploy Amazon Managed Streaming for Apache Kafka (Amazon MSK) to handle website event ingestion, process data with Amazon Kinesis Data Analytics, and store results in Amazon Redshift for further analysis.

D) Set up Amazon Kinesis Data Firehose to capture website event ingestion, process data with Amazon Kinesis Data Analytics, and store results in Amazon S3, utilizing Amazon Athena for querying.

E) Use AWS AppSync to integrate website data with Amazon Neptune graph database for real-time analysis, with Amazon QuickSight for visualization.

QUESTION 45

A software development company is storing source code repositories in Amazon S3 and requires encryption of the data at rest. The company wants to maintain full control over the encryption keys and access to audit logs. Which option would provide the most suitable solution for this scenario?

A) Utilize server-side encryption with Amazon S3 managed keys (SSE-S3) to encrypt the data on Amazon S3

B) Implement client-side encryption with customer-provided keys (SSE-C) and upload the encrypted data to Amazon S3

C) Use server-side encryption with AWS Key Management Service (SSE-KMS) keys to encrypt the data on Amazon S3

D) Use server-side encryption with customer-provided keys (SSE-C) to encrypt the data on Amazon S3

E) Enable AWS CloudTrail to monitor S3 bucket activities for auditing purposes

QUESTION 46

You are tasked with designing a high-performing IoT solution for a manufacturing company that produces sensors for monitoring industrial machinery. The solution must efficiently process real-time data from thousands of sensors, ensure low latency for critical alerts, and comply with industry regulations. Which combination of AWS services and features would best meet these requirements?

A) Configure AWS IoT Core for data ingestion, implement AWS Lambda for edge processing, set up Amazon Kinesis Data Streams for real-time data processing, integrate with Amazon DynamoDB for real-time data storage, and utilize Amazon S3 for long-term data archival.

B) Deploy Amazon API Gateway for data ingestion, utilize AWS Fargate for edge processing, configure

Amazon Kinesis Data Analytics for real-time data analysis, connect with Amazon RDS for real-time data storage, and employ Amazon Glacier for long-term data archival.

C) Utilize AWS IoT Greengrass for data ingestion, leverage AWS Lambda for edge processing, employ Amazon Kinesis Data Streams for real-time data processing, store real-time data in Amazon DynamoDB, and archive long-term data in Amazon S3.

D) Implement AWS IoT Events for data ingestion, set up AWS Lambda for edge processing, use Amazon Kinesis Data Streams for real-time data processing, deploy Amazon Aurora for real-time data storage, and employ Amazon S3 Glacier for long-term data archival.

E) Utilize AWS IoT Core for data ingestion, configure AWS Greengrass for edge computing, implement Amazon Kinesis Data Streams for real-time data processing, utilize AWS Lambda for serverless processing, and store real-time data in Amazon DynamoDB.

QUESTION 47

You are designing a high-performance edge computing solution for a retail company that operates a chain of stores worldwide. The company wants to deploy applications on edge devices to reduce latency for customer-facing services such as inventory management and personalized recommendations. Which architecture would best meet these requirements?

A) Utilize AWS Wavelength to deploy applications on edge devices located within telecommunication providers' data centers, leverage AWS IoT Greengrass for edge data processing, and integrate with AWS DynamoDB for real-time data storage.

B) Implement applications on Amazon EC2 instances deployed in AWS Outposts located near retail stores, utilize AWS IoT Greengrass for edge data processing, and integrate with Amazon RDS for real-time data storage.

C) Deploy applications on edge devices using AWS Snow Family devices placed in retail stores, leverage AWS IoT Greengrass for edge data processing, and integrate with Amazon S3 for real-time data storage.

D) Utilize AWS Lambda@Edge for deploying applications on edge devices located in retail stores, leverage AWS IoT Greengrass for edge data processing, and integrate with Amazon Aurora for real-time data storage.

E) Implement applications on Amazon EC2 instances deployed in AWS Local Zones located near retail stores, utilize AWS IoT Greengrass for edge data processing, and integrate with Amazon Redshift for real-time data storage.

QUESTION 48

A healthcare startup is developing a mobile application to facilitate real-time health monitoring and advice. The application will collect data from various health devices, analyze this data to provide personalized health recommendations, and securely store user health records. Given the need for scalability, security, and low latency, which AWS services should be utilized to design and deploy scalable and high-performance APIs for this application?

A) Amazon API Gateway for managing APIs, AWS Lambda for serverless data processing, Amazon DynamoDB for storing health records, and Amazon Cognito for authentication.

B) Amazon ECS for containerized microservice management, Amazon RDS for relational data storage, AWS WAF for security, and Amazon CloudFront for content delivery.

C) AWS Direct Connect for dedicated connectivity, Amazon S3 for data storage, Amazon EC2 for compute resources, and AWS IAM for managing access permissions.

D) Amazon Kinesis for real-time data streaming, Amazon EMR for data analysis, Amazon EBS for block storage, and Amazon CloudWatch for monitoring.

E) AWS Fargate for running containers without managing servers, Amazon Redshift for data warehousing, AWS Shield for DDoS protection, and AWS Step Functions for orchestrating serverless workflows.

QUESTION 49

A software development company operates a continuous integration and continuous deployment (CI/CD) pipeline for its applications. The pipeline requires compute resources for short-duration build and test jobs throughout the day. The company wants to minimize infrastructure costs while ensuring quick turnaround times for development cycles. Which pricing option for Amazon EC2 instances would be the most suitable choice for this scenario?

A) Utilize reserved instances (RI) for the entire duration of operation
B) Implement on-demand instances for the entire duration of operation
C) Utilize spot instances for the entire duration of operation
D) Employ a combination of reserved instances (RI) and spot instances
E) Implement a mix of reserved instances (RI) and on-demand instances

QUESTION 50

You are designing a high-performing architecture for a data analytics platform that requires processing large volumes of streaming data in real-time. The platform needs to balance performance with cost optimization while ensuring scalability and resilience. Which approach would best meet the requirements?

A) Utilize Amazon Kinesis Data Firehose to ingest streaming data, and configure it to deliver data directly to Amazon S3 for storage and further processing. Implement Amazon Athena to query the data directly from S3, ensuring cost-effective performance optimization.

B) Deploy Amazon Kinesis Data Streams to ingest and process streaming data in real-time, utilizing AWS Lambda to perform data transformations and analysis. Configure auto-scaling for Lambda functions based on incoming data volume to optimize resource utilization and costs.

C) Implement Amazon Kinesis Data Analytics to process streaming data in real-time, utilizing SQL queries to perform aggregations and transformations. Configure auto-scaling for Kinesis Data Analytics to dynamically adjust resources based on workload demands, ensuring high performance and cost efficiency.

D) Deploy Amazon Managed Streaming for Apache Kafka (Amazon MSK) to handle streaming data ingestion and processing, leveraging Apache Kafka's scalability and resilience features. Implement

QUESTION 51

You are designing a high-performing architecture for a financial services company that requires low-latency access to real-time financial data, high availability, and stringent security measures. The company operates globally, serving millions of customers who rely on instant access to their financial information. What AWS solution would best meet these requirements?

A) Utilize Amazon CloudFront with custom SSL certificates for global content delivery, Amazon DynamoDB for high-performance data storage, AWS Lambda for processing transactions, and AWS WAF for application security.

B) Implement AWS Global Accelerator to route user traffic, Amazon EC2 Auto Scaling for compute scalability, Amazon EFS for shared file storage, and AWS Shield Advanced for DDoS protection.

C) Deploy Amazon Route 53 for DNS routing, Amazon API Gateway for secure API management, Amazon RDS with encryption for data storage, and Amazon Cognito for user authentication.

D) Leverage AWS Direct Connect for dedicated network connections, Amazon Aurora for scalable database needs, AWS AppSync for real-time data synchronization, and Amazon GuardDuty for threat detection.

E) Use AWS Fargate for running containerized applications, Amazon DynamoDB for high-performance data storage, AWS Step Functions for orchestrating transaction processes, and Amazon Macie for data security and privacy.

QUESTION 52

A multinational e-commerce company wants to ensure high availability for its website, which serves customers globally. The company wants to minimize downtime and ensure resilience across AWS Regions and Availability Zones. Additionally, they want to leverage Amazon Route 53 for health checking and DNS failover strategies to direct traffic to healthy endpoints in case of failures. What solution architecture best meets these requirements?

A) Implement an auto-scaling group of Amazon EC2 instances across multiple Availability Zones, using Amazon Route 53 health checks and DNS failover for traffic redirection in case of failures.

B) Deploy a multi-region architecture with AWS Global Accelerator for load balancing and failover, using Amazon Route 53 for DNS resolution.

C) Utilize Amazon EC2 instances with AWS Auto Scaling across multiple Regions, implementing Amazon Route 53 latency-based routing for traffic distribution.

D) Configure an Amazon CloudFront distribution with origin failover to multiple S3 buckets across different Regions, leveraging Amazon Route 53 for DNS routing.

E) Implement an Amazon ECS cluster with tasks deployed across multiple Availability Zones, using Amazon Route 53 health checks for failover.

QUESTION 53

A global e-commerce company requires its Amazon EC2-hosted application to serve customers with the lowest latency possible. What strategy should be employed to ensure this?

A) Deploy EC2 instances in a single, centrally-located region.
B) Utilize Amazon CloudFront with EC2 instances as origin servers.
C) Implement Global Accelerator to route traffic to the nearest EC2 instances.
D) Configure EC2 instances across multiple regions without any traffic management.
E) Place EC2 instances behind an Application Load Balancer with cross-zone load balancing enabled.

QUESTION 54

Your company operates a web application that experiences fluctuating traffic patterns throughout the day. You need to design a cost-effective database solution that can handle variable workloads while minimizing costs during periods of low activity. Which option would best meet these requirements while considering the need for automated scaling and cost optimization?

A) Utilize Amazon RDS Multi-AZ configuration for MySQL
B) Deploy Amazon Aurora Serverless for automatic scaling based on workload demand
C) Implement Amazon DynamoDB with On-Demand capacity for NoSQL needs
D) Opt for Amazon RDS Provisioned IOPS for improved performance
E) Use Amazon Redshift for data warehousing needs

QUESTION 55

For a global online retail company, product information is stored in an Amazon Aurora database. The company wants to ensure that product details are globally consistent, but pricing information needs to be specific to each region to accommodate local taxes and currency exchange rates. What is the most efficient way to structure this database solution?

A) Utilize Amazon Aurora Global Database for product details and separate Aurora instances for regional pricing.

B) Use Amazon DynamoDB global tables for product details and Amazon Aurora for regional pricing.
C) Implement Amazon Aurora with cross-region replication for product details and regional tables for pricing.

D) Deploy separate Amazon Aurora instances for both product details and pricing in each region.
E) Use Amazon DynamoDB global tables for both product details and pricing, with application logic to handle regional differences.

QUESTION 56

Your company operates a large-scale data analytics platform on AWS, utilizing Amazon S3 for storing raw data and Amazon Redshift for data warehousing. The company wants to implement a cost-effective backup and archival solution for its data lake, ensuring long-term retention while minimizing storage costs. Which approach aligns with best practices for designing the backup and archival solution?

A) Implement AWS Backup to automate and manage backups of Amazon S3 data
B) Configure lifecycle policies to transition data from Amazon S3 to Amazon S3 Glacier
C) Utilize AWS DataSync to replicate data from Amazon S3 to on-premises storage

D) Leverage AWS Storage Gateway for seamless integration between Amazon S3 and on-premises storage

E) Deploy AWS Snow Family for offline transfer of data from Amazon S3 to physical devices

QUESTION 57

Your company operates a global e-commerce platform with customers in multiple regions. You need to distribute product images stored in Amazon S3 to users worldwide while minimizing data transfer costs and ensuring fast delivery. What would be the most suitable approach to achieve these objectives?

A) Use Amazon CloudFront with the S3 bucket containing product images set as the origin to cache images at edge locations

B) Implement Amazon S3 Transfer Acceleration to optimize data transfer speeds for product images

C) Set up cross-region replication for the S3 bucket hosting product images to automatically replicate objects to edge locations

D) Utilize AWS DataSync to synchronize product images between multiple S3 buckets in different regions

E) Deploy AWS Snowball to physically distribute product images to AWS data centers in different regions

QUESTION 58

Your company operates a global e-commerce platform that experiences seasonal spikes in traffic, particularly during holiday sales events. To ensure optimal performance and availability during peak periods, you decide to implement Amazon CloudFront for cost-effective global content delivery. Which of the following configurations would best optimize costs while maintaining performance during peak traffic?

A) Utilize Amazon CloudFront with dynamic content caching to deliver personalized product recommendations

B) Configure Amazon CloudFront with custom SSL certificate for enhanced security and trust

C) Implement Amazon CloudFront with origin failover to ensure high availability of content delivery

D) Enable Amazon CloudFront cache invalidation to quickly update content changes across edge locations

E) Integrate Amazon CloudFront with AWS Shield to protect against DDoS attacks

QUESTION 59

Your company operates a data analytics platform that processes large volumes of data from various sources. As part of a cost optimization initiative, you need to design a solution for automating data lifecycle management while minimizing expenses. Which approach would best achieve this goal?

A) Implement Amazon S3 lifecycle policies to automate tiering and deletions based on object age and access patterns

B) Utilize Amazon Glacier for long-term data archival and manual deletion of obsolete data

C) Deploy Amazon CloudWatch Events to trigger Lambda functions for manual data lifecycle management

D) Leverage AWS Backup to schedule regular backups and manage data retention policies

E) Use Amazon S3 Intelligent-Tiering to automatically move objects between storage tiers based on access patterns

QUESTION 60

A manufacturing company wants to ensure that its IoT devices deployed in various factories can securely communicate with AWS services for data collection and processing. What solution should the solutions architect recommend to establish secure communication between IoT devices and AWS?

A) Open the necessary ports on the factory firewalls to allow direct communication between IoT devices and AWS services.

B) Implement IAM policies to grant IoT devices access to AWS services based on their unique identifiers.

C) Configure AWS IoT Core to authenticate and authorize IoT devices before allowing communication with AWS services.

D) Share AWS account access keys with each IoT device for direct access to AWS services.

E) Utilize AWS Direct Connect to establish dedicated network connections between IoT devices and AWS services.

QUESTION 61

Your company is designing a cost-optimized architecture for a web application that experiences variable traffic throughout the day. The application must automatically scale to handle increases in traffic while minimizing costs during periods of low activity. Which solution should you recommend for this scenario?

A) Utilize Amazon EC2 Auto Scaling with Amazon CloudWatch alarms to adjust capacity based on traffic patterns

B) Implement Amazon Elastic Container Service (Amazon ECS) with AWS Fargate to automatically scale containerized workloads

C) Use AWS Lambda with Amazon API Gateway to run serverless functions in response to incoming requests

D) Deploy AWS AppSync with GraphQL resolvers to handle traffic fluctuations and automatically adjust capacity

E) Utilize Amazon DynamoDB On-Demand capacity mode to automatically scale read and write capacity based on traffic patterns

QUESTION 62

You are designing a global e-commerce platform that requires low-latency access to product images and videos while optimizing costs. The solution should ensure high availability and performance for users worldwide. Which approach should you recommend for this scenario?

A) Implement Amazon S3 Transfer Acceleration to optimize data transfers and reduce latency for media uploads

B) Use Amazon CloudFront with Lambda@Edge to cache and deliver multimedia content at edge locations

C) Deploy Amazon Elastic File System (Amazon EFS) to store multimedia files and enable fast access from multiple regions

D) Utilize Amazon Kinesis Video Streams to ingest and process live streaming multimedia content

E) Implement AWS Direct Connect with AWS Transit Gateway to establish private connectivity between on-premises data centers and AWS regions

QUESTION 63

Your company operates a hybrid cloud environment with on-premises infrastructure and AWS resources. The data transfer costs between your on-premises data center and AWS have been escalating, impacting the overall operational budget. To address this issue, you need to design a solution that optimizes data transfer costs while ensuring efficient connectivity. What approach should you recommend?

A) Implement AWS Direct Connect to establish a dedicated connection between your on-premises data center and AWS

B) Utilize AWS Snow Family devices to transfer large volumes of data between your on-premises environment and AWS

C) Deploy AWS Storage Gateway to cache frequently accessed data locally and reduce data transfer costs

D) Leverage Amazon S3 Transfer Acceleration to optimize data transfer speeds and reduce costs

E) Configure AWS VPN to establish secure and cost-effective connectivity between your on-premises network and AWS

QUESTION 64

Your company operates a global e-commerce platform that experiences fluctuating traffic throughout the year. To optimize costs while ensuring high availability, you are tasked with designing a solution that dynamically scales resources based on demand. What approach should you recommend?

A) Utilize AWS Auto Scaling with Amazon EC2 Spot Instances to automatically adjust capacity based on demand fluctuations

B) Implement AWS Fargate with Amazon ECS to automatically scale containers based on traffic patterns

C) Leverage AWS Lambda with Amazon API Gateway to build serverless applications that scale automatically based on incoming requests

D) Deploy Amazon Aurora Global Database to replicate data across regions and ensure low-latency access for read-heavy workloads

E) Utilize Amazon S3 Transfer Acceleration to optimize data transfer speeds and reduce costs associated with cross-region replication

QUESTION 65

Your company is planning to optimize AWS costs by enhancing visibility and accountability across teams. As a solutions architect, you need to recommend a solution that provides comprehensive cost insights and accountability measures.

A) Implement AWS Cost Explorer with custom reporting to analyze cost trends and anomalies
B) Utilize AWS Budgets to set and track cost limits for individual teams and projects
C) Implement AWS IAM policies to restrict access to costly services and features based on user roles
D) Leverage AWS Service Catalog to standardize and control provisioned resources to minimize cost
E) Utilize AWS Trusted Advisor to identify cost optimization opportunities and best practices

PRACTICE TEST 1 - ANSWERS ONLY

QUESTION 1

Answer - B) Enforce MFA for both IAM users and the root account, and implement IAM roles for EC2 instances accessing S3 buckets.

A) Incorrect - Enabling MFA for both IAM users and the root account enhances security and is a recommended best practice. Ignoring MFA for the root account leaves a critical security gap.

B) Correct - Enforcing MFA for both IAM users and the root account significantly enhances account security. Implementing IAM roles for EC2 instances allows secure access to AWS services like S3 without needing to store AWS credentials on the instances.

C) Incorrect - IAM roles are crucial for secure access management, but relying solely on roles and avoiding MFA disregards the security benefits of multi-factor authentication.

D) Incorrect - Disabling IAM user accounts and relying only on the root account, even with MFA, is highly discouraged due to the broad access rights of the root account.

E) Incorrect - While it's important to secure access to databases, implementing MFA only for RDS access misses the broader security benefits of MFA across all sensitive services and accounts.

QUESTION 2

Answer - C) Deploy the application on EC2 instances across multiple Regions, using Amazon Route 53 for region health checks.

A) - Incorrect, because while Amazon CloudFront and AWS Shield provide DDoS protection and content distribution, they don't directly address cross-region deployment for high availability and disaster recovery.

B) - Incorrect, as this option only covers data redundancy within a single Region and does not involve multiple Regions for true geographic diversity and resilience.

C) - Correct, because deploying EC2 instances across multiple Regions with Amazon Route 53 health checks aligns with best practices for designing secure, resilient applications. This ensures high availability and facilitates disaster recovery.

D) - Incorrect, because AWS Wavelength Zones are designed to minimize latency for mobile and edge devices, not specifically for inter-region security and disaster recovery.

E) - Incorrect, as AWS Outposts is meant for hybrid cloud scenarios, offering AWS infrastructure, services, APIs, and tools to virtually any datacenter, co-location space, or on-premises facility, but it does not specifically address the question's focus on multiple AWS Regions and global infrastructure security.

QUESTION 3

Answer - A) AWS Shield Advanced for DDoS protection, AWS WAF for filtering malicious web traffic, and Amazon Inspector for security assessments.

A) Correct - This combination of services provides a comprehensive security approach. AWS Shield

Advanced offers DDoS protection, AWS WAF helps protect web applications from common web exploits, and Amazon Inspector provides automated security assessments to help identify vulnerabilities or deviations from best practices.

B) Incorrect - While Amazon CloudFront, Amazon Cognito, and AWS IAM are important for overall security, they do not specifically address the comprehensive needs of DDoS protection, SQL injection prevention, and vulnerability assessments.

C) Incorrect - AWS Lambda, AWS Systems Manager, and AWS CloudTrail are valuable for automation, management, and logging, but they do not directly provide protections against DDoS attacks, SQL injections, or perform web application vulnerability assessments.

D) Incorrect - Amazon GuardDuty, AWS Config, and Amazon Macie are crucial for threat detection, compliance, and data security but do not cover the specific combination of DDoS protection, web traffic filtering, and security assessments provided by Shield Advanced, WAF, and Inspector.

E) Incorrect - Amazon Route 53, AWS Fargate, and AWS KMS focus on DNS security, serverless application security, and encryption management, which are important but not directly aligned with the question's scenario focusing on DDoS, SQL injection, and security assessments.

QUESTION 4

Answer - [C] Set up a VPN connection between the on-premises network and Amazon VPC for encrypted communication. Utilize AWS PrivateLink to securely access the database without exposing it to the internet, and configure AWS KMS for encryption of data at rest and in transit.

Option C - Correct. This solution ensures secure communication between the on-premises network and Amazon VPC via VPN, utilizes AWS PrivateLink for secure access to the database, and implements AWS KMS for encryption of data at rest and in transit.

Option A - VPN connection and AWS Direct Connect provide secure network connectivity but may not address the requirement for minimizing latency. SSL/TLS encryption and security groups are valid components but do not fully meet the requirements.

Option B - While AWS Direct Connect and encryption at rest and in transit are mentioned, the solution lacks VPN for encrypted communication and may not fully meet the latency requirement.

Option D - AWS VPN CloudHub and AWS Transit Gateway offer network connectivity options but may not be the most suitable for the given requirements. AWS Certificate Manager is mentioned but may not fully address encryption needs.

Option E - AWS Site-to-Site VPN and security groups are mentioned, but AWS PrivateLink and encryption using AWS KMS are more appropriate for this scenario.

QUESTION 5

Answer - [A] Allow s3:GetObject, s3:PutObject, s3:GetObjectVersion for the specified bucket.]

Option A is correct because it grants read (s3:GetObject) and write (s3:PutObject) access to objects in the specified bucket, as well as access to object versions (s3:GetObjectVersion), meeting the requirement. It does not include permissions to delete objects.

Option B is incorrect because it includes s3:DeleteObject, which allows the deletion of objects, violating the requirement.

Option C is incorrect because it grants additional permissions to delete objects and list the bucket contents, which are not required and may pose a security risk.

Option D is incorrect because it lacks the s3:DeleteObject permission required for write access to the bucket, and it includes unnecessary s3:ListBucket permission.

Option E is incorrect because although it includes all the necessary permissions, it then restricts the s3:DeleteObject permission, which contradicts the requirement for write access.

QUESTION 6

Answer - [A] Implement Amazon Cognito user pools for user authentication and authorization. Use Amazon API Gateway with IAM authorization for API access control.

Option A - Correct. Amazon Cognito user pools provide secure authentication and authorization for users, and IAM authorization with API Gateway ensures fine-grained access control for APIs.

Option B - While IAM roles and Lambda authorizers are valid options, using Cognito user pools provides additional features specifically designed for user authentication and authorization.

Option C - Implementing custom logic may introduce security risks and complexity. Cognito user pools offer a more standardized and secure solution for user management.

Option D - While integrating third-party IdPs with Cognito is possible, it may introduce additional complexity and dependencies. Cognito user pools alone can fulfill the authentication and authorization requirements.

Option E - OAuth 2.0 with API Gateway and Secrets Manager may provide authentication and authorization but may not offer the same level of user management features and security as Cognito user pools.

QUESTION 7

Answer - A) Use AWS KMS with customer-managed keys (CMKs) and enable automatic rotation.

A) Use AWS KMS with customer-managed keys (CMKs) and enable automatic rotation. - Correct because it meets the requirement for secure key management, supports HIPAA compliance by providing encryption at rest and in transit, and offers automatic rotation to enhance security.

B) Use instance store volumes with Amazon EC2 and manage encryption keys manually. - Incorrect because manual key management increases the risk of security breaches and does not inherently support HIPAA compliance requirements for encryption.

C) Store encryption keys in Amazon S3 and apply S3 server-side encryption. - Incorrect because while S3 encryption provides data security, storing keys alongside data without a dedicated management system does not comply with best practices for key management.

D) Implement AWS CloudHSM to manage keys outside of AWS managed services. - Incorrect for this scenario as it introduces complexity and higher cost without additional benefits over AWS KMS for the given requirements.

E) Use AWS KMS with AWS managed keys (default) for encryption and manually rotate them annually. - Incorrect because relying on AWS managed keys limits the control over the encryption keys and manual rotation annually may not meet compliance requirements for certain regulations.

QUESTION 8

Answer - C) and E)

A) Use AWS IAM Identity Center for monitoring and alerts. - Incorrect because IAM Identity Center primarily manages identities and federations, not real-time threat detection.

B) Implement AWS CloudWatch for real-time threat detection. - Incorrect because CloudWatch is mainly used for monitoring and operational data collection, not specifically for threat detection.

C) Utilize Amazon GuardDuty for intelligent threat detection and alerts. - Correct because GuardDuty offers intelligent threat detection and continuous monitoring.

D) Deploy AWS WAF for real-time threat detection. - Incorrect as WAF protects web applications from web exploits, not general threat detection.

E) Set up AWS Security Hub for centralized security and compliance monitoring. - Correct because Security Hub gives a comprehensive view of high-priority security alerts and compliance status across AWS accounts.

QUESTION 9

Answer - [A] Implementing AWS WAF with rules to filter incoming web traffic, ensuring compliance with regulatory standards.

A) Implementing AWS WAF (Web Application Firewall) with rules to filter incoming web traffic is crucial for protecting against common web-based attacks like SQL injection and XSS. By ensuring compliance with regulatory standards, the company can meet data protection requirements.

B) Amazon Cognito provides user authentication and authorization, but it may not directly address protection against web-based attacks or compliance with regulatory standards.

C) While Amazon API Gateway provides secure access to APIs, it may not offer the same level of protection against web-based attacks as AWS WAF, nor does it explicitly ensure compliance with regulatory standards.

D) AWS Shield Advanced provides DDoS protection but may not directly address web application security or compliance with data protection regulations.

E) AWS KMS encrypts data at rest, which is important for data protection but may not specifically address protection against web-based attacks or compliance with regulatory standards.

QUESTION 10

Answer - C) Use Amazon SQS FIFO queue with a batch mode of 10 messages per operation.

C) Use Amazon SQS FIFO queue with a batch mode of 10 messages per operation - This option ensures real-time processing of package status updates while efficiently handling sudden spikes in tracking requests during promotional events by processing multiple updates in a batch. The FIFO guarantees order accuracy, and batch processing enhances efficiency, meeting the company's requirements for real-time updates and scalability.

A) Use Amazon SQS FIFO queue with exactly-once processing enabled - While ensuring order accuracy, it may not efficiently handle sudden spikes in tracking requests due to sequential processing.

B) Use Amazon SQS FIFO queue with message deduplication enabled - While avoiding duplicate messages, it doesn't guarantee order processing, and may not efficiently handle sudden spikes in tracking requests.

D) Use Amazon SQS standard queue to process the messages - Standard queues lack message ordering, which is crucial for maintaining package status order, and may not efficiently handle sudden spikes in tracking requests.

E) Use Amazon SQS FIFO queue with default settings - Default settings may not ensure real-time processing and order accuracy, especially during sudden spikes in tracking requests.

QUESTION 11

Answer - B) Amazon CloudFront, AWS Shield Advanced, and AWS WAF

A) AWS Shield Standard, Amazon S3, and AWS Auto Scaling - Incorrect because AWS Shield Standard provides basic DDoS protection which might not be adequate for sophisticated attacks. S3 and Auto Scaling do not address the CDN or application layer protection.

B) Amazon CloudFront, AWS Shield Advanced, and AWS WAF - Correct because CloudFront provides a global CDN service, Shield Advanced offers enhanced DDoS protection, and WAF provides application layer protection.

C) AWS Global Accelerator, Amazon Inspector, and Amazon CloudWatch - Incorrect because these services do not offer an integrated solution for DDoS protection, CDN, and application layer security. Inspector is for security assessments, not real-time protection.

D) Amazon Route 53, AWS Network Firewall, and AWS Lambda - Incorrect because this combination lacks a CDN solution and does not offer the same level of DDoS protection as Shield Advanced.

E) Amazon API Gateway, AWS Direct Connect, and AWS Fargate - Incorrect because they focus on API management, dedicated network connections, and container management, respectively, not on DDoS protection or global content delivery.

QUESTION 12

Answer - B) Implement AWS IAM Identity Center (SSO) with SAML 2.0 federation to on-premises AD.

A) Configure AWS Directory Service AD Connector for direct AD integration. - Incorrect because AD Connector is designed for leveraging AD credentials in AWS but does not provide a seamless SSO experience for AWS service access as IAM Identity Center does.

B) Implement AWS IAM Identity Center (SSO) with SAML 2.0 federation to on-premises AD. - Correct because it allows for the integration of on-premises AD with AWS, enabling SSO capabilities for developers to access AWS resources based on their AD group memberships, without replicating identities.

C) Utilize Amazon Cognito with federation to on-premises AD for developer authentication. - Incorrect for enterprise-wide identity management across multiple AWS services, as Cognito is more suited for application-level user identity and access management.

D) Deploy AWS Lambda functions to synchronize identities from on-premises AD to AWS IAM users. - Incorrect because this approach involves replicating identities into AWS, which contradicts the scenario requirements.

E) Set up an AWS VPN tunnel to connect on-premises AD with AWS IAM roles for access control. - Incorrect as VPN tunnels are for network connectivity, not for identity federation or management.

QUESTION 13

Answer - [A) Integrating AWS WAF with Amazon API Gateway for advanced protection.]

A) Integrating AWS WAF with Amazon API Gateway for advanced protection - AWS WAF provides a web application firewall that helps protect web applications and APIs from common web exploits. Integrating it with API Gateway adds an extra layer of security by filtering and monitoring HTTP requests.

B) Implementing AWS IAM for user authentication - While IAM provides user authentication, it does not directly address API security concerns related to protection against common web exploits.

C) Configuring AWS CloudFront with AWS Shield for DDoS protection - While CloudFront and AWS Shield provide DDoS protection, they are not specifically tailored for securing APIs against common web exploits.

D) Enabling AWS Lambda authorizers for API Gateway authentication - Lambda authorizers control access to APIs based on custom authentication logic but do not provide protection against common web exploits.

E) Utilizing Amazon Inspector for continuous security monitoring - Amazon Inspector is used for vulnerability assessment and continuous security monitoring but does not actively protect APIs from common web exploits.

QUESTION 14

Answer - A) Utilize AWS Config and AWS Audit Manager for continuous compliance monitoring and reporting.

A) Utilize AWS Config and AWS Audit Manager for continuous compliance monitoring and reporting. - Correct because AWS Config provides detailed visibility into resource configurations and changes, while AWS Audit Manager helps automate evidence collection for audits, together offering a comprehensive solution for managing HIPAA compliance.

B) Implement AWS CloudTrail and Amazon Inspector for real-time security analysis and HIPAA compliance auditing. - Incorrect as CloudTrail and Inspector are more focused on security analysis and vulnerability assessments, not specifically designed for compliance monitoring and reporting.

C) Leverage Amazon Macie for PHI data discovery and classification, integrated with AWS Lambda for automated remediation of non-compliant configurations. - Incorrect because, while Macie is essential for PHI management, it doesn't provide a comprehensive compliance reporting mechanism as AWS Config and Audit Manager do.

D) Deploy AWS Systems Manager to automate patch management and use AWS Trusted Advisor for best practices and compliance checks. - Incorrect as they offer patch management and best practice checks but lack the specific compliance reporting and monitoring capabilities required for HIPAA.

E) Configure Amazon GuardDuty for threat detection and AWS Security Hub for centralized compliance management, focusing on HIPAA benchmarks. - Incorrect because, although Security Hub centralizes compliance data, the combination of AWS Config and Audit Manager more directly addresses the need for automated compliance reporting and remediation for HIPAA.

QUESTION 15

Answer - B) Implement Amazon S3 Intelligent-Tiering to automatically optimize storage costs. and D) Opt for multipart uploads to Amazon S3, followed by lifecycle policies to transition to Amazon S3 Glacier Deep Archive.

A) Use AWS Snowball for initial data transfer, then store data using Amazon S3 Glacier. - Incorrect. While Snowball is effective for large data transfers, it doesn't address the ongoing need for cost optimization.

B) Implement Amazon S3 Intelligent-Tiering to automatically optimize storage costs. - Correct. This option provides a cost-effective solution by automatically moving data to the most cost-effective access tier without sacrificing data integrity or security.

C) Leverage Amazon DataSync for ongoing data uploads and Amazon S3 Standard-Infrequent Access for storage. - Incorrect. This doesn't fully optimize for the lowest possible storage costs over the long term.

D) Opt for multipart uploads to Amazon S3, followed by lifecycle policies to transition to Amazon S3 Glacier Deep Archive. - Correct. This approach minimizes costs by leveraging Glacier Deep Archive for the lowest storage cost and ensures data durability.

E) Configure AWS Transfer for SFTP directly into Amazon S3 Glacier for secure uploads. - Incorrect. While secure, this method lacks the flexibility and cost optimization provided by Intelligent-Tiering and lifecycle policies.

QUESTION 16

Answer - [A, E] Utilize AWS Organizations to centrally manage multiple AWS accounts and enforce service control policies. Implement AWS Control Tower to automatically provision and configure a multi-account environment with pre-established security baselines.

Option B is incorrect because while IAM roles with cross-account access can enable resource sharing, they do not provide centralized management and enforcement of policies.

Option C is incorrect because AWS RAM is used for resource sharing, not security enforcement, across accounts.

Option D is incorrect because AWS SSO provides access management, but it does not enforce segregation of duties across multiple accounts.

Options A and E are the correct choices as they advocate for utilizing AWS Organizations to centrally manage multiple AWS accounts and enforce service control policies, and implementing AWS Control Tower to automatically provision and configure a multi-account environment with pre-established security baselines, ensuring segregation of duties and improved security and compliance across business units.

QUESTION 17

Answer - B) Set up AWS Direct Connect for high data throughput and AWS Transit Gateway for simplified network management.

A) Establish an AWS Site-to-Site VPN for secure connectivity and Amazon CloudFront for reduced latency - Incorrect because, while it ensures secure connectivity, Site-to-Site VPN does not match the high throughput requirement.

B) Set up AWS Direct Connect for high data throughput and AWS Transit Gateway for simplified network management - Correct because Direct Connect provides high data throughput necessary for disaster recovery scenarios, and Transit Gateway simplifies network management across multiple VPCs and connections.

C) Implement AWS Direct Connect along with Amazon S3 Transfer Acceleration for high-speed data transfer - Incorrect because, although it accelerates transfers to S3, this combination doesn't address the full scope of connectivity and network management needs.

D) Use multiple AWS Direct Connect connections with AWS Global Accelerator to enhance network performance - Incorrect because Global Accelerator is focused on improving internet-facing application performance, not internal connectivity for disaster recovery.

E) Configure AWS Direct Connect with AWS Backup for seamless data replication and disaster recovery - Incorrect as it doesn't specifically address the latency and throughput requirements compared to the combination of Direct Connect and Transit Gateway.

QUESTION 18

Answer - B) Employ AWS Snowmobile for large-scale video data transfer, AWS Elemental MediaConvert for video processing, and Amazon Cognito for user authentication.

A) Incorrect because Elastic Transcoder and CloudFront address video processing and delivery, but IAM, while providing access control, doesn't directly address the high throughput and dynamic scaling requirements for video processing.

B) Correct as Snowmobile facilitates the transfer of vast amounts of video data, Elemental MediaConvert offers scalable and secure video processing, and Cognito provides robust user authentication, aligning with the security and performance needs.

C) Incorrect because DataSync, Lambda, and WAF cater to data transfer, serverless processing, and security, but do not specifically support the high throughput required for video processing or comprehensive access controls.

D) Incorrect as Step Functions, S3, and GuardDuty offer workflow orchestration, storage, and security monitoring, but do not fully meet the high throughput and dynamic resource scaling needs for video content management.

E) Incorrect because Kinesis Video Streams and Auto Scaling address real-time processing and resource scaling, but Shield's focus on DDoS protection doesn't contribute to the specific requirements of access control and throughput for video processing.

QUESTION 19

Answer - [A] Use AWS AppConfig to store application configurations and leverage AWS Lambda triggers for automatic updates. Implement IAM roles with fine-grained permissions to control access to AppConfig configurations.

Option B - Storing configurations directly in Lambda environment variables lacks centralized management and may lead to security vulnerabilities.

Option C - Storing configuration files in plaintext within S3 introduces security risks and lacks built-in management features like rotation.

Option D - While Parameter Store can manage configurations centrally, it may not offer the same level of integration and automation as AppConfig.

Option E - Implementing a custom solution with DynamoDB introduces complexity and may not offer the same level of integration with AWS services as AppConfig.

QUESTION 20

Answer - B) Suspend the ReplaceUnhealthy process type for the Auto Scaling group and apply the maintenance patch to the instance. Once the instance is ready, manually set the instance's health status back to healthy and activate the ReplaceUnhealthy process type again.

B) Suspend the ReplaceUnhealthy process type for the Auto Scaling group and apply the maintenance patch to the instance - This option effectively addresses the maintenance challenge by suspending the process responsible for replacing unhealthy instances, allowing the maintenance to proceed without triggering Auto Scaling actions.

A) Suspend the Launch process type for the Auto Scaling group and apply the maintenance patch to the instance - Suspending the launch process may not prevent instance replacement and may not efficiently address the maintenance challenge.

C) Stop the instance, apply the maintenance patch, and then start the instance - Stopping the instance may disrupt application availability, and manually starting it again may not align with the requirement for uninterrupted maintenance.

D) Temporarily suspend the AddToLoadBalancer process type for the Auto Scaling group and apply the maintenance patch to the instance - Suspending processes related to load balancer integration may not efficiently address the maintenance challenge and may not prevent instance replacement during maintenance.

E) Take a snapshot of the instance, create a new Amazon Machine Image (AMI), and then launch a new instance using this AMI - Creating a new instance from a snapshot introduces complexity and may not efficiently address the maintenance challenge, especially in scenarios where immediate fixes are required.

QUESTION 21

Answer - D) Configure AWS App Runner for easy deployment and scaling, Amazon DynamoDB with On-Demand Capacity for flexible database management, Amazon CloudFront for global content delivery, and AWS Auto Scaling for compute resources.

A) Incorrect because while EC2 Auto Scaling and Aurora provide scalability and resilience, they require more manual management compared to App Runner and DynamoDB On-Demand, which automatically scale with demand without provisioning or capacity planning.

B) Incorrect as Lambda and API Gateway offer serverless scalability and API management, but ElastiCache might not offer the same level of flexibility and scalability as DynamoDB On-Demand, and Global Accelerator is more suited for improving application performance rather than handling sudden surges in user registrations and ride requests.

C) Incorrect because ECS, RDS Multi-AZ, Direct Connect, and Route 53 provide scalability and resilience but might require more manual configuration and management compared to the fully managed services like App Runner and DynamoDB On-Demand.

D) Correct as App Runner simplifies deployment and scaling, DynamoDB On-Demand adjusts capacity automatically, CloudFront accelerates content delivery globally, and Auto Scaling adjusts compute resources dynamically, offering a comprehensive and automated solution for handling increased demand with minimal downtime and optimal user experience.

E) Incorrect because EKS and Redshift offer scalability but might be more complex to manage compared to App Runner and DynamoDB On-Demand, and S3 Glacier is designed for archival storage rather than handling real-time user registrations and ride requests for a ride-sharing platform.

QUESTION 22

Answer - [A) Utilize Amazon Kinesis Data Analytics for processing real-time transactions with SQL queries.]

A) Kinesis Data Analytics allows for real-time processing of streaming data using SQL queries, suitable for processing transactions.
B) Amazon MQ is more for enterprise messaging, not real-time transaction processing.
C) Step Functions are for workflow orchestration, not real-time analytics.
D) While S3 can store transaction data, it doesn't provide real-time processing capabilities like Kinesis Data Analytics.
E) Glue is for ETL processing, not real-time analytics.

QUESTION 23

Answer - [C) Deploy Amazon Aurora for relational database storage with Multi-AZ deployment for automated failover and cost-efficient scaling to maintain high availability with minimal expenses.]

Option C) is correct as it involves utilizing Amazon Aurora for relational database storage with Multi-AZ deployment for automated failover and cost-efficient scaling, ensuring fault tolerance and scalability while optimizing costs.

Option A) involves deployment and scaling but may not emphasize cost efficiency or database reliability effectively.

Option B) involves static content storage but does not directly address application availability or database scalability.

Option D) and E) involve serverless and containerized deployment but may not provide the same level of database reliability or cost optimization as Multi-AZ deployment.

QUESTION 24

Answer - [B) Amazon CloudFront and C) Amazon Aurora]

Option B involves Amazon CloudFront for content delivery, leveraging edge locations to cache and serve content with low latency to global customers.

Option C involves Amazon Aurora for a highly available relational database, ensuring scalability and reliability for transactional data storage.

Option A involves Amazon EC2 for compute capacity, but it may not provide the same level of scalability and global reach as CloudFront and Aurora.

Option D involves Amazon SQS for decoupling application components, which is important for scalability but not directly related to global content delivery or database requirements.

Option E involves Amazon Route 53 for DNS resolution, which is necessary but does not directly address the scalability or low-latency access requirements of the platform.

QUESTION 25

Answer - B) Create an Amazon CloudWatch metric filter to process AWS CloudTrail logs containing API call details. Establish an alarm based on this metric's rate to send an Amazon SNS notification to the required team.

B) Create an Amazon CloudWatch metric filter to process AWS CloudTrail logs containing API call details. Establish an alarm based on this metric's rate to send an Amazon SNS notification to the required team. - This option directly addresses the scenario by analyzing CloudTrail logs for unauthorized API queries and triggering real-time alerts using CloudWatch alarms and Amazon SNS notifications.

A) Implement AWS Config Rules to monitor API activity and define rules to detect unauthorized API calls. Configure AWS Config to trigger an AWS Lambda function upon rule evaluation to notify relevant stakeholders. - While AWS Config can monitor API activity, it may not provide real-time alerting capabilities for immediate incident response as required in this scenario.

C) Leverage AWS Trusted Advisor to publish metrics about check results to Amazon CloudWatch. Set up an alarm to track status changes for checks in the Service Limits category for the APIs, triggering notifications when service quotas are exceeded. - While Trusted Advisor offers valuable insights, it may not directly address the need for real-time detection of unauthorized API queries.

D) Use Amazon Athena SQL queries against AWS CloudTrail log files stored in Amazon S3 buckets. Generate reports using Amazon QuickSight for managerial dashboards. - While this option provides insights, it may not offer real-time alerting capabilities as required in this scenario.

E) Configure AWS CloudTrail to stream event data to Amazon Kinesis. Utilize Amazon Kinesis stream-level metrics in Amazon CloudWatch to trigger an AWS Lambda function that will initiate an error workflow. - While this option utilizes streaming data, it may introduce complexity and latency compared to directly analyzing CloudTrail logs for real-time alerts.

QUESTION 26

Answer - E) Use Amazon EventBridge to build event-driven architectures and enable seamless communication between microservices via events.

Option E is correct because Amazon EventBridge is designed to facilitate event-driven architectures, allowing seamless communication between microservices via events. This ensures low latency and high availability while promoting decoupling and scalability in a microservices environment.

Option A is incorrect because while Amazon SQS decouples microservices, it may not offer the same level of low latency and high availability for inter-service communication as Amazon EventBridge.

Option B is incorrect because while AWS Step Functions orchestrate microservices, they may not be the most suitable option for handling inter-service communication in terms of low latency and high availability.

Option C is incorrect because while Amazon API Gateway manages HTTP endpoints, it may not provide the same level of efficiency for inter-service communication as Amazon EventBridge.

Option D is incorrect because while AWS AppSync provides a GraphQL API layer, it may not be the most suitable option for ensuring low latency and high availability in inter-service communication.

QUESTION 27

Answer - A) Utilize AWS Step Functions for orchestrating workflow tasks

Option A - AWS Step Functions provide a reliable way to coordinate multiple AWS services into serverless workflows, ensuring resilience and fault tolerance.
Option B - Amazon SQS can handle message queuing but lacks the orchestration capabilities needed for complex workflows.
Option C - AWS Lambda is suitable for event-driven processing but does not provide the workflow orchestration features needed for resilience.
Option D - Amazon ECS offers container management but is not designed for orchestrating serverless workflows.
Option E - Amazon EKS is a managed Kubernetes service and is not the best fit for serverless workflow orchestration.

QUESTION 28

Answer - D) Implement AWS Step Functions for orchestrating video processing workflows, use AWS Lambda for transcoding, Amazon Rekognition for compliance analysis, Amazon S3 for storage, and AWS IAM for access control.

A) Correct for leveraging serverless services and secure storage, but does not provide an orchestrated workflow solution.

B) Incorrect because EC2 is not serverless and EFS may not offer the best cost and scalability for video storage. Amazon Inspector is for security assessments, not content compliance.

C) Incorrect as it doesn't leverage serverless services optimally for this use case. Amazon Glacier is for long-term archival, not immediate processing and access.

D) Correct because it offers a fully serverless, scalable, cost-efficient solution with appropriate services for processing, analysis, security, and storage. Step Functions provide the orchestrated workflow needed.

E) Incorrect due to the use of Fargate which, while serverless, is not as cost-effective for processing tasks as Lambda. S3 Glacier is not suitable for scenarios where quick access to processed videos is needed.

QUESTION 29

Answer - B) Deploy an Application Load Balancer (ALB) with Target Groups for dynamic traffic routing.

A) Amazon Route 53 with Latency routing policy is more suitable for routing traffic based on latency, not for handling dynamic traffic patterns.

B) ALB with Target Groups can efficiently distribute traffic to multiple instances across AZs and adapt to changing traffic loads.

C) Classic Load Balancer is not recommended for new deployments due to its limitations.

D) CloudFront with Lambda@Edge is primarily used for content delivery optimization, not for load balancing.

E) NLB operates at the transport layer and does not provide dynamic traffic routing capabilities.

QUESTION 30

Answer - A) Use Amazon Route 53 based geolocation routing policy to restrict access to attendees located in the authorized countries

A) By utilizing Amazon Route 53's geolocation routing policy, the conference organizer can restrict access to the live-streamed keynote sessions to attendees only in the authorized countries, ensuring compliance with speaker agreements.

B, C, D, E) These options do not directly address the requirement of restricting access to attendees from specific countries for the live-streamed keynote sessions. Weighted routing, latency-based routing, failover routing, and geoproximity routing do not provide the necessary geographic control needed for this scenario.

QUESTION 31

Answer - A) Utilize Amazon S3 for data storage, AWS Lake Formation for building and securing the data lake, Amazon Athena for querying data, and AWS Glue for data cataloging and preparation.

A) Correct, because it outlines a comprehensive, scalable solution for a data lake on AWS that meets the requirements for analytics, security, and compliance. Amazon S3 provides secure, scalable object storage. AWS Lake Formation simplifies and secures data lake setup. Amazon Athena allows serverless querying, and AWS Glue offers data preparation and cataloging.

B) Incorrect, RDS and Redshift focus on relational data storage and warehousing, not on creating a flexible data lake. KMS and QuickSight are useful for encryption and visualization but don't address the full scope of data lake requirements.

C) Incorrect, as EBS and EC2 are not optimized for data lake storage and analytics. CloudFront and WAF are more focused on content delivery and web security, not on data analytics or lake formation.

D) Incorrect, while DynamoDB, EMR, and Kinesis are powerful AWS services, they are best suited for specific use cases rather than a comprehensive data lake solution. Macie provides data security but doesn't fulfill all specified requirements.

E) Incorrect, Storage Gateway and Direct Connect focus on hybrid cloud and network connection, not directly on data lake or analytics capabilities. Redshift Spectrum and GuardDuty offer querying and security but don't provide a complete data lake solution.

QUESTION 32

Answer - [C) Deploy Amazon Aurora with multi-master replication and fast failover for real-time updates and continuous availability.]

Option A) - Incorrect because while Amazon DynamoDB provides scalability and multi-region availability, it lacks the real-time updates and continuous availability features provided by Amazon Aurora with multi-master replication.

Option B) - Incorrect because while Aurora Serverless offers cost optimization and automated scaling, it may not provide the same level of real-time updates and continuous availability as Amazon Aurora with multi-master replication.

Option C) - Correct because Amazon Aurora with multi-master replication and fast failover ensures real-time updates and continuous availability, making it suitable for the corporation's requirements.

Option D) - Incorrect because Amazon Redshift is optimized for analytics and may not offer the same level of real-time updates and continuous availability as Amazon Aurora.

Option E) - Incorrect because while Amazon DocumentDB provides encryption and fine-grained access control, it lacks the multi-master replication and fast failover features required for real-time updates and continuous availability.

QUESTION 33

Answer - D) Implement Amazon VPC with private subnets for EC2 instances, using AWS Direct Connect for hybrid cloud connectivity. Deploy AWS Network Firewall for network security, supplemented with Security Groups and NACLs for additional layers of security.

A) - Incorrect. While using Amazon VPC with public and private subnets and establishing a VPN connection is a good practice for hybrid connectivity, this option does not leverage the bandwidth and consistent latency benefits of AWS Direct Connect, which is critical for financial institutions requiring smooth data synchronization.

B) - Incorrect. Deploying all EC2 instances in public subnets exposes them unnecessarily to the internet, which is not a recommended practice for sensitive financial applications. Furthermore, relying on Security Groups alone does not provide the layered security approach recommended by AWS best practices.

C) - Incorrect. Utilizing public subnets for all EC2 instances and ignoring NACLs omits critical layers of security. While AWS Network Firewall provides robust network security, combining it with NACLs and Security Groups offers a more comprehensive security posture.

D) - Correct. This option aligns with best practices by deploying EC2 instances in private subnets for enhanced security, using AWS Direct Connect for reliable, high-bandwidth connectivity between AWS and the on-premises data center, and incorporating AWS Network Firewall alongside Security Groups and NACLs for multi-layered network security.

E) - Incorrect. Setting up a fully public VPC and relying solely on AWS Shield for network security is not suitable for an application handling sensitive financial data. This option lacks the necessary network isolation and comprehensive security measures required for such applications.

QUESTION 34

Answer - B) Utilize Amazon Aurora Serverless with multi-AZ deployment for the database layer.

A) Incorrect - While DynamoDB with global tables offers high availability and scalability, it is a NoSQL database and may not support the relational database features required by the application.

B) Correct - Amazon Aurora Serverless with multi-AZ deployment provides a relational database with automatic failover, scalable storage, and the ability to handle complex queries, meeting all the application's requirements.

C) Incorrect - Amazon RDS for MySQL with a single-AZ deployment lacks automatic failover across multiple availability zones, which is crucial for high availability.

D) Incorrect - Amazon S3 and Athena provide scalable storage and querying capabilities but are not suitable for applications requiring relational database features and automatic failover.

E) Incorrect - Amazon DocumentDB offers scalability and multi-region replication but, being a NoSQL database, might not fulfill the relational database requirements of the application.

QUESTION 35

Answer - B) Implement WebSocket APIs on Amazon API Gateway with Amazon DynamoDB for real-time communication

B) Leveraging WebSocket APIs on Amazon API Gateway with Amazon DynamoDB enables real-time communication features like in-game chat and live updates, ensuring high concurrency and low-latency communication required for multiplayer games.

A, C, D, E) These options either do not provide support for real-time communication or involve using services not suitable for handling high concurrency and low-latency requirements.

QUESTION 36

Answer - [A, B]

A) Correct - Redshift with Auto Scaling ensures scalability and cost optimization.
B) Correct - S3 with Intelligent-Tiering optimizes storage costs for the data warehouse.
C) Incorrect - Glue for ETL processes is relevant but not directly related to scalability or cost optimization.
D) Incorrect - CloudWatch monitoring is relevant but not directly related to scalability or cost optimization.
E) Incorrect - Athena for ad-hoc queries doesn't directly relate to data warehouse scalability or cost optimization.

QUESTION 37

Answer - [A, B]

A) Incorrect - While streaming logs from ECS instances to CloudWatch Logs is relevant, X-Ray is used for tracing, not logging, and does not directly address monitoring Lambda functions.

B) Correct - CloudWatch Container Insights collects ECS performance metrics, CloudTrail captures API activity, and S3 provides long-term storage, ensuring comprehensive monitoring and logging for ECS and Lambda.

C) Incorrect - Multi-region logging with CloudTrail and CloudWatch Alarms for ECS CPU utilization are relevant, but this option lacks tracing for Lambda functions and ECS.

D) Incorrect - Integrating X-Ray with ECS and Lambda for tracing is relevant, but CloudWatch Events are primarily for event-driven architectures, not monitoring, and logging.

E) Incorrect - While CloudWatch Logs Insights allows real-time log querying, AWS Config is for configuration changes tracking, not monitoring, and logging, and SNS notifications are not mentioned in the context of this scenario.

QUESTION 38

Answer - A) Utilize Amazon EC2 Auto Scaling to automatically adjust compute capacity based on traffic fluctuations.

B) Implement AWS Lambda for serverless execution of code in response to events, reducing costs for sporadic workloads.

D) Utilize Amazon ECS for containerized microservices, providing scalability and cost optimization through efficient resource allocation.

Option A - Amazon EC2 Auto Scaling is suitable for adjusting compute capacity based on variable traffic patterns, ensuring scalability while optimizing costs.

Option B - AWS Lambda is ideal for handling sporadic workloads with its serverless execution model, reducing costs by only paying for actual usage.

Option D - Amazon ECS offers containerized microservices, allowing efficient resource allocation and optimization, aligning with the requirements of the architecture.

Options C and E may not be the most suitable choices for the given scenario as they may not provide the required level of flexibility or cost optimization.

QUESTION 39

Answer - D) Deploy Amazon Route 53 with AWS Global Accelerator for efficient DNS routing and global application acceleration.

Option A - Implement Amazon CloudFront with AWS Shield for DDoS protection and Amazon Route 53 for DNS routing - This choice lacks the use of AWS Global Accelerator for global application acceleration.

Option B - Utilize Amazon VPC with public and private subnets, employing AWS Direct Connect for dedicated network connections, and AWS VPN for secure hybrid connectivity - While this option addresses security and connectivity, it does not optimize global application performance effectively.

Option C - Configure Amazon CloudFront with AWS WAF for global content delivery and protection against web attacks - This choice focuses on web attack protection but does not optimize global application performance.

Option D - Deploy Amazon Route 53 with AWS Global Accelerator for efficient DNS routing and global application acceleration - This option provides the best solution by leveraging Route 53 with Global Accelerator for efficient DNS routing and global application acceleration, ensuring high availability and low latency.

Option E - Use AWS Transit Gateway for scalable and efficient network connectivity across multiple VPCs - While Transit Gateway offers scalable network connectivity, it does not specifically address global application performance optimization.

QUESTION 40

Answer - C) Ingest tracking data into Amazon Kinesis Data Streams, which triggers an AWS Lambda function for processing and stores notification data in Amazon DynamoDB

C) Ingesting tracking data into Amazon Kinesis Data Streams with AWS Lambda allows for real-time processing and timely delivery of notifications. Storing notification data in Amazon DynamoDB ensures scalability and low-latency access.

A) Processing tracking data with AWS Lambda and Amazon S3 may introduce latency and is not suitable for real-time processing.

B) Using Amazon Kinesis Data Firehose may not provide the necessary real-time processing capabilities for delivering timely notifications.

D) Amazon SQS is not optimized for real-time processing of tracking data, and storing notification data in Amazon Redshift may introduce delays.

E) Using Amazon API Gateway and an EC2 instance for processing lacks the scalability and real-time processing capabilities required for real-time package tracking systems.

QUESTION 41

Answer - A) Configure Amazon CloudFront with AWS Global Accelerator to optimize content delivery and ensure low-latency access globally.

Option A - Amazon CloudFront with AWS Global Accelerator optimizes content delivery by using the AWS global network infrastructure, providing low-latency access to customers worldwide.

Option B - AWS Direct Connect establishes dedicated network connections, but it may not optimize content delivery or provide low-latency access globally.

Option C - AWS Transit Gateway creates a hub for network connectivity but may not directly optimize content delivery or ensure low-latency access.

Option D - AWS PrivateLink provides secure access to AWS services but is not specifically designed for optimizing content delivery or ensuring low-latency access globally.

Option E - Amazon Route 53 with latency-based routing directs traffic based on geographic location but may not optimize content delivery as effectively as Amazon CloudFront with AWS Global Accelerator.

QUESTION 42

Answer - [A] Implement Amazon RDS with read replicas in multiple Availability Zones (AZs).]

Option A) provides a highly available solution by deploying Amazon RDS with read replicas across multiple AZs. This architecture ensures redundancy and improves performance by distributing read traffic.

Option B) does not provide automatic scalability and high availability compared to managed database services like Amazon RDS with multi-AZ deployments.

Option C) While DynamoDB offers scalability, it might not be the best fit for traditional SQL database requirements.

Option D) Amazon Aurora Serverless is ideal for unpredictable workloads, but may not offer the same level of performance as provisioned instances under heavy, predictable loads.

Option E) Amazon ElastiCache is suitable for caching, but may not directly address database performance bottlenecks.

QUESTION 43

Answer - [A] Implement AWS Lake Formation to build a secure data lake and manage data access.]

Option A) AWS Lake Formation is specifically designed for building secure data lakes and managing data access, making it an ideal choice for the e-commerce company's requirements.

Option B) Amazon S3 is indeed a suitable option for cost-effective storage, but it alone does not provide the necessary features for building a data lake.

Option C) AWS Glue is used for data ingestion, which aligns with the requirements for automating the process of loading data into the data lake.

Option D) Amazon Athena is chosen to ensure fast and interactive querying of transaction data, which is crucial for real-time analysis.

Option E) Ensuring data lake security and compliance with AWS policies and practices is essential but does not address the need for building the data lake itself.

QUESTION 44

Answer - [C] Deploy Amazon Managed Streaming for Apache Kafka (Amazon MSK) to handle website event ingestion, process data with Amazon Kinesis Data Analytics, and store results in Amazon Redshift for further analysis.

Option A lacks scalability with DynamoDB and introduces latency with Lambda.
Option B's use of EC2 instances and Redshift may not be cost-efficient or scalable.
Option D's storage in S3 is not ideal for real-time access, and Athena may introduce latency.
Option E's use of Neptune and QuickSight may not be optimized for real-time analytics on high-volume data streams. Amazon MSK offers scalable and durable event streaming with advanced analytics capabilities through Kinesis Data Analytics, while Redshift provides a powerful data warehousing solution for further analysis, making option C the most suitable choice.

QUESTION 45

Answer - C) Use server-side encryption with AWS Key Management Service (SSE-KMS) keys to encrypt the data on Amazon S3

C) Server-side encryption with AWS Key Management Service (SSE-KMS) allows the software development company to maintain full control over the encryption keys and access to audit logs.

A) Server-side encryption with Amazon S3 managed keys (SSE-S3) encrypts the data at rest but does not provide the level of control required by the company.

B) Client-side encryption with customer-provided keys (SSE-C) may not offer the desired control and auditing features for encryption keys.

D) Using server-side encryption with customer-provided keys (SSE-C) also lacks the centralized control and auditing capabilities provided by AWS KMS.

E) Enabling AWS CloudTrail provides auditing capabilities but does not directly address the encryption requirement for data at rest in Amazon S3.

QUESTION 46

Answer - [C] Utilize AWS IoT Greengrass for data ingestion, leverage AWS Lambda for edge processing, employ Amazon Kinesis Data Streams for real-time data processing, store real-time data in Amazon DynamoDB, and archive long-term data in Amazon S3.

Option A is incorrect because although it utilizes AWS IoT Core for data ingestion and AWS Lambda for edge processing, Amazon Kinesis Data Streams and Amazon DynamoDB are better suited for real-time data processing and storage, respectively, than Amazon RDS. Additionally, S3 is more suitable for long-term data archival than Amazon Glacier.

Option B is incorrect because it utilizes Amazon API Gateway, which is not typically used for IoT data ingestion, and AWS Fargate, which is not optimal for edge processing in IoT scenarios. Amazon RDS and Amazon Glacier are also not the best choices for real-time data storage and long-term data archival in IoT solutions.

Option D is incorrect because AWS IoT Events is not commonly used for data ingestion in IoT solutions, and Amazon Aurora is not the ideal database service for real-time data storage in this context. Amazon S3 Glacier is also not well-suited for long-term data archival in IoT scenarios.

Option E is incorrect because although it uses AWS IoT Core and AWS Greengrass, it employs AWS Lambda for serverless processing instead of edge processing, which may introduce latency issues in real-time data processing for IoT applications.

QUESTION 47

Answer - [A] Utilize AWS Wavelength to deploy applications on edge devices located within telecommunication providers' data centers, leverage AWS IoT Greengrass for edge data processing, and integrate with AWS DynamoDB for real-time data storage.

Option A is the correct choice because AWS Wavelength provides low-latency edge computing within telecommunication providers' data centers, ideal for reducing latency for customer-facing services. AWS IoT Greengrass enables edge data processing, and DynamoDB offers real-time data storage, meeting the requirements effectively.

Options B, C, D, and E either lack the same level of latency reduction, suitable edge computing solutions, or appropriate real-time data storage services.

QUESTION 48

Answer - A) Amazon API Gateway for managing APIs, AWS Lambda for serverless data processing, Amazon DynamoDB for storing health records, and Amazon Cognito for authentication.

A) Correct - Amazon API Gateway provides a robust platform for creating, managing, and securing APIs. AWS Lambda enables scalable, serverless computing for real-time data processing. DynamoDB offers a high-performance database solution for storing health records, and Amazon Cognito provides secure user authentication, making this combination ideal for the application's requirements.

B) Incorrect - While ECS, RDS, WAF, and CloudFront are powerful services, they do not offer the same level of serverless scalability or the direct API management capabilities as API Gateway and Lambda for real-time processing.

C) Incorrect - Direct Connect, S3, EC2, and IAM focus on connectivity, storage, compute, and access management but lack the serverless architecture and API management provided by API Gateway and Lambda for dynamic, real-time data processing.

D) Incorrect - Kinesis, EMR, EBS, and CloudWatch offer solutions for data streaming, analysis, storage, and monitoring but do not directly address API management or serverless processing of health data as effectively as the chosen services.

E) Incorrect - Fargate, Redshift, Shield, and Step Functions focus on container management, data warehousing, security, and workflow orchestration, which are not as directly relevant to building scalable and high-performance APIs for real-time health monitoring.

QUESTION 49

Answer - C) Utilize spot instances for the entire duration of operation

C) Utilizing spot instances for the entire duration allows the software development company to benefit from significantly lower costs for short-duration compute jobs, optimizing infrastructure expenses without compromising on turnaround times.

A) Using reserved instances (RI) for the entire duration may result in underutilization of resources for short-duration jobs and could lead to higher costs.

B) Implementing on-demand instances for the entire duration may result in higher costs for short-duration jobs without the benefit of cost savings offered by spot instances.

D) Employing a combination of reserved instances (RI) and spot instances may introduce complexity and may not align with the company's goal of minimizing costs for short-duration jobs.

E) Implementing a mix of reserved instances (RI) and on-demand instances may not provide the same level of cost optimization for short-duration compute jobs as spot instances.

QUESTION 50

Answer - C) Implement Amazon Kinesis Data Analytics to process streaming data in real-time, utilizing SQL queries to perform aggregations and transformations. Configure auto-scaling for Kinesis Data Analytics to dynamically adjust resources based on workload demands, ensuring high performance and cost efficiency.

Option A introduces unnecessary overhead by storing data in S3 before processing, impacting performance.
Option B relies on AWS Lambda, which might not be the most cost-effective solution for large data volumes.
Option D introduces complexity with Apache Kafka, potentially increasing costs and management overhead.
Option C is the best choice as it directly processes data in real-time with Amazon Kinesis Data Analytics, utilizing SQL queries for efficient aggregations and transformations, while also providing auto-scaling capabilities for cost optimization.

QUESTION 51

Answer - A) Utilize Amazon CloudFront with custom SSL certificates for global content delivery, Amazon DynamoDB for high-performance data storage, AWS Lambda for processing transactions, and AWS WAF for application security.

Option A - Correct: Amazon CloudFront provides low-latency access to real-time financial data globally. DynamoDB offers high-performance data storage. AWS Lambda enables serverless transaction processing. AWS WAF ensures application security.

Option B - Incorrect: AWS Global Accelerator and EC2 Auto Scaling provide performance and scalability but may not offer the same level of security and optimization as CloudFront with DynamoDB and Lambda.

Option C - Incorrect: Route 53, API Gateway, RDS, and Cognito offer a robust infrastructure but lack the content delivery optimization provided by CloudFront for global low-latency access.

Option D - Incorrect: Direct Connect, Aurora, AppSync, and GuardDuty focus on connectivity, database scalability, data synchronization, and security but do not address global content delivery and transaction processing as effectively as option A.

Option E - Incorrect: Fargate, DynamoDB, Step Functions, and Macie support container management, data storage, process orchestration, and data protection but fall short in providing a cohesive solution for global web application delivery and security as A does.

QUESTION 52

Answer - B) Deploy a multi-region architecture with AWS Global Accelerator for load balancing and failover, using Amazon Route 53 for DNS resolution.

A) Incorrect - While deploying EC2 instances across multiple AZs is a good practice for high availability, it does not address resilience across Regions or utilize Route 53 for DNS failover.

B) Correct - Utilizing a multi-region architecture with Global Accelerator for load balancing and failover, along with Route 53 for DNS resolution, ensures high availability and resilience across Regions and AZs.

C) Incorrect - Although using EC2 instances with Auto Scaling across multiple Regions can enhance availability, it does not provide the same level of resilience as a multi-region architecture with Global Accelerator.

D) Incorrect - CloudFront with origin failover and Route 53 DNS routing may improve availability, but it does not offer the same level of resilience across Regions as a multi-region architecture.
E) Incorrect - While ECS tasks across AZs provide some level of fault tolerance, it does not ensure resilience across Regions, which is crucial for high availability.

QUESTION 53

Answer - C) Implement Global Accelerator to route traffic to the nearest EC2 instances.

A) A single region can't ensure low latency globally.
B) CloudFront is optimal for static content, not dynamic application traffic.
C) Correct, as Global Accelerator improves global application availability and performance by routing users to the closest endpoint.
D) Multiple regions without traffic management may not effectively reduce latency.
E) Cross-zone load balancing optimizes traffic distribution within a region, not globally.

QUESTION 54

Answer - [B] Deploy Amazon Aurora Serverless for automatic scaling based on workload demand.

Option A - Multi-AZ configuration focuses on high availability, not automated scaling based on workload demand.

Option B - Correct. Amazon Aurora Serverless automatically adjusts capacity, scaling up or down based on workload demand, ensuring cost-effectiveness during low activity periods.

Option C - While DynamoDB offers On-Demand capacity, it may not be suitable for relational database workloads and does not provide automatic scaling.

Option D - Provisioned IOPS enhances performance but does not address automated scaling requirements.

Option E - Redshift is a data warehousing solution and may not be suitable for transactional relational database workloads with variable workloads.

QUESTION 55

Answer - B) Use Amazon DynamoDB global tables for product details and Amazon Aurora for regional pricing.

A) Aurora Global Database is suitable for global consistency but may not offer the best flexibility for regional pricing.

B) Correct, because DynamoDB global tables ensure product information consistency, while Aurora allows for tailored regional pricing.

C) Cross-region replication in Aurora is more suited to disaster recovery than to handling regional pricing models.

D) Separate instances would complicate global consistency for product details.

E) DynamoDB global tables alone would not efficiently manage regional pricing nuances without complex application logic.

QUESTION 56

Answer - [B] Configure lifecycle policies to transition data from Amazon S3 to Amazon S3 Glacier.

Option A - Implementing AWS Backup for Amazon S3 may offer automation but does not address long-term storage cost optimization.

Option B - Correct. Configuring lifecycle policies to transition data from Amazon S3 to Amazon S3 Glacier ensures cost-effective long-term storage while maintaining data accessibility.

Option C - Utilizing AWS DataSync for replication may facilitate data transfer but does not specifically address cost optimization for long-term storage.

Option D - Leveraging AWS Storage Gateway focuses on integration but does not directly address the cost optimization aspect of long-term storage.

Option E - Deploying AWS Snow Family for offline transfer may assist in data migration but is not the most cost-effective solution for long-term archival storage.

QUESTION 57

Answer - [A] Implement Amazon CloudFront with the S3 bucket containing product images set as the origin to cache images at edge locations.

Option A - Correct. Implementing Amazon CloudFront with the S3 bucket containing product images set as the origin allows caching of images at edge locations, reducing data transfer costs and ensuring fast delivery to users worldwide.

Option B - Amazon S3 Transfer Acceleration optimizes data transfer speeds but may not offer the same level of content delivery capabilities as Amazon CloudFront for this scenario.

Option C - Cross-region replication for S3 buckets may replicate objects between regions but does not directly address the requirement for fast delivery to users worldwide.

Option D - While AWS DataSync can synchronize data between S3 buckets, it may not offer the same level of content delivery capabilities as Amazon CloudFront for this scenario.

Option E - AWS Snowball involves physical data transfer and may not be as efficient or cost-effective as using Amazon CloudFront for distributing product images to users worldwide.

QUESTION 58

Answer - [A] Utilize Amazon CloudFront with dynamic content caching to deliver personalized product recommendations.

Option A - Correct. Utilizing Amazon CloudFront with dynamic content caching for personalized product recommendations optimizes costs by efficiently delivering frequently accessed dynamic content during peak traffic periods.

Option B - Configuring Amazon CloudFront with a custom SSL certificate enhances security but does not directly optimize costs associated with content delivery.

Option C - Implementing Amazon CloudFront with origin failover ensures high availability but may not directly optimize costs during peak traffic periods.

Option D - Enabling Amazon CloudFront cache invalidation helps update content changes but does not directly address cost optimization concerns.

Option E - Integrating Amazon CloudFront with AWS Shield enhances DDoS protection but may not directly optimize costs associated with content delivery.

QUESTION 59

Answer - [A] Implement Amazon S3 lifecycle policies to automate tiering and deletions based on object age and access patterns.

Option A - Correct. Implementing Amazon S3 lifecycle policies allows for automated tiering and deletions based on predefined rules, ensuring cost-effective data lifecycle management.

Option B - Utilizing Amazon Glacier for long-term data archival may be suitable but does not address automated lifecycle management or cost optimization.

Option C - Deploying Amazon CloudWatch Events to trigger Lambda functions for manual data lifecycle management introduces complexity and may not be as cost-effective as automated solutions.

Option D - Leveraging AWS Backup for regular backups and data retention policies is relevant but does not specifically address data lifecycle management within Amazon S3.

Option E - Using Amazon S3 Intelligent-Tiering for automatic tiering based on access patterns is relevant but does not address data deletion or comprehensive lifecycle management.

QUESTION 60

Answer - [C] Configure AWS IoT Core to authenticate and authorize IoT devices before allowing communication with AWS services.

A) Incorrect - Opening ports on factory firewalls exposes IoT devices to security risks and does not provide centralized authentication and authorization mechanisms.

B) Incorrect - Implementing IAM policies for IoT devices based on their unique identifiers may not provide robust authentication and authorization mechanisms required for secure communication with AWS services.

C) Correct - Configuring AWS IoT Core to authenticate and authorize IoT devices ensures secure communication with AWS services, with centralized management of device identities and permissions.

D) Incorrect - Sharing AWS account access keys with IoT devices poses security risks and compromises the integrity of access control mechanisms.

E) Incorrect - Utilizing AWS Direct Connect for IoT device communication introduces unnecessary complexity and may not be suitable for securely managing communication with multiple devices across various locations.

QUESTION 61

Answer - [A] Utilize Amazon EC2 Auto Scaling with Amazon CloudWatch alarms to adjust capacity based on traffic patterns.

Option A - Correct. Amazon EC2 Auto Scaling with Amazon CloudWatch alarms allows for automatic adjustment of EC2 instances based on traffic patterns, ensuring the application can scale to handle increased demand while minimizing costs during periods of low activity.

Option B - While Amazon ECS with AWS Fargate can automatically scale containerized workloads, it may not provide the same level of flexibility and cost optimization as EC2 Auto Scaling.

Option C - AWS Lambda with API Gateway is suitable for serverless functions but may not offer the same level of control and optimization for variable traffic patterns as EC2 Auto Scaling.

Option D - AWS AppSync with GraphQL resolvers may handle traffic fluctuations but does not offer the same scalability and cost optimization features as EC2 Auto Scaling.

Option E - While DynamoDB On-Demand capacity mode can automatically scale capacity, it may not provide the same cost optimization benefits as EC2 Auto Scaling for variable traffic patterns.

QUESTION 62

Answer - [B] Use Amazon CloudFront with Lambda@Edge to cache and deliver multimedia content at edge locations.

Option A - Amazon S3 Transfer Acceleration optimizes data transfers but may not provide the same low-latency access as CloudFront with Lambda@Edge for multimedia content delivery.

Option B - Correct. Amazon CloudFront with Lambda@Edge allows for caching and delivering multimedia content at edge locations, ensuring low-latency access and optimizing costs for a global e-commerce platform.

Option C - Amazon EFS may provide fast access from multiple regions but may not offer the same content delivery and caching capabilities as CloudFront with Lambda@Edge.

Option D - Amazon Kinesis Video Streams is suitable for live streaming multimedia content but may not address the requirement for optimizing costs and reducing latency for static product images and videos.

Option E - AWS Direct Connect with AWS Transit Gateway provides private connectivity but may not optimize content delivery and reduce latency for multimedia content as effectively as CloudFront with Lambda@Edge.

QUESTION 63

Answer - [C] Deploy AWS Storage Gateway to cache frequently accessed data locally and reduce data transfer costs.

Option A - AWS Direct Connect provides dedicated connectivity but may not directly address the need for optimizing data transfer costs.

Option B - AWS Snow Family devices are used for offline data transfer and may not be the most cost-effective solution for reducing ongoing data transfer costs.

Option C - Correct. Deploying AWS Storage Gateway allows for caching frequently accessed data locally, reducing the need for data transfers between the on-premises environment and AWS, thus optimizing costs.

Option D - Amazon S3 Transfer Acceleration improves transfer speeds but may not directly reduce data transfer costs in hybrid environments.

Option E - AWS VPN provides secure connectivity but may not offer the same level of cost optimization as AWS Storage Gateway for reducing data transfer costs.

QUESTION 64

Answer - [A] Utilize AWS Auto Scaling with Amazon EC2 Spot Instances to automatically adjust capacity based on demand fluctuations.

Option A - Correct. Utilizing AWS Auto Scaling with Amazon EC2 Spot Instances allows for automatic adjustment of capacity based on demand fluctuations, optimizing costs while ensuring high availability.

Option B - AWS Fargate with Amazon ECS allows for container scaling but may not directly address the cost optimization aspect related to fluctuating traffic.

Option C - AWS Lambda with Amazon API Gateway enables serverless scalability but may not be suitable for all types of workloads, especially those requiring EC2 instances.

Option D - Amazon Aurora Global Database ensures data replication across regions but may not directly address dynamic scaling requirements for application resources.

Option E - Amazon S3 Transfer Acceleration improves transfer speeds but may not directly address the need for dynamic scaling of application resources based on demand.

QUESTION 65

Answer - [A] Implement AWS Cost Explorer with custom reporting to analyze cost trends and anomalies.

Option A - Correct. Implementing AWS Cost Explorer with custom reporting provides comprehensive cost insights and allows for analysis of cost trends and anomalies, enhancing visibility and accountability.

Option B - AWS Budgets helps track cost limits but may not provide the same level of comprehensive cost insights and analysis as AWS Cost Explorer with custom reporting.

Option C - While AWS IAM policies can restrict access to services, they primarily focus on security rather than providing cost insights and accountability.

Option D - AWS Service Catalog helps standardize resource provisioning but may not directly address cost insights and accountability across teams.

Option E - AWS Trusted Advisor identifies cost optimization opportunities but may not offer the same level of detailed cost analysis and reporting as AWS Cost Explorer.

PRACTICE TEST 2 - QUESTIONS ONLY

QUESTION 1

An e-commerce platform is expanding its operations globally and requires a robust AWS infrastructure that ensures secure, resilient, and high-performing architecture. The company is particularly focused on designing IAM policies and roles that adhere to the principle of least privilege access. How should the company structure its IAM policies to effectively manage permissions for its development and operations teams, who need different levels of access to resources like Amazon EC2 instances, Amazon S3 buckets, and AWS Lambda functions?

A) Create a single IAM policy for all users, granting full access to EC2, S3, and Lambda to simplify management.

B) Implement individual IAM policies for each service and assign them to groups corresponding to each team's responsibilities.

C) Grant all users administrative access and rely on AWS CloudTrail logs for auditing and compliance.

D) Use AWS Organizations to create separate accounts for development and operations teams, applying service control policies (SCPs) to manage permissions at the account level.

E) Assign direct permissions to each user based on their job role, avoiding the use of IAM groups or roles.

QUESTION 2

An online gaming company wants to use AWS to launch a new game globally. They need a network architecture that maximizes security and minimizes latency for players around the world. What AWS services and design principles should be emphasized to meet these requirements?

A) Deploy the game's backend on Amazon EC2 instances across multiple Availability Zones and use AWS Shield for DDoS protection.

B) Leverage Amazon CloudFront for content delivery, Amazon Route 53 for traffic management, and Amazon GuardDuty for threat detection.

C) Utilize a single AWS region for centralized management and deploy AWS WAF for web application firewall protection.

D) Implement AWS Direct Connect for dedicated gaming traffic between players' locations and AWS, ignoring other AWS networking services.

E) Focus on Amazon VPC for network isolation, ignoring the benefits of deploying across multiple regions and availability zones.

QUESTION 3

As a healthcare application hosted on AWS faces stringent compliance and security requirements, the company seeks to implement a solution that not only detects threats but also helps in preventing data breaches and ensuring patient data is protected in accordance with HIPAA guidelines. Which AWS services should be integrated to ensure both compliance and security?

A) Amazon Macie for sensitive data discovery and classification, AWS IAM for fine-grained access control, and Amazon GuardDuty for continuous monitoring and malicious activity detection.

B) AWS Config for tracking resource configurations, AWS CloudTrail for logging API calls, and AWS KMS for managing cryptographic keys.

C) AWS WAF to protect against web exploits, AWS Shield for infrastructure protection, and AWS Fargate for running containers securely.

D) Amazon RDS for encrypted database services, AWS Certificate Manager for managing SSL/TLS certificates, and Amazon Inspector for automated security assessments.

E) AWS Systems Manager for application configuration management, Amazon Cognito for user identity and data synchronization, and AWS Lambda for automated security response.

QUESTION 4

Your organization is designing a new microservices architecture on AWS to improve scalability and agility. As part of the design, you need to implement secure network connectivity and content delivery for the microservices. The architecture should ensure that communication between microservices is encrypted, and content delivery is optimized for low latency and high availability. Which solution should you recommend?

A) Deploy microservices in separate Amazon VPCs and establish VPC peering connections for communication. Use AWS CloudFront with custom SSL certificates to deliver content securely and improve latency.

B) Utilize AWS App Mesh to manage communication between microservices and enforce encryption using mutual TLS (mTLS). Implement Amazon CloudFront with AWS Shield Advanced for DDoS protection and Amazon Route 53 for global DNS resolution.

C) Implement AWS PrivateLink to securely access microservices without traversing the public internet. Deploy Amazon CloudFront with AWS WAF to protect against common web attacks and improve content delivery performance.

D) Configure microservices in a single Amazon VPC with separate subnets for each service. Use AWS Direct Connect for dedicated network connectivity and Amazon S3 Transfer Acceleration for fast content delivery.

E) Deploy microservices on Amazon ECS clusters and use AWS Transit Gateway for inter-cluster communication. Utilize AWS Global Accelerator to improve content delivery performance and reduce latency.

QUESTION 5

Your organization has multiple AWS accounts, each representing different departments. You need to ensure that a specific Amazon S3 bucket in the central security account can be accessed by the billing department's AWS Lambda functions to process billing data. However, the Lambda functions should not be able to modify the bucket's existing content. Which IAM policy configuration should you implement to meet this requirement?

A) Allow s3:GetObject, s3:GetObjectVersion for the specified bucket.

B) Allow s3:GetObject, s3:GetObjectVersion, s3:PutObject for the specified bucket.

C) Allow s3:GetObject, s3:GetObjectVersion, s3:PutObject, s3:DeleteObject for the specified bucket.

D) Allow s3:GetObject, s3:GetObjectVersion, s3:ListBucket for the specified bucket.

E) Allow s3:GetObject, s3:GetObjectVersion, s3:ListBucket, except s3:PutObject, s3:DeleteObject for the specified bucket.

QUESTION 6

Your company is migrating its legacy monolithic application to a serverless architecture on AWS. Security is a top priority, and you need to ensure that sensitive data is protected both in transit and at rest. Which combination of services should you use to achieve this goal?

A) Utilize AWS Lambda for compute, Amazon API Gateway for API management, and Amazon RDS for database storage. Enable encryption at rest for RDS using AWS Key Management Service (KMS) and implement TLS encryption for API Gateway.

B) Implement AWS Fargate for compute, Amazon Aurora for database storage, and AWS Elastic Load Balancing for load distribution. Enable encryption at rest for Aurora using AWS KMS and use AWS Certificate Manager (ACM) for TLS encryption with Fargate.

C) Deploy AWS Lambda for compute, Amazon DynamoDB for database storage, and Amazon API Gateway for API management. Enable encryption at rest for DynamoDB using AWS KMS and configure API Gateway to use TLS encryption.

D) Utilize AWS Elastic Beanstalk for compute, Amazon S3 for object storage, and Amazon CloudFront for content delivery. Enable encryption at rest for S3 using AWS KMS and use CloudFront with ACM for TLS encryption.

E) Implement Amazon ECS for compute, Amazon Redshift for data warehousing, and Amazon VPC for network isolation. Enable encryption at rest for Redshift using AWS KMS and implement VPN connections for secure data transfer.

QUESTION 7

An e-commerce company is expanding its operations globally and needs to ensure that its customer data is encrypted across all regions while minimizing latency in key retrieval for decryption operations. The solution architect needs to design a multi-region key management solution that optimizes for performance and security. Which of the following approaches should the architect consider?

A) Use a single AWS KMS CMK in the primary region and replicate the encrypted data to other regions.

B) Deploy AWS KMS CMKs in each region where data is stored and use AWS Global Accelerator to reduce latency.

C) Implement AWS CloudHSM in each region and manually synchronize keys across regions.

D) Utilize Amazon S3 Cross-Region Replication with default S3 encryption in each target region.

E) Store keys in Amazon DynamoDB global tables and encrypt data client-side before storing in any region.

QUESTION 8

You are designing a secure architecture for a financial services company that requires comprehensive security monitoring and compliance. The architecture includes multiple AWS services such as Amazon EC2, Amazon S3, and AWS Lambda. Which approach should you take to implement effective security monitoring and compliance?

A) Integrate AWS CloudWatch Logs with AWS CloudTrail for centralized log analysis. Configure AWS Config rules to assess resource compliance.

B) Implement Amazon GuardDuty to detect and respond to security threats automatically. Configure Amazon Macie to classify and protect sensitive data stored in Amazon S3.

C) Set up AWS Security Hub to aggregate security findings from multiple AWS services. Implement AWS Config rules to monitor resource configuration changes.

D) Utilize AWS CloudTrail for logging API activity and AWS Config for tracking resource changes. Configure AWS Trusted Advisor to provide real-time recommendations for security best practices.

E) Configure AWS Config to track resource inventory and changes. Implement AWS Artifact to access compliance reports and agreements.

QUESTION 9

Your organization is developing a microservices-based application that requires secure communication between services. Each microservice needs to authenticate and authorize requests from other services. Additionally, the application must comply with industry regulations for data privacy and security. Which of the following options provides the most suitable solution for implementing secure API strategies while ensuring compliance?

A) Utilizing AWS IAM roles and policies for service-to-service authentication, ensuring adherence to industry regulations

B) Configuring AWS Lambda authorizers in Amazon API Gateway for request validation and authorization, ensuring secure communication between microservices

C) Implementing OAuth 2.0 authentication with Amazon Cognito for API access control, ensuring compliance with industry standards

D) Deploying AWS Certificate Manager (ACM) for SSL/TLS encryption of API endpoints, ensuring data privacy and security

E) Enabling AWS AppMesh for managing communication between microservices, ensuring compliance with industry regulations for data privacy

QUESTION 10

A healthcare provider is migrating its medical records system to AWS and requires a solution that ensures patient records are processed accurately and efficiently while also providing the ability to handle high volumes of record updates during peak hours. Which option should the company choose to implement this requirement?

A) Use Amazon SQS FIFO queue with a batch mode of 5 messages per operation.
B) Use Amazon SQS FIFO queue with exactly-once processing enabled.
C) Use Amazon SQS FIFO queue with default settings to process the messages.
D) Use Amazon SQS standard queue to process the messages.
E) Use Amazon SQS FIFO queue with message deduplication enabled.

QUESTION 11

A finance corporation with stringent regulatory compliance requirements needs to safeguard its customer data transactions over its network. They seek an AWS solution that offers stateful and stateless packet inspection, web request filtering, and the ability to integrate with their existing Virtual Private Cloud (VPC) setup for granular control over inbound and outbound traffic.

A) AWS WAF, AWS Shield Advanced, and AWS Network Firewall
B) Amazon CloudFront, Amazon S3, and AWS Lambda
C) AWS Global Accelerator, Amazon GuardDuty, and AWS IAM
D) Amazon VPC, Amazon CloudWatch, and Amazon Inspector
E) AWS Direct Connect, AWS Fargate, and AWS Step Functions

QUESTION 12

In preparation for a global product launch, a software company requires a robust solution to manage access to their AWS-hosted environments for hundreds of temporary marketing consultants worldwide. The solution must enable quick onboarding and offboarding of consultant access to specific AWS resources, based on the project they are assigned to, and must integrate with the company's existing identity provider (IdP) to leverage existing user credentials.

A) Deploy AWS IAM users and groups for each consultant, manually managing permissions.
B) Use AWS Directory Service with AWS IAM roles for external identity provider access.

C) Implement AWS IAM Identity Center (SSO) integrated with the existing IdP for dynamic access management.

D) Configure Amazon Cognito user pools to manage consultant identities and access permissions.
E) Establish AWS Resource Access Manager with shared VPCs for controlled environment access.

QUESTION 13

A financial services company wants to securely expose their payment API to third-party developers. They require a secure, scalable solution using Amazon API Gateway. What should the Solutions Architect recommend to ensure authentication and authorization, rate limiting, and protection against common web exploits?

A) Use Amazon Cognito for authentication, AWS IAM for authorization, apply API Gateway throttling, and integrate AWS WAF.

B) Implement Lambda authorizers for authentication, Amazon Cognito for authorization, use API Gateway's default rate limiting, and rely on API Gateway's native DDoS protection.

C) Utilize Amazon Cognito for both authentication and authorization, set custom rate limits in API Gateway, and enable AWS Shield Advanced.

D) Employ API Gateway resource policies for authentication, use AWS IAM roles for authorization, configure API Gateway custom throttling, and attach AWS WAF to the API Gateway.

E) Implement AWS IAM for both authentication and authorization, use Amazon CloudFront in front of API Gateway for rate limiting, and deploy Amazon Inspector for attack detection.

QUESTION 14

An international bank using AWS needs to ensure continuous compliance with GDPR across its cloud infrastructure. They require a solution to automatically assess and enforce GDPR compliance standards, including data protection and privacy controls.

A) Implement AWS CloudFormation for infrastructure as code, ensuring GDPR compliance in template configurations.

B) Use AWS Config rules to automatically assess compliance with GDPR standards and AWS Lambda for enforcement actions.

C) Deploy Amazon QuickSight for GDPR compliance reporting based on AWS CloudTrail logs.

D) Configure AWS WAF and AWS Shield for protecting web applications and data from breaches, aligned with GDPR requirements.

E) Leverage AWS Security Hub custom insights for GDPR compliance, integrating AWS IAM Access Analyzer for analyzing permission levels and risk.

QUESTION 15

A software development firm is working on a large-scale IoT project that generates terabytes of sensor data daily. This data needs to be uploaded to Amazon S3 for analysis and future machine learning projects. Given the volume of data and the need for timely analysis, which AWS service combination offers the best performance and cost efficiency for uploading and processing this data?

A) Leverage AWS Direct Connect and Amazon S3 multipart uploads for fast, secure data transfer.
B) Utilize Amazon Kinesis Data Firehose for real-time data streaming into Amazon S3.
C) Use Amazon S3 Transfer Acceleration for quick uploads and AWS Lambda for data processing.
D) Implement AWS Snowball Edge for bulk data transfer, followed by Amazon S3 for storage.
E) Opt for AWS DataSync to automate and accelerate data transfer to Amazon S3.

QUESTION 16

A company is designing a new application that will be hosted on AWS. The application requires access to multiple AWS services, including Amazon S3 for storage, Amazon DynamoDB for databases, and AWS Lambda for serverless computing. The security team wants to ensure that the principle of least privilege is applied. What should the Solutions Architect recommend?

A) Create an IAM user for the application with full access permissions.

B) Use IAM roles with specific policies for S3, DynamoDB, and Lambda that grant only the necessary permissions.

C) Utilize AWS Organizations to manage policies at the account level.
D) Enable IAM Access Analyzer across all services to automatically apply the necessary permissions.
E) Apply a single blanket IAM policy directly to the application's EC2 instances for simplicity.

QUESTION 17

A multinational enterprise is deploying a new application across multiple AWS regions and requires a highly available, secure network architecture that minimizes inter-region latency. The application must access a centralized database securely with minimal latency and without traversing the public internet.

A) Use inter-region VPC peering for connectivity and Amazon RDS with read replicas in each region.

B) Implement AWS Transit Gateway for inter-region connectivity and host the database in Amazon Aurora Global Database.

C) Configure AWS Direct Connect between regions and use Amazon DynamoDB with global tables.
D) Establish AWS VPN CloudHub for networking and Amazon Neptune for the database.

E) Leverage AWS Global Accelerator for performance and Amazon DocumentDB with cross-region replication.

QUESTION 18

A multinational e-commerce company is experiencing high costs associated with its AWS usage due to inefficient resource utilization and lack of optimized architectures. The company wants to implement automated cost management strategies while ensuring security best practices.

A) Utilize AWS Budgets to set cost thresholds and alerts for different departments within the organization. Implement AWS Cost Explorer to analyze usage patterns and identify cost-saving opportunities.

B) Deploy AWS Trusted Advisor to analyze AWS usage and recommend cost optimization opportunities. Set up AWS Config Rules to enforce tagging policies for cost allocation and tracking.

C) Implement AWS Lambda functions triggered by CloudWatch Events to automatically shut down idle resources outside of business hours. Utilize AWS Cost and Usage Report for detailed billing analysis and optimization insights.

D) Utilize AWS Savings Plans to reduce costs for long-term commitments. Set up AWS CloudFormation templates for infrastructure as code to ensure consistency and cost-effective resource provisioning.

E) Deploy AWS Auto Scaling to dynamically adjust resource capacity based on demand. Utilize AWS Compute Optimizer to recommend instance types for cost and performance optimization.

QUESTION 19

A multinational e-commerce company is developing a serverless application on AWS Lambda to process customer orders. They need to securely manage API keys and other sensitive information while ensuring compliance with industry regulations. Which of the following strategies would best meet the company's requirements?

A) Store API keys directly in environment variables within Lambda functions. Implement strict IAM policies to control access to Lambda functions.

B) Utilize AWS Secrets Manager to securely store API keys and sensitive information. Integrate AWS Lambda with Secrets Manager for automated retrieval of secrets at runtime.

C) Maintain a plaintext configuration file within the application codebase stored in an encrypted Amazon S3 bucket. Use IAM roles to restrict access to the S3 bucket.

D) Implement AWS Systems Manager Parameter Store to centrally manage API keys and configurations. Develop custom Lambda functions to retrieve configuration settings from Parameter Store.

E) Store sensitive information in plaintext files within an Amazon EFS file system. Implement IAM policies to control access to the EFS file system.

QUESTION 20

A retail company is encountering challenges in managing maintenance tasks on specific Amazon EC2 instances within an Auto Scaling group. Each time maintenance patches are applied, the instances briefly show as out of service, leading to Auto Scaling provisioning replacements. What strategies would you recommend as a solutions architect to efficiently handle this issue?

A) Suspend the Terminate process type for the Auto Scaling group and apply the maintenance patch to the instance. Once the instance is ready, manually set the instance's health status back to healthy and activate the Terminate process type again.

B) Suspend the ReplaceUnhealthy process type for the Auto Scaling group and apply the maintenance patch to the instance. Once the instance is ready, manually set the instance's health status back to healthy and activate the ReplaceUnhealthy process type again.

C) Put the instance into the Detached state and then update the instance by applying the maintenance patch. Once the instance is ready, exit the Detached state and then return the instance to service.

D) Temporarily suspend the AddToLoadBalancer process type for the Auto Scaling group and apply the maintenance patch to the instance. Once the instance is ready, manually set the instance's health status back to healthy and activate the AddToLoadBalancer process type again.

E) Take a snapshot of the instance, create a new Amazon Machine Image (AMI), and then launch a new instance using this AMI. Apply the maintenance patch to this new instance and then add it back to the Auto Scaling Group by using the manual scaling policy. Terminate the earlier instance that had the maintenance issue.

QUESTION 21

A global e-commerce platform is redesigning its product recommendation system to provide personalized recommendations to users based on their browsing history and previous purchases. The architecture needs to support real-time data processing and scale dynamically based on traffic fluctuations.

A) Utilize Amazon Kinesis Data Streams for ingesting real-time user data, AWS Lambda for processing events, Amazon DynamoDB for storing user profiles, and Amazon ElastiCache for caching frequently accessed data.

B) Deploy Amazon SQS to decouple components, Amazon SNS for event notification, AWS Step Functions for orchestrating workflows, Amazon Aurora for storing user data, and Amazon CloudFront for content delivery.

C) Implement Amazon EventBridge for event-driven architecture, Amazon EMR for processing large datasets, Amazon Neptune for graph database storage, and Amazon RDS for relational database management.

D) Configure Amazon S3 for data storage, AWS Glue for data transformation, AWS AppSync for real-time GraphQL APIs, and Amazon RDS for managing user metadata.

E) Leverage Amazon ECS for containerized microservices, Amazon S3 for storing recommendation models, Amazon API Gateway for managing APIs, and Amazon ElastiCache for session management.

QUESTION 22

You are tasked with designing a highly resilient architecture for a new e-commerce platform. The platform is expected to experience variable traffic throughout the day, with occasional spikes during flash sales. The architecture needs to ensure high availability, scalability, and cost efficiency. What solution would best meet these requirements?

A) Utilize AWS Lambda for handling occasional spikes in traffic.
B) Deploy the application on Amazon EC2 instances with Auto Scaling to handle variable traffic.
C) Implement AWS Fargate for serverless container deployments to ensure scalability.
D) Leverage Amazon EKS for container orchestration to manage variable workloads.
E) Use AWS Step Functions to automate workflows and ensure efficient resource utilization.

QUESTION 23

A retail company is experiencing unexpectedly high costs for its e-commerce website hosted on AWS and wants to identify the underlying reasons to optimize expenses. The company needs to ensure cost efficiency while maintaining high performance and scalability. Which AWS service should the company investigate to analyze cost drivers and optimize expenses while meeting business requirements?

A) Utilize Amazon CloudWatch with AWS Cost Explorer for monitoring and analyzing resource utilization to identify cost drivers and optimize expenses while ensuring high performance

B) Implement AWS Trusted Advisor for cost optimization recommendations and AWS Budgets for cost tracking to identify areas of overspending and improve cost efficiency while maintaining scalability

C) Deploy AWS X-Ray for tracing and debugging application performance issues with a focus on reducing resource consumption and improving efficiency while minimizing costs

D) Utilize Amazon Inspector for security assessments and AWS Service Catalog for resource provisioning to enhance data security and compliance with regulatory requirements while optimizing expenses

E) Implement AWS Artifact for regulatory compliance and AWS Config for configuration management to ensure adherence to industry regulations and optimize expenses while meeting business requirements

QUESTION 24

Your organization is planning to migrate its on-premises data warehouse to the cloud to improve scalability and reduce operational overhead. The data warehouse must handle large volumes of structured and unstructured data, support complex queries, and provide high availability. Which AWS services should you include in this cloud-based data warehouse solution?

A) Amazon Redshift for petabyte-scale data warehousing
B) Amazon S3 for scalable and durable object storage
C) Amazon Athena for serverless querying of S3 data
D) Amazon Aurora for high-performance relational database
E) AWS Glue for data catalog and ETL processing

QUESTION 25

A media streaming company has observed a sudden increase in unauthorized AWS API queries during non-operational hours, with no discernible impact on system performance. The management requires an automated solution to promptly alert relevant teams during such occurrences. Which approach would be most effective in this scenario?

A) Create an Amazon CloudWatch metric filter to process AWS CloudTrail logs containing API call details. Establish an alarm based on this metric's rate to send an Amazon SNS notification to the required team.

B) Implement AWS Config Rules to monitor API activity and define rules to detect unauthorized API calls. Configure AWS Config to trigger an AWS Lambda function upon rule evaluation to notify relevant stakeholders.

C) Leverage AWS Trusted Advisor to publish metrics about check results to Amazon CloudWatch. Set up an alarm to track status changes for checks in the Service Limits category for the APIs, triggering notifications when service quotas are exceeded.

D) Use Amazon Athena SQL queries against AWS CloudTrail log files stored in Amazon S3 buckets. Generate reports using Amazon QuickSight for managerial dashboards.

E) Configure AWS CloudTrail to stream event data to Amazon Kinesis. Utilize Amazon Kinesis stream-level metrics in Amazon CloudWatch to trigger an AWS Lambda function that will initiate an error workflow.

QUESTION 26

A software company is designing a microservices architecture on AWS for its new application. The company requires a solution to manage and secure APIs effectively while also ensuring scalability and resilience. Which option would best fulfill these requirements?

A) Implement Amazon API Gateway with IAM authentication to manage and secure APIs, and leverage AWS Lambda for serverless execution of microservices.

B) Deploy Amazon MQ to enable message queuing and ensure reliable communication between microservices while maintaining security through encryption.

C) Utilize Amazon EventBridge to build event-driven architectures and enable seamless communication between microservices via events, ensuring scalability and resilience.

D) Configure AWS AppMesh to provide service mesh capabilities for microservices, allowing fine-grained control over traffic routing and policy enforcement.

E) Set up Amazon EKS Anywhere to deploy microservices in on-premises environments, ensuring data residency compliance and security.

QUESTION 27

A financial institution is designing a serverless workflow for processing loan applications. The workflow must incorporate error handling and retry mechanisms to ensure the reliability of the application processing. Which of the following options provides the most suitable approach for implementing error handling and retries in the workflow?

A) Implement AWS Step Functions with built-in retry and error handling features
B) Utilize Amazon S3 event notifications to trigger Lambda functions for error processing

C) Deploy Amazon SQS for queuing loan application data and use Lambda to process messages asynchronously

D) Leverage Amazon Kinesis Data Streams for real-time processing of loan applications and use Lambda to handle errors

QUESTION 28

A health tech startup wants to design a serverless application that allows for real-time patient monitoring and analysis. The system must be highly available, scale automatically to handle variable loads, and ensure patient data is managed securely and compliantly. What architecture should the startup implement?

A) Use Amazon Kinesis Data Streams for real-time data ingestion, AWS Lambda for data processing, Amazon DynamoDB for data storage, and secure data with AWS KMS.

B) Deploy AWS Fargate for data ingestion, Amazon RDS for data storage, leverage Amazon EC2 for data processing, and manage security with Amazon GuardDuty.

C) Implement Amazon MQ for data ingestion, use AWS Batch for processing, store data in Amazon RDS, and secure with AWS IAM policies.

D) Utilize Amazon SQS for data ingestion, AWS Lambda for data processing, Amazon S3 for data storage, and encrypt data using Amazon Cognito.

E) Use AWS AppSync for real-time data management, AWS Lambda for data processing, Amazon DynamoDB for data storage, and AWS IAM for access control and security.

QUESTION 29

A healthcare provider is building a telemedicine platform that requires low-latency and highly available communication between patients and healthcare professionals globally. Which combination of AWS services would best meet the provider's requirements?

A) Utilize Amazon Route 53 with Geolocation routing policy for directing traffic based on patient locations

B) Deploy Amazon Elastic Load Balancing (ELB) with Network Load Balancer (NLB) for efficient network routing

C) Implement Amazon CloudFront with Lambda@Edge for real-time content delivery optimization
D) Configure an Amazon Global Accelerator with accelerator endpoints for global application availability
E) Set up Amazon AppStream 2.0 for secure application streaming

QUESTION 30

A regional sports league is live-streaming matches to fans in specific cities within a country. They need to ensure that only fans from those cities can access the live streams. How can they effectively enforce this restriction?

A) Use Amazon Route 53 based geolocation routing policy to restrict access to fans located in the designated cities

B) Implement Amazon Route 53 based weighted routing policy to distribute traffic evenly across the designated cities

C) Utilize Amazon Route 53 based latency-based routing policy to direct fans to the nearest regional streaming server for improved performance

D) Employ Amazon Route 53 based failover routing policy to redirect traffic to alternative servers in case of server failures

E) Apply Amazon Route 53 based geoproximity routing policy to direct traffic based on the proximity of fans to regional streaming servers

QUESTION 31

An online retail company is looking to leverage their sales data to gain insights into customer behavior and preferences. They require a solution that allows for real-time analytics and the ability to scale during peak shopping periods. What AWS services and features should they implement to meet these requirements?

A) Implement Amazon Kinesis for real-time data streaming, Amazon S3 for data storage, AWS Glue for ETL operations, and Amazon Athena for querying data.

B) Use Amazon DynamoDB for NoSQL data storage, AWS Lambda for serverless computing, Amazon QuickSight for analytics, and AWS Elastic Beanstalk for application deployment.

C) Deploy Amazon Redshift for data warehousing, Amazon Redshift Spectrum for querying exabytes of data across S3, AWS Data Pipeline for data movement, and Amazon QuickSight for visualization.

D) Utilize AWS Fargate for running containerized microservices, Amazon RDS for relational data storage, Amazon CloudWatch for monitoring, and AWS Step Functions for orchestrating microservices workflows.

E) Choose Amazon EC2 for compute resources, Amazon EBS for block storage, Amazon EMR for big data processing, and Amazon Kinesis Data Analytics for real-time analytics.

QUESTION 32

A healthcare provider needs to design a resilient architecture for its patient records database. The architecture must support disaster recovery across multiple AWS Regions while maintaining low recovery point objectives (RPOs) and recovery time objectives (RTOs). Which combination of AWS services and features should the provider use to meet these requirements?

A) Implement Amazon RDS with cross-Region read replicas and use AWS Backup for automated backups and cross-Region replication of backups.

B) Utilize Amazon Aurora with global databases for multi-master replication and fast failover, coupled with Amazon S3 cross-Region replication for backups.

C) Deploy Amazon DynamoDB with global tables for multi-Region replication and use AWS Direct Connect for low-latency connectivity between Regions.

D) Migrate to Amazon Redshift for analytics and scalability and configure cross-Region snapshots for disaster recovery with Amazon S3 replication.

E) Implement Amazon DocumentDB with point-in-time recovery enabled and utilize AWS Snowball for cross-Region data transfer and offline backup.

QUESTION 33

A company is designing a highly available and fault-tolerant architecture for its web application hosted on AWS. They need to ensure optimal network performance and security for their application. Which option provides the most appropriate solution for implementing advanced networking architectures in this scenario?

A) Configure an Amazon VPC with public and private subnets, use network ACLs for stateless filtering, and implement security groups for stateful filtering

B) Utilize AWS Direct Connect to establish a dedicated network connection between the company's data center and AWS, ensuring consistent network performance and enhanced security

C) Implement AWS Transit Gateway to simplify network connectivity between multiple VPCs and on-premises networks, enabling centralized network management and routing

D) Deploy Amazon Route 53 with latency-based routing policies to route traffic to the nearest AWS region, optimizing latency and improving application performance

E) Leverage AWS Global Accelerator to improve the availability and performance of the application by directing user traffic to the closest AWS edge location

QUESTION 34

An e-commerce platform is experiencing unpredictable spikes in traffic, leading to potential service degradation. They want to ensure their web application remains highly available and performs consistently under varying loads. Which configuration should be implemented to meet this objective?

A) Use Amazon EC2 instances with Amazon CloudWatch for monitoring and manual scaling.
B) Implement Elastic Load Balancing with Amazon EC2 Auto Scaling and Amazon CloudWatch.
C) Deploy the application on AWS Elastic Beanstalk with AWS Lambda for traffic handling.

D) Utilize Amazon S3 for static web hosting and Amazon CloudFront for global content delivery.
E) Configure Amazon API Gateway for traffic management and AWS Fargate for container management.

QUESTION 35

A financial services company is developing a mobile banking application and needs to expose APIs for account management, transaction history, and fund transfers. They require a solution that ensures security, compliance, and high availability. Which configuration should they implement using Amazon API Gateway to meet these requirements effectively?

A) Utilize RESTful APIs on Amazon API Gateway with AWS Lambda authorizers for authentication and authorization

B) Implement WebSocket APIs on Amazon API Gateway with API Gateway API keys for secure access

C) Create HTTP APIs on Amazon API Gateway and integrate with AWS IAM for user authentication and access control

D) Deploy GraphQL APIs on Amazon API Gateway with Amazon Cognito for user authentication and authorization

E) Configure RESTful APIs on Amazon API Gateway with Amazon API Gateway resource policies for access control and compliance

QUESTION 36

Your company operates a real-time analytics platform on AWS that processes a large volume of streaming data from various sources. You need to ensure the platform can handle varying loads while maintaining high performance and reliability. Which combination of AWS services and strategies should you implement to achieve these objectives effectively? Select THREE.

A) Utilize Amazon Kinesis Data Streams for ingesting and processing real-time data streams.
B) Implement Amazon DynamoDB Accelerator (DAX) for caching frequently accessed data for low-latency responses.
C) Configure AWS Lambda functions triggered by Kinesis events for real-time data processing.
D) Utilize Amazon EMR with Apache Spark for batch processing of historical data.
E) Set up Amazon CloudWatch alarms to monitor Kinesis stream metrics and trigger scaling actions.

QUESTION 37

Your organization is experiencing intermittent performance issues with its AWS-hosted applications, resulting in increased latency and occasional service disruptions. As the solutions architect, you need to design a troubleshooting strategy that enables quick identification and resolution of performance bottlenecks. How would you approach the implementation of a monitoring and troubleshooting solution to address the performance issues effectively? Select TWO.

A) Deploy AWS CloudTrail to capture API calls and integrate with AWS Lambda to trigger notifications for significant events. Configure Amazon CloudWatch Metrics to monitor application-level performance metrics.

B) Utilize AWS X-Ray to trace requests across application components and identify performance bottlenecks. Implement Amazon CloudWatch Alarms to alert on predefined thresholds for key metrics such as CPU utilization and latency.

C) Set up Amazon CloudWatch Logs agent on EC2 instances to collect log data and create metric filters to monitor specific patterns indicative of performance issues. Leverage AWS Config to track resource configurations for potential misconfigurations impacting performance.

D) Implement Amazon CloudWatch Container Insights to collect and analyze performance metrics from ECS clusters. Utilize AWS Trusted Advisor to review recommendations for optimizing application performance and cost.

E) Configure AWS CloudFormation templates to automatically provision resources with monitoring enabled, including CloudWatch Metrics and Alarms. Integrate AWS X-Ray with Lambda for tracing and use CloudWatch Logs Insights for real-time log analysis.

QUESTION 38

Your company is developing a new e-commerce platform that expects a surge in traffic during sales events. You need to design a solution that automatically adjusts resources based on demand to ensure a smooth shopping experience while minimizing costs. Which AWS services would you incorporate into your architecture to achieve this? Select THREE.

A) Implement Amazon CloudFront to cache content at edge locations and reduce latency during traffic spikes.

B) Leverage Amazon EC2 Auto Scaling to adjust compute capacity dynamically based on traffic patterns.

C) Utilize Amazon SQS to decouple components of the architecture and handle traffic surges efficiently.

D) Deploy AWS Lambda for serverless execution of code in response to events, reducing costs during low-traffic periods.

E) Utilize AWS Auto Scaling to automatically adjust resources across various AWS services based on configurable policies.

QUESTION 39

A multinational corporation wants to optimize its network architecture for high throughput and low latency to support its globally distributed users. Which solution would be most suitable for this scenario?

A) Utilize Amazon CloudFront with AWS Shield for DDoS protection and Amazon Route 53 for DNS routing.

B) Deploy Amazon Route 53 with AWS Global Accelerator for efficient DNS routing and global application acceleration.

C) Implement Amazon VPC with public and private subnets, employing AWS Direct Connect for dedicated network connections, and AWS VPN for secure hybrid connectivity.

D) Leverage multi-AZ configuration of Amazon RDS for Oracle that allows the Database Administrator (DBA) to access and customize the database environment and the underlying operating system.

E) Use AWS Transit Gateway for scalable and efficient network connectivity across multiple VPCs.

QUESTION 40

A social media platform intends to develop a real-time sentiment analysis system to analyze user posts and comments. They require a solution that can process streaming data rapidly and analyze sentiment without delays or manual intervention. Which configuration should they implement using AWS serverless components to meet these requirements effectively?

A) Utilize AWS Lambda with Amazon S3 for processing streaming data and Amazon RDS for storing sentiment analysis results

B) Implement Amazon Kinesis Data Firehose with AWS Lambda for processing streaming data and Amazon ElastiCache for storing sentiment analysis results

C) Ingest streaming data into Amazon Kinesis Data Streams, which triggers an AWS Lambda function for processing and stores sentiment analysis results in Amazon DynamoDB

D) Ingest streaming data into Amazon SQS, which triggers an AWS Lambda function for processing and stores sentiment analysis results in Amazon Redshift

E) Use Amazon API Gateway to ingest streaming data, which is processed by an application running on an Amazon EC2 instance, and store sentiment analysis results in Amazon Elasticsearch Service

QUESTION 41

A financial services company operates multiple data centers in different regions and wants to ensure disaster recovery and data sovereignty compliance. They need a solution that replicates their data across regions while minimizing network latency. Which AWS service should the company use to meet these requirements?

A) Configure Amazon S3 Cross-Region Replication to replicate data across regions with minimal network latency.

B) Implement AWS Direct Connect to establish dedicated connections between data centers for low-latency replication.

C) Utilize Amazon Route 53 with latency-based routing to direct traffic to the nearest data center for disaster recovery.

D) Deploy AWS Global Accelerator to improve the availability and performance of applications by using the AWS global network.

E) Implement AWS Snowball to transfer large volumes of data securely between data centers.

QUESTION 42

Your company operates a data-intensive application where frequent database reads are necessary for real-time analytics. However, the current database infrastructure struggles to keep up with the increasing read requests, impacting application performance. Which solution should you recommend to optimize database performance?

A) Implement Amazon Aurora Serverless for on-demand scalability.
B) Configure Amazon RDS with Multi-AZ deployment for high availability.
C) Leverage Amazon DynamoDB Accelerator (DAX) for caching frequently accessed data.

D) Deploy Amazon Neptune for graph database capabilities.

E) Utilize Amazon Redshift for data warehousing and analytics.

QUESTION 43

Your company is planning to migrate its on-premises data warehouse to AWS to improve performance and scalability. As part of the migration, you need to design a high-performance data lake architecture that can handle large volumes of data from multiple sources. What solution should you recommend to achieve this?

A) Utilize Amazon Redshift for the data warehouse and AWS Lake Formation to build a secure data lake for storing and analyzing data from various sources.

B) Implement Amazon Aurora Serverless for the data warehouse and Amazon S3 for cost-effective storage of data lake content.

C) Design a hybrid architecture with Amazon RDS for the data warehouse and Amazon Kinesis for real-time data ingestion into the data lake.

D) Deploy Amazon DynamoDB for the data warehouse and Amazon S3 Glacier for long-term archival storage of data lake content.

E) Leverage Amazon Neptune for the data warehouse and Amazon S3 for real-time storage and analysis of data lake content.

QUESTION 44

Your company operates a fleet of IoT devices generating telemetry data continuously. They require a real-time analytics solution to monitor device health and trigger alerts for anomalies. Which architecture would best suit this requirement?

A) Use AWS IoT Core to ingest device data, process it with AWS Glue for transformation, and store results in Amazon Redshift for analysis and alerting.

B) Deploy Amazon Kinesis Data Streams to ingest telemetry data, process it using AWS Lambda functions, and store results in Amazon RDS for real-time access.

C) Utilize Amazon Managed Streaming for Apache Kafka (Amazon MSK) for device data ingestion, process it with Amazon Kinesis Data Analytics, and trigger alerts using Amazon CloudWatch.

D) Implement AWS AppSync to connect IoT devices to Amazon Neptune graph database, analyze data in real-time, and trigger alerts with Amazon SNS.

E) Set up Amazon Kinesis Data Firehose to capture telemetry data, process it using Amazon EMR, and store results in Amazon S3 for further analysis and alerting.

QUESTION 45

A healthcare organization needs to securely store patient medical records in Amazon S3 while ensuring compliance with HIPAA regulations. The organization wants to use encryption keys that are managed by AWS and provide additional control and auditing capabilities. Which option would be the most suitable choice for this scenario?

A) Implement client-side encryption with customer-provided keys (SSE-C) and upload the encrypted data to Amazon S3

B) Use server-side encryption with AWS Key Management Service (SSE-KMS) keys to encrypt the data on Amazon S3

C) Utilize server-side encryption with Amazon S3 managed keys (SSE-S3) to encrypt the data on Amazon S3

D) Use server-side encryption with customer-provided keys (SSE-C) to encrypt the data on Amazon S3

E) Enable AWS CloudTrail to monitor S3 bucket activities for auditing purposes

QUESTION 46

You are designing an IoT solution for a smart city project that aims to collect real-time data from various sensors deployed across the city for traffic management, environmental monitoring, and public safety. The solution must be scalable, resilient, and capable of handling large volumes of data with minimal latency. Which architecture would you recommend to achieve these objectives?

A) Deploy Amazon API Gateway for data ingestion, utilize AWS Fargate for edge processing, configure Amazon Kinesis Data Analytics for real-time data analysis, connect with Amazon RDS for real-time data storage, and employ Amazon Glacier for long-term data archival.

B) Utilize AWS IoT Greengrass for data ingestion, leverage AWS Lambda for edge processing, employ Amazon Kinesis Data Streams for real-time data processing, store real-time data in Amazon DynamoDB, and archive long-term data in Amazon S3.

C) Implement AWS IoT Events for data ingestion, set up AWS Lambda for edge processing, use Amazon Kinesis Data Streams for real-time data processing, deploy Amazon Aurora for real-time data storage, and employ Amazon S3 Glacier for long-term data archival.

D) Configure AWS IoT Core for data ingestion, implement AWS Lambda for edge processing, set up Amazon Kinesis Data Streams for real-time data processing, integrate with Amazon RDS for real-time data storage, and utilize Amazon S3 for long-term data archival.

E) Utilize AWS IoT Core for data ingestion, configure AWS Greengrass for edge computing, implement Amazon Kinesis Data Streams for real-time data processing, utilize AWS Lambda for serverless processing, and store real-time data in Amazon DynamoDB.

QUESTION 47

You are tasked with designing an edge computing solution for a transportation company that operates a fleet of autonomous vehicles. The company requires a solution capable of processing large volumes of sensor data in real-time to enable autonomous navigation and vehicle-to-vehicle communication. Which architecture would best meet these requirements?

A) Deploy applications on edge devices using AWS Snow Family devices installed in each autonomous vehicle, leverage AWS IoT Greengrass for edge data processing, and integrate with Amazon DynamoDB for real-time data storage.

B) Utilize AWS Wavelength to deploy applications on edge devices located within telecommunication providers' data centers, leverage AWS IoT Greengrass for edge data processing, and integrate with Amazon S3 for real-time data storage.

C) Implement applications on Amazon EC2 instances deployed in AWS Outposts located near vehicle hubs, utilize AWS IoT Greengrass for edge data processing, and integrate with Amazon RDS for real-time data storage.

D) Utilize AWS Lambda@Edge for deploying applications on edge devices located in each autonomous vehicle, leverage AWS IoT Greengrass for edge data processing, and integrate with Amazon Aurora for real-time data storage.

E) Deploy applications on edge devices using AWS Local Zones located near vehicle hubs, leverage AWS IoT Greengrass for edge data processing, and integrate with Amazon Redshift for real-time data storage.

QUESTION 48

A multinational corporation is deploying a new IoT product line that includes smart thermostats, light bulbs, and security cameras. The devices will be deployed globally and require a scalable solution to handle millions of device connections, process real-time data for immediate actions, and perform predictive maintenance analysis. Security, low latency, and compliance with international data protection laws are critical.

A) Use AWS IoT Core for device connectivity, Amazon Kinesis for real-time data streaming, AWS Lambda for event-driven data processing, Amazon DynamoDB for data storage, and AWS IoT Device Defender for security.

B) Deploy Amazon EC2 instances for device connectivity, AWS Direct Connect for low-latency data processing, Amazon RDS for data storage, Amazon GuardDuty for security, and AWS CloudTrail for compliance auditing.

C) Implement AWS Greengrass for edge computing and data processing, Amazon S3 for data storage, Amazon EC2 Auto Scaling for backend processing, Amazon CloudFront for distributing updates, and Amazon Inspector for security.

D) Leverage Amazon MQ for messaging between devices, AWS Fargate for serverless compute resources, Amazon EFS for shared data storage, AWS WAF for web application firewall, and AWS Shield for DDoS protection.

E) Utilize AWS IoT Core for device management, AWS Global Accelerator for performance, Amazon Redshift for data warehousing, Amazon SageMaker for predictive maintenance analysis, and AWS Certificate Manager for SSL/TLS certificates.

QUESTION 49

A digital marketing agency operates a platform for running online advertising campaigns. The platform experiences variable demand throughout the day, with peak usage during specific hours when campaigns are active. The agency aims to minimize infrastructure costs while ensuring the scalability and performance of its advertising platform. Which pricing option for Amazon EC2 instances would be the most appropriate choice for this scenario?

A) Use reserved instances (RI) for the entire duration of operation
B) Implement on-demand instances for the entire duration of operation
C) Utilize spot instances for the entire duration of operation
D) Employ a combination of reserved instances (RI) and spot instances

E) Implement a mix of reserved instances (RI) and on-demand instances

QUESTION 50

You are tasked with designing a cost-effective solution for optimizing the performance of a web application hosted on Amazon EC2 instances. The application experiences varying levels of traffic throughout the day, requiring a scalable and efficient infrastructure. Which approach would be most suitable for achieving the desired outcome?

A) Implement Amazon EC2 Auto Scaling to automatically adjust the number of EC2 instances based on demand, utilizing Amazon CloudWatch alarms to trigger scaling actions. Configure Amazon RDS with provisioned IOPS to ensure consistent database performance.

B) Utilize AWS Lambda functions to handle incoming requests and process data asynchronously, reducing the need for constantly running EC2 instances. Store application data in Amazon DynamoDB for low-latency access and scalability.

C) Deploy Amazon EC2 Spot Instances to leverage unused EC2 capacity at a lower cost, combined with Amazon Elastic Load Balancing (ELB) to distribute traffic across instances. Implement Amazon ElastiCache for caching frequently accessed data, reducing database load and improving application performance.

D) Utilize AWS Fargate to run containers without managing the underlying infrastructure, ensuring optimal resource allocation and cost efficiency. Integrate Amazon CloudFront as a content delivery network (CDN) to cache and serve static assets, reducing latency and improving application responsiveness.

QUESTION 51

An online gaming company is planning to launch a new game globally, requiring high-speed content delivery, real-time player interaction, and a scalable backend. The game is expected to attract millions of players worldwide who expect seamless gameplay and social interaction features. Which AWS architecture would best support these requirements?

A) Deploy Amazon GameLift for managed game sessions, Amazon CloudFront for content delivery, AWS Lambda for real-time backend processing, and Amazon GuardDuty for security monitoring.

B) Use AWS Global Accelerator for improving network performance, Amazon ECS for container management, Amazon DynamoDB for player data storage, and AWS WAF for application-level protection.

C) Implement Amazon S3 for storing game assets, AWS Direct Connect for reducing latency, Amazon API Gateway for managing game APIs, and Amazon Cognito for player authentication and data security.

D) Utilize Amazon CloudFront with AWS Shield for DDoS protection, Amazon Aurora for high-performance database needs, AWS AppSync for data synchronization, and AWS IAM for managing access permissions.

E) Leverage Amazon Route 53 for DNS management, AWS Fargate for running serverless containers, Amazon Kinesis for real-time data processing, and AWS Certificate Manager for managing SSL/TLS certificates.

QUESTION 52

A software development company needs to design a highly available architecture for its web application, which involves managing state across multiple instances. They want to ensure data durability and availability using Amazon S3 and Glacier. What architecture should they implement?

A) Deploy the application on Amazon EC2 instances across multiple Regions, using Amazon S3 for stateful data storage and Glacier for long-term archival.

B) Utilize Amazon RDS Multi-AZ deployment for database management, coupled with Amazon S3 for state management across EC2 instances in different Availability Zones.

C) Implement an Amazon EFS file system shared across EC2 instances for state management, with regular backups to Amazon S3 for durability.

D) Configure an AWS Lambda function triggered by Amazon S3 events to manage state across EC2 instances, using Glacier for long-term storage.

E) Deploy the application on AWS Fargate containers across multiple Availability Zones, using Amazon S3 for state management and Glacier for backup.

QUESTION 53

To enhance the security of a web application deployed on EC2 instances, a company wants to ensure only authenticated users can access certain API endpoints. Which solution is most effective?

A) Implement API keys for each user in the application code.
B) Use AWS WAF with custom rules to validate user authentication tokens.
C) Configure Security Groups to allow access only from authenticated user IPs.
D) Deploy Amazon Cognito for user authentication and integrate with the application.
E) Utilize AWS IAM roles and policies to grant access to the EC2 instances.

QUESTION 54

Your organization requires a highly available and scalable database solution for its e-commerce platform. However, you also need to ensure cost optimization without compromising performance. Which option would be the most suitable considering the need for scalability, availability, and cost-effectiveness?

A) Deploy Amazon Aurora with Multi-AZ configuration for high availability
B) Utilize Amazon RDS Provisioned IOPS for guaranteed performance
C) Implement Amazon DynamoDB with auto-scaling and on-demand capacity
D) Opt for Amazon RDS with read replicas for improved read performance
E) Use Amazon Redshift Spectrum for querying data directly from S3

QUESTION 55

A global news platform stores articles in an Amazon Aurora database. To optimize for reader engagement, the platform wishes to analyze reading trends in real-time and adjust article recommendations accordingly. This requires a fast, scalable solution for analytics that spans multiple regions. How should they implement this analytics solution?

A) Integrate Amazon Aurora with Amazon Redshift for global analytics.

B) Use Amazon Aurora with Amazon ElastiCache for real-time analytics.
C) Implement Amazon Aurora Global Database with AWS Glue for data integration and analytics.
D) Utilize Amazon DynamoDB streams with Amazon Aurora for real-time trend analysis.
E) Deploy Amazon Aurora and use Amazon Athena for querying and analyzing data across regions.

QUESTION 56

Your organization is managing a high-traffic web application on AWS, utilizing Amazon S3 for storing user-generated content and Amazon RDS for database storage. As part of cost optimization efforts, the company wants to implement a backup strategy that minimizes storage costs while ensuring data durability. Which solution aligns with best practices for achieving this objective?

A) Configure Amazon S3 versioning to maintain multiple versions of user-generated content
B) Implement Amazon RDS automated backups with a retention period of 30 days
C) Utilize Amazon S3 Cross-Region Replication for disaster recovery purposes
D) Enable Amazon S3 Transfer Acceleration to improve data transfer speed
E) Leverage Amazon S3 Lifecycle policies to transition older user-generated content to Amazon Glacier

QUESTION 57

Your organization is planning to distribute a large software update package to users globally. The update package is stored in an Amazon S3 bucket and needs to be downloaded by users with minimal latency. What would be the most efficient and cost-effective solution to achieve this?

A) Set up cross-region replication for the S3 bucket to automatically replicate the update package to edge locations
B) Deploy AWS Snowball to physically distribute the update package to AWS data centers in different regions
C) Utilize Amazon S3 Transfer Acceleration to optimize data transfer speeds for the update package
D) Implement Amazon CloudFront with the S3 bucket containing the update package set as the origin to cache the package at edge locations
E) Use AWS DataSync to synchronize the update package between multiple S3 buckets in different regions

QUESTION 58

Your organization is managing a high-traffic web application that relies on Amazon S3 to store and serve static content such as images, videos, and JavaScript files. To optimize costs, you plan to serve this static content through Amazon CloudFront. Which of the following strategies would best minimize costs while maximizing performance for serving static content?

A) Utilize Amazon CloudFront with multi-region replication to ensure high availability and durability of static content
B) Implement Amazon CloudFront with custom origin headers to control caching behavior and improve performance
C) Configure Amazon CloudFront with origin access identity to restrict access to S3 buckets and enhance security
D) Enable Amazon CloudFront with real-time logs to analyze viewer access patterns and optimize cache

hit rates

E) Integrate Amazon CloudFront with AWS WAF to protect against common web exploits and malicious attacks

QUESTION 59

Your organization is migrating its legacy data storage infrastructure to AWS to improve scalability and cost-effectiveness. The data includes both frequently accessed and infrequently accessed records, and you need to implement a solution that optimizes storage costs. What approach should you recommend?

A) Use Amazon S3 Standard storage class for all data and manually move infrequently accessed records to Amazon Glacier

B) Implement Amazon S3 Intelligent-Tiering to automatically move data between storage classes based on access patterns

C) Deploy Amazon S3 One Zone-IA storage class for frequently accessed records and Amazon S3 Glacier for infrequently accessed records

D) Leverage Amazon S3 Reduced Redundancy Storage (RRS) for frequently accessed records and Amazon S3 Glacier for infrequently accessed records

E) Utilize Amazon S3 Standard-Infrequent Access (S3 Standard-IA) storage class for frequently accessed records and Amazon S3 Glacier for infrequently accessed records

QUESTION 60

A software development company wants to implement role-based access control (RBAC) for its AWS resources to ensure that developers, testers, and operations teams have appropriate permissions based on their roles. What solution should the solutions architect recommend to enforce RBAC in AWS?

A) Utilize AWS Identity and Access Management (IAM) policies to assign permissions directly to individual team members' IAM user accounts.

B) Implement IAM groups for developers, testers, and operations teams and assign permissions to these groups based on their roles.

C) Share AWS account access keys with team members and rely on team leads to manage permissions for their respective teams.

D) Configure AWS Organizations to enforce RBAC across all member accounts within the organization.

E) Utilize AWS Single Sign-On (SSO) to authenticate team members and assign roles with corresponding permissions.

QUESTION 61

Your organization is migrating an on-premises database to AWS and requires a cost-optimized solution that can scale to meet growing demand. The database must maintain high availability and performance while minimizing costs. Which solution should you recommend for this scenario?

A) Utilize Amazon RDS with Provisioned IOPS to ensure consistent performance and scale storage capacity as needed

B) Implement Amazon Aurora Serverless with Aurora Global Database to automatically adjust compute and storage capacity based on demand

C) Deploy Amazon Redshift with RA3 instances and managed storage to optimize performance and cost-effectively scale compute and storage separately

D) Use Amazon ElastiCache for Redis with replication to maintain high availability and horizontally scale read capacity

E) Utilize Amazon DynamoDB with On-Demand capacity mode to automatically scale read and write capacity based on demand

QUESTION 62

Your organization operates a distributed team across multiple geographic locations, and you need to ensure efficient collaboration and data sharing while minimizing costs. Employees frequently access large files stored in Amazon S3 buckets for their work. Which solution should you recommend to optimize data transfer costs for this scenario?

A) Utilize Amazon S3 Transfer Acceleration to optimize data transfers and reduce latency for accessing large files

B) Implement Amazon CloudFront with Lambda@Edge to cache and deliver multimedia content at edge locations

C) Configure Amazon S3 Cross-Region Replication to replicate frequently accessed data to regions closer to users

D) Use AWS DataSync to transfer data between on-premises storage systems and Amazon S3 buckets

E) Deploy Amazon S3 Glacier for long-term storage of large files and retrieve data as needed

QUESTION 63

Your organization is planning to expand its hybrid cloud architecture by integrating AWS Outposts into its existing on-premises infrastructure. Cost optimization is a key consideration, and you need to design a solution that minimizes expenses while ensuring seamless integration between on-premises and cloud resources. What approach should you recommend?

A) Utilize AWS Outposts to host all workload components, minimizing data transfer costs between on-premises and cloud environments

B) Implement AWS Direct Connect to establish dedicated connectivity between on-premises data centers and AWS Outposts

C) Leverage AWS VPN to establish secure and cost-effective connectivity between on-premises networks and AWS Outposts

D) Deploy AWS Storage Gateway to facilitate efficient data transfer and storage optimization between on-premises infrastructure and AWS Outposts

E) Utilize AWS Snow Family devices to transfer large volumes of data between on-premises environments and AWS Outposts

QUESTION 64

Your organization operates a data-intensive application that requires efficient data processing and analytics. However, the finance department is concerned about escalating costs associated with data storage and processing. As a solutions architect, you need to design a cost-efficient solution that meets the organization's data processing needs while minimizing expenses. What approach should you recommend?

A) Utilize Amazon Kinesis with AWS Lambda to process and analyze streaming data in real-time, reducing storage costs

B) Implement Amazon Redshift Spectrum with Amazon S3 to analyze data directly from S3 storage without the need to load it into Redshift, optimizing costs

C) Leverage Amazon RDS with Amazon Aurora Serverless to automatically adjust database capacity based on demand, reducing operational costs

D) Deploy Amazon Elasticsearch Service with Amazon OpenSearch Service to analyze log data and perform text-based search queries, minimizing data processing costs

E) Utilize Amazon S3 Intelligent-Tiering to automatically move data between storage classes based on access patterns, optimizing storage costs

QUESTION 65

Your organization is seeking to implement strategies to reduce AWS costs while maintaining performance and availability. As a solutions architect, you need to recommend a solution that optimizes costs without compromising performance.

A) Utilize AWS Auto Scaling to dynamically adjust resources based on traffic patterns and optimize cost
B) Implement Amazon CloudFront to cache content closer to end users and reduce data transfer costs

C) Leverage AWS Compute Optimizer to analyze resource utilization and right-size EC2 instances for cost savings

D) Utilize Amazon EBS Provisioned IOPS SSD volumes to improve performance and cost efficiency for database workloads

E) Implement AWS Lambda with provisioned concurrency to reduce cold starts and optimize costs for serverless workloads

PRACTICE TEST 2 - ANSWERS ONLY

QUESTION 1

Answer - B) Implement individual IAM policies for each service and assign them to groups corresponding to each team's responsibilities.

A) Incorrect - Granting full access to all users violates the principle of least privilege and exposes the architecture to unnecessary risk.

B) Correct - Implementing individual IAM policies for each service and assigning them to groups based on team responsibilities aligns with the principle of least privilege, ensuring that team members have access only to the resources necessary for their roles.

C) Incorrect - Granting all users administrative access is a security risk and does not adhere to the principle of least privilege. Relying solely on CloudTrail for oversight is not a proactive security strategy.

D) Incorrect - While using AWS Organizations and SCPs is a good practice for managing permissions across multiple accounts, it does not replace the need for detailed IAM policies within each account to enforce least privilege access.

E) Incorrect - Assigning direct permissions to each user can be cumbersome to manage and does not take advantage of the benefits of grouping users with similar access needs. It also increases the risk of errors in permission assignment.

QUESTION 2

Answer - B) Leverage Amazon CloudFront for content delivery, Amazon Route 53 for traffic management, and Amazon GuardDuty for threat detection.

A) Incorrect - While deploying across multiple Availability Zones and using AWS Shield are important, they do not address global latency reduction as effectively as a content delivery network like Amazon CloudFront.

B) Correct - This approach minimizes latency for a global audience by delivering content closer to users (Amazon CloudFront), intelligently routing traffic for optimal performance (Amazon Route 53), and enhancing security with continuous monitoring for malicious activity (Amazon GuardDuty).

C) Incorrect - Centralizing the infrastructure in a single region may simplify management but will likely increase latency for users far from that region. AWS WAF is important for protection but does not address the global latency issue.

D) Incorrect - AWS Direct Connect reduces latency between on-premises environments and AWS but is not practical for globally distributed players and should be complemented with other services for security and content delivery.

E) Incorrect - Amazon VPC provides network isolation but focusing solely on it without considering multi-region deployment and content delivery services like Amazon CloudFront does not effectively address global accessibility and latency concerns.

QUESTION 3

Answer - A) Amazon Macie for sensitive data discovery and classification, AWS IAM for fine-grained access control, and Amazon GuardDuty for continuous monitoring and malicious activity detection.

A) Correct - This combination targets compliance and security effectively. Amazon Macie is ideal for identifying and protecting sensitive data to comply with HIPAA, AWS IAM provides detailed access control to ensure that only authorized personnel can access sensitive information, and Amazon GuardDuty offers continuous security monitoring and threat detection, crucial for maintaining the integrity and confidentiality of patient data.

B) Incorrect - While AWS Config, AWS CloudTrail, and AWS KMS are important for compliance and security, they do not offer the same direct benefits for sensitive data protection, access control, and continuous monitoring as Macie, IAM, and GuardDuty.

C) Incorrect - AWS WAF, AWS Shield, and AWS Fargate focus on web security, DDoS protection, and container security respectively. They are essential in a broad security strategy but less focused on HIPAA compliance and sensitive data protection.

D) Incorrect - Amazon RDS, AWS Certificate Manager, and Amazon Inspector provide database encryption, certificate management, and security assessments but do not offer comprehensive protection for sensitive data, fine-grained access control, and continuous threat detection.

E) Incorrect - AWS Systems Manager, Amazon Cognito, and AWS Lambda are valuable for management, authentication, and automation but do not specifically address the combination of data discovery, access control, and continuous monitoring for threats and compliance.

QUESTION 4

Answer - [B] Utilize AWS App Mesh to manage communication between microservices and enforce encryption using mutual TLS (mTLS). Implement Amazon CloudFront with AWS Shield Advanced for DDoS protection and Amazon Route 53 for global DNS resolution.

Option B - Correct. AWS App Mesh provides service mesh capabilities, including encryption using mutual TLS, while Amazon CloudFront with AWS Shield Advanced offers DDoS protection and low latency content delivery. Amazon Route 53 ensures global DNS resolution.

Option A - VPC peering connections and CloudFront with custom SSL certificates offer secure communication and content delivery but lack DDoS protection and global DNS resolution.

Option C - AWS PrivateLink and CloudFront with AWS WAF provide secure access and protection against web attacks but may not fully meet the requirements for DDoS protection and global DNS resolution.

Option D - Using a single VPC with separate subnets and AWS Direct Connect provides network connectivity but may not offer the same level of scalability and agility as AWS App Mesh and may lack DDoS protection.

Option E - Amazon ECS clusters with AWS Transit Gateway and AWS Global Accelerator offer some benefits, but they may not provide the same level of security and management capabilities as AWS App Mesh and CloudFront with AWS Shield Advanced.

QUESTION 5

Answer - [A] Allow s3:GetObject, s3:GetObjectVersion for the specified bucket.]

Option A is correct because it grants read-only access (s3:GetObject) to objects in the specified bucket, including object versions (s3:GetObjectVersion), meeting the requirement of accessing billing data without modification permissions.

Option B is incorrect because it includes s3:PutObject, which allows the Lambda functions to modify the bucket's content, violating the requirement.

Option C is incorrect because it grants unnecessary delete permissions in addition to write permissions, which are not required and may pose a security risk.

Option D is incorrect because it lacks the s3:PutObject permission required for writing data to the bucket, and it includes unnecessary s3:ListBucket permission.

Option E is incorrect because although it includes all the necessary read permissions, it then restricts the s3:PutObject and s3:DeleteObject permissions, which contradicts the requirement for processing billing data.

QUESTION 6

Answer - [C] Deploy AWS Lambda for compute, Amazon DynamoDB for database storage, and Amazon API Gateway for API management. Enable encryption at rest for DynamoDB using AWS KMS and configure API Gateway to use TLS encryption.

Option C - Correct. AWS Lambda, DynamoDB, and API Gateway are suitable for serverless architectures, and enabling encryption at rest and TLS encryption ensures data protection.

Option A - While Lambda and API Gateway are suitable, RDS may not be the best choice for a serverless architecture, and enabling encryption for RDS does not address data in transit.

Option B - Fargate and Aurora may not align well with a serverless architecture, and while encryption at rest is enabled for Aurora, TLS encryption for Fargate is not mentioned.

Option D - Elastic Beanstalk, S3, and CloudFront are not typically used in a serverless architecture, and while encryption at rest is enabled for S3, TLS encryption for CloudFront is not mentioned.

Option E - ECS, Redshift, and VPC are not typically used in a serverless architecture, and while encryption at rest is enabled for Redshift, VPN connections do not address data in transit within the serverless architecture.

QUESTION 7

Answer - B) Deploy AWS KMS CMKs in each region where data is stored and use AWS Global Accelerator to reduce latency.

A) Use a single AWS KMS CMK in the primary region and replicate the encrypted data to other regions. - Incorrect because this approach can introduce latency due to key retrieval from a single region.

B) Deploy AWS KMS CMKs in each region where data is stored and use AWS Global Accelerator to reduce latency. - Correct as it ensures data is encrypted locally in each region, minimizing latency in key retrieval, and AWS Global Accelerator optimizes the path to the nearest region, improving performance.

C) Implement AWS CloudHSM in each region and manually synchronize keys across regions. - Incorrect due to the operational overhead of manual synchronization and the potential for synchronization errors.

D) Utilize Amazon S3 Cross-Region Replication with default S3 encryption in each target region. - Incorrect because it doesn't address the key management strategy or the optimization of key retrieval latency across regions.

E) Store keys in Amazon DynamoDB global tables and encrypt data client-side before storing in any region. - Incorrect because managing encryption keys within DynamoDB does not utilize AWS's dedicated key management services and introduces potential security risks.

QUESTION 8

Answer - [C] Set up AWS Security Hub to aggregate security findings from multiple AWS services. Implement AWS Config rules to monitor resource configuration changes.

Option C - Correct. Setting up AWS Security Hub to aggregate security findings and using AWS Config rules to monitor resource configuration changes ensures effective security monitoring and compliance for the architecture.

Option A - While integrating CloudWatch Logs with CloudTrail and configuring Config rules for compliance assessment are valid, they may not provide the same level of centralized security monitoring as Security Hub.

Option B - While GuardDuty and Macie are effective for threat detection and data protection, Security Hub provides centralized security monitoring across multiple AWS services.

Option D - While CloudTrail and Config are useful for logging API activity and tracking resource changes, Security Hub offers a more comprehensive solution for security monitoring.

Option E - While Config can track resource inventory and changes, and Artifact provides compliance reports, Security Hub aggregates security findings from multiple services, offering a more comprehensive solution.

QUESTION 9

Answer - [B] Configuring AWS Lambda authorizers in Amazon API Gateway for request validation and authorization, ensuring secure communication between microservices.

A) AWS IAM roles and policies provide service-to-service authentication but may not integrate seamlessly with API Gateway for secure API strategies.

B) AWS Lambda authorizers in Amazon API Gateway allow for custom authorization logic, ensuring secure communication between microservices and compliance with industry regulations for data privacy and security.

C) While OAuth 2.0 authentication with Amazon Cognito can control API access, it may not directly address secure communication between microservices or compliance with industry standards.

D) ACM provides SSL/TLS encryption for API endpoints, enhancing data privacy and security, but may not directly handle authorization for service-to-service communication or compliance with industry regulations.

E) AWS AppMesh manages communication between microservices but may not directly ensure secure API strategies or compliance with industry regulations for data privacy.

QUESTION 10

Answer - A) Use Amazon SQS FIFO queue with a batch mode of 5 messages per operation.

A) Use Amazon SQS FIFO queue with a batch mode of 5 messages per operation - This option ensures accurate and efficient processing of patient records by processing multiple updates in a batch, meeting the company's requirement for timely processing and scalability during peak hours. The FIFO guarantees order accuracy, and batch processing enhances efficiency.

B) Use Amazon SQS FIFO queue with exactly-once processing enabled - While ensuring order accuracy, it may not efficiently handle high volumes of record updates during peak hours due to sequential processing.

C) Use Amazon SQS FIFO queue with default settings - Default settings may not ensure record accuracy and efficient processing, especially during peak hours, and may not efficiently handle batch processing.

D) Use Amazon SQS standard queue to process the messages - Standard queues lack message ordering, which is crucial for maintaining record order, and may not efficiently handle high volumes of record updates.

E) Use Amazon SQS FIFO queue with message deduplication enabled - While avoiding duplicate messages, it doesn't guarantee order processing, and may not efficiently handle high volumes of record updates during peak hours.

QUESTION 11

Answer - A) AWS WAF, AWS Shield Advanced, and AWS Network Firewall

A) AWS WAF, AWS Shield Advanced, and AWS Network Firewall - Correct because AWS WAF provides web request filtering, AWS Shield Advanced offers protection against DDoS attacks, and AWS Network Firewall allows for stateful and stateless packet inspection within a VPC.

B) Amazon CloudFront, Amazon S3, and AWS Lambda - Incorrect because this combination focuses on content delivery, storage, and compute functions without specifically addressing network security and packet inspection.

C) AWS Global Accelerator, Amazon GuardDuty, and AWS IAM - Incorrect as they are focused on improving global application performance, threat detection, and identity management, respectively, not directly on network security or compliance.

D) Amazon VPC, Amazon CloudWatch, and Amazon Inspector - Incorrect because, while important for monitoring and security assessments, they do not offer the specific network protection features like stateful and stateless inspection or web request filtering.

E) AWS Direct Connect, AWS Fargate, and AWS Step Functions - Incorrect as they focus on network connections, container management, and workflow automation, respectively, not on integrated network security or compliance measures.

QUESTION 12

Answer - C) Implement AWS IAM Identity Center (SSO) integrated with the existing IdP for dynamic access management.

A) Deploy AWS IAM users and groups for each consultant, manually managing permissions. - Incorrect due to the manual effort required for onboarding and offboarding, which is not scalable for hundreds of consultants.

B) Use AWS Directory Service with AWS IAM roles for external identity provider access. - Incorrect because it's less efficient for temporary consultant access management compared to IAM Identity Center with SSO.

C) Implement AWS IAM Identity Center (SSO) integrated with the existing IdP for dynamic access management. - Correct as it allows for seamless integration with the existing IdP, enabling scalable and efficient access management for temporary consultants based on their assignments.

D) Configure Amazon Cognito user pools to manage consultant identities and access permissions. - Incorrect for this scenario as Cognito is better suited for customer-facing apps rather than temporary employee access.

E) Establish AWS Resource Access Manager with shared VPCs for controlled environment access. - Incorrect because it focuses on resource sharing across AWS accounts, not on managing temporary consultant access.

QUESTION 13

Answer - A) Use Amazon Cognito for authentication, AWS IAM for authorization, apply API Gateway throttling, and integrate AWS WAF.

A) Use Amazon Cognito for authentication, AWS IAM for authorization, apply API Gateway throttling, and integrate AWS WAF - Correct. This option fully addresses authentication, authorization, rate limiting, and protection against common web exploits using the recommended AWS services.

B) Implement Lambda authorizers for authentication, Amazon Cognito for authorization, use API Gateway's default rate limiting, and rely on API Gateway's native DDoS protection - Incorrect because Lambda authorizers and Cognito cannot be used together in this manner for authentication and authorization, and API Gateway's native DDoS protection is not sufficient for advanced protection.

C) Utilize Amazon Cognito for both authentication and authorization, set custom rate limits in API Gateway, and enable AWS Shield Advanced - Incorrect because AWS Shield Advanced is more suited for DDoS protection than specific API exploit protection.

D) Employ API Gateway resource policies for authentication, use AWS IAM roles for authorization, configure API Gateway custom throttling, and attach AWS WAF to the API Gateway - Incorrect because resource policies are not used for authentication in the context of third-party developers accessing payment APIs.

E) Implement AWS IAM for both authentication and authorization, use Amazon CloudFront in front of API Gateway for rate limiting, and deploy Amazon Inspector for attack detection - Incorrect because Amazon Inspector is not designed for real-time attack detection on APIs and CloudFront is not the primary tool for rate limiting API requests.

QUESTION 14

Answer - B) Use AWS Config rules to automatically assess compliance with GDPR standards and AWS Lambda for enforcement actions.

A) Implement AWS CloudFormation for infrastructure as code, ensuring GDPR compliance in template configurations. - Incorrect because, while CloudFormation supports infrastructure as code, it does not provide automatic compliance assessment or enforcement specific to GDPR.

B) Use AWS Config rules to automatically assess compliance with GDPR standards and AWS Lambda for enforcement actions. - Correct as AWS Config offers the capability to continuously monitor and record AWS resource configurations, assessing them against GDPR-specific requirements, while Lambda allows for automated response actions to address non-compliance.

C) Deploy Amazon QuickSight for GDPR compliance reporting based on AWS CloudTrail logs. - Incorrect because QuickSight is primarily a business intelligence tool and, although useful for compliance reporting, does not offer automated compliance assessment or enforcement capabilities.

D) Configure AWS WAF and AWS Shield for protecting web applications and data from breaches, aligned with GDPR requirements. - Incorrect as WAF and Shield focus on security and protection rather than compliance monitoring and enforcement.

E) Leverage AWS Security Hub custom insights for GDPR compliance, integrating AWS IAM Access Analyzer for analyzing permission levels and risk. - Incorrect because, while Security Hub and IAM Access Analyzer provide security insights and risk assessment, they do not offer the automated compliance assessment and enforcement mechanism provided by AWS Config and Lambda.

QUESTION 15

Answer - B) Utilize Amazon Kinesis Data Firehose for real-time data streaming into Amazon S3. and C) Use Amazon S3 Transfer Acceleration for quick uploads and AWS Lambda for data processing.

A) Leverage AWS Direct Connect and Amazon S3 multipart uploads for fast, secure data transfer. - Incorrect. While this option provides a secure and reliable method for data transfer, it may not offer the best cost efficiency for the high volume of IoT data.

B) Utilize Amazon Kinesis Data Firehose for real-time data streaming into Amazon S3. - Correct. Kinesis Data Firehose is ideal for efficiently handling high-volume, real-time data streams, making it suitable for IoT scenarios.

C) Use Amazon S3 Transfer Acceleration for quick uploads and AWS Lambda for data processing. - Correct. This combination allows for rapid data uploads from any location and serverless processing, optimizing both performance and cost.

D) Implement AWS Snowball Edge for bulk data transfer, followed by Amazon S3 for storage. - Incorrect. Snowball Edge is suited for occasional, large-scale data transfers, not continuous data streams from IoT devices.

E) Opt for AWS DataSync to automate and accelerate data transfer to Amazon S3. - Incorrect. While DataSync provides automation and acceleration, it doesn't specifically cater to the real-time processing needs of IoT data like Kinesis Data Firehose does.

QUESTION 16

Answer - B) Use IAM roles with specific policies for S3, DynamoDB, and Lambda that grant only the necessary permissions.

A) Create an IAM user for the application with full access permissions - Incorrect because assigning full access to an IAM user violates the principle of least privilege.

B) Use IAM roles with specific policies for S3, DynamoDB, and Lambda that grant only the necessary permissions - Correct as it aligns with the principle of least privilege by granting only necessary permissions.

C) Utilize AWS Organizations to manage policies at the account level - Incorrect because this does not directly apply the principle of least privilege to individual services.

D) Enable IAM Access Analyzer across all services to automatically apply the necessary permissions - Incorrect as IAM Access Analyzer helps identify unintended permissions but does not automatically apply permissions.

E) Apply a single blanket IAM policy directly to the application's EC2 instances for simplicity - Incorrect because a blanket policy does not adhere to the principle of least privilege.

QUESTION 17

Answer - B) Implement AWS Transit Gateway for inter-region connectivity and host the database in Amazon Aurora Global Database.

A) Incorrect as VPC peering does not support inter-region peering directly and introduces complexity when connecting multiple regions. RDS read replicas improve read performance but do not address the application's centralized data access requirement.

B) Correct because AWS Transit Gateway simplifies network management across regions, and Amazon Aurora Global Database offers low-latency, cross-region reads and writes, meeting the application's needs.

C) Incorrect because AWS Direct Connect links on-premises to AWS and does not provide inter-region connectivity. DynamoDB global tables provide multi-region redundancy but might not meet specific latency requirements for centralized data access.

D) Incorrect as AWS VPN CloudHub is designed for connecting multiple sites, not for high-performance inter-region application connectivity. Neptune is a graph database and might not fit all database requirements of the application.

E) Incorrect because AWS Global Accelerator improves internet-facing service performance, not internal AWS connectivity. DocumentDB with cross-region replication adds complexity and might not be the most efficient solution for centralized data access.

QUESTION 18

Answer - [A] Utilize AWS Budgets to set cost thresholds and alerts for different departments within the organization. Implement AWS Cost Explorer to analyze usage patterns and identify cost-saving opportunities.

Option B - While Trusted Advisor provides cost optimization recommendations, it does not directly address setting cost thresholds and alerts.

Option C - While Lambda can automate resource shutdown, it may not cover all cost-saving opportunities, and Cost and Usage Report provides detailed billing but may not be as user-friendly as Cost Explorer.

Option D - While Savings Plans reduce costs, CloudFormation is more focused on infrastructure provisioning rather than cost management.

Option E - While Auto Scaling and Compute Optimizer help with performance and cost optimization, they do not directly address cost threshold setting and analysis like AWS Budgets and Cost Explorer.

QUESTION 19

Answer - [B] Utilize AWS Secrets Manager to securely store API keys and sensitive information. Integrate AWS Lambda with Secrets Manager for automated retrieval of secrets at runtime.

Option A - Storing API keys directly in environment variables within Lambda functions is not recommended for security reasons and lacks centralized management and rotation capabilities.

Option C - Storing plaintext configurations in an S3 bucket introduces security risks and lacks automation for retrieval and rotation.

Option D - While Parameter Store can centrally manage configurations, Secrets Manager is specifically designed for securely storing and rotating secrets like API keys.

Option E - Storing sensitive information in plaintext files within EFS lacks encryption and may expose data to unauthorized access. Explanation for Choice B: Utilizing AWS Secrets Manager provides secure storage and rotation of secrets like API keys. Integrating with Lambda allows for automated retrieval at runtime, enhancing security and compliance.

QUESTION 20

Answer - B) Suspend the ReplaceUnhealthy process type for the Auto Scaling group and apply the maintenance patch to the instance. Once the instance is ready, manually set the instance's health status back to healthy and activate the ReplaceUnhealthy process type again.

B) Suspend the ReplaceUnhealthy process type for the Auto Scaling group and apply the maintenance patch to the instance - This option effectively addresses the maintenance challenge by suspending the process responsible for replacing unhealthy instances, allowing the maintenance to proceed without triggering Auto Scaling actions.

A) Suspend the Terminate process type for the Auto Scaling group and apply the maintenance patch to the instance - Suspending termination processes may not prevent instance replacement and may not efficiently address the maintenance challenge.

C) Put the instance into the Detached state and then update the instance by applying the maintenance patch - Detaching instances may disrupt application availability and may not align with the requirement for uninterrupted maintenance.

D) Temporarily suspend the AddToLoadBalancer process type for the Auto Scaling group and apply the maintenance patch to the instance - Suspending processes related to load balancer integration may not efficiently address the maintenance challenge and may not prevent instance replacement during maintenance.

E) Take a snapshot of the instance, create a new Amazon Machine Image (AMI), and then launch a new instance using this AMI - Creating a new instance from a snapshot introduces complexity and may not efficiently address the maintenance challenge, especially in scenarios where immediate fixes are required.

QUESTION 21

Answer - A) Utilize Amazon Kinesis Data Streams for ingesting real-time user data, AWS Lambda for processing events, Amazon DynamoDB for storing user profiles, and Amazon ElastiCache for caching frequently accessed data.

A) Correct because Kinesis Data Streams enables real-time data ingestion, Lambda handles event processing, DynamoDB offers fast and scalable storage, and ElastiCache improves performance with caching, aligning with the requirement for real-time processing and dynamic scalability.

B) Incorrect because while SQS and SNS offer decoupling and event notification, Step Functions might not be suitable for real-time processing, Aurora is more focused on relational data rather than user profiles, and CloudFront is for content delivery rather than user data storage.

C) Incorrect as EventBridge and EMR provide event-driven and big data processing capabilities, but Neptune and RDS might not be the optimal choices for storing and managing user profiles for personalized recommendations, which require fast retrieval and scalability.

D) Incorrect because S3, Glue, and RDS offer data storage and processing capabilities but might not provide the same level of real-time processing and dynamic scalability as Kinesis, Lambda, and DynamoDB, essential for the personalized recommendation system.

E) Incorrect as ECS, S3, and API Gateway offer microservices architecture and API management, but may not provide the same level of real-time processing and dynamic scalability as Kinesis, Lambda, and ElastiCache required for the e-commerce platform's recommendation system.

QUESTION 22

Answer - [C] Implement AWS Fargate for serverless container deployments to ensure scalability.

A) AWS Lambda is suitable for handling event-driven workloads but may not be the best choice for long-running tasks or containerized applications.

B) While Amazon EC2 instances with Auto Scaling can handle variable traffic, they require management overhead and may not offer the same level of scalability and cost efficiency as serverless or containerized solutions.

C) AWS Fargate provides serverless container deployments, offering scalability and cost efficiency without the need to manage infrastructure directly. This aligns well with the requirements of the e-commerce platform.

D) Amazon EKS is suitable for container orchestration but may introduce additional complexity and management overhead compared to serverless container deployments.

E) AWS Step Functions automate workflows but may not directly address the scalability and cost efficiency requirements of the architecture.

QUESTION 23

Answer - [B) Implement AWS Trusted Advisor for cost optimization recommendations and AWS Budgets for cost tracking to identify areas of overspending and improve cost efficiency while maintaining scalability.]

Option B) is correct as it involves utilizing AWS Trusted Advisor for cost optimization recommendations and AWS Budgets for cost tracking, enabling the company to identify cost drivers and optimize expenses while maintaining scalability.

Option A) involves monitoring but does not specifically address cost optimization or scalability.

Option C) and D) focus on performance and security, respectively, which may not directly relate to cost optimization.

Option E) involves regulatory compliance but may not address the cost optimization requirements effectively.

QUESTION 24

Answer - [A) Amazon Redshift and E) AWS Glue]

Option A involves Amazon Redshift for petabyte-scale data warehousing, offering high-performance analytics and scalability for structured data.

Option E involves AWS Glue for data catalog and ETL processing, facilitating data ingestion, transformation, and loading tasks.

Option B involves Amazon S3 for object storage, which is important for storing large volumes of data but not directly related to data warehouse querying or processing.

Option C involves Amazon Athena for serverless querying of S3 data, which is useful for ad-hoc analytics but may not provide the same performance or scalability as Redshift.

Option D involves Amazon Aurora for high-performance relational database, which is not typically used as a data warehousing solution for large volumes of unstructured data.

QUESTION 25

Answer - A) Create an Amazon CloudWatch metric filter to process AWS CloudTrail logs containing API call details. Establish an alarm based on this metric's rate to send an Amazon SNS notification to the required team.

A) Create an Amazon CloudWatch metric filter to process AWS CloudTrail logs containing API call details. Establish an alarm based on this metric's rate to send an Amazon SNS notification to the required team. - This option directly addresses the scenario by analyzing CloudTrail logs for unauthorized API queries and triggering real-time alerts using CloudWatch alarms and Amazon SNS notifications.

B) Implement AWS Config Rules to monitor API activity and define rules to detect unauthorized API calls.

Configure AWS Config to trigger an AWS Lambda function upon rule evaluation to notify relevant stakeholders. - While AWS Config can monitor API activity, it may not provide real-time alerting capabilities for immediate incident response as required in this scenario.

C) Leverage AWS Trusted Advisor to publish metrics about check results to Amazon CloudWatch. Set up an alarm to track status changes for checks in the Service Limits category for the APIs, triggering notifications when service quotas are exceeded. - While Trusted Advisor offers valuable insights, it may not directly address the need for real-time detection of unauthorized API queries.

D) Use Amazon Athena SQL queries against AWS CloudTrail log files stored in Amazon S3 buckets. Generate reports using Amazon QuickSight for managerial dashboards. - While this option provides insights, it may not offer real-time alerting capabilities as required in this scenario.

E) Configure AWS CloudTrail to stream event data to Amazon Kinesis. Utilize Amazon Kinesis stream-level metrics in Amazon CloudWatch to trigger an AWS Lambda function that will initiate an error workflow. - While this option utilizes streaming data, it may introduce complexity and latency compared to directly analyzing CloudTrail logs for real-time alerts.

QUESTION 26

Answer - A) Implement Amazon API Gateway with IAM authentication to manage and secure APIs, and leverage AWS Lambda for serverless execution of microservices.

Option A is correct because implementing Amazon API Gateway with IAM authentication allows effective management and security of APIs, while leveraging AWS Lambda for serverless execution ensures scalability and resilience for microservices. This aligns with the requirements of managing and securing APIs effectively while ensuring scalability and resilience in a microservices architecture.

Option B is incorrect because while Amazon MQ enables message queuing, it may not provide the same level of API management and security as Amazon API Gateway with IAM authentication.

Option C is incorrect because while Amazon EventBridge facilitates event-driven architectures, it may not be the most suitable option for managing and securing APIs in a microservices environment.

Option D is incorrect because while AWS AppMesh offers service mesh capabilities, it may introduce complexity and overhead that are unnecessary for managing and securing APIs in a microservices architecture.

Option E is incorrect because while Amazon EKS Anywhere enables on-premises deployment, it does not directly address the requirement for managing and securing APIs effectively in a microservices architecture on AWS.

QUESTION 27

Answer - A) Implement AWS Step Functions with built-in retry and error handling features

Option A - AWS Step Functions provide built-in retry and error handling features, allowing for reliable and resilient serverless workflow orchestration.

Option B - While Amazon S3 event notifications and Lambda can handle errors, they do not provide the comprehensive workflow orchestration capabilities offered by Step Functions.

Option C - Amazon SQS and Lambda are suitable for asynchronous processing but do not provide the advanced error handling and retry mechanisms needed for complex workflows.

Option D - Amazon Kinesis Data Streams and Lambda can handle real-time processing but are not designed for orchestrating serverless workflows with built-in error handling and retries.

QUESTION 28

Answer - A) Use Amazon Kinesis Data Streams for real-time data ingestion, AWS Lambda for data processing, Amazon DynamoDB for data storage, and secure data with AWS KMS.

A) Correct because it provides a highly scalable, serverless architecture suitable for real-time processing, with secure and compliant data management through encryption.

B) Incorrect because it involves managed services that are not serverless, potentially leading to higher costs and more management overhead. GuardDuty is a threat detection service, not directly related to data compliance.

C) Incorrect as it doesn't offer the real-time processing capabilities required for patient monitoring. AWS IAM policies are for access control, not for encrypting data.

D) Incorrect due to SQS being more suited for decoupling components rather than real-time data ingestion. S3 is not the optimal choice for the kind of structured, quickly accessible data storage required here. Cognito is for identity management, not encryption.

E) Incorrect because AppSync is ideal for mobile and web applications but not specifically designed for real-time data ingestion and processing as required in this scenario.

QUESTION 29

Answer - D) Configure an Amazon Global Accelerator with accelerator endpoints for global application availability.

A) Route 53 with Geolocation routing policy routes traffic based on geographic location, but it does not optimize for low latency between patients and healthcare professionals.

B) NLB operates at the transport layer and is not optimized for low-latency communication.

C) CloudFront with Lambda@Edge is primarily used for content delivery optimization, not for real-time communication.

D) Global Accelerator improves global application availability and optimizes for low-latency communication between users and endpoints.

E) AppStream 2.0 is used for application streaming and does not optimize for low-latency communication.

QUESTION 30

Answer - A) Use Amazon Route 53 based geolocation routing policy to restrict access to fans located in the designated cities

A) By using Amazon Route 53's geolocation routing policy, the sports league can ensure that only fans from the specified cities can access the live streams, effectively managing traffic and complying with regional restrictions.

B, C, D, E) These options do not directly address the requirement of restricting access to fans from specific cities for the live streams. Weighted routing, latency-based routing, failover routing, and geoproximity routing do not provide the necessary geographic control needed for this scenario.

QUESTION 31

Answer - A) Implement Amazon Kinesis for real-time data streaming, Amazon S3 for data storage, AWS Glue for ETL operations, and Amazon Athena for querying data.

A) Correct, as this combination of services enables real-time data analytics and scalable data storage and querying, meeting the company's needs for insights into customer behavior. Kinesis supports real-time data streaming, S3 offers scalable storage, Glue facilitates ETL processes, and Athena allows for serverless querying.

B) Incorrect, DynamoDB, Lambda, and Elastic Beanstalk offer robust solutions for storage, computing, and deployment but don't specifically address real-time analytics or scalable querying as well as option A.

C) Incorrect, Redshift and Data Pipeline are powerful for warehousing and data movement, but this setup isn't optimized for real-time streaming analytics.

D) Incorrect, Fargate, RDS, CloudWatch, and Step Functions focus more on application deployment and orchestration rather than on analytics and data scaling.

E) Incorrect, EC2, EBS, and EMR are suited for compute, storage, and processing but don't provide the same real-time analytics capabilities as Kinesis Data Analytics combined with the other services in option A.

QUESTION 32

Answer - [A) Implement Amazon RDS with cross-Region read replicas and use AWS Backup for automated backups and cross-Region replication of backups.]

Option A) - Correct because Amazon RDS with cross-Region read replicas and AWS Backup ensures automated backups and cross-Region replication, meeting the healthcare provider's requirements for disaster recovery with low RPOs and RTOs effectively.

Option B) - Incorrect because while Aurora with global databases offers multi-master replication and fast failover, it lacks integration with AWS Backup for automated backups and cross-Region replication essential for disaster recovery.

Option C) - Incorrect because although DynamoDB supports global tables for multi-Region replication, it lacks integration with AWS Backup for automated backups required for disaster recovery.

Option D) - Incorrect because Amazon Redshift is optimized for analytics and may not offer the same level of backup and disaster recovery features as Amazon RDS.

Option E) - Incorrect because Amazon DocumentDB lacks cross-Region replication and automated backup features, which are essential for disaster recovery across multiple AWS Regions.

QUESTION 33

Answer - C) Implement AWS Transit Gateway to simplify network connectivity between multiple VPCs and on-premises networks, enabling centralized network management and routing.

Option C - AWS Transit Gateway simplifies network connectivity by acting as a hub that connects multiple VPCs and on-premises networks, allowing for centralized management and routing. This solution ensures optimal network performance and security for the highly available and fault-tolerant architecture.

Option A - While configuring an Amazon VPC with subnets and network ACLs is essential, it may not provide the centralized management and routing capabilities needed for this scenario.

Option B - AWS Direct Connect offers a dedicated network connection but may not be necessary for this scenario and could add complexity without significant benefits.

Option D - Route 53 with latency-based routing improves performance but may not provide the centralized management and routing capabilities required for the scenario.

Option E - AWS Global Accelerator improves availability and performance but focuses on directing traffic to AWS edge locations and may not address the need for centralized network management and routing.

QUESTION 34

Answer - B) Implement Elastic Load Balancing with Amazon EC2 Auto Scaling and Amazon CloudWatch.

A) Incorrect - Amazon EC2 instances with CloudWatch for monitoring can offer insights into application performance but lack the automatic scaling needed for handling unpredictable traffic spikes.

B) Correct - Elastic Load Balancing distributes incoming traffic across multiple targets, Amazon EC2 Auto Scaling adjusts capacity to maintain steady performance, and CloudWatch provides monitoring and alarming, together ensuring high availability and consistent performance.

C) Incorrect - AWS Elastic Beanstalk simplifies deployment and operations but using AWS Lambda for traffic handling isn't directly applicable to e-commerce platform scaling needs.

D) Incorrect - Amazon S3 and CloudFront can serve static content efficiently but don't address dynamic content scaling and performance consistency needs for a web application.

E) Incorrect - Amazon API Gateway and AWS Fargate are suitable for managing APIs and containers, respectively, but don't directly address the need for automatic scaling and load balancing for high availability.

QUESTION 35

Answer - A) Utilize RESTful APIs on Amazon API Gateway with AWS Lambda authorizers for authentication and authorization

A) Leveraging RESTful APIs on Amazon API Gateway with AWS Lambda authorizers provides robust authentication and authorization mechanisms, ensuring security, compliance, and high availability for the mobile banking application.

B, C, D, E) These options either do not provide adequate security measures or are not suitable for ensuring compliance and high availability in a mobile banking application.

QUESTION 36

Answer - [A, C, E]

A) Correct - Kinesis Data Streams efficiently handles real-time data ingestion and processing.
B) Incorrect - DAX is suitable for caching but not directly related to real-time data processing performance or reliability.
C) Correct - Lambda for real-time processing ensures scalability and responsiveness.
D) Incorrect - EMR with Spark is suitable for batch processing but not real-time analytics platform optimization.
E) Correct - CloudWatch alarms for monitoring and scaling actions maintain performance under varying loads.

QUESTION 37

Answer - [B, C]

A) Incorrect - While CloudTrail captures API calls and CloudWatch Metrics monitors performance, Lambda notifications are not sufficient for troubleshooting performance issues, and no mention of tracing for root cause analysis.

B) Correct - X-Ray traces requests and identifies bottlenecks, while CloudWatch Alarms alert on predefined thresholds for CPU utilization and latency, ensuring effective performance issue identification and resolution.

C) Correct - CloudWatch Logs agent collects log data, and AWS Config tracks resource configurations, aiding in identifying misconfigurations affecting performance. No mention of ECS or Container Insights, which may not be relevant in this scenario.

D) Incorrect - Container Insights is mentioned, but Trusted Advisor focuses on cost optimization, not troubleshooting performance issues, and no mention of CloudTrail for capturing API activity.

E) Incorrect - While CloudFormation templates enable resource provisioning with monitoring, X-Ray and CloudWatch Logs Insights are more relevant for troubleshooting performance issues. CloudTrail and Trusted Advisor are not directly related to real-time monitoring and troubleshooting.

QUESTION 38

Answer - A) Implement Amazon CloudFront to cache content at edge locations and reduce latency during traffic spikes.
B) Leverage Amazon EC2 Auto Scaling to adjust compute capacity dynamically based on traffic patterns.
C) Utilize Amazon SQS to decouple components of the architecture and handle traffic surges efficiently.

Option A - Amazon CloudFront helps reduce latency and offload traffic from origin servers during traffic spikes, ensuring a smooth shopping experience for users.

Option B - Amazon EC2 Auto Scaling dynamically adjusts compute capacity, ensuring scalability and cost-effectiveness during sales events.

Option C - Amazon SQS enables decoupling of components and handles traffic surges efficiently by providing scalable message queues.

Options D and E may not directly address the scalability and cost optimization requirements for handling traffic spikes in the e-commerce platform architecture.

QUESTION 39

Answer - B) Deploy Amazon Route 53 with AWS Global Accelerator for efficient DNS routing and global application acceleration.

Option A - Implement Amazon CloudFront with AWS Shield for DDoS protection and Amazon Route 53 for DNS routing - This choice focuses on content delivery and DNS routing but may not optimize network performance as effectively as Global Accelerator.

Option B - Deploy Amazon Route 53 with AWS Global Accelerator for efficient DNS routing and global application acceleration - This option provides the best solution by leveraging Global Accelerator for efficient DNS routing and global application acceleration, ensuring high throughput and low latency.

Option C - Implementing VPC with Direct Connect and VPN addresses network connectivity but does not specifically optimize for global application performance.

Option D - This choice is unrelated to optimizing network performance.

Option E - AWS Transit Gateway offers scalable connectivity but does not specifically address the requirement for high throughput and low latency.

QUESTION 40

Answer - C) Ingest streaming data into Amazon Kinesis Data Streams, which triggers an AWS Lambda function for processing and stores sentiment analysis results in Amazon DynamoDB

C) Ingesting streaming data into Amazon Kinesis Data Streams with AWS Lambda allows for real-time sentiment analysis without delays. Storing sentiment analysis results in Amazon DynamoDB ensures low-latency access and scalability.

A) Processing streaming data with AWS Lambda and Amazon S3 may introduce latency and is not suitable for real-time sentiment analysis systems.

B) Using Amazon Kinesis Data Firehose may not provide the necessary real-time processing capabilities for sentiment analysis systems.

D) Amazon SQS is not optimized for real-time processing of streaming data, and storing sentiment analysis results in Amazon Redshift may introduce delays.

E) Using Amazon API Gateway and an EC2 instance for processing lacks the scalability and real-time processing capabilities required for real-time sentiment analysis systems.

QUESTION 41

Answer - A) Configure Amazon S3 Cross-Region Replication to replicate data across regions with minimal network latency.

Option A - Amazon S3 Cross-Region Replication replicates data across regions with minimal network latency, ensuring disaster recovery and data sovereignty compliance.

Option B - AWS Direct Connect establishes dedicated connections but may not optimize data replication latency across regions.

Option C - Amazon Route 53 with latency-based routing directs traffic based on geographic location but may not optimize data replication latency across regions.

Option D - AWS Global Accelerator improves application availability and performance but may not directly address data replication latency across regions.

Option E - AWS Snowball is used for data transfer but may not provide continuous data replication across regions with minimal latency.

QUESTION 42

Answer - [C) Leverage Amazon DynamoDB Accelerator (DAX) for caching frequently accessed data.]

Option C) Using Amazon DynamoDB Accelerator (DAX) for caching frequently accessed data can significantly improve read performance by reducing the need to query the database directly for commonly accessed data.

Option A) While Aurora Serverless offers scalability, it may not provide the same level of performance as caching frequently accessed data with DAX.

Option B) Multi-AZ deployment enhances availability but may not directly address read performance issues.

Option D) Amazon Neptune is not designed for optimizing read performance in real-time analytics scenarios.

Option E) Amazon Redshift is a data warehousing solution and may not be suitable for real-time analytics read requirements.

QUESTION 43

Answer - [A) Utilize Amazon Redshift for the data warehouse and AWS Lake Formation to build a secure data lake for storing and analyzing data from various sources.]

Option A) Amazon Redshift provides a powerful data warehousing solution, and AWS Lake Formation allows for building a secure data lake, making this combination ideal for the migration requirements.

Option B) Amazon Aurora Serverless and Amazon S3 are suitable for certain workloads but may not offer the same level of performance and scalability for a data warehouse and data lake, respectively.

Option C) While Amazon RDS and Amazon Kinesis are viable options, they may not provide the same level of integration and performance as Amazon Redshift and AWS Lake Formation for this scenario.

Option D) Amazon DynamoDB and Amazon S3 Glacier serve different purposes and may not meet the requirements for a high-performance data warehouse and data lake architecture.

Option E) Amazon Neptune is a graph database service and may not be the best choice for a data warehouse, and Amazon S3 alone may not provide the necessary features for a comprehensive data lake solution.

QUESTION 44

Answer - [C] Utilize Amazon Managed Streaming for Apache Kafka (Amazon MSK) for device data ingestion, process it with Amazon Kinesis Data Analytics, and trigger alerts using Amazon CloudWatch.

Option A introduces unnecessary complexity with Glue and Redshift and may not provide real-time analytics.
Option B lacks scalability with Lambda and may face latency issues.
Option D's use of AppSync and Neptune may not be suitable for real-time analytics on IoT telemetry data.
Option E's use of Firehose and EMR may not provide the real-time processing required for timely alerts on device health anomalies. Amazon MSK provides a durable and scalable solution for ingesting and processing streaming data, while Kinesis Data Analytics offers real-time analytics capabilities, making option C the most appropriate choice.

QUESTION 45

Answer - B) Use server-side encryption with AWS Key Management Service (SSE-KMS) keys to encrypt the data on Amazon S3

B) Server-side encryption with AWS Key Management Service (SSE-KMS) provides the required encryption of data at rest while offering additional control and auditing capabilities suitable for compliance with HIPAA regulations.

A) Client-side encryption with customer-provided keys (SSE-C) shifts the responsibility of encryption to the client, which may not align with HIPAA compliance requirements.

C) Server-side encryption with Amazon S3 managed keys (SSE-S3) encrypts the data at rest but may not provide the additional control and auditing capabilities required for HIPAA compliance.

D) Using server-side encryption with customer-provided keys (SSE-C) also lacks the centralized control and auditing capabilities provided by AWS KMS.

E) Enabling AWS CloudTrail provides auditing capabilities but does not directly address the encryption requirement for data at rest in Amazon S3.

QUESTION 46

Answer - [B] Utilize AWS IoT Greengrass for data ingestion, leverage AWS Lambda for edge processing, employ Amazon Kinesis Data Streams for real-time data processing, store real-time data in Amazon DynamoDB, and archive long-term data in Amazon S3.

Option A is incorrect because it uses Amazon API Gateway for data ingestion, which is not typically used in IoT solutions for sensor data collection. AWS Fargate is also not the ideal choice for edge processing in IoT scenarios. Additionally, Amazon RDS and Amazon Glacier are not the most suitable options for real-time data storage and long-term data archival in IoT solutions.

Option C is incorrect because AWS IoT Events is not commonly used for data ingestion in IoT solutions, and Amazon Aurora is not the optimal database service for real-time data storage in this context.

Amazon S3 Glacier is also not well-suited for long-term data archival in IoT scenarios.

Option D is incorrect because it uses AWS IoT Core for data ingestion but does not leverage edge processing capabilities provided by AWS Greengrass.

Option E is incorrect because although it uses AWS IoT Core and AWS Greengrass, it employs AWS Lambda for serverless processing instead of edge processing, which may introduce latency issues in real-time data processing for IoT applications.

QUESTION 47

Answer - [A] Deploy applications on edge devices using AWS Snow Family devices installed in each autonomous vehicle, leverage AWS IoT Greengrass for edge data processing, and integrate with Amazon DynamoDB for real-time data storage.

Option A is the correct choice because deploying Snow Family devices in autonomous vehicles ensures edge computing capability, which is crucial for processing large volumes of sensor data in real-time. AWS IoT Greengrass facilitates edge data processing, and DynamoDB offers real-time data storage, meeting the requirements effectively.

Options B, C, D, and E either lack the same level of edge computing capability, suitable edge data processing solutions, or appropriate real-time data storage services.

QUESTION 48

Answer - A) Use AWS IoT Core for device connectivity, Amazon Kinesis for real-time data streaming, AWS Lambda for event-driven data processing, Amazon DynamoDB for data storage, and AWS IoT Device Defender for security.

Option A - Correct. This solution provides a comprehensive and secure architecture for IoT devices with AWS IoT Core at the core for device management, Kinesis for data streaming, Lambda for processing, DynamoDB for storage, and IoT Device Defender for security, addressing all key requirements.

Option B - Incorrect. While EC2, Direct Connect, RDS, GuardDuty, and CloudTrail provide necessary components, this setup lacks the specialized IoT services that offer better scalability and integration for IoT solutions.

Option C - Incorrect. Greengrass, S3, EC2 Auto Scaling, CloudFront, and Inspector address several aspects but do not provide the optimized device connectivity and real-time processing as efficiently as AWS IoT Core and Kinesis.

Option D - Incorrect. MQ, Fargate, EFS, WAF, and Shield focus on messaging, compute, storage, and security but lack the IoT-specific capabilities provided by AWS IoT Core and the real-time data processing needed for IoT devices.

Option E - Incorrect. While IoT Core, Global Accelerator, Redshift, SageMaker, and Certificate Manager cover many requirements, this combination does not offer the streamlined real-time data processing and event-driven actions enabled by AWS Lambda and Kinesis in option A.

QUESTION 49

Answer - D) Employ a combination of reserved instances (RI) and spot instances

D) Employing a combination of reserved instances (RI) and spot instances allows the digital marketing agency to benefit from cost savings with RIs during predictable usage periods while leveraging the scalability and cost-effectiveness of spot instances during peak usage hours.

A) Using reserved instances (RI) for the entire duration may result in underutilization of resources during non-peak hours, leading to higher costs.

B) Implementing on-demand instances for the entire duration may result in higher costs, especially during peak usage hours when campaigns are active.

C) Utilizing spot instances for the entire duration may be risky as spot instances can be terminated with short notice, potentially affecting platform availability during peak hours.

E) Implementing a mix of reserved instances (RI) and on-demand instances may not provide the same level of cost optimization and scalability needed for handling variable demand throughout the day.

QUESTION 50

Answer - C) Deploy Amazon EC2 Spot Instances to leverage unused EC2 capacity at a lower cost, combined with Amazon Elastic Load Balancing (ELB) to distribute traffic across instances. Implement Amazon ElastiCache for caching frequently accessed data, reducing database load and improving application performance.

Option A relies on provisioned EC2 instances, which may not be the most cost-effective solution for variable traffic.

Option B introduces complexity with AWS Lambda and might not be suitable for all application workloads.

Option D, while providing a serverless solution, does not address the variable traffic requirement directly.

Option C is the best choice as it leverages cost-effective EC2 Spot Instances for scalability, combined with ELB for traffic distribution and ElastiCache for performance optimization.

QUESTION 51

Answer - A) Deploy Amazon GameLift for managed game sessions, Amazon CloudFront for content delivery, AWS Lambda for real-time backend processing, and Amazon GuardDuty for security monitoring.

Option A - Correct: Amazon GameLift optimizes session management for global multiplayer games. CloudFront ensures fast content delivery. Lambda allows for scalable, serverless computing for game logic, and GuardDuty provides intelligent threat detection, meeting the game's performance, scalability, and security requirements.

Option B - Incorrect: Global Accelerator and ECS offer performance and management benefits, DynamoDB provides fast data storage, and WAF secures against web exploits, but this combination lacks the dedicated game session management provided by GameLift.

Option C - Incorrect: S3, Direct Connect, API Gateway, and Cognito address storage, latency reduction, API management, and security but do not offer the comprehensive gaming architecture and real-time processing capabilities as effectively as option A.

Option D - Incorrect: CloudFront with Shield, Aurora, AppSync, and IAM provide a secure and scalable environment but lack specific services for managing real-time multiplayer game sessions as GameLift does.

Option E - Incorrect: Route 53, Fargate, Kinesis, and Certificate Manager offer DNS management, container execution, real-time data streaming, and SSL/TLS management but fall short in delivering a specialized gaming solution with session management and threat detection capabilities provided in A.

QUESTION 52

Answer - C) Implement an Amazon EFS file system shared across EC2 instances for state management, with regular backups to Amazon S3 for durability.

A) Incorrect - Deploying on EC2 instances across Regions does not ensure high availability and durability, and it does not leverage S3 and Glacier effectively for state management and archival.

B) Incorrect - While RDS Multi-AZ deployment enhances availability for databases, it does not address state management across instances or utilize S3 and Glacier effectively.

C) Correct - Utilizing Amazon EFS for shared state management across instances ensures high availability and durability, with regular backups to S3 providing additional data protection.

D) Incorrect - Using Lambda and S3 events for state management may not provide the necessary durability and availability, especially for shared state across instances.

E) Incorrect - Fargate containers may offer scalability, but they do not inherently address state management and durability concerns across instances.

QUESTION 53

Answer - B) Use AWS WAF with custom rules to validate user authentication tokens.

A) API keys provide basic security but don't handle dynamic authentication scenarios well.

B) Correct, as AWS WAF can inspect HTTP headers for authentication tokens, providing a scalable and secure method to protect APIs.

C) IP-based access control is not practical for users with dynamic IPs.

D) Amazon Cognito provides authentication services but does not directly secure API endpoints.

E) IAM roles control access to AWS resources, not application-level authentication.

QUESTION 54

Answer - [C] Implement Amazon DynamoDB with auto-scaling and on-demand capacity.

Option A - Aurora with Multi-AZ configuration focuses on high availability but may not offer the same cost-effectiveness as DynamoDB with auto-scaling.

Option B - While Provisioned IOPS ensures performance, it may not be the most cost-effective option for scalability.

Option C - Correct. DynamoDB with auto-scaling and on-demand capacity provides scalability, high availability, and cost optimization, making it suitable for e-commerce platforms.

Option D - RDS with read replicas enhances read performance but may not provide the same scalability and cost-effectiveness as DynamoDB.

Option E - Redshift Spectrum allows querying data from S3 but may not offer the same real-time scalability and availability as DynamoDB.

QUESTION 55

Answer - D) Utilize Amazon DynamoDB streams with Amazon Aurora for real-time trend analysis.

A) Redshift is powerful for analytics but may not offer the real-time performance required for trend analysis.

B) ElastiCache enhances data retrieval speeds but is not an analytics solution.

C) AWS Glue is a data integration service, not specifically tailored for real-time analytics.

D) Correct, as DynamoDB streams provide real-time data processing capabilities, making it ideal for analyzing trends and adjusting recommendations dynamically.

E) Athena is suitable for querying large datasets but may not deliver the real-time analysis needed for dynamic content recommendations.

QUESTION 56

Answer - [E] Leverage Amazon S3 Lifecycle policies to transition older user-generated content to Amazon Glacier.

Option A - Configuring Amazon S3 versioning increases storage costs without directly optimizing for long-term archival.

Option B - Implementing Amazon RDS automated backups ensures data durability but does not address cost optimization for user-generated content stored in Amazon S3.

Option C - Utilizing Amazon S3 Cross-Region Replication focuses on disaster recovery and redundancy, not on cost optimization for backups.

Option D - Enabling Amazon S3 Transfer Acceleration improves data transfer speed but does not specifically address backup storage costs.

Option E - Correct. Leveraging Amazon S3 Lifecycle policies to transition older user-generated content to Amazon Glacier ensures cost-effective long-term archival while maintaining data durability.

QUESTION 57

Answer - [D] Implement Amazon CloudFront with the S3 bucket containing the update package set as the origin to cache the package at edge locations.

Option D - Correct. Implementing Amazon CloudFront with the S3 bucket containing the update package set as the origin allows caching of the package at edge locations, reducing latency and ensuring efficient delivery to users globally.

Option A - Cross-region replication for S3 buckets may replicate objects between regions but does not directly address the requirement for minimal latency for global users.

Option B - AWS Snowball involves physical data transfer and may not be as efficient or cost-effective as using Amazon CloudFront for distributing software updates globally.

Option C - While Amazon S3 Transfer Acceleration optimizes data transfer speeds, it may not offer the same level of content delivery capabilities as Amazon CloudFront for this scenario.

Option E - AWS DataSync can synchronize data between S3 buckets but may not offer the same level of content delivery capabilities as Amazon CloudFront for distributing software updates globally.

QUESTION 58

Answer - [B] Implement Amazon CloudFront with custom origin headers to control caching behavior and improve performance.

Option A - Utilizing Amazon CloudFront with multi-region replication enhances availability and durability but may not directly optimize costs for serving static content.

Option B - Correct. Implementing Amazon CloudFront with custom origin headers allows for controlling caching behavior, optimizing cache hit rates, and improving performance while minimizing costs.

Option C - Configuring Amazon CloudFront with origin access identity enhances security but does not directly focus on cost optimization for serving static content.

Option D - Enabling Amazon CloudFront with real-time logs helps analyze viewer access patterns but may not directly optimize costs associated with serving static content.

Option E - Integrating Amazon CloudFront with AWS WAF enhances security but may not directly optimize costs for serving static content.

QUESTION 59

Answer - [B] Implement Amazon S3 Intelligent-Tiering to automatically move data between storage classes based on access patterns.

Option B - Correct. Implementing Amazon S3 Intelligent-Tiering allows for automatic data movement between storage classes based on access patterns, optimizing storage costs for both frequently and infrequently accessed records.

Option A - Manually moving infrequently accessed records to Amazon Glacier introduces complexity and may not be as efficient as automated solutions.

Option C - Deploying different storage classes for frequently and infrequently accessed records may require manual management and may not optimize costs as effectively as automated tiering.

Option D - Utilizing Amazon S3 Reduced Redundancy Storage (RRS) for frequently accessed records may compromise durability, and using Amazon S3 Glacier for infrequently accessed records may not be as cost-effective as other options.

Option E - Using Amazon S3 Standard-Infrequent Access (S3 Standard-IA) for frequently accessed records and Amazon S3 Glacier for infrequently accessed records does not provide automatic tiering based on access patterns.

QUESTION 60

Answer - [B] Implement IAM groups for developers, testers, and operations teams and assign permissions to these groups based on their roles.

A) Incorrect - Assigning permissions directly to individual team members' IAM user accounts does not provide a scalable and centralized approach for managing permissions based on roles.

B) Correct - Implementing IAM groups for developers, testers, and operations teams and assigning permissions to these groups based on their roles ensures a centralized and scalable approach to enforcing RBAC in AWS.

C) Incorrect - Sharing AWS account access keys with team members is highly discouraged due to security risks and lack of centralized control over permissions.

D) Incorrect - Configuring AWS Organizations focuses on managing multiple AWS accounts within an organization and may not directly address RBAC enforcement at the resource level.

E) Incorrect - Utilizing AWS Single Sign-On (SSO) for authentication does not inherently enforce RBAC; it may simplify authentication but does not address permissions management at the resource level.

QUESTION 61

Answer - [B] Implement Amazon Aurora Serverless with Aurora Global Database to automatically adjust compute and storage capacity based on demand.

Option B - Correct. Amazon Aurora Serverless with Aurora Global Database automatically adjusts compute and storage capacity based on demand, providing a cost-effective and scalable solution while maintaining high availability and performance.

Option A - While Amazon RDS with Provisioned IOPS can scale storage capacity, it may not offer the same cost optimization benefits as Aurora Serverless.

Option C - Amazon Redshift with RA3 instances and managed storage is suitable for data warehousing but may not provide the same scalability and cost optimization as Aurora Serverless for database workloads.

Option D - Amazon ElastiCache for Redis with replication offers high availability and scalability for caching but may not be the most cost-effective solution for database migration.

Option E - While DynamoDB On-Demand capacity mode can automatically scale capacity, it may not provide the same cost optimization benefits as Aurora Serverless for database workloads.

QUESTION 62

Answer - [C] Configure Amazon S3 Cross-Region Replication to replicate frequently accessed data to regions closer to users.

Option A - Amazon S3 Transfer Acceleration optimizes data transfers but may not be the most cost-effective solution for frequent access to large files across multiple geographic locations.

Option B - Amazon CloudFront with Lambda@Edge is suitable for multimedia content delivery but may not be optimized for large file data transfer and collaboration.

Option C - Correct. Amazon S3 Cross-Region Replication replicates frequently accessed data to regions closer to users, optimizing data transfer costs and improving access speed for large files.

Option D - AWS DataSync is designed for data transfer but may not provide the same cost optimization for frequently accessed large files as cross-region replication.

Option E - Amazon S3 Glacier is suitable for long-term storage but may not offer the same level of accessibility and cost optimization for frequently accessed large files as cross-region replication.

QUESTION 63

Answer - [D] Deploy AWS Storage Gateway to facilitate efficient data transfer and storage optimization between on-premises infrastructure and AWS Outposts.

Option A - Hosting all workload components on AWS Outposts may not be the most cost-effective solution and may not fully leverage existing on-premises infrastructure.

Option B - AWS Direct Connect provides dedicated connectivity but may not directly address the need for seamless integration and cost optimization in a hybrid cloud environment with AWS Outposts.

Option C - AWS VPN offers secure connectivity but may not provide the same level of optimization as AWS Storage Gateway for data transfer and storage between on-premises infrastructure and AWS Outposts.

Option D - Correct. Deploying AWS Storage Gateway facilitates efficient data transfer and storage optimization, ensuring seamless integration and cost optimization between on-premises infrastructure and AWS Outposts.

Option E - AWS Snow Family devices are used for offline data transfer and may not be the most suitable solution for optimizing ongoing data transfer between on-premises environments and AWS Outposts.

QUESTION 64

Answer - [B] Implement Amazon Redshift Spectrum with Amazon S3 to analyze data directly from S3 storage without the need to load it into Redshift, optimizing costs.

Option A - Amazon Kinesis with AWS Lambda processes streaming data but may not directly address the cost efficiency of data storage and processing.

Option B - Correct. Implementing Amazon Redshift Spectrum with Amazon S3 allows for analyzing data directly from S3 storage, optimizing costs by eliminating the need to load data into Redshift.

Option C - Amazon RDS with Amazon Aurora Serverless adjusts database capacity but may not directly optimize costs related to data processing.

Option D - Amazon Elasticsearch Service with Amazon OpenSearch Service analyzes log data but may not directly address cost optimization for data processing.

Option E - Amazon S3 Intelligent-Tiering moves data between storage classes based on access patterns but may not directly optimize costs for data analysis and processing.

QUESTION 65

Answer - [A] Utilize AWS Auto Scaling to dynamically adjust resources based on traffic patterns and optimize cost.

Option A - Correct. Utilizing AWS Auto Scaling allows for dynamic resource adjustment based on traffic patterns, optimizing costs without compromising performance.

Option B - Amazon CloudFront improves content delivery but may not directly optimize costs for compute resources.

Option C - AWS Compute Optimizer analyzes resource utilization but may not provide the same level of dynamic cost optimization as AWS Auto Scaling.

Option D - Amazon EBS Provisioned IOPS SSD volumes improve performance but may not directly optimize costs for compute resources.

Option E - AWS Lambda with provisioned concurrency reduces cold starts but may not address cost optimization for other types of workloads.

PRACTICE TEST 3 - QUESTIONS ONLY

QUESTION 1

A multinational corporation is deploying a new application across multiple AWS accounts to enhance global availability and disaster recovery capabilities. The application requires cross-account access to resources like Amazon S3 buckets for storage and AWS Lambda for serverless computing. Which strategy should the company implement to manage cross-account access securely?

A) Use AWS IAM roles with external ID to grant cross-account access and enforce least privilege access.

B) Share the root account credentials across accounts to ensure seamless access to all resources.

C) Create IAM users in each account and use access keys for cross-account resource sharing.

D) Implement cross-account access by enabling public access to S3 buckets and using API keys for Lambda.

E) Utilize AWS Control Tower to automate the setup of cross-account access with service control policies (SCPs).

QUESTION 2

A healthcare organization, subject to strict data residency regulations, plans to migrate its patient data to AWS. The organization wants to ensure compliance with these regulations while leveraging the AWS global infrastructure for high availability and disaster recovery. Which strategy should be prioritized?

A) Store all patient data in Amazon S3 with default encryption enabled and use Amazon Macie for data security and compliance.

B) Use AWS Outposts to host sensitive patient data on-premises while utilizing AWS services for processing and analytics.

C) Deploy patient data across multiple AWS regions to ensure high availability, disregarding specific data residency requirements.

D) Implement data residency controls by selecting AWS regions that comply with local regulations for data storage, and use Amazon RDS for database services.

E) Focus solely on AWS CloudHSM for encryption, assuming it addresses all data residency and compliance concerns.

QUESTION 3

An international news outlet uses AWS to host its content delivery platform. Given the high profile of the organization and the geopolitical sensitivity of its content, the platform is a constant target for state-sponsored cyber attacks, including sophisticated DDoS attacks and advanced persistent threats (APTs). Which AWS services should be employed to enhance the platform's resilience against these specific types of threats?

A) AWS Shield Advanced for comprehensive DDoS protection, Amazon GuardDuty for intelligent threat detection, and AWS WAF for custom web traffic filtering rules.

B) Amazon CloudFront for global content delivery, AWS Direct Connect for a dedicated network connection, and AWS IAM for managing access.

C) AWS Fargate for running containerized applications, Amazon Inspector for security assessments, and Amazon VPC for network isolation.

D) AWS Lambda for executing security functions, AWS Systems Manager for infrastructure automation, and Amazon RDS for database security.

E) AWS Global Accelerator for improving application performance, Amazon Macie for data security and privacy, and Amazon S3 for secure object storage.

QUESTION 4

Your company operates a highly available web application hosted on Amazon EC2 instances distributed across multiple Availability Zones (AZs). As the solutions architect, you are tasked with enhancing the security posture of the application's network infrastructure. The company wants to implement a solution that provides real-time visibility into network traffic, detects malicious activity, and automatically blocks unauthorized access attempts. Which solution should you recommend?

A) Deploy AWS Network Firewall to inspect and filter incoming and outgoing traffic at the subnet level. Utilize Amazon CloudWatch Logs and Amazon CloudWatch Events to monitor network activity and trigger automated responses based on predefined rules.

B) Implement AWS WAF on Amazon CloudFront to protect against common web attacks such as SQL injection and cross-site scripting (XSS). Enable AWS Shield Advanced for DDoS protection and real-time threat intelligence.

C) Configure AWS GuardDuty to continuously monitor AWS accounts for malicious activity and unauthorized behavior. Utilize AWS Config to assess resource configurations for compliance with security best practices.

D) Utilize AWS Security Hub to centrally manage security findings from multiple AWS services. Implement AWS Firewall Manager to enforce security policies and automate rule enforcement across AWS accounts and resources.

E) Deploy AWS VPC Traffic Mirroring to capture and inspect network traffic at the Elastic Network Interface (ENI) level. Use Amazon Inspector to analyze traffic patterns and identify potential security vulnerabilities.

QUESTION 5

A retail company is expanding its online presence and wants to revamp its order fulfillment system by migrating it to AWS. The company needs to ensure that orders placed during peak hours are processed promptly while maintaining order accuracy. Additionally, they require a solution that allows for easy scalability to accommodate fluctuating order volumes. Which option should the company choose to implement this requirement?

A) Use Amazon SQS FIFO queue with exactly-once processing enabled.
B) Use Amazon SQS FIFO queue with message deduplication enabled.
C) Use Amazon SQS FIFO queue with a batch mode of 10 messages per operation.

D) Use Amazon SQS standard queue to process the messages.
E) Use Amazon SQS FIFO queue with default settings to process the messages.

QUESTION 6

Your company is developing a new serverless application that requires real-time processing of streaming data from IoT devices. Security is a primary concern, and you need to ensure that only authorized devices can send data to the application. Which combination of services should you use to achieve secure ingestion of data?

A) Utilize Amazon Kinesis Data Streams for data ingestion, AWS Lambda for real-time processing, and Amazon API Gateway for API management. Implement AWS IoT Core with device certificates for secure device authentication.

B) Implement Amazon Kinesis Data Firehose for data ingestion, AWS Lambda for real-time processing, and Amazon API Gateway for API management. Use AWS IoT Core with IAM roles for secure device authentication.

C) Deploy Amazon Kinesis Data Analytics for data ingestion, AWS Lambda for real-time processing, and Amazon API Gateway for API management. Enable AWS IoT Device Defender for monitoring and security assessment of IoT devices.

D) Utilize Amazon Kinesis Video Streams for data ingestion, AWS Lambda for real-time processing, and Amazon API Gateway for API management. Implement AWS IoT Core with custom authentication logic for secure device authentication.

E) Implement Amazon Managed Streaming for Apache Kafka (Amazon MSK) for data ingestion, AWS Lambda for real-time processing, and Amazon API Gateway for API management. Use AWS IoT Core with Amazon Cognito for secure device authentication.

QUESTION 7

A financial services firm wants to implement a key management solution that allows them to maintain full control over the encryption keys while leveraging AWS services for storing sensitive financial data. Compliance regulations require that the keys used for encrypting data must be stored with hardware security modules. What is the most suitable AWS service for this requirement?

A) Use AWS KMS with customer-managed keys and enable hardware security module (HSM) protection.
B) Deploy AWS CloudHSM and manage the encryption keys within the HSM.
C) Utilize Amazon S3 with server-side encryption and integrate with AWS CloudHSM.
D) Implement AWS Secrets Manager for storing and managing encryption keys with HSM-backed encryption.
E) Use Amazon EBS volumes encrypted with AWS managed keys and AWS KMS integration.

QUESTION 8

A financial services company requires a solution to ensure their AWS environment complies with industry regulations by continuously monitoring and auditing their cloud resources. Which set of AWS services should they integrate for compliance monitoring and reporting? Select Two.

A) AWS Config and AWS CloudTrail
B) Amazon QuickSight and AWS Glue
C) AWS KMS and Amazon Macie
D) AWS Audit Manager and AWS Security Hub
E) Amazon Detective and AWS IAM Identity Center

QUESTION 9

You are tasked with designing a highly available and scalable architecture for a real-time messaging application. Security is a top priority, and the architecture must protect against unauthorized access and data breaches. Additionally, the application needs to adhere to industry compliance standards for data protection. Which of the following strategies best addresses these security requirements while ensuring compliance?

A) Utilizing AWS Secrets Manager for managing API keys and credentials, ensuring secure access control and compliance with industry regulations

B) Implementing end-to-end encryption using AWS Key Management Service (KMS) for securing data in transit and at rest, ensuring compliance with industry standards

C) Configuring Amazon GuardDuty for continuous threat detection and monitoring, ensuring real-time security analytics and compliance monitoring

D) Enabling Amazon Cognito for user authentication and access control, ensuring secure access to the messaging application and compliance with data protection regulations

E) Deploying AWS Network Firewall to filter traffic and prevent unauthorized access, ensuring compliance with industry regulations for data protection

QUESTION 10

A media company is migrating its video editing platform to AWS and needs a solution that ensures low-latency access to video files stored on a file system service. The platform must be able to seamlessly access these files during and after migration. Which option is the most suitable solution to meet this requirement?

A) Use Amazon FSx File Gateway to provide low-latency, on-premises access to fully managed file shares in Amazon EFS. The applications deployed on AWS can access this data directly from Amazon EFS.

B) Use Amazon Storage Gateway's File Gateway to provide low-latency, on-premises access to fully managed file shares in Amazon FSx for Windows File Server. The applications deployed on AWS can access this data directly from Amazon FSx in AWS.

C) Use AWS Storage Gateway's File Gateway to provide low-latency, on-premises access to fully managed file shares in Amazon S3. The applications deployed on AWS can access this data directly from Amazon S3.

D) Use Amazon FSx File Gateway to provide low-latency, on-premises access to fully managed file shares in Amazon FSx for Windows File Server. The applications deployed on AWS can access this data directly from Amazon FSx in AWS.

QUESTION 11

A multinational corporation with operations in multiple countries wants to secure its AWS-hosted applications against region-specific cyber threats while maintaining compliance with local data sovereignty laws. The solution must dynamically adapt to emerging threats and offer detailed visibility into network traffic.

A) Amazon VPC with AWS Network Firewall, Amazon GuardDuty for threat detection, and AWS CloudTrail for logging

B) AWS Shield Advanced with AWS WAF for application layer protection, and Amazon CloudWatch for monitoring

C) AWS Lambda for custom threat response automation, AWS Fargate for container management, and Amazon S3 for logging

D) AWS Direct Connect for dedicated network connections, Amazon Route 53 for traffic management, and AWS IAM for access control

E) Amazon CloudFront for global content delivery, AWS Global Accelerator for performance optimization, and Amazon Inspector for security assessments

QUESTION 12

An international banking institution, adhering to strict financial compliance regulations, requires a solution to extend their on-premises privilege access management system to control and audit access to AWS resources. They need detailed logging of all actions taken by privileged users and the ability to enforce multi-factor authentication (MFA) for these users when accessing critical AWS resources.

A) Integrate AWS CloudTrail with on-premises SIEM systems for auditing privileged actions.

B) Configure AWS IAM roles for privileged users with enforced MFA, leveraging AWS CloudTrail for logging.

C) Utilize AWS IAM Identity Center (SSO) for centralized access, integrating with AWS KMS for enhanced security.

D) Implement AWS Directory Service integration with on-premises systems, enabling MFA via AWS IAM policies.

E) Establish federated access with AWS IAM and on-premises LDAP, using Amazon GuardDuty for anomaly detection and AWS CloudTrail for activity logging.

QUESTION 13

An e-commerce platform is developing a new microservice for handling product reviews, deployed using AWS Lambda and API Gateway. They need to ensure that only authenticated users can post reviews, and the system should scale automatically to handle varying loads. Additionally, they want to protect the API from SQL injection and XSS attacks. Which of the following setups would meet these requirements?

A) Use Amazon Cognito User Pools for authentication, deploy AWS WAF with SQL injection and XSS rules on API Gateway, and rely on Lambda's automatic scaling.

B) Implement API keys in API Gateway for authentication, use Amazon Inspector for SQL injection and XSS detection, and enable Lambda concurrency controls for scaling.

C) Employ Amazon Cognito Identity Pools for authentication, attach AWS Shield to API Gateway for attack protection, and use AWS Auto Scaling with Lambda.

D) Utilize AWS IAM roles for user authentication, enable Amazon GuardDuty for SQL injection and XSS detection, and rely on Lambda's built-in scaling capabilities.

E) Implement AWS IAM authentication with API Gateway, use AWS WAF with custom rules for SQL injection and XSS protection on API Gateway, and allow Lambda to handle scaling.

QUESTION 14

A fintech startup on AWS requires a compliance automation solution to adhere to PCI DSS requirements for their payment processing system. The solution must continuously monitor the environment for any deviations from PCI DSS standards and automate the process of bringing resources back into compliance.

A) Configure AWS Shield and Amazon Inspector to automatically protect against threats and assess for PCI DSS compliance.

B) Use AWS Systems Manager for automated patch management and AWS Config for PCI DSS compliance monitoring and auto-remediation.

C) Leverage AWS Step Functions for orchestrating compliance workflows and AWS Audit Manager for PCI DSS assessments.

D) Implement AWS Lambda for custom compliance checks and remediation scripts, integrated with Amazon CloudWatch for monitoring.

E) Deploy AWS WAF for real-time threat protection and AWS Trusted Advisor for continuous PCI DSS compliance scanning and recommendations.

QUESTION 15

A software development company is facing challenges in performing maintenance work on specific Amazon EC2 instances that are part of an Auto Scaling group. The company observes that every time maintenance patches are deployed, the instance health check status shows as out of service for a few minutes, triggering the provision of replacement instances by the Auto Scaling group. As a solutions architect, which steps would you recommend to efficiently complete the maintenance work? (Select two)

A) Suspend the ScheduledActions process type for the Auto Scaling group and apply the maintenance patch to the instance. Once the instance is ready, manually set the instance's health status back to healthy and activate the ScheduledActions process type again.

B) Suspend the ReplaceUnhealthy process type for the Auto Scaling group and apply the maintenance patch to the instance. Once the instance is ready, manually set the instance's health status back to healthy and activate the ReplaceUnhealthy process type again.

C) Delete the Auto Scaling group and apply the maintenance fix to the given instance. Create a new Auto Scaling group and add all the instances again using the manual scaling policy.

D) Put the instance into the Standby state and then update the instance by applying the maintenance patch. Once the instance is ready, exit the Standby state and then return the instance to service.

E) Take a snapshot of the instance, create a new Amazon Machine Image (AMI), and then launch a new instance using this AMI. Apply the maintenance patch to this new instance and then add it back to the Auto Scaling Group by using the manual scaling policy. Terminate the earlier instance that had the maintenance issue.

QUESTION 16

Your company plans to deploy a new application on AWS that must interact securely with existing AWS resources without embedding access keys or credentials. Which approach ensures the application can securely access the necessary AWS resources while adhering to AWS best practices?

A) Embed the AWS Access and Secret Keys in the application code.
B) Use environment variables to store AWS Access and Secret Keys on the EC2 instances.
C) Assign an IAM role to the EC2 instances where the application runs.
D) Store AWS Access and Secret Keys in a public GitHub repository for easy access.
E) Create an IAM user for each service the application accesses, and rotate keys weekly.

QUESTION 17

An online gaming company wants to design a secure, scalable VPC for their AWS-hosted gaming servers, with the ability to scale based on user demand and ensure secure, low-latency connections to players worldwide. The architecture must segregate public-facing services from backend systems and provide detailed network traffic visibility for security monitoring.

A) Deploy public and private subnets within a VPC, utilize ELB for scalability, and enable VPC flow logs for traffic monitoring.

B) Configure multiple VPCs for each game server, use AWS Global Accelerator for global traffic routing, and Amazon CloudWatch for monitoring.

C) Implement a single VPC with AWS Shield for DDoS protection, AWS Direct Connect for dedicated gaming traffic, and use AWS Config for network monitoring.

D) Use AWS App Mesh to manage traffic between services, Amazon S3 for game data storage, and enable AWS WAF for security monitoring.

E) Establish VPC peering between gaming server VPCs, leverage Amazon Route 53 for DNS queries, and Amazon Inspector for security assessments.

QUESTION 18

A healthcare organization is migrating sensitive patient data to AWS and needs to ensure robust security measures are in place to protect against potential threats. Additionally, the organization requires cost-effective solutions to manage its AWS expenses.

A) Implement AWS IAM roles with strict permissions to control access to patient data. Utilize AWS KMS for encryption of sensitive data at rest and in transit. Set up AWS Cost Explorer to analyze usage patterns and identify cost-saving opportunities.

B) Deploy Amazon GuardDuty for threat detection and implement AWS Config Rules to enforce security best practices. Utilize AWS Budgets to set cost thresholds and alerts for different departments within the organization.

C) Utilize AWS CloudTrail for logging API activity and integrate with AWS CloudWatch for real-time monitoring. Implement AWS WAF to protect against common web exploits. Set up AWS Trusted Advisor to monitor cost optimization opportunities.

D) Implement Amazon Macie for data discovery and classification. Configure AWS S3 bucket policies to restrict access and enable server-side encryption. Utilize AWS Savings Plans to reduce costs for long-term commitments.

E) Deploy AWS Security Hub for centralized security monitoring and compliance checking. Integrate AWS Lambda functions for automated incident response. Set up AWS Cost and Usage Report for detailed billing analysis and optimization insights.

QUESTION 19

A technology startup is building a microservices architecture on AWS using AWS Fargate for container orchestration. They need to implement secure management of secrets and sensitive data within their containerized applications. Which of the following approaches would best suit the startup's requirements?

A) Embed secrets directly within Docker containers as environment variables. Utilize IAM roles with least privilege access for containers to retrieve secrets at runtime.

B) Implement AWS Secrets Manager to securely store and rotate secrets. Integrate applications running on Fargate with Secrets Manager for secure retrieval of secrets.

C) Store secrets in plaintext files within Docker volumes attached to containers. Implement IAM policies to control access to the Docker volumes.

D) Utilize AWS Systems Manager Parameter Store to manage secrets centrally. Develop custom scripts within containers to fetch secrets from Parameter Store.

E) Maintain a spreadsheet containing sensitive information stored in an encrypted Amazon S3 bucket. Use IAM policies to control access to the S3 bucket and retrieve secrets at runtime.

QUESTION 20

A media streaming platform observed an unusual surge in unauthorized AWS API queries during peak usage hours, which did not impact system performance. To proactively address such incidents, the management seeks an automated solution to trigger real-time alerts. What would be the most effective solution in this scenario?

A) Run Amazon Athena SQL queries against AWS CloudTrail log files stored in Amazon S3 buckets. Use Amazon QuickSight to generate reports for managerial dashboards.

B) Configure AWS CloudTrail to stream event data to Amazon Kinesis. Utilize Amazon Kinesis stream-level metrics in Amazon CloudWatch to trigger an AWS Lambda function that will initiate an error workflow.

C) AWS Trusted Advisor publishes metrics about check results to Amazon CloudWatch. Create an alarm to track status changes for checks in the Service Limits category for the APIs. The alarm will then notify when the service quota is reached or exceeded.

D) Create an Amazon CloudWatch metric filter that processes AWS CloudTrail logs containing API call details and identifies any errors by factoring in all the error codes that need to be tracked. Establish an alarm based on this metric's rate to send an Amazon SNS notification to the required team.

E) Implement AWS Config Rules to monitor API activity and define rules to detect unauthorized API calls. Configure AWS Config to trigger an AWS Lambda function upon rule evaluation to notify relevant stakeholders.

QUESTION 21

A financial institution is migrating its legacy monolithic application to a cloud-native architecture to improve agility and scalability. The new architecture should decouple components, allow independent scaling, and ensure high availability.

A) Implement Amazon SQS for inter-service communication, AWS Lambda for microservices, Amazon Aurora Serverless for database management, and Amazon CloudFront for global content delivery.

B) Deploy Amazon EKS for Kubernetes-based orchestration, Amazon RDS Multi-AZ for database resilience, AWS Step Functions for workflow automation, and Amazon Route 53 for DNS management.

C) Utilize Amazon SNS for event notification, Amazon API Gateway for managing APIs, AWS Fargate for serverless compute, and Amazon DynamoDB for NoSQL data storage.

D) Configure Amazon EventBridge for event-driven architecture, Amazon ECS for container orchestration, Amazon Neptune for graph database storage, and AWS Direct Connect for dedicated network connectivity.

E) Leverage Amazon Kinesis for data streaming, AWS Lambda for serverless computing, Amazon RDS for relational database management, and Amazon EFS for shared storage among microservices.

QUESTION 22

Your company is planning to migrate its monolithic application to a microservices architecture to improve scalability and maintainability. The architecture should support continuous integration and deployment. Which AWS services would facilitate this transition effectively?

A) Use Amazon ECS with AWS CodePipeline and AWS CodeBuild for container orchestration.

B) Employ AWS Lambda with Amazon API Gateway and AWS CodeCommit for serverless application deployment.

C) Implement AWS Fargate with AWS CodeDeploy and Amazon ECR for serverless container deployments.

D) Leverage Amazon EKS with AWS CodeArtifact and AWS CodeDeploy for Kubernetes-based microservices deployment.

E) Utilize AWS Batch with Amazon S3 for batch processing and deployment.

QUESTION 23

An educational technology startup is developing a new online learning platform and wants to optimize costs for its cloud infrastructure on AWS while ensuring high availability and performance. The company requires a cost-efficient solution that meets the demands of a growing user base. Which AWS service would be most suitable to achieve this goal?

A) Utilize Amazon EC2 Spot Instances for cost-effective hosting with Amazon RDS for database storage and automatic backups to ensure high availability and cost efficiency

B) Implement AWS Lambda for serverless application components with Amazon API Gateway for HTTP API management to achieve high scalability and cost optimization

C) Deploy Amazon EKS with AWS Fargate for containerized application deployment and scaling based on workload demand to optimize costs while ensuring high availability and performance

D) Utilize Amazon S3 for static content storage with Amazon CloudFront for content delivery and caching to achieve high performance and cost efficiency

E) Implement Amazon RDS Multi-AZ deployment combined with Amazon Route 53 DNS failover for automated failover in case of database or server failures to ensure high availability and cost optimization

QUESTION 24

Your team is tasked with designing a serverless application for processing real-time data streams from IoT devices. The application must analyze incoming data for anomalies and trigger alerts based on predefined thresholds. Additionally, the solution should scale automatically to handle fluctuations in data volume. Which AWS services should you include in this serverless architecture?

A) Amazon Kinesis Data Streams for real-time data ingestion
B) AWS Lambda for serverless event-driven processing
C) Amazon DynamoDB for NoSQL database with single-digit millisecond latency
D) Amazon SNS for push notifications to alerting systems
E) AWS Glue for ETL processing of streaming data

QUESTION 25

A financial services company uses Amazon Aurora for transaction processing. To enhance database availability and read throughput, the company deployed multiple Aurora read replicas across different availability zones. The replicas are configured with varying instance sizes and failover priorities. Given the scenario where a primary instance failure occurs, which replica will Aurora promote as the new primary?

A) Tier-1 (8 terabytes)
B) Tier-2 (16 terabytes)
C) Tier-5 (32 terabytes)
D) Tier-10 (8 terabytes)
E) Tier-15 (16 terabytes)

QUESTION 26

A financial services company is building a microservices-based application on AWS and needs a solution for service discovery and inter-service communication that supports both HTTP and non-HTTP protocols. The solution must also be highly available and scalable. Which option would best meet these requirements?

A) Deploy Amazon API Gateway to manage and expose HTTP endpoints for microservices, enabling synchronous communication between them.

B) Utilize AWS AppMesh to provide service mesh capabilities for microservices, allowing fine-grained control over traffic routing and policy enforcement for both HTTP and non-HTTP protocols.

C) Implement Amazon MQ to enable message queuing and reliable communication between microservices, supporting both HTTP and non-HTTP protocols.

D) Configure AWS AppSync to provide a GraphQL API layer for microservices, allowing efficient data fetching and real-time updates over both HTTP and non-HTTP protocols.

E) Use AWS Step Functions to orchestrate the execution of microservices and handle inter-service communication, supporting both HTTP and non-HTTP protocols.

QUESTION 27

An e-learning platform is developing a serverless workflow to manage course enrollment and content delivery. The platform requires the ability to handle failures gracefully and retry failed tasks. Which of the following options is the most appropriate for implementing fault tolerance and error handling in the workflow?

A) Utilize AWS Step Functions with automatic retries and error handling for orchestrating course enrollment and content delivery tasks

B) Implement Amazon SNS for event notification and Lambda for processing course enrollment and content delivery events

C) Deploy Amazon SQS for queuing enrollment and delivery tasks and use Lambda to process messages asynchronously

D) Leverage Amazon EventBridge for triggering Lambda functions based on course enrollment and content delivery events

QUESTION 28

A media company is designing a serverless architecture to transcode video files uploaded by users. They want to ensure high performance and scalability while minimizing costs. Which option provides the most cost-efficient solution for video transcoding in a serverless architecture using AWS services?

A) Utilize AWS Lambda to trigger Amazon Elastic Transcoder jobs for video transcoding, leveraging on-demand pricing for serverless execution

B) Implement Amazon ECS Fargate with spot instances for running containerized transcoding jobs, optimizing costs based on instance availability

C) Use Amazon S3 event notifications to trigger AWS Elemental MediaConvert jobs for video transcoding, paying only for the resources consumed during job execution

D) Deploy a fleet of EC2 instances with auto scaling groups to accommodate fluctuating transcoding workloads

E) Leverage Amazon Redshift to process video files in parallel, taking advantage of its distributed computing capabilities to optimize performance and reduce costs

QUESTION 29

A media streaming company wants to enhance its platform's user experience by dynamically adjusting video quality based on network conditions and device capabilities. Which option would support this requirement effectively?

A) Deploy an Application Load Balancer (ALB) with Target Groups for traffic distribution
B) Implement Amazon CloudFront with Lambda@Edge for real-time content optimization
C) Utilize Amazon Route 53 with Geoproximity routing policy for geographic-based routing
D) Configure Amazon Elastic Load Balancing (ELB) with Classic Load Balancer for legacy compatibility
E) Set up Amazon Elastic Load Balancing (ELB) with Network Load Balancer (NLB) for network-level routing

QUESTION 30

A multinational retail corporation aims to revolutionize its customer experience by leveraging real-time data analytics to optimize product recommendations and promotions. They require a solution capable of processing high volumes of customer interaction data across various touchpoints, including online, mobile, and in-store, to deliver personalized experiences. Which AWS service combination should they implement to achieve this while ensuring scalability and real-time processing?

A) Utilize a Spark Streaming cluster on Amazon EMR to process customer interaction data before storing it in Amazon RDS

B) Implement Amazon Kinesis Data Analytics to analyze streaming customer interaction data and store it in Amazon Redshift for further analysis

C) Employ Amazon Kinesis Data Firehose to ingest data and use AWS Lambda to filter and transform before storing it in Amazon DynamoDB

D) Utilize Amazon Kinesis Data Streams with AWS Lambda for real-time data processing and store it in Amazon S3

E) Ingest data directly into Amazon S3 using Amazon Kinesis Data Firehose without intermediate processing

QUESTION 31

A healthcare analytics company wants to build a secure, compliant data lake on AWS to store and analyze large volumes of sensitive health records. Compliance with HIPAA and GDPR is a must. Which architecture would ensure data security, compliance, and the ability to perform complex analyses on health data?

A) Use Amazon S3 for storage, AWS Lake Formation to manage data lake security and access, Amazon Athena for serverless querying, and AWS KMS for encryption.

B) Deploy Amazon DynamoDB for secure NoSQL data storage, Amazon Redshift for analysis, AWS IAM for managing access permissions, and Amazon Macie for data privacy.

C) Implement Amazon EFS for file storage, Amazon EMR for data processing, AWS Shield for DDoS protection, and Amazon GuardDuty for threat detection.

D) Utilize Amazon RDS for relational data storage, Amazon QuickSight for BI and analytics, AWS CloudTrail for governance, and AWS WAF for web application firewall security.

E) Choose AWS Fargate for containerized data processing, Amazon S3 Glacier for long-term data archiving, Amazon Kinesis for real-time data processing, and AWS Config for configuration management.

QUESTION 32

A global retail company is experiencing high traffic during seasonal sales and needs a solution to ensure its database can handle sudden spikes in workload while maintaining high availability. Which combination of AWS services and features should the company utilize to address this requirement?

A) Implement Amazon RDS with Multi-AZ deployment and use Amazon Aurora Global Database for read scalability across Regions.

B) Utilize Amazon DynamoDB with auto-scaling enabled and DynamoDB Accelerator (DAX) for in-memory caching to handle sudden traffic spikes.

C) Deploy Amazon Redshift with Concurrency Scaling and utilize Redshift Spectrum for querying external data without loading into Redshift.

D) Migrate to Amazon DocumentDB with provisioned IOPS and use Amazon ElastiCache for Redis for caching frequently accessed data.

E) Implement Amazon Neptune with read replicas across multiple Availability Zones and use AWS Database Migration Service (DMS) for continuous data replication.

QUESTION 33

A healthcare company is migrating its patient records management system to AWS. The system must comply with strict data privacy and security regulations. It requires a resilient architecture that can automatically scale to meet varying loads while ensuring data is encrypted both in transit and at rest. Which solution should the Solutions Architect recommend to achieve these objectives?

A) Deploy the application on Amazon EC2 instances with Auto Scaling groups across multiple Availability Zones. Use Amazon RDS with encryption for database storage. Implement SSL/TLS for data in transit.

B) Utilize AWS Fargate for running the application without managing servers, and Amazon Aurora Serverless for a scalable, encrypted database. Use AWS VPN for data in transit encryption.

C) Use Amazon S3 for storing patient records, enabling default encryption for data at rest. Deploy the application using AWS Elastic Beanstalk for easy scaling. Rely on Amazon CloudFront for securing data in transit.

D) Implement a serverless architecture using AWS Lambda for the application, coupled with Amazon DynamoDB with encryption at rest for storing patient records. Use Amazon API Gateway with SSL/TLS encryption for data in transit.

E) Host the application on a single, large Amazon EC2 instance for simplicity, using Amazon EBS with encryption for data storage. Employ AWS Direct Connect for secure, private connectivity to AWS.

QUESTION 34

A global media company wants to ensure their video content is delivered with minimal latency to their worldwide audience. What AWS service should primarily be used to optimize their content delivery network?

A) Use Amazon S3 for content storage and Amazon CloudFront as a CDN.
B) Deploy content on Amazon EBS volumes and use Amazon Route 53 for DNS services.
C) Store videos in Amazon Glacier for archival and use AWS Direct Connect for dedicated network connections.
D) Utilize AWS Storage Gateway for on-premises storage integration and Amazon Kinesis Video Streams for content delivery.
E) Implement Amazon Elastic File System (EFS) for storage and AWS Global Accelerator to improve internet traffic flow.

QUESTION 35

A healthcare organization wants to develop a telemedicine platform to facilitate remote consultations between patients and doctors. They need a solution that supports real-time video streaming and secure transmission of patient data. Which setup should they configure using Amazon API Gateway to meet these requirements effectively?

A) Utilize RESTful APIs on Amazon API Gateway with Amazon Kinesis Video Streams for real-time video streaming and AWS Lambda for secure transmission of patient data

B) Implement WebSocket APIs on Amazon API Gateway with Amazon S3 for real-time video streaming and Amazon Cognito for secure transmission of patient data

C) Create HTTP APIs on Amazon API Gateway and integrate with Amazon CloudFront for real-time video streaming and AWS IAM for secure transmission of patient data

D) Deploy GraphQL APIs on Amazon API Gateway with Amazon Rekognition for real-time video streaming and Amazon SNS for secure transmission of patient data

E) Configure RESTful APIs on Amazon API Gateway with Amazon ECS for real-time video streaming and Amazon SNS for secure transmission of patient data

QUESTION 36

You are designing an architecture for a high-traffic web application that requires resilient performance under varying loads. The application must handle sudden spikes in traffic without degradation in performance. Which combination of AWS services and best practices should you implement to ensure reliable performance? Select THREE.

A) Utilize Amazon CloudFront for content delivery acceleration.

B) Implement Amazon DynamoDB with auto-scaling enabled for database management.

C) Configure Amazon EC2 instances with AWS Auto Scaling to adjust capacity based on demand.

D) Deploy AWS Lambda functions triggered by Amazon S3 events for asynchronous processing.

E) Set up Amazon Route 53 with latency-based routing for efficient traffic distribution.

QUESTION 37

Your company operates a highly dynamic AWS environment with frequent updates to infrastructure and application configurations. As a result, you need to ensure proactive monitoring and alerting to detect any unauthorized changes or deviations from the intended state. How would you design a monitoring solution to achieve this goal, considering the need for continuous compliance monitoring and rapid incident response? Select TWO.

A) Implement AWS Config Rules to define desired configurations and detect any non-compliant resources. Utilize Amazon CloudWatch Events to trigger AWS Lambda functions for automated remediation actions based on rule violations.

B) Deploy AWS CloudTrail to track API activity and integrate with Amazon GuardDuty for threat detection. Use AWS Config to assess resource configuration compliance against predefined rules and leverage AWS Security Hub for centralized security insights.

C) Utilize Amazon Inspector to assess the security and compliance of EC2 instances and Lambda functions. Set up CloudWatch Alarms to monitor CPU and memory utilization thresholds for performance optimization.

D) Implement AWS Service Catalog to define standardized resource configurations and enforce compliance. Configure AWS Config to track changes and notify stakeholders via Amazon SNS for any unauthorized modifications. Integrate AWS Detective for security incident analysis and response orchestration.

E) Set up AWS CloudWatch Logs agent on all instances to collect log data and analyze using CloudWatch Logs Insights. Implement AWS AppConfig to manage application configurations centrally and ensure consistency across deployments.

QUESTION 38

You are tasked with designing a microservices architecture for a media streaming platform that needs to handle bursts of traffic from users accessing different types of media content. The architecture should be cost-efficient while maintaining high availability and scalability. Which AWS service or services would you recommend for this scenario? Select TWO.

A) Deploy Amazon Kinesis for real-time data processing of streaming data at scale, ensuring efficient handling of traffic bursts.

B) Utilize Amazon ECS for deploying and managing containers at scale, providing flexibility and cost optimization.

C) Implement AWS Lambda for serverless execution of code in response to events, reducing costs during low-traffic periods.

D) Leverage Amazon CloudFront to cache media content at edge locations and reduce latency for users.

E) Utilize AWS Fargate for serverless containers, ensuring efficient resource utilization without managing underlying infrastructure.

QUESTION 39

A startup company needs to design a network architecture that can efficiently distribute traffic across its resources while ensuring scalability and security. What solution would meet these requirements?

A) Deploy Amazon Route 53 with AWS Global Accelerator for efficient DNS routing and global application acceleration.

B) Implement Amazon VPC with public and private subnets, employing AWS Direct Connect for dedicated network connections, and AWS VPN for secure hybrid connectivity.

C) Utilize Elastic Load Balancing (ELB) for distributing traffic across resources.

D) Configure Amazon CloudFront with AWS WAF for global content delivery and protection against web attacks.

E) Use AWS Transit Gateway for scalable and efficient network connectivity across multiple VPCs.

QUESTION 40

A healthcare organization wants to develop a patient monitoring system to track vital signs in real-time and alert healthcare providers of any abnormalities. They require a solution that can process streaming data from medical devices continuously and trigger alerts promptly. Which configuration should they implement using AWS serverless components to meet these requirements effectively?

A) Utilize AWS Lambda with Amazon S3 for processing streaming data and Amazon RDS for storing alert data

B) Implement Amazon Kinesis Data Firehose with AWS Lambda for processing streaming data and Amazon ElastiCache for storing alert data

C) Ingest streaming data into Amazon Kinesis Data Streams, which triggers an AWS Lambda function for processing and stores alert data in Amazon DynamoDB

D) Ingest streaming data into Amazon SQS, which triggers an AWS Lambda function for processing and stores alert data in Amazon Redshift

E) Use Amazon API Gateway to ingest streaming data, which is processed by an application running on an Amazon EC2 instance, and store alert data in Amazon Elasticsearch Service

QUESTION 41

A media streaming company wants to ensure high availability and low-latency access to its content for users worldwide. They need a solution that optimizes content delivery and ensures resilience against regional failures. Which AWS service should the company use to achieve these objectives?

A) Implement Amazon CloudFront with AWS Global Accelerator to optimize content delivery and improve availability by using the AWS global network.

B) Utilize Amazon Route 53 with latency-based routing to direct user traffic to the nearest AWS edge location for low-latency access.

C) Deploy AWS Direct Connect to establish dedicated connections between data centers and AWS regions for low-latency content delivery.

D) Configure Amazon S3 Cross-Region Replication to replicate content across regions and ensure resilience against regional failures.

E) Implement Amazon CloudWatch with custom metrics to monitor content delivery performance and availability.

QUESTION 42

Your team is designing a solution for a social media platform that requires efficient handling of high concurrency. The platform experiences spikes in user activity during peak hours, leading to performance issues with the current database setup. What strategy should you employ to ensure optimal database performance under high concurrency?

A) Implement Amazon RDS with Multi-AZ deployment for fault tolerance.
B) Utilize Amazon Aurora Serverless for automatic scaling based on demand.
C) Configure database sharding to horizontally partition data across multiple instances.
D) Deploy Amazon DynamoDB with on-demand capacity to handle sudden spikes in traffic.
E) Use Amazon ElastiCache to cache frequently accessed data and reduce database load.

QUESTION 43

A multinational corporation aims to integrate real-time analytics into their global operations to enhance decision-making and operational efficiency. They require a solution that can ingest, store, and analyze vast amounts of structured and unstructured data from diverse sources including IoT devices, social media, and transactional systems. The solution must offer both batch and real-time analytics capabilities, ensure data security, and comply with international data protection regulations. Additionally, the corporation seeks to minimize operational costs while ensuring scalability and high availability across multiple regions.

A) Utilize AWS Lake Formation for data lake creation, Amazon S3 for data storage, Amazon Kinesis for real-time data streaming, Amazon Athena for querying data, and AWS Glue for data preparation and loading.

B) Deploy Amazon EC2 instances with Apache Hadoop for batch processing, Amazon EFS for data storage, Amazon MQ for messaging, Amazon RDS for transactional data management, and Amazon CloudWatch for monitoring.

C) Implement Amazon DynamoDB for NoSQL data storage, Amazon EMR for big data processing, AWS Data Pipeline for data orchestration, Amazon QuickSight for business intelligence, and AWS IAM for security.

D) Use Amazon Redshift for data warehousing, Amazon S3 for archiving, AWS DataSync for data transfer, Amazon Lex for building conversational interfaces, and Amazon CloudFront for global content delivery.

E) Leverage Amazon Managed Streaming for Apache Kafka (Amazon MSK) for data streaming, AWS

Fargate for running containers, Amazon Athena for serverless querying, Amazon S3 for data lake storage, and AWS Lambda for event-driven data processing.

QUESTION 44

Your company is building a real-time fraud detection system for financial transactions. The system must analyze transaction data promptly to identify suspicious activities and trigger alerts. Which architecture would be most effective for this scenario?

A) Utilize Amazon Kinesis Data Firehose for transaction data ingestion, process it with AWS Glue, and store results in Amazon Aurora for real-time analysis and alerting.

B) Implement Amazon Kinesis Data Streams for transaction data, process it using AWS Lambda functions, and store results in Amazon DynamoDB for real-time access.

C) Deploy Amazon Managed Streaming for Apache Kafka (Amazon MSK) for transaction data ingestion, process it with Amazon Kinesis Data Analytics, and trigger alerts using Amazon SNS.

D) Utilize AWS AppSync to integrate transaction data with Amazon Neptune graph database, analyze data in real-time, and trigger alerts with Amazon SQS.

E) Set up Amazon Kinesis Data Firehose to capture transaction data, process it using Amazon EMR, and store results in Amazon S3 for further analysis and alerting.

QUESTION 45

A media company wants to securely store video content in Amazon S3 while ensuring encryption of the data at rest. The company requires the ability to rotate encryption keys periodically without disrupting access to the stored data. Which option would be the most suitable choice for this scenario?

A) Utilize server-side encryption with Amazon S3 managed keys (SSE-S3) to encrypt the data on Amazon S3

B) Implement server-side encryption with AWS Key Management Service (SSE-KMS) and enable automatic key rotation

C) Use client-side encryption with customer-provided keys (SSE-C) and upload the encrypted data to Amazon S3

D) Implement server-side encryption with customer-provided keys (SSE-C) and manually rotate encryption keys

E) Enable AWS CloudTrail to monitor S3 bucket activities for auditing purposes

QUESTION 46

You are designing an IoT solution for a fleet management company that wants to track the location, status, and performance of its vehicles in real-time. The solution should be cost-effective while ensuring high availability and reliability. Which combination of AWS services and features would you recommend for this scenario?

A) Implement AWS IoT Events for data ingestion, set up AWS Lambda for edge processing, use Amazon

Kinesis Data Streams for real-time data processing, deploy Amazon Aurora for real-time data storage, and employ Amazon S3 Glacier for long-term data archival.

B) Utilize AWS IoT Greengrass for data ingestion, leverage AWS Lambda for edge processing, employ Amazon Kinesis Data Streams for real-time data processing, store real-time data in Amazon DynamoDB, and archive long-term data in Amazon S3.

C) Deploy Amazon API Gateway for data ingestion, utilize AWS Fargate for edge processing, configure Amazon Kinesis Data Analytics for real-time data analysis, connect with Amazon RDS for real-time data storage, and employ Amazon Glacier for long-term data archival.

D) Utilize AWS IoT Core for data ingestion, configure AWS Greengrass for edge computing, implement Amazon Kinesis Data Streams for real-time data processing, utilize AWS Lambda for serverless processing, and store real-time data in Amazon DynamoDB.

E) Configure AWS IoT Core for data ingestion, implement AWS Lambda for edge processing, set up Amazon Kinesis Data Streams for real-time data processing, integrate with Amazon RDS for real-time data storage, and utilize Amazon S3 for long-term data archival.

QUESTION 47

You are designing an edge computing solution for a healthcare provider that wants to process patient health data in real-time to enable remote monitoring and diagnosis. The solution must comply with strict regulatory requirements for data privacy and security. Which architecture would best meet these requirements?

A) Utilize AWS Lambda@Edge to deploy applications on edge devices located in hospitals and clinics, leverage AWS IoT Greengrass for edge data processing, and integrate with Amazon DynamoDB for real-time data storage.

B) Deploy applications on edge devices using AWS Snow Family devices installed in hospitals and clinics, leverage AWS IoT Greengrass for edge data processing, and integrate with Amazon Aurora for real-time data storage.

C) Implement applications on Amazon EC2 instances deployed in AWS Outposts located within hospitals and clinics, utilize AWS IoT Greengrass for edge data processing, and integrate with Amazon RDS for real-time data storage.

D) Utilize AWS Wavelength to deploy applications on edge devices located within telecommunication providers' data centers, leverage AWS IoT Greengrass for edge data processing, and integrate with Amazon S3 for real-time data storage.

E) Deploy applications on edge devices using AWS Local Zones located within hospitals and clinics, leverage AWS IoT Greengrass for edge data processing, and integrate with Amazon Redshift for real-time data storage.

QUESTION 48

For a FinTech company offering real-time stock trading services, ensuring low latency and secure API transactions is paramount. The company needs to efficiently manage thousands of transactions per second, enforce strict access controls, and provide traders with real-time market data. Considering AWS services, how should the company architect its API to meet these high-performance and security demands?

A) Implement Amazon API Gateway for high-performance API management, AWS Lambda for real-time transaction processing, Amazon DynamoDB for storing transaction records, and AWS IAM for access control.

B) Use Amazon Kinesis for handling real-time data streams, Amazon ECS for microservice management, Amazon EFS for durable storage, and Amazon Cognito for user authentication.

C) Deploy AWS AppSync for data synchronization, Amazon RDS for transaction data storage, AWS Fargate for serverless container execution, and AWS Shield for DDoS protection.

D) Leverage Amazon SQS for message queuing, AWS Step Functions for transaction workflow orchestration, Amazon S3 for data storage, and Amazon Macie for data security and privacy.

E) Utilize AWS Global Accelerator to improve API performance, Amazon Aurora for high-throughput database needs, AWS WAF for web application firewall protection, and AWS X-Ray for monitoring and tracing.

QUESTION 49

An e-commerce company operates a web application for handling customer orders and inventory management. The application experiences consistent traffic during business hours and occasional spikes during sales events and promotions. The company wants to optimize infrastructure costs while ensuring reliable performance during peak times. Which pricing option for Amazon EC2 instances would be the most suitable choice for this scenario?

A) Utilize reserved instances (RI) for the entire duration of operation
B) Implement on-demand instances for the entire duration of operation
C) Utilize spot instances for the entire duration of operation
D) Employ a combination of reserved instances (RI) and spot instances
E) Implement a mix of reserved instances (RI) and on-demand instances

QUESTION 50

Your company is migrating its data analytics platform to AWS and is looking to optimize costs while maintaining high performance. The platform processes large datasets and requires scalable compute resources. Which approach would be most effective for achieving cost-effective performance optimization?

A) Utilize Amazon Redshift Spectrum to query data directly from Amazon S3 without loading it into Redshift, reducing storage costs. Implement Amazon Athena for interactive query processing, paying only for the queries executed.

B) Deploy Amazon EMR with spot instances to process data stored in Amazon S3, leveraging the cost savings of spot instances for compute-intensive workloads. Integrate Amazon QuickSight for visualization and reporting, enabling cost-effective analytics.

C) Implement a combination of AWS Kinesis Data Firehose for real-time data streaming, AWS Glue for data preparation, and AWS Lambda for serverless data processing. This setup aims to optimize costs by paying only for the resources used without provisioning or managing servers.

D) Use Amazon RDS for database services paired with AWS Data Pipeline for orchestration of data transfers and transformations. This approach focuses on automating workflows between different AWS services but may not provide the scalability needed for large datasets.

E) Opt for a serverless architecture using AWS Lambda for data processing, coupled with Amazon S3 for data storage and Amazon DynamoDB for NoSQL database needs. This method minimizes costs by automatically scaling with the workload and charging only for the compute time used.

QUESTION 51

A multinational corporation is deploying a global contact center with AI capabilities for real-time language translation, sentiment analysis, and personalized responses. The contact center serves customers from diverse linguistic backgrounds, requiring seamless communication and personalized support. What AWS architecture would best meet these requirements?

A) Use Amazon Connect for the contact center, Amazon Lex for conversational interfaces and sentiment analysis, AWS Lambda for scalability and integration with CRM/ERP systems, and Amazon Translate for real-time language translation.

B) Deploy AWS Direct Connect for dedicated network connections to CRM and ERP, Amazon Polly for text-to-speech functionality, Amazon S3 for data storage, and Amazon RDS for transactional data management.

C) Implement Amazon API Gateway for secure API integration, Amazon Kinesis for real-time data streaming, Amazon SageMaker for building personalized AI responses, and AWS Fargate for running containerized workloads.

D) Utilize Amazon SQS for message queuing, AWS Step Functions for orchestration of customer service workflows, Amazon Comprehend for sentiment analysis, and Amazon Aurora Serverless for scalable database needs.

E) Leverage AWS AppSync for real-time data synchronization, AWS Elastic Beanstalk for application deployment, Amazon Rekognition for image and sentiment analysis, and Amazon DynamoDB for storing customer data.

QUESTION 52

A financial services company needs to design a high-performing architecture for its real-time trading platform, which serves customers worldwide. The platform requires low-latency access to financial data and must ensure data durability and availability. What architecture should they implement?

A) Deploy the platform on Amazon EC2 instances with an Amazon RDS database, utilizing Amazon S3 for data backup and AWS Global Accelerator for low-latency access.

B) Utilize Amazon Redshift for data analytics and Amazon DynamoDB for low-latency access to trading data, with Amazon S3 for data archival.

C) Implement an Amazon EMR cluster for real-time data processing, using Amazon S3 for data storage and Glacier for long-term archival.

D) Configure an Amazon Kinesis Data Streams pipeline for real-time data ingestion, with Amazon RDS Multi-AZ deployment for transactional data and Amazon S3 for data backup.

E) Deploy the platform on AWS Lambda functions triggered by Amazon API Gateway events, utilizing Amazon DynamoDB for low-latency access and S3 for data archival.

QUESTION 53

A software company needs to ensure its Amazon EC2 instances automatically recover from hardware failures. Which feature should be implemented to meet this requirement?

A) Use Elastic Load Balancers to reroute traffic in case of instance failure.
B) Implement EC2 Auto Scaling groups to replace unhealthy instances.
C) Configure EC2 Instance Recovery for automatic instance recovery.
D) Apply AWS Lambda functions to monitor and replace failed instances.
E) Utilize Amazon CloudWatch alarms and EC2 Auto Recovery actions.

QUESTION 54

Your company needs to design a data storage solution for its IoT devices, which will generate a large volume of data with variable ingestion rates. The solution should ensure low-latency access to the data and cost optimization. Which approach would best fulfill these requirements considering the need for real-time data ingestion, low-latency access, and cost-effectiveness?

A) Utilize Amazon S3 for data storage and query data using Amazon Athena
B) Deploy Amazon Redshift with Concurrency Scaling for high-performance analytics
C) Implement Amazon Kinesis Data Streams for real-time data ingestion and analytics
D) Opt for Amazon RDS Multi-AZ configuration for relational data storage
E) Use Amazon DynamoDB for its flexible and scalable NoSQL capabilities

QUESTION 55

An online education platform uses Amazon Aurora for storing course content and student records. The platform is expanding globally and needs to ensure that course content is consistent worldwide, but student records should be region-specific to comply with local data protection laws. Which database architecture should be used?

A) Deploy Amazon Aurora Global Database for course content and use Amazon RDS for student records in each region.

B) Use Amazon DynamoDB global tables for course content and Amazon Aurora for regional student records.

C) Implement separate Amazon Aurora instances in each region for both course content and student records.

D) Utilize Amazon Aurora Global Database for both course content and student records, with region-specific access controls.

E) Use Amazon S3 for global course content storage and Amazon Aurora for regional student records.

QUESTION 56

Your company operates a media streaming platform on AWS, utilizing Amazon S3 for storing video files and Amazon CloudFront for content delivery. The company wants to implement a backup solution for its media assets, ensuring high durability and availability while minimizing costs. Which approach aligns with best practices for designing the backup solution?

A) Utilize Amazon S3 Cross-Region Replication to replicate media assets to a secondary AWS region
B) Implement AWS Backup to automate and manage backups of Amazon S3 data
C) Configure Amazon S3 Object Lock to prevent accidental deletion of media assets
D) Leverage Amazon S3 Transfer Acceleration for faster data transfer during backups
E) Utilize Amazon S3 Intelligent-Tiering to optimize storage costs based on access patterns

QUESTION 57

Your organization is migrating a large volume of data from an on-premises data center to AWS. The data transfer needs to be completed within a specific timeframe while minimizing costs. What would be the most appropriate solution for this scenario?

A) Utilize AWS Direct Connect to establish a dedicated network connection between the on-premises data center and AWS
B) Deploy AWS Snowmobile to physically transfer the data from the on-premises data center to AWS
C) Implement AWS DataSync to transfer data directly from on-premises storage to Amazon S3
D) Set up Amazon S3 Transfer Acceleration to optimize data transfer speeds for the migration
E) Use AWS Transfer Family to set up an SFTP server for secure data transfer to Amazon S3

QUESTION 58

Your company operates a global media streaming platform that delivers high-quality video content to millions of users worldwide. As part of cost optimization efforts, you decide to leverage Amazon CloudFront for content delivery. Which of the following configurations would best optimize costs while ensuring high-quality video streaming performance for users across different regions?

A) Utilize Amazon CloudFront with signed URLs to restrict access to video content and prevent unauthorized sharing

B) Implement Amazon CloudFront with Lambda@Edge functions to customize content delivery based on viewer device characteristics

C) Configure Amazon CloudFront with regional edge caches to reduce latency for viewers in specific geographic regions

D) Enable Amazon CloudFront with field-level encryption to protect sensitive data in transit and enhance security

E) Integrate Amazon CloudFront with AWS Elemental MediaPackage for packaging and origination of video content

QUESTION 59

Your company's data storage costs have been increasing due to the accumulation of obsolete data in

Amazon S3 buckets. You need to implement a solution to automatically identify and delete data that is no longer needed, reducing storage costs. What approach should you take?

A) Implement Amazon S3 Cross-Region Replication to replicate data to a secondary bucket and manually delete obsolete data from the primary bucket

B) Leverage Amazon S3 Storage Class Analysis to identify infrequently accessed data and manually delete obsolete records

C) Deploy AWS Lambda functions triggered by Amazon CloudWatch Events to analyze object metadata and delete data based on predefined criteria

D) Utilize Amazon S3 Batch Operations to schedule regular clean-up tasks and delete obsolete data from S3 buckets

E) Enable Amazon S3 Object Lock to prevent accidental deletion of data and manually review and delete obsolete records periodically

QUESTION 60

A financial services company wants to implement fine-grained access control for its AWS resources to ensure compliance with regulatory requirements. What solution should the solutions architect recommend to enforce granular permissions management?

A) Implement AWS Resource Access Manager (RAM) to share AWS resources across accounts while maintaining control over resource access.

B) Utilize AWS Identity and Access Management (IAM) policies with condition keys to restrict access based on various attributes, such as IP address or time of day.

C) Configure AWS Service Control Policies (SCPs) to establish permission guardrails for the entire AWS organization.

D) Enable AWS Key Management Service (KMS) to encrypt sensitive data and manage access through encryption key policies.

E) Implement AWS Identity Federation to grant temporary access to AWS resources based on external identity providers.

QUESTION 61

Your team is designing a global application architecture that requires low-latency access to data and services across multiple regions. Cost optimization is a key consideration, and you need to ensure that the architecture can scale efficiently while minimizing costs. Which approach should you recommend for this scenario?

A) Utilize Amazon CloudFront with AWS Lambda@Edge to cache and deliver content at edge locations
B) Implement Amazon Route 53 with latency-based routing to direct users to the nearest AWS region

C) Use AWS Global Accelerator to optimize the path to AWS services and improve global application performance

D) Deploy Amazon S3 Transfer Acceleration to accelerate data transfers to and from Amazon S3

E) Utilize AWS Direct Connect with AWS Transit Gateway to establish private connectivity between on-premises data centers and AWS regions

QUESTION 62

Your company operates a media streaming platform that serves users globally. To minimize costs while ensuring high availability and low latency for streaming content, you need to design a cost-effective solution for content delivery. Which approach should you recommend for this scenario?

A) Use Amazon CloudFront with AWS WAF to protect against DDoS attacks and optimize content delivery

B) Implement Amazon Route 53 with latency-based routing to direct users to the nearest AWS edge location

C) Utilize Amazon S3 Transfer Acceleration to optimize data transfers and reduce latency for media uploads

D) Deploy Amazon CloudFront with Lambda@Edge to cache and deliver streaming content at edge locations

E) Use AWS Direct Connect with AWS Transit Gateway to establish private connectivity between on-premises data centers and AWS regions

QUESTION 63

Your company is migrating its on-premises database workloads to AWS using a hybrid cloud approach. Cost optimization is a priority, and you need to design a solution that minimizes expenses while ensuring efficient data transfer and storage. What approach should you recommend?

A) Utilize AWS DataSync to transfer data from on-premises databases to Amazon S3 and then migrate the databases to Amazon RDS

B) Implement AWS Database Migration Service (DMS) to replicate on-premises databases to Amazon RDS instances for seamless migration

C) Deploy AWS Snowball Edge to transfer large volumes of on-premises database backups to Amazon S3 for long-term storage

D) Leverage AWS Storage Gateway to cache frequently accessed on-premises database data locally and reduce data transfer costs to AWS

E) Utilize AWS Data Pipeline to automate the transfer of on-premises database backups to Amazon S3 and then restore them to Amazon RDS

QUESTION 64

Your company operates a serverless architecture for its application, leveraging AWS Lambda extensively. However, the finance department has noticed an increase in costs associated with Lambda function invocations. As a solutions architect, you need to design a cost-efficient solution that maintains the benefits of serverless architecture while reducing expenses. What approach should you recommend?

A) Implement AWS Lambda provisioned concurrency to reduce cold starts and optimize costs associated with function invocations

B) Utilize Amazon API Gateway caching to reduce the number of Lambda function invocations and lower costs

C) Leverage AWS Step Functions to orchestrate Lambda function workflows and optimize costs by minimizing function invocations

D) Deploy AWS Fargate with Amazon ECS to run containerized workloads and reduce costs compared to serverless functions

E) Utilize AWS Batch to manage batch processing workloads and lower costs by optimizing resource utilization

QUESTION 65

Your company is experiencing challenges in controlling AWS costs across various departments and projects. As a solutions architect, you need to recommend a solution that enables granular cost control and accountability.

A) Utilize AWS Organizations to implement consolidated billing and cost allocation tags for detailed cost tracking

B) Implement AWS Budgets to set and monitor cost limits for specific services and projects

C) Leverage AWS Cost and Usage Report with Amazon Athena for custom cost analysis and reporting

D) Utilize AWS Resource Access Manager (RAM) to share AWS resources across accounts and track usage for cost allocation

E) Implement AWS Service Catalog to standardize and control provisioned resources to minimize cost

PRACTICE TEST 3 - ANSWERS ONLY

QUESTION 1

Answer - A) Use AWS IAM roles with external ID to grant cross-account access and enforce least privilege access.

A) Correct - Using IAM roles with an external ID is a secure way to grant cross-account access. It allows for precise control over permissions and adheres to the principle of least privilege.

B) Incorrect - Sharing root account credentials is extremely risky and violates AWS security best practices. It should be avoided at all costs.

C) Incorrect - Creating IAM users in each account and using access keys for cross-account sharing is not as secure or manageable as using IAM roles.

D) Incorrect - Enabling public access to S3 buckets and using API keys for Lambda functions introduces significant security risks and is not a recommended practice for cross-account access.

E) Incorrect - While AWS Control Tower can automate the setup of multiple AWS accounts and enforce security baselines with SCPs, it is not directly used for managing cross-account access to specific resources like S3 and Lambda. IAM roles with external IDs are the standard approach for this scenario.

QUESTION 2

Answer - D) Implement data residency controls by selecting AWS regions that comply with local regulations for data storage, and use Amazon RDS for database services.

A) Incorrect - While Amazon S3 and Amazon Macie are important for data security, this choice does not address the specific requirement for data residency compliance.

B) Incorrect - AWS Outposts is a solution for extending AWS infrastructure on-premises, but it may not be the most cost-effective or scalable solution for data residency compliance for all types of data and does not leverage AWS's global infrastructure for availability.

C) Incorrect - Deploying data across multiple regions without considering data residency requirements could result in non-compliance with local regulations.

D) Correct - This strategy ensures compliance with data residency regulations by storing data in appropriate regions while leveraging AWS global infrastructure for high availability and disaster recovery. Amazon RDS supports this approach by providing managed relational database services that can be deployed within specific regions.

E) Incorrect - While AWS CloudHSM provides hardware-based key storage for encryption, relying solely on it does not ensure compliance with data residency regulations. This approach overlooks the necessity to strategically select AWS regions for data storage.

QUESTION 3

Answer - A) AWS Shield Advanced for comprehensive DDoS protection, Amazon GuardDuty for intelligent threat detection, and AWS WAF for custom web traffic filtering rules.

A) Correct - This selection addresses the outlined threats directly. AWS Shield Advanced offers protection against large-scale DDoS attacks, Amazon GuardDuty provides intelligent threat detection capabilities that can help identify APTs and other sophisticated attacks, and AWS WAF allows the creation of custom rules to filter out malicious web traffic, offering a robust defense mechanism for the platform.

B) Incorrect - Amazon CloudFront, AWS Direct Connect, and AWS IAM are important for content delivery, network optimization, and access management, but they do not specifically provide the level of threat protection and detection needed against state-sponsored attacks.

C) Incorrect - AWS Fargate, Amazon Inspector, and Amazon VPC provide infrastructure security and assessment tools, but they do not offer the specialized protection against DDoS and advanced persistent threats as the services in choice A.

D) Incorrect - While AWS Lambda, AWS Systems Manager, and Amazon RDS offer automation, management, and database security, they do not specifically address the sophisticated nature of state-sponsored cyber attacks.

E) Incorrect - AWS Global Accelerator, Amazon Macie, and Amazon S3 focus on performance optimization, data security, and storage. While important, these services do not directly counter the specific threats of sophisticated DDoS attacks and APTs.

QUESTION 4

Answer - [A] Deploy AWS Network Firewall to inspect and filter incoming and outgoing traffic at the subnet level. Utilize Amazon CloudWatch Logs and Amazon CloudWatch Events to monitor network activity and trigger automated responses based on predefined rules.

Option A - Correct. AWS Network Firewall provides inspection and filtering capabilities, while CloudWatch Logs and CloudWatch Events enable monitoring and automated responses to network activity.

Option B - AWS WAF and AWS Shield Advanced offer protection against web attacks and DDoS, but they may not provide the same level of visibility and automation for network traffic monitoring.

Option C - AWS GuardDuty and AWS Config focus more on monitoring for malicious activity and compliance rather than real-time network traffic inspection and automated response.

Option D - AWS Security Hub and AWS Firewall Manager are more focused on central management of security findings and policy enforcement, rather than real-time network traffic monitoring and response.

Option E - While AWS VPC Traffic Mirroring and Amazon Inspector offer network traffic inspection capabilities, they may not provide the same level of automated response as AWS Network Firewall and CloudWatch Events.

QUESTION 5

Answer - C) Use Amazon SQS FIFO queue with a batch mode of 10 messages per operation.

C) Use Amazon SQS FIFO queue with a batch mode of 10 messages per operation - This option allows for processing multiple orders in a batch, ensuring prompt handling during peak hours. The FIFO ensures order accuracy, and batch processing enhances scalability by reducing the number of API calls needed to process orders, thus meeting the company's requirements for prompt order processing and scalability.

A) Use Amazon SQS FIFO queue with exactly-once processing enabled - While ensuring order accuracy, exactly-once processing may not offer the scalability needed during peak hours, as it processes messages sequentially.

B) Use Amazon SQS FIFO queue with message deduplication enabled - While ensuring order accuracy by avoiding duplicate messages, it doesn't address the scalability requirement during peak hours.

D) Use Amazon SQS standard queue to process the messages - Standard queues lack message ordering, which is crucial for maintaining order accuracy, and may not meet the scalability requirement during peak hours.

E) Use Amazon SQS FIFO queue with default settings - Default settings may not ensure scalability during peak hours, and the absence of batch processing may hinder prompt order processing.

QUESTION 6

Answer - [A] Utilize Amazon Kinesis Data Streams for data ingestion, AWS Lambda for real-time processing, and Amazon API Gateway for API management. Implement AWS IoT Core with device certificates for secure device authentication.

Option A - Correct. Amazon Kinesis Data Streams, AWS Lambda, and API Gateway are suitable for real-time data processing, and AWS IoT Core with device certificates ensures secure device authentication.

Option B - While Kinesis Data Firehose, Lambda, and API Gateway are suitable, using IAM roles with IoT Core for device authentication may not provide the same level of security as device certificates.

Option C - Kinesis Data Analytics may not be suitable for data ingestion, and while AWS IoT Device Defender provides monitoring and security assessment, it does not handle device authentication.

Option D - Kinesis Video Streams may not align well with data ingestion from IoT devices, and custom authentication logic with IoT Core may introduce complexity and security risks.

Option E - Amazon MSK, while suitable for Apache Kafka, may not be the best choice for data ingestion from IoT devices, and using Cognito with IoT Core for device authentication may not provide the same level of security as device certificates.

QUESTION 7

Answer - B) Deploy AWS CloudHSM and manage the encryption keys within the HSM.

A) Use AWS KMS with customer-managed keys and enable hardware security module (HSM) protection. - Incorrect because while AWS KMS supports HSMs, it does not offer the same level of control and exclusivity over the hardware that some compliance regulations might require.

B) Deploy AWS CloudHSM and manage the encryption keys within the HSM. - Correct as it provides the firm with full control over their encryption keys and the hardware security modules, meeting strict compliance requirements.

C) Utilize Amazon S3 with server-side encryption and integrate with AWS CloudHSM. - Incorrect because this option doesn't specify how keys are managed within CloudHSM, and S3's integration is not the primary key management solution.

D) Implement AWS Secrets Manager for storing and managing encryption keys with HSM-backed encryption. - Incorrect because AWS Secrets Manager is primarily used for managing secrets, not specifically for compliance-focused key management with HSMs.

E) Use Amazon EBS volumes encrypted with AWS managed keys and AWS KMS integration. - Incorrect because it does not provide the level of control over the HSMs that compliance regulations may require for a financial services firm.

QUESTION 8

Answer - A) and D)

A) AWS Config and AWS CloudTrail - Correct because Config provides AWS resource inventory, configuration history, and configuration change notifications, while CloudTrail logs events and API calls, both essential for compliance monitoring.

B) Amazon QuickSight and AWS Glue - Incorrect as these services are used for business intelligence and data integration, respectively, not compliance monitoring.

C) AWS KMS and Amazon Macie - Incorrect because they focus on key management and data protection/security, respectively.

D) AWS Audit Manager and AWS Security Hub - Correct because Audit Manager helps continuously audit AWS usage to ensure compliance with regulations, and Security Hub provides comprehensive security insights.

E) Amazon Detective and AWS IAM Identity Center - Incorrect because these are for in-depth analysis of security findings and identity management, respectively.

QUESTION 9

Answer - [D] Enabling Amazon Cognito for user authentication and access control, ensuring secure access to the messaging application and compliance with data protection regulations.

A) AWS Secrets Manager is suitable for managing credentials but may not directly address user authentication or compliance with industry standards for data protection.

B) While end-to-end encryption using AWS KMS enhances data security, it may not provide user authentication or access control mechanisms required for compliance with industry regulations.

C) Amazon GuardDuty offers threat detection and monitoring but may not directly handle user authentication or access control, nor does it ensure compliance with data protection regulations.

D) Amazon Cognito provides user authentication, access control, and compliance features, making it suitable for securing access to the messaging application and meeting industry standards for data protection.

E) AWS Network Firewall filters traffic but may not directly provide user authentication or compliance features required for securing a messaging application and ensuring adherence to industry regulations.

QUESTION 10

Answer - A) Use Amazon FSx File Gateway to provide low-latency, on-premises access to fully managed file shares in Amazon EFS. The applications deployed on AWS can access this data directly from Amazon EFS.

A) Use Amazon FSx File Gateway to provide low-latency, on-premises access to fully managed file shares in Amazon EFS. The applications deployed on AWS can access this data directly from Amazon EFS - This option aligns with the requirement by suggesting the use of Amazon FSx File Gateway with Amazon EFS, ensuring low-latency access to video files during and after migration.

B) Use Amazon Storage Gateway's File Gateway to provide low-latency, on-premises access to fully managed file shares in Amazon FSx for Windows File Server. The applications deployed on AWS can access this data directly from Amazon FSx in AWS - This option does not align with the requirement as it suggests using FSx for Windows File Server instead of Amazon EFS, which may not meet the low-latency access requirement.

C) Use AWS Storage Gateway's File Gateway to provide low-latency, on-premises access to fully managed file shares in Amazon S3. The applications deployed on AWS can access this data directly from Amazon S3 - This option does not align with the requirement as it suggests using Amazon S3 instead of Amazon EFS, which may not meet the low-latency access requirement.

D) Use Amazon FSx File Gateway to provide low-latency, on-premises access to fully managed file shares in Amazon FSx for Windows File Server. The applications deployed on AWS can access this data directly from Amazon FSx in AWS - This option does not align with the requirement as it suggests using FSx for Windows File Server instead of Amazon EFS, which may not meet the low-latency access requirement.

QUESTION 11

Answer - A) Amazon VPC with AWS Network Firewall, Amazon GuardDuty for threat detection, and AWS CloudTrail for logging

A) Amazon VPC with AWS Network Firewall, Amazon GuardDuty for threat detection, and AWS CloudTrail for logging - Correct because this combination allows for granular network control with VPC, dynamic threat detection with GuardDuty, and detailed access and event logging with CloudTrail, catering to both security and compliance needs across regions.

B) AWS Shield Advanced with AWS WAF for application layer protection, and Amazon CloudWatch for monitoring - Incorrect as it focuses on DDoS and application layer protection without addressing regional cyber threats or compliance with data sovereignty laws specifically.

C) AWS Lambda for custom threat response automation, AWS Fargate for container management, and Amazon S3 for logging - Incorrect because, while offering a degree of flexibility and logging, it doesn't provide the integrated, comprehensive network protection or compliance assurance required.

D) AWS Direct Connect for dedicated network connections, Amazon Route 53 for traffic management, and AWS IAM for access control - Incorrect as these services focus more on connectivity, DNS management, and identity access management rather than dynamic threat defense and compliance.

E) Amazon CloudFront for global content delivery, AWS Global Accelerator for performance optimization, and Amazon Inspector for security assessments - Incorrect because, while useful for performance and assessment, this set does not specifically address dynamic regional threat protection or compliance with local data laws.

QUESTION 12

Answer - B) Configure AWS IAM roles for privileged users with enforced MFA, leveraging AWS CloudTrail for logging.

A) Integrate AWS CloudTrail with on-premises SIEM systems for auditing privileged actions. - Incorrect as it only covers the auditing aspect, not the enforcement of MFA or the integration with a privilege access management system.

B) Configure AWS IAM roles for privileged users with enforced MFA, leveraging AWS CloudTrail for logging. - Correct because it addresses the need for detailed logging of privileged actions and enforces MFA for enhanced security compliance, aligning with financial regulations.

C) Utilize AWS IAM Identity Center (SSO) for centralized access, integrating with AWS KMS for enhanced security. - Incorrect because, while it provides centralized access management, it does not specifically mention MFA enforcement or direct integration with privilege access management systems.

D) Implement AWS Directory Service integration with on-premises systems, enabling MFA via AWS IAM policies. - Incorrect as it lacks the direct connection to logging and auditing of privileged actions that CloudTrail provides.

E) Establish federated access with AWS IAM and on-premises LDAP, using Amazon GuardDuty for anomaly detection and AWS CloudTrail for activity logging. - Incorrect because it doesn't specifically address the enforcement of MFA for privileged access, despite providing a comprehensive security monitoring setup.

QUESTION 13

Answer - A) Use Amazon Cognito User Pools for authentication, deploy AWS WAF with SQL injection and XSS rules on API Gateway, and rely on Lambda's automatic scaling.

A) Use Amazon Cognito User Pools for authentication, deploy AWS WAF with SQL injection and XSS rules on API Gateway, and rely on Lambda's automatic scaling - Correct. This setup provides a secure authentication mechanism, protection against specific web attacks, and automatic scaling.

B) Implement API keys in API Gateway for authentication, use Amazon Inspector for SQL injection and XSS detection, and enable Lambda concurrency controls for scaling - Incorrect because API keys are not an authentication mechanism for users, and Amazon Inspector does not provide real-time web attack protection.

C) Employ Amazon Cognito Identity Pools for authentication, attach AWS Shield to API Gateway for attack protection, and use AWS Auto Scaling with Lambda - Incorrect because Identity Pools provide access to AWS services and are not used directly for user authentication. AWS Shield is primarily for DDoS protection, not specific web attacks like SQL injection or XSS.

D) Utilize AWS IAM roles for user authentication, enable Amazon GuardDuty for SQL injection and XSS detection, and rely on Lambda's built-in scaling capabilities - Incorrect because IAM roles are not suitable for individual user authentication in this context, and GuardDuty is a threat detection service, not a web application firewall.

E) Implement AWS IAM authentication with API Gateway, use AWS WAF with custom rules for SQL injection and XSS protection on API Gateway, and allow Lambda to handle scaling - Incorrect because while the WAF setup is suitable, IAM authentication in this context doesn't apply to individual end-users directly interacting with APIs.

QUESTION 14

Answer - B) Use AWS Systems Manager for automated patch management and AWS Config for PCI DSS compliance monitoring and auto-remediation.

A) Configure AWS Shield and Amazon Inspector to automatically protect against threats and assess for PCI DSS compliance. - Incorrect because Shield focuses on DDoS protection and Inspector on security assessments, neither directly automating PCI DSS compliance monitoring and remediation.

B) Use AWS Systems Manager for automated patch management and AWS Config for PCI DSS compliance monitoring and auto-remediation. - Correct as Systems Manager aids in maintaining the security of EC2 instances through automated patching, and AWS Config continuously monitors and automatically remediates non-compliant configurations against PCI DSS requirements.

C) Leverage AWS Step Functions for orchestrating compliance workflows and AWS Audit Manager for PCI DSS assessments. - Incorrect because, while useful for assessment and workflow orchestration, this combination doesn't provide the same level of automation in monitoring and remediation as AWS Config with Systems Manager.

D) Implement AWS Lambda for custom compliance checks and remediation scripts, integrated with Amazon CloudWatch for monitoring. - Incorrect as this requires custom development and may not offer the comprehensive, out-of-the-box compliance solution that AWS Config and Systems Manager provide.

E) Deploy AWS WAF for real-time threat protection and AWS Trusted Advisor for continuous PCI DSS compliance scanning and recommendations. - Incorrect because WAF focuses on application layer protection, and Trusted Advisor offers best practices recommendations, not automated compliance remediation.

QUESTION 15

Answer - [B, D]

B) Suspend the ReplaceUnhealthy process type for the Auto Scaling group and apply the maintenance patch to the instance - This option efficiently addresses the maintenance challenge by suspending the process that replaces unhealthy instances, allowing uninterrupted maintenance work on the affected instance.

D) Put the instance into the Standby state and then update the instance by applying the maintenance patch - Placing the instance in the Standby state allows for maintenance without triggering Auto Scaling actions, ensuring the continuity of the maintenance process without disruption to the application's availability.

A) Suspend the ScheduledActions process type for the Auto Scaling group and apply the maintenance patch to the instance - Suspending scheduled actions may not prevent instance replacement triggered by health status changes, leading to potential disruptions during maintenance.

C) Delete the Auto Scaling group and apply the maintenance fix to the given instance - Deleting and recreating the Auto Scaling group is a drastic measure and may result in unnecessary downtime and loss of configuration settings.

E) Take a snapshot of the instance, create a new Amazon Machine Image (AMI), and then launch a new instance using this AMI - Creating a new instance from a snapshot introduces complexity and may not efficiently address the maintenance challenge, especially in scenarios where immediate fixes are required.

QUESTION 16

Answer - C) Assign an IAM role to the EC2 instances where the application runs.

A) Embed the AWS Access and Secret Keys in the application code - Incorrect because it is not secure and does not comply with AWS best practices.

B) Use environment variables to store AWS Access and Secret Keys on the EC2 instances - Incorrect because, while better than embedding in code, it still poses a risk if the instance is compromised.

C) Assign an IAM role to the EC2 instances where the application runs - Correct because it allows secure access without embedding credentials and adheres to best practices.

D) Store AWS Access and Secret Keys in a public GitHub repository for easy access - Incorrect and poses a significant security risk.

E) Create an IAM user for each service the application accesses, and rotate keys weekly - Incorrect because managing users for each service is cumbersome and does not leverage IAM roles' advantages.

QUESTION 17

Answer - A) Deploy public and private subnets within a VPC, utilize ELB for scalability, and enable VPC flow logs for traffic monitoring.

A) Correct because it aligns with best practices for VPC design, segregating public and private resources effectively, using ELB for dynamic scaling, and VPC flow logs for detailed network traffic visibility.

B) Incorrect as configuring multiple VPCs for each server increases complexity and does not inherently improve scalability or security. Global Accelerator and CloudWatch address different aspects but not the core scenario requirements.

C) Incorrect because Shield and Direct Connect address specific concerns (DDoS protection and dedicated connectivity) but don't fully meet the scalability and internal segmentation needs. Config monitors configuration changes, not real-time traffic.

D) Incorrect as App Mesh is service mesh, not a VPC design tool. S3 and WAF are critical but don't address the core network design and scalability requirements.

E) Incorrect because VPC peering is used for connecting VPCs, not for scalability or segregation of gaming architecture. Route 53 and Inspector offer DNS management and security assessments but do not address the primary network architecture design challenge.

QUESTION 18

Answer - [B] Deploy Amazon GuardDuty for threat detection and implement AWS Config Rules to enforce security best practices. Utilize AWS Budgets to set cost thresholds and alerts for different departments within the organization.

Option A - While IAM roles and KMS encryption address security concerns, they do not directly provide threat detection and cost management capabilities like GuardDuty and Budgets.

Option C - While CloudTrail, CloudWatch, and WAF address security concerns, they may not cover all aspects of threat detection like GuardDuty, and Trusted Advisor focuses on cost optimization rather than setting cost thresholds.

Option D - While Macie and S3 policies address data security concerns, they do not provide threat detection capabilities like GuardDuty.

Option E - While Security Hub provides centralized security monitoring, it does not directly address setting cost thresholds and alerts like AWS Budgets.

QUESTION 19

Answer - [B] Implement AWS Secrets Manager to securely store and rotate secrets. Integrate applications running on Fargate with Secrets Manager for secure retrieval of secrets.

Option A - Embedding secrets directly within Docker containers is not recommended for security reasons and lacks centralized management and rotation capabilities.

Option C - Storing secrets in plaintext files within Docker volumes poses security risks and lacks automation for rotation and retrieval.

Option D - While Parameter Store can centrally manage configurations, Secrets Manager is specifically designed for securely storing and rotating secrets.

Option E - Managing sensitive information in a spreadsheet within an S3 bucket lacks automation for rotation and retrieval and introduces unnecessary complexity.

Explanation for Choice B: Implementing AWS Secrets Manager allows for secure storage and rotation of secrets. Integrating with Fargate enables automated retrieval within containerized applications, enhancing security and compliance.

QUESTION 20

Answer - D) Create an Amazon CloudWatch metric filter that processes AWS CloudTrail logs containing API call details and identifies any errors by factoring in all the error codes that need to be tracked. Establish an alarm based on this metric's rate to send an Amazon SNS notification to the required team.

D) Create an Amazon CloudWatch metric filter that processes AWS CloudTrail logs containing API call details and identifies any errors by factoring in all the error codes that need to be tracked. Establish an alarm based on this metric's rate to send an Amazon SNS notification to the required team. - This option presents the most suitable solution by leveraging CloudTrail logs to detect unauthorized API calls in near real-time and triggering alerts via CloudWatch alarms and Amazon SNS notifications.

A) Run Amazon Athena SQL queries against AWS CloudTrail log files stored in Amazon S3 buckets. Use

Amazon QuickSight to generate reports for managerial dashboards. - While Athena and QuickSight provide insights, they may not offer real-time alerting capabilities as required in this scenario.

B) Configure AWS CloudTrail to stream event data to Amazon Kinesis. Utilize Amazon Kinesis stream-level metrics in Amazon CloudWatch to trigger an AWS Lambda function that will initiate an error workflow. - While this option leverages streaming data for monitoring, it may introduce complexity and latency compared to directly analyzing CloudTrail logs.

C) AWS Trusted Advisor publishes metrics about check results to Amazon CloudWatch. Create an alarm to track status changes for checks in the Service Limits category for the APIs. The alarm will then notify when the service quota is reached or exceeded. - While Trusted Advisor offers valuable insights, it may not directly address the need for real-time detection of unauthorized API queries.

E) Implement AWS Config Rules to monitor API activity and define rules to detect unauthorized API calls. Configure AWS Config to trigger an AWS Lambda function upon rule evaluation to notify relevant stakeholders. - While AWS Config can monitor API activity, it may not provide real-time alerting capabilities for immediate incident response as required in this scenario.

QUESTION 21

Answer - C) Utilize Amazon SNS for event notification, Amazon API Gateway for managing APIs, AWS Fargate for serverless compute, and Amazon DynamoDB for NoSQL data storage.

C) Correct because SNS provides event notification, API Gateway manages APIs, Fargate enables serverless compute, and DynamoDB offers NoSQL storage, aligning with the requirement for decoupling, independent scaling, and high availability in the cloud-native architecture.

B) Incorrect because while EKS and RDS Multi-AZ offer scalability and resilience, Step Functions and Route 53 are not directly related to decoupling and independent scaling of microservices, which are essential for a cloud-native architecture.

C) Incorrect as SQS, Lambda, Aurora Serverless, and CloudFront do not offer the same level of decoupling and independent scaling capabilities as SNS, API Gateway, Fargate, and DynamoDB required for a cloud-native architecture.

D) Incorrect because EventBridge, ECS, Neptune, and Direct Connect may provide scalability and resilience, but they may not offer the same level of simplicity and flexibility as SNS, API Gateway, Fargate, and DynamoDB in achieving decoupling and independent scaling in a cloud-native architecture.

E) Incorrect as Kinesis, Lambda, RDS, and EFS offer streaming, serverless compute, relational database management, and shared storage, respectively, but may not provide the same level of simplicity and scalability as SNS, API Gateway, Fargate, and DynamoDB for achieving decoupling and independent scaling in a cloud-native architecture.

QUESTION 22

Answer - A) Use Amazon ECS with AWS CodePipeline and AWS CodeBuild for container orchestration.

Option A combines Amazon ECS for container orchestration with AWS CodePipeline and AWS CodeBuild for continuous integration and deployment, aligning with the requirements for transitioning to a microservices architecture with CI/CD support.

Options B, C, D, and E do not provide an appropriate combination of services for the specified architecture and deployment needs.

QUESTION 23

Answer - [D) Utilize Amazon S3 for static content storage with Amazon CloudFront for content delivery and caching to achieve high performance and cost efficiency.]

Option D) is correct as it involves utilizing Amazon S3 for static content storage with Amazon CloudFront for content delivery and caching, ensuring high performance and cost efficiency.

Option A) involves Spot Instances but may not provide the same level of stability or cost efficiency as static content hosting.

Option B) involves serverless processing but may not provide the same level of performance as traditional hosting.

Option C) involves containerized deployment but may not provide the same level of cost optimization as static content hosting.

Option E) involves database deployment but does not directly address cost optimization.

QUESTION 24

Answer - [A) Amazon Kinesis Data Streams and B) AWS Lambda]

Option A involves Amazon Kinesis Data Streams for real-time data ingestion, enabling processing of streaming data from IoT devices.

Option B involves AWS Lambda for serverless event-driven processing, allowing automatic scaling and execution of code in response to incoming data.

Option C involves Amazon DynamoDB for NoSQL database, which provides low-latency storage for processed data but is not directly involved in real-time data processing.

Option D involves Amazon SNS for push notifications, which may be used for alerting but is not essential for real-time data processing.

Option E involves AWS Glue for ETL processing, which is more suitable for batch processing than real-time stream processing.

QUESTION 25

Answer - A) Tier-1 (8 terabytes)

A) Tier-1 (8 terabytes) - Correct. Amazon Aurora promotes the read replica with the highest priority (lowest tier number) as the new primary instance, regardless of instance size.
B) Tier-2 (16 terabytes) - Incorrect. Although this instance has a large size, its failover tier is lower than Tier-1.
C) Tier-5 (32 terabytes) - Incorrect. This instance has the largest size but does not have the highest priority for failover.
D) Tier-10 (8 terabytes) - Incorrect. This instance has a lower priority compared to Tier-1.

E) Tier-15 (16 terabytes) - Incorrect. This instance has the lowest priority among the options provided.

QUESTION 26

Answer - B) Utilize AWS AppMesh to provide service mesh capabilities for microservices, allowing fine-grained control over traffic routing and policy enforcement for both HTTP and non-HTTP protocols

Option B is correct because AWS AppMesh provides service mesh capabilities for microservices, allowing fine-grained control over traffic routing and policy enforcement for both HTTP and non-HTTP protocols. This ensures high availability, scalability, and support for various communication protocols in a microservices architecture.

Option A is incorrect because while Amazon API Gateway manages HTTP endpoints, it may not support non-HTTP protocols and may not offer the same level of fine-grained control as AWS AppMesh.

Option C is incorrect because while Amazon MQ enables message queuing, it may not provide the same level of traffic control and policy enforcement as AWS AppMesh for inter-service communication.

Option D is incorrect because while AWS AppSync provides a GraphQL API layer, it may not support non-HTTP protocols and may not offer the same level of traffic control as AWS AppMesh.

Option E is incorrect because while AWS Step Functions orchestrate microservices, they may not provide the same level of traffic control and policy enforcement as AWS AppMesh for inter-service communication.

QUESTION 27

Answer - A) Utilize AWS Step Functions with automatic retries and error handling for orchestrating course enrollment and content delivery tasks

Option A - AWS Step Functions offer automatic retries and error handling, providing fault tolerance and ensuring the reliability of serverless workflows.

Option B - While Amazon SNS and Lambda can handle event notifications and processing, they do not offer the comprehensive workflow orchestration features provided by Step Functions.

Option C - Amazon SQS and Lambda are suitable for asynchronous processing but lack the built-in retry and error handling capabilities needed for fault tolerance.

Option D - Amazon EventBridge and Lambda can handle event triggers but do not provide the advanced workflow orchestration features required for fault tolerance and error handling.

QUESTION 28

Answer - C) Use Amazon S3 event notifications to trigger AWS Elemental MediaConvert jobs for video transcoding, paying only for the resources consumed during job execution.

Option C - Amazon S3 event notifications coupled with AWS Elemental MediaConvert enable cost-efficient video transcoding by only paying for the resources used during job execution. This approach ensures scalability and performance while minimizing costs.

Option A - While AWS Lambda can trigger transcoding jobs, using Amazon Elastic Transcoder may not be the most cost-efficient solution compared to MediaConvert.

Option B - Amazon ECS Fargate with spot instances offers cost optimization but may not be as cost-effective as using MediaConvert with S3 event notifications.

Option D - Using EC2 instances requires managing infrastructure and may not offer the same level of scalability and cost efficiency as serverless options like MediaConvert.

Option E - Amazon Redshift is a data warehousing solution and is not optimized for video transcoding tasks, making it less suitable for this use case.

QUESTION 29

Answer - B) Implement Amazon CloudFront with Lambda@Edge for real-time content optimization.

A) ALB with Target Groups is used for application-level routing and does not provide dynamic video quality adjustments.

B) CloudFront with Lambda@Edge allows real-time optimization of content delivery, enabling dynamic adjustment of video quality based on network conditions and device capabilities.

C) Route 53 with Geoproximity routing policy routes traffic based on geographic proximity but does not optimize content delivery.

D) Classic Load Balancer is not recommended for new deployments due to its limitations.

E) NLB operates at the transport layer and does not provide content optimization capabilities.

QUESTION 30

Answer - D) Utilize Amazon Kinesis Data Streams with AWS Lambda for real-time data processing and store it in Amazon S3

D) Amazon Kinesis Data Streams combined with AWS Lambda offers real-time data processing capabilities suitable for analyzing customer interaction data across multiple touchpoints, delivering personalized experiences, and ensuring scalability with real-time processing.

A, B) These options involve storing data in relational databases or data warehouses, which may not be suitable for real-time processing and scalability required for optimizing product recommendations and promotions.

C, E) While these options involve using AWS Lambda and Amazon DynamoDB or S3, they may not provide the real-time processing capabilities required for delivering personalized experiences and optimizing promotions.

QUESTION 31

Answer - A) Use Amazon S3 for storage, AWS Lake Formation to manage data lake security and access, Amazon Athena for serverless querying, and AWS KMS for encryption.

A) Correct, as it provides a comprehensive, secure, and compliant solution for storing and analyzing sensitive health records. S3 offers scalable storage, Lake Formation secures the data lake, Athena allows complex analyses, and KMS ensures data encryption.

B) Incorrect, DynamoDB and Redshift are powerful for storage and analysis, but this combination lacks the data lake management and specific compliance capabilities provided by Lake Formation in option A.

C) Incorrect, EFS and EMR are useful for storage and processing, but Shield and GuardDuty, while enhancing security, don't directly address the compliance and data lake management needs for healthcare data.

D) Incorrect, RDS and QuickSight provide strong database and analytics tools, but CloudTrail and WAF focus more on governance and web security, not on the comprehensive data lake security and compliance required for healthcare data.

E) Incorrect, Fargate and Kinesis address processing and real-time data handling, but Glacier and Config are not optimized for the immediate, secure analysis of sensitive health records required in this scenario.

QUESTION 32

Answer - [B) Utilize Amazon DynamoDB with auto-scaling enabled and DynamoDB Accelerator (DAX) for in-memory caching to handle sudden traffic spikes.]

Option B) - Correct because Amazon DynamoDB with auto-scaling and DynamoDB Accelerator (DAX) efficiently handles sudden traffic spikes with in-memory caching, meeting the requirements of the global retail company effectively.

Option A) - Incorrect because while Amazon RDS with Multi-AZ deployment offers high availability, it lacks in-memory caching capabilities provided by DynamoDB Accelerator (DAX) required for handling sudden traffic spikes.

Option C) - Incorrect because Amazon Redshift is optimized for analytics and may not handle sudden spikes in workload effectively, as required by the retail company.

Option D) - Incorrect because although Amazon DocumentDB provides provisioned IOPS, it may not offer the same level of auto-scaling and in-memory caching capabilities as Amazon DynamoDB.

Option E) - Incorrect because Amazon Neptune is a graph database and may not be suitable for handling sudden traffic spikes in a retail environment, lacking the necessary capabilities provided by Amazon DynamoDB with auto-scaling and DynamoDB Accelerator (DAX).

QUESTION 33

Answer - D) Implement a serverless architecture using AWS Lambda for the application, coupled with Amazon DynamoDB with encryption at rest for storing patient records. Use Amazon API Gateway with SSL/TLS encryption for data in transit.

A) - Incorrect. While this option provides scalability and data encryption, it does not fully leverage the benefits of a serverless architecture for automatic scaling and operational efficiency. Also, it requires managing servers, which increases operational complexity.

B) - Incorrect. AWS Fargate and Amazon Aurora Serverless are good choices for server management and scalable databases. However, using AWS VPN for data in transit encryption does not directly apply to the application layer and is more suited for network connectivity.

C) - Incorrect. Amazon S3 and AWS Elastic Beanstalk provide scalability and data at rest encryption. However, relying on Amazon CloudFront for securing data in transit is more suited for content delivery scenarios, not application data flow.

D) - Correct. This option best meets the requirements by employing a serverless architecture with AWS Lambda, which provides automatic scaling and operational efficiency. Amazon DynamoDB offers scalability and encryption at rest, while Amazon API Gateway secures data in transit with SSL/TLS encryption, aligning with the healthcare company's compliance requirements.

E) - Incorrect. Hosting the application on a single, large EC2 instance does not provide the required scalability or high availability. Additionally, while Amazon EBS encryption and AWS Direct Connect offer secure data storage and connectivity, they do not address the need for automatic scaling or operational efficiency provided by a serverless approach.

QUESTION 34

Answer - A) Use Amazon S3 for content storage and Amazon CloudFront as a CDN.

A) Correct - Amazon S3 provides secure, durable, and highly-scalable object storage. Amazon CloudFront is a fast content delivery network (CDN) service that securely delivers data, videos, applications, and APIs to customers globally with low latency and high transfer speeds. This combination is ideal for global media content delivery.

B) Incorrect - Amazon EBS and Route 53 do not provide a CDN solution necessary for global content delivery with minimal latency.

C) Incorrect - Amazon Glacier is for long-term archival, not for fast content delivery. AWS Direct Connect does provide a dedicated network but does not optimize content delivery to end users globally.

D) Incorrect - AWS Storage Gateway and Amazon Kinesis Video Streams serve different purposes and do not primarily address global content delivery optimization.

E) Incorrect - While AWS Global Accelerator improves internet traffic flow, it does not specifically optimize video content delivery without the use of a CDN like Amazon CloudFront.

QUESTION 35

Answer - B) Implement WebSocket APIs on Amazon API Gateway with Amazon S3 for real-time video streaming and Amazon Cognito for secure transmission of patient data

B) Implementing WebSocket APIs on Amazon API Gateway allows for real-time video streaming, while leveraging Amazon S3 ensures secure transmission of patient data. Amazon Cognito provides user authentication and access control, ensuring secure transmission of patient data.

A) Using RESTful APIs with Amazon Kinesis Video Streams may support real-time video streaming but doesn't address secure data transmission effectively.

C, D, E) These options either do not provide suitable services for real-time video streaming or involve using services not ideal for secure transmission of patient data.

QUESTION 36

Answer - [A, B, C]

A) Correct - CloudFront accelerates content delivery, improving performance and reliability.
B) Correct - DynamoDB with auto-scaling adjusts capacity dynamically, ensuring performance under varying loads.
C) Correct - AWS Auto Scaling adjusts EC2 capacity, maintaining performance during traffic fluctuations.
D) Incorrect - Lambda for asynchronous processing doesn't directly address performance under varying loads.
E) Incorrect - Latency-based routing with Route 53 doesn't directly relate to handling traffic spikes.

QUESTION 37

Answer - [A, B]

A) Correct - AWS Config Rules define desired configurations and trigger automated remediation actions via CloudWatch Events and Lambda functions, ensuring continuous compliance monitoring and rapid incident response.

B) Correct - CloudTrail tracks API activity, GuardDuty detects threats, and Config assesses resource configuration compliance. Security Hub provides centralized security insights, enabling proactive monitoring and incident response.

C) Incorrect - While Inspector assesses security and compliance, CloudWatch Alarms monitor performance, not compliance. This option lacks the automation and centralized monitoring needed for continuous compliance monitoring and rapid incident response.

D) Incorrect - Service Catalog enforces standardized configurations, but Detective focuses on security incident analysis, not configuration monitoring. CloudWatch Logs and AppConfig are not directly related to continuous compliance monitoring.

E) Incorrect - While CloudWatch Logs and AppConfig are mentioned, this option lacks the integration with other services for compliance monitoring and rapid incident response. AWS Config Rules and CloudTrail with GuardDuty provide a more comprehensive solution for the given requirements.

QUESTION 38

Answer - A) Deploy Amazon Kinesis for real-time data processing of streaming data at scale, ensuring efficient handling of traffic bursts.
 B) Utilize Amazon ECS for deploying and managing containers at scale, providing flexibility and cost optimization.

Option A - Amazon Kinesis enables real-time data processing of streaming data at scale, making it suitable for handling bursts of incoming media streaming data efficiently.

 Option B - Amazon ECS allows deploying and managing containers at scale, providing flexibility and cost optimization through efficient resource utilization.

 Options C, D, and E may not directly address the scalability and cost efficiency requirements for handling bursts of traffic in the media streaming platform architecture.

QUESTION 39

Answer - C) Utilize Elastic Load Balancing (ELB) for distributing traffic across resources.

Option A - Deploying Amazon Route 53 with AWS Global Accelerator is focused on DNS routing and global application acceleration but does not directly address traffic distribution across resources.

Option B - While implementing VPC with Direct Connect and VPN provides secure hybrid connectivity, it does not specifically address traffic distribution requirements.

Option C - Utilizing Elastic Load Balancing (ELB) is the correct choice as it efficiently distributes traffic across resources, ensuring scalability and security.

Option D - Configuring CloudFront with WAF focuses on content delivery and web attack protection but does not address traffic distribution as directly as ELB.

Option E - AWS Transit Gateway offers scalable connectivity but does not specifically focus on traffic distribution across resources.

QUESTION 40

Answer - C) Ingest streaming data into Amazon Kinesis Data Streams, which triggers an AWS Lambda function for processing and stores alert data in Amazon DynamoDB

C) Ingesting streaming data into Amazon Kinesis Data Streams with AWS Lambda allows for real-time processing and timely alerts. Storing alert data in Amazon DynamoDB ensures low-latency access and scalability.

A) Processing streaming data with AWS Lambda and Amazon S3 may introduce latency and is not suitable for real-time monitoring systems.

B) Using Amazon Kinesis Data Firehose may not provide the necessary real-time processing capabilities for triggering alerts promptly.

D) Amazon SQS is not optimized for real-time processing of streaming data, and storing alert data in Amazon Redshift may introduce delays.

E) Using Amazon API Gateway and an EC2 instance for processing lacks the scalability and real-time processing capabilities required for patient monitoring systems.

QUESTION 41

Answer - A) Implement Amazon CloudFront with AWS Global Accelerator to optimize content delivery and improve availability by using the AWS global network.

Option A - Amazon CloudFront with AWS Global Accelerator optimizes content delivery and improves availability by leveraging the AWS global network, ensuring high availability and low-latency access worldwide.

Option B - Amazon Route 53 with latency-based routing directs traffic based on geographic location but may not optimize content delivery as effectively as Amazon CloudFront with AWS Global Accelerator.

Option C - AWS Direct Connect establishes dedicated connections but may not optimize content delivery or improve availability as effectively as Amazon CloudFront with AWS Global Accelerator.

Option D - Amazon S3 Cross-Region Replication replicates data for resilience but may not directly optimize content delivery or improve availability.

Option E - Amazon CloudWatch with custom metrics monitors performance but may not directly optimize content delivery or improve availability as effectively as Amazon CloudFront with AWS Global Accelerator.

QUESTION 42

Answer - [C) Configure database sharding to horizontally partition data across multiple instances.]

Option C) Database sharding involves horizontally partitioning data across multiple instances, enabling better scalability and performance under high concurrency scenarios.

Option A) Multi-AZ deployment enhances fault tolerance but may not directly address performance issues under high concurrency.

Option B) Aurora Serverless provides scalability, but may not offer the same level of performance as sharding for high concurrency scenarios.

Option D) DynamoDB on-demand capacity can handle spikes, but may not provide the same level of scalability as sharding for high concurrency.

Option E) ElastiCache helps with caching but may not directly address performance issues under high concurrency.

QUESTION 43

Answer - E) Leverage Amazon Managed Streaming for Apache Kafka (Amazon MSK) for data streaming, AWS Fargate for running containers, Amazon Athena for serverless querying, Amazon S3 for data lake storage, and AWS Lambda for event-driven data processing.

Option A - Correct. AWS Lake Formation, S3, Kinesis, Athena, and Glue provide a comprehensive solution for building secure, scalable, and cost-efficient data lakes that support both real-time and batch processing.

Option B - Incorrect. While this combination includes big data processing and storage solutions, it lacks the integration and serverless capabilities of AWS services specifically designed for data lakes and real-time analytics.

Option C - Incorrect. This option focuses on NoSQL storage and big data processing but does not offer an optimal solution for real-time data streaming and lacks the specific AWS services for cost-effective data lake creation and management.

Option D - Incorrect. Redshift and S3 are valuable for warehousing and archiving, but this option does not provide the comprehensive real-time analytics and serverless data processing capabilities required for the scenario.

Option E - Correct. MSK, Fargate, Athena, S3, and Lambda form an ideal combination for a scalable, secure, and cost-efficient solution for real-time and batch processing in a data lake environment, aligning with the corporation's needs.

QUESTION 44

Answer - [C] Deploy Amazon Managed Streaming for Apache Kafka (Amazon MSK) for transaction data ingestion, process it with Amazon Kinesis Data Analytics, and trigger alerts using Amazon SNS.

Option A introduces complexity with Glue and Aurora and may not be optimized for real-time analytics.

Option B lacks scalability with Lambda and may face latency issues.
Option D's use of AppSync and Neptune may not be suitable for real-time analytics on financial transaction data.

Option E's use of Firehose and EMR may not provide the real-time processing required for timely alerts on fraudulent activities. Amazon MSK offers a scalable and durable event streaming platform, and Kinesis Data Analytics provides real-time analytics capabilities, making option C the most effective choice for building a fraud detection system.

QUESTION 45

Answer - B) Implement server-side encryption with AWS Key Management Service (SSE-KMS) and enable automatic key rotation

B) Implementing server-side encryption with AWS Key Management Service (SSE-KMS) allows for automatic key rotation without disrupting access to the stored data, meeting the media company's requirement.

A) Server-side encryption with Amazon S3 managed keys (SSE-S3) encrypts the data at rest but does not support automatic key rotation.

C) Client-side encryption with customer-provided keys (SSE-C) shifts the responsibility of encryption to the client and may not align with the company's key rotation requirement.

D) Implementing server-side encryption with customer-provided keys (SSE-C) and manually rotating encryption keys introduces operational overhead and potential disruptions to data access.

E) Enabling AWS CloudTrail provides auditing capabilities but does not directly address the encryption and key rotation requirements for data at rest in Amazon S3.

QUESTION 46

Answer - [B] Utilize AWS IoT Greengrass for data ingestion, leverage AWS Lambda for edge processing, employ Amazon Kinesis Data Streams for real-time data processing, store real-time data in Amazon DynamoDB, and archive long-term data in Amazon S3.

Option A is incorrect because AWS IoT Events is not commonly used for data ingestion in IoT solutions, and Amazon Aurora is not the optimal database service for real-time data storage in this context. Amazon S3 Glacier is also not well-suited for long-term data archival in IoT scenarios.

Option C is incorrect because it uses Amazon API Gateway for data ingestion, which is not typically used in IoT solutions for sensor data collection. AWS Fargate is also not the ideal choice for edge processing in IoT scenarios. Additionally, Amazon RDS and Amazon Glacier are not the most suitable options for real-time data storage and long-term data archival in IoT solutions.

Option D is incorrect because although it uses AWS IoT Core and AWS Greengrass, it employs AWS

Lambda for serverless processing instead of edge processing, which may introduce latency issues in real-time data processing for IoT applications.

Option E is incorrect because it uses AWS IoT Core for data ingestion but does not leverage edge processing capabilities provided by AWS Greengrass.

QUESTION 47

Answer - [B] Deploy applications on edge devices using AWS Snow Family devices installed in hospitals and clinics, leverage AWS IoT Greengrass for edge data processing, and integrate with Amazon Aurora for real-time data storage.

Option B is the correct choice because deploying Snow Family devices in hospitals and clinics ensures edge computing capability while complying with strict regulatory requirements for data privacy and security. AWS IoT Greengrass facilitates edge data processing, and Aurora provides real-time data storage, meeting the requirements effectively.

Options A, C, D, and E either lack the same level of compliance with regulatory requirements, suitable edge computing solutions, or appropriate real-time data storage services.

QUESTION 48

Answer - A) Implement Amazon API Gateway for high-performance API management, AWS Lambda for real-time transaction processing, Amazon DynamoDB for storing transaction records, and AWS IAM for access control.

A) Correct - Amazon API Gateway offers scalable API management tailored for high-throughput scenarios like stock trading, AWS Lambda enables scalable, real-time processing, DynamoDB provides fast and scalable storage for transactions, and IAM ensures robust access control, making this setup ideal for the company's needs.

B) Incorrect - Kinesis, ECS, EFS, and Cognito are suited for real-time data streaming, microservices, storage, and authentication but may not offer the same level of API management and transaction-specific scalability and security as API Gateway, Lambda, and IAM.

C) Incorrect - AppSync, RDS, Fargate, and Shield offer data synchronization, storage, container execution, and DDoS protection but lack the direct API scalability and real-time processing capabilities required for stock trading services provided by API Gateway and Lambda.

D) Incorrect - SQS, Step Functions, S3, and Macie provide messaging, workflow orchestration, storage, and security but do not offer the comprehensive API management, real-time processing, and access control necessary for high-frequency trading APIs.

E) Incorrect - Global Accelerator, Aurora, WAF, and X-Ray enhance performance, security, and monitoring but do not specifically address the real-time API management and transaction processing demands as effectively as the services in A.

QUESTION 49

Answer - D) Employ a combination of reserved instances (RI) and spot instances

D) Employing a combination of reserved instances (RI) and spot instances allows the e-commerce company to benefit from cost savings with RIs during predictable usage periods while leveraging the scalability and cost-effectiveness of spot instances during sales events and promotions.

A) Using reserved instances (RI) for the entire duration may not accommodate sudden spikes in traffic efficiently and could lead to over-provisioning.

B) Implementing on-demand instances for the entire duration may result in higher costs, especially during peak traffic times.

C) Utilizing spot instances for the entire duration may be risky as spot instances can be terminated with short notice, potentially affecting application availability during peak times.

E) Implementing a mix of reserved instances (RI) and on-demand instances may not provide the same level of cost optimization and scalability needed for handling both consistent traffic and occasional spikes effectively.

QUESTION 50

Answer - B) Deploy Amazon EMR with spot instances to process data stored in Amazon S3, leveraging the cost savings of spot instances for compute-intensive workloads. Integrate Amazon QuickSight for visualization and reporting, enabling cost-effective analytics.

Option B is the correct choice as it leverages Amazon EMR with spot instances, which offer significant cost savings for compute-intensive workloads. Integrating Amazon QuickSight further enhances cost-effectiveness by providing visualization and reporting capabilities.

Option A, while utilizing Redshift Spectrum and Athena, may not be the most cost-effective solution for large datasets.

Option C introduces unnecessary complexity with Kinesis Data Firehose and AWS Glue, potentially increasing costs.

Option D focuses on RDS and Data Pipeline, which may not provide the required scalability and cost optimization for large datasets.

QUESTION 51

Answer - A) Use Amazon Connect for the contact center, Amazon Lex for conversational interfaces and sentiment analysis, AWS Lambda for scalability and integration with CRM/ERP systems, and Amazon Translate for real-time language translation.

Option A - Correct: Amazon Connect provides a cloud-based contact center service that scales with demand. Amazon Lex offers natural language understanding and sentiment analysis. AWS Lambda allows for seamless integration with existing systems and scalability. Amazon Translate enables real-time language translation, meeting the requirements for seamless communication and personalized support in a global contact center.

Option B - Incorrect: Direct Connect, Polly, S3, and RDS focus on network connectivity, text-to-speech, data storage, and relational databases but do not provide the same level of integration and AI capabilities as Connect, Lex, Lambda, and Translate.

Option C - Incorrect: API Gateway, Kinesis, SageMaker, and Fargate are valuable services, but they are not tailored for contact center operations and real-time language translation as A does.

Option D - Incorrect: SQS, Step Functions, Comprehend, and Aurora Serverless support workflow orchestration and data analysis but do not cover the AI-driven contact center requirements specified in the scenario.

Option E - Incorrect: AppSync, Elastic Beanstalk, Rekognition, and DynamoDB offer useful features but lack the specialized capabilities for real-time language translation and sentiment analysis in a contact center context as provided by Amazon Connect, Lex, Lambda, and Translate.

QUESTION 52

Answer - D) Configure an Amazon Kinesis Data Streams pipeline for real-time data ingestion, with Amazon RDS Multi-AZ deployment for transactional data and Amazon S3 for data backup.

A) Incorrect - While EC2 instances and RDS may provide some performance benefits, they may not meet the low-latency requirements, and Global Accelerator may not be the optimal solution for real-time trading.

B) Incorrect - Redshift and DynamoDB offer different data storage solutions, but they may not provide the necessary performance and data durability for real-time trading.

C) Incorrect - EMR clusters are suitable for big data processing, but they may introduce latency and complexity that are not ideal for real-time trading platforms.

D) Correct - Configuring Kinesis for real-time data ingestion, coupled with RDS Multi-AZ deployment for transactional data and S3 for backup, ensures high performance, durability, and availability for the trading platform.

E) Incorrect - While Lambda functions offer scalability, they may not meet the performance requirements of a real-time trading platform, and DynamoDB alone may not provide sufficient durability for data archival.

QUESTION 53

Answer - E) Utilize Amazon CloudWatch alarms and EC2 Auto Recovery actions.

A) ELBs distribute traffic but don't address instance recovery.
B) Auto Scaling groups replace instances, but the process isn't instant.
C) Instance Recovery is a feature, but it's CloudWatch alarms that trigger the recovery action.
D) Lambda can automate recovery, but it requires custom scripting.
E) Correct, as CloudWatch alarms with Auto Recovery actions enable automatic detection and recovery of impaired instances, minimizing downtime.

QUESTION 54

Answer - [C] Implement Amazon Kinesis Data Streams for real-time data ingestion and analytics.

Option A - While S3 allows storing data and querying with Athena, it may not offer real-time ingestion and analytics capabilities.

Option B - Redshift with Concurrency Scaling focuses on analytics and may not provide the real-time ingestion and low-latency access required for IoT data.

Option C - Correct. Kinesis Data Streams enables real-time data ingestion and analytics with low-latency access, meeting the requirements for IoT data processing.

Option D - RDS Multi-AZ configuration focuses on high availability for relational data but may not offer real-time ingestion and low-latency access. Option E - DynamoDB provides scalable NoSQL capabilities but may not offer the same real-time ingestion and analytics features as Kinesis.

QUESTION 55

Answer - B) Use Amazon DynamoDB global tables for course content and Amazon Aurora for regional student records.

A) Aurora Global Database for course content doesn't address the need for global consistency as efficiently as DynamoDB global tables.

B) Correct, because DynamoDB global tables ensure global consistency for course content, while Aurora provides the necessary regional segregation for student records.

C) Separate Aurora instances would unnecessarily duplicate course content across regions.

D) Using Aurora Global Database with access controls complicates management and does not leverage the strengths of DynamoDB for global data.

E) While S3 can store content, it's not optimized for database operations like DynamoDB for course content management.

QUESTION 56

Answer - [A] Utilize Amazon S3 Cross-Region Replication to replicate media assets to a secondary AWS region.

Option A - Correct. Utilizing Amazon S3 Cross-Region Replication ensures high durability and availability by replicating media assets to a secondary AWS region, while minimizing costs.

Option B - Implementing AWS Backup offers automation but may not be the most cost-effective solution for large-scale media assets.

Option C - Configuring Amazon S3 Object Lock enhances data protection but does not directly address backup requirements.

Option D - Leveraging Amazon S3 Transfer Acceleration improves data transfer speed but does not specifically optimize backup costs.

Option E - Utilizing Amazon S3 Intelligent-Tiering may optimize storage costs but does not directly address backup requirements for media assets.

QUESTION 57

Answer - [C] Implement AWS DataSync to transfer data directly from on-premises storage to Amazon S3.

Option C - Correct. Implementing AWS DataSync allows direct transfer of data from on-premises storage to Amazon S3, ensuring timely completion of the migration while minimizing costs.

Option A - AWS Direct Connect provides a dedicated network connection but may not directly address the requirement for transferring large volumes of data within a specific timeframe.

Option B - AWS Snowmobile is suitable for large-scale data migrations but may not be as cost-effective or efficient as AWS DataSync for this scenario.

Option D - Amazon S3 Transfer Acceleration optimizes data transfer speeds but may not significantly reduce costs for large volume data transfers from an on-premises data center.

Option E - AWS Transfer Family provides secure file transfer protocols but may not offer the same level of efficiency or cost-effectiveness as AWS DataSync for large-scale data migration.

QUESTION 58

Answer - [C] Configure Amazon CloudFront with regional edge caches to reduce latency for viewers in specific geographic regions.

Option A - Utilizing Amazon CloudFront with signed URLs restricts access but may not directly optimize costs for content delivery.

Option B - Implementing Amazon CloudFront with Lambda@Edge functions allows for customization but may not directly focus on cost optimization for video streaming performance.

Option C - Correct. Configuring Amazon CloudFront with regional edge caches reduces latency for viewers in specific geographic regions, optimizing costs while ensuring high-quality video streaming performance.

Option D - Enabling Amazon CloudFront with field-level encryption enhances security but may not directly address cost optimization concerns for content delivery.

Option E - Integrating Amazon CloudFront with AWS Elemental MediaPackage focuses on packaging and origination but may not directly optimize costs for content delivery.

QUESTION 59

Answer - [D] Utilize Amazon S3 Batch Operations to schedule regular clean-up tasks and delete obsolete data from S3 buckets.

Option D - Correct. Utilizing Amazon S3 Batch Operations allows for scheduling regular clean-up tasks and deleting obsolete data from S3 buckets, automating the process and reducing storage costs.

Option A - Implementing Amazon S3 Cross-Region Replication introduces complexity and may not efficiently identify and delete obsolete data.

Option B - Leveraging Amazon S3 Storage Class Analysis to identify infrequently accessed data requires manual deletion of obsolete records and may not be as automated as other solutions.

Option C - Deploying AWS Lambda functions triggered by Amazon CloudWatch Events to analyze object metadata and delete data may require significant development effort and ongoing maintenance.

Option E - Enabling Amazon S3 Object Lock prevents accidental deletion but does not provide an automated solution for identifying and deleting obsolete data.

QUESTION 60

Answer - [B] Utilize AWS Identity and Access Management (IAM) policies with condition keys to restrict access based on various attributes, such as IP address or time of day.

A) Incorrect - Implementing AWS Resource Access Manager (RAM) allows sharing of AWS resources but does not directly enforce fine-grained access control at the resource level.

B) Correct - Utilizing IAM policies with condition keys enables fine-grained access control by restricting access based on various attributes, such as IP address or time of day, ensuring compliance with regulatory requirements.

C) Incorrect - Configuring AWS Service Control Policies (SCPs) focuses on setting permission guardrails for the entire AWS organization and may not provide granular permissions management at the resource level.

D) Incorrect - Enabling AWS Key Management Service (KMS) encrypts sensitive data but does not directly enforce fine-grained access control over AWS resources.

E) Incorrect - Implementing AWS Identity Federation grants temporary access based on external identity providers but may not provide the level of granularity required for fine-grained access control over AWS resources.

QUESTION 61

Answer - [A] Utilize Amazon CloudFront with AWS Lambda@Edge to cache and deliver content at edge locations.

Option A - Correct. Amazon CloudFront with Lambda@Edge allows for low-latency content delivery by caching content at edge locations, reducing the load on origin servers and minimizing costs associated with data transfer and origin fetches.

Option B - While Amazon Route 53 with latency-based routing can direct users to the nearest AWS region, it may not provide the same level of performance optimization and cost efficiency as CloudFront with Lambda@Edge.

Option C - AWS Global Accelerator improves global application performance but may not offer the same cost optimization benefits as CloudFront with Lambda@Edge for content delivery.

Option D - Amazon S3 Transfer Acceleration accelerates data transfers to and from S3 but may not address the requirement for low-latency access to services across multiple regions.

Option E - AWS Direct Connect with AWS Transit Gateway provides private connectivity but may not optimize content delivery and reduce costs as effectively as CloudFront with Lambda@Edge.

QUESTION 62

Answer - [D] Deploy Amazon CloudFront with Lambda@Edge to cache and deliver streaming content at edge locations.

Option A - Amazon CloudFront with AWS WAF provides security but may not offer the same content delivery and caching capabilities as CloudFront with Lambda@Edge for media streaming.

Option B - Latency-based routing with Route 53 directs users to the nearest edge location but may not optimize content delivery and reduce latency as effectively as CloudFront with Lambda@Edge.

Option C - Amazon S3 Transfer Acceleration optimizes data transfers but may not provide the same low-latency access as CloudFront with Lambda@Edge for streaming content delivery.

Option D - Correct. Amazon CloudFront with Lambda@Edge allows for caching and delivering streaming content at edge locations, ensuring high availability, low latency, and cost optimization for global users.

Option E - AWS Direct Connect with AWS Transit Gateway provides private connectivity but may not optimize content delivery and reduce latency for streaming content as effectively as CloudFront with Lambda@Edge.

QUESTION 63

Answer - [D] Leverage AWS Storage Gateway to cache frequently accessed on-premises database data locally and reduce data transfer costs to AWS.

Option A - AWS DataSync is suitable for data transfer but may not directly address the need for cost optimization in a hybrid cloud migration scenario.

Option B - AWS Database Migration Service (DMS) replicates databases but may not optimize data transfer costs or storage efficiency for hybrid cloud migrations.

Option C - AWS Snowball Edge is used for offline data transfer and may not be the most cost-effective solution for ongoing data transfer and storage optimization in a hybrid cloud environment.

Option D - Correct. Leveraging AWS Storage Gateway allows for caching frequently accessed on-premises database data locally, reducing data transfer costs to AWS and optimizing storage efficiency.

Option E - AWS Data Pipeline automates data transfer but may not provide the same level of cost optimization as AWS Storage Gateway for hybrid cloud migrations involving on-premises databases.

QUESTION 64

Answer - [A] Implement AWS Lambda provisioned concurrency to reduce cold starts and optimize costs associated with function invocations.

Option A - Correct. Implementing AWS Lambda provisioned concurrency reduces cold starts and optimizes costs associated with function invocations.

Option B - Amazon API Gateway caching may reduce function invocations but may not directly address cost efficiency related to Lambda function invocations.

Option C - AWS Step Functions orchestrate workflows but may not directly optimize costs associated with Lambda function invocations.

Option D - AWS Fargate with Amazon ECS runs containerized workloads but may not directly provide the benefits of serverless architecture.

Option E - AWS Batch manages batch processing workloads but may not directly optimize costs for serverless functions like Lambda.

QUESTION 65

Answer - [A] Utilize AWS Organizations to implement consolidated billing and cost allocation tags for detailed cost tracking.

Option A - Correct. Utilizing AWS Organizations enables consolidated billing and cost allocation tags, allowing for granular cost control and accountability across departments and projects.

Option B - AWS Budgets helps monitor cost limits but may not provide the same level of granularity and accountability as AWS Organizations.

Option C - AWS Cost and Usage Report with Amazon Athena allows for custom analysis but may not offer the same level of centralized cost control as AWS Organizations.

Option D - AWS Resource Access Manager (RAM) shares resources but may not directly address cost control and accountability requirements.

Option E - AWS Service Catalog standardizes provisioning but may not provide the same level of cost tracking and accountability as AWS Organizations.

PRACTICE TEST 4 - QUESTIONS ONLY

QUESTION 1

As part of a security strategy overhaul, a healthcare company using AWS wants to implement a centralized management system for overseeing security across its multiple AWS accounts. The company has sensitive patient data and is subject to strict compliance regulations. Which AWS service should the company utilize to enhance its security posture by providing a unified view of security alerts and compliance status across all accounts?

A) Use Amazon GuardDuty for intelligent threat detection and continuous monitoring.
B) Implement AWS Control Tower for centralized governance across multiple AWS accounts.
C) Leverage AWS Security Hub for a comprehensive view of security alerts and compliance status.
D) Utilize Amazon Inspector for automated security assessment and compliance reporting.
E) Deploy AWS IAM Identity Center (AWS Single Sign-On) for centralized access management.

QUESTION 2

Considering AWS's global infrastructure, what strategy should an organization adopt to ensure data residency compliance while leveraging AWS services for processing and storing sensitive data?

A) Use AWS DataSync for transferring data to the nearest AWS Region that complies with data residency laws.

B) Implement Amazon S3 Cross-Region Replication to replicate data across Regions that meet compliance requirements.

C) Deploy AWS Snowball devices in each location where data is collected, ensuring data is processed locally.

D) Select AWS Regions and Availability Zones that adhere to local data residency requirements for data storage and processing.

E) Configure AWS CloudHSM in multiple Regions to keep encrypted data within specific geographical boundaries.

QUESTION 3

Your company is planning to enhance the security posture of its web applications hosted on Amazon EC2 instances. You need to recommend a solution to mitigate common web vulnerabilities and ensure robust protection against external threats.

A) Implement AWS WAF with managed rule sets to filter web traffic and protect against common web vulnerabilities

B) Utilize AWS Shield Advanced to protect against DDoS attacks and provide real-time threat intelligence

C) Configure AWS CloudFront with AWS Lambda@Edge to inspect and filter incoming web requests for malicious content

D) Deploy Amazon Inspector to continuously assess the security posture of EC2 instances and remediate any vulnerabilities

E) Utilize AWS Firewall Manager to centrally configure and manage WAF rules across multiple AWS accounts and resources

QUESTION 4

Your company is designing a disaster recovery (DR) solution for its critical workloads hosted on AWS. As part of the design, you need to ensure secure connectivity between the primary and DR environments with minimal latency. The DR environment should be isolated from the internet and accessible only through a secure channel. Additionally, the solution should support failover testing without disrupting the production environment. Which architecture should you recommend?

A) Set up a VPN connection between the primary and DR environments for encrypted communication. Utilize AWS Direct Connect for dedicated network connectivity, and configure VPC peering between the environments for seamless failover testing.

B) Deploy a private connectivity solution such as AWS Site-to-Site VPN or AWS Direct Connect Gateway to establish secure communication between the primary and DR environments. Implement AWS Transit Gateway to route traffic between the environments and isolate the DR environment from the internet.

C) Utilize AWS Direct Connect to establish dedicated private network connectivity between the primary and DR environments. Configure AWS Global Accelerator to improve network performance and latency, and implement VPC endpoints to access services without internet exposure.

D) Implement AWS Client VPN to provide secure remote access to the DR environment for failover testing. Use AWS PrivateLink to access resources in the DR environment securely, and configure AWS WAF to protect against common web attacks.

E) Set up AWS Direct Connect with AWS Transit Gateway to establish private network connectivity between the primary and DR environments. Utilize AWS PrivateLink for secure access to services in the DR environment, and implement AWS Shield Advanced for DDoS protection.

QUESTION 5

A software development company is migrating its project management system to AWS. They require a solution that ensures each task update is processed exactly once and in the order it was submitted, while also providing efficient handling of bulk task updates. Which option should the company choose to implement this requirement?

A) Use Amazon SQS FIFO queue with exactly-once processing enabled.
B) Use Amazon SQS FIFO queue with a batch mode of 100 messages per operation.
C) Use Amazon SQS FIFO queue with default settings to process the messages.
D) Use Amazon SQS standard queue to process the messages.
E) Use Amazon SQS FIFO queue with message deduplication enabled.

QUESTION 6

Your company is developing a serverless application that requires integration with various third-party APIs for data processing. Security and compliance are critical, and you need to ensure that sensitive data is transmitted securely between the application and external APIs. Which approach should you take to achieve this goal?

A) Utilize AWS Lambda for serverless compute, Amazon API Gateway for API management, and AWS Secrets Manager for securely storing API keys and secrets. Implement OAuth 2.0 authorization with API Gateway for secure access to external APIs.

B) Implement AWS Fargate for serverless compute, Amazon API Gateway for API management, and AWS Key Management Service (KMS) for encrypting sensitive data. Use API Gateway with IAM authorization for secure access to external APIs.

C) Deploy AWS Lambda for serverless compute, Amazon API Gateway for API management, and AWS Key Management Service (KMS) for encrypting sensitive data. Use AWS Lambda authorizers with API Gateway for secure access to external APIs.

D) Utilize Amazon ECS for serverless compute, Amazon API Gateway for API management, and AWS Secrets Manager for securely storing API keys and secrets. Implement OAuth 2.0 authorization with API Gateway for secure access to external APIs.

E) Implement AWS Fargate for serverless compute, Amazon API Gateway for API management, and AWS Systems Manager Parameter Store for securely storing API keys and secrets. Use API Gateway with OAuth 2.0 authorization for secure access to external APIs.

QUESTION 7

Your company is designing a highly secure serverless application that requires fine-grained access control for various AWS resources. The architecture includes AWS Lambda functions, Amazon S3 buckets, and Amazon DynamoDB tables. As the solutions architect, you need to implement a comprehensive IAM strategy to ensure secure access to these resources. Which approach should you take to achieve this goal?

A) Create IAM roles with specific permissions for each Lambda function, and use IAM policies to control access to S3 buckets and DynamoDB tables.

B) Implement IAM users with custom policies for each AWS resource, and configure IAM groups for role-based access control.

C) Utilize IAM policies attached to S3 buckets and DynamoDB tables to control access, and use IAM roles for cross-service authentication between Lambda functions and other AWS services.

D) Set up IAM policies at the account level to manage access control for all AWS resources, and use IAM roles for temporary access to resources by Lambda functions.

E) Implement IAM policies with condition keys to control access based on specific criteria, and use IAM roles for federated access to AWS services by external users.

QUESTION 8

Your company operates a critical healthcare application on AWS that requires robust security monitoring and compliance to protect sensitive patient data. As the solutions architect, you need to design a solution that effectively meets these requirements. What approach should you take to implement security monitoring and compliance?

A) Implement AWS CloudTrail to log API activity and store the logs in Amazon S3. Configure Amazon GuardDuty to continuously monitor for malicious activity and unauthorized behavior.

B) Utilize AWS Config to assess resource configurations and detect changes in resource configurations. Integrate Amazon CloudWatch Events with AWS Lambda to automate responses to security incidents based on predefined rules.

C) Deploy AWS Security Hub to centrally manage security compliance checks and provide insights into security posture. Use AWS Config to monitor resource configurations and detect deviations from desired configurations.

D) Configure Amazon CloudWatch Logs to capture and analyze log data from Amazon EC2 instances and other AWS services. Integrate Amazon Inspector with Amazon S3 for vulnerability assessment and compliance checks.

E) Set up AWS Config Rules to automatically evaluate the configuration of AWS resources against industry standards. Implement AWS CloudTrail with Amazon CloudWatch Logs for comprehensive logging and monitoring of API activity.

QUESTION 9

Your company is developing a serverless application that processes sensitive financial data. Compliance regulations mandate strict access control and audit logging for all data transactions. Additionally, the application must comply with industry standards for data encryption. Which of the following options provides the most suitable solution for meeting these compliance requirements?

A) Configuring AWS CloudTrail for logging all API calls and actions taken on AWS resources, ensuring comprehensive audit logging and compliance monitoring

B) Utilizing AWS IAM roles with fine-grained permissions for accessing financial data, ensuring strict access control and compliance with industry regulations

C) Implementing AWS Key Management Service (KMS) for encrypting sensitive data at rest, ensuring compliance with data encryption standards

D) Enabling AWS Config for tracking changes to AWS resource configurations and compliance monitoring, ensuring adherence to industry regulations

E) Deploying AWS Security Hub for centralized security posture management and compliance monitoring, ensuring compliance with industry standards for data protection

QUESTION 10

A research institute is migrating its data analysis platform to AWS and requires a solution that ensures low-latency access to large datasets stored on a file system service. The platform must be able to access these datasets without disruption after migration. Which option is the most suitable solution to meet this requirement?

A) Use Amazon FSx File Gateway to provide low-latency, on-premises access to fully managed file shares in Amazon EFS. The applications deployed on AWS can access this data directly from Amazon EFS.

B) Use Amazon Storage Gateway's File Gateway to provide low-latency, on-premises access to fully managed file shares in Amazon FSx for Windows File Server. The applications deployed on AWS can access this data directly from Amazon FSx in AWS.

C) Use AWS Storage Gateway's File Gateway to provide low-latency, on-premises access to fully managed file shares in Amazon S3. The applications deployed on AWS can access this data directly from Amazon S3.

D) Use Amazon FSx File Gateway to provide low-latency, on-premises access to fully managed file shares in Amazon FSx for Windows File Server. The applications deployed on AWS can access this data directly from Amazon FSx in AWS.

QUESTION 11

A rapidly growing online gaming company requires a solution to protect its real-time multiplayer games from DDoS attacks, which have become increasingly frequent during peak hours. The company also seeks to implement an elastic architecture that automatically scales to accommodate the number of online players, ensuring uninterrupted gaming experience without over-provisioning resources.

A) Amazon Route 53 for DNS services, AWS Auto Scaling for resource management, and AWS Shield Advanced for DDoS protection

B) AWS WAF for web request filtering, Amazon CloudFront for content delivery, and Amazon EC2 Auto Scaling for compute scaling

C) AWS Network Firewall for stateful packet inspection, AWS Lambda for backend automation, and Amazon DynamoDB for player data storage

D) AWS Global Accelerator for improved global access, AWS Fargate for serverless container deployment, and AWS Shield Standard for basic DDoS protection

E) Amazon VPC for network isolation, Amazon GuardDuty for threat detection, and AWS CloudFormation for infrastructure as code deployment

QUESTION 12

A fast-growing tech startup is leveraging AWS to scale their operations rapidly. They need to implement a secure, efficient way to manage and automate access for their expanding development team to AWS services and resources. The solution must support automatic role-based access control and integrate with their continuous integration/continuous deployment (CI/CD) pipelines to ensure developers have the necessary permissions as their roles evolve within the company.

A) Use AWS IAM Access Analyzer to automatically assign roles based on usage patterns.
B) Implement AWS IAM Identity Center (SSO) with role-based access control and integration with CI/CD pipelines.

C) Configure Amazon Cognito with user groups for role-based access in AWS, linked to the CI/CD system.
D) Leverage AWS CodePipeline to manage IAM roles and permissions within AWS based on deployment needs.

E) Establish AWS Lambda functions to update IAM policies and roles dynamically based on developer activity and project assignments.

QUESTION 13

A media streaming company is developing a new API to deliver content to its users across various platforms. The company wants to ensure high performance and scalability while protecting against potential security threats. Which approach would be most effective in achieving these goals?

A) Implementing API caching using Amazon CloudFront.
B) Deploying AWS Shield Advanced for comprehensive DDoS protection.
C) Configuring Amazon RDS for database optimization.
D) Enabling AWS Lambda authorizers for API Gateway authentication.
E) Utilizing AWS Direct Connect for low-latency connectivity.

QUESTION 14

A multinational corporation is migrating its operations to AWS and needs to ensure compliance with multiple international regulations, including GDPR, HIPAA, and SOC 2. They are looking for a scalable solution to manage compliance across different regions and services within AWS.

A) Utilize AWS Control Tower to set up a multi-account environment with pre-configured compliance blueprints for GDPR, HIPAA, and SOC 2.

B) Implement Amazon RDS with encryption and Amazon VPC with private subnets for data protection and network isolation, respectively.

C) Configure AWS CloudTrail and AWS Security Hub for centralized logging and compliance management, focusing on international regulations.

D) Deploy AWS Audit Manager to automate evidence collection and reporting for GDPR, HIPAA, and SOC 2 compliance.

E) Leverage AWS Config conformance packs with custom AWS Lambda functions for continuous compliance monitoring and remediation across multiple regulations.

QUESTION 15

A healthcare organization is experiencing difficulties in managing maintenance tasks on specific Amazon EC2 instances within an Auto Scaling group. Whenever maintenance patches are applied, the instances briefly show as out of service, triggering Auto Scaling to provision replacements. As a solutions architect, which approach would you suggest to optimize the maintenance process?

A) Temporarily suspend the Launch process type for the Auto Scaling group and apply the maintenance patch to the instance. Once the instance is ready, manually set the instance's health status back to healthy and activate the Launch process type again.

B) Suspend the Terminate process type for the Auto Scaling group and apply the maintenance patch to the instance. Once the instance is ready, manually set the instance's health status back to healthy and activate the Terminate process type again.

C) Stop the instance, apply the maintenance patch, and then start the instance.

D) Suspend the ReplaceUnhealthy process type for the Auto Scaling group and apply the maintenance patch to the instance. Once the instance is ready, manually set the instance's health status back to healthy and activate the ReplaceUnhealthy process type again.

 E) Take a snapshot of the instance, create a new Amazon Machine Image (AMI), and then launch a new instance using this AMI. Apply the maintenance patch to this new instance and then add it back to the Auto Scaling Group by using the manual scaling policy. Terminate the earlier instance that had the maintenance issue.

QUESTION 16

A financial services company needs to ensure that their AWS resources are only accessible by users during business hours from the company's network. Which IAM policy condition should the Solutions Architect recommend to meet this requirement?

A) Use the "aws:MultiFactorAuthAge" condition to enforce MFA before granting access.
B) Apply the "aws:Requester" condition to restrict access to specific roles.
C) Implement the "aws:CurrentTime" condition to restrict access based on time.
D) Utilize the "aws:SourceIp" condition to restrict access from the company's network.
E) Combine "aws:CurrentTime" and "aws:SourceIp" conditions to restrict access based on time and IP address.

QUESTION 17

A global retail company is restructuring its AWS environment to improve the security and efficiency of its e-commerce platform. They require a network architecture that allows for private connectivity to AWS services, isolates development environments from production, and provides a mechanism for auditing network traffic to detect potential security threats.

A) Utilize AWS PrivateLink for private access to AWS services, separate VPCs for development and production environments, and implement Amazon GuardDuty for threat detection.

B) Implement a centralized AWS Transit Gateway to manage inter-VPC connectivity, use AWS VPN for private service access, and AWS CloudTrail for auditing.

C) Configure Amazon VPC endpoints for private AWS service access, VPC peering for environment isolation, and enable VPC flow logs for network traffic auditing.

D) Deploy AWS Direct Connect for connecting on-premises to AWS, use AWS Organizations for account management, and Amazon Macie for data security and threat detection.

E) Establish AWS WAF at the VPC edge, use Amazon S3 for data storage with VPC Endpoint Gateway for private access, and AWS Lambda for automated threat response.

QUESTION 18

A financial institution is expanding its AWS footprint to accommodate increased customer demand for online banking services. The institution requires solutions to ensure the security and resilience of its AWS infrastructure while optimizing costs to remain competitive.

A) Implement AWS Shield Advanced for DDoS protection and AWS WAF for web application firewall. Set up Amazon CloudWatch Alarms to monitor resource usage and trigger automated scaling actions.

B) Deploy AWS Transit Gateway to connect multiple VPCs and ensure consistent network security policies across the organization. Utilize AWS Savings Plans to reduce costs for long-term commitments.

C) Utilize Amazon RDS Multi-AZ deployment for database high availability and implement Amazon Aurora Serverless for cost-effective database scaling. Set up AWS Config Rules to enforce security and compliance best practices.

D) Implement AWS Direct Connect for dedicated network connectivity between on-premises infrastructure and AWS. Set up AWS CodePipeline for automated deployment and integrate AWS CodeCommit for version control.

E) Deploy Amazon Kinesis for real-time data streaming and analysis. Utilize AWS Lambda functions for event-driven processing and AWS Auto Scaling to optimize resource utilization and cost.

QUESTION 19

A financial institution is migrating its legacy applications to AWS ECS for containerized deployment. They need to ensure that sensitive information, such as database credentials, is securely managed within their ECS tasks. Which of the following strategies would best address the institution's requirements?

A) Store database credentials directly in Dockerfiles as environment variables. Use IAM roles with strict access policies for ECS tasks to access the environment variables.

B) Implement AWS Secrets Manager to securely store database credentials. Integrate ECS tasks with Secrets Manager for automated retrieval of credentials at runtime.

C) Maintain plaintext configuration files containing database credentials within Docker images. Implement IAM policies to control access to the Docker images in the Amazon ECR repository.

D) Utilize AWS Systems Manager Parameter Store to centrally manage database credentials. Develop custom logic within ECS tasks to retrieve credentials from Parameter Store.

E) Store database credentials in plaintext files within an encrypted Amazon EFS file system. Implement IAM policies to control access to the EFS file system for ECS tasks.

QUESTION 20

A finance company detected an unexpected increase in illicit AWS API requests during non-peak hours, with no visible system impact. The management seeks an automated solution to promptly notify relevant teams in such instances. Which solution would best address this requirement?

A) Configure AWS CloudTrail to stream event data to Amazon Kinesis. Utilize Amazon Kinesis stream-level metrics in Amazon CloudWatch to trigger an AWS Lambda function that will initiate an error workflow.

B) Use Amazon Athena SQL queries against AWS CloudTrail log files stored in Amazon S3 buckets. Generate reports using Amazon QuickSight for managerial dashboards.

C) Create an Amazon CloudWatch metric filter to process AWS CloudTrail logs containing API call details. Establish an alarm based on this metric's rate to send an Amazon SNS notification to the required team.

D) Implement AWS Config Rules to monitor API activity and define rules to detect unauthorized API calls. Configure AWS Config to trigger an AWS Lambda function upon rule evaluation to notify relevant stakeholders.

E) Leverage AWS Trusted Advisor to publish metrics about check results to Amazon CloudWatch. Set up an alarm to track status changes for checks in the Service Limits category for the APIs, triggering notifications when service quotas are exceeded.

QUESTION 21

A media streaming platform is redesigning its backend architecture to support millions of concurrent users accessing video content globally. The architecture needs to ensure low-latency streaming, high availability, and scalability to handle sudden spikes in user demand during peak hours.

A) Deploy Amazon EC2 instances with Auto Scaling, Amazon RDS Multi-AZ for database management, Amazon CloudFront for content delivery, and Amazon ElastiCache for caching frequently accessed data.

B) Utilize AWS Lambda for serverless backend logic, Amazon API Gateway for managing APIs, Amazon Kinesis Video Streams for video ingestion, and Amazon CloudWatch for monitoring performance.

C) Implement Amazon ECS for containerized microservices, Amazon RDS Read Replicas for database scaling, AWS Direct Connect for dedicated network connectivity, and Amazon S3 for storing video assets.

D) Configure Amazon EKS for Kubernetes-based orchestration, Amazon DynamoDB for NoSQL data storage, Amazon CloudFront for global content delivery, and Amazon Redshift for analyzing user viewing patterns.

E) Leverage Amazon Managed Streaming for Apache Kafka (Amazon MSK) for real-time data streaming, AWS Lambda for processing video metadata, Amazon S3 Glacier for archival storage, and Amazon CloudFront for low-latency content delivery.

QUESTION 22

You are designing a real-time analytics platform that processes streaming data from IoT devices. The platform needs to scale automatically based on incoming data volume and ensure low latency processing. Which AWS service would be most suitable for this use case?

A) Utilize AWS Lambda with Amazon Kinesis for real-time data processing.
B) Deploy the application on Amazon EC2 instances with Amazon SQS for message queuing.
C) Implement AWS Fargate with AWS Step Functions for serverless workflow management.
D) Leverage Amazon Redshift with AWS Glue for data analytics and ETL processing.
E) Utilize Amazon EMR with Amazon S3 for big data processing and analysis.

QUESTION 23

A travel agency is developing a new booking platform on AWS and wants to ensure high availability and fault tolerance while optimizing costs. The company requires a solution that minimizes expenses while providing uninterrupted service to customers. Which AWS service would best support this requirement?

A) Utilize Amazon EC2 instances across multiple Availability Zones with AWS Auto Scaling for automated scaling based on traffic patterns to ensure high availability and cost efficiency

B) Implement Amazon S3 for static content storage with Amazon CloudFront for global content delivery to reduce latency and improve performance while minimizing costs

C) Deploy Amazon Aurora for relational database storage with Multi-AZ deployment for automated failover and cost-efficient scaling to maintain high availability with minimal expenses

D) Utilize AWS Lambda with Amazon DynamoDB for serverless application components and data storage to achieve high scalability with low operational costs

E) Implement Amazon ECS with AWS Fargate for containerized deployment and scaling of application components to optimize costs while ensuring fault tolerance and scalability

QUESTION 24

Your company operates a content delivery network (CDN) for streaming video content to global audiences. You need to improve the performance and reliability of the CDN while reducing costs. Additionally, you want to implement security measures to protect against DDoS attacks. Which AWS services should you use to enhance the CDN infrastructure?

A) Amazon CloudFront for content delivery with edge locations
B) AWS Shield for DDoS protection
C) Amazon CloudWatch for monitoring CDN performance
D) AWS WAF for web application firewall
E) Amazon S3 for origin storage of video content

QUESTION 25

An online retail company uses Amazon Aurora for managing inventory and customer orders. The company requires high availability and read scalability. To achieve this, they have configured Aurora replicas with various failover priorities and storage capacities. In case the primary instance fails, which replica will be promoted based on the company's failover strategy?

A) Tier-3 (24 terabytes)
B) Tier-4 (12 terabytes)
C) Tier-6 (18 terabytes)
D) Tier-8 (24 terabytes)
E) Tier-9 (12 terabytes)

QUESTION 26

A transportation company is developing a microservices-based application on AWS to track vehicle locations in real-time. The company requires a solution for collecting and processing location data from vehicles distributed across different regions. The solution must ensure low latency and high availability. Which option would best fulfill these requirements?

A) Implement Amazon Kinesis Data Streams to ingest real-time data from vehicles and process it using AWS Lambda functions for real-time analytics and updates.

B) Utilize Amazon S3 Transfer Acceleration to optimize upload and download speeds for vehicle location data, and trigger AWS Lambda functions for processing and updates.

C) Deploy Amazon Managed Streaming for Apache Kafka (Amazon MSK) to ingest and process vehicle location data in real-time across different regions, ensuring low latency and high availability.

D) Configure Amazon SQS to decouple the collection and processing of vehicle location data, enabling asynchronous communication between microservices while ensuring scalability and resilience.

E) Set up Amazon EventBridge to capture and process events from vehicles, enabling seamless communication between microservices and ensuring low latency and high availability.

QUESTION 27

A media streaming company is building a serverless workflow for processing and transcoding video files. The company needs to ensure that the workflow can recover from failures automatically and resume processing without manual intervention. Which of the following options offers the best approach for achieving fault tolerance and automated error recovery in the workflow?

A) Utilize AWS Step Functions with automatic retries and AWS Lambda for processing and transcoding video files

B) Implement Amazon SQS for message queuing and Amazon SNS for event notification to trigger Lambda functions for video processing

C) Deploy Amazon S3 event notifications to trigger Lambda functions for video processing and leverage Amazon CloudWatch Alarms for error monitoring and recovery

D) Leverage Amazon EventBridge for orchestrating video processing tasks and use Amazon S3 for storing intermediate results

QUESTION 28

For a global online retailer, ensuring low latency and high availability for its e-commerce platform is crucial. The company seeks a serverless architecture that scales dynamically with user demand across different regions. Security and data consistency are also paramount. Which architecture would best meet these requirements?

A) Deploy Amazon CloudFront with AWS Lambda@Edge for content delivery and compute tasks, Amazon DynamoDB Global Tables for database, and secure with AWS WAF.

B) Use AWS Global Accelerator with Amazon EC2 instances for compute, Amazon RDS with Read Replicas for database, and secure with Amazon GuardDuty.

C) Implement Amazon API Gateway for regional request routing, AWS Lambda for compute, Amazon S3 for storage, and Amazon Cognito for user authentication.

D) Utilize AWS AppSync for data synchronization across regions, Amazon Aurora Serverless for the database, AWS Lambda for backend processes, and secure with AWS IAM policies.

E) Leverage Amazon SNS for cross-region message delivery, AWS Fargate for compute tasks, Amazon DynamoDB for storage, and AWS Secrets Manager for security.

QUESTION 29

A gaming company is launching a new multiplayer online game that requires low-latency communication and high availability for players worldwide. Which option provides the most suitable load balancing solution for this scenario?

A) Deploy Amazon Elastic Load Balancing (ELB) with Network Load Balancer (NLB) for efficient network routing

B) Utilize Amazon Route 53 with Latency routing policy for global traffic distribution
C) Implement Amazon CloudFront with Lambda@Edge for real-time content optimization
D) Set up an Amazon Global Accelerator with accelerator endpoints for global application availability
E) Configure an Application Load Balancer (ALB) with Target Groups for dynamic traffic routing

QUESTION 30

A healthcare organization wants to enhance patient care by analyzing real-time medical sensor data from IoT devices. They require a solution capable of processing streaming data efficiently and triggering alerts based on predefined medical thresholds. Which AWS service combination should they utilize to achieve this while ensuring reliability and scalability?

A) Utilize a Spark Streaming cluster on Amazon EMR to process medical sensor data before storing it in Amazon RDS

B) Implement Amazon Kinesis Data Analytics to analyze streaming medical sensor data and store it in Amazon Redshift for further analysis

C) Employ Amazon Kinesis Data Firehose to ingest data and use AWS Lambda to filter and transform before storing it in Amazon DynamoDB

D) Utilize Amazon Kinesis Data Streams with AWS Lambda for real-time data processing and store it in Amazon S3

E) Ingest data directly into Amazon S3 using Amazon Kinesis Data Firehose without intermediate processing

QUESTION 31

An entertainment company is building a content recommendation system to enhance user experience on their streaming platform. They need a solution that allows for the analysis of user interactions in real-time to offer personalized content recommendations. Which AWS architecture would best support these requirements?

A) Implement Amazon Kinesis for real-time data streaming, AWS Lambda for processing data streams, Amazon DynamoDB for storing user interactions, and Amazon Personalize for generating content recommendations.

B) Use Amazon SQS for messaging between services, Amazon EC2 for data processing, Amazon RDS for storing user data, and AWS Glue for data integration.

C) Deploy Amazon S3 for data storage, Amazon Redshift for data warehousing, AWS Data Pipeline for data orchestration, and Amazon QuickSight for data visualization.

D) Utilize AWS Fargate for running containerized applications, Amazon ECR for container management, AWS Step Functions for orchestrating workflows, and Amazon SageMaker for building recommendation models.

E) Choose Amazon EMR for big data processing, Amazon S3 for storing logs, Amazon Athena for querying data, and AWS Lake Formation for managing the data lake environment.

QUESTION 32

A financial institution requires a resilient architecture for its database to ensure data integrity and availability, especially during peak trading hours. Which approach should the institution take to meet its requirements while optimizing costs?

A) Implement Amazon RDS with Multi-AZ deployment and utilize read replicas for scaling read operations during peak hours.

B) Utilize Amazon Aurora Serverless with auto-scaling and provisioned Aurora Capacity Units (ACUs) for predictable performance during peak trading hours.

C) Deploy Amazon DynamoDB with on-demand scaling and utilize DynamoDB Streams for real-time data processing and analysis.

D) Migrate to Amazon Redshift for analytics and scalability and use Redshift Concurrency Scaling for handling concurrent queries during peak hours.

E) Implement Amazon DocumentDB with MongoDB compatibility and use DocumentDB global clusters for cross-Region replication and failover.

QUESTION 33

An online gaming company wants to create a globally distributed, highly available game backend that can scale automatically and maintain low latency for players around the world. The backend needs to process and store large volumes of game state data in real-time. Which AWS services should be utilized to meet these requirements?

A) Implement Amazon DynamoDB Global Tables for distributed data storage, Amazon ElastiCache for Redis to reduce latency for frequently accessed data, and Amazon CloudFront to distribute static game content globally.

B) Use Amazon RDS with Read Replicas across multiple regions, AWS Lambda for backend processing, and AWS Global Accelerator to improve application responsiveness worldwide.

C) Deploy Amazon ECS with Fargate for serverless container management, Amazon Aurora Global Database for relational data storage, and Amazon S3 with Transfer Acceleration for fast global data transfers.

D) Utilize Amazon DynamoDB with on-demand capacity mode for scalable data storage, Amazon Kinesis for real-time data processing, and AWS Global Accelerator to optimize connectivity and reduce latency for players globally.

E) Set up Amazon S3 for storing game state data, AWS AppSync for real-time data synchronization across clients, and Elastic Load Balancing (ELB) to distribute incoming game traffic across multiple Amazon EC2 instances.

QUESTION 34

Considering a financial organization needs to comply with regulatory requirements for data sovereignty while utilizing cloud resources, which AWS feature should be prioritized to ensure data does not leave the specified geographic area?

A) Enable AWS CloudTrail geo-fencing.
B) Implement Amazon S3 Cross-Region Replication with location constraints.
C) Use AWS WAF regional rules for data traffic.
D) Apply AWS IAM policies to restrict data access based on geographic location.
E) Configure Amazon VPC to use endpoints within a specific region only.

QUESTION 35

A logistics company is developing a tracking system for monitoring the movement of goods in real-time. They require a solution that can handle a high volume of tracking requests and provide accurate location data. Which configuration should they implement using Amazon API Gateway to meet these requirements effectively?

A) Utilize RESTful APIs on Amazon API Gateway with Amazon DynamoDB for storing tracking data and AWS Lambda for processing tracking requests

B) Implement WebSocket APIs on Amazon API Gateway with Amazon S3 for storing tracking data and Amazon SQS for processing tracking requests

C) Create HTTP APIs on Amazon API Gateway and integrate with Amazon Aurora for storing tracking data and Amazon ECS for processing tracking requests

D) Deploy GraphQL APIs on Amazon API Gateway with Amazon Redshift for storing tracking data and Amazon Kinesis for processing tracking requests

E) Configure RESTful APIs on Amazon API Gateway with Amazon ElastiCache for storing tracking data and Amazon EMR for processing tracking requests

QUESTION 36

Your company operates a highly available, scalable architecture on AWS. During peak hours, there's a surge in traffic resulting in increased demand on your Amazon RDS databases. You need to optimize the performance of your RDS instances to handle the load efficiently. Which strategies should you employ to achieve this goal while maintaining reliability? Select TWO.

A) Implement read replicas in different Availability Zones for load distribution.
B) Utilize Amazon RDS Performance Insights for real-time database performance monitoring.
C) Configure Enhanced Monitoring on Amazon RDS instances to collect detailed system metrics.
D) Use Amazon RDS Multi-AZ deployment to ensure high availability and automatic failover.
E) Apply Amazon RDS Storage Auto Scaling to dynamically adjust storage capacity based on usage.

QUESTION 37

Your e-commerce platform, hosted on AWS, experienced a sudden surge in traffic due to a promotional campaign, resulting in increased load on your application servers. As a solutions architect, you need to ensure the scalability and availability of your application during such traffic spikes while minimizing costs. How would you design an auto-scaling solution to dynamically adjust resources based on demand and optimize costs without compromising performance? Select TWO.

A) Utilize Amazon EC2 Auto Scaling groups with target tracking scaling policies to automatically adjust the number of instances based on CPU utilization. Implement Amazon CloudWatch Alarms to trigger notifications for capacity increases.

B) Deploy AWS Lambda functions to handle sudden traffic spikes and integrate with Amazon API Gateway for serverless scalability. Configure Amazon CloudFront with AWS Shield for DDoS protection and cache optimization.

C) Implement Amazon ECS with service auto-scaling to manage containerized applications dynamically. Utilize AWS Fargate to automatically provision and scale container resources based on workload demands.

D) Utilize Amazon RDS Aurora Serverless for the database layer, allowing automatic scaling based on traffic patterns. Set up Amazon ElastiCache for caching frequently accessed data to reduce database load and improve application performance.

E) Deploy AWS Lambda@Edge to run serverless code closer to end-users, reducing latency and improving scalability. Configure Amazon CloudFront with Lambda@Edge functions to customize content delivery and handle traffic spikes effectively.

QUESTION 38

Your company is developing a new data processing pipeline that requires executing various tasks in response to different events, such as file uploads or database changes. The architecture needs to be highly scalable, cost-effective, and easily maintainable. Which AWS service or services would you recommend for building this serverless data processing pipeline? Select TWO.

A) Utilize AWS Lambda for serverless execution of code in response to events, ensuring scalability and cost-effectiveness.

B) Implement Amazon SQS to decouple components and handle event-driven workflows efficiently.

C) Leverage AWS Step Functions for orchestrating serverless workflows, ensuring smooth execution and easy maintenance.

D) Deploy Amazon EMR for processing large volumes of data cost-effectively using managed Hadoop clusters.

E) Utilize Amazon S3 for storing input and output data, ensuring durability and scalability.

QUESTION 39

A company is looking to establish secure hybrid network connectivity between its on-premises data center and AWS cloud resources. What solution should the company choose to meet this requirement?

A) Deploy Amazon Route 53 with AWS Global Accelerator for efficient DNS routing and global application acceleration.

B) Utilize Amazon CloudFront with AWS Shield for DDoS protection and Amazon Route 53 for DNS routing.

C) Implement Amazon VPC with public and private subnets, employing AWS Direct Connect for dedicated network connections, and AWS VPN for secure hybrid connectivity.

D) Configure Amazon CloudFront with AWS WAF for global content delivery and protection against web attacks.

E) Use AWS Transit Gateway for scalable and efficient network connectivity across multiple VPCs.

QUESTION 40

A retail company aims to develop a dynamic pricing engine to adjust product prices based on demand and competitor pricing in real-time. They require a solution that can process market data continuously and update prices promptly without manual intervention. Which setup should they configure using AWS serverless components to meet these requirements effectively?

A) Utilize AWS Lambda with Amazon S3 for processing market data and Amazon RDS for storing price updates

B) Implement Amazon Kinesis Data Firehose with AWS Lambda for processing market data and Amazon ElastiCache for storing price updates

C) Ingest market data into Amazon Kinesis Data Streams, which triggers an AWS Lambda function for processing and stores price updates in Amazon DynamoDB

D) Ingest market data into Amazon SQS, which triggers an AWS Lambda function for processing and stores price updates in Amazon Redshift

E) Use Amazon API Gateway to ingest market data, which is processed by an application running on an Amazon EC2 instance, and store price updates in Amazon Elasticsearch Service

QUESTION 41

A gaming company is developing a real-time multiplayer game that requires low-latency communication between players distributed across different regions. They need a solution that ensures consistent performance and minimal lag for players. Which AWS service should the company use to achieve these objectives?

A) Implement Amazon GameLift to deploy, operate, and scale dedicated game servers for low-latency multiplayer gaming experiences.

B) Utilize Amazon Route 53 with latency-based routing to direct player traffic to the nearest game server for minimal lag.

C) Deploy AWS Global Accelerator to improve the availability and performance of game servers by using the AWS global network.

D) Configure Amazon DynamoDB Accelerator (DAX) to cache frequently accessed game data and reduce read latency for players.

E) Implement AWS Direct Connect to establish dedicated connections between game servers and AWS regions for low-latency communication.

QUESTION 42

Your company operates a global online gaming platform with users from around the world. To ensure low-latency access for all users, the database must be optimized for speed and performance. Which solution would best meet this requirement?

A) Implement Amazon RDS with Multi-AZ deployment for high availability.
B) Deploy the database layer on Amazon EC2 instances using EFS for shared storage.
C) Leverage Amazon Aurora with its performance optimizations and global replication.
D) Utilize Amazon Redshift for data warehousing and analytics.
E) Configure Amazon DynamoDB with provisioned capacity to handle global traffic.

QUESTION 43

An online retail company is planning to launch a new service that leverages customer data to provide personalized shopping experiences. They aim to analyze customer behavior, purchase history, and social media interactions in real-time to offer personalized product recommendations. The solution must scale dynamically to handle varying loads, especially during peak shopping seasons, and ensure compliance with data privacy regulations. Additionally, the company seeks to implement this solution with minimal infrastructure management overhead and cost-effectiveness.

A) Deploy Amazon Personalize for creating personalized user recommendations, Amazon Kinesis for real-time data processing, AWS Lambda for serverless computing, Amazon S3 for data storage, and AWS IAM for managing access permissions.

B) Use Amazon Redshift for data warehousing, AWS Data Pipeline for data movement, Amazon QuickSight for data visualization, Amazon EC2 Auto Scaling for compute scaling, and Amazon GuardDuty for security monitoring.

C) Implement Amazon SageMaker for building machine learning models, Amazon DynamoDB for storing user data, AWS AppSync for real-time data synchronization, Amazon EKS for container orchestration, and AWS WAF for web application firewall.

D) Leverage AWS Glue for data integration and ETL, Amazon Athena for querying data, Amazon S3 for data lake storage, AWS Fargate for running containers without managing servers, and Amazon Cognito for user authentication.

E) Utilize Amazon Elastic Container Service (Amazon ECS) for container management, AWS Batch for batch processing, Amazon ElastiCache for caching, Amazon CloudFront for content delivery, and Amazon Macie for data security and privacy.

QUESTION 44

Your company is developing a real-time recommendation engine for a video streaming platform. The engine needs to analyze user behavior instantly and suggest relevant content. Which architecture would be most suitable for this use case?

A) Use Amazon Kinesis Data Firehose for streaming user events, process them with AWS Glue, and store results in Amazon RDS for real-time access.

B) Implement Amazon Kinesis Data Streams for user behavior data, process it using Apache Flink on

Amazon EC2 instances, and store results in Amazon Redshift for analysis and recommendation.

C) Deploy Amazon Managed Streaming for Apache Kafka (Amazon MSK) for user event ingestion, process data with Amazon Kinesis Data Analytics, and trigger recommendations using AWS Lambda.

D) Utilize AWS AppSync to connect user devices to Amazon Neptune graph database, analyze data in real-time, and trigger recommendations with Amazon Pinpoint.

E) Set up Amazon Kinesis Data Firehose to capture user events, process them using Amazon EMR, and store results in Amazon S3 for further analysis and recommendation.

QUESTION 45

A retail company is planning to migrate its customer database to Amazon S3 and requires encryption of the data at rest. The company wants to maintain control over the encryption keys and ensure that only authorized users can access the data. Which option would provide the most suitable solution for this scenario?

A) Utilize server-side encryption with Amazon S3 managed keys (SSE-S3) to encrypt the data on Amazon S3

B) Implement server-side encryption with AWS Key Management Service (SSE-KMS) and define fine-grained access policies

C) Use client-side encryption with customer-provided keys (SSE-C) and upload the encrypted data to Amazon S3

D) Implement server-side encryption with customer-provided keys (SSE-C) and restrict access through IAM policies

E) Enable AWS CloudTrail to monitor S3 bucket activities for auditing purposes

QUESTION 46

You are tasked with designing an IoT solution for an agricultural company that aims to monitor soil moisture levels, temperature, and humidity in its fields to optimize irrigation and crop yield. The solution should be scalable, cost-effective, and capable of processing data from thousands of sensors distributed across vast farmlands. Which architecture would best meet these requirements?

A) Utilize AWS IoT Core for data ingestion, configure AWS Greengrass for edge computing, implement Amazon Kinesis Data Streams for real-time data processing, utilize AWS Lambda for serverless processing, and store real-time data in Amazon DynamoDB.

B) Deploy Amazon API Gateway for data ingestion, utilize AWS Fargate for edge processing, configure Amazon Kinesis Data Analytics for real-time data analysis, connect with Amazon RDS for real-time data storage, and employ Amazon Glacier for long-term data archival.

C) Configure AWS IoT Core for data ingestion, implement AWS Lambda for edge processing, set up Amazon Kinesis Data Streams for real-time data processing, integrate with Amazon RDS for real-time data storage, and utilize Amazon S3 for long-term data archival.

D) Implement AWS IoT Events for data ingestion, set up AWS Lambda for edge processing, use Amazon Kinesis Data Streams for real-time data processing, deploy Amazon Aurora for real-time data storage, and employ Amazon S3 Glacier for long-term data archival.

E) Utilize AWS IoT Greengrass for data ingestion, leverage AWS Lambda for edge processing, employ Amazon Kinesis Data Streams for real-time data processing, store real-time data in Amazon DynamoDB, and archive long-term data in Amazon S3.

QUESTION 47

You are designing an edge computing solution for a manufacturing company that operates multiple factories worldwide. The company wants to process sensor data from production lines in real-time to optimize manufacturing processes and minimize downtime. Which architecture would best meet these requirements?

A) Deploy applications on edge devices using AWS Local Zones located near factory locations, leverage AWS IoT Greengrass for edge data processing, and integrate with Amazon DynamoDB for real-time data storage.

B) Utilize AWS Wavelength to deploy applications on edge devices located within telecommunication providers' data centers, leverage AWS IoT Greengrass for edge data processing, and integrate with Amazon S3 for real-time data storage.

C) Implement applications on Amazon EC2 instances deployed in AWS Outposts located near factory locations, utilize AWS IoT Greengrass for edge data processing, and integrate with Amazon RDS for real-time data storage.

D) Utilize AWS Lambda@Edge for deploying applications on edge devices located in each factory, leverage AWS IoT Greengrass for edge data processing, and integrate with Amazon Aurora for real-time data storage.

E) Deploy applications on edge devices using AWS Snow Family devices placed in factory locations, leverage AWS IoT Greengrass for edge data processing, and integrate with Amazon Redshift for real-time data storage.

QUESTION 48

An online retail company is expanding its services to include an API that allows third-party vendors to upload product catalogs, manage inventory, and process orders. The API must be highly available, scale according to demand, and secure sensitive data against breaches. Furthermore, the company seeks to monitor API usage patterns to optimize vendor experiences. Which AWS architecture would best suit these requirements?

A) Utilize Amazon API Gateway for API management, AWS Lambda for scalable computing, Amazon RDS for data storage, and Amazon QuickSight for usage analytics.

B) Deploy Amazon S3 for storing product information, AWS Direct Connect for dedicated connectivity, Amazon DynamoDB for inventory management, and AWS IAM for securing API access.

C) Implement AWS Fargate for running serverless containers, Amazon CloudFront for content delivery, AWS WAF for protecting APIs, and Amazon Kinesis for monitoring data streams.

D) Use AWS AppSync for application data synchronization, Amazon Aurora for scalable database needs, AWS Shield for advanced DDoS protection, and AWS CloudTrail for API activity logging.

E) Leverage Amazon SQS for decoupling incoming requests, Amazon ECS with Auto Scaling for microservice management, Amazon ElastiCache for caching, and Amazon CloudWatch for operational monitoring.

QUESTION 49

A company needs to grant permissions for a team to read objects from an Amazon S3 bucket and write objects to a specific folder within the bucket. However, the team should not be allowed to delete objects or modify the bucket's properties. Which IAM policy statement should be added to address this requirement?

A) {
"Action": [
"s3:GetObject",
"s3:PutObject"
],
"Resource": "arn:aws:s3:::example-bucket/",
"Effect": "Allow"
}

B) {
"Action": [
"s3:GetObject",
"s3:PutObject",
"s3:DeleteObject",
"s3:PutBucketPolicy"
],
"Resource": "arn:aws:s3:::example-bucket/",
"Effect": "Allow"
}

C) {
"Action": [
"s3:GetObject",
"s3:PutObject"
],
"Resource": "arn:aws:s3:::example-bucket/",
"Effect": "Allow"
}

D) {
"Action": [
"s3:GetObject",
"s3:PutObject",
"s3:DeleteBucket",

```
"s3:PutBucketPolicy"
],
"Resource": "arn:aws:s3:::example-bucket/",
"Effect": "Allow"
}


E) {
"Action": [
"s3:GetObject",
"s3:PutObject",
"s3:DeleteBucket",
"s3:PutBucketPolicy"
],
"Resource": "arn:aws:s3:::example-bucket",
"Effect": "Allow"
}
```

QUESTION 50

You are designing a solution for a media streaming platform that requires high availability and low latency for delivering content to users worldwide. The platform must optimize costs while maintaining excellent performance. Which approach would best meet the requirements?

A) Utilize Amazon CloudFront as a content delivery network (CDN) to cache and distribute media content globally, reducing latency for users. Implement Amazon S3 for storing media files and enable cross-region replication for high availability.

B) Deploy Amazon EC2 instances in multiple AWS regions to ensure global availability, utilizing Amazon Route 53 for DNS routing and failover. Implement Amazon ElastiCache for caching frequently accessed media content, reducing latency and improving performance.

C) Utilize Amazon Aurora Global Database to replicate data across multiple AWS regions for high availability and disaster recovery. Integrate Amazon CloudFront as a CDN to cache and serve media content, optimizing content delivery and reducing latency for users.

D) Implement Amazon API Gateway to manage API requests from client applications, with AWS Lambda functions to process requests and retrieve media content from Amazon S3. Deploy Amazon CloudFront as a CDN to cache and distribute media content, ensuring low latency and high availability for users worldwide.

QUESTION 51

A large e-commerce company is migrating its monolithic application to a microservices architecture on AWS to improve scalability, agility, and reliability. Which AWS services should be leveraged to ensure efficient resource allocation and optimal performance for each microservice?

A) Implement AWS Fargate for running containerized microservices, Amazon EKS for managing Kubernetes clusters, Amazon EFS for shared storage, and AWS X-Ray for distributed tracing.

B) Use AWS Lambda for serverless microservices, Amazon API Gateway for API management, Amazon DynamoDB for NoSQL data storage, and AWS Step Functions for workflow orchestration.

C) Deploy Amazon ECS for container management, Amazon EKS for Kubernetes clusters, Amazon RDS for relational databases, and Amazon S3 for object storage.

D) Utilize AWS Batch for batch processing workloads, AWS App Mesh for service mesh management, Amazon ElastiCache for caching, and AWS CodePipeline for continuous integration and delivery.

E) Leverage AWS Glue for ETL operations, AWS CodeDeploy for automating application deployments, Amazon Kinesis for real-time data streaming, and Amazon SQS for message queuing between microservices.

QUESTION 52

A healthcare provider needs to design a resilient architecture for its patient management system, which stores sensitive medical records. The system must ensure data confidentiality, integrity, and availability. What architecture should they implement?

A) Deploy the system on Amazon EC2 instances with Amazon RDS for database management, utilizing AWS Shield for DDoS protection and AWS WAF for web application firewall.

B) Utilize AWS Managed Services for automated infrastructure management, coupled with Amazon Aurora for high availability and Amazon S3 for data storage.

C) Implement an AWS Lambda function for processing patient data, using Amazon API Gateway for secure API access and Amazon DynamoDB for data storage.

D) Configure an Amazon VPC with private subnets for backend services, using Amazon CloudFront for content delivery and Amazon Macie for data security.

E) Deploy the system on AWS Fargate containers with Amazon EKS for orchestration, utilizing Amazon S3 for data storage and Amazon Inspector for security assessments.

QUESTION 53

A healthcare application uses an Amazon Aurora database for patient records. The application is deployed in North America and plans to expand to Europe, requiring patient data to be stored locally due to compliance regulations. Which strategy allows for regional data compliance while ensuring global access to application configurations stored in a separate table?

A) Use Amazon Aurora Global Database for patient records and Amazon DynamoDB global tables for application configurations.

B) Use Amazon Aurora Multi-Master in both regions for all tables.

C) Implement Amazon Aurora Global Database for all tables and restrict access based on region.
D) Use Amazon Aurora in each region for patient records and Amazon DynamoDB global tables for application configurations.

E) Implement separate Amazon Aurora instances in each region for patient records and a single Amazon RDS instance for application configurations.

QUESTION 54

Your organization is planning to migrate its on-premises data warehouse to AWS to achieve better scalability and cost optimization. The new solution should support complex analytical queries and ensure high availability. Which option would be the most suitable considering the need for scalability, cost optimization, and availability?

A) Deploy Amazon Redshift Spectrum for querying external data sources
B) Utilize Amazon S3 for data storage and query data using Athena
C) Implement Amazon RDS for PostgreSQL with Multi-AZ configuration
D) Opt for Amazon Redshift with Concurrency Scaling for high-performance analytics
E) Use Amazon Aurora for its high availability and scalable relational database capabilities

QUESTION 55

An e-commerce company wants to grant temporary access to a group of contractors from a third-party vendor to manage product listings on their website. Which approach should the solutions architect recommend to ensure secure access management?

A) Create IAM users for each contractor and provide them with long-term access credentials.

B) Generate temporary IAM roles with restricted permissions for the contractors to assume during their assignment.

C) Share the root account credentials with the contractors for direct access.
D) Utilize IAM groups and assign permissions directly to the contractors' email addresses.
E) Implement IAM policies directly on the EC2 instances hosting the website.

QUESTION 56

Your organization is managing a data warehousing solution on AWS, utilizing Amazon Redshift for analytics and Amazon S3 for storing raw data. The company wants to implement a backup strategy for its data warehouse, ensuring data durability and compliance with regulatory requirements. Which approach aligns with best practices for designing the backup strategy?

A) Implement AWS Backup to automate and manage backups of Amazon Redshift data
B) Configure Amazon S3 Cross-Region Replication to replicate raw data to a secondary AWS region
C) Utilize Amazon S3 Object Lock to prevent accidental deletion of data in Amazon S3
D) Implement Amazon Redshift automated snapshots with a retention period of 30 days
E) Leverage Amazon S3 Glacier for long-term archival of historical data

QUESTION 57

Your company operates a global video streaming platform that delivers high-definition content to users worldwide. You need to ensure minimal buffering and latency while optimizing data transfer costs. Which AWS service would best meet these requirements?

A) Implement Amazon CloudFront with the S3 bucket containing video content set as the origin to cache videos at edge locations

B) Use Amazon Kinesis to stream video content to users in real-time

C) Set up Amazon S3 Transfer Acceleration to optimize data transfer speeds for video content delivery

D) Utilize AWS Elemental MediaConvert to transcode video content into multiple formats for optimized delivery

E) Deploy AWS Snowball to physically distribute video content to AWS data centers in different regions

QUESTION 58

Your organization manages a portfolio of web applications hosted on Amazon EC2 instances across multiple AWS Regions. To improve user experience and reduce latency, you plan to implement Amazon CloudFront as a content delivery network (CDN). Which of the following strategies would best optimize costs while enhancing performance for delivering dynamic web content?

A) Utilize Amazon CloudFront with AWS Lambda@Edge functions to dynamically generate personalized content based on user preferences

B) Implement Amazon CloudFront with origin request policies to customize request routing and optimize caching behavior

C) Configure Amazon CloudFront with real-time logs to monitor viewer traffic patterns and optimize cache hit rates

D) Enable Amazon CloudFront with SSL/TLS certificate management to ensure secure communication between viewers and the CDN

E) Integrate Amazon CloudFront with Amazon Route 53 for global DNS resolution and traffic routing

QUESTION 59

Your organization's data storage costs have been steadily increasing, and you have been tasked with designing a cost-effective solution for data archival. The solution should automatically move infrequently accessed data to a more cost-efficient storage tier. What would you recommend?

A) Implement Amazon S3 Intelligent-Tiering with a single-tier storage strategy for all data

B) Utilize Amazon S3 Standard-Infrequent Access (S3 Standard-IA) storage class for all data and manually move infrequently accessed data to Amazon S3 Glacier

C) Deploy Amazon S3 Lifecycle policies to transition infrequently accessed data to Amazon S3 Glacier

D) Leverage Amazon S3 Cross-Region Replication to replicate infrequently accessed data to a secondary bucket in Amazon S3 Glacier

E) Enable Amazon S3 Object Lock to prevent modification of infrequently accessed data and manually move it to Amazon S3 Glacier

QUESTION 60

A multinational e-commerce company is experiencing fluctuating traffic patterns on its website, resulting in occasional performance issues during peak hours. The company wants to implement an Auto Scaling solution to ensure optimal performance and cost efficiency. What should the solutions architect recommend to achieve this?

A) Configure the Auto Scaling group to use a scheduled scaling policy triggered at specific times of peak traffic.

B) Implement an Auto Scaling group with a target tracking scaling policy based on the average CPU utilization across instances.

C) Configure the Auto Scaling group to use a step scaling policy triggered by sudden increases in traffic.
D) Utilize an Auto Scaling group with a simple scaling policy based on manual adjustments to instance counts.

E) Implement an Auto Scaling group with a predictive scaling policy based on machine learning algorithms analyzing traffic patterns.

QUESTION 61

Your company is designing a scalable architecture for a new social media application that expects rapid user growth. Cost optimization is a priority, and you need to ensure that the architecture can handle spikes in user activity while minimizing costs. Which solution should you recommend for this scenario?

A) Utilize Amazon DynamoDB with on-demand capacity mode to automatically scale read and write capacity based on demand

B) Implement Amazon ElastiCache with Redis to cache frequently accessed data and reduce database load

C) Use Amazon Aurora with provisioned capacity and Aurora Multi-Master to scale read and write capacity across multiple database instances

D) Deploy AWS Lambda with Amazon API Gateway to run serverless functions in response to incoming requests

E) Utilize Amazon S3 with Transfer Acceleration to optimize data transfers and reduce latency for media uploads

QUESTION 62

Your organization manages a large dataset stored in Amazon S3 across multiple regions. Data is frequently replicated between regions for disaster recovery purposes, leading to high data transfer costs. You need to design a cost-effective solution to minimize data transfer costs while ensuring data integrity and availability. What should you recommend for this scenario?

A) Utilize AWS Snow Family to transfer large amounts of data between regions at a lower cost

B) Implement AWS DataSync to automate and optimize data transfers between Amazon S3 buckets in different regions

C) Configure Amazon S3 Cross-Region Replication to replicate data only for critical datasets between regions

D) Use Amazon S3 Transfer Acceleration to optimize data transfers and reduce latency for cross-region replication

E) Deploy Amazon S3 Glacier for long-term storage of replicated data to reduce data transfer costs

QUESTION 63

Your organization has implemented AWS Outposts to extend its on-premises infrastructure to the AWS Cloud. However, you've noticed an increase in data transfer costs between the on-premises environment and AWS Outposts. To address this issue, you need to design a solution that optimizes data transfer costs while maintaining efficient connectivity. What approach should you recommend?

A) Utilize AWS Direct Connect to establish dedicated connectivity between on-premises data centers and AWS Outposts

B) Implement AWS Storage Gateway to cache frequently accessed data locally and reduce data transfer costs between on-premises infrastructure and AWS Outposts

C) Deploy AWS Snow Family devices to transfer large volumes of data between on-premises environments and AWS Outposts

D) Leverage Amazon S3 Transfer Acceleration to optimize data transfer speeds and reduce costs associated with data transfer to AWS Outposts

E) Utilize AWS VPN to establish secure and cost-effective connectivity between on-premises networks and AWS Outposts

QUESTION 64

Your organization operates a microservices architecture deployed on AWS, with each microservice communicating with other services over the network. However, the operations team has noticed high costs associated with data transfer between microservices within the same AWS region. As a solutions architect, you need to design a cost-efficient solution that reduces expenses while maintaining inter-service communication. What approach should you recommend?

A) Utilize AWS PrivateLink to establish private connectivity between microservices within the same VPC, reducing data transfer costs

B) Implement Amazon CloudFront with AWS Global Accelerator to optimize content delivery and reduce data transfer costs between microservices

C) Leverage AWS Direct Connect with AWS Transit Gateway to establish private connectivity between regions and reduce data transfer costs

D) Deploy Amazon ElastiCache to cache frequently accessed data between microservices, reducing the need for data transfer

E) Utilize AWS App Mesh to manage and monitor communication between microservices, optimizing data transfer costs

QUESTION 65

Your organization is looking to optimize costs by identifying and eliminating unused or underutilized AWS resources. As a solutions architect, you need to recommend a solution that automates resource optimization and provides actionable insights.

A) Implement AWS Trusted Advisor to analyze resource utilization and recommend cost optimization opportunities

B) Utilize AWS Cost Explorer to identify unused resources and analyze cost trends over time

C) Leverage AWS Config to track resource configuration changes and identify unused resources

D) Utilize AWS Lambda with AWS CloudTrail to automate resource cleanup based on predefined rules

E) Implement AWS Systems Manager Automation to schedule resource optimization tasks and generate cost reports

PRACTICE TEST 4 - ANSWERS ONLY

QUESTION 1

Answer - C) Leverage AWS Security Hub for a comprehensive view of security alerts and compliance status.

A) Incorrect - While Amazon GuardDuty offers intelligent threat detection, it does not provide a unified view of security alerts and compliance status across multiple accounts.

B) Incorrect - AWS Control Tower is great for setting up and governing a secure, multi-account AWS environment, but it does not specifically focus on providing a unified view of security alerts and compliance status.

C) Correct - AWS Security Hub is designed to give users a comprehensive view of their high-priority security alerts and compliance status across all their AWS accounts, making it the best choice for this scenario.

D) Incorrect - Amazon Inspector is useful for automated security assessments but does not offer a centralized view of security alerts and compliance across multiple accounts.

E) Incorrect - AWS IAM Identity Center provides centralized access management but does not offer visibility into security alerts and compliance status.

QUESTION 2

Answer - D) Select AWS Regions and Availability Zones that adhere to local data residency requirements for data storage and processing.

A) - Incorrect, because AWS DataSync is a data transfer service and does not inherently ensure compliance with data residency requirements.

B) - Incorrect, Amazon S3 Cross-Region Replication does allow for data replication across Regions, but the key is selecting the initial and replication Regions based on compliance needs, which is not explicitly stated.

C) - Incorrect, as AWS Snowball is a data transport solution and, while it processes data locally, it doesn't address continuous operational requirements for data residency within the cloud infrastructure.

D) - Correct, because actively selecting AWS Regions and Availability Zones that comply with local data residency laws for storing and processing data is the direct approach to meeting compliance requirements.

E) - Incorrect, AWS CloudHSM provides hardware security modules in the cloud, and while it's important for encryption and key management, it's the selection of Regions and AZs that primarily ensures compliance with data residency regulations.

QUESTION 3

Answer - [A] Implement AWS WAF with managed rule sets to filter web traffic and protect against common web vulnerabilities.

Option A - Correct. Implementing AWS WAF with managed rule sets provides protection against common web vulnerabilities by filtering web traffic.

Option B - AWS Shield Advanced protects against DDoS attacks but may not directly mitigate common web vulnerabilities.

Option C - While AWS CloudFront with Lambda@Edge can inspect and filter web requests, it may not provide the same level of comprehensive protection against common web vulnerabilities as AWS WAF.

Option D - Amazon Inspector assesses security posture but may not focus specifically on mitigating common web vulnerabilities.

Option E - AWS Firewall Manager centrally manages WAF rules but may not directly mitigate common web vulnerabilities on EC2 instances.

QUESTION 4

Answer - [B] Deploy a private connectivity solution such as AWS Site-to-Site VPN or AWS Direct Connect Gateway to establish secure communication between the primary and DR environments. Implement AWS Transit Gateway to route traffic between the environments and isolate the DR environment from the internet.

Option B - Correct. This solution provides secure communication between the primary and DR environments using private connectivity options like AWS Site-to-Site VPN or AWS Direct Connect Gateway. AWS Transit Gateway isolates the DR environment from the internet and facilitates traffic routing between the environments.

Option A - While VPN connection and AWS Direct Connect offer secure communication, VPC peering may not provide the desired isolation for the DR environment from the internet.

Option C - AWS Direct Connect and AWS Global Accelerator offer dedicated connectivity and improved performance but may not provide the necessary isolation for the DR environment. VPC endpoints alone do not address the requirement for secure connectivity between environments.

Option D - AWS Client VPN and AWS PrivateLink provide secure access options but may not fully meet the requirements for private connectivity and isolation of the DR environment. AWS WAF is not directly related to the connectivity between environments.

Option E - While AWS Direct Connect with AWS Transit Gateway offers private network connectivity and isolation, AWS PrivateLink and AWS Shield Advanced are not necessary components for this scenario.

QUESTION 5

Answer - B) Use Amazon SQS FIFO queue with a batch mode of 100 messages per operation.

B) Use Amazon SQS FIFO queue with a batch mode of 100 messages per operation - This option ensures each task update is processed in the order it was submitted while efficiently handling bulk updates with batch processing. The FIFO guarantees exactly-once processing, meeting the company's requirements for order and accuracy while efficiently managing bulk updates.

A) Use Amazon SQS FIFO queue with exactly-once processing enabled - While ensuring order accuracy, it may not efficiently handle bulk updates as it processes messages sequentially.

C) Use Amazon SQS FIFO queue with default settings - Default settings may not ensure exactly-once processing and may not efficiently handle bulk updates.

D) Use Amazon SQS standard queue to process the messages - Standard queues lack message ordering, which is essential for maintaining task order, and may not efficiently handle bulk updates.

E) Use Amazon SQS FIFO queue with message deduplication enabled - While avoiding duplicate messages, it doesn't guarantee order processing, and may not efficiently handle bulk updates.

QUESTION 6

Answer - [A] Utilize AWS Lambda for serverless compute, Amazon API Gateway for API management, and AWS Secrets Manager for securely storing API keys and secrets. Implement OAuth 2.0 authorization with API Gateway for secure access to external APIs.

Option A - Correct. AWS Lambda, API Gateway, and Secrets Manager provide a secure serverless architecture, and OAuth 2.0 with API Gateway ensures secure access to external APIs.

Option B - Fargate is not typically used for serverless compute, and using IAM authorization with API Gateway may not provide the same level of security for external API access as OAuth 2.0.

Option C - While Lambda, API Gateway, and KMS are suitable, Lambda authorizers with API Gateway may not provide the same level of security for external API access as OAuth 2.0.

Option D - ECS is not typically used for serverless compute, and using OAuth 2.0 with API Gateway may not be possible with ECS.

Option E - Fargate is not typically used for serverless compute, and Parameter Store may not provide the same level of security for storing API keys and secrets as Secrets Manager.

QUESTION 7

Answer - [A] Create IAM roles with specific permissions for each Lambda function, and use IAM policies to control access to S3 buckets and DynamoDB tables.

Option A - Correct. Creating IAM roles with specific permissions for each Lambda function and using IAM policies to control access to S3 buckets and DynamoDB tables ensures fine-grained access control for the serverless application.

Option B - Using IAM users with custom policies and IAM groups may lead to unnecessary complexity and does not align with best practices for serverless architectures.

Option C - While IAM policies can be attached to S3 buckets and DynamoDB tables, using IAM roles for cross-service authentication is the recommended approach for Lambda functions accessing other AWS services.

Option D - Setting up IAM policies at the account level may result in over-permissioned roles and does not provide fine-grained access control for individual resources.

Option E - While IAM policies with condition keys and IAM roles for federated access are valid, they may not provide the same level of control and granularity required for a serverless application's security needs.

QUESTION 8

Answer - [C] Deploy AWS Security Hub to centrally manage security compliance checks and provide insights into security posture. Use AWS Config to monitor resource configurations and detect deviations from desired configurations.

Option C - Correct. Deploying AWS Security Hub for centralized security compliance checks and AWS Config for monitoring resource configurations aligns with the requirements for robust security monitoring and compliance in a critical healthcare application.

Option A - While AWS CloudTrail and Amazon GuardDuty provide monitoring capabilities, AWS Security Hub offers centralized security compliance checks and insights into security posture.

Option B - While AWS Config can detect changes in resource configurations, Amazon CloudWatch Events with AWS Lambda may not provide the same level of centralized security compliance checks as AWS Security Hub.

Option D - Although Amazon CloudWatch Logs and Amazon Inspector offer monitoring and vulnerability assessment capabilities, they may not provide centralized security compliance checks like AWS Security Hub.

Option E - While AWS Config Rules and AWS CloudTrail with Amazon CloudWatch Logs offer monitoring and compliance evaluation, they may not provide centralized insights into security posture like AWS Security Hub.

QUESTION 9

Answer - [A] Configuring AWS CloudTrail for logging all API calls and actions taken on AWS resources, ensuring comprehensive audit logging and compliance monitoring.

A) AWS CloudTrail provides detailed logging of API calls and actions on AWS resources, enabling comprehensive audit logging and compliance monitoring required for sensitive financial data processing.

B) While AWS IAM roles provide access control, they may not offer the same level of audit logging as AWS CloudTrail, and may not directly address compliance with data encryption standards.

C) AWS KMS encrypts sensitive data at rest, enhancing data security, but may not provide the comprehensive audit logging required for compliance with industry regulations.

D) AWS Config tracks changes to resource configurations but may not offer the same level of audit logging as AWS CloudTrail, nor does it directly address compliance with data encryption standards.

E) AWS Security Hub offers centralized security management but may not provide the detailed audit logging required for compliance with industry regulations regarding data transactions and may not directly address data encryption compliance standards.

QUESTION 10

Answer - A) Use Amazon FSx File Gateway to provide low-latency, on-premises access to fully managed file shares in Amazon EFS. The applications deployed on AWS can access this data directly from Amazon EFS.

A) Use Amazon FSx File Gateway to provide low-latency, on-premises access to fully managed file shares in Amazon EFS. The applications deployed on AWS can access this data directly from Amazon EFS - This option meets the requirement by suggesting the use of Amazon FSx File Gateway with Amazon EFS, ensuring low-latency access to large datasets during and after migration.

B) Use Amazon Storage Gateway's File Gateway to provide low-latency, on-premises access to fully managed file shares in Amazon FSx for Windows File Server. The applications deployed on AWS can access this data directly from Amazon FSx in AWS - This option does not align with the requirement as it suggests using FSx for Windows File Server instead of Amazon EFS, which may not meet the low-latency access requirement.

C) Use AWS Storage Gateway's File Gateway to provide low-latency, on-premises access to fully managed file shares in Amazon S3. The applications deployed on AWS can access this data directly from Amazon S3 - This option does not align with the requirement as it suggests using Amazon S3 instead of Amazon EFS, which may not meet the low-latency access requirement.

D) Use Amazon FSx File Gateway to provide low-latency, on-premises access to fully managed file shares in Amazon FSx for Windows File Server. The applications deployed on AWS can access this data directly from Amazon FSx in AWS - This option does not align with the requirement as it suggests using FSx for Windows File Server instead of Amazon EFS, which may not meet the low-latency access requirement.

QUESTION 11

Answer - A) Amazon Route 53 for DNS services, AWS Auto Scaling for resource management, and AWS Shield Advanced for DDoS protection

A) Amazon Route 53 for DNS services, AWS Auto Scaling for resource management, and AWS Shield Advanced for DDoS protection - Correct because Route 53 can efficiently manage DNS requests, AWS Auto Scaling adjusts resources based on demand, and Shield Advanced offers comprehensive DDoS protection, ensuring both scalability and security.

B) AWS WAF for web request filtering, Amazon CloudFront for content delivery, and Amazon EC2 Auto Scaling for compute scaling - Incorrect because, while it addresses scaling and content delivery, it lacks specialized DDoS protection that Shield Advanced provides.

C) AWS Network Firewall for stateful packet inspection, AWS Lambda for backend automation, and Amazon DynamoDB for player data storage - Incorrect as it focuses on data management and serverless computing without addressing the direct need for DDoS protection.

D) AWS Global Accelerator for improved global access, AWS Fargate for serverless container deployment, and AWS Shield Standard for basic DDoS protection - Incorrect because Shield Standard might not offer sufficient protection against sophisticated or large-scale DDoS attacks targeted at online gaming.

E) Amazon VPC for network isolation, Amazon GuardDuty for threat detection, and AWS CloudFormation for infrastructure as code deployment - Incorrect as this setup focuses on infrastructure management and monitoring without directly addressing the scalability and DDoS protection required.

QUESTION 12

Answer - B) Implement AWS IAM Identity Center (SSO) with role-based access control and integration with CI/CD pipelines.

A) Use AWS IAM Access Analyzer to automatically assign roles based on usage patterns. - Incorrect because Access Analyzer is used for analyzing and identifying permissions, not for automating role assignment or integration with CI/CD pipelines.

B) Implement AWS IAM Identity Center (SSO) with role-based access control and integration with CI/CD pipelines. - Correct as it allows for centralized access management, supports role-based access control, and can be integrated with CI/CD pipelines to automate access based on evolving roles.

C) Configure Amazon Cognito with user groups for role-based access in AWS, linked to the CI/CD system. - Incorrect for internal development team management as Cognito is primarily aimed at managing app user identities.

D) Leverage AWS CodePipeline to manage IAM roles and permissions within AWS based on deployment needs. - Incorrect because CodePipeline automates code deployment, not IAM role management or access control.

E) Establish AWS Lambda functions to update IAM policies and roles dynamically based on developer activity and project assignments. - Incorrect as this approach would require significant custom development and may not offer the seamless integration and management provided by IAM Identity Center.

QUESTION 13

Answer - [A) Implementing API caching using Amazon CloudFront.]

A) Implementing API caching using Amazon CloudFront - CloudFront can cache API responses at edge locations, reducing the load on backend servers, improving latency, and providing scalability.

B) Deploying AWS Shield Advanced for comprehensive DDoS protection - While effective against DDoS attacks, AWS Shield Advanced may not directly address performance and scalability concerns related to API delivery.

C) Configuring Amazon RDS for database optimization - Database optimization may improve overall application performance but may not directly address API performance and scalability concerns.

D) Enabling AWS Lambda authorizers for API Gateway authentication - Lambda authorizers control access to APIs based on custom authentication logic but do not directly optimize API performance and scalability.

E) Utilizing AWS Direct Connect for low-latency connectivity - Direct Connect provides dedicated network connections but may not directly optimize API performance and scalability.

QUESTION 14

Answer - D) Deploy AWS Audit Manager to automate evidence collection and reporting for GDPR, HIPAA, and SOC 2 compliance.

A) Utilize AWS Control Tower to set up a multi-account environment with pre-configured compliance blueprints for GDPR, HIPAA, and SOC 2. - Incorrect because, while Control Tower provides governance for multi-account environments, it does not specifically automate evidence collection and reporting for compliance.

B) Implement Amazon RDS with encryption and Amazon VPC with private subnets for data protection and network isolation, respectively. - Incorrect as these are infrastructure security measures, not compliance management solutions.

C) Configure AWS CloudTrail and AWS Security Hub for centralized logging and compliance management, focusing on international regulations. - Incorrect because, although they provide important compliance management features, they do not offer the automated evidence collection and reporting capabilities of AWS Audit Manager.

D) Deploy AWS Audit Manager to automate evidence collection and reporting for GDPR, HIPAA, and SOC 2 compliance. - Correct as Audit Manager is designed specifically to help with compliance audits by automating the collection of evidence and helping to manage the audit workflow, making it ideal for dealing with multiple regulations.

E) Leverage AWS Config conformance packs with custom AWS Lambda functions for continuous compliance monitoring and remediation across multiple regulations. - Incorrect as this requires more setup and maintenance compared to the out-of-the-box solutions provided by AWS Audit Manager for compliance reporting and evidence management.

QUESTION 15

Answer - D) Suspend the ReplaceUnhealthy process type for the Auto Scaling group and apply the maintenance patch to the instance. Once the instance is ready, manually set the instance's health status back to healthy and activate the ReplaceUnhealthy process type again.

D) Suspend the ReplaceUnhealthy process type for the Auto Scaling group and apply the maintenance patch to the instance - This option effectively addresses the maintenance challenge by suspending the process responsible for replacing unhealthy instances, allowing the maintenance to proceed without triggering Auto Scaling actions.

A) Temporarily suspend the Launch process type for the Auto Scaling group and apply the maintenance patch to the instance - Suspending the launch process may not prevent instance replacement triggered by health status changes, potentially leading to disruptions during maintenance.

B) Suspend the Terminate process type for the Auto Scaling group and apply the maintenance patch to the instance - Suspending termination processes may not prevent instance replacement and may not efficiently address the maintenance challenge.

C) Stop the instance, apply the maintenance patch, and then start the instance - Stopping the instance may disrupt application availability, and manually starting it again may not align with the requirement for uninterrupted maintenance.

E) Take a snapshot of the instance, create a new Amazon Machine Image (AMI), and then launch a new instance using this AMI - Creating a new instance from a snapshot introduces complexity and may not efficiently address the maintenance challenge, especially in scenarios where immediate fixes are required.

QUESTION 16

Answer - E) Combine "aws:CurrentTime" and "aws:SourceIp" conditions to restrict access based on time and IP address.

A) Use the "aws:MultiFactorAuthAge" condition to enforce MFA before granting access - Incorrect because it relates to MFA, not access based on time or IP.

B) Apply the "aws:Requester" condition to restrict access to specific roles - Incorrect as it does not limit access by time or IP address.

C) Implement the "aws:CurrentTime" condition to restrict access based on time - Partially correct but does not restrict access by network.

D) Utilize the "aws:SourceIp" condition to restrict access from the company's network - Partially correct but does not restrict access by time.

E) Combine "aws:CurrentTime" and "aws:SourceIp" conditions to restrict access based on time and IP address - Correct because it meets both requirements of time-based and network-based access restrictions.

QUESTION 17

Answer - C) Configure Amazon VPC endpoints for private AWS service access, VPC peering for environment isolation, and enable VPC flow logs for network traffic auditing.

A) Incorrect as PrivateLink and GuardDuty address specific aspects of the scenario but separating environments into different VPCs without a clear connectivity strategy may hinder efficiency.

B) Incorrect because Transit Gateway and VPN address connectivity efficiently but CloudTrail monitors API activity, not network traffic, thus not fully addressing the threat detection requirement.

C) Correct as VPC endpoints provide private connectivity to AWS services, peering offers isolation between development and production, and flow logs enable auditing of all network traffic for security analysis.

D) Incorrect because Direct Connect and Organizations focus on connectivity and account management, respectively, but do not address the isolation or auditing needs directly. Macie is focused on data protection, not network traffic auditing.

E) Incorrect as WAF protects against web exploits, and while S3 with VPC Endpoint Gateway offers private storage access, and Lambda can automate responses, this setup doesn't address the core requirements of environment isolation and comprehensive network traffic auditing.

QUESTION 18

Answer - [A] Implement AWS Shield Advanced for DDoS protection and AWS WAF for web application firewall. Set up Amazon CloudWatch Alarms to monitor resource usage and trigger automated scaling actions.

Option B - While Transit Gateway facilitates network connectivity, it does not directly address security measures like Shield and WAF, and Savings Plans focus on cost optimization rather than monitoring resource usage.

Option C - While RDS Multi-AZ and Aurora Serverless provide high availability and cost-effective scaling, they do not directly address DDoS protection and web application firewall needs.

Option D - While Direct Connect provides dedicated network connectivity, it does not directly address security measures and automated scaling actions like Shield, WAF, and CloudWatch Alarms.

Option E - While Kinesis and Lambda facilitate real-time data processing, they do not directly address DDoS protection, web application firewall, and resource usage monitoring like Shield, WAF, and CloudWatch Alarms.

QUESTION 19

Answer - [B] Implement AWS Secrets Manager to securely store database credentials. Integrate ECS tasks with Secrets Manager for automated retrieval of credentials at runtime.

Option A - Storing credentials directly in Dockerfiles as environment variables is not recommended for security reasons and lacks centralized management and rotation capabilities.

Option C - Maintaining plaintext credentials within Docker images poses security risks and lacks automation for rotation and retrieval.

Option D - While Parameter Store can centrally manage configurations, Secrets Manager is specifically designed for securely storing and rotating secrets like database credentials.

Option E - Storing credentials in plaintext files within EFS lacks encryption and may expose data to unauthorized access.

Explanation for Choice B: Utilizing AWS Secrets Manager provides secure storage and rotation of database credentials. Integrating with ECS tasks allows for automated retrieval at runtime, enhancing security and compliance.

QUESTION 20

Answer - C) Create an Amazon CloudWatch metric filter to process AWS CloudTrail logs containing API call details. Establish an alarm based on this metric's rate to send an Amazon SNS notification to the required team.

C) Create an Amazon CloudWatch metric filter to process AWS CloudTrail logs containing API call details. Establish an alarm based on this metric's rate to send an Amazon SNS notification to the required team. - This option efficiently addresses the requirement by directly analyzing CloudTrail logs, setting up CloudWatch alarms, and triggering SNS notifications in near real-time upon detecting unauthorized API requests.

A) Configure AWS CloudTrail to stream event data to Amazon Kinesis. Utilize Amazon Kinesis stream-level metrics in Amazon CloudWatch to trigger an AWS Lambda function that will initiate an error workflow. - While this option utilizes streaming data, it may introduce complexity and latency compared to directly analyzing CloudTrail logs for real-time alerts.

B) Use Amazon Athena SQL queries against AWS CloudTrail log files stored in Amazon S3 buckets. Generate reports using Amazon QuickSight for managerial dashboards. - While Athena and QuickSight provide insights, they may not offer real-time alerting capabilities as required in this scenario.

D) Implement AWS Config Rules to monitor API activity and define rules to detect unauthorized API calls. Configure AWS Config to trigger an AWS Lambda function upon rule evaluation to notify relevant stakeholders. - While AWS Config can monitor API activity, it may not provide real-time alerting capabilities for immediate incident response as required in this scenario.

E) Leverage AWS Trusted Advisor to publish metrics about check results to Amazon CloudWatch. Set up an alarm to track status changes for checks in the Service Limits category for the APIs, triggering notifications when service quotas are exceeded. - While Trusted Advisor offers valuable insights, it may not directly address the need for real-time detection of unauthorized API queries.

QUESTION 21

Answer - B) Utilize AWS Lambda for serverless backend logic, Amazon API Gateway for managing APIs, Amazon Kinesis Video Streams for video ingestion, and Amazon CloudWatch for monitoring performance.

B) Correct because Lambda offers serverless backend logic, API Gateway manages APIs, Kinesis Video Streams handles video ingestion, and CloudWatch monitors performance, aligning with the requirement for low-latency streaming, high availability, and scalability in the backend architecture of a media streaming platform.

A) Incorrect because while EC2 Auto Scaling and RDS Multi-AZ offer scalability and resilience, they may not provide the same level of simplicity and flexibility as Lambda, API Gateway, and Kinesis Video Streams in handling sudden spikes in user demand and ensuring low-latency streaming.

C) Incorrect as ECS, RDS Read Replicas, Direct Connect, and S3 offer scalability and network connectivity, but they may not provide the same level of serverless scalability and real-time ingestion capabilities as Lambda, API Gateway, and Kinesis Video Streams for a media streaming platform.

D) Incorrect because while EKS, DynamoDB, CloudFront, and Redshift offer scalability and analytics capabilities, they may not provide the same level of serverless processing and real-time ingestion capabilities as Lambda, API Gateway, Kinesis Video Streams, and CloudWatch for a media streaming platform.

E) Incorrect as MSK, Lambda, S3 Glacier, and CloudFront offer streaming, serverless processing, archival storage, and content delivery, respectively, but they may not provide the same level of simplicity and scalability as Lambda, API Gateway, Kinesis Video Streams, and CloudWatch for handling millions of concurrent users and ensuring low-latency streaming in a media streaming platform.

QUESTION 22

Answer - A) Utilize AWS Lambda with Amazon Kinesis for real-time data processing.

Option A combines AWS Lambda with Amazon Kinesis to process streaming data in real-time, ensuring scalability and low latency processing, which aligns with the requirements of the real-time analytics platform. Options B, C, D, and E do not provide the same level of real-time processing and scalability as Lambda with Kinesis.

QUESTION 23

Answer - [C) Deploy Amazon Aurora for relational database storage with Multi-AZ deployment for automated failover and cost-efficient scaling to maintain high availability with minimal expenses.]

Option C) is correct as it involves utilizing Amazon Aurora for relational database storage with Multi-AZ deployment for automated failover and cost-efficient scaling, ensuring fault tolerance and scalability

while optimizing costs.
Option A) and E) involve deployment and scaling but may not emphasize cost efficiency or database reliability effectively.

Option B) involves static content storage but does not directly address application availability or database scalability.

Option D) involves serverless processing but may not provide the same level of database reliability or cost optimization as Multi-AZ deployment.

QUESTION 24

Answer - [A) Amazon CloudFront, B) AWS Shield, and D) AWS WAF]

Option A involves Amazon CloudFront for content delivery, utilizing edge locations to improve performance and reliability.

Option B involves AWS Shield for DDoS protection, safeguarding the CDN infrastructure against malicious attacks.

Option D involves AWS WAF for web application firewall, providing additional security by filtering and monitoring incoming traffic.

Option C involves Amazon CloudWatch for monitoring performance, which is important but does not directly address security or reliability concerns.

Option E involves Amazon S3 for origin storage, which is essential for content delivery but does not directly enhance CDN performance or security.

QUESTION 25

Answer - A) Tier-3 (24 terabytes)

A) Tier-3 (24 terabytes) - Correct. In Aurora's failover mechanism, the replica with the highest priority (the lowest tier number) is promoted as the new primary instance. Size is not a consideration for failover priority.

B) Tier-4 (12 terabytes) - Incorrect. Despite being a viable option, this replica has a lower failover priority compared to Tier-3.

C) Tier-6 (18 terabytes) - Incorrect. This option is neither the highest priority nor the largest size.
D) Tier-8 (24 terabytes) - Incorrect. This instance has a larger size but is not the highest priority for failover.
E) Tier-9 (12 terabytes) - Incorrect. This is the lowest priority among the given options.

QUESTION 26

Answer - A) Implement Amazon Kinesis Data Streams to ingest real-time data from vehicles and process it using AWS Lambda functions for real-time analytics and updates.

Option A is correct because implementing Amazon Kinesis Data Streams to ingest real-time data from vehicles and processing it using AWS Lambda functions ensures low latency and high availability for collecting and processing vehicle location data in real-time across different regions. This aligns with the requirement for tracking vehicle locations in real-time with low latency and high availability.

Option B is incorrect because while Amazon S3 Transfer Acceleration optimizes upload and download speeds, it may not offer the same level of real-time processing and low latency as Amazon Kinesis Data Streams with AWS Lambda.

Option C is incorrect because while Amazon MSK ingests and processes data in real-time, it may introduce additional complexity and overhead that are unnecessary for collecting and processing vehicle location data.

Option D is incorrect because while Amazon SQS decouples collection and processing, it may not provide the same level of real-time processing and low latency as Amazon Kinesis Data Streams with AWS Lambda.

Option E is incorrect because while Amazon EventBridge captures and processes events, it may not offer the same level of real-time processing and low latency as Amazon Kinesis Data Streams with AWS Lambda.

QUESTION 27

Answer - A) Utilize AWS Step Functions with automatic retries and AWS Lambda for processing and transcoding video files

Option A - AWS Step Functions provide automatic retries and fault tolerance, ensuring the resilience of serverless workflows. Combined with AWS Lambda, it offers a robust solution for fault-tolerant video processing.

Option B - While Amazon SQS and SNS can handle queuing and event notification, they do not provide the workflow orchestration features and automatic retries needed for fault tolerance and error recovery.

Option C - Amazon S3 event notifications and CloudWatch Alarms can monitor errors but lack the comprehensive fault tolerance and automated recovery features provided by Step Functions.

Option D - Amazon EventBridge can orchestrate tasks, but it does not offer the built-in error handling and automatic retry capabilities needed for fault tolerance and automated error recovery in serverless workflows.

QUESTION 28

Answer - A) Deploy Amazon CloudFront with AWS Lambda@Edge for content delivery and compute tasks, Amazon DynamoDB Global Tables for database, and secure with AWS WAF.

A) Correct as it provides a globally distributed architecture with low latency and high availability through CloudFront and Lambda@Edge. DynamoDB Global Tables ensure data consistency across regions, and AWS WAF secures the application.

B) Incorrect because EC2 and RDS, while capable, do not offer a serverless solution that can scale automatically without manual intervention. GuardDuty is for threat detection, not for application-level security.

C) Incorrect due to the lack of a global data consistency solution. S3 is suitable for storage but doesn't address the low latency requirement for dynamic content. Cognito is for authentication, not overall security.

D) Incorrect because, while it offers serverless components, AppSync focuses on data synchronization for mobile and web applications and may not provide the low-latency content delivery needed.

E) Incorrect as it does not offer a coherent solution for low latency and high availability across regions. SNS is for notifications, not content delivery.

QUESTION 29

Answer - A) Deploy Amazon Elastic Load Balancing (ELB) with Network Load Balancer (NLB) for efficient network routing.

A) NLB operates at the transport layer and is optimized for low-latency communication and high availability, making it suitable for multiplayer online games.

B) Route 53 with Latency routing policy routes traffic based on latency, but NLB provides more efficient network routing for real-time gaming.

C) CloudFront with Lambda@Edge is primarily used for content delivery optimization, not for real-time communication in gaming applications.

D) Global Accelerator improves global application availability but does not optimize for low-latency gaming communication.

E) ALB with Target Groups is suitable for dynamic traffic routing but may not provide the same level of performance as NLB for gaming applications.

QUESTION 30

Answer - D) Utilize Amazon Kinesis Data Streams with AWS Lambda for real-time data processing and store it in Amazon S3

D) Amazon Kinesis Data Streams combined with AWS Lambda offers real-time data processing capabilities suitable for analyzing medical sensor data from IoT devices, triggering alerts based on predefined thresholds, ensuring reliability, and scalability.

A, B) These options involve storing data in relational databases or data warehouses, which may not be suitable for real-time processing and scalability required for enhancing patient care.

C, E) While these options involve using AWS Lambda and Amazon DynamoDB or S3, they may not provide the real-time processing capabilities required for triggering alerts based on medical thresholds.

QUESTION 31

Answer - A) Implement Amazon Kinesis for real-time data streaming, AWS Lambda for processing data streams, Amazon DynamoDB for storing user interactions, and Amazon Personalize for generating content recommendations.

A) Correct, as this solution directly addresses the need for analyzing user interactions in real-time and providing personalized content recommendations. Kinesis captures real-time user interactions, Lambda processes the data, DynamoDB stores the interactions, and Personalize offers the recommendation engine.

B) Incorrect, SQS, EC2, RDS, and Glue offer a robust infrastructure but don't specifically cater to real-time analysis or personalized recommendations as effectively as option A.

C) Incorrect, S3, Redshift, Data Pipeline, and QuickSight focus on data storage, warehousing, and visualization, not on real-time processing or personalized content recommendations.

D) Incorrect, while Fargate, ECR, Step Functions, and SageMaker provide powerful tools for application deployment and machine learning models, they don't offer the integrated, real-time recommendation system capabilities as seamlessly as option A.

E) Incorrect, EMR, S3, Athena, and Lake Formation are suited for big data processing and data lake management but don't provide the immediate, personalized recommendation capabilities required for a streaming platform.

QUESTION 32

Answer - [A) Implement Amazon RDS with Multi-AZ deployment and utilize read replicas for scaling read operations during peak hours.]

Option A) - Correct because Amazon RDS with Multi-AZ deployment and read replicas efficiently scales read operations during peak trading hours, ensuring data integrity and availability while optimizing costs for the financial institution.

Option B) - Incorrect because although Aurora Serverless offers auto-scaling, it may not provide the same level of performance and scalability as Amazon RDS with Multi-AZ deployment and read replicas required during peak trading hours.

Option C) - Incorrect because Amazon DynamoDB is a NoSQL database and may not offer the relational data support required by a financial institution for data integrity and availability during peak trading hours.

Option D) - Incorrect because Amazon Redshift is optimized for analytics and may not offer the same level of transactional support and data integrity as Amazon RDS required by the financial institution during peak trading hours.

Option E) - Incorrect because Amazon DocumentDB may not offer the same level of cost optimization and scalability as Amazon RDS with Multi-AZ deployment and read replicas required by the financial institution during peak trading hours.

QUESTION 33

Answer - D) Utilize Amazon DynamoDB with on-demand capacity mode for scalable data storage, Amazon Kinesis for real-time data processing, and AWS Global Accelerator to optimize connectivity and reduce latency for players globally.

A) - Incorrect. While Amazon DynamoDB Global Tables, Amazon ElastiCache for Redis, and Amazon CloudFront are excellent for global distribution and reducing latency, they lack the real-time data processing capabilities required for a gaming backend.

B) - Incorrect. Amazon RDS with Read Replicas and AWS Lambda are solid choices for data storage and processing, but AWS Global Accelerator offers more direct benefits for global gaming experiences in terms of connectivity and latency reduction.

C) - Incorrect. Although Amazon ECS with Fargate and Amazon Aurora Global Database provide scalable and serverless options for container management and relational data storage, they do not specifically address the need for real-time data processing and global latency optimization as effectively as other options.

D) - Correct. This option offers a comprehensive solution for a global gaming backend. Amazon DynamoDB with on-demand capacity ensures scalable, low-latency data storage. Amazon Kinesis facilitates real-time data processing, which is crucial for maintaining game state. AWS Global Accelerator improves global application performance, reducing latency for a seamless player experience.

E) - Incorrect. While Amazon S3, AWS AppSync, and Elastic Load Balancing (ELB) provide components of the solution, this combination does not fully address the requirements for scalable real-time data processing and global latency reduction as effectively as Option D.

QUESTION 34

Answer - E) Configure Amazon VPC to use endpoints within a specific region only.

A) Incorrect - AWS CloudTrail geo-fencing is not a feature; CloudTrail is used for logging and monitoring account activity.

B) Incorrect - Amazon S3 Cross-Region Replication does not prevent data from leaving a geographic area; it replicates data across regions.

C) Incorrect - AWS WAF regional rules are for traffic filtering based on web requests, not for ensuring data sovereignty.

D) Incorrect - AWS IAM policies restrict access to resources based on user permissions, not geographic location.

E) Correct - Configuring Amazon VPC to use endpoints within a specific region ensures that the data remains within the geographic boundaries set by regulatory requirements, thereby maintaining compliance with data sovereignty laws.

QUESTION 35

Answer - A) Utilize RESTful APIs on Amazon API Gateway with Amazon DynamoDB for storing tracking data and AWS Lambda for processing tracking requests

A) Utilizing RESTful APIs on Amazon API Gateway with Amazon DynamoDB enables efficient handling of a high volume of tracking requests and provides accurate location data for the logistics company.

B, C, D, E) These options either do not provide efficient storage and processing capabilities or involve using services not suitable for real-time tracking systems.

QUESTION 36

Answer - [A, B]

A) Correct - Read replicas distribute the load, improving performance and reliability.

B) Correct - Performance Insights provides real-time database monitoring for optimization.

C) Incorrect - Enhanced Monitoring collects detailed metrics but doesn't directly optimize performance under varying loads.

D) Incorrect - Multi-AZ deployment ensures availability but doesn't directly optimize performance under varying loads.

E) Incorrect - Storage Auto Scaling adjusts storage capacity but doesn't directly optimize database performance.

QUESTION 37

Answer - [A, D]

A) Correct - EC2 Auto Scaling with target tracking scaling policies adjusts instance count based on CPU utilization, ensuring scalability and cost optimization. CloudWatch Alarms notify of capacity increases, facilitating proactive resource management.

B) Incorrect - While Lambda functions and API Gateway provide serverless scalability, this option lacks auto-scaling for compute resources and database scalability, essential for handling traffic spikes effectively.

C) Incorrect - ECS service auto-scaling is relevant for containerized applications, but it does not address the auto-scaling of compute resources for the application layer. Fargate manages container resources but does not optimize costs during traffic spikes.

D) Correct - Aurora Serverless scales database capacity based on traffic patterns, and ElastiCache reduces database load by caching frequently accessed data, ensuring both scalability and cost optimization during traffic spikes.

E) Incorrect - Lambda@Edge improves content delivery but does not address auto-scaling of compute resources or database scalability, essential for handling traffic spikes effectively. CloudFront configuration with Lambda@Edge is not sufficient to ensure scalability and cost optimization during traffic surges.

QUESTION 38

Answer - A) Utilize AWS Lambda for serverless execution of code in response to events, ensuring scalability and cost-effectiveness.

C) Leverage AWS Step Functions for orchestrating serverless workflows, ensuring smooth execution and easy maintenance.

Option A - AWS Lambda allows for serverless execution of code in response to events, providing scalability and cost-effectiveness for the data processing pipeline.

Option C - AWS Step Functions orchestrates serverless workflows, ensuring smooth execution and easy maintenance of the data processing pipeline.

Options B, D, and E may not directly address the requirements for a highly scalable, cost-effective, and easily maintainable serverless data processing pipeline.

QUESTION 39

Answer - C) Implement Amazon VPC with public and private subnets, employing AWS Direct Connect for dedicated network connections, and AWS VPN for secure hybrid connectivity.

Option A - Deploying Amazon Route 53 with AWS Global Accelerator is focused on DNS routing and global application acceleration, not hybrid network connectivity.

Option B - Utilizing CloudFront with Shield and Route 53 addresses content delivery and DNS routing but does not provide secure hybrid connectivity.

Option C - Implementing VPC with Direct Connect and VPN is the correct choice for secure hybrid network connectivity between on-premises data center and AWS cloud resources.

Option D - Configuring CloudFront with WAF focuses on content delivery and web attack protection, not hybrid network connectivity.

Option E - AWS Transit Gateway offers scalable connectivity but does not specifically address the requirement for secure hybrid connectivity between on-premises and AWS resources.

QUESTION 40

Answer - C) Ingest market data into Amazon Kinesis Data Streams, which triggers an AWS Lambda function for processing and stores price updates in Amazon DynamoDB

C) Ingesting market data into Amazon Kinesis Data Streams with AWS Lambda allows for real-time processing and dynamic price updates. Storing price updates in Amazon DynamoDB ensures low-latency access and scalability.

A) Processing market data with AWS Lambda and Amazon S3 may introduce latency and is not suitable for real-time pricing engines.

B) Using Amazon Kinesis Data Firehose may not provide the necessary real-time processing capabilities for updating prices promptly.

D) Amazon SQS is not optimized for real-time processing of market data, and storing price updates in Amazon Redshift may introduce delays.

E) Using Amazon API Gateway and an EC2 instance for processing lacks the scalability and real-time processing capabilities required for dynamic pricing engines.

QUESTION 41

Answer - A) Implement Amazon GameLift to deploy, operate, and scale dedicated game servers for low-latency multiplayer gaming experiences.

Option A - Amazon GameLift provides dedicated game servers for low-latency multiplayer gaming experiences, ensuring consistent performance and minimal lag for players.

Option B - Amazon Route 53 with latency-based routing directs traffic based on geographic location but may not optimize game server performance as effectively as Amazon GameLift.

Option C - AWS Global Accelerator improves application availability and performance but may not directly optimize game server performance as effectively as Amazon GameLift.

Option D - Amazon DynamoDB Accelerator (DAX) caches data for reduced latency but may not be suitable for real-time multiplayer gaming communication.

Option E - AWS Direct Connect establishes dedicated connections but may not optimize game server communication latency as effectively as Amazon GameLift.

QUESTION 42

Answer - [C) Leverage Amazon Aurora with its performance optimizations and global replication.]

Option C) Amazon Aurora is specifically designed for high performance and offers global replication for low-latency access across regions.

Option A) Multi-AZ deployment enhances availability but may not directly address speed and performance requirements.

Option B) Deploying on EC2 instances with EFS may not provide the same level of performance as managed database services like Aurora.

Option D) Amazon Redshift is not optimized for low-latency access and is primarily used for data warehousing and analytics.

Option E) While DynamoDB offers scalability, it may not provide the same level of performance optimization as Aurora for global access.

QUESTION 43

Answer - A) Deploy Amazon Personalize for creating personalized user recommendations, Amazon Kinesis for real-time data processing, AWS Lambda for serverless computing, Amazon S3 for data storage, and AWS IAM for managing access permissions.

Option A - Correct. This combination effectively addresses the need for real-time data processing, personalized recommendations, serverless architecture, secure data storage, and access management, making it highly suitable for the scenario.

Option B - Incorrect. While Redshift and EC2 Auto Scaling provide data warehousing and compute scaling, this option lacks the real-time processing and personalized recommendation capabilities offered by Amazon Personalize.

Option C - Incorrect. SageMaker and DynamoDB are powerful for machine learning and data storage, but this setup requires more management overhead and doesn't focus on personalized recommendations as directly as Amazon Personalize.

Option D - Incorrect. Glue, Athena, and S3 form a solid foundation for a data lake, but this option doesn't provide the real-time personalized recommendation capabilities needed for the scenario.

Option E - Incorrect. ECS, Batch, ElastiCache, and CloudFront offer valuable services for container management, processing, caching, and delivery, but they do not directly address the need for personalized recommendations and real-time data processing as effectively as option A.

QUESTION 44

Answer - [C] Deploy Amazon Managed Streaming for Apache Kafka (Amazon MSK) for user event ingestion, process data with Amazon Kinesis Data Analytics, and trigger recommendations using AWS Lambda.

Option A introduces complexity with Glue and RDS and may not provide real-time analytics.

Option B's use of EC2 instances and Redshift may not be cost-efficient or scalable.

Option D's use of AppSync and Neptune may not be suitable for real-time analytics on user behavior data.

Option E's use of Firehose and EMR may not provide the real-time processing required for instant recommendations on video streaming platforms. Amazon MSK offers a scalable and durable event streaming platform, and Kinesis Data Analytics provides real-time analytics capabilities, making option C the most suitable choice for building a real-time recommendation engine.

QUESTION 45

Answer - B) Implement server-side encryption with AWS Key Management Service (SSE-KMS) and define fine-grained access policies

B) Implementing server-side encryption with AWS Key Management Service (SSE-KMS) allows the retail company to maintain control over encryption keys and define fine-grained access policies, ensuring only authorized users can access the data.

A) Server-side encryption with Amazon S3 managed keys (SSE-S3) encrypts the data at rest but may not provide the desired control over encryption keys and access policies.

C) Client-side encryption with customer-provided keys (SSE-C) shifts the responsibility of encryption to the client and may not align with the company's requirement for centralized control.

D) Implementing server-side encryption with customer-provided keys (SSE-C) and restricting access through IAM policies may introduce complexity and potential security risks.

E) Enabling AWS CloudTrail provides auditing capabilities but does not directly address the encryption and access control requirements for data at rest in Amazon S3.

QUESTION 46

Answer - [A] Utilize AWS IoT Core for data ingestion, configure AWS Greengrass for edge computing, implement Amazon Kinesis Data Streams for real-time data processing, utilize AWS Lambda for serverless processing, and store real-time data in Amazon DynamoDB.

Option B is incorrect because it uses Amazon API Gateway for data ingestion, which is not typically used in IoT solutions for sensor data collection. AWS Fargate is also not the ideal choice for edge processing in IoT scenarios. Additionally, Amazon RDS and Amazon Glacier are not the most suitable options for real-time data storage and long-term data archival in IoT solutions.

Option C is incorrect because it does not utilize AWS Greengrass for edge computing, which is essential for processing data closer to the source in IoT scenarios. Amazon S3 is also not ideal for real-time data storage compared to Amazon DynamoDB.

Option D is incorrect because AWS IoT Events is not commonly used for data ingestion in IoT solutions, and Amazon Aurora is not the optimal database service for real-time data storage in this context. Amazon S3 Glacier is also not well-suited for long-term data archival in IoT scenarios.

Option E is incorrect because although it uses AWS IoT Greengrass, it employs AWS Lambda for serverless processing instead of edge processing, which may introduce latency issues in real-time data processing for IoT applications.

QUESTION 47

Answer - [A] Deploy applications on edge devices using AWS Local Zones located near factory locations, leverage AWS IoT Greengrass for edge data processing, and integrate with Amazon DynamoDB for real-time data storage.

Option A is the correct choice because deploying applications on edge devices in Local Zones near factory locations ensures low-latency edge computing capability, ideal for processing sensor data in real-time. AWS IoT Greengrass facilitates edge data processing, and DynamoDB provides real-time data storage.

Options B, C, D, and E either lack the same level of latency reduction, suitable edge computing solutions, or appropriate real-time data storage services.

QUESTION 48

Answer - A) Utilize Amazon API Gateway for API management, AWS Lambda for scalable computing, Amazon RDS for data storage, and Amazon QuickSight for usage analytics.

A) Correct - Amazon API Gateway provides robust API management capabilities, AWS Lambda offers scalable serverless computing for processing vendor requests, Amazon RDS serves as a reliable data storage solution, and QuickSight enables detailed analysis of API usage, aligning with the online retail company's goals for scalability, security, and analytics.

B) Incorrect - S3, Direct Connect, DynamoDB, and IAM offer solutions for storage, connectivity, data management, and security but lack the comprehensive API management and scalable computing capabilities needed for vendor interaction as provided by API Gateway and Lambda.

C) Incorrect - Fargate, CloudFront, WAF, and Kinesis are powerful for container management, content delivery, security, and data monitoring but do not offer the same level of API integration, scalability, and usage analytics as API Gateway, Lambda, and QuickSight.

D) Incorrect - AppSync, Aurora, Shield, and CloudTrail provide data synchronization, database scalability, protection, and logging but miss out on the direct API management and serverless computing framework necessary for handling dynamic vendor interactions.

E) Incorrect - SQS, ECS with Auto Scaling, ElastiCache, and CloudWatch support decoupling, microservice scaling, caching, and monitoring but do not specifically address API management or the analytic requirements for optimizing vendor experiences as effectively as option A.

QUESTION 49

Answer - C)

C) Adding the statement with actions s3:GetObject and s3:PutObject and restricting the resource to arn:aws:s3:::example-bucket/* allows the team to read objects from the bucket and write objects to the specific folder, meeting the requirement.

A) While this option allows reading and writing objects, it does not restrict deleting objects or modifying bucket properties, violating the requirement.

B) This option grants excessive permissions by allowing deleting objects and modifying bucket policies, which are not required and violate the least privilege principle.

D) This option grants permissions to delete the entire bucket and modify bucket policies, which are beyond the scope of the requirement and violate the least privilege principle.

E) Similar to option D, this choice grants unnecessary permissions to delete the bucket and modify bucket policies, which are not aligned with the requirement.

QUESTION 50

Answer - A) Utilize Amazon CloudFront as a content delivery network (CDN) to cache and distribute media content globally, reducing latency for users. Implement Amazon S3 for storing media files and enable cross-region replication for high availability.

Option A is the correct choice as it leverages Amazon CloudFront as a CDN to distribute media content globally, reducing latency for users. Storing media files in Amazon S3 with cross-region replication ensures high availability and disaster recovery.

Option B introduces unnecessary complexity with EC2 instances and ElastiCache, which may not provide the required scalability and cost optimization.

Option C focuses on database replication but lacks the direct content delivery optimization offered by CloudFront.

Option D, while utilizing API Gateway and Lambda, does not directly address global content distribution requirements.

QUESTION 51

Answer - A) Implement AWS Fargate for running containerized microservices, Amazon EKS for managing Kubernetes clusters, Amazon EFS for shared storage, and AWS X-Ray for distributed tracing.

Option A - Correct: Fargate offers serverless container management, EKS manages Kubernetes clusters, EFS provides scalable shared storage, and X-Ray offers distributed tracing, ensuring efficient resource allocation and optimal performance for each microservice in the e-commerce company's migration to a microservices architecture.

Option B - Incorrect: Lambda, API Gateway, DynamoDB, and Step Functions support serverless and API-driven microservices but may not provide the same level of control and scalability as Fargate and EKS for containerized microservices in a microservices architecture migration.

Option C - Incorrect: ECS, EKS, RDS, and S3 offer container management, Kubernetes clusters, relational databases, and object storage, but they may not align with the agility and scalability needs of a microservices architecture migration as A does.

Option D - Incorrect: Batch, App Mesh, ElastiCache, and CodePipeline focus on batch processing, service mesh management, caching, and CI/CD, which are essential but not specific to efficient resource allocation and performance optimization for microservices as in A.

Option E - Incorrect: Glue, CodeDeploy, Kinesis, and SQS address ETL, deployment automation, real-time streaming, and message queuing, but they may not be as well-suited for efficient resource allocation and performance optimization in a microservices architecture as A.

QUESTION 52

Answer - D) Configure an Amazon VPC with private subnets for backend services, using Amazon CloudFront for content delivery and Amazon Macie for data security.

A) Incorrect - While EC2 instances and RDS offer flexibility, they may not provide the necessary security and resilience for sensitive medical records.

B) Incorrect - Managed Services and Aurora offer convenience, but they may not address the specific security and resilience requirements of healthcare data.

C) Incorrect - Lambda functions and DynamoDB may offer scalability, but they may not provide the necessary control and security measures for sensitive medical records.

D) Correct - Configuring a VPC with private subnets, CloudFront for content delivery, and Macie for data security ensures confidentiality, integrity, and availability of medical records.

E) Incorrect - While Fargate containers and EKS offer scalability, they may introduce additional complexity and may not address the specific security requirements of healthcare data.

QUESTION 53

Answer - D) Use Amazon Aurora in each region for patient records and Amazon DynamoDB global tables for application configurations.

A) Aurora Global Database is not needed for application configurations which are global by nature.

B) Aurora Multi-Master is designed for write scalability, not compliance with data residency.

C) Global Database doesn't inherently restrict access based on region; additional configuration would be needed.

D) Correct, because it meets compliance by using Aurora regionally for patient data and DynamoDB for globally accessible configurations.

E) Using a single RDS instance for global configurations could become a bottleneck and doesn't leverage global distribution.

QUESTION 54

Answer - [D] Opt for Amazon Redshift with Concurrency Scaling for high-performance analytics.

Option A - Redshift Spectrum allows querying external data sources but may not provide the same performance and scalability as Redshift.

Option B - While S3 with Athena offers cost optimization, it may not meet the complex analytical query and high availability requirements of a data warehouse.

Option C - RDS with Multi-AZ configuration provides high availability for relational data but may not offer the same scalability and performance as Redshift.

Option D - Correct. Redshift with Concurrency Scaling ensures high-performance analytics, scalability, and cost optimization, making it suitable for migrating on-premises data warehouses.

Option E - Aurora offers high availability and scalability but may not provide the same analytical query performance as Redshift for data warehousing needs.

QUESTION 55

Answer - [B] Generate temporary IAM roles with restricted permissions for the contractors to assume during their assignment.

A) Incorrect - Creating IAM users with long-term access credentials is not recommended for temporary access, as it poses security risks in case credentials are compromised.

B) Correct - Generating temporary IAM roles with restricted permissions ensures secure access management for contractors, limiting their access to only what is necessary during their assignment.

C) Incorrect - Sharing root account credentials is highly discouraged due to security concerns, as it provides unrestricted access to the entire AWS account.

D) Incorrect - Assigning permissions directly to contractors' email addresses is not a recommended approach, as it bypasses IAM best practices and complicates access management.

E) Incorrect - Implementing IAM policies directly on EC2 instances is not scalable and does not provide centralized access control, making it challenging to manage access for multiple contractors.

QUESTION 56

Answer - [D] Implement Amazon Redshift automated snapshots with a retention period of 30 days.

Option A - Implementing AWS Backup may offer automation but does not specifically address backup requirements for Amazon Redshift.

Option B - Configuring Amazon S3 Cross-Region Replication focuses on redundancy but does not directly address backup requirements for Amazon Redshift.

Option C - Utilizing Amazon S3 Object Lock enhances data protection but does not specifically address backup requirements for Amazon Redshift.

Option D - Correct. Implementing Amazon Redshift automated snapshots with a retention period of 30 days ensures data durability and compliance with regulatory requirements for the data warehousing solution.

Option E - Leveraging Amazon S3 Glacier for long-term archival may be suitable for historical data but does not specifically address backup requirements for Amazon Redshift.

QUESTION 57

Answer - [A] Implement Amazon CloudFront with the S3 bucket containing video content set as the origin to cache videos at edge locations.

Option A - Correct. Implementing Amazon CloudFront with the S3 bucket containing video content set as the origin allows caching of videos at edge locations, minimizing buffering and latency while optimizing data transfer costs.

Option B - Amazon Kinesis is used for real-time data streaming and may not directly address the requirement for delivering high-definition video content with minimal buffering and latency.

Option C - While Amazon S3 Transfer Acceleration optimizes data transfer speeds, it may not offer the same level of content delivery capabilities as Amazon CloudFront for video streaming.

Option D - AWS Elemental MediaConvert is used for video transcoding but may not directly address the requirement for minimizing buffering and latency in video streaming.

Option E - AWS Snowball involves physical data transfer and may not be as efficient or cost-effective as using Amazon CloudFront for delivering video content to users worldwide.

QUESTION 58

Answer - [B] Implement Amazon CloudFront with origin request policies to customize request routing and optimize caching behavior.

Option A - Utilizing Amazon CloudFront with Lambda@Edge functions for dynamic content generation may enhance user experience but may not directly optimize costs for delivering dynamic web content.

Option B - Correct. Implementing Amazon CloudFront with origin request policies allows for customizing request routing and optimizing caching behavior, thereby optimizing costs while enhancing performance for dynamic content delivery.

Option C - Configuring Amazon CloudFront with real-time logs helps monitor traffic patterns but may not directly focus on cost optimization for dynamic content delivery.

Option D - Enabling Amazon CloudFront with SSL/TLS certificate management enhances security but may not directly address cost optimization concerns for content delivery.

Option E - Integrating Amazon CloudFront with Amazon Route 53 enhances DNS resolution but may not directly optimize costs for delivering dynamic web content.

QUESTION 59

Answer - [C] Deploy Amazon S3 Lifecycle policies to transition infrequently accessed data to Amazon S3 Glacier.

Option C - Correct. Deploying Amazon S3 Lifecycle policies allows for automatic transitioning of infrequently accessed data to Amazon S3 Glacier, ensuring cost-effective data archival without manual intervention.

Option A - Implementing Amazon S3 Intelligent-Tiering with a single-tier storage strategy may not effectively optimize costs for infrequently accessed data.

Option B - Utilizing Amazon S3 Standard-Infrequent Access (S3 Standard-IA) for all data and manually moving infrequently accessed data to Amazon S3 Glacier introduces manual effort and may not be as automated as lifecycle policies.

Option D - Leveraging Amazon S3 Cross-Region Replication to replicate infrequently accessed data to Amazon S3 Glacier may introduce complexity and may not be as cost-effective as lifecycle policies.

Option E - Enabling Amazon S3 Object Lock prevents modification but does not automate the process of transitioning infrequently accessed data to Amazon S3 Glacier.

QUESTION 60

Answer - [B] Implement an Auto Scaling group with a target tracking scaling policy based on the average CPU utilization across instances.

A) Incorrect - Using a scheduled scaling policy based on specific times does not dynamically respond to fluctuating traffic patterns, potentially leading to under or over-provisioning of resources.

B) Correct - Implementing a target tracking scaling policy based on CPU utilization ensures that the Auto Scaling group adjusts the number of instances to maintain a desired average CPU utilization, optimizing performance and cost efficiency.

C) Incorrect - Configuring a step scaling policy triggered by sudden increases in traffic may not provide the fine-grained adjustments needed for optimal performance during fluctuating traffic patterns.

D) Incorrect - Utilizing a simple scaling policy based on manual adjustments lacks automation and may result in delayed responses to changing traffic conditions.

E) Incorrect - Implementing a predictive scaling policy based on machine learning algorithms may introduce unnecessary complexity and may not be as effective in responding to immediate traffic fluctuations compared to a target tracking policy based on real-time metrics.

QUESTION 61

Answer - [A] Utilize Amazon DynamoDB with on-demand capacity mode to automatically scale read and write capacity based on demand.

Option A - Correct. Amazon DynamoDB with on-demand capacity mode automatically scales capacity based on demand, allowing the architecture to handle spikes in user activity while minimizing costs by only paying for resources consumed.

Option B - Amazon ElastiCache with Redis can cache data to reduce database load but may not provide the same level of scalability and cost optimization as DynamoDB on-demand capacity mode.

Option C - Amazon Aurora with provisioned capacity and Aurora Multi-Master offers scalability but may not offer the same level of cost optimization and simplicity as DynamoDB on-demand capacity mode.

Option D - While AWS Lambda with API Gateway can handle serverless functions, it may not address the scalability requirements for the database layer as effectively as DynamoDB on-demand capacity mode.

Option E - Amazon S3 with Transfer Acceleration optimizes data transfers but may not directly address the scalability requirements for the database layer.

QUESTION 62

Answer - [C] Configure Amazon S3 Cross-Region Replication to replicate data only for critical datasets between regions.

Option A - AWS Snow Family is suitable for transferring large amounts of data but may not provide continuous replication and real-time data transfer optimization between regions.

Option B - AWS DataSync automates data transfers but may not offer the same cost optimization for continuous replication between regions as cross-region replication.

Option C - Correct. Amazon S3 Cross-Region Replication allows for replicating data only for critical datasets between regions, minimizing data transfer costs while ensuring data integrity and availability.

Option D - Amazon S3 Transfer Acceleration optimizes data transfers but may not address the specific requirement for minimizing data transfer costs between regions for disaster recovery purposes.

Option E - Amazon S3 Glacier is suitable for long-term storage but may not provide real-time data replication and low-latency access required for disaster recovery scenarios.

QUESTION 63

Answer - [B] Implement AWS Storage Gateway to cache frequently accessed data locally and reduce data transfer costs between on-premises infrastructure and AWS Outposts.

Option A - AWS Direct Connect provides dedicated connectivity but may not directly address the need for optimizing data transfer costs to AWS Outposts.

Option B - Correct. Implementing AWS Storage Gateway allows for caching frequently accessed data locally, reducing data transfer costs between on-premises infrastructure and AWS Outposts.

Option C - AWS Snow Family devices are used for offline data transfer and may not be the most suitable solution for optimizing ongoing data transfer costs to AWS Outposts.

Option D - Amazon S3 Transfer Acceleration improves transfer speeds but may not directly reduce data transfer costs in a hybrid cloud environment with AWS Outposts.

Option E - AWS VPN provides secure connectivity but may not offer the same level of cost optimization as AWS Storage Gateway for reducing data transfer costs to AWS Outposts.

QUESTION 64

Answer - [A] Utilize AWS PrivateLink to establish private connectivity between microservices within the same VPC, reducing data transfer costs.

Option A - Correct. Utilizing AWS PrivateLink establishes private connectivity between microservices within the same VPC, reducing data transfer costs.

Option B - Amazon CloudFront with AWS Global Accelerator optimizes content delivery but may not directly address data transfer costs between microservices within the same region.

Option C - AWS Direct Connect with AWS Transit Gateway establishes private connectivity between regions but may not directly reduce data transfer costs between microservices within the same region.

Option D - Amazon ElastiCache caches data but may not directly reduce data transfer costs between microservices.

Option E - AWS App Mesh manages communication between microservices but may not directly optimize data transfer costs.

QUESTION 65

Answer - [D] Utilize AWS Lambda with AWS CloudTrail to automate resource cleanup based on predefined rules.

Option D - Correct. Utilizing AWS Lambda with AWS CloudTrail allows for automation of resource cleanup based on predefined rules, optimizing costs by eliminating unused resources.

Option A - AWS Trusted Advisor analyzes resource utilization but may not provide automated resource cleanup capabilities.

Option B - AWS Cost Explorer identifies unused resources but may not automate resource cleanup as efficiently as AWS Lambda with AWS CloudTrail.

Option C - AWS Config tracks configuration changes but may not directly automate resource cleanup for cost optimization.

Option E - AWS Systems Manager Automation schedules tasks but may not offer the same level of automation and integration with AWS CloudTrail for cost optimization.

PRACTICE TEST 5 - QUESTIONS ONLY

QUESTION 1

A multinational corporation wants to ensure that their AWS root account is secured with multi-factor authentication (MFA) and that IAM users have the least privilege access for their job functions. What combination of actions adheres best to the AWS Well-Architected Framework?

A) Enable MFA for root account only. Design IAM policies based on job functions.

B) Utilize AWS Control Tower to manage security and SCPs for MFA enforcement on all accounts.

C) Implement MFA for IAM users only. Use AWS Organizations to manage permissions.

D) Enable MFA for both root and IAM users. Use AWS IAM to create policies for least privilege access and AWS STS for cross-account access.

E) Apply service control policies to enforce MFA on root accounts. Rely on AWS IAM roles for cross-account access.

QUESTION 2

A software development company is building a global web application hosted on AWS. They aim to optimize the application's security, performance, and compliance with data protection laws across different regions. What best practices should they follow when deploying their application on AWS's global infrastructure?

A) Host the application in a single AWS region closest to the majority of the users and use Amazon CloudFront for global content delivery.

B) Distribute the application across multiple AWS regions, using Amazon CloudFront for content delivery and AWS WAF for web application firewall protection.

C) Keep all sensitive data in Amazon S3 buckets in one region, using default encryption and ignoring the application's distribution across regions.

D) Utilize AWS Global Accelerator to improve application performance worldwide without considering specific regional deployment strategies.

E) Implement a multi-region deployment strategy, ensuring data is stored and processed in compliance with regional data protection laws, and use Amazon CloudFront and AWS WAF for global security and performance.

QUESTION 3

Your organization is experiencing an increase in security incidents related to unauthorized access attempts and data breaches. You need to recommend a solution that provides continuous monitoring and threat detection to identify and respond to security threats effectively.

A) Implement Amazon GuardDuty to continuously monitor AWS accounts for malicious activity and unauthorized behavior

B) Utilize AWS Config to assess resource configurations for compliance with security best practices and detect unauthorized changes

C) Deploy AWS CloudTrail with Amazon CloudWatch Events to log and monitor API activity for potential security threats

D) Configure AWS IAM Access Analyzer to identify and remediate unintended access to AWS resources

E) Utilize AWS Security Hub to centrally manage security findings from multiple AWS services and automate compliance checks

QUESTION 4

Your organization is planning to migrate its on-premises data warehouse to Amazon Redshift for better scalability and performance. As the solutions architect, you need to design a secure architecture for the data warehouse that meets industry compliance standards. The solution should encrypt data at rest and in transit, enforce fine-grained access control, and provide auditing capabilities for compliance monitoring. Which architecture should you recommend?

A) Deploy Amazon Redshift in a single VPC subnet with encrypted EBS volumes for data at rest encryption. Utilize AWS IAM roles and groups to enforce fine-grained access control, and enable Amazon Redshift audit logging for compliance monitoring.

B) Configure Amazon Redshift Spectrum to query data directly from Amazon S3, enabling data encryption using AWS KMS-managed keys. Implement AWS Glue for data cataloging and enforcing row-level access control, and utilize AWS CloudTrail for auditing API activity.

C) Set up Amazon Redshift cross-region replication for disaster recovery and scalability. Encrypt data in transit using SSL/TLS, and utilize Amazon Redshift Enhanced VPC Routing for network traffic isolation. Implement AWS Lake Formation for centralized data governance and access control, and enable AWS CloudTrail logging for compliance auditing.

D) Utilize Amazon Redshift Concurrency Scaling to handle fluctuating query workloads efficiently. Enable Amazon Redshift automatic snapshots for data backup and recovery. Implement AWS Secrets Manager for managing database credentials securely, and configure AWS IAM policies for access control.

E) Deploy Amazon Redshift clusters in separate VPCs across multiple AWS accounts for isolation. Use AWS Key Management Service (KMS) for encryption of data at rest and in transit, and implement AWS Identity and Access Management (IAM) policies for fine-grained access control. Enable Amazon Redshift audit logging and integrate with Amazon CloudWatch for compliance monitoring.

QUESTION 5

A manufacturing company is migrating its inventory management system to AWS and requires a solution that ensures inventory updates are processed in the order they are received while also providing the ability to process multiple updates simultaneously for different product categories. Which option should the company choose to implement this requirement?

A) Use Amazon SQS FIFO queue with a batch mode of 5 messages per operation.
B) Use Amazon SQS FIFO queue with default settings to process the messages.
C) Use Amazon SQS FIFO queue with exactly-once processing enabled.

D) Use Amazon SQS standard queue to process the messages.

E) Use Amazon SQS FIFO queue with message deduplication enabled.

QUESTION 6

Your company is developing a serverless application that requires secure access to data stored in Amazon S3 buckets. You need to ensure that only authorized users can read and write data to the S3 buckets while maintaining high availability and reliability. Which combination of services should you use to achieve this goal?

A) Utilize AWS Lambda for serverless compute, Amazon API Gateway for API management, and Amazon S3 for object storage. Implement IAM policies on S3 buckets to control access and use API Gateway with IAM authorization for secure API access.

B) Deploy AWS Fargate for serverless compute, Amazon API Gateway for API management, and Amazon S3 for object storage. Configure S3 bucket policies to control access and use API Gateway with IAM authorization for secure API access.

C) Implement AWS Lambda for serverless compute, Amazon API Gateway for API management, and Amazon S3 for object storage. Configure S3 bucket policies to control access and use API Gateway with OAuth 2.0 authorization for secure API access.

D) Utilize Amazon ECS for serverless compute, Amazon API Gateway for API management, and Amazon S3 for object storage. Implement IAM policies on S3 buckets to control access and use API Gateway with OAuth 2.0 authorization for secure API access.

E) Implement AWS Fargate for serverless compute, Amazon API Gateway for API management, and Amazon S3 for object storage. Configure S3 bucket policies to control access and use API Gateway with OAuth 2.0 authorization for secure API access.

QUESTION 7

A global enterprise is migrating its on-premises applications to AWS and needs to ensure that the encryption keys used for data encryption can be managed centrally but applied locally within each region to comply with regional data protection laws. The solution must also allow for the keys to be disabled instantly in case of a security breach. Which setup would best meet these requirements?

A) Centralize key management with AWS KMS and use resource-based policies for regional control.

B) Deploy regional AWS CloudHSM clusters and manage keys locally with synchronization for central oversight.

C) Use AWS KMS with multi-region keys and enable key deactivation features for immediate action.

D) Implement a custom solution using Amazon DynamoDB for storing keys and AWS Lambda for regional distribution and management.

E) Store and manage keys in AWS Secrets Manager with replication across regions for local application.

QUESTION 8

A media company uses AWS to host its globally distributed content delivery network. They want to ensure that their infrastructure is protected from both internal and external threats while maintaining compliance with media industry standards. Which services are best suited for this purpose? Select

THREE.

A) AWS Shield and Amazon CloudFront
B) AWS WAF and AWS Firewall Manager
C) Amazon GuardDuty and AWS Security Hub
D) AWS IAM Identity Center and Amazon Inspector
E) Amazon VPC and AWS Direct Connect

QUESTION 9

You are designing an architecture for a healthcare application that requires secure access to patient records stored in a database. Compliance regulations mandate strong authentication and encryption for protecting sensitive health information. Additionally, the application needs to ensure high availability and scalability to handle peak loads. Which of the following options provides the most suitable solution for meeting these requirements?

A) Deploying Amazon RDS with encryption at rest and AWS IAM database authentication, ensuring secure access control and compliance with data protection regulations

B) Utilizing AWS Lambda for serverless processing of patient data, ensuring high availability and scalability during peak loads

C) Implementing Amazon S3 with server-side encryption and access control policies for storing patient records, ensuring compliance with data encryption standards

D) Configuring Amazon CloudFront with AWS Shield for DDoS protection, ensuring high availability and scalability for accessing patient records

E) Enabling Amazon Elasticsearch Service with fine-grained access control and encryption, ensuring secure search and retrieval of patient records and compliance with data protection regulations

QUESTION 10

A software development company is migrating its code repository to AWS and needs a solution that ensures low-latency access to source code files stored on a file system service. The developers must be able to access these files without disruption after migration. Which option is the most suitable solution to meet this requirement?

A) Use Amazon FSx File Gateway to provide low-latency, on-premises access to fully managed file shares in Amazon EFS. The applications deployed on AWS can access this data directly from Amazon EFS.

B) Use Amazon Storage Gateway's File Gateway to provide low-latency, on-premises access to fully managed file shares in Amazon FSx for Windows File Server. The applications deployed on AWS can access this data directly from Amazon FSx in AWS.

C) Use AWS Storage Gateway's File Gateway to provide low-latency, on-premises access to fully managed file shares in Amazon S3. The applications deployed on AWS can access this data directly from Amazon S3.

D) Use Amazon FSx File Gateway to provide low-latency, on-premises access to fully managed file shares in Amazon FSx for Windows File Server. The applications deployed on AWS can access this data directly from Amazon FSx in AWS.

QUESTION 11

An enterprise-level SaaS provider specializing in data analytics services for retail companies is seeking to enhance the security posture of its AWS infrastructure. The goal is to implement a solution that not only secures the network perimeter but also provides in-depth monitoring and analytics of network traffic for advanced threat detection and mitigation, all while ensuring compliance with GDPR and other privacy regulations.

A) AWS Network Firewall for granular network controls, Amazon Kinesis for real-time data processing, and AWS CloudTrail for governance

B) Amazon Inspector for vulnerability assessments, Amazon Macie for data privacy, and AWS WAF for application layer security

C) AWS Shield Advanced for DDoS protection, AWS Fargate for application isolation, and Amazon Athena for querying logs

D) Amazon CloudFront for content delivery, AWS Direct Connect for a private network connection, and AWS Lambda for executing custom security scripts

E) Amazon VPC for network isolation, AWS IAM for access management, and Amazon GuardDuty for threat detection and monitoring

QUESTION 12

For a highly sensitive government project, a defense contractor must ensure that access to AWS resources is strictly controlled and monitored. The solution must allow access only from designated secure facilities and enforce strong multi-factor authentication mechanisms. Additionally, the contractor seeks to integrate this system with their existing hardware MFA devices and government identity management system.

A) Configure AWS IAM policies to restrict access based on IP address and enforce hardware MFA.

B) Use AWS IAM Identity Center (SSO) with conditional access policies and hardware MFA integration.

C) Implement Amazon Cognito with custom authentication flows for hardware MFA and IP restrictions.

D) Establish VPN connections from secure facilities to AWS, with AWS Directory Service managing hardware MFA devices.

E) Leverage AWS Network Firewall for IP whitelisting and AWS IAM for MFA, integrating with the government's identity management system.

QUESTION 13

A healthcare application uses Amazon API Gateway to manage access to its APIs. The application needs to ensure compliance with health data protection regulations by logging all access to its APIs, including the identity of the API caller, and monitoring for unusual patterns of access. Which solution meets these compliance requirements while ensuring scalability and security?

A) Enable Amazon CloudWatch Logs and Amazon CloudWatch Events for API Gateway, use AWS IAM for authentication, and AWS Lambda for access pattern analysis.

B) Implement Amazon API Gateway access logging to an Amazon S3 bucket, use Amazon Cognito for user authentication, and Amazon GuardDuty for monitoring access patterns.

C) Utilize API Gateway execution logging with AWS CloudTrail, employ Amazon Cognito and IAM for dual authentication, and AWS WAF for monitoring.

D) Enable API Gateway to log to Amazon CloudWatch, use AWS IAM roles for service-to-service authentication, and Amazon Inspector for real-time access monitoring.

E) Implement AWS CloudTrail for logging API calls, Amazon Cognito for authentication, and AWS Lambda for custom access pattern analysis.

QUESTION 14

An online education platform needs to automate compliance with the Children's Online Privacy Protection Act (COPPA) across its AWS-hosted services. The platform requires a solution that not only monitors for compliance but also automatically corrects any configurations that might lead to violations of COPPA requirements.

A) Deploy Amazon Cognito for user authentication and age verification, integrated with AWS Lambda for automating compliance actions based on user age.

B) Utilize AWS Config and AWS Service Catalog to enforce COPPA-compliant resource configurations and automatically correct violations.

C) Implement AWS CloudTrail for logging user actions and AWS Macie for identifying and protecting sensitive information related to children.

D) Configure AWS KMS for encryption of sensitive data and Amazon GuardDuty for detecting potential threats to children's data.

E) Leverage AWS IAM policies to restrict access to children's data and Amazon QuickSight for visualizing compliance status with COPPA regulations.

QUESTION 15

An education institution faces challenges in performing maintenance activities on specific Amazon EC2 instances within an Auto Scaling group. Each time maintenance patches are applied, the instances briefly show as out of service, prompting Auto Scaling to provision replacements. What steps would you recommend as a solutions architect to address this issue effectively?

A) Suspend the AlarmNotifications process type for the Auto Scaling group and apply the maintenance patch to the instance. Once the instance is ready, manually set the instance's health status back to healthy and activate the AlarmNotifications process type again.

B) Suspend the ReplaceUnhealthy process type for the Auto Scaling group and apply the maintenance patch to the instance. Once the instance is ready, manually set the instance's health status back to healthy and activate the ReplaceUnhealthy process type again.

C) Put the instance into the Detached state and then update the instance by applying the maintenance patch. Once the instance is ready, exit the Detached state and then return the instance to service.

D) Suspend the AddToLoadBalancer process type for the Auto Scaling group and apply the maintenance patch to the instance. Once the instance is ready, manually set the instance's health status back to healthy and activate the AddToLoadBalancer process type again.

E) Take a snapshot of the instance, create a new Amazon Machine Image (AMI), and then launch a new instance using this AMI. Apply the maintenance patch to this new instance and then add it back to the Auto Scaling Group by using the manual scaling policy. Terminate the earlier instance that had the maintenance issue.

QUESTION 16

Your company operates a global e-commerce platform hosted on Amazon EC2 instances behind an Application Load Balancer (ALB). You need to implement a solution to mitigate DDoS attacks and ensure high availability of the platform. Which combination of AWS services and features should you use to achieve this?

A) Utilize AWS Shield Standard and enable AWS WAF with rate-based rules on the ALB to mitigate DDoS attacks and protect against web application layer attacks.

B) Deploy AWS Shield Advanced to protect against DDoS attacks and configure AWS Global Accelerator to distribute incoming traffic across multiple AWS regions for high availability.

C) Enable AWS WAF with IP match conditions on the ALB to block traffic from known malicious IP addresses and configure Amazon CloudFront with AWS Shield Standard to absorb DDoS attacks.

D) Implement Amazon GuardDuty to monitor for DDoS threats and configure AWS Shield Advanced to provide additional protection against DDoS attacks on the ALB.

E) Deploy AWS Shield Standard with AWS WAF on the ALB to protect against DDoS attacks and configure Amazon Route 53 with health checks and failover routing policies for high availability.

QUESTION 17

In preparation for regulatory compliance audits, a healthcare application hosted on AWS must ensure that its network architecture supports strict access controls, encrypted data transmission, and detailed logging for all network traffic involving patient data. The solution must also be resilient to DDoS attacks.

A) Design the VPC with dedicated subnets for sensitive data, employ AWS Shield Advanced for DDoS resilience, and activate AWS CloudTrail and VPC flow logs for logging.

B) Use Amazon VPC with Network ACLs and Security Groups for granular access control, Amazon CloudFront with AWS Certificate Manager (ACM) for encryption, and Amazon GuardDuty for traffic logging.

C) Configure AWS WAF and AWS Shield Standard on Internet Gateways, implement Amazon Route 53 for encrypted DNS queries, and use Amazon Athena to query VPC flow logs.

D) Establish AWS Client VPN for encrypted access, deploy AWS Firewall Manager for centralized security management, and utilize AWS KMS with Amazon RDS for data encryption.

E) Implement Amazon Cognito for user authentication, AWS Direct Connect for private, encrypted connectivity, and enable Amazon CloudWatch Logs for network traffic monitoring.

QUESTION 18

A technology startup is developing a new mobile application that requires backend infrastructure on AWS. The startup aims to ensure the security and scalability of its application while managing costs efficiently to support rapid growth.

A) Deploy Amazon API Gateway for backend API management and AWS Lambda for serverless computing. Utilize Amazon DynamoDB for NoSQL database storage and enable DynamoDB Auto Scaling for automatic throughput adjustments.

B) Implement Amazon ECS for containerized application deployment and AWS Fargate for serverless container management. Set up Amazon Aurora for relational database storage and enable Aurora Auto Scaling for automatic scaling based on workload demand.

C) Utilize AWS Amplify for building and deploying mobile applications with built-in security features. Implement Amazon Cognito for user authentication and authorization. Set up AWS AppSync for scalable GraphQL APIs.

D) Deploy Amazon S3 for storing static assets and enable server-side encryption. Utilize Amazon CloudFront for content delivery and set up AWS Lambda@Edge for serverless computing at the edge.

E) Implement AWS App Mesh for microservices communication and monitoring. Deploy Amazon EKS for container orchestration and utilize AWS EBS for persistent block storage. Set up AWS Auto Scaling to automatically adjust the capacity of the Kubernetes cluster.

QUESTION 19

A software development company is designing a CI/CD pipeline for deploying serverless applications on AWS Lambda. They need to implement secure management of environment-specific configurations and secrets during the deployment process. Which of the following approaches would best meet the company's requirements?

A) Embed configuration settings directly within deployment packages. Utilize AWS CodePipeline with IAM roles to restrict access to deployment artifacts.

B) Implement AWS Systems Manager Parameter Store to centrally manage environment-specific configurations and secrets. Use AWS CodePipeline with Parameter Store integration for retrieving configurations during deployments.

C) Store secrets in plaintext files within version-controlled repositories. Implement AWS CodePipeline with IAM roles to control access to the repositories and retrieve secrets during deployments.

D) Utilize AWS Secrets Manager to store and rotate secrets. Develop custom Lambda functions within the CI/CD pipeline to fetch secrets from Secrets Manager during deployments.

E) Maintain configuration settings within AWS Lambda environment variables. Use AWS CodePipeline with Lambda environment variable integration for retrieving configurations during deployments.

QUESTION 20

An online education platform encountered an unusual surge in unauthorized AWS API queries during low-traffic hours, with no noticeable impact on system performance. The management seeks an automated solution to promptly alert relevant teams in such occurrences. Which approach would be most effective in this scenario?

A) Use Amazon Athena SQL queries against AWS CloudTrail log files stored in Amazon S3 buckets. Generate reports using Amazon QuickSight for managerial dashboards.

B) Configure AWS CloudTrail to stream event data to Amazon Kinesis. Utilize Amazon Kinesis stream-level metrics in Amazon CloudWatch to trigger an AWS Lambda function that will initiate an error workflow.

C) Implement AWS Config Rules to monitor API activity and define rules to detect unauthorized API calls. Configure AWS Config to trigger an AWS Lambda function upon rule evaluation to notify relevant stakeholders.

D) Leverage AWS Trusted Advisor to publish metrics about check results to Amazon CloudWatch. Set up an alarm to track status changes for checks in the Service Limits category for the APIs, triggering notifications when service quotas are exceeded.

E) Create an Amazon CloudWatch metric filter to process AWS CloudTrail logs containing API call details. Establish an alarm based on this metric's rate to send an Amazon SNS notification to the required team.

QUESTION 21

A healthcare application is being developed to provide real-time patient monitoring and alerting for critical health conditions. The architecture must ensure high availability, low-latency data processing, and compliance with healthcare regulations.

A) Implement Amazon SQS for message queuing, Amazon SNS for event notification, AWS Lambda for serverless processing, and Amazon Aurora for HIPAA-compliant database storage.

B) Deploy Amazon Kinesis Data Streams for real-time data ingestion, Amazon RDS Multi-AZ for database resilience, Amazon CloudFront for content delivery, and AWS Fargate for containerized processing.

C) Utilize Amazon EventBridge for event-driven architecture, Amazon API Gateway for managing APIs, Amazon DynamoDB for NoSQL data storage, and AWS Glue for data transformation.

D) Configure Amazon Managed Streaming for Apache Kafka (Amazon MSK) for real-time data streaming, AWS Lambda for processing health data, Amazon S3 for storing patient records, and Amazon RDS for relational database management.

E) Leverage Amazon S3 for data storage, Amazon Redshift for data analytics, AWS AppSync for real-time GraphQL APIs, and Amazon ElastiCache for caching frequently accessed data.

QUESTION 22

Your company is developing a new e-commerce application that requires high availability and the ability to handle sudden spikes in traffic during promotional events. The application should also minimize operational overhead. Which AWS service would be most suitable for this scenario?

A) Utilize AWS Lambda with Amazon DynamoDB for serverless scalability.
B) Deploy the application on Amazon EC2 instances with Amazon RDS for traditional scalability.
C) Implement AWS Fargate with Amazon Aurora for serverless container deployment.

D) Leverage AWS Elastic Beanstalk with Amazon Redshift for auto-scaling.

E) Utilize Amazon ECS with Amazon S3 for container orchestration and storage.

QUESTION 23

A multinational e-commerce company is designing a disaster recovery (DR) strategy for its critical application hosted on AWS. The company aims to achieve a low Recovery Point Objective (RPO) and Recovery Time Objective (RTO) while minimizing costs. Which AWS service should the company consider for implementing a pilot light architecture as part of its DR strategy?

A) Utilize Amazon S3 with cross-region replication enabled for storing application backups and data snapshots, ensuring low RPO and RTO

B) Implement AWS Backup with lifecycle policies for automated backup and restore operations, minimizing recovery time and cost

C) Deploy AWS Lambda with Amazon DynamoDB Streams for real-time data replication and failover, achieving near-zero RPO and RTO at scale

D) Utilize Amazon EC2 Auto Scaling with a minimum number of instances in a separate AWS Region for rapid application scaling during disaster recovery

E) Implement Amazon Route 53 with latency-based routing policies for DNS failover between multiple AWS Regions, ensuring high availability and fault tolerance with minimal downtime and cost

QUESTION 24

Your organization is developing a microservices-based application that requires centralized authentication and authorization for user access. The application should support multiple identity providers and enforce fine-grained access controls based on user roles. Additionally, you want to implement logging and auditing capabilities for user activities. Which AWS services should you include in this application architecture?

A) Amazon Cognito for authentication and authorization
B) AWS IAM for fine-grained access control
C) Amazon API Gateway for RESTful API integration
D) Amazon CloudTrail for logging API calls
E) AWS Lambda for serverless execution of custom authorization logic

QUESTION 25

A media streaming service utilizes Amazon Aurora to store vast amounts of media metadata. To ensure low latency reads and high availability, they've deployed Aurora replicas in various sizes and with distinct failover tiers. If the primary instance encounters an issue, which of the following replicas would Aurora automatically promote to maintain service continuity?

A) Tier-2 (20 terabytes)
B) Tier-2 (10 terabytes)
C) Tier-7 (15 terabytes)
D) Tier-11 (20 terabytes)

E) Tier-11 (10 terabytes)

QUESTION 26

A retail company is developing a microservices-based application on AWS to manage its inventory across multiple regions. The company requires a solution for ensuring fault tolerance and high availability of its microservices, with minimal operational overhead. Which option would best meet these requirements? Select TWO.

A) Utilize AWS Fargate to deploy containerized microservices, enabling automatic scaling and managing infrastructure resources efficiently without the need for manual intervention.

B) Implement Amazon RDS Multi-AZ deployment for the database tier of microservices, ensuring automatic failover and high availability of database instances across multiple Availability Zones.

C) Deploy microservices on Amazon EC2 instances within Auto Scaling groups, enabling automatic scaling and replacing unhealthy instances to maintain fault tolerance and high availability.

D) Configure Amazon DynamoDB global tables for microservices, enabling automatic replication of data across multiple regions and ensuring fault tolerance and high availability of data access.

E) Set up Amazon S3 cross-region replication for microservices, ensuring fault tolerance and high availability of data storage with minimal operational overhead.

QUESTION 27

A healthcare organization is developing a serverless workflow for processing patient data. The organization requires the workflow to adhere to HIPAA compliance regulations, including data encryption and auditability. Which of the following options ensures compliance with HIPAA requirements while orchestrating the serverless workflow?

A) Utilize AWS Step Functions with AWS Key Management Service (KMS) for encrypting patient data at rest and in transit

B) Implement Amazon S3 versioning for maintaining data integrity and AWS CloudTrail for auditing workflow activities

C) Deploy Amazon RDS with encryption for storing patient data and leverage Amazon SNS for event notification to trigger Lambda functions for workflow tasks

D) Leverage Amazon EventBridge for orchestrating workflow tasks and use AWS CloudWatch Logs for capturing workflow execution logs and analyzing compliance metrics

QUESTION 28

A financial services company is planning to deploy a serverless application for real-time fraud detection. The application must process transactions in milliseconds, scale automatically, and ensure data is encrypted in transit and at rest. Which set of AWS services should the company use to achieve these requirements?

A) Use Amazon Kinesis Data Streams for transaction ingestion, AWS Lambda for processing, Amazon DynamoDB with DAX for storage, and AWS Certificate Manager for managing encryption keys.

B) Implement Amazon SQS for transaction ingestion, AWS Fargate for processing, Amazon RDS for storage, and Amazon Macie for data security.

C) Deploy AWS AppSync for real-time data handling, Amazon Aurora Serverless for storage, AWS Lambda for backend processing, and AWS KMS for key management and encryption.

D) Utilize Amazon SNS for transaction notifications, Amazon EC2 Auto Scaling for processing, Amazon EFS for storage, and AWS CloudHSM for cryptographic operations.

E) Leverage Amazon MQ for transaction messaging, AWS Batch for processing, Amazon QLDB for storage, and Amazon GuardDuty for monitoring security threats.

QUESTION 29

A financial institution is migrating its trading platform to the cloud and requires a load balancing solution that can handle sudden spikes in trading activity while ensuring minimal latency for executing trades. Which combination of AWS services provides the most suitable solution for this scenario?

A) Implement Amazon CloudFront with Lambda@Edge for real-time content optimization
B) Set up Amazon Elastic Load Balancing (ELB) with Classic Load Balancer for legacy compatibility
C) Configure an Application Load Balancer (ALB) with Target Groups for dynamic traffic routing
D) Utilize Amazon Route 53 with Geolocation routing policy for directing traffic based on trader locations

E) Deploy an Amazon Elastic Load Balancer (ELB) with Network Load Balancer (NLB) for efficient network routing

QUESTION 30

A financial institution intends to detect fraudulent transactions in real-time to mitigate risks and ensure compliance with regulatory standards. They require a solution capable of processing streaming transaction data efficiently and flagging suspicious activities promptly. Which AWS service combination should they deploy to achieve this while ensuring accuracy and scalability?

A) Utilize a Spark Streaming cluster on Amazon EMR to process transaction data before storing it in Amazon RDS

B) Implement Amazon Kinesis Data Analytics to analyze streaming transaction data and store it in Amazon Redshift for further analysis

C) Employ Amazon Kinesis Data Firehose to ingest data and use AWS Lambda to filter and transform before storing it in Amazon DynamoDB

D) Utilize Amazon Kinesis Data Streams with AWS Lambda for real-time data processing and store it in Amazon S3

E) Ingest data directly into Amazon S3 using Amazon Kinesis Data Firehose without intermediate processing

QUESTION 31

A financial services firm is looking to analyze historical trading data to predict future market trends. They require a scalable solution that can handle large datasets and complex computations. Which AWS services would best fit their needs for data analysis and scalable computing?

A) Utilize Amazon S3 for storing trading data, Amazon Athena for querying historical data, AWS Lambda for executing computation-heavy tasks, and Amazon Forecast for predictive analytics.

B) Deploy Amazon EC2 instances for computational tasks, Amazon EBS for data storage, Amazon RDS for transactional data management, and Amazon QuickSight for visualization.

C) Implement Amazon Redshift for data warehousing, AWS Glue for data preparation, Amazon Machine Learning for predictive analytics, and AWS Data Pipeline for data movement.

D) Use AWS Fargate for containerized data processing, Amazon ECR for container image storage, AWS Batch for batch processing tasks, and Amazon SageMaker for building predictive models.

E) Choose Amazon Kinesis for real-time data processing, Amazon DynamoDB for storing time-series trading data, AWS Step Functions for coordinating tasks, and Amazon EMR for big data analytics.

QUESTION 32

A media streaming company wants to improve the performance and scalability of its content delivery system by optimizing database operations. Which combination of AWS services and features should the company implement to achieve these objectives while minimizing costs?

A) Implement Amazon RDS with Provisioned IOPS and utilize Amazon CloudFront for content caching and distribution to users.

B) Utilize Amazon DynamoDB with global tables for multi-Region replication and use Amazon ElastiCache for Redis for caching frequently accessed data.

C) Deploy Amazon Aurora Serverless with auto-scaling and provisioned Aurora Capacity Units (ACUs) for predictable performance and scalability.

D) Migrate to Amazon Redshift for analytics and scalability and utilize Redshift Spectrum for querying external data without loading into Redshift.

E) Implement Amazon DocumentDB with point-in-time recovery enabled and utilize AWS Snowball for cross-Region data transfer and offline backup.

QUESTION 33

A media company is designing a content management system (CMS) on AWS to manage and deliver digital content to users worldwide. The system must support rapid content updates and ensure that content is delivered with low latency to users regardless of their location. Additionally, the architecture should be cost-effective and scalable to accommodate fluctuating traffic patterns. Which architectural design should the Solutions Architect recommend?

A) Utilize Amazon S3 for content storage, Amazon CloudFront as the CDN to distribute content globally, and Amazon EC2 Auto Scaling to dynamically adjust compute resources based on demand.

B) Deploy the CMS on AWS Elastic Beanstalk for easy application management, use Amazon RDS for content database storage, and Amazon Route 53 for DNS services to route users to the nearest server.

C) Implement AWS Lambda for serverless content management logic, Amazon DynamoDB for scalable content storage, and AWS Global Accelerator to ensure low latency content delivery to users worldwide.

D) Set up Amazon ECS with Fargate for containerized content management, Amazon EFS for shared content storage across containers, and utilize Amazon CloudFront for global content delivery.

E) Configure Amazon S3 for storing digital content, with Amazon CloudFront for content delivery. Use AWS AppSync to manage real-time content updates and synchronization across devices.

QUESTION 34

A multinational corporation is planning to migrate its on-premises data center to AWS to improve scalability and resilience. They want to ensure secure communication between their on-premises network and AWS resources. Which option offers the best approach for implementing hybrid cloud architectures in this scenario?

A) Set up an AWS Client VPN to establish encrypted connections between the on-premises network and AWS VPCs, providing secure access to resources over the internet

B) Deploy AWS Site-to-Site VPN to establish secure IPsec tunnels between the on-premises network and AWS, enabling private communication over the internet

C) Utilize AWS Direct Connect to establish a dedicated network connection between the on-premises data center and AWS, ensuring private and consistent network performance

D) Implement AWS PrivateLink to securely expose selected AWS services to the on-premises network without traversing the internet, maintaining data privacy and security

E) Configure AWS Transit Gateway with VPN attachments to establish secure and scalable connectivity between the on-premises network and multiple VPCs in AWS, simplifying network management and routing

QUESTION 35

An online retail platform wants to integrate a recommendation engine into its website to personalize product recommendations for users. They need a solution that analyzes user behavior in real-time and generates personalized recommendations. Which setup should they configure using Amazon API Gateway to meet these requirements effectively?

A) Utilize RESTful APIs on Amazon API Gateway with Amazon SNS for real-time event notifications and AWS Lambda for generating personalized recommendations

B) Implement WebSocket APIs on Amazon API Gateway with Amazon Kinesis for real-time data streaming and Amazon SageMaker for generating personalized recommendations

C) Create HTTP APIs on Amazon API Gateway and integrate with Amazon SQS for real-time event processing and Amazon Comprehend for generating personalized recommendations

D) Deploy GraphQL APIs on Amazon API Gateway with Amazon EventBridge for real-time event routing and Amazon Personalize for generating personalized recommendations

E) Configure RESTful APIs on Amazon API Gateway with Amazon DynamoDB for real-time data storage and Amazon ECS for generating personalized recommendations

QUESTION 36

Your company is designing a serverless architecture on AWS for a new application that requires high availability and scalability. The application must handle sudden spikes in traffic without manual intervention. Which combination of AWS services and best practices should you incorporate into the architecture to achieve these objectives while optimizing costs? Select THREE.

A) Implement AWS Lambda with provisioned concurrency to ensure consistent performance under varying loads.

B) Use Amazon API Gateway for HTTP API endpoints and leverage caching to reduce latency and cost.

C) Utilize Amazon DynamoDB with on-demand capacity mode for flexible scalability without capacity planning.

D) Set up Amazon CloudWatch alarms to trigger AWS Lambda auto-scaling based on predefined thresholds.

E) Deploy AWS Fargate for containerized workload management without provisioning or managing servers.

QUESTION 37

Your organization operates a critical financial application on AWS that must adhere to strict compliance requirements for data encryption and access control. As a solutions architect, you need to design a secure and compliant architecture for the application's data storage layer. How would you implement encryption and access control mechanisms to ensure data security and compliance with regulatory standards? Select TWO.

A) Deploy Amazon RDS with encryption at rest enabled and utilize AWS IAM database authentication for secure access control. Implement AWS KMS for centralized key management and rotation.

B) Utilize Amazon S3 with server-side encryption enabled and enforce fine-grained access control using IAM policies. Set up AWS CloudTrail to monitor S3 bucket access and API activity.

C) Implement Amazon DynamoDB with client-side encryption enabled to encrypt data at rest. Use AWS IAM roles for granular access control and enforce least privilege principles.

D) Utilize Amazon Redshift with encryption at rest enabled and implement AWS Secrets Manager for secure storage and rotation of database credentials. Configure IAM policies to control access to Redshift clusters and data.

E) Deploy Amazon DocumentDB with encryption at rest enabled and leverage AWS Certificate Manager for SSL/TLS certificate management. Implement AWS CloudHSM for secure key storage and access control using IAM policies.

QUESTION 38

Your company operates a web application that experiences frequent peaks in traffic during specific hours of the day. To ensure a consistent user experience, you need to design a scalable and resilient architecture that can handle these traffic spikes while minimizing costs. Which AWS service or services would you recommend to achieve this objective? Select TWO.

A) Deploy Amazon CloudFront to cache static content and reduce latency during traffic spikes.
B) Utilize Amazon EC2 Auto Scaling to automatically adjust compute capacity based on traffic patterns.

C) Implement Amazon Route 53 for intelligent DNS routing to distribute traffic across multiple endpoints.

D) Leverage Amazon RDS Multi-AZ configuration for database scalability and high availability.

E) Utilize AWS Lambda for serverless execution of code in response to events, reducing costs during low-traffic periods.

QUESTION 39

A gaming company requires a network architecture that can efficiently handle fluctuating traffic loads, ensure low latency, and provide global application performance. What solution would best meet these requirements?

A) Use AWS Transit Gateway for scalable and efficient network connectivity across multiple VPCs.
B) Deploy Amazon Route 53 with AWS Global Accelerator for efficient DNS routing and global application acceleration.
C) Configure Amazon CloudFront with AWS WAF for global content delivery and protection against web attacks.
D) Implement Amazon VPC with public and private subnets, employing AWS Direct Connect for dedicated network connections, and AWS VPN for secure hybrid connectivity.
E) Utilize Elastic Load Balancing (ELB) for distributing traffic across resources.

QUESTION 40

An educational institution wants to develop a student performance analytics system to monitor academic progress and identify students at risk of falling behind. They require a solution that can process student data from various sources continuously and generate alerts promptly. Which configuration should they implement using AWS serverless components to meet these requirements effectively?

A) Utilize AWS Lambda with Amazon S3 for processing student data and Amazon RDS for storing alert data

B) Implement Amazon Kinesis Data Firehose with AWS Lambda for processing student data and Amazon ElastiCache for storing alert data

C) Ingest student data into Amazon Kinesis Data Streams, which triggers an AWS Lambda function for processing and stores alert data in Amazon DynamoDB

D) Ingest student data into Amazon SQS, which triggers an AWS Lambda function for processing and stores alert data in Amazon Redshift

E) Use Amazon API Gateway to ingest student data, which is processed by an application running on an Amazon EC2 instance, and store alert data in Amazon Elasticsearch Service

QUESTION 41

A software development company is migrating its microservices architecture to AWS and needs a solution for inter-service communication that ensures low latency and high throughput. They want to adopt a serverless approach to manage scalability and reduce operational overhead. Which AWS service should the company use to achieve these objectives?

A) Utilize Amazon API Gateway to create RESTful APIs for microservices communication with low latency and high throughput.

B) Implement AWS Step Functions to orchestrate microservices workflows and manage inter-service communication with serverless scalability.

C) Deploy Amazon MQ to enable messaging between microservices with support for multiple protocols and low-latency communication.

D) Configure Amazon Elastic Load Balancing (ELB) to distribute incoming microservices traffic across multiple EC2 instances for improved scalability and low latency.

E) Implement Amazon EventBridge to build event-driven architectures for microservices communication with low-latency event delivery and automatic scaling.

QUESTION 42

Your team is tasked with optimizing database performance for a large-scale IoT platform that generates a high volume of real-time data. The current database infrastructure struggles to handle the influx of data, leading to latency issues. What solution should you implement to improve database performance in this scenario?

A) Utilize Amazon RDS with Multi-AZ deployment for fault tolerance.
B) Deploy Amazon Neptune for graph database capabilities to handle interconnected IoT data.
C) Leverage Amazon DynamoDB with on-demand capacity to handle variable IoT data ingestion rates.

D) Implement Amazon RDS with read replicas in multiple Availability Zones (AZs) for scalable read performance.

E) Configure Amazon Aurora Serverless for auto-scaling based on IoT data volume.

QUESTION 43

A global sports analytics company wants to enhance its platform by incorporating real-time analysis of sports data from various sources, including sensors on players, video feeds, and social media. The solution must provide insights into player performance, game trends, and fan engagement in real-time. It should also be capable of scaling to accommodate large, fluctuating volumes of data during major sporting events and ensure data security and compliance with international regulations. Furthermore, the company aims to minimize infrastructure maintenance and operational costs while maximizing data processing speed and analytical capabilities.

A) Utilize AWS Lambda for serverless data processing, Amazon Kinesis for real-time data streaming, Amazon S3 for scalable data storage, Amazon Athena for querying data, and AWS Glue for data cataloging.

B) Deploy Amazon EC2 instances for compute resources, Amazon RDS for relational data storage, AWS Direct Connect for reduced latency, Amazon QuickSight for data visualization, and Amazon GuardDuty for security monitoring.

C) Implement Amazon DynamoDB for NoSQL data storage, Amazon EMR for big data processing, AWS Data Pipeline for data orchestration, Amazon SageMaker for machine learning insights, and AWS IAM for security.

D) Use Amazon Redshift for data warehousing, AWS DataSync for data transfer, Amazon Lex for building conversational interfaces, Amazon CloudFront for global content delivery, and AWS Shield for DDoS protection.

E) Leverage Amazon Managed Streaming for Apache Kafka (Amazon MSK) for data streaming, AWS Fargate for container management, Amazon Athena for serverless querying, Amazon S3 for data lake storage, and Amazon QuickSight for business intelligence.

QUESTION 44

Your company needs to build a real-time log analysis system for monitoring application performance. The system should process log data immediately and generate alerts for anomalies. Which architecture would be most appropriate for this requirement?

A) Utilize Amazon Kinesis Data Firehose to ingest log events, process them with AWS Glue, and store results in Amazon Aurora for real-time analysis and alerting.

B) Implement Amazon Kinesis Data Streams for log data ingestion, process it using AWS Lambda functions, and store results in Amazon DynamoDB for real-time access.

C) Deploy Amazon Managed Streaming for Apache Kafka (Amazon MSK) for log event ingestion, process data with Amazon Kinesis Data Analytics, and trigger alerts using Amazon CloudWatch.

D) Utilize AWS AppSync to integrate log data with Amazon Neptune graph database, analyze data in real-time, and trigger alerts with Amazon CloudTrail.

E) Set up Amazon Kinesis Data Firehose to capture log events, process them using Amazon EMR, and store results in Amazon S3 for further analysis and alerting.

QUESTION 45

A legal firm is storing sensitive documents in Amazon S3 and requires encryption of the data at rest to comply with regulatory requirements. The firm wants to ensure that only authorized individuals with specific roles can access the data, and also track any changes made to the encryption keys. Which option would be the most appropriate solution for this requirement?

A) Utilize server-side encryption with Amazon S3 managed keys (SSE-S3) to encrypt the data on Amazon S3

B) Implement server-side encryption with AWS Key Management Service (SSE-KMS) and configure IAM roles for access control

C) Use client-side encryption with customer-provided keys (SSE-C) and upload the encrypted data to Amazon S3

D) Implement server-side encryption with customer-provided keys (SSE-C) and monitor access using AWS CloudTrail

E) Enable AWS CloudTrail to monitor S3 bucket activities for auditing purposes

QUESTION 46

You are designing an IoT solution for a logistics company that wants to track the location and condition of its shipments in real-time to ensure timely delivery and product quality. The solution must be highly available, scalable, and capable of handling data from thousands of sensors installed on shipping containers. Which architecture would you recommend for this scenario?

A) Deploy Amazon API Gateway for data ingestion, utilize AWS Fargate for edge processing, configure Amazon Kinesis Data Analytics for real-time data analysis, connect with Amazon RDS for real-time data storage, and employ Amazon Glacier for long-term data archival.

B) Utilize AWS IoT Core for data ingestion, configure AWS Greengrass for edge computing, implement Amazon Kinesis Data Streams for real-time data processing, integrate with Amazon RDS for real-time data storage, and utilize Amazon S3 for long-term data archival.

C) Implement AWS IoT Events for data ingestion, set up AWS Lambda for edge processing, use Amazon Kinesis Data Streams for real-time data processing, deploy Amazon Aurora for real-time data storage, and employ Amazon S3 Glacier for long-term data archival.

D) Utilize AWS IoT Greengrass for data ingestion, leverage AWS Lambda for edge processing, employ Amazon Kinesis Data Streams for real-time data processing, store real-time data in Amazon DynamoDB, and archive long-term data in Amazon S3.

E) Configure AWS IoT Core for data ingestion, implement AWS Lambda for edge processing, set up Amazon Kinesis Data Streams for real-time data processing, integrate with Amazon RDS for real-time data storage, and utilize Amazon S3 for long-term data archival.

QUESTION 47

You are designing an edge computing solution for a gaming company that wants to reduce latency for multiplayer online games. The company requires a solution capable of processing real-time player interactions and game events at the edge to provide a seamless gaming experience. Which architecture would best meet these requirements?

A) Utilize AWS Lambda@Edge to deploy applications on edge devices located in gaming server locations, leverage AWS IoT Greengrass for edge data processing, and integrate with Amazon DynamoDB for real-time data storage.

B) Deploy applications on edge devices using AWS Snow Family devices installed in gaming server locations, leverage AWS IoT Greengrass for edge data processing, and integrate with Amazon Aurora for real-time data storage.

C) Implement applications on Amazon EC2 instances deployed in AWS Outposts located near gaming server locations, utilize AWS IoT Greengrass for edge data processing, and integrate with Amazon RDS for real-time data storage.

D) Utilize AWS Wavelength to deploy applications on edge devices located within telecommunication providers' data centers, leverage AWS IoT Greengrass for edge data processing, and integrate with Amazon S3 for real-time data storage.

E) Deploy applications on edge devices using AWS Local Zones located near gaming server locations, leverage AWS IoT Greengrass for edge data processing, and integrate with Amazon Redshift for real-time data storage.

QUESTION 48

A sports analytics company is developing a platform to deliver live game statistics and performance analytics to fans via a highly responsive API. The platform will aggregate data in real-time from multiple sources, apply complex analytical models, and present insights through a user-friendly API. Security, scalability, and the ability to handle large, fluctuating volumes of requests during major sporting events are critical. What AWS service configuration would optimally support these requirements?

A) Combine Amazon Kinesis for real-time data ingestion, AWS Lambda for data processing, Amazon DynamoDB for scalable data storage, and Amazon API Gateway for secure API exposure.

B) Use Amazon EC2 with Auto Scaling for compute resources, Amazon S3 for data storage, AWS Direct Connect for minimizing latency, and AWS IAM for access management.

C) Deploy Amazon ECS with Fargate for containerized workload management, Amazon RDS for relational data storage, Amazon CloudFront for data distribution, and AWS WAF for API protection.

D) Implement AWS Global Accelerator to improve application performance, Amazon Redshift for analytics database, Amazon SQS for message queuing, and Amazon Cognito for user authentication.

E) Leverage AWS AppSync for managing backend data synchronization, Amazon EBS for persistent storage, AWS Step Functions for orchestration of data processing workflows, and AWS Shield for DDoS protection.

QUESTION 49

A software development team requires access to an Amazon S3 bucket to read, write, and delete objects as part of their CI/CD pipeline. However, they should not be allowed to modify the bucket policy or change the bucket's versioning settings. Which IAM policy statement should be added to meet these requirements?

```
A) {
"Action": [
"s3:GetObject",
"s3:PutObject",
"s3:DeleteObject"
],
"Resource": "arn:aws:s3:::example-bucket/",
"Effect": "Allow"
```

```
}

B) {
 "Action": [
 "s3:GetObject",
 "s3:PutObject",
 "s3:DeleteObject",
 "s3:PutBucketPolicy"
 ],
 "Resource": "arn:aws:s3:::example-bucket/",
 "Effect": "Allow"
 }


C) {
 "Action": [
 "s3:GetObject",
 "s3:PutObject",
 "s3:DeleteObject",
 "s3:PutBucketVersioning"
 ],
 "Resource": "arn:aws:s3:::example-bucket/*",
 "Effect": "Allow"
 }


D) {
 "Action": [
 "s3:GetObject",
 "s3:PutObject",
 "s3:DeleteObject",
 "s3:PutBucketPolicy"
 ],
 "Resource": "arn:aws:s3:::example-bucket",
 "Effect": "Allow"
 }


E) {
 "Action": [
 "s3:GetObject",
 "s3:PutObject",
 "s3:DeleteObject",
 "s3:PutBucketVersioning"
 ],
 "Resource": "arn:aws:s3:::example-bucket",
 "Effect": "Allow"
```

}

QUESTION 50

Your company operates a web application that experiences significant fluctuations in traffic throughout the day. During peak hours, the application needs to scale dynamically to accommodate increased user demand while maintaining cost efficiency. Which approach would be most suitable for optimizing performance and cost during peak traffic periods?

A) Utilize Amazon EC2 Spot Instances to handle peak traffic periods, leveraging the cost savings of Spot Instances for temporary compute capacity. Implement Amazon CloudWatch alarms to trigger scaling actions based on CPU utilization, ensuring optimal resource allocation.

B) Deploy Amazon RDS Multi-AZ deployment for a managed relational database service, ensuring high availability and durability during peak traffic periods. Utilize Amazon ElastiCache for caching frequently accessed data, reducing database load and improving application performance.

C) Implement Amazon DynamoDB with provisioned capacity to handle peak traffic periods, ensuring consistent performance and scalability. Configure auto-scaling for DynamoDB read and write capacity, dynamically adjusting resources based on workload demands.

D) Utilize AWS Lambda functions to handle incoming requests during peak traffic periods, reducing the need for constantly running EC2 instances. Store application data in Amazon Aurora Serverless for on-demand scalability, optimizing resource utilization and cost efficiency.

QUESTION 51

A healthcare organization is modernizing its patient management system to ensure high availability, data privacy, and compliance with healthcare regulations. Which AWS architecture would best meet these requirements?

A) Utilize Amazon EC2 Auto Scaling for application scalability, Amazon RDS for patient data storage, Amazon S3 for backup and disaster recovery, and AWS IAM for access control.

B) Deploy AWS Lambda for serverless compute, Amazon DynamoDB for NoSQL patient data storage, Amazon S3 for file storage, and AWS Certificate Manager for SSL/TLS certificate management.

C) Implement Amazon ECS for containerized applications, Amazon Aurora Serverless for on-demand relational database needs, Amazon S3 Glacier for long-term data archiving, and AWS CloudTrail for auditing.

D) Leverage Amazon API Gateway for secure API management, AWS Step Functions for workflow automation, Amazon Redshift for analytics, and AWS KMS for encryption of sensitive data.

E) Use AWS Fargate for running containerized workloads, Amazon Aurora for high-performance relational databases, Amazon Glacier for cold storage, and AWS Config for compliance monitoring and auditing.

QUESTION 52

An online gaming company is designing an architecture for its multiplayer gaming platform, which requires real-time communication and high availability. The platform must ensure minimal latency and optimal performance for players worldwide. What architecture should they implement?

A) Deploy the platform on Amazon EC2 instances with Amazon RDS for backend database management, utilizing Amazon Route 53 for DNS routing and AWS Direct Connect for low-latency connectivity.

B) Utilize Amazon DynamoDB for storing player data, coupled with AWS Lambda functions for serverless game logic and Amazon API Gateway for secure API access.

C) Implement an Amazon ECS cluster for hosting game servers, using Amazon ElastiCache for caching frequently accessed data and Amazon S3 for storing game assets.

D) Configure an Amazon SQS queue for handling player requests asynchronously, with Amazon Aurora for backend data storage and Amazon CloudFront for content delivery.

E) Deploy the platform on AWS Fargate containers with Amazon EKS for orchestration, utilizing Amazon SNS for real-time notifications and Amazon CloudWatch for monitoring.

QUESTION 53

A multinational corporation wants to migrate its internal finance application to AWS, requiring the employees' payroll information to be accessible only within the region where they are employed, while maintaining a global report of finances in all regions. Which database configuration meets these requirements?

A) Use Amazon Aurora Global Database for payroll information and a separate Aurora instance for global financial reports.

B) Utilize Amazon DynamoDB global tables for payroll information and Amazon Aurora for global financial reports.

C) Implement Amazon Aurora in each region for payroll information and Amazon DynamoDB global tables for financial reports.

D) Deploy Amazon Aurora Global Database for both payroll information and global financial reports, with regional replication.

E) Use separate Amazon Aurora instances in each region for payroll information and Amazon S3 for storing and accessing global financial reports.

QUESTION 54

Your company operates a real-time analytics platform that processes streaming data from various sources. As the Solutions Architect, you aim to design a cost-effective solution while ensuring high performance and scalability. Which approach would best fulfill these requirements considering the need for real-time analytics, cost optimization, and scalability?

A) Deploy Amazon Kinesis Data Analytics for real-time data analysis
B) Utilize Amazon Redshift Spectrum for querying data directly from S3
C) Implement Amazon Athena for querying data stored in Amazon S3

D) Opt for Amazon EMR with Apache Spark for batch processing

E) Use Amazon RDS Multi-AZ configuration for high availability

QUESTION 55

A software development company wants to streamline access to their AWS resources for developers working on different projects. The solutions architect needs to recommend a solution that allows developers to access only the resources relevant to their projects while minimizing administrative overhead. What approach should the solutions architect suggest?

A) Grant full administrative access to all developers and rely on their discretion to access only relevant resources.

B) Create IAM roles for each project and assign developers to these roles based on their project assignments.

C) Utilize IAM policies to grant access to specific AWS resources and attach these policies directly to individual developers' IAM user accounts.

D) Establish IAM groups for each project and assign developers to these groups with the necessary permissions.

E) Implement cross-account IAM roles and delegate access to developers based on project requirements.

QUESTION 56

Your company is migrating its legacy data storage solution to AWS, aiming to improve scalability and cost efficiency. The current solution involves periodic backups to tape storage for long-term retention. The company wants to implement a cloud-native backup solution on AWS that minimizes costs while ensuring data durability. Which approach aligns with best practices for designing the backup solution?

A) Utilize AWS Backup to automate and manage backups of on-premises data to Amazon S3

B) Implement AWS Storage Gateway Tape Gateway for seamless integration with existing tape-based backup workflows

C) Configure AWS DataSync to replicate on-premises data to Amazon S3 Glacier for long-term archival

D) Leverage AWS Snowball Edge for offline transfer of on-premises data to Amazon S3

E) Utilize Amazon S3 Intelligent-Tiering to automatically optimize storage costs based on access patterns

QUESTION 57

Your organization has a requirement to transfer large datasets between Amazon S3 buckets located in different regions on a regular basis. The data transfer process needs to be automated and optimized for cost efficiency. What would be the most suitable solution to achieve this?

A) Utilize AWS DataSync to automate and optimize data transfer between S3 buckets in different regions

B) Set up cross-region replication for the S3 buckets to automatically replicate objects between regions

C) Deploy AWS Snowball to physically transfer the datasets between S3 buckets in different regions

D) Implement Amazon S3 Transfer Acceleration to optimize data transfer speeds for the datasets

E) Use AWS Transfer Family to automate SFTP-based data transfers between S3 buckets in different regions

QUESTION 58

Your company operates a social media platform that experiences unpredictable spikes in user-generated content uploads. To optimize costs while maintaining scalability and performance, you plan to use Amazon CloudFront for content delivery. Which of the following configurations would best align with your cost optimization objectives while ensuring efficient content delivery during peak upload periods?

A) Utilize Amazon CloudFront with Lambda@Edge functions to analyze user content uploads and apply real-time transformations

B) Implement Amazon CloudFront with cache behaviors to control caching duration and optimize cache hit rates

C) Configure Amazon CloudFront with custom error pages to provide a consistent user experience during service disruptions

D) Enable Amazon CloudFront with cookie forwarding to personalize content delivery based on user preferences

E) Integrate Amazon CloudFront with AWS Direct Connect to establish private connectivity between the origin server and edge locations

QUESTION 59

Your company operates a media streaming platform that stores a vast amount of video content in Amazon S3 buckets. The storage costs have become a concern, and you need to implement a solution for cost-effective data lifecycle management. Which approach should you recommend?

A) Use Amazon S3 Intelligent-Tiering with a single-tier storage strategy for all video content

B) Implement Amazon S3 Object Lock to prevent modification of video content and manually move infrequently accessed videos to Amazon S3 Glacier

C) Deploy Amazon S3 Lifecycle policies to transition infrequently accessed video content to Amazon S3 Glacier

D) Leverage Amazon S3 Cross-Region Replication to replicate video content to a secondary bucket in Amazon S3 Glacier

E) Utilize Amazon S3 Standard-Infrequent Access (S3 Standard-IA) storage class for all video content and manually move infrequently accessed videos to Amazon S3 Glacier

QUESTION 60

A media streaming company wants to ensure that its video streaming service maintains consistent performance levels during peak usage periods. What Auto Scaling configuration should the solutions architect recommend to achieve this?

A) Configure the Auto Scaling group to use a target tracking scaling policy based on network throughput across instances.

B) Implement an Auto Scaling group with a scheduled scaling policy triggered at specific times of peak usage.

C) Configure the Auto Scaling group to use a step scaling policy triggered by sudden increases in the number of requests.

D) Utilize an Auto Scaling group with a simple scaling policy based on manual adjustments to instance counts.

E) Implement an Auto Scaling group with a predictive scaling policy based on machine learning algorithms analyzing user behavior.

QUESTION 61

Your organization is planning to migrate its data center to AWS and requires a cost-effective solution for disaster recovery. The solution must provide high availability and minimize costs while ensuring data integrity and durability. Which approach should you recommend for this scenario?

A) Utilize AWS Backup to automate and centralize backups of AWS resources and on-premises applications

B) Implement AWS DataSync to transfer data between on-premises storage systems and AWS storage services

C) Use AWS Snowball to transfer large amounts of data to AWS for disaster recovery purposes

D) Deploy AWS Storage Gateway with volume gateways to integrate on-premises applications with AWS storage

E) Utilize AWS Transfer Family to securely transfer files over SFTP, FTPS, and FTP protocols

QUESTION 62

Your organization is migrating its on-premises application to AWS to improve scalability and reduce costs. The application requires low-latency access to a large dataset stored in Amazon S3, and you need to design a cost-effective solution for data access. Which approach should you recommend for this scenario?

A) Implement AWS Direct Connect to establish a dedicated network connection between on-premises infrastructure and AWS regions

B) Use Amazon S3 Transfer Acceleration to optimize data transfers and reduce latency for accessing the dataset

C) Deploy Amazon FSx for Windows File Server to store the dataset and enable fast access from on-premises and AWS environments

D) Configure AWS DataSync to synchronize the dataset between on-premises storage systems and Amazon S3 buckets

E) Utilize Amazon CloudFront with Lambda@Edge to cache and deliver the dataset at edge locations

QUESTION 63

Your company operates a hybrid cloud architecture with on-premises resources and AWS services. You've observed that the data transfer costs between your on-premises environment and AWS have been higher than anticipated, impacting the overall operational budget. To address this issue, you need to design a solution that optimizes data transfer costs while ensuring efficient connectivity. What approach should you recommend?

A) Deploy AWS VPN to establish secure and cost-effective connectivity between on-premises networks and AWS

B) Utilize AWS Snow Family devices to transfer large volumes of data between on-premises environments and AWS

C) Implement AWS Direct Connect to establish dedicated connectivity between on-premises data centers and AWS

D) Leverage Amazon S3 Transfer Acceleration to optimize data transfer speeds and reduce costs associated with data transfer to AWS

E) Deploy AWS Storage Gateway to cache frequently accessed data locally and reduce data transfer costs between on-premises infrastructure and AWS

QUESTION 64

Your company operates a global application that serves customers in different geographic regions. However, the finance department has noticed escalating costs associated with cross-region data transfers. As a solutions architect, you need to design a cost-efficient architecture that maintains global availability while reducing expenses related to data transfer. What approach should you recommend?

A) Implement Amazon CloudFront with AWS Global Accelerator to cache content at edge locations and minimize data transfer between regions

B) Utilize Amazon S3 Transfer Acceleration to optimize data transfer speeds between regions and reduce costs

C) Deploy Amazon DynamoDB global tables to replicate data across regions and ensure low-latency access for users

D) Leverage AWS Direct Connect with AWS Transit Gateway to establish private connectivity between regions and reduce data transfer costs

E) Utilize Amazon Route 53 latency-based routing to route traffic to the nearest AWS region and minimize data transfer distances

QUESTION 65

Your company is seeking to implement cost-effective data transfer solutions between on-premises data centers and AWS cloud resources. As a solutions architect, you need to recommend a solution that minimizes data transfer costs while ensuring reliable connectivity.

A) Utilize AWS Direct Connect to establish dedicated network connections between on-premises data centers and AWS regions

B) Implement AWS DataSync to automate data transfers between on-premises storage and Amazon S3

C) Leverage AWS Transfer Family to enable secure FTP, FTPS, and SFTP transfers to and from Amazon S3

D) Utilize Amazon S3 Transfer Acceleration to optimize data transfer speeds for large-scale uploads to Amazon S3

E) Implement AWS VPN CloudHub to establish VPN connections between multiple on-premises data centers and AWS regions

PRACTICE TEST 5 - ANSWERS ONLY

QUESTION 1

Answer - D) Enable MFA for both root and IAM users. Use AWS IAM to create policies for least privilege access and AWS STS for cross-account access.

A) - Incorrect because it suggests enabling MFA only for the root account, neglecting IAM users.

B) - Incorrect as it implies AWS Control Tower alone can enforce MFA, which is not enough without specific policies for IAM users.

C) - Incorrect because MFA is implemented for IAM users only, leaving the root account vulnerable.

D) - Correct because it provides a comprehensive approach by enabling MFA for both root and IAM users, and uses AWS IAM and AWS STS for least privilege and cross-account access management, aligning with the AWS Well-Architected Framework for security.

E) - Incorrect because it only mentions SCPs for MFA enforcement on root accounts and does not address MFA for IAM users or least privilege access.

QUESTION 2

Answer - E) Implement a multi-region deployment strategy, ensuring data is stored and processed in compliance with regional data protection laws, and use Amazon CloudFront and AWS WAF for global security and performance.

A) Incorrect - While hosting in a single region may simplify deployment, it does not optimize performance for global users as effectively as a multi-region approach, nor does it address compliance with data protection laws in different regions.

B) Incorrect - This option improves security and performance but lacks specific consideration for compliance with regional data protection laws regarding data storage and processing.

C) Incorrect - Storing all sensitive data in one region could violate data protection laws in regions where the data originates or is accessed. Default encryption is essential but not sufficient for compliance.

D) Incorrect - AWS Global Accelerator improves application performance but is not a comprehensive solution for security or compliance with data protection laws.

E) Correct - This approach balances security, performance, and compliance needs. A multi-region deployment ensures data is handled according to local laws, while Amazon CloudFront and AWS WAF enhance global performance and security.

QUESTION 3

Answer - [A] Implement Amazon GuardDuty to continuously monitor AWS accounts for malicious activity and unauthorized behavior.

Option A - Correct. Implementing Amazon GuardDuty provides continuous monitoring and threat detection for identifying malicious activity and unauthorized behavior in AWS accounts.

Option B - AWS Config assesses configurations but may not provide the same level of continuous threat detection as Amazon GuardDuty.

Option C - AWS CloudTrail logs API activity but may not directly provide continuous monitoring and threat detection like Amazon GuardDuty.

Option D - AWS IAM Access Analyzer identifies unintended access but may not offer continuous monitoring for security threats like Amazon GuardDuty.

Option E - AWS Security Hub centrally manages security findings but may not provide the same level of continuous threat detection as Amazon GuardDuty.

QUESTION 4

Answer - [B] Configure Amazon Redshift Spectrum to query data directly from Amazon S3, enabling data encryption using AWS KMS-managed keys. Implement AWS Glue for data cataloging and enforcing row-level access control, and utilize AWS CloudTrail for auditing API activity.

Option B - Correct. This solution leverages Amazon Redshift Spectrum for querying data from Amazon S3 with encryption using AWS KMS-managed keys. AWS Glue provides data cataloging and access control enforcement, while AWS CloudTrail offers auditing capabilities.

Option A - While deploying Amazon Redshift in a single VPC with encrypted EBS volumes and using IAM roles for access control are valid, it may lack the flexibility and scalability provided by Amazon Redshift Spectrum and AWS Glue.

Option C - Cross-region replication, SSL/TLS encryption, and enhanced VPC routing offer some benefits, but AWS Lake Formation and CloudTrail may not be necessary components for this scenario.

Option D - While Amazon Redshift Concurrency Scaling and automatic snapshots offer scalability and data backup capabilities, AWS Secrets Manager and IAM policies alone may not address all encryption and access control requirements.

Option E - Deploying Amazon Redshift clusters in separate VPCs across multiple AWS accounts may introduce complexity without significant benefits. Additionally, AWS IAM policies alone may not provide the fine-grained access control needed for compliance.

QUESTION 5

Answer - A) Use Amazon SQS FIFO queue with a batch mode of 5 messages per operation.

A) Use Amazon SQS FIFO queue with a batch mode of 5 messages per operation - This option processes inventory updates in the order they are received while allowing for simultaneous processing of multiple updates for different product categories through batch mode. It ensures order accuracy and scalability, meeting the company's requirements for sequential updates and parallel processing.

B) Use Amazon SQS FIFO queue with default settings - Default settings may not ensure order accuracy and efficient parallel processing for different product categories.

C) Use Amazon SQS FIFO queue with exactly-once processing enabled - While ensuring order accuracy, it may not efficiently handle simultaneous updates due to sequential processing.

D) Use Amazon SQS standard queue to process the messages - Standard queues lack message ordering, which is crucial for maintaining inventory order, and may not efficiently handle simultaneous updates.

E) Use Amazon SQS FIFO queue with message deduplication enabled - While avoiding duplicate messages, it doesn't guarantee order processing, and may not efficiently handle simultaneous updates.

QUESTION 6

Answer - [A] Utilize AWS Lambda for serverless compute, Amazon API Gateway for API management, and Amazon S3 for object storage. Implement IAM policies on S3 buckets to control access and use API Gateway with IAM authorization for secure API access.

Option A - Correct. AWS Lambda, API Gateway, and S3 with IAM policies provide a secure serverless architecture, and IAM authorization with API Gateway ensures secure API access.

Option B - Fargate is not typically used for serverless compute, and using IAM authorization with API Gateway may be more suitable than OAuth 2.0.

Option C - While Lambda, API Gateway, and S3 are suitable, OAuth 2.0 may not be the best choice for controlling access to S3 buckets.

Option D - ECS is not typically used for serverless compute, and OAuth 2.0 may not be the best choice for controlling access to S3 buckets.

Option E - Fargate is not typically used for serverless compute, and OAuth 2.0 may not be the best choice for controlling access to S3 buckets.

QUESTION 7

Answer - C) Use AWS KMS with multi-region keys and enable key deactivation features for immediate action

A) Centralize key management with AWS KMS and use resource-based policies for regional control. - Incorrect because it does not fully support the requirement for local application of keys in compliance with regional laws without specifying the use of multi-region keys.

B) Deploy regional AWS CloudHSM clusters and manage keys locally with synchronization for central oversight. - Incorrect due to the complexity and potential for synchronization issues, which might not offer the instant key disablement required in case of a breach.

C) Use AWS KMS with multi-region keys and enable key deactivation features for immediate action. - Correct because it allows for centralized management with local application of keys and provides the ability to instantly disable keys, meeting the enterprise's requirements for compliance and security.

D) Implement a custom solution using Amazon DynamoDB for storing keys and AWS Lambda for regional distribution and management. - Incorrect because this approach introduces unnecessary complexity and security risks compared to using AWS's dedicated key management services.

E) Store and manage keys in AWS Secrets Manager with replication across regions for local application. - Incorrect as Secrets Manager is not primarily intended for encryption key management and does not provide the same level of control or instant deactivation features as KMS for this scenario.

QUESTION 8

Answer - B), C), and D)

A) AWS Shield and Amazon CloudFront - Incorrect because, while they provide DDoS protection and content delivery network services respectively, they don't directly address internal threats or compliance.

B) AWS WAF and AWS Firewall Manager - Correct because they protect web applications from common web exploits and manage firewall rules across accounts and applications, respectively.

C) Amazon GuardDuty and AWS Security Hub - Correct because GuardDuty offers intelligent threat detection, and Security Hub aggregates security and compliance findings across accounts.

D) AWS IAM Identity Center and Amazon Inspector - Correct because IAM Identity Center manages access, while Inspector assesses applications for vulnerabilities.

E) Amazon VPC and AWS Direct Connect - Incorrect as they are primarily for networking and not specific to security monitoring or compliance.

QUESTION 9

Answer - [A] Deploying Amazon RDS with encryption at rest and AWS IAM database authentication, ensuring secure access control and compliance with data protection regulations.

A) Amazon RDS with encryption at rest and AWS IAM database authentication provides secure access control and compliance with data protection regulations required for healthcare applications.

B) While AWS Lambda offers high availability and scalability, it may not directly address secure access control or compliance with data protection regulations.

C) Amazon S3 with server-side encryption and access control policies secures data storage but may not directly address database access control or compliance with data protection regulations for patient records.

D) Amazon CloudFront with AWS Shield provides DDoS protection for web applications but may not directly address database access control or compliance requirements for patient record security.

E) Amazon Elasticsearch Service with fine-grained access control and encryption is suitable for search and retrieval but may not provide the same level of database access control or compliance with data protection regulations as Amazon RDS with IAM database authentication.

QUESTION 10

Answer - A) Use Amazon FSx File Gateway to provide low-latency, on-premises access to fully managed file shares in Amazon EFS. The applications deployed on AWS can access this data directly from Amazon EFS.

A) Use Amazon FSx File Gateway to provide low-latency, on-premises access to fully managed file shares in Amazon EFS. The applications deployed on AWS can access this data directly from Amazon EFS - This option aligns with the requirement by suggesting the use of Amazon FSx File Gateway with Amazon EFS, ensuring low-latency access to source code files during and after migration.

B) Use Amazon Storage Gateway's File Gateway to provide low-latency, on-premises access to fully managed file shares in Amazon FSx for Windows File Server. The applications deployed on AWS can access this data directly from Amazon FSx in AWS - This option does not align with the requirement as it suggests using FSx for Windows File Server instead of Amazon EFS, which may not meet the low-latency access requirement.

C) Use AWS Storage Gateway's File Gateway to provide low-latency, on-premises access to fully managed file shares in Amazon S3. The applications deployed on AWS can access this data directly from Amazon S3 - This option does not align with the requirement as it suggests using Amazon S3 instead of Amazon EFS, which may not meet the low-latency access requirement.

D) Use Amazon FSx File Gateway to provide low-latency, on-premises access to fully managed file shares in Amazon FSx for Windows File Server. The applications deployed on AWS can access this data directly from Amazon FSx in AWS - This option does not align with the requirement as it suggests using FSx for Windows File Server instead of Amazon EFS, which may not meet the low-latency access requirement.

QUESTION 11

Answer - A) AWS Network Firewall for granular network controls, Amazon Kinesis for real-time data processing, and AWS CloudTrail for governance

A) AWS Network Firewall for granular network controls, Amazon Kinesis for real-time data processing, and AWS CloudTrail for governance - Correct because this combination offers robust network security, the ability to analyze network traffic in real-time for threat detection, and comprehensive governance and auditing capabilities, aligning with GDPR requirements.

B) Amazon Inspector for vulnerability assessments, Amazon Macie for data privacy, and AWS WAF for application layer security - Incorrect because, while providing security assessments, data protection, and application layer security, it lacks the real-time network monitoring and control that the scenario demands.

C) AWS Shield Advanced for DDoS protection, AWS Fargate for application isolation, and Amazon Athena for querying logs - Incorrect as it focuses more on DDoS protection and application isolation without addressing granular network control or real-time data processing for threat detection.

D) Amazon CloudFront for content delivery, AWS Direct Connect for a private network connection, and AWS Lambda for executing custom security scripts - Incorrect because this setup emphasizes content delivery and private connectivity, missing comprehensive network monitoring and real-time threat analysis.

E) Amazon VPC for network isolation, AWS IAM for access management, and Amazon GuardDuty for threat detection and monitoring - Incorrect as it provides a basic security foundation but lacks the detailed network traffic analysis and real-time processing required for advanced threat detection and compliance.

QUESTION 12

Answer - B) Use AWS IAM Identity Center (SSO) with conditional access policies and hardware MFA integration.

A) Configure AWS IAM policies to restrict access based on IP address and enforce hardware MFA. -

Incorrect because while IAM policies can enforce MFA, they are not as comprehensive for integrating with external identity systems or hardware MFA devices as IAM Identity Center.

B) Use AWS IAM Identity Center (SSO) with conditional access policies and hardware MFA integration. - Correct as it offers a robust solution for integrating with external identity systems and hardware MFA devices, while also providing the ability to enforce conditional access policies based on secure facility locations.

C) Implement Amazon Cognito with custom authentication flows for hardware MFA and IP restrictions. - Incorrect for complex enterprise or government environments requiring integration with existing hardware MFA devices and stringent access controls.

D) Establish VPN connections from secure facilities to AWS, with AWS Directory Service managing hardware MFA devices. - Incorrect because it focuses on network connectivity rather than the comprehensive identity and access management solution required.

E) Leverage AWS Network Firewall for IP whitelisting and AWS IAM for MFA, integrating with the government's identity management system. - Incorrect as it doesn't provide the seamless integration with hardware MFA and conditional access controls offered by IAM Identity Center.

QUESTION 13

Answer - B) Implement Amazon API Gateway access logging to an Amazon S3 bucket, use Amazon Cognito for user authentication, and Amazon GuardDuty for monitoring access patterns.

A) Enable Amazon CloudWatch Logs and Amazon CloudWatch Events for API Gateway, use AWS IAM for authentication, and AWS Lambda for access pattern analysis - Incorrect because while this provides logging and potential for custom analysis, it doesn't directly address user authentication or standard monitoring for compliance.

B) Implement Amazon API Gateway access logging to an Amazon S3 bucket, use Amazon Cognito for user authentication, and Amazon GuardDuty for monitoring access patterns - Correct. This combination ensures compliance with health data protection regulations by logging all accesses and monitoring for unusual patterns effectively.

C) Utilize API Gateway execution logging with AWS CloudTrail, employ Amazon Cognito and IAM for dual authentication, and AWS WAF for monitoring - Incorrect because AWS WAF is focused on web security, not access pattern monitoring for compliance purposes.

D) Enable API Gateway to log to Amazon CloudWatch, use AWS IAM roles for service-to-service authentication, and Amazon Inspector for real-time access monitoring - Incorrect because Inspector is focused on security assessments of EC2 instances, not API access monitoring.

E) Implement AWS CloudTrail for logging API calls, Amazon Cognito for authentication, and AWS Lambda for custom access pattern analysis - Incorrect because, while it provides a foundation for logging and authentication, it lacks the integrated monitoring solution offered by GuardDuty for unusual access patterns.

QUESTION 14

Answer - B) Utilize AWS Config and AWS Service Catalog to enforce COPPA-compliant resource configurations and automatically correct violations.

A) Deploy Amazon Cognito for user authentication and age verification, integrated with AWS Lambda for automating compliance actions based on user age. - Incorrect because, while important for age verification, it doesn't provide comprehensive monitoring or automatic correction of COPPA violations across AWS resources.

B) Utilize AWS Config and AWS Service Catalog to enforce COPPA-compliant resource configurations and automatically correct violations. - Correct as AWS Config continuously monitors and records AWS resource configurations, allowing for automatic detection and correction of non-compliant configurations; while AWS Service Catalog allows for the creation and management of COPPA-compliant resources, ensuring compliance is maintained.

C) Implement AWS CloudTrail for logging user actions and AWS Macie for identifying and protecting sensitive information related to children. - Incorrect because these services focus on logging and data protection but do not offer the automated correction of configuration violations.

D) Configure AWS KMS for encryption of sensitive data and Amazon GuardDuty for detecting potential threats to children's data. - Incorrect as encryption and threat detection are important, but they do not address the need for continuous compliance monitoring and automated correction of violations.

E) Leverage AWS IAM policies to restrict access to children's data and Amazon QuickSight for visualizing compliance status with COPPA regulations. - Incorrect because, while these tools are useful for access control and visualization, they do not provide the automated compliance enforcement and correction capabilities offered by AWS Config and Service Catalog.

QUESTION 15

Answer - [B, E]

B) Suspend the ReplaceUnhealthy process type for the Auto Scaling group and apply the maintenance patch to the instance - This option effectively addresses the maintenance challenge by suspending the process responsible for replacing unhealthy instances, allowing the maintenance to proceed without triggering Auto Scaling actions.

E) Take a snapshot of the instance, create a new Amazon Machine Image (AMI), and then launch a new instance using this AMI - Creating a new instance from a snapshot introduces complexity and may not efficiently address the maintenance challenge, especially in scenarios where immediate fixes are required.

A) Suspend the AlarmNotifications process type for the Auto Scaling group and apply the maintenance patch to the instance - Suspending alarm notifications may not prevent instance replacement triggered by health status changes, potentially leading to disruptions during maintenance.

C) Put the instance into the Detached state and then update the instance by applying the maintenance patch - Detaching instances may disrupt application availability and may not align with the requirement for uninterrupted maintenance.

D) Suspend the AddToLoadBalancer process type for the Auto Scaling group and apply the maintenance patch to the instance - Suspending processes related to load balancer integration may not efficiently address the maintenance challenge and may not prevent instance replacement during maintenance.

QUESTION 16

Answer - [A) Utilize AWS Shield Standard and enable AWS WAF with rate-based rules on the ALB to mitigate DDoS attacks and protect against web application layer attacks.]

Option A is correct because it combines AWS Shield Standard for DDoS protection with AWS WAF, specifically using rate-based rules on the ALB, to mitigate DDoS attacks and protect against web application layer attacks, aligning with best practices for security and high availability.

Option B is incorrect because although it mentions AWS Shield Advanced for DDoS protection, it does not include specific measures for protecting the ALB against DDoS attacks or ensuring high availability. Option C is incorrect because it lacks AWS Shield Standard for overall DDoS protection and relies solely on AWS WAF with IP match conditions, which may not be sufficient against all types of attacks.

Option D is incorrect because although it includes AWS Shield Advanced, it does not mention specific protection measures for the ALB, and GuardDuty is more focused on threat detection rather than mitigation.

Option E is incorrect because although it includes AWS Shield Standard and AWS WAF, it does not mention specific configurations for mitigating DDoS attacks on the ALB, and Route 53 is primarily used for DNS routing, not DDoS protection or high availability of the ALB.

QUESTION 17

Answer - A) Design the VPC with dedicated subnets for sensitive data, employ AWS Shield Advanced for DDoS resilience, and activate AWS CloudTrail and VPC flow logs for logging.

A) Correct as it meets all specified requirements: dedicated subnets isolate sensitive data, Shield Advanced offers DDoS protection, CloudTrail provides API activity logging, and VPC flow logs capture all network traffic for auditing purposes.

B) Incorrect because, while CloudFront and ACM offer encrypted content delivery, and NACLs/Security Groups provide access control, GuardDuty is for threat detection, not traffic logging, and does not address DDoS resilience directly.

C) Incorrect as WAF and Shield Standard protect against web exploits and basic DDoS attacks, but Athena querying flow logs, while useful, doesn't provide real-time logging or encryption of data in transit per the scenario requirements.

D) Incorrect because Client VPN and Firewall Manager address aspects of secure access and management, and KMS/RDS encrypt data at rest, but this does not comprehensively cover network traffic logging or dedicated subnetting for patient data.

E) Incorrect as Cognito and Direct Connect address user authentication and private connectivity, but CloudWatch Logs primarily monitor operational data, not detailed network traffic involving sensitive patient information, and do not address DDoS resilience directly.

QUESTION 18

Answer - [A] Deploy Amazon API Gateway for backend API management and AWS Lambda for serverless computing. Utilize Amazon DynamoDB for NoSQL database storage and enable DynamoDB Auto Scaling for automatic throughput adjustments.

Option B - While ECS and Fargate provide containerized deployment options, Aurora Auto Scaling, and DynamoDB Auto Scaling are more suitable for serverless computing with Lambda.

Option C - While Amplify, Cognito, and AppSync are suitable for mobile application development, they do not directly address backend infrastructure requirements like API management and serverless computing.

Option D - While S3, CloudFront, and Lambda@Edge address content storage and delivery, they do not directly address backend API management and serverless computing needs.

Option E - While App Mesh, EKS, and EBS are suitable for microservices architecture, they are not directly related to backend infrastructure requirements like API management and serverless computing.

QUESTION 19

Answer - [B] Implement AWS Systems Manager Parameter Store to centrally manage environment-specific configurations and secrets. Use AWS CodePipeline with Parameter Store integration for retrieving configurations during deployments.

Option A - Embedding configuration settings within deployment packages lacks flexibility and may expose sensitive information.

Option C - Storing secrets in plaintext files within version-controlled repositories poses security risks and lacks centralized management and rotation capabilities.

Option D - While Secrets Manager can securely store and rotate secrets, using custom Lambda functions within the CI/CD pipeline introduces complexity and may not align with best practices for deployment automation.

Option E - Storing configuration settings within Lambda environment variables lacks centralized management and may lead to inconsistency across environments.

Explanation for Choice B: Implementing Parameter Store allows for centralized management of configurations and secrets. Integrating with CodePipeline enables secure retrieval during deployments, enhancing automation and compliance.

QUESTION 20

Answer - E) Create an Amazon CloudWatch metric filter to process AWS CloudTrail logs containing API call details. Establish an alarm based on this metric's rate to send an Amazon SNS notification to the required team.

E) Create an Amazon CloudWatch metric filter to process AWS CloudTrail logs containing API call details. Establish an alarm based on this metric's rate to send an Amazon SNS notification to the required team. - This option directly addresses the scenario by analyzing CloudTrail logs for unauthorized API queries and triggering real-time alerts using CloudWatch alarms and Amazon SNS notifications.

A) Use Amazon Athena SQL queries against AWS CloudTrail log files stored in Amazon S3 buckets. Generate reports using Amazon QuickSight for managerial dashboards. - While this option provides insights, it may not offer real-time alerting capabilities as required in this scenario.

B) Configure AWS CloudTrail to stream event data to Amazon Kinesis. Utilize Amazon Kinesis stream-level metrics in Amazon CloudWatch to trigger an AWS Lambda function that will initiate an error workflow. - While this option utilizes streaming data, it may introduce complexity and latency compared to directly analyzing CloudTrail logs for real-time alerts.

C) Implement AWS Config Rules to monitor API activity and define rules to detect unauthorized API calls. Configure AWS Config to trigger an AWS Lambda function upon rule evaluation to notify relevant stakeholders. - While AWS Config can monitor API activity, it may not provide real-time alerting capabilities for immediate incident response as required in this scenario.

D) Leverage AWS Trusted Advisor to publish metrics about check results to Amazon CloudWatch. Set up an alarm to track status changes for checks in the Service Limits category for the APIs, triggering notifications when service quotas are exceeded. - While Trusted Advisor offers valuable insights, it may not directly address the need for real-time detection of unauthorized API queries.

QUESTION 21

Answer - A) Implement Amazon SQS for message queuing, Amazon SNS for event notification, AWS Lambda for serverless processing, and Amazon Aurora for HIPAA-compliant database storage.

A) Correct because SQS provides message queuing, SNS offers event notification, Lambda handles serverless processing, and Aurora provides HIPAA-compliant database storage, aligning with the requirement for high availability, low-latency processing, and healthcare compliance in the architecture of a healthcare application.

B) Incorrect because while Kinesis, RDS Multi-AZ, CloudFront, and Fargate offer scalability and resilience, they may not provide the same level of HIPAA compliance and simplicity as SQS, SNS, Lambda, and Aurora for real-time patient monitoring and alerting in a healthcare application.

C) Incorrect as EventBridge, API Gateway, DynamoDB, and Glue offer event-driven architecture and data storage, but they may not provide the same level of HIPAA compliance and real-time processing as SQS, SNS, Lambda, and Aurora for real-time patient monitoring and alerting in a healthcare application.

D) Incorrect because while MSK, Lambda, S3, and RDS offer streaming, processing, storage, and database management, respectively, they may not provide the same level of HIPAA compliance and simplicity as SQS, SNS, Lambda, and Aurora for real-time patient monitoring and alerting in a healthcare application.

E) Incorrect as S3, Redshift, AppSync, and ElastiCache offer storage, analytics, GraphQL APIs, and caching, respectively, but they may not provide the same level of HIPAA compliance and real-time processing as SQS, SNS, Lambda, and Aurora for real-time patient monitoring and alerting in a healthcare application.

QUESTION 22

Answer - A) Utilize AWS Lambda with Amazon DynamoDB for serverless scalability.

Option A offers serverless scalability with AWS Lambda and Amazon DynamoDB, allowing the application to handle sudden spikes in traffic without provisioning or managing servers. This approach minimizes operational overhead while ensuring high availability.

Options B, C, D, and E do not provide the same level of scalability or operational simplicity as a serverless architecture with Lambda and DynamoDB.

QUESTION 23

Answer - [D) Utilize Amazon EC2 Auto Scaling with a minimum number of instances in a separate AWS Region for rapid application scaling during disaster recovery.]

Option D) is correct as it involves implementing a pilot light architecture, which maintains a minimal version of the application in a separate AWS Region, allowing for rapid scaling during disaster recovery while minimizing costs.

Option A) involves cross-region replication for backup but may not address rapid application scaling.

Option B) involves automated backup but may not provide the same level of scalability during disaster recovery.

Option C) involves real-time replication but may not achieve the required RPO and RTO objectives.

Option E) involves DNS failover but may not provide the same level of application scalability during disaster recovery.

QUESTION 24

Answer - [A) Amazon Cognito, B) AWS IAM, and D) Amazon CloudTrail]

Option A involves Amazon Cognito for authentication and authorization, supporting multiple identity providers and user roles.

Option B involves AWS IAM for fine-grained access control, ensuring secure access to application resources.

Option D involve Amazon CloudTrail for logging API calls, enabling auditing and monitoring of user activities.

Option C involves Amazon API Gateway for API integration, which is important but not directly related to authentication or authorization mechanisms.

Option E involves AWS Lambda for serverless execution, which could be used for custom authorization logic but is not as integral to centralized authentication as Cognito and IAM.

QUESTION 25

Answer - A) Tier-2 (20 terabytes)

A) Tier-2 (20 terabytes) - Correct. Aurora will promote the read replica with the highest priority (the lowest tier number). When tiers are equal, other factors such as instance size do not directly affect failover priority, but here it indicates a misconfiguration to be clarified.

B) Tier-2 (10 terabytes) - Incorrect due to a misunderstanding in the options provided; Aurora does not prioritize based on instance size for failover, and duplicate tier numbers suggest a need for clarification.

C) Tier-7 (15 terabytes) - Incorrect as it has a lower priority compared to Tier-2.

D) Tier-11 (20 terabytes) - Incorrect due to its lower failover priority.

E) Tier-11 (10 terabytes) - Incorrect as it combines both a lower priority and a smaller size, though size is not a primary consideration for failover.

QUESTION 26

Answer - [A, B]

Option A is correct because utilizing AWS Fargate to deploy containerized microservices allows automatic scaling and efficient management of infrastructure resources without the need for manual intervention, ensuring fault tolerance and high availability with minimal operational overhead.

Option B is correct because implementing Amazon RDS Multi-AZ deployment for the database tier ensures automatic failover and high availability of database instances across multiple Availability Zones, contributing to fault tolerance and high availability with minimal operational overhead.

Option C is incorrect because while deploying microservices on Amazon EC2 instances within Auto Scaling groups enables automatic scaling and replacement of unhealthy instances, it may involve more operational overhead compared to AWS Fargate.

Option D is incorrect because while configuring Amazon DynamoDB global tables enables automatic replication of data, it may not provide the same level of operational simplicity and fault tolerance as AWS Fargate and Amazon RDS Multi-AZ deployment.

Option E is incorrect because while setting up Amazon S3 cross-region replication ensures fault tolerance and high availability of data storage, it may not address fault tolerance and high availability requirements for microservices themselves.

QUESTION 27

Answer - A) Utilize AWS Step Functions with AWS Key Management Service (KMS) for encrypting patient data at rest and in transit

Option A - AWS Step Functions provide workflow orchestration with built-in support for AWS KMS encryption, ensuring compliance with HIPAA requirements for data encryption.

Option B - While Amazon S3 versioning and AWS CloudTrail provide data integrity and auditing capabilities, they do not offer the workflow orchestration features needed for compliance.

Option C - Amazon RDS encryption and SNS event notifications lack the comprehensive workflow orchestration and compliance features provided by Step Functions.

Option D - Amazon EventBridge and CloudWatch Logs offer orchestration and logging but do not provide the encryption features required for HIPAA compliance in serverless workflows.

QUESTION 28

Answer - A) Use Amazon Kinesis Data Streams for transaction ingestion, AWS Lambda for processing, Amazon DynamoDB with DAX for storage, and AWS Certificate Manager for managing encryption keys.

A) Correct because it provides a seamless, scalable, and secure serverless solution for real-time processing. Kinesis for real-time data ingestion, Lambda for processing, DynamoDB with DAX for fast data retrieval, and Certificate Manager for encryption ensure high performance and security.

B) Incorrect because SQS and Fargate are not optimized for real-time processing as required in this scenario. RDS does not provide the same level of scalability and performance as DynamoDB with DAX. Macie is focused on data discovery and security, not encryption management.

C) Incorrect because AppSync is not designed for high-volume, real-time transaction processing. Aurora Serverless and Lambda are good choices but do not match the performance needs for real-time fraud detection. KMS is suitable for encryption but does not cover the whole requirement.

D) Incorrect as it lacks the serverless scalability required for real-time processing. EFS does not provide the performance needed for this application, and CloudHSM, while secure, is overkill for managing encryption in this context.

E) Incorrect due to the lack of a real-time processing solution. MQ and Batch are not suitable for real-time applications, and QLDB, while secure, does not offer the real-time performance required. GuardDuty is for threat detection, not encryption or key management.

QUESTION 29

Answer - C) Configure an Application Load Balancer (ALB) with Target Groups for dynamic traffic routing.

A) CloudFront with Lambda@Edge is primarily used for content delivery optimization, not for handling sudden spikes in trading activity.

B) Classic Load Balancer is not recommended for new deployments due to its limitations.

C) ALB with Target Groups can efficiently handle dynamic traffic patterns and adapt to spikes in trading activity while ensuring minimal latency.

D) Route 53 with Geolocation routing policy routes traffic based on geographic location but does not optimize for trading activity spikes. E) NLB operates at the transport layer and may not provide the same level of flexibility as ALB for handling dynamic traffic patterns in trading applications.

QUESTION 30

Answer - D) Utilize Amazon Kinesis Data Streams with AWS Lambda for real-time data processing and store it in Amazon S3

D) Amazon Kinesis Data Streams combined with AWS Lambda offers real-time data processing capabilities suitable for analyzing transaction data, detecting fraudulent activities, ensuring compliance, and scalability with real-time processing.

A, B) These options involve storing data in relational databases or data warehouses, which may not be suitable for real-time processing and scalability required for detecting fraudulent transactions.

C, E) While these options involve using AWS Lambda and Amazon DynamoDB or S3, they may not provide the real-time processing capabilities required for flagging suspicious activities promptly.

QUESTION 31

Answer - C) Implement Amazon Redshift for data warehousing, AWS Glue for data preparation, Amazon Machine Learning for predictive analytics, and AWS Data Pipeline for data movement.

C) Correct, as this combination offers a comprehensive solution for analyzing large datasets and performing complex computations, with Redshift providing a powerful data warehousing solution, Glue for data preparation, Machine Learning for predictive analytics, and Data Pipeline for efficient data movement.

A) Incorrect, while S3, Athena, and Lambda support data storage and querying, Forecast is specifically for time-series forecasting, which may not fully meet the complex computational requirements for market trend analysis.

B) Incorrect, EC2, EBS, and RDS offer robust computing and storage options, but QuickSight, while useful for visualization, doesn't provide the same level of predictive analytics or scalable computing as the combination in option C.

D) Incorrect, Fargate, ECR, Batch, and SageMaker are powerful for containerized processing and machine learning models, but this setup lacks the integrated data warehousing and preparation capabilities provided by Redshift and Glue.

E) Incorrect, Kinesis, DynamoDB, Step Functions, and EMR are suited for real-time processing and big data analytics but don't offer the focused predictive analytics or data warehousing capabilities as effectively as option C.

QUESTION 32

Answer - [B) Utilize Amazon DynamoDB with global tables for multi-Region replication and use Amazon ElastiCache for Redis for caching frequently accessed data.]

Option B) - Correct because Amazon DynamoDB with global tables and Amazon ElastiCache for Redis efficiently handles performance and scalability of database operations while minimizing costs for the media streaming company.

Option A) - Incorrect because while Amazon RDS with Provisioned IOPS offers performance optimization, it may not provide the same level of scalability and cost efficiency as Amazon DynamoDB and ElastiCache.

Option C) - Incorrect because Aurora Serverless may not offer the same level of scalability and cost optimization as Amazon DynamoDB and ElastiCache required by the media streaming company.

Option D) - Incorrect because Amazon Redshift is optimized for analytics and may not offer the same level of performance and scalability as Amazon DynamoDB and ElastiCache required by the media streaming company.

Option E) - Incorrect because Amazon DocumentDB may not offer the same level of multi-Region replication and caching features as Amazon DynamoDB and ElastiCache required by the media streaming company.

QUESTION 33

Answer - E) Configure Amazon S3 for storing digital content, with Amazon CloudFront for content delivery. Use AWS AppSync to manage real-time content updates and synchronization across devices.

A) - Incorrect. While this option leverages Amazon S3 and Amazon CloudFront effectively for content storage and distribution, it relies on Amazon EC2 Auto Scaling for compute resources, which may not be as cost-effective or scalable for content management systems as serverless options.

B) - Incorrect. AWS Elastic Beanstalk and Amazon RDS provide a managed application and database environment but may not offer the best cost-efficiency or scalability needed for fluctuating traffic patterns, nor the lowest latency content delivery as effectively as other options.

C) - Incorrect. AWS Lambda and Amazon DynamoDB are highly scalable and cost-effective, but AWS Global Accelerator, while improving global performance, may not be as effective for content delivery needs as Amazon CloudFront.

D) - Incorrect. Amazon ECS with Fargate and Amazon EFS offer scalable container management and shared storage, but this setup may not be the most cost-effective or efficient for delivering content globally compared to leveraging a CDN like Amazon CloudFront.

E) - Correct. This option provides a scalable, cost-effective solution for managing and delivering digital content. Amazon S3 and Amazon CloudFront ensure efficient global content distribution. AWS AppSync enhances the architecture by enabling real-time content updates and synchronization, addressing the need for rapid content changes and low latency delivery to users worldwide.

QUESTION 34

Answer - E) Configure AWS Transit Gateway with VPN attachments to establish secure and scalable connectivity between the on-premises network and multiple VPCs in AWS, simplifying network management and routing.

Option E - Configuring AWS Transit Gateway with VPN attachments enables secure and scalable connectivity between the on-premises network and AWS VPCs, simplifying network management and routing while maintaining security.

Option A - While AWS Client VPN provides encrypted connections, it may not offer the scalability and centralized management needed for large-scale hybrid cloud architectures.

Option B - AWS Site-to-Site VPN establishes secure IPsec tunnels but may not provide the scalability and centralized management capabilities of AWS Transit Gateway.

Option C - AWS Direct Connect offers dedicated network connections but may be cost-prohibitive and less scalable compared to VPN-based solutions like AWS Transit Gateway.

Option D - AWS PrivateLink allows secure access to AWS services but is more focused on service integration rather than hybrid network connectivity.

QUESTION 35

Answer - D) Deploy GraphQL APIs on Amazon API Gateway with Amazon EventBridge for real-time event routing and Amazon Personalize for generating personalized recommendations

D) Leveraging GraphQL APIs on Amazon API Gateway with Amazon EventBridge allows for real-time event routing, while utilizing Amazon Personalize enables the generation of personalized recommendations for the online retail platform.

A, B, C, E) These options either do not provide support for real-time event processing or involve using services not suitable for generating personalized recommendations.

QUESTION 36

Answer - [B, C, D]

A) Incorrect - Provisioned concurrency doesn't directly relate to handling varying loads.
B) Correct - API Gateway with caching optimizes latency and cost for HTTP APIs.
C) Correct - DynamoDB on-demand mode allows flexible scalability without capacity planning.
D) Correct - CloudWatch alarms trigger Lambda auto-scaling, ensuring performance under varying loads.
E) Incorrect - Fargate provides serverless container management but doesn't directly optimize costs or performance under varying loads.

QUESTION 37

Answer - [A, B]

A) Correct - RDS with encryption at rest and IAM database authentication ensures data security and access control, meeting compliance requirements. AWS KMS provides centralized key management and rotation.

B) Correct - S3 server-side encryption and IAM policies enforce data security and access control. CloudTrail monitoring enhances visibility into S3 bucket access and activity, facilitating compliance monitoring and auditing.

C) Incorrect - While DynamoDB client-side encryption and IAM roles provide security and access control, this option lacks centralized key management and rotation, essential for compliance with regulatory standards.

D) Incorrect - Redshift encryption at rest and Secrets Manager for database credentials storage are relevant, but IAM policies alone may not provide granular access control required for compliance. SSL/TLS certificate management with ACM is not directly related to data encryption compliance.

E) Incorrect - DocumentDB encryption at rest and AWS CloudHSM for key storage are relevant, but IAM policies may not provide granular access control required for compliance. Certificate Manager with CloudHSM is not typically used for encryption at rest in DocumentDB.

QUESTION 38

Answer - A) Deploy Amazon CloudFront to cache static content and reduce latency during traffic spikes.
B) Utilize Amazon EC2 Auto Scaling to automatically adjust compute capacity based on traffic patterns.

Option A - Amazon CloudFront caches static content and reduces latency during traffic spikes, ensuring a consistent user experience.

Option B - Amazon EC2 Auto Scaling automatically adjusts compute capacity, ensuring scalability and cost optimization during peak traffic hours.

Options C, D, and E may not directly address the scalability and cost optimization requirements for handling traffic spikes in the web application architecture.

QUESTION 39

Answer - B) Deploy Amazon Route 53 with AWS Global Accelerator for efficient DNS routing and global application acceleration.

Option A - Using AWS Transit Gateway provides scalable connectivity but does not specifically address the requirement for global application performance optimization.

Option B - Deploying Amazon Route 53 with AWS Global Accelerator is the correct choice as it optimizes DNS routing and global application performance, ensuring low latency and efficient handling of fluctuating traffic loads.

Option C - Configuring CloudFront with WAF focuses on content delivery and web attack protection but may not optimize global application performance as effectively as Global Accelerator.

Option D - Implementing VPC with Direct Connect and VPN provides secure hybrid connectivity but does not specifically optimize for global application performance.

Option E - Utilizing Elastic Load Balancing (ELB) distributes traffic across resources but does not specifically address global application performance optimization.

QUESTION 40

Answer - C) Ingest student data into Amazon Kinesis Data Streams, which triggers an AWS Lambda function for processing and stores alert data in Amazon DynamoDB

C) Ingesting student data into Amazon Kinesis Data Streams with AWS Lambda allows for real-time processing and timely alerts. Storing alert data in Amazon DynamoDB ensures low-latency access and scalability.

A) Processing student data with AWS Lambda and Amazon S3 may introduce latency and is not suitable for real-time analytics systems.

B) Using Amazon Kinesis Data Firehose may not provide the necessary real-time processing capabilities for generating alerts promptly.

D) Amazon SQS is not optimized for real-time processing of student data, and storing alert data in Amazon Redshift may introduce delays.

E) Using Amazon API Gateway and an EC2 instance for processing lacks the scalability and real-time processing capabilities required for student performance analytics systems.

QUESTION 41

Answer - A) Utilize Amazon API Gateway to create RESTful APIs for microservices communication with low latency and high throughput.

Option A - Amazon API Gateway creates RESTful APIs for microservices communication, providing low latency, high throughput, and serverless scalability.

Option B - AWS Step Functions orchestrate workflows but may not directly optimize microservices communication latency or throughput as effectively as Amazon API Gateway.

Option C - Amazon MQ enables messaging but may not be as suitable for low-latency microservices communication as Amazon API Gateway.

Option D - Amazon Elastic Load Balancing (ELB) distributes traffic but may not optimize microservices communication latency or throughput as effectively as Amazon API Gateway.

Option E - Amazon EventBridge supports event-driven architectures but may not directly optimize microservices communication latency or throughput as effectively as Amazon API Gateway.

QUESTION 42

Answer - [D) Implement Amazon RDS with read replicas in multiple Availability Zones (AZs) for scalable read performance.]

Option D) Implementing Amazon RDS with read replicas in multiple AZs allows for scalable read performance, crucial for handling the high volume of real-time data in an IoT platform.

Option A) Multi-AZ deployment enhances fault tolerance but may not directly address performance issues with data ingestion and read access.

Option B) Amazon Neptune is not specifically optimized for handling high volume IoT data and may not offer the same level of performance as a relational database with read replicas.

Option C) While DynamoDB offers scalability, it may not provide the same level of performance optimization for real-time data ingestion as RDS with read replicas.

Option E) Aurora Serverless may not offer the same level of control and performance as RDS with read replicas for real-time IoT data.

QUESTION 43

Answer - A) Utilize AWS Lambda for serverless data processing, Amazon Kinesis for real-time data streaming, Amazon S3 for scalable data storage, Amazon Athena for querying data, and AWS Glue for data cataloging.

Option A - Correct. This solution offers a comprehensive, scalable, and cost-effective approach to real-time sports data analysis, with serverless processing, scalable storage, and efficient data querying and cataloging.

Option B - Incorrect. While EC2, RDS, and QuickSight provide compute, storage, and visualization, they lack the serverless, scalable architecture and real-time streaming capabilities required for handling fluctuating sports data volumes.

Option C - Incorrect. DynamoDB, EMR, and SageMaker offer strong NoSQL storage, big data processing, and machine learning capabilities, but this setup does not provide the optimal real-time data streaming and serverless processing required for the scenario.

Option D - Incorrect. Redshift, DataSync, and CloudFront focus on warehousing, data transfer, and content delivery but lack the real-time streaming and serverless processing capabilities necessary for real-time sports analytics.

Option E - Incorrect. While MSK and QuickSight are strong for data streaming and business intelligence, this option does not offer the same level of serverless processing and data cataloging efficiency as option A.

QUESTION 44

Answer - [C] Deploy Amazon Managed Streaming for Apache Kafka (Amazon MSK) for log event ingestion, process data with Amazon Kinesis Data Analytics, and trigger alerts using Amazon CloudWatch.

Option A introduces complexity with Glue and Aurora and may not be optimized for real-time analytics.
Option B lacks scalability with Lambda and may face latency issues.
Option D's use of AppSync and Neptune may not be suitable for real-time log analysis.

Option E's use of Firehose and EMR may not provide the real-time processing required for immediate alerts on application performance anomalies. Amazon MSK offers a scalable and durable event streaming platform, and Kinesis Data Analytics provides real-time analytics capabilities, making option C the most appropriate choice for building a real-time log analysis system.

QUESTION 45

Answer - B) Implement server-side encryption with AWS Key Management Service (SSE-KMS) and configure IAM roles for access control

B) Implementing server-side encryption with AWS Key Management Service (SSE-KMS) allows the legal firm to configure IAM roles for access control and track changes to encryption keys, meeting both compliance and security requirements.

A) Server-side encryption with Amazon S3 managed keys (SSE-S3) encrypts the data at rest but may not provide the necessary control over access and key management.

C) Client-side encryption with customer-provided keys (SSE-C) shifts the responsibility of encryption to the client and may not align with the firm's requirement for centralized key management.

D) Implementing server-side encryption with customer-provided keys (SSE-C) and monitoring access using AWS CloudTrail may not offer the same level of control and granularity provided by AWS KMS.
E) Enabling AWS CloudTrail provides auditing capabilities but does not directly address the encryption and access control requirements for data at rest in Amazon S3.

QUESTION 46

Answer - [B] Utilize AWS IoT Core for data ingestion, configure AWS Greengrass for edge computing, implement Amazon Kinesis Data Streams for real-time data processing, integrate with Amazon RDS for real-time data storage, and utilize Amazon S3 for long-term data archival.

Option A is incorrect because it uses Amazon API Gateway for data ingestion, which is not typically used in IoT solutions for sensor data collection. AWS Fargate is also not the ideal choice for edge processing in IoT scenarios. Additionally, Amazon RDS and Amazon Glacier are not the most suitable options for real-time data storage and long-term data archival in IoT solutions.

Option C is incorrect because AWS IoT Events is not commonly used for data ingestion in IoT solutions, and Amazon Aurora is not the optimal database service for real-time data storage in this context. Amazon S3 Glacier is also not well-suited for long-term data archival in IoT scenarios.

Option D is incorrect because although it uses AWS IoT Greengrass, it employs AWS Lambda for edge processing instead of utilizing Greengrass capabilities, which are better suited for processing data at the edge.

Option E is incorrect because it does not leverage AWS Greengrass for edge computing, which is essential for processing data closer to the source in IoT scenarios. Additionally, Amazon S3 is not ideal for real-time data storage compared to Amazon RDS.

QUESTION 47

Answer - [A] Utilize AWS Lambda@Edge to deploy applications on edge devices located in gaming server locations, leverage AWS IoT Greengrass for edge data processing, and integrate with Amazon DynamoDB for real-time data storage.

Option A is the correct choice because deploying applications on edge devices in gaming server locations using Lambda@Edge ensures low-latency edge computing capability, ideal for processing real-time player interactions and game events. AWS IoT Greengrass facilitates edge data processing, and DynamoDB provides real-time data storage.

Options B, C, D, and E either lack the same level of latency reduction, suitable edge computing solutions, or appropriate real-time data storage services.

QUESTION 48

Answer - A) Combine Amazon Kinesis for real-time data ingestion, AWS Lambda for data processing, Amazon DynamoDB for scalable data storage, and Amazon API Gateway for secure API exposure.

A) Correct - Amazon Kinesis facilitates the real-time ingestion of game data, AWS Lambda processes this data efficiently in a serverless manner, Amazon DynamoDB provides a scalable database for storing analytics, and Amazon API Gateway securely exposes the processed data through APIs, perfectly meeting the platform's requirements for real-time analytics delivery.

B) Incorrect - EC2 with Auto Scaling, S3, Direct Connect, and IAM offer compute scaling, data storage, reduced latency, and access management but lack the real-time processing and API management capabilities of Kinesis, Lambda, and API Gateway for live sports analytics.

C) Incorrect - ECS with Fargate, RDS, CloudFront, and WAF provide a solid foundation for running containers, data storage, content distribution, and security but do not specifically address the real-time data aggregation and analytics needs as efficiently as the combination in A.

D) Incorrect - Global Accelerator, Redshift, SQS, and Cognito enhance performance, provide analytics storage, support messaging, and manage user authentication but are not as aligned with the need for real-time data processing and API management for sports analytics.

E) Incorrect - AppSync, EBS, Step Functions, and Shield focus on data synchronization, storage, workflow orchestration, and DDoS protection but do not offer the integrated solution for real-time sports data analysis and API delivery as effectively as the services in A.

QUESTION 49

Answer - A) {
"Action": [
"s3:GetObject",
"s3:PutObject",
"s3:DeleteObject"
],
"Resource": "arn:aws:s3:::example-bucket/",
"Effect": "Allow"
}

A) This option allows the team to read, write, and delete objects within the bucket while restricting access to modifying the bucket policy, aligning with the requirement.

B) Allowing the team to modify the bucket policy violates the requirement as they should not have permissions to alter the policy.

C) Granting permissions to modify the bucket's versioning settings is unnecessary and exceeds the requirement.

D) This option grants the team permissions to modify the bucket policy, which is not in line with the requirement.

E) Similar to option C, allowing the team to change the bucket's versioning settings is beyond the scope of the requirement.

QUESTION 50

Answer - A) Utilize Amazon EC2 Spot Instances to handle peak traffic periods, leveraging the cost savings of Spot Instances for temporary compute capacity. Implement Amazon CloudWatch alarms to trigger scaling actions based on CPU utilization, ensuring optimal resource allocation.

Option A is the correct choice as it leverages Amazon EC2 Spot Instances for temporary compute capacity during peak traffic periods, optimizing cost efficiency. CloudWatch alarms ensure timely scaling actions based on CPU utilization, ensuring optimal resource allocation.

Option B focuses on database deployment and caching but does not address compute capacity optimization.

Option C relies on DynamoDB, which may not be the most cost-effective solution for variable traffic.

Option D, while utilizing Lambda and Aurora Serverless, may not provide the required performance and scalability during peak traffic periods.

QUESTION 51

Answer - C) Implement Amazon ECS for containerized applications, Amazon Aurora Serverless for on-demand relational database needs, Amazon S3 Glacier for long-term data archiving, and AWS CloudTrail for auditing.

Option C - Correct: ECS offers container management, Aurora Serverless provides on-demand relational databases, S3 Glacier offers cost-effective long-term data archiving, and CloudTrail ensures compliance with auditing, aligning with the high availability, data privacy, and compliance needs of the healthcare organization's patient management system modernization.

Option A - Incorrect: EC2 Auto Scaling, RDS, S3, and IAM provide scalability, data storage, backup, and access control but may not offer the same level of cost-effectiveness and compliance assurance as ECS, Aurora Serverless, S3 Glacier, and CloudTrail.

Option B - Incorrect: Lambda, DynamoDB, S3, and Certificate Manager support serverless compute, NoSQL storage, file storage, and SSL/TLS management but may not offer the same level of database scalability and auditing capabilities as ECS, Aurora Serverless, S3 Glacier, and CloudTrail.

Option D - Incorrect: API Gateway, Step Functions, Redshift, and KMS provide secure API management, workflow automation, analytics, and encryption but may not be as well-suited for containerized applications and long-term data archiving as ECS, Aurora Serverless, S3 Glacier, and CloudTrail.

Option E - Incorrect: Fargate, Aurora, Glacier, and Config offer containerized workloads, high-performance databases, cold storage, and compliance monitoring but may not provide the same level of flexibility and cost-effectiveness for containerized applications and long-term data archiving as ECS, Aurora Serverless, S3 Glacier, and CloudTrail.

QUESTION 52

Answer - C) Implement an Amazon ECS cluster for hosting game servers, using Amazon ElastiCache for caching frequently accessed data and Amazon S3 for storing game assets.

A) Incorrect - While EC2 instances and RDS offer flexibility, they may not provide the low-latency and scalability required for real-time gaming.

B) Incorrect - DynamoDB and Lambda functions may offer scalability, but they may not provide the necessary performance for real-time communication in multiplayer gaming.

C) Correct - Deploying an ECS cluster for game servers, coupled with ElastiCache for caching and S3 for asset storage, ensures high availability and optimal performance for multiplayer gaming.

D) Incorrect - SQS queues and Aurora may introduce latency and complexity, which are not ideal for real-time communication in online gaming.

E) Incorrect - While Fargate containers and EKS offer scalability, they may not provide the real-time communication capabilities required for multiplayer gaming, and SNS and CloudWatch are not directly relevant to this use case.

QUESTION 53

Answer - C) Implement Amazon Aurora in each region for payroll information and Amazon DynamoDB global tables for financial reports.

A) Aurora Global Database does not suit region-specific access needs for payroll information.

B) DynamoDB global tables do not meet the regional data residency requirement for payroll.

C) Correct, as Aurora provides the needed data residency for payroll, and DynamoDB global tables offer a globally accessible solution for financial reports.

D) This does not address regional data access restrictions required for payroll information.

E) While S3 provides global access, it is not an optimal solution for dynamic financial reporting needs.

QUESTION 54

Answer - [A] Deploy Amazon Kinesis Data Analytics for real-time data analysis.

Option A - Correct. Amazon Kinesis Data Analytics provides real-time data analysis capabilities, ensuring high performance and scalability while optimizing costs.

Option B - Redshift Spectrum allows querying data from S3 but may not offer the real-time analytics capabilities needed for streaming data.

Option C - While Athena can query data in S3, it may not provide real-time analytics capabilities for streaming data.

Option D - EMR with Spark is more suitable for batch processing and may not offer real-time analytics capabilities.

Option E - RDS Multi-AZ configuration focuses on high availability but may not provide the same scalability and cost optimization as Kinesis Data Analytics for real-time analytics.

QUESTION 55

Answer - [D] Establish IAM groups for each project and assign developers to these groups with the necessary permissions.

A) Incorrect - Granting full administrative access to all developers increases the risk of unauthorized access and compromises security by providing unnecessary permissions.

B) Incorrect - While creating IAM roles for each project could work, it adds complexity and administrative overhead, especially as the number of projects and developers grows.

C) Incorrect - Attaching IAM policies directly to individual developers' IAM user accounts is not scalable and makes it challenging to manage permissions, especially for developers working on multiple projects.

D) Correct - Establishing IAM groups for each project and assigning developers to these groups with the necessary permissions minimizes administrative overhead and ensures developers only have access to resources relevant to their projects.

E) Incorrect - Implementing cross-account IAM roles adds unnecessary complexity and may not align with the organization's structure and access control requirements.

QUESTION 56

Answer - [A] Utilize AWS Backup to automate and manage backups of on-premises data to Amazon S3.

Option A - Correct. Utilizing AWS Backup automates and manages backups of on-premises data to Amazon S3, ensuring cost efficiency and data durability in a cloud-native environment.

Option B - Implementing AWS Storage Gateway Tape Gateway maintains reliance on tape-based workflows, which may not fully leverage the benefits of cloud-native storage.

Option C - Configuring AWS DataSync for replication may facilitate data transfer but does not directly address backup requirements.

Option D - Leveraging AWS Snowball Edge for offline transfer may assist in migration but is not the most cost-effective solution for ongoing backups.

Option E - Utilizing Amazon S3 Intelligent-Tiering may optimize storage costs but does not specifically address backup requirements for on-premises data.

QUESTION 57

Answer - [A] Utilize AWS DataSync to automate and optimize data transfer between S3 buckets in different regions.

Option A - Correct. AWS DataSync can automate and optimize data transfer between S3 buckets in different regions, ensuring efficient and cost-effective transfers of large datasets.

Option B - Cross-region replication for S3 buckets may replicate objects between regions but may not offer the same level of automation or cost efficiency as AWS DataSync for this scenario.

Option C - AWS Snowball involves physical data transfer and may not be suitable for automating regular data transfers between S3 buckets in different regions.

Option D - While Amazon S3 Transfer Acceleration optimizes data transfer speeds, it may not offer the same level of automation or cost efficiency as AWS DataSync for transferring large datasets between S3 buckets.

Option E - AWS Transfer Family provides SFTP-based data transfers but may not offer the same level of automation or cost efficiency as AWS DataSync for transferring large datasets between S3 buckets in different regions.

QUESTION 58

Answer - [B] Implement Amazon CloudFront with cache behaviors to control caching duration and optimize cache hit rates.

Option A - Utilizing Amazon CloudFront with Lambda@Edge functions for real-time transformations may enhance user experience but may not directly optimize costs for content delivery during peak upload periods.

Option B - Correct. Implementing Amazon CloudFront with cache behaviors allows for controlling caching duration and optimizing cache hit rates, aligning with cost optimization objectives while ensuring efficient content delivery during peak upload periods.

Option C - Configuring Amazon CloudFront with custom error pages enhances user experience but may not directly focus on cost optimization for content delivery.

Option D - Enabling Amazon CloudFront with cookie forwarding personalizes content delivery but may not directly address cost optimization concerns during peak upload periods.

Option E - Integrating Amazon CloudFront with AWS Direct Connect enhances connectivity but may not directly optimize costs for content delivery during peak upload periods.

QUESTION 59

Answer - [C] Deploy Amazon S3 Lifecycle policies to transition infrequently accessed video content to Amazon S3 Glacier.

Option C - Correct. Deploying Amazon S3 Lifecycle policies allows for automatic transitioning of infrequently accessed video content to Amazon S3 Glacier, reducing storage costs without manual intervention.

Option A - Using Amazon S3 Intelligent-Tiering with a single-tier storage strategy may not effectively optimize costs for infrequently accessed video content.

Option B - Implementing Amazon S3 Object Lock prevents modification but does not automate the process of transitioning infrequently accessed videos to Amazon S3 Glacier.

Option D - Leveraging Amazon S3 Cross-Region Replication to replicate video content to Amazon S3 Glacier may introduce complexity and may not be as cost-effective as lifecycle policies.

Option E - Utilizing Amazon S3 Standard-Infrequent Access (S3 Standard-IA) for all video content and manually moving infrequently accessed videos to Amazon S3 Glacier introduces manual effort and may not be as automated as lifecycle policies.

QUESTION 60

Answer - [A] Configure the Auto Scaling group to use a target tracking scaling policy based on network throughput across instances.

A) Correct - Using a target tracking scaling policy based on network throughput ensures that the Auto Scaling group adjusts the number of instances to maintain a desired level of network performance, crucial for video streaming services.

B) Incorrect - Implementing a scheduled scaling policy triggered at specific times may not accurately align with peak usage periods, potentially resulting in under or over-provisioning of resources.

C) Incorrect - Configuring a step scaling policy triggered by sudden increases in the number of requests may not provide the fine-grained adjustments needed to maintain consistent performance levels during peak usage.

D) Incorrect - Utilizing a simple scaling policy based on manual adjustments lacks automation and may result in delayed responses to changing traffic conditions, impacting performance.

E) Incorrect - Implementing a predictive scaling policy based on machine learning algorithms may introduce unnecessary complexity and may not be as effective in responding to immediate traffic fluctuations compared to a target tracking policy based on real-time metrics.

QUESTION 61

Answer - [A] Utilize AWS Backup to automate and centralize backups of AWS resources and on-premises applications.

Option A - Correct. AWS Backup automates and centralizes backups of AWS resources and on-premises applications, providing a cost-effective solution for disaster recovery while ensuring data integrity and durability.

Option B - AWS DataSync transfers data between on-premises storage systems and AWS but may not offer the same level of automation and centralized management as AWS Backup for disaster recovery purposes.

Option C - AWS Snowball transfers large amounts of data to AWS but may not provide the same level of automation and cost-effectiveness as AWS Backup for disaster recovery.

Option D - AWS Storage Gateway integrates on-premises applications with AWS storage but may not offer the same level of disaster recovery capabilities and centralized management as AWS Backup.

Option E - AWS Transfer Family securely transfers files over various protocols but may not be the most suitable solution for disaster recovery and centralized backup management as AWS Backup.

QUESTION 62

Answer - [E] Utilize Amazon CloudFront with Lambda@Edge to cache and deliver the dataset at edge locations.

Option A - AWS Direct Connect provides private connectivity but may not optimize content delivery and reduce latency for accessing a large dataset as effectively as CloudFront with Lambda@Edge.

Option B - Amazon S3 Transfer Acceleration optimizes data transfers but may not provide the same low-latency access as CloudFront with Lambda@Edge for accessing a large dataset.

Option C - Amazon FSx for Windows File Server may provide fast access but may not offer the same content delivery and caching capabilities as CloudFront with Lambda@Edge.

Option D - AWS DataSync is designed for data synchronization but may not optimize content delivery and reduce latency for accessing a large dataset as effectively as CloudFront with Lambda@Edge.

Option E - Correct. Amazon CloudFront with Lambda@Edge allows for caching and delivering the dataset at edge locations, ensuring low-latency access and cost-effective content delivery for migrating on-premises applications to AWS.

QUESTION 63

Answer - [E] Deploy AWS Storage Gateway to cache frequently accessed data locally and reduce data transfer costs between on-premises infrastructure and AWS.

Option A - AWS VPN provides connectivity but may not directly address the need for optimizing data transfer costs in a hybrid cloud architecture.

Option B - AWS Snow Family devices are used for offline data transfer and may not be the most suitable solution for ongoing data transfer cost optimization.

Option C - AWS Direct Connect provides dedicated connectivity but may not directly reduce data transfer costs in a hybrid cloud environment.

Option D - Amazon S3 Transfer Acceleration improves transfer speeds but may not directly reduce data transfer costs between on-premises environments and AWS.

Option E - Correct. Deploying AWS Storage Gateway allows for caching frequently accessed data locally, reducing data transfer costs between on-premises infrastructure and AWS.

QUESTION 64

Answer - [A] Implement Amazon CloudFront with AWS Global Accelerator to cache content at edge locations and minimize data transfer between regions.

Option A - Correct. Implementing Amazon CloudFront with AWS Global Accelerator allows for caching content at edge locations, reducing data transfer between regions while ensuring high availability.

Option B - Amazon S3 Transfer Acceleration improves transfer speeds but may not directly reduce data transfer costs between regions.

Option C - Amazon DynamoDB global tables ensure data replication across regions but may not directly address the issue of reducing data transfer costs between regions.

Option D - AWS Direct Connect with AWS Transit Gateway can establish private connectivity between regions but may not directly minimize data transfer costs.

Option E - Amazon Route 53 latency-based routing optimizes traffic routing but may not directly reduce data transfer costs between regions.

QUESTION 65

Answer - [B] Implement AWS DataSync to automate data transfers between on-premises storage and Amazon S3.

Option B - Correct. Implementing AWS DataSync automates data transfers between on-premises storage and Amazon S3, minimizing data transfer costs and ensuring reliable connectivity.

Option A - AWS Direct Connect provides dedicated network connections but may not directly address cost-effective data transfer requirements.

Option C - AWS Transfer Family enables secure transfers but may not be the most cost-effective solution for large-scale data transfers.

Option D - Amazon S3 Transfer Acceleration optimizes speed but may not minimize data transfer costs for on-premises data centers.

Option E - AWS VPN CloudHub establishes VPN connections but may not be the most cost-effective solution for data transfer between on-premises data centers and AWS.

PRACTICE TEST 6 - QUESTIONS ONLY

QUESTION 1

A global retail company wants to simplify access for developers and operators working across multiple AWS accounts without compromising security. They are considering federating access using IAM roles and an external directory service. What approach should they take to implement federated access securely?

A) Use AWS IAM Identity Center to establish trust between AWS accounts and the external directory service.

B) Directly attach IAM policies to users in the external directory service for access to AWS resources.

C) Store access credentials in Amazon S3 and grant access to users through IAM roles.

D) Use AWS Lambda to automate the creation of IAM users based on external directory service membership.

E) Implement an Amazon Cognito user pool to federate access to AWS Management Console.

QUESTION 2

A financial institution is launching a new application that requires high security for its transaction data. The application will be hosted on AWS, and the company is focused on securing the application configuration and credentials effectively. Considering AWS best practices, how should the company manage its application configuration and secrets to ensure the highest level of security?

A) Store secrets in environment variables within Amazon EC2 instances.
B) Utilize AWS Secrets Manager for storing and rotating credentials and secrets.
C) Keep application configuration files in an Amazon S3 bucket with public access to allow easy retrieval.
D) Embed credentials directly in the application code for convenience.
E) Use AWS Systems Manager Parameter Store to manage secrets and application configuration.

QUESTION 3

Your company is migrating its on-premises databases to Amazon RDS to leverage cloud scalability and availability. You need to ensure that the migrated databases are secure against external threats and comply with industry regulations.

A) Configure AWS Key Management Service (KMS) to encrypt data at rest and manage encryption keys for Amazon RDS instances

B) Implement Amazon RDS Enhanced Monitoring to collect and analyze performance metrics for database instances

C) Utilize AWS Database Migration Service (DMS) to securely migrate on-premises databases to Amazon RDS

D) Deploy AWS Certificate Manager (ACM) to provision SSL/TLS certificates for secure communication with Amazon RDS instances

E) Enable Amazon RDS database encryption at the instance level to encrypt data in transit and ensure compliance with industry regulations

QUESTION 4

Your company operates a critical web application that requires high availability and fault tolerance. The application currently runs on Amazon EC2 instances distributed across multiple Availability Zones (AZs). As the solutions architect, you need to design a resilient architecture that ensures the application remains available even in the event of AZ failures. Which solution should you recommend?

A) Utilize Amazon EC2 Auto Scaling with target tracking scaling policies to maintain the desired capacity across multiple AZs. Implement Amazon RDS Multi-AZ deployment for database redundancy and failover.

B) Configure Amazon EC2 instances in separate regions to distribute the workload and ensure high availability. Utilize Amazon Aurora Global Database for multi-region replication and automatic failover.

C) Implement Amazon EC2 instances in an Auto Scaling group across multiple AZs. Utilize Amazon RDS Read Replicas for read scalability and fault tolerance.

D) Utilize AWS Elastic Beanstalk to automatically manage the deployment, scaling, and load balancing of the application across multiple AZs. Implement Amazon RDS Multi-AZ deployment for database redundancy and failover.

E) Deploy Amazon EC2 instances in a single AZ with Elastic Load Balancing to distribute traffic. Utilize Amazon RDS Multi-AZ deployment for database redundancy and failover.

QUESTION 5

A transportation company is migrating its logistics tracking system to AWS and needs a solution that ensures shipment status updates are processed promptly and accurately while also supporting high volumes of updates during peak times. Which option should the company choose to implement this requirement?

A) Use Amazon SQS FIFO queue with exactly-once processing enabled.
B) Use Amazon SQS FIFO queue with message deduplication enabled.
C) Use Amazon SQS FIFO queue with a batch mode of 10 messages per operation.
D) Use Amazon SQS standard queue to process the messages.
E) Use Amazon SQS FIFO queue with default settings to process the messages.

QUESTION 6

Your company is designing a highly secure serverless application that requires fine-grained access control for various AWS resources. The architecture includes AWS Lambda functions, Amazon S3 buckets, and Amazon DynamoDB tables. As the solutions architect, you need to implement a comprehensive IAM strategy to ensure secure access to these resources. Which approach should you take to achieve this goal?

A) Create IAM roles with specific permissions for each Lambda function, and use IAM policies to control access to S3 buckets and DynamoDB tables.

B) Implement IAM users with custom policies for each AWS resource, and configure IAM groups for role-based access control.

C) Utilize IAM policies attached to S3 buckets and DynamoDB tables to control access, and use IAM roles for cross-service authentication between Lambda functions and other AWS services.

D) Set up IAM policies at the account level to manage access control for all AWS resources, and use IAM roles for temporary access to resources by Lambda functions.

E) Implement IAM policies with condition keys to control access based on specific criteria, and use IAM roles for federated access to AWS services by external users.

QUESTION 7

You are designing a highly secure architecture for a financial institution's cloud infrastructure on AWS. The architecture requires advanced network security measures. Which of the following options provides the most effective solution for implementing advanced network security?

A) Implementing a combination of security groups and network ACLs
B) Configuring AWS Network Firewall with custom rules
C) Utilizing AWS WAF in conjunction with AWS Shield
D) Deploying AWS Firewall Manager to manage security policies
E) Utilizing AWS Transit Gateway with AWS VPN

QUESTION 8

You are designing a secure architecture for a web application that handles sensitive user data. The application must protect against common web-based attacks, such as SQL injection and cross-site scripting (XSS). Which of the following strategies is most effective for integrating AWS services to achieve this security goal?

A) Implementing AWS WAF with rules to filter incoming web traffic
B) Utilizing Amazon Cognito for user authentication and authorization
C) Configuring Amazon API Gateway with rate limiting and authentication mechanisms
D) Enabling AWS Shield Advanced for DDoS protection
E) Deploying AWS Key Management Service (KMS) for encrypting user data at rest

QUESTION 9

Your company is developing a microservices architecture for a high-traffic e-commerce platform. Security is a top concern, and you need to ensure secure communication between microservices. Additionally, compliance regulations mandate encryption for data in transit. Which option best addresses these requirements?

A) Implementing mutual TLS authentication between microservices in Amazon ECS, ensuring secure communication and compliance with encryption standards

B) Utilizing AWS App Mesh to manage traffic between microservices, ensuring encryption and compliance with industry regulations

C) Configuring AWS Lambda authorizers in Amazon API Gateway for authentication and authorization, ensuring secure communication and compliance with encryption standards

D) Enabling AWS PrivateLink for private communication between microservices, ensuring encryption and compliance with industry standards

E) Deploying AWS WAF in front of microservices to filter and inspect incoming traffic, ensuring secure communication and compliance with encryption standards

QUESTION 10

A financial institution is migrating its document management system to AWS and requires a solution that ensures low-latency access to client files stored on a file system service. The employees must be able to access these files without disruption after migration. Which option is the most suitable solution to meet this requirement?

A) Use Amazon FSx File Gateway to provide low-latency, on-premises access to fully managed file shares in Amazon EFS. The applications deployed on AWS can access this data directly from Amazon EFS.

B) Use Amazon Storage Gateway's File Gateway to provide low-latency, on-premises access to fully managed file shares in Amazon FSx for Windows File Server. The applications deployed on AWS can access this data directly from Amazon FSx in AWS.

C) Use AWS Storage Gateway's File Gateway to provide low-latency, on-premises access to fully managed file shares in Amazon S3. The applications deployed on AWS can access this data directly from Amazon S3.

D) Use Amazon FSx File Gateway to provide low-latency, on-premises access to fully managed file shares in Amazon FSx for Windows File Server. The applications deployed on AWS can access this data directly from Amazon FSx in AWS.

QUESTION 11

A healthcare application stores patient records and must comply with HIPAA regulations. The application needs a scalable and secure storage solution on AWS, capable of encrypting data both at rest and in transit, with fine-grained access control for sensitive patient records.

A) Use Amazon S3 with default encryption, S3 bucket policies for access control, and Amazon Macie for data classification and protection.

B) Deploy Amazon EFS with encryption at rest enabled, IAM policies for access control, and AWS KMS for key management.

C) Implement Amazon FSx for Windows File Server with automatic backups, AWS Shield for DDoS protection, and VPC endpoints for secure data transit.

D) Utilize AWS Backup with cross-region backup capabilities, Amazon GuardDuty for threat detection, and AWS IAM roles for access management.

E) Configure Amazon S3 with server-side encryption (SSE) using AWS KMS, S3 access points for managing data access, and S3 lifecycle policies for data retention.

QUESTION 12

A startup is deploying a new web application on AWS and wants to ensure that the deployment process is as secure as possible. They plan to use AWS Elastic Beanstalk for easy management and scaling but are concerned about securing the application environment and managing configuration changes over time.

A) Use AWS Elastic Beanstalk with environment properties for secret management and enable AWS CloudTrail for monitoring configuration changes.

B) Implement AWS CloudFormation to automate secure deployment and AWS Config to track environment changes.

C) Deploy the application using AWS CodeDeploy, integrate AWS Key Management Service for encryption, and use Amazon CloudWatch for real-time monitoring.

D) Leverage AWS CodePipeline for continuous integration/continuous delivery (CI/CD), AWS WAF for application security, and AWS Shield for DDoS protection.

E) Configure AWS Elastic Beanstalk to use custom AMIs hardened according to AWS best practices, and establish IAM roles with limited permissions for application deployment.

QUESTION 13

A global financial services firm is developing an AWS-based application that requires strict compliance with industry regulations. They need a robust incident response plan that includes the ability to detect unauthorized access or anomalies quickly and to take automated actions to mitigate potential threats.

A) Utilize Amazon CloudWatch for monitoring, AWS Lambda for automated response, and AWS CloudTrail for logging and detecting anomalies.

B) Deploy AWS Shield Advanced for DDoS protection, Amazon Inspector for vulnerability assessments, and AWS Config for configuration tracking.

C) Implement Amazon GuardDuty for threat detection, AWS Security Hub for security monitoring, and AWS Step Functions for automated remediation workflows.

D) Configure Amazon S3 event notifications to trigger AWS Lambda functions for incident responses, and use Amazon Macie for sensitive data discovery and protection.

E) Leverage AWS WAF for real-time web traffic monitoring, AWS IAM Access Analyzer for analyzing permissions, and AWS Key Management Service (AWS KMS) for data encryption management.

QUESTION 14

You are designing a secure architecture for a healthcare application that needs to store and process sensitive patient data. The architecture must comply with strict regulatory requirements for data encryption and key management. Which approach should you recommend to ensure compliance and security?

A) Utilize AWS Key Management Service (KMS) for encryption and key management, implementing envelope encryption with AWS KMS customer master keys (CMKs) and AWS CloudHSM for hardware-based key storage.

B) Implement server-side encryption with Amazon S3 and manage encryption keys using AWS IAM policies.

C) Use AWS Lambda to encrypt and decrypt data at rest in Amazon DynamoDB, and manage encryption keys securely in an Amazon S3 bucket with restricted access permissions.

D) Leverage AWS CloudTrail for auditing and monitoring, and configure AWS IAM roles to enforce strict access controls on sensitive data stored in Amazon RDS.

E) Deploy AWS Secrets Manager to manage encryption keys and automatically rotate them based on predefined policies, ensuring compliance with regulatory requirements.

QUESTION 15

A financial services company is encountering difficulties in managing maintenance tasks on specific Amazon EC2 instances within an Auto Scaling group. Whenever maintenance patches are applied, the instances briefly show as out of service, leading to Auto Scaling provisioning replacements. What actions would you recommend as a solutions architect to address this issue efficiently?

A) Suspend the Terminate process type for the Auto Scaling group and apply the maintenance patch to the instance. Once the instance is ready, manually set the instance's health status back to healthy and activate the Terminate process type again.

B) Suspend the ReplaceUnhealthy process type for the Auto Scaling group and apply the maintenance patch to the instance. Once the instance is ready, manually set the instance's health status back to healthy and activate the ReplaceUnhealthy process type again.

C) Stop the instance, apply the maintenance patch, and then start the instance.

D) Temporarily suspend the AddToLoadBalancer process type for the Auto Scaling group and apply the maintenance patch to the instance. Once the instance is ready, manually set the instance's health status back to healthy and activate the AddToLoadBalancer process type again.

E) Take a snapshot of the instance, create a new Amazon Machine Image (AMI), and then launch a new instance using this AMI. Apply the maintenance patch to this new instance and then add it back to the Auto Scaling Group by using the manual scaling policy. Terminate the earlier instance that had the maintenance issue.

QUESTION 16

A Solutions Architect is designing a multi-tier web application on AWS. The application requires different IAM roles for Amazon EC2 instances, AWS Lambda functions, and Amazon RDS databases to interact with each other securely. What is the most secure way to manage these roles and permissions?

A) Create a single IAM role with permissions for EC2, Lambda, and RDS, and attach it to each service.

B) Generate IAM roles for each service with minimum necessary permissions and establish trust relationships.

C) Utilize AWS Service Catalog to automatically assign roles based on the service template.

D) Implement an IAM users group for the services and manually assign permissions as needed.

E) Enable cross-account access between services using IAM roles with broad permissions.

QUESTION 17

An online education platform is optimizing its AWS-based video streaming service to accommodate a growing global user base. They require a network design that supports efficient content delivery, robust security measures to protect user data, and scalable infrastructure to handle peak traffic loads.

A) Implement Amazon CloudFront with AWS WAF for content delivery and security, use Auto Scaling groups within a VPC for scalability, and enable Amazon CloudWatch for monitoring.

B) Deploy Amazon Route 53 for global traffic management, establish AWS Fargate for containerized video processing, and configure Amazon GuardDuty for security monitoring.

C) Utilize AWS Global Accelerator for performance optimization, set up AWS Lambda for backend processing, and apply Amazon S3 bucket policies for data security.

D) Configure Elastic Load Balancing (ELB) across multiple Availability Zones, use Amazon RDS with Multi-AZ deployments for data storage, and Amazon Inspector for security assessments.

E) Establish VPC peering for inter-region connectivity, leverage AWS Direct Connect for dedicated content delivery, and enable AWS Config for configuration and security governance.

QUESTION 18

A retail company with a global presence is looking to improve the performance and availability of its e-commerce platform on AWS. The company also wants to ensure that costs are optimized to maximize profit margins.

A) Utilize Amazon CloudFront for content delivery and set up AWS Lambda@Edge for serverless computing at edge locations. Implement Amazon Aurora Multi-Master for database high availability and scalability.

B) Deploy Amazon ECS for containerized application deployment and utilize AWS EFS for shared file storage across multiple containers. Set up Amazon RDS Multi-AZ deployment for database high availability and automatic failover.

C) Implement AWS Global Accelerator for improving global application performance and availability. Utilize Amazon S3 for storing static website assets and enable server-side encryption.

D) Deploy Amazon EC2 instances across multiple Availability Zones and configure Elastic Load Balancing for distributing incoming traffic. Utilize Amazon RDS Read Replicas for database scalability and read-heavy workloads.

E) Utilize Amazon Route 53 for DNS routing and load balancing. Implement Amazon CloudFront with Lambda@Edge for caching and dynamic content delivery. Set up Amazon Aurora Serverless for database storage to automatically scale based on demand.

QUESTION 19

A retail company is developing a microservices-based architecture on AWS Lambda for its e-commerce platform. They need to ensure secure management of API keys and other sensitive information within their serverless applications. Which of the following approaches would best suit the company's requirements?

A) Store secrets as Kubernetes secrets within the cluster. Implement RBAC (Role-Based Access Control) to restrict access to secrets based on service identities.

B) Utilize AWS Secrets Manager to securely store API keys and sensitive information. Integrate AWS Lambda with Secrets Manager for automated retrieval of secrets at runtime.

C) Maintain plaintext secrets within Kubernetes pods. Implement network policies to control access to secrets based on pod identities.

D) Utilize AWS Key Management Service (KMS) to encrypt secrets stored within etcd, the Kubernetes cluster's datastore. Use IAM roles to control access to KMS encryption keys.

E) Store secrets directly in Docker images and distribute them using Amazon ECR. Implement IAM policies to control access to Docker images in ECR based on pod identities.

QUESTION 20

A healthcare organization noticed an increase in unauthorized AWS API queries during off-peak hours, with no apparent impact on system performance. The management seeks an automated solution to promptly alert relevant teams during such occurrences. Which solution would be most suitable in this scenario?

A) Configure AWS CloudTrail to stream event data to Amazon Kinesis. Utilize Amazon Kinesis stream-level metrics in Amazon CloudWatch to trigger an AWS Lambda function that will initiate an error workflow.

B) Leverage AWS Trusted Advisor to publish metrics about check results to Amazon CloudWatch. Set up an alarm to track status changes for checks in the Service Limits category for the APIs, triggering notifications when service quotas are exceeded.

C) Use Amazon Athena SQL queries against AWS CloudTrail log files stored in Amazon S3 buckets. Generate reports using Amazon QuickSight for managerial dashboards.

D) Create an Amazon CloudWatch metric filter to process AWS CloudTrail logs containing API call details. Establish an alarm based on this metric's rate to send an Amazon SNS notification to the required team.

E) Implement AWS Config Rules to monitor API activity and define rules to detect unauthorized API calls. Configure AWS Config to trigger an AWS Lambda function upon rule evaluation to notify relevant stakeholders.

QUESTION 21

An e-learning platform is redesigning its architecture to support interactive live streaming sessions with hundreds of participants simultaneously. The architecture needs to ensure low-latency streaming, high availability, and scalability to accommodate varying numbers of participants dynamically.

A) Deploy Amazon EC2 instances with Auto Scaling, Amazon RDS Multi-AZ for database management, Amazon CloudFront for content delivery, and Amazon ElastiCache for caching frequently accessed data.

B) Utilize AWS Lambda for serverless backend logic, Amazon API Gateway for managing APIs, Amazon Kinesis Video Streams for video ingestion, and Amazon CloudWatch for monitoring performance.

C) Implement Amazon ECS for containerized microservices, Amazon RDS Read Replicas for database scaling, AWS Direct Connect for dedicated network connectivity, and Amazon S3 for storing video assets.

D) Configure Amazon EKS for Kubernetes-based orchestration, Amazon DynamoDB for NoSQL data storage, Amazon CloudFront for global content delivery, and Amazon Redshift for analyzing user viewing patterns.

E) Leverage Amazon Managed Streaming for Apache Kafka (Amazon MSK) for real-time data streaming, AWS Lambda for processing video metadata, Amazon S3 Glacier for archival storage, and Amazon CloudFront for low-latency content delivery.

QUESTION 22

Your company is launching a global e-commerce platform that requires high availability and low latency for users worldwide. Additionally, the platform must handle sudden spikes in traffic during peak shopping seasons. Which combination of AWS services should you utilize to meet these requirements?

A) Amazon Route 53 for DNS routing with latency-based routing
B) Amazon CloudFront for content delivery with edge caching
C) AWS Global Accelerator for optimized global networking with traffic flow management
D) Amazon DynamoDB for scalable and low-latency NoSQL database
E) Amazon EC2 Auto Scaling for dynamically adjusting compute capacity with predictive scaling

QUESTION 23

A financial institution is designing a disaster recovery (DR) solution for its core banking application hosted on AWS. The company aims to ensure high availability and fault tolerance while optimizing costs. Which AWS service should the company consider to implement a warm standby architecture for its DR strategy?

A) Utilize Amazon Route 53 with health checks and DNS failover between active and standby environments, ensuring seamless failover and high availability

B) Implement Amazon RDS Multi-AZ deployment with automated failover for database redundancy and minimal downtime during DR events

C) Deploy Amazon EC2 instances in an AWS Region with automated backups and AMI snapshots for quick recovery and minimal data loss

D) Utilize AWS Lambda with Amazon DynamoDB Streams for real-time data replication and failover, achieving near-zero RPO and RTO at scale

E) Implement Amazon S3 with versioning and lifecycle policies for data replication and archive storage, ensuring data durability and compliance with regulatory requirements during DR scenarios

QUESTION 24

A multinational financial institution, operating across several continents, requires a robust networking architecture to securely connect its on-premises data center with AWS cloud infrastructure. The architecture must ensure high availability, scalability, and security while minimizing latency for mission-critical applications. Which AWS solution would best address these requirements?

A) Implement AWS Direct Connect with VPN for secure hybrid connectivity
B) Utilize Amazon Route 53 with AWS Global Accelerator for optimized routing
C) Configure AWS Transit Gateway with Direct Connect for scalable network management
D) Set up AWS Client VPN with AWS Site-to-Site VPN for remote access
E) Deploy AWS PrivateLink with AWS Transit Gateway for private connectivity

QUESTION 25

A software development firm uses Amazon Aurora for its development and testing environments. They rely on Aurora for its failover capabilities to ensure the database remains available during testing phases. Considering their setup with read replicas of different sizes and failover tiers, which replica would be prioritized for promotion in the event of a primary instance failure?

A) Tier-1 (4 terabytes)
B) Tier-3 (8 terabytes)
C) Tier-3 (4 terabytes)
D) Tier-5 (8 terabytes)
E) Tier-5 (4 terabytes)

QUESTION 26

A financial institution is redesigning its application infrastructure on AWS to ensure high availability and resilience. The company wants to implement immutable infrastructure to achieve these goals. Which solution should the architect recommend for achieving immutable infrastructure on AWS?

A) Utilize AWS CodeDeploy to automate the deployment of application updates and rollbacks.

B) Implement AWS CloudFormation to define infrastructure as code and manage the deployment of AWS resources in a declarative manner.

C) Use Amazon EKS Anywhere to deploy Kubernetes clusters on-premises and ensure consistent infrastructure across environments.

D) Leverage AWS Elastic Beanstalk to deploy and manage applications in an environment that automatically handles the deployment, from capacity provisioning to load balancing.

E) Configure AWS Lambda to automatically scale and execute code in response to HTTP requests or in-app activity.

QUESTION 27

A global e-commerce company is designing a microservices architecture for its online platform. The company needs to secure its APIs with fine-grained access control. Which option provides the best approach for securing microservices with Amazon API Gateway authorizers?

A) Utilize JWT authorizers with Amazon API Gateway to validate JWT tokens against an identity provider

B) Implement AWS Lambda authorizers to execute custom authorization logic before allowing access to APIs

C) Configure IAM role-based authorizers to authenticate users and control access to APIs

D) Use OAuth 2.0 authorizers with Amazon Cognito user pools to manage user authentication and authorization

E) Implement custom authorizers with AWS Lambda to perform token validation and authorization checks

QUESTION 28

An e-commerce company is planning to deploy a microservices-based application on AWS to handle seasonal traffic spikes. They are considering Amazon EKS and Amazon ECS for container orchestration. The architecture should be scalable, secure, and cost-effective. Which service should they use, and what features should be implemented to meet these requirements?

A) Deploy on Amazon EKS with Auto Scaling, use Amazon RDS with Multi-AZ deployments for the database, and Amazon CloudFront for content delivery.

B) Use Amazon ECS with Fargate launch type, implement Amazon EFS for shared storage, and leverage AWS WAF for security at the edge.

C) Opt for Amazon EKS with AWS Fargate for serverless compute, Amazon ECR for container image management, and AWS Shield for DDoS protection.

D) Implement Amazon ECS with EC2 launch type, use Amazon DynamoDB for scalable NoSQL storage, and Amazon API Gateway for secure API management.

E) Choose Amazon EKS, use AWS App Mesh for service mesh capabilities, Amazon ECR for container image management, and Elastic Load Balancing (ELB) for traffic distribution.

QUESTION 29

A multinational e-commerce company is expanding its operations to multiple regions to improve global reach. They require a resilient architecture that can withstand regional failures while maintaining low latency for customers. Which solution meets the company's requirements?

A) Deploy an Amazon Aurora Global Database for cross-region replication and automatic failover
B) Utilize Amazon RDS Multi-AZ deployment with read replicas in different regions for redundancy
C) Implement Amazon DynamoDB Global Tables for multi-region replication and automatic failover
D) Set up Amazon ElastiCache with automatic failover across regions for caching data
E) Configure Amazon Redshift cross-region snapshots for disaster recovery and data synchronization

QUESTION 30

A logistics company needs to track shipment movements in real-time to optimize delivery routes and ensure on-time deliveries. They require a solution capable of processing GPS data efficiently and providing insights into route optimization. Which AWS service combination should they implement to achieve this while ensuring accuracy and scalability?

A) Utilize a Spark Streaming cluster on Amazon EMR to process GPS data before storing it in Amazon RDS

B) Implement Amazon Kinesis Data Analytics to analyze streaming GPS data and store it in Amazon Redshift for further analysis

C) Employ Amazon Kinesis Data Firehose to ingest data and use AWS Lambda to filter and transform before storing it in Amazon DynamoDB

D) Utilize Amazon Kinesis Data Streams with AWS Lambda for real-time data processing and store it in Amazon S3

E) Ingest data directly into Amazon S3 using Amazon Kinesis Data Firehose without intermediate processing

QUESTION 31

A financial institution is looking to automate compliance and security for their AWS environment. They need to ensure that their AWS resources comply with industry standards and internal policies, particularly for sensitive data protection and access management. Which combination of AWS services should they use to automate compliance checks and security monitoring?

A) Use AWS Config for continuous compliance monitoring, AWS CloudTrail for governance, AWS Lambda for automated security responses, and Amazon GuardDuty for threat detection.

B) Implement Amazon Inspector for security assessments, AWS WAF for application security, Amazon Macie for data privacy, and AWS IAM for access management.

C) Deploy AWS Shield for DDoS protection, Amazon Cognito for user identity management, AWS KMS for encryption, and AWS Trusted Advisor for best practices recommendations.

D) Utilize Amazon VPC for network isolation, Amazon S3 Glacier for encrypted data storage, AWS Direct Connect for secure, private connectivity, and AWS Fargate for running containers without managing servers.

E) Choose AWS AppSync for data synchronization, Amazon DynamoDB for secure NoSQL database services, AWS Step Functions for serverless orchestration, and Amazon SNS for notification services.

QUESTION 32

A multinational financial institution is designing a disaster recovery (DR) solution for its critical database. The architecture must ensure minimal data loss and rapid recovery in case of a disaster. Which approach should the institution take to meet these requirements while optimizing costs?

A) Implement Amazon RDS with Multi-AZ deployment and utilize read replicas for scaling read operations during peak hours.

B) Utilize Amazon Aurora Serverless with auto-scaling and provisioned Aurora Capacity Units (ACUs) for predictable performance during peak trading hours.

C) Deploy Amazon DynamoDB with on-demand scaling and utilize DynamoDB Streams for real-time data processing and analysis.

D) Migrate to Amazon Redshift for analytics and scalability and use Redshift Concurrency Scaling for handling concurrent queries during peak hours.

E) Implement Amazon DocumentDB with MongoDB compatibility and use DocumentDB global clusters for cross-Region replication and failover.

QUESTION 33

Your company is developing a new e-commerce platform that consists of multiple microservices handling various functionalities such as user authentication, product catalog management, and order processing. Security is a top priority, and you need to ensure secure API communication between these microservices. What approach would best achieve this goal?

A) Configure API Gateway with AWS IAM authorization.
B) Implement OAuth 2.0 authentication with Amazon Cognito.
C) Use AWS WAF to protect API endpoints.
D) Secure API communication with AWS Shield.
E) Store sensitive data in plaintext within Lambda environment variables.

QUESTION 34

You are designing a highly available and resilient architecture for a web application that requires scalable compute resources and storage. The application experiences variable traffic throughout the day, with peak usage during certain hours. You need to select the most cost-effective solution for the compute resources while ensuring resilience and scalability. Which option should you choose?

A) Utilize Amazon EC2 instances with Auto Scaling groups and Amazon EBS volumes
B) Implement AWS Lambda functions triggered by Amazon API Gateway
C) Deploy containers using Amazon ECS with AWS Fargate
D) Utilize AWS Outposts for on-premises compute resources
E) Deploy the application on AWS Wavelength for ultra-low latency

QUESTION 35

A travel booking platform wants to implement a notification system to alert users about flight delays or cancellations in real-time. They require a solution that can send timely notifications to users based on updates from airline APIs. Which configuration should they implement using Amazon API Gateway to meet these requirements effectively?

A) Utilize RESTful APIs on Amazon API Gateway with Amazon RDS for storing flight information and AWS Lambda for sending notifications to users

B) Implement WebSocket APIs on Amazon API Gateway with Amazon DynamoDB for storing flight information and Amazon SNS for sending notifications to users

C) Create HTTP APIs on Amazon API Gateway and integrate with Amazon Aurora for storing flight information and Amazon SES for sending notifications to users

D) Deploy GraphQL APIs on Amazon API Gateway with Amazon Redshift for storing flight information and Amazon Pinpoint for sending notifications to users

E) Configure RESTful APIs on Amazon API Gateway with Amazon ElastiCache for storing flight information and Amazon Simple Notification Service (SNS) for sending notifications to users

QUESTION 36

Your company, a leading e-commerce platform, is planning to migrate its data infrastructure to AWS. The platform handles a vast amount of customer data, including personal and payment information. As the solution architect, you need to design a robust encryption strategy to ensure data security and compliance with regulatory standards. Considering the sensitivity of the data, which approach should you take to encrypt the data effectively? Select TWO.

A) Utilize Amazon RDS with encryption at rest enabled and encrypt data in transit using AWS Certificate Manager (ACM).

B) Implement Amazon S3 server-side encryption with AWS Key Management Service (KMS) managed keys and enforce SSL/TLS for encrypting data in transit.

C) Deploy Amazon Aurora with encryption at rest enabled and leverage AWS CloudHSM for secure key storage.

D) Utilize Amazon DynamoDB with client-side encryption enabled and use AWS Secrets Manager for key management policies.

E) Configure Amazon Redshift with encryption at rest enabled and utilize AWS KMS for managing encryption keys securely.

QUESTION 37

A media company requires a highly available storage solution for their global content delivery network (CDN) to serve media files with minimal latency. The solution must be scalable, secure, and cost-effective, with the ability to handle sudden spikes in demand. Which storage solution meets these criteria?

A) Amazon EBS volumes attached to EC2 instances behind an Elastic Load Balancer.
B) Amazon S3 with Transfer Acceleration enabled and lifecycle policies configured.
C) Amazon EFS mounted to multiple EC2 instances across different regions.
D) Amazon RDS with read replicas to serve media files stored in blob storage.
E) AWS Storage Gateway with cached volumes to store and retrieve media files.

QUESTION 38

You are designing a high-performing database solution for a large e-commerce platform that experiences heavy traffic during peak hours. The database needs to handle simultaneous read requests efficiently while ensuring data consistency. Which AWS service or feature combination would you recommend for optimizing database read performance in this scenario?

A) Implement Amazon RDS Multi-AZ deployment with read replicas to distribute read traffic across multiple availability zones.

B) Deploy Amazon ElastiCache for Redis to cache frequently accessed data and reduce database load.

C) Utilize Amazon Aurora Multi-Master for simultaneous write operations across multiple database instances.

D) Configure Amazon DynamoDB global tables to replicate data across multiple AWS regions for low-latency reads.

E) Deploy Amazon Redshift Spectrum to offload read queries to the data lake stored in Amazon S3.

QUESTION 39

A multinational financial institution needs to design a scalable data ingestion pipeline to process real-time financial transactions securely. The system must be capable of efficiently handling fluctuating data loads and ensuring high availability. What solution would best meet these requirements?

A) Utilize AWS DataSync to transfer data from on-premises servers to Amazon S3, and configure Amazon Kinesis Data Streams to process real-time financial transactions.

B) Implement AWS Transfer Family to securely ingest data from external partners, and leverage AWS Glue for data transformation and preparation.

C) Configure Amazon CloudFront with AWS Shield for DDoS protection, and use AWS Step Functions to orchestrate the data ingestion process.

D) Deploy AWS Direct Connect to establish dedicated network connections between on-premises servers and Amazon S3, and leverage Amazon QuickSight for real-time analytics.

E) Utilize Amazon S3 Glacier for long-term storage of financial transaction data, and implement AWS AppSync for real-time data synchronization.

QUESTION 40

A manufacturing company wants to develop a predictive maintenance system to monitor equipment health in real-time and schedule maintenance proactively. They require a solution that can process sensor data continuously and predict equipment failures without delays. Which setup should they configure using AWS serverless components to meet these requirements effectively?

A) Utilize AWS Lambda with Amazon S3 for processing sensor data and Amazon RDS for storing maintenance schedules

B) Implement Amazon Kinesis Data Firehose with AWS Lambda for processing sensor data and Amazon ElastiCache for storing maintenance schedules

C) Ingest sensor data into Amazon Kinesis Data Streams, which triggers an AWS Lambda function for processing and stores maintenance schedules in Amazon DynamoDB

D) Ingest sensor data into Amazon SQS, which triggers an AWS Lambda function for processing and stores maintenance schedules in Amazon Redshift

E) Use Amazon API Gateway to ingest sensor data, which is processed by an application running on an

Amazon EC2 instance, and store maintenance schedules in Amazon Elasticsearch Service

QUESTION 41

A fintech startup is building a high-frequency trading platform to analyze market trends in real-time and execute trades based on algorithmic strategies. The solution requires ultra-low latency for data processing, high scalability for handling spikes in market data, and robust security measures to protect sensitive financial information. Which serverless architecture would best meet these stringent requirements?

A) AWS Lambda for data processing, Amazon Kinesis for real-time data streaming, and Amazon DynamoDB for secure and scalable storage.

B) Amazon EC2 Auto Scaling for compute scalability, Amazon S3 for data storage, and AWS Shield for security.

C) Amazon SNS for notifications, AWS Step Functions for workflow management, and Amazon RDS with Multi-AZ deployment for data storage.

D) Amazon API Gateway for RESTful API management, AWS Lambda for backend processing, and Amazon Cognito for authentication.

E) AWS Fargate for container management, Amazon SQS for message queuing, and AWS KMS for encryption.

QUESTION 42

Your company operates a hybrid cloud environment, with critical applications running both on-premises and in AWS. You need to ensure seamless connectivity between these environments while maintaining high performance and security. Which solution would best meet these requirements?

A) Implement AWS Direct Connect to establish a dedicated network connection between your on-premises data center and AWS.

B) Deploy AWS VPN to create a secure encrypted connection over the internet between your on-premises network and AWS.

C) Utilize AWS Transit Gateway to simplify network connectivity and routing between your on-premises data center and AWS.

D) Configure AWS Site-to-Site VPN to establish VPN tunnels over the internet between your on-premises network and AWS.

E) Implement AWS Global Accelerator to improve the availability and performance of your applications across regions.

QUESTION 43

A global e-commerce company plans to expand its services to new regions across the world. To ensure a seamless user experience, they require a robust deployment strategy that addresses high availability, low latency, and compliance with regional data protection laws. The company's architecture must efficiently handle dynamic content such as user profiles, shopping carts, and real-time product recommendations, as well as static content like product images and descriptions. The solution should also provide resilience against DDoS attacks and scale automatically to manage traffic spikes during major sales events.

A) Utilize Amazon CloudFront with AWS Shield for content delivery and DDoS protection, Amazon S3 for storing static content, AWS Lambda@Edge for dynamic content processing, and Amazon Route 53 for DNS management.

B) Deploy Amazon EC2 instances across multiple Availability Zones with Auto Scaling, use Amazon RDS for user data storage, Amazon CloudFront for global content delivery, and AWS WAF for web application firewall.

C) Implement AWS Global Accelerator to improve application performance, Elastic Load Balancing across multiple regions, Amazon EFS for shared file storage, and Amazon Cognito for user authentication and data compliance.

D) Leverage Amazon CloudFront with custom SSL certificates for secure content delivery, AWS Fargate for serverless container management, Amazon DynamoDB for low latency data access, and AWS Outposts for local data processing in regions with strict data sovereignty laws.

E) Use AWS Direct Connect and VPN for dedicated network connections, Amazon S3 and Amazon Glacier for data storage and archiving, AWS AppSync for managing backend data synchronization, and Amazon GuardDuty for threat detection.

QUESTION 44

Your company is developing a high-performance machine learning model using Amazon SageMaker to analyze large datasets and make real-time predictions. The model must provide low-latency predictions to support time-sensitive applications. Which architecture would best suit this requirement?

A) Utilize Amazon SageMaker for model training and inference, leveraging Amazon S3 for data storage and Amazon CloudWatch for monitoring.

B) Implement Amazon SageMaker for distributed training and inference, utilizing Amazon EFS for shared model storage and Amazon CloudWatch for monitoring.

C) Deploy Amazon SageMaker for real-time inference with AWS Lambda, storing model artifacts in Amazon RDS for quick access.

D) Utilize Amazon SageMaker for batch inference, integrating Amazon S3 for input data storage and Amazon CloudWatch for performance monitoring.

E) Implement Amazon SageMaker for distributed training with Amazon EBS for model storage and Amazon CloudWatch for monitoring and optimization.

QUESTION 45

A technology startup is developing a mobile application that will store user-generated content in Amazon S3. The startup requires encryption of the data at rest and wants to manage encryption keys programmatically via an API. Additionally, the startup wants to integrate key usage with its existing logging and monitoring systems. Which option would provide the most suitable solution for this scenario?

A) Utilize server-side encryption with Amazon S3 managed keys (SSE-S3) to encrypt the data on Amazon S3

B) Implement server-side encryption with AWS Key Management Service (SSE-KMS) and utilize AWS CloudTrail for monitoring

C) Use client-side encryption with customer-provided keys (SSE-C) and upload the encrypted data to Amazon S3

D) Implement server-side encryption with customer-provided keys (SSE-C) and develop custom logging and monitoring solutions

E) Enable AWS CloudTrail to monitor S3 bucket activities and integrate with custom logging systems

QUESTION 46

You are tasked with designing a highly scalable and resilient web application for a popular e-commerce platform. The application must handle unpredictable traffic spikes during seasonal sales events and ensure minimal latency for users worldwide. Which combination of AWS services and features would best meet these requirements?

A) Deploy the web application on Amazon EC2 instances with Auto Scaling groups, utilize Amazon ElastiCache for caching frequently accessed data, configure Amazon CloudFront for content delivery, and leverage Amazon Route 53 for global DNS routing.

B) Utilize AWS Lambda for serverless compute, store dynamic data in Amazon DynamoDB, cache frequently accessed data in Amazon ElastiCache, leverage Amazon CloudFront for content delivery, and implement Amazon Route 53 for global DNS routing.

C) Implement the web application as Docker containers using Amazon ECS, configure Amazon RDS for relational data storage, utilize Amazon ElastiCache for caching, leverage Amazon CloudFront for content delivery, and implement Amazon Route 53 for global DNS routing.

D) Deploy the web application on AWS Fargate for serverless compute, store dynamic data in Amazon DynamoDB, cache frequently accessed data in Amazon ElastiCache, configure Amazon CloudFront for content delivery, and leverage Amazon Route 53 for global DNS routing.

E) Utilize Amazon EC2 instances with Amazon Aurora for relational data storage, implement Amazon ElastiCache for caching, configure Amazon CloudFront for content delivery, and leverage Amazon Route 53 for global DNS routing.

QUESTION 47

You are designing a scalable architecture for a social media platform that experiences unpredictable spikes in user activity. The architecture must automatically adjust to varying loads while ensuring high availability and performance. Which approach would best meet these requirements?

A) Utilize Amazon EC2 Auto Scaling groups with Amazon RDS Multi-AZ deployment for database resilience, and Amazon ElastiCache for caching frequently accessed data.

B) Implement serverless functions with AWS Lambda for handling user requests, Amazon DynamoDB for storing user data, and Amazon S3 for static content storage.

C) Deploy applications on AWS Outposts to maintain consistency with on-premises infrastructure, use AWS Fargate for container orchestration, and leverage AWS Direct Connect for secure connectivity.

D) Utilize AWS Wavelength to deploy applications on edge devices for low-latency processing, AWS Global Accelerator for optimized routing, and Amazon Aurora for high-performance database needs.

E) Implement a microservices architecture with Amazon ECS for container management, Amazon MQ for message queuing, and Amazon Aurora Serverless for database scalability.

QUESTION 48

You are tasked with enhancing the security posture of a gaming company's AWS environment. The company stores sensitive player data in Amazon S3 buckets and runs game servers on Amazon EC2 instances. Which approach should you take to monitor for malicious activity and vulnerabilities effectively?

A) Utilize Amazon Inspector to monitor any malicious activity on data stored in Amazon S3. Use security assessments provided by Amazon GuardDuty to check for vulnerabilities on Amazon EC2 instances.

B) Deploy Amazon Inspector to monitor any malicious activity on data stored in Amazon RDS. Use security assessments provided by Amazon Inspector to check for vulnerabilities on Amazon RDS instances.

C) Leverage Amazon GuardDuty to monitor any malicious activity on data stored in Amazon S3. Use security assessments provided by Amazon GuardDuty to check for vulnerabilities on Amazon RDS instances.

D) Use Amazon GuardDuty to monitor any malicious activity on data stored in Amazon S3. Use security assessments provided by Amazon Inspector to check for vulnerabilities on Amazon EC2 instances.

E) Implement AWS Security Hub to monitor any malicious activity on data stored in Amazon S3. Use security assessments provided by AWS Security Hub to check for vulnerabilities on Amazon RDS instances.

QUESTION 49

An organization wants to grant access to a specific folder within an Amazon S3 bucket to a third-party vendor for data exchange. The vendor needs permissions to read, write, and delete objects within that folder only, without any access to other objects or settings in the bucket. Which IAM policy statement should be added to fulfill this requirement?

A) {
"Action": [
"s3:GetObject",
"s3:PutObject",
"s3:DeleteObject"
],
"Resource": "arn:aws:s3:::example-bucket/specific-folder/",
"Effect": "Allow"
}

```
B) {
 "Action": [
 "s3:GetObject",
 "s3:PutObject",
 "s3:DeleteObject",
 "s3:PutBucketPolicy"
 ],
 "Resource": "arn:aws:s3:::example-bucket/specific-folder/",
 "Effect": "Allow"
 }


C) {
 "Action": [
 "s3:GetObject",
 "s3:PutObject",
 "s3:DeleteObject",
 "s3:ListBucket"
 ],
 "Resource": "arn:aws:s3:::example-bucket/specific-folder/",
 "Effect": "Allow"
 }


D) {
 "Action": [
 "s3:GetObject",
 "s3:PutObject",
 "s3:DeleteObject",
 "s3:PutBucketPolicy"
 ],
 "Resource": "arn:aws:s3:::example-bucket/",
 "Effect": "Allow"
 }


E) {
 "Action": [
 "s3:GetObject",
 "s3:PutObject",
 "s3:DeleteObject",
 "s3:PutBucketPolicy"
 ],
 "Resource": "arn:aws:s3:::example-bucket",
 "Effect": "Allow"
 }
```

QUESTION 50

You are designing a data replication strategy for a multinational e-commerce company that operates in multiple regions. The company requires real-time synchronization of product inventory data across all regions to ensure consistent availability for customers. Which approach would best meet the company's requirements for high availability and performance?

A) Utilize AWS DataSync to replicate product inventory data between Amazon S3 buckets in each region, ensuring low-latency synchronization and efficient data transfer.

B) Implement Amazon Kinesis Data Streams to capture inventory updates in real-time, and then use AWS Lambda to process and distribute the data to regional databases deployed on Amazon RDS for high availability and scalability.

C) Deploy Amazon Aurora Global Database to replicate inventory data across multiple regions with minimal replication lag, ensuring read consistency and high availability for global customers.

D) Utilize Amazon DynamoDB global tables to replicate product inventory data across AWS regions, enabling multi-master replication for real-time updates and ensuring low-latency access for customers worldwide.

E) Implement AWS Database Migration Service (DMS) to continuously replicate product inventory data from the primary database to read replicas deployed in each region, ensuring high availability and scalability for global access.

QUESTION 51

A global e-commerce company wants to improve their website's performance worldwide by leveraging Amazon CloudFront and AWS Lambda@Edge. The primary goal is to reduce latency for end-users and handle dynamic content personalization. Which configuration will most effectively meet these requirements?

A) Use Amazon CloudFront with default cache settings and Lambda@Edge for dynamic content.

B) Configure Amazon CloudFront with geolocation routing and integrate AWS WAF for security, using Lambda@Edge for content personalization.

C) Deploy multiple Amazon EC2 instances across regions and use Amazon Route 53 for geolocation routing.

D) Use Amazon CloudFront with optimized cache settings based on user location and Lambda@Edge for both dynamic content personalization and security enhancements.

E) Implement an Amazon S3 bucket for static content delivery and Amazon EC2 for dynamic content without Amazon CloudFront.

QUESTION 52

A company wants to enforce a data retention policy that requires certain objects in an S3 bucket to be automatically deleted after a specified period. Which feature of S3 should be utilized to implement this policy?

A) "Action": ["s3:GetObject"], "Resource": ["arn:aws:s3:::example-bucket/"], "Effect": "Allow" (Read-Only Policy)

B) "Action": ["s3:PutObject"], "Resource": ["arn:aws:s3:::example-bucket/"], "Effect": "Deny" (Deny Modification)

C) "Action": ["s3:GetObject"], "s3:PutObject"], "Resource": ["arn:aws:s3:::example-bucket/"], "Effect": "Allow" (Read and Write Access)

D) "Action": ["s3:ListBucket"], "s3:GetObject"], "Resource": ["arn:aws:s3:::example-bucket/"], "Effect": "Allow" (List and Read Access)

E) "Action": ["s3:GetObject"], "s3:DeleteObject"], "Resource": ["arn:aws:s3:::example-bucket/*"], "Effect": "Allow" (Read and Delete Access)

QUESTION 53

Your company is launching a new e-commerce platform that expects fluctuating traffic patterns throughout the day. As the Solutions Architect, you aim to design a cost-effective solution to handle these variations efficiently. Which approach would best fulfill this requirement while leveraging AWS services?

A) Utilize Amazon EC2 Reserved Instances
B) Implement auto-scaling with Amazon EC2
C) Use Amazon Aurora for database hosting
D) Migrate the application to AWS Lambda
E) Utilize Amazon DynamoDB for NoSQL database needs

QUESTION 54

Your company operates a global e-commerce platform with customers in various regions. You need to design a cost-effective solution to ensure low-latency access for customers while minimizing data transfer costs. Which approach should you recommend?

A) Utilize Amazon CloudFront with AWS Global Accelerator for low-latency access
B) Implement AWS Direct Connect with Amazon Route 53 for optimized global routing
C) Deploy Amazon S3 Transfer Acceleration for faster data uploads
D) Opt for Amazon VPC Endpoint for Amazon S3 to reduce data transfer costs
E) Leverage AWS Transit Gateway for efficient routing between regions

QUESTION 55

A healthcare organization needs to ensure that only authorized personnel can access sensitive patient data stored in an Amazon S3 bucket. What solution should the solutions architect recommend to enforce secure access control?

A) Make the S3 bucket publicly accessible and rely on AWS Trusted Advisor to monitor access.
B) Enable server-side encryption for the S3 bucket to protect patient data at rest.
C) Implement IAM policies to restrict access to the S3 bucket based on the role of each user.
D) Create a VPN connection to the S3 bucket and grant access to authorized users through the VPN.
E) Configure S3 bucket policies to allow access only from specific IP addresses associated with authorized users.

QUESTION 56

Your company operates a web application that experiences highly variable traffic throughout the day. You need to design a cost-optimized compute scaling solution that can efficiently handle these fluctuations in demand. What approach should you take?

A) Utilize Amazon EC2 Auto Scaling with a target tracking scaling policy
B) Implement AWS Batch to dynamically scale compute resources based on workload demands
C) Leverage AWS Lambda with provisioned concurrency to handle peak traffic efficiently
D) Deploy Amazon ECS with capacity providers for automatic scaling of containerized workloads
E) Utilize AWS Outposts for on-premises compute scaling alongside AWS CloudWatch alarms

QUESTION 57

Your company operates a large e-commerce platform that heavily relies on a multi-tiered architecture. The database tier, powered by Amazon RDS, hosts critical customer data. However, recent performance analysis indicates that database costs are escalating due to inefficient resource allocation. As a solutions architect, you are tasked with optimizing Amazon RDS costs without compromising performance. What would be the most effective strategy in this scenario?

A) Implement Amazon RDS Multi-AZ deployment to enhance fault tolerance and reduce costs

B) Utilize Amazon RDS Reserved Instances to commit to a predefined usage period and receive a significant discount

C) Integrate Amazon RDS with Amazon ElastiCache to leverage in-memory caching and minimize database load

D) Configure Amazon RDS Performance Insights to analyze database performance metrics and identify cost-saving opportunities

E) Use Amazon RDS Automated Backups to streamline backup processes and lower storage costs

QUESTION 58

Your company is planning to migrate its web application to AWS to optimize costs while ensuring high availability and performance. The application experiences variable traffic throughout the day. As a solutions architect, you are tasked with designing a cost-effective architecture that can dynamically scale based on demand. Which of the following instance purchasing options would best meet the requirements?

A) Utilize AWS EC2 Reserved Instances for baseline capacity and supplement with AWS Spot Instances for additional capacity during traffic spikes

B) Implement AWS Savings Plans to ensure a consistent discount on all instance usage regardless of demand fluctuations

C) Combine AWS EC2 On-Demand Instances with AWS Lambda for serverless processing to eliminate the need for manual scaling

D) Deploy a mix of AWS EC2 On-Demand Instances and AWS Spot Instances, dynamically adjusting the ratio based on traffic patterns

E) Leverage AWS EC2 Dedicated Hosts to guarantee isolated hardware resources for the web application

QUESTION 59

Your company is running a web application that experiences variable traffic throughout the day. You are tasked with optimizing costs for the application's compute resources while ensuring performance. Which approach would best achieve this goal?

A) Utilize Amazon EC2 On-Demand Instances for consistent performance
B) Implement Amazon EC2 Spot Instances for cost savings during periods of low demand
C) Use a combination of Amazon EC2 On-Demand Instances and Spot Instances with Auto Scaling
D) Reserve Amazon EC2 instances for long-term cost predictability
E) Deploy AWS Fargate for serverless container management

QUESTION 60

A software development company is deploying a web application that experiences varying levels of traffic throughout the day. The company wants to ensure that the application can handle sudden traffic spikes without compromising performance. What Auto Scaling strategy should the solutions architect recommend?

A) Configure the Auto Scaling group to use a scheduled scaling policy triggered at specific times of peak traffic.

B) Implement an Auto Scaling group with a target tracking scaling policy based on the number of incoming HTTP requests.

C) Configure the Auto Scaling group to use a step scaling policy triggered by sudden increases in the number of requests per minute.

D) Utilize an Auto Scaling group with a simple scaling policy based on manual adjustments to instance counts.

E) Implement an Auto Scaling group with a predictive scaling policy based on historical traffic patterns.

QUESTION 61

Your company operates a global e-commerce platform that experiences high traffic volumes during seasonal sales events. To optimize costs while ensuring low-latency access to product images and videos worldwide, you need to design a solution that efficiently delivers multimedia content. Which approach should you recommend for this scenario?

A) Implement Amazon S3 Transfer Acceleration to optimize data transfers and reduce latency for media uploads

B) Use Amazon CloudFront with Lambda@Edge to cache and deliver multimedia content at edge locations

C) Deploy Amazon Elastic File System (Amazon EFS) to store multimedia files and enable fast access from multiple regions

D) Utilize AWS Direct Connect with AWS Transit Gateway to establish private connectivity between on-premises data centers and AWS regions

E) Implement Amazon Kinesis Video Streams to ingest and process live streaming multimedia content

QUESTION 62

Your company is developing a new web application that requires frequent testing and development in AWS. Cost optimization is crucial, and you need to design a solution that minimizes expenses while providing efficient testing environments. Which approach should you recommend?

A) Use AWS CloudFormation to create and manage development and testing environments
B) Deploy Amazon EC2 instances with On-Demand pricing for consistent testing environments
C) Utilize Amazon RDS for database testing with provisioned IOPS for optimal performance
D) Implement Amazon S3 Glacier for long-term storage of test data
E) Leverage AWS Direct Connect for dedicated network connectivity between development and testing environments

QUESTION 63

Your company is planning to expand its operations globally and wants to deploy its application in multiple AWS regions to ensure high availability and disaster recovery. However, the finance team is concerned about the potential increase in costs associated with deploying resources across multiple regions. As a solutions architect, you need to design a cost-efficient multi-region architecture that meets the company's requirements while minimizing expenses. What approach should you recommend?

A) Utilize Amazon Route 53 latency-based routing and AWS Global Accelerator to distribute traffic efficiently across multiple AWS regions

B) Deploy Amazon CloudFront with AWS Global Accelerator to optimize content delivery and reduce data transfer costs between regions

C) Implement Amazon DynamoDB global tables to replicate data across regions and ensure low-latency access for users

D) Leverage AWS Direct Connect with AWS Transit Gateway to establish private connectivity between regions and reduce data transfer costs

E) Utilize Amazon S3 cross-region replication to automatically replicate data between regions and ensure data durability and availability

QUESTION 64

Your company is planning to deploy a large-scale web application on AWS, which will serve millions of users worldwide. The application requires high availability, scalability, and cost efficiency. As a solutions architect, you need to recommend a cost-efficient deployment strategy for the application's backend services.

A) Utilize Amazon EC2 instances with AWS Auto Scaling to dynamically adjust capacity based on traffic patterns

B) Implement AWS Lambda functions with Amazon API Gateway to create a serverless backend that scales automatically

C) Deploy microservices using Amazon ECS Anywhere across on-premises servers and AWS to optimize resource utilization

D) Utilize Amazon RDS with Amazon Aurora Serverless to automatically adjust database capacity based on demand

E) Leverage Amazon S3 for static content storage and Amazon CloudFront for content delivery to reduce data transfer costs

QUESTION 65

Your company is looking to optimize costs by identifying and eliminating unused or underutilized AWS resources. As a solutions architect, you need to recommend a solution that automates resource optimization and provides actionable insights.

A) Utilize AWS Trusted Advisor to analyze resource utilization and recommend cost optimization opportunities

B) Utilize AWS Compute Optimizer to analyze resource utilization and recommend right-sizing of EC2 instances

C) Implement AWS Cost Explorer to identify unused resources and analyze cost trends over time

D) Utilize AWS Lambda with AWS CloudTrail to automate resource cleanup based on predefined rules

E) Leverage AWS Budgets to set and monitor cost limits for specific services and projects

PRACTICE TEST 6 - ANSWERS ONLY

QUESTION 1

Answer - A) Use AWS IAM Identity Center to establish trust between AWS accounts and the external directory service.

A) Correct - AWS IAM Identity Center (formerly AWS Single Sign-On) enables secure access to AWS accounts and business applications, using trust relationships with external identity providers. It streamlines access management across multiple AWS accounts without compromising security.

B) Incorrect - IAM policies cannot be directly attached to users in external directory services. AWS IAM Identity Center is the correct solution for federating access from an external directory.

C) Incorrect - Storing access credentials in Amazon S3 is not a secure or recommended method for managing federated access.

D) Incorrect - Automating the creation of IAM users with AWS Lambda does not leverage federation and complicates access management.

E) Incorrect - Amazon Cognito is primarily used for mobile and web application sign-in, not for managing federated access across multiple AWS accounts in this context.

QUESTION 2

Answer - B) Utilize AWS Secrets Manager for storing and rotating credentials and secrets.

A) Incorrect - Storing secrets in environment variables is less secure as they can be exposed to anyone who has access to the instances.

B) Correct - AWS Secrets Manager is specifically designed for securely storing and rotating sensitive credentials and secrets, which aligns with the security requirements of a financial institution's application.

C) Incorrect - Storing sensitive application configuration files in an Amazon S3 bucket with public access poses a significant security risk.

D) Incorrect - Embedding credentials directly in the application code is a poor security practice, making them hard to rotate and vulnerable to exposure.

E) Incorrect - While AWS Systems Manager Parameter Store is a viable option for managing configuration data and secrets, AWS Secrets Manager offers enhanced features specifically for the rotation of secrets, making it a better choice for handling credentials and secrets for high-security applications.

QUESTION 3

Answer - [A] Configure AWS Key Management Service (KMS) to encrypt data at rest and manage encryption keys for Amazon RDS instances.

Option A - Correct. Configuring AWS KMS to encrypt data at rest and manage encryption keys for Amazon RDS instances ensures security and compliance with industry regulations.

Option B - Amazon RDS Enhanced Monitoring collects performance metrics but may not directly address security and compliance requirements.

Option C - AWS Database Migration Service securely migrates databases but may not directly ensure security and compliance for Amazon RDS instances.

Option D - AWS Certificate Manager provisions SSL/TLS certificates but may not directly address data encryption and compliance for Amazon RDS instances.

Option E - Enabling Amazon RDS database encryption at the instance level helps encrypt data in transit but may not cover data encryption at rest and compliance requirements as comprehensively as AWS KMS.

QUESTION 4

Answer - [D] Utilize AWS Elastic Beanstalk to automatically manage the deployment, scaling, and load balancing of the application across multiple AZs. Implement Amazon RDS Multi-AZ deployment for database redundancy and failover.

Option D - Correct. AWS Elastic Beanstalk automates the deployment and management of the application across multiple AZs, providing high availability. Amazon RDS Multi-AZ deployment ensures database redundancy and failover.

Option A - While EC2 Auto Scaling and RDS Multi-AZ deployment provide some level of fault tolerance, Elastic Beanstalk offers a more automated and comprehensive solution for managing application deployment and scaling.

Option B - Deploying EC2 instances in separate regions may introduce additional latency and complexity, and Aurora Global Database is not necessary for AZ-level fault tolerance.

Option C - While EC2 instances in an Auto Scaling group and RDS Read Replicas offer scalability, they do not provide the same level of fault tolerance as Elastic Beanstalk and RDS Multi-AZ deployment.

Option E - Deploying EC2 instances in a single AZ with Elastic Load Balancing introduces a single point of failure and does not provide sufficient fault tolerance for AZ failures.

QUESTION 5

Answer - C) Use Amazon SQS FIFO queue with a batch mode of 10 messages per operation.

C) Use Amazon SQS FIFO queue with a batch mode of 10 messages per operation - This option ensures prompt and accurate processing of shipment status updates by processing multiple updates in a batch, meeting the company's requirement for timely processing and scalability during peak times. The FIFO guarantees order accuracy, and batch processing enhances efficiency.

A) Use Amazon SQS FIFO queue with exactly-once processing enabled - While ensuring order accuracy, it may not efficiently handle high volumes of updates due to sequential processing.

B) Use Amazon SQS FIFO queue with message deduplication enabled - While avoiding duplicate messages, it doesn't guarantee order processing, and may not efficiently handle high volumes of updates.

D) Use Amazon SQS standard queue to process the messages - Standard queues lack message ordering, which is crucial for maintaining shipment order, and may not efficiently handle high volumes of updates.

 E) Use Amazon SQS FIFO queue with default settings - Default settings may not ensure prompt and accurate processing of updates, especially during peak times, and may not efficiently handle high volumes of updates.

QUESTION 6

Answer - [A] Create IAM roles with specific permissions for each Lambda function, and use IAM policies to control access to S3 buckets and DynamoDB tables.

Option A - Correct. Creating IAM roles with specific permissions for each Lambda function and using IAM policies to control access to S3 buckets and DynamoDB tables ensures fine-grained access control for the serverless application.

 Option B - Using IAM users with custom policies and IAM groups may lead to unnecessary complexity and does not align with best practices for serverless architectures.

 Option C - While IAM policies can be attached to S3 buckets and DynamoDB tables, using IAM roles for cross-service authentication is the recommended approach for Lambda functions accessing other AWS services.

 Option D - Setting up IAM policies at the account level may result in over-permissioned roles and does not provide fine-grained access control for individual resources.

 Option E - While IAM policies with condition keys and IAM roles for federated access are valid, they may not provide the same level of control and granularity required for a serverless application's security needs.

QUESTION 7

Answer - [B] Configuring AWS Network Firewall with custom rules.

A) Incorrect - Security groups and network ACLs offer basic network security measures but lack the advanced capabilities required for highly secure architectures.

B) Correct - Configuring AWS Network Firewall with custom rules provides advanced network security measures, allowing fine-grained control over traffic filtering and protection against various types of threats.

C) Incorrect - AWS WAF and AWS Shield primarily focus on web application security and DDoS protection, respectively, which may not address all aspects of advanced network security.

D) Incorrect - AWS Firewall Manager helps manage security policies across multiple AWS accounts and resources but may not provide the level of granular control needed for advanced network security.

E) Incorrect - AWS Transit Gateway with AWS VPN provides scalable and secure connectivity between on-premises networks and AWS, but it's not specifically designed for implementing advanced network security measures.

QUESTION 8

Answer - [A] Implementing AWS WAF with rules to filter incoming web traffic.

A) Correct - AWS WAF (Web Application Firewall) is specifically designed to protect web applications against common attacks by allowing you to create rules to filter incoming web traffic and mitigate threats such as SQL injection and XSS.

B) Incorrect - Amazon Cognito is primarily used for user authentication and authorization and may not directly address protection against web-based attacks.

C) Incorrect - Amazon API Gateway is used for creating and managing APIs, and while it can provide some security features like rate limiting and authentication, it may not offer the same level of protection against web-based attacks as AWS WAF.

D) Incorrect - AWS Shield Advanced provides DDoS protection but does not specifically address web application security.

E) Incorrect - AWS KMS is used for encrypting data at rest and does not directly address protection against web-based attacks.

QUESTION 9

Answer - [A] Implementing mutual TLS authentication between microservices in Amazon ECS, ensuring secure communication and compliance with encryption standards.

A) Implementing mutual TLS authentication between microservices in Amazon ECS ensures secure communication by verifying the identity of each service and encrypting data in transit, meeting compliance requirements for encryption standards.

B) While AWS App Mesh manages traffic between microservices, it may not directly enforce encryption or address compliance with encryption standards for data in transit.

C) AWS Lambda authorizers in Amazon API Gateway handle authentication and authorization for APIs but may not directly address secure communication between microservices or compliance with encryption standards.

D) AWS PrivateLink provides private communication between services but may not explicitly enforce encryption or compliance with encryption standards for data in transit.

E) AWS WAF filters traffic but does not directly handle secure communication between microservices or ensure compliance with encryption standards for data in transit.

QUESTION 10

Answer - A) Use Amazon FSx File Gateway to provide low-latency, on-premises access to fully managed file shares in Amazon EFS. The applications deployed on AWS can access this data directly from Amazon EFS.

A) Use Amazon FSx File Gateway to provide low-latency, on-premises access to fully managed file shares in Amazon EFS. The applications deployed on AWS can access this data directly from Amazon EFS - This option aligns with the requirement by suggesting the use of Amazon FSx File Gateway with Amazon EFS, ensuring low-latency access to client files during and after migration.

B) Use Amazon Storage Gateway's File Gateway to provide low-latency, on-premises access to fully managed file shares in Amazon FSx for Windows File Server. The applications deployed on AWS can access this data directly from Amazon FSx in AWS - This option does not align with the requirement as it suggests using FSx for Windows File Server instead of Amazon EFS, which may not meet the low-latency access requirement.

C) Use AWS Storage Gateway's File Gateway to provide low-latency, on-premises access to fully managed file shares in Amazon S3. The applications deployed on AWS can access this data directly from Amazon S3 - This option does not align with the requirement as it suggests using Amazon S3 instead of Amazon EFS, which may not meet the low-latency access requirement.

D) Use Amazon FSx File Gateway to provide low-latency, on-premises access to fully managed file shares in Amazon FSx for Windows File Server. The applications deployed on AWS can access this data directly from Amazon FSx in AWS - This option does not align with the requirement as it suggests using FSx for Windows File Server instead of Amazon EFS, which may not meet the low-latency access requirement.

QUESTION 11

Answer - A) Use Amazon S3 with default encryption, S3 bucket policies for access control, and Amazon Macie for data classification and protection.

A) Use Amazon S3 with default encryption, S3 bucket policies for access control, and Amazon Macie for data classification and protection. - Correct because S3 provides scalable storage, default encryption, and access control policies align with HIPAA requirements. Macie enhances security by classifying and protecting sensitive data.

B) Deploy Amazon EFS with encryption at rest enabled, IAM policies for access control, and AWS KMS for key management. - Incorrect because EFS is optimized for file storage and might not offer the same level of data classification and protection as Macie for patient records.

C) Implement Amazon FSx for Windows File Server with automatic backups, AWS Shield for DDoS protection, and VPC endpoints for secure data transit. - Incorrect as FSx provides file storage for Windows applications and its features do not directly address HIPAA compliance for patient records as well as Macie does.

D) Utilize AWS Backup with cross-region backup capabilities, Amazon GuardDuty for threat detection, and AWS IAM roles for access management. - Incorrect because, while it ensures data protection and security monitoring, it does not offer the specific data classification and protection capabilities of Macie.

E) Configure Amazon S3 with server-side encryption (SSE) using AWS KMS, S3 access points for managing data access, and S3 lifecycle policies for data retention. - Incorrect because, although it provides secure and managed data access, it lacks the explicit mention of data classification and additional protection that Macie offers.

QUESTION 12

Answer - B) Implement AWS CloudFormation to automate secure deployment and AWS Config to track environment changes.

A) Use AWS Elastic Beanstalk with environment properties for secret management and enable AWS CloudTrail for monitoring configuration changes. - Incorrect because, while Elastic Beanstalk and

CloudTrail provide application management and monitoring, this option doesn't fully address the automation of secure deployment practices.

B) Implement AWS CloudFormation to automate secure deployment and AWS Config to track environment changes. - Correct as CloudFormation allows for the infrastructure to be defined as code, ensuring consistent and repeatable deployments, while AWS Config tracks changes, aiding in security and compliance.

C) Deploy the application using AWS CodeDeploy, integrate AWS Key Management Service for encryption, and use Amazon CloudWatch for real-time monitoring. - Incorrect because, although this combination secures deployment and monitors the application, it lacks the comprehensive environment and configuration management provided by CloudFormation and AWS Config.

D) Leverage AWS CodePipeline for continuous integration/continuous delivery (CI/CD), AWS WAF for application security, and AWS Shield for DDoS protection. - Incorrect as it focuses on CI/CD and protection mechanisms but does not address infrastructure as code and configuration tracking.

E) Configure AWS Elastic Beanstalk to use custom AMIs hardened according to AWS best practices, and establish IAM roles with limited permissions for application deployment. - Incorrect because, while using hardened AMIs and restricted IAM roles is a good practice, it doesn't offer the same level of deployment automation and change tracking as CloudFormation and AWS Config.

QUESTION 13

Answer - C) Implement Amazon GuardDuty for threat detection, AWS Security Hub for security monitoring, and AWS Step Functions for automated remediation workflows.

A) Utilize Amazon CloudWatch for monitoring, AWS Lambda for automated response, and AWS CloudTrail for logging and detecting anomalies. - Incorrect because, while these services are critical for monitoring and automation, they do not provide the comprehensive threat detection and security posture management offered by GuardDuty and Security Hub.

B) Deploy AWS Shield Advanced for DDoS protection, Amazon Inspector for vulnerability assessments, and AWS Config for configuration tracking. - Incorrect as these services focus on specific aspects of security, such as DDoS protection and vulnerability assessments, without offering the integrated threat detection and automated response workflow required.

C) Implement Amazon GuardDuty for threat detection, AWS Security Hub for security monitoring, and AWS Step Functions for automated remediation workflows. - Correct because GuardDuty and Security Hub offer comprehensive monitoring and threat detection, while Step Functions allow for the orchestration of automated response actions, aligning with the firm's need for a robust incident response plan.

D) Configure Amazon S3 event notifications to trigger AWS Lambda functions for incident responses, and use Amazon Macie for sensitive data discovery and protection. - Incorrect because, although effective for specific scenarios like data protection, this option doesn't provide the broader incident detection and response capabilities required.

E) Leverage AWS WAF for real-time web traffic monitoring, AWS IAM Access Analyzer for analyzing permissions, and AWS Key Management Service (AWS KMS) for data encryption management. - Incorrect as these tools focus more on perimeter defense, permission analysis, and encryption, not on the comprehensive incident response and forensic analysis capabilities needed.

QUESTION 14

Answer - [A] Utilize AWS Key Management Service (KMS) for encryption and key management, implementing envelope encryption with AWS KMS customer master keys (CMKs) and AWS CloudHSM for hardware-based key storage.

Option A - Correct. Utilizing AWS KMS for encryption and key management, implementing envelope encryption with AWS KMS CMKs, and integrating AWS CloudHSM for hardware-based key storage aligns with the requirement for compliance and security in handling sensitive patient data.

Option B - Server-side encryption with Amazon S3 may provide encryption at rest, but it does not address the need for key management and hardware-based key storage as required by strict regulatory requirements.

Option C - While encrypting data in Amazon DynamoDB is essential, managing encryption keys in an S3 bucket with restricted access permissions may not meet the stringent requirements for compliance and security.

Option D - Using AWS CloudTrail for auditing and monitoring, along with IAM roles for access control, is important but does not specifically address encryption and key management for sensitive patient data.

Option E - While AWS Secrets Manager can manage encryption keys and automate rotation, it may not provide the same level of control and compliance as utilizing AWS KMS and AWS CloudHSM for encryption and key management.

QUESTION 15

Answer - B) Suspend the ReplaceUnhealthy process type for the Auto Scaling group and apply the maintenance patch to the instance. Once the instance is ready, manually set the instance's health status back to healthy and activate the ReplaceUnhealthy process type again.

B) Suspend the ReplaceUnhealthy process type for the Auto Scaling group and apply the maintenance patch to the instance - This option effectively addresses the maintenance challenge by suspending the process responsible for replacing unhealthy instances, allowing the maintenance to proceed without triggering Auto Scaling actions.

A) Suspend the Terminate process type for the Auto Scaling group and apply the maintenance patch to the instance - Suspending termination processes may not prevent instance replacement and may not efficiently address the maintenance challenge.

C) Stop the instance, apply the maintenance patch, and then start the instance - Stopping the instance may disrupt application availability, and manually starting it again may not align with the requirement for uninterrupted maintenance.

D) Temporarily suspend the AddToLoadBalancer process type for the Auto Scaling group and apply the maintenance patch to the instance - Suspending processes related to load balancer integration may not efficiently address the maintenance challenge and may not prevent instance replacement during maintenance.

E) Take a snapshot of the instance, create a new Amazon Machine Image (AMI), and then launch a new instance using this AMI - Creating a new instance from a snapshot introduces complexity and may not efficiently address the maintenance challenge, especially in scenarios where immediate fixes are required.

QUESTION 16

Answer - B) Generate IAM roles for each service with minimum necessary permissions and establish trust relationships.

A) Create a single IAM role with permissions for EC2, Lambda, and RDS, and attach it to each service - Incorrect because it does not follow the principle of least privilege.

B) Generate IAM roles for each service with minimum necessary permissions and establish trust relationships - Correct as it ensures that each service has only the permissions it needs, adhering to the principle of least privilege.

C) Utilize AWS Service Catalog to automatically assign roles based on the service template - Incorrect because it does not specifically address managing permissions securely.

D) Implement an IAM users group for the services and manually assign permissions as needed - Incorrect as it does not leverage the benefits of IAM roles for services.

E) Enable cross-account access between services using IAM roles with broad permissions - Incorrect due to not following the least privilege principle.

QUESTION 17

Answer - A) Implement Amazon CloudFront with AWS WAF for content delivery and security, use Auto Scaling groups within a VPC for scalability, and enable Amazon CloudWatch for monitoring.

A) Correct because CloudFront provides efficient global content delivery, AWS WAF offers robust web application security, Auto Scaling handles load variability, and CloudWatch enables comprehensive monitoring.

B) Incorrect as Route 53 and Fargate address DNS and container management, respectively, but do not provide a complete solution for scalable content delivery and security specific to user data within a video streaming service.

C) Incorrect because Global Accelerator improves application performance and S3 policies secure data, but this setup lacks a detailed approach to scalable infrastructure specifically tailored for video streaming.

D) Incorrect as ELB and RDS Multi-AZ support high availability, but do not specifically address efficient global content delivery or the platform's scalability needs for video streaming. Inspector offers security insights but is not focused on web application security.

E) Incorrect because VPC peering and Direct Connect focus on network connectivity, not global content delivery efficiency or scalability for peak loads. AWS Config governs resource configuration but does not directly contribute to the core requirements of efficient content delivery and user data protection.

QUESTION 18

Answer - [D] Deploy Amazon EC2 instances across multiple Availability Zones and configure Elastic Load Balancing for distributing incoming traffic. Utilize Amazon RDS Read Replicas for database scalability and read-heavy workloads.

Option A - While CloudFront and Lambda@Edge improve content delivery, Aurora Multi-Master does not directly address database scalability for read-heavy workloads.

Option B - While ECS and EFS facilitate containerized deployment and shared file storage, RDS Multi-AZ is more suitable for database high availability.

Option C - While Global Accelerator improves application performance and availability, it does not directly address database scalability like RDS Read Replicas.

Option E - While Route 53 and CloudFront with Lambda@Edge improve DNS routing and content delivery, Aurora Serverless does not directly address database scalability for read-heavy workloads.

QUESTION 19

Answer - [A] Store secrets as Kubernetes secrets within the cluster. Implement RBAC (Role-Based Access Control) to restrict access to secrets based on service identities.

Option B - While Secrets Manager can securely store and rotate secrets, managing Kubernetes secrets within the cluster is a more native approach and aligns with best practices for Kubernetes security.

Option C - Storing plaintext secrets within Kubernetes pods poses security risks and lacks encryption. Option D - Utilizing KMS for encrypting secrets within etcd is complex and may not align with standard Kubernetes practices for secret management.

Option E - Storing secrets directly in Docker images and using IAM policies for access control introduces security risks and lacks dynamic secret management capabilities.

Explanation for Choice A: Storing secrets as Kubernetes secrets within the cluster provides native support for secret management. Implementing RBAC allows for granular access control, enhancing security and compliance within the Kubernetes environment.

QUESTION 20

Answer - D) Create an Amazon CloudWatch metric filter to process AWS CloudTrail logs containing API call details. Establish an alarm based on this metric's rate to send an Amazon SNS notification to the required team.

D) Create an Amazon CloudWatch metric filter to process AWS CloudTrail logs containing API call details. Establish an alarm based on this metric's rate to send an Amazon SNS notification to the required team. - This option directly addresses the scenario by analyzing CloudTrail logs for unauthorized API queries and triggering real-time alerts using CloudWatch alarms and Amazon SNS notifications.

 A) Configure AWS CloudTrail to stream event data to Amazon Kinesis. Utilize Amazon Kinesis stream-level metrics in Amazon CloudWatch to trigger an AWS Lambda function that will initiate an error workflow. - While this option utilizes streaming data, it may introduce complexity and latency compared to directly analyzing CloudTrail logs for real-time alerts.

B) Leverage AWS Trusted Advisor to publish metrics about check results to Amazon CloudWatch. Set up an alarm to track status changes for checks in the Service Limits category for the APIs, triggering notifications when service quotas are exceeded. - While Trusted Advisor offers valuable insights, it may not directly address the need for real-time detection of unauthorized API queries.

C) Use Amazon Athena SQL queries against AWS CloudTrail log files stored in Amazon S3 buckets. Generate reports using Amazon QuickSight for managerial dashboards. - While this option provides insights, it may not offer real-time alerting capabilities as required in this scenario.

E) Implement AWS Config Rules to monitor API activity and define rules to detect unauthorized API calls. Configure AWS Config to trigger an AWS Lambda function upon rule evaluation to notify relevant stakeholders. - While AWS Config can monitor API activity, it may not provide real-time alerting capabilities for immediate incident response as required in this scenario.

QUESTION 21

Answer - B) Utilize AWS Lambda for serverless backend logic, Amazon API Gateway for managing APIs, Amazon Kinesis Video Streams for video ingestion, and Amazon CloudWatch for monitoring performance.

B) Correct because Lambda offers serverless backend logic, API Gateway manages APIs, Kinesis Video Streams handles video ingestion, and CloudWatch monitors performance, aligning with the requirement for low-latency streaming, high availability, and scalability in supporting interactive live streaming sessions with hundreds of participants simultaneously on an e-learning platform.

A) Incorrect because while EC2 Auto Scaling and RDS Multi-AZ offer scalability and resilience, they may not provide the same level of simplicity and flexibility as Lambda, API Gateway, and Kinesis Video Streams in handling varying numbers of participants dynamically and ensuring low-latency streaming.

C) Incorrect as ECS, RDS Read Replicas, Direct Connect, and S3 offer scalability and network connectivity, but they may not provide the same level of serverless scalability and real-time ingestion capabilities as Lambda, API Gateway, and Kinesis Video Streams for supporting interactive live streaming sessions with hundreds of participants simultaneously on an e-learning platform.

D) Incorrect because while EKS, DynamoDB, CloudFront, and Redshift offer scalability and analytics capabilities, they may not provide the same level of serverless processing and real-time ingestion capabilities as Lambda, API Gateway, Kinesis Video Streams, and CloudWatch for supporting interactive live streaming sessions with hundreds of participants simultaneously on an e-learning platform.

E) Incorrect as MSK, Lambda, S3 Glacier, and CloudFront offer streaming, serverless processing, archival storage, and content delivery, respectively, but they may not provide the same level of simplicity and scalability as Lambda, API Gateway, Kinesis Video Streams, and CloudWatch for supporting interactive live streaming sessions with hundreds of participants simultaneously on an e-learning platform.

QUESTION 22

Answer - [C) AWS Global Accelerator]

Option A involves Amazon Route 53 for DNS routing and latency-based routing, but it does not address optimized global networking for low latency.

Option B involves Amazon CloudFront for content delivery and edge caching, but it does not optimize global networking for low latency.

Option C is correct as AWS Global Accelerator provides optimized global networking with traffic flow management, reducing latency and improving availability.

Option D involves Amazon DynamoDB for a scalable NoSQL database but does not directly address global networking.

Option E involves Amazon EC2 Auto Scaling for adjusting compute capacity but does not optimize global networking for low latency.

QUESTION 23

Answer - [B] Implement Amazon RDS Multi-AZ deployment with automated failover for database redundancy and minimal downtime during DR events.]

Option B) is correct as it involves implementing a warm standby architecture using Amazon RDS Multi-AZ deployment, ensuring database redundancy and minimal downtime during DR events.

Option A) involves DNS failover but may not provide the same level of database redundancy and failover capabilities.

Option C) involves EC2 instances but may not provide automated failover for the database.
Option D) involves real-time replication but may not achieve the same level of database redundancy as Multi-AZ deployment.
Option E) involves S3 for data storage but may not address database failover requirements effectively.

QUESTION 24

Answer - B) Utilize Amazon Route 53 with AWS Global Accelerator for optimized routing

Option A: Implementing Direct Connect with VPN provides secure hybrid connectivity but does not optimize routing for global operations.

Option C: Configuring Transit Gateway with Direct Connect offers scalable network management but does not optimize routing for global operations.

Option D: Setting up Client VPN with Site-to-Site VPN provides remote access but does not optimize routing for global operations.

Option E: Deploying PrivateLink with Transit Gateway provides private connectivity but does not optimize routing for global operations.

QUESTION 25

Answer - A) Tier-1 (4 terabytes)

A) Tier-1 (4 terabytes) - Correct. Aurora prioritizes the failover based on tier numbers, with the lowest number being the highest priority, independent of storage size.

B) Tier-3 (8 terabytes) - Incorrect. Despite having more storage, it has a lower priority due to its tier number.

C) Tier-3 (4 terabytes) - Incorrect. It shares the same tier as another option but has less storage, although storage size is not the deciding factor for failover.

D) Tier-5 (8 terabytes) - Incorrect. This tier has a lower priority for failover compared to tiers 1 and 3.

E) Tier-5 (4 terabytes) - Incorrect. It is the least preferred option based on the combination of its failover tier and storage size, despite size not affecting failover priority.

QUESTION 26

Answer - B) Implement AWS CloudFormation to define infrastructure as code and manage the deployment of AWS resources in a declarative manner.

Option A is incorrect because while AWS CodeDeploy automates application deployment, it does not inherently support the principles of immutable infrastructure where the infrastructure is immutable and replaced rather than updated.

Option B is correct because AWS CloudFormation allows defining infrastructure as code, enabling the creation of immutable infrastructure and managing the deployment of AWS resources in a declarative manner, aligning with the goal of achieving immutable infrastructure on AWS.

Option C is incorrect because while Amazon EKS Anywhere facilitates Kubernetes deployment on-premises, it does not directly address the goal of achieving immutable infrastructure on AWS.

Option D is incorrect because while AWS Elastic Beanstalk automates application deployment, it may not inherently support the principles of immutable infrastructure.

Option E is incorrect because while AWS Lambda scales and executes code, it does not directly address the goal of achieving immutable infrastructure on AWS.

QUESTION 27

Answer - A) Utilize JWT authorizers with Amazon API Gateway to validate JWT tokens against an identity provider

Option A - JWT authorizers with Amazon API Gateway validate JWT tokens against an identity provider, providing fine-grained access control to microservices.

Option B - AWS Lambda authorizers execute custom logic but may not offer the simplicity and scalability of JWT authorizers for token validation.

Option C - IAM role-based authorizers authenticate users based on IAM roles, which may not be suitable for fine-grained access control in microservices.

Option D - OAuth 2.0 authorizers with Amazon Cognito are more focused on user authentication and may not offer the flexibility needed for microservices authorization.

Option E - Custom authorizers with AWS Lambda require additional complexity and may not offer the out-of-the-box functionality provided by JWT authorizers.

QUESTION 28

Answer - C) Opt for Amazon EKS with AWS Fargate for serverless compute, Amazon ECR for container image management, and AWS Shield for DDoS protection.

A) Incorrect because, while EKS is highly scalable and secure, RDS Multi-AZ and CloudFront are not directly related to container orchestration's scalability and cost-effectiveness.

B) Partially correct, ECS with Fargate is cost-effective and scalable, but EFS might not be the optimal choice for all container storage needs, and WAF, while important for security, doesn't cover the scalability aspect of container orchestration.

C) Correct, EKS with Fargate offers serverless compute, removing the need to manage servers and scaling automatically, ECR provides a secure location to store and manage container images, and AWS Shield offers DDoS protection, enhancing the architecture's security.

D) Incorrect, ECS with EC2 launch type requires managing servers, which might not be as cost-effective or scalable as a serverless option. DynamoDB and API Gateway are useful but don't fully address the question's requirements regarding container orchestration.

E) Incorrect, while EKS and ECR are suitable choices, App Mesh and ELB focus more on networking and less on the scalability and cost-effectiveness of container orchestration.

QUESTION 29

Answer - C) Implement Amazon DynamoDB Global Tables for multi-region replication and automatic failover.

A) Aurora Global Database offers cross-region replication but may not provide the same level of automatic failover as DynamoDB Global Tables.

B) RDS Multi-AZ deployment only provides redundancy within the same region.

D) ElastiCache supports replication but may not offer automatic failover across regions.

E) Redshift cross-region snapshots are for disaster recovery and data synchronization but do not provide automatic failover for active workloads.

QUESTION 30

Answer - D) Utilize Amazon Kinesis Data Streams with AWS Lambda for real-time data processing and store it in Amazon S3

D) Amazon Kinesis Data Streams combined with AWS Lambda offers real-time data processing capabilities suitable for analyzing GPS data, optimizing delivery routes, ensuring on-time deliveries, and providing insights into route optimization with accuracy and scalability.

A, B) These options involve storing data in relational databases or data warehouses, which may not be suitable for real-time processing and scalability required for tracking shipment movements.

C, E) While these options involve using AWS Lambda and Amazon DynamoDB or S3, they may not provide the real-time processing capabilities required for optimizing delivery routes and ensuring on-time deliveries.

QUESTION 31

Answer - A) Use AWS Config for continuous compliance monitoring, AWS CloudTrail for governance, AWS Lambda for automated security responses, and Amazon GuardDuty for threat detection.

A) Correct, as this combination offers comprehensive security and compliance automation. AWS Config and CloudTrail provide visibility into resource configuration and activity for compliance monitoring and governance. Lambda enables automated security responses, and GuardDuty offers intelligent threat detection.

 B) Incorrect because, while these services enhance security, they do not offer a comprehensive solution for compliance automation and real-time security incident response as efficiently as the services listed in A.

 C) Incorrect as these services focus on specific security and encryption needs but do not provide the overall compliance monitoring and automated response system necessary for a financial institution's requirements.

 D) Incorrect because these services are more focused on infrastructure and storage rather than the comprehensive security, compliance, and automation needs of a financial institution.

 E) Incorrect as these services are geared towards application development and do not directly address the compliance and security automation requirements.

QUESTION 32

Answer - [A] Implement Amazon RDS with Multi-AZ deployment and utilize read replicas for scaling read operations during peak hours.]

Option A - Correct because Amazon RDS with Multi-AZ deployment ensures high availability and minimal data loss, while read replicas help scale read operations, meeting the institution's requirements for disaster recovery.

Option B - Incorrect because Aurora Serverless may not provide the necessary performance and scalability for critical database workloads during a disaster recovery scenario.

Option C - Incorrect because DynamoDB, while offering scalability, may not provide the same level of features for disaster recovery and rapid recovery as Amazon RDS Multi-AZ deployment.

Option D - Incorrect because Redshift is optimized for analytics and may not offer the same level of disaster recovery features as Amazon RDS Multi-AZ deployment.

Option E - Incorrect because DocumentDB may not offer the same level of disaster recovery capabilities as Amazon RDS Multi-AZ deployment.

QUESTION 33

Answer - [B] Implement OAuth 2.0 authentication with Amazon Cognito.

Option A is incorrect as API Gateway with AWS IAM authorization does not provide user authentication. Option C is incorrect because while AWS WAF can protect API endpoints, it's not directly related to authentication.

Option D is incorrect as AWS Shield is focused on DDoS protection, not API authentication.

Option E is incorrect as storing sensitive data in plaintext within Lambda environment variables is a security risk.

Option B is correct because OAuth 2.0 authentication with Amazon Cognito is a recommended approach for securing API communication in a microservices architecture. This approach provides robust user authentication and authorization mechanisms.

QUESTION 34

Answer - [A) Utilize Amazon EC2 instances with Auto Scaling groups and Amazon EBS volumes.]

Option A provides a cost-effective solution by using Amazon EC2 instances with Auto Scaling groups, which automatically adjust the number of instances based on traffic, ensuring scalability. Amazon EBS volumes provide persistent storage for the instances.

Option B, while serverless, may not be the most cost-effective for variable traffic.
Option C introduces unnecessary complexity and may not be the most cost-efficient.

Option D, AWS Outposts, is not typically used for variable workloads.
Option E, AWS Wavelength, is designed for ultra-low latency and may not be the most cost-effective solution for this scenario.

QUESTION 35

Answer - E) Configure RESTful APIs on Amazon API Gateway with Amazon ElastiCache for storing flight information and Amazon Simple Notification Service (SNS) for sending notifications to users

E) Configuring RESTful APIs on Amazon API Gateway with Amazon ElastiCache for storing flight information and utilizing Amazon SNS ensures timely notifications to users about flight delays or cancellations, meeting the requirements of the travel booking platform.

A, B, C, D) These options either do not provide efficient storage and notification capabilities or involve using services not suitable for real-time notification systems.

QUESTION 36

Answer - [B, E]

A) Incorrect - While RDS encryption at rest is relevant, ACM is used for SSL/TLS certificates but not directly for encrypting data in transit.

B) Correct - S3 server-side encryption with KMS managed keys covers data at rest, and SSL/TLS ensures data in transit encryption, meeting the requirements effectively.

C) Incorrect - Aurora encryption at rest is relevant, but CloudHSM is not typically used for Aurora encryption key storage.

D) Incorrect - DynamoDB client-side encryption is suitable for data at rest, and Secrets Manager manages secrets but doesn't directly address data encryption.

E) Correct - Redshift encryption at rest coupled with KMS for key management ensures data security at rest and in transit, aligning with compliance and security requirements.

QUESTION 37

Answer - B) Amazon S3 with Transfer Acceleration enabled and lifecycle policies configured.

A) Incorrect - EBS volumes provide block storage for EC2 instances but aren't designed for global content delivery or to handle sudden spikes in demand without additional configuration.

B) Correct - Amazon S3 with Transfer Acceleration improves the upload speed of media files globally, and lifecycle policies help manage costs by automating transitions to less expensive storage classes or deleting outdated content. It's scalable, secure, and cost-effective, suitable for global CDN requirements.

C) Incorrect - EFS provides a scalable file storage solution but is more suited for use cases requiring shared access to files, and it doesn't inherently optimize for global content delivery latency.

D) Incorrect - RDS is a managed relational database service for structured data, not optimized for serving media files as a CDN.

E) Incorrect - AWS Storage Gateway extends on-premises storage to AWS, but it's not optimized for global media file delivery and lacks the scalability required for sudden demand spikes.

QUESTION 38

Answer - A) Implement Amazon RDS Multi-AZ deployment with read replicas to distribute read traffic across multiple availability zones.

Option A - Amazon RDS Multi-AZ deployment with read replicas ensures high availability and efficient distribution of read traffic, optimizing database read performance.

Option B - Amazon ElastiCache for Redis caches frequently accessed data, reducing database load and improving read performance.

Option C - Amazon Aurora Multi-Master allows simultaneous write operations across multiple database instances but does not directly address read performance optimization.

Option D - Amazon DynamoDB global tables replicate data for disaster recovery and high availability but may not be the best choice for optimizing read performance in this scenario.

Option E - Amazon Redshift Spectrum offloads read queries to data stored in Amazon S3, which may not be suitable for optimizing real-time database read performance.

QUESTION 39

Answer - A) Utilize AWS DataSync to transfer data from on-premises servers to Amazon S3, and configure Amazon Kinesis Data Streams to process real-time financial transactions.

Option A - AWS DataSync provides scalable data transfer capabilities from on-premises to Amazon S3, while Amazon Kinesis Data Streams enables real-time processing of financial transactions, meeting the requirements for scalability, security, and high availability.

Option B - While AWS Transfer Family and AWS Glue are relevant services, they do not directly address the need for real-time processing of financial transactions.

Option C - Amazon CloudFront with AWS Shield and AWS Step Functions are not designed for real-time data processing, making this option less suitable for the scenario.

QUESTION 40

Answer - C) Ingest sensor data into Amazon Kinesis Data Streams, which triggers an AWS Lambda function for processing and stores maintenance schedules in Amazon DynamoDB

C) Ingesting sensor data into Amazon Kinesis Data Streams with AWS Lambda allows for real-time processing and proactive scheduling of maintenance. Storing maintenance schedules in Amazon DynamoDB ensures low-latency access and scalability.

A) Processing sensor data with AWS Lambda and Amazon S3 may introduce latency and is not suitable for real-time predictive maintenance systems.

B) Using Amazon Kinesis Data Firehose may not provide the necessary real-time processing capabilities for scheduling maintenance proactively.

D) Amazon SQS is not optimized for real-time processing of sensor data, and storing maintenance schedules in Amazon Redshift may introduce delays.

E) Using Amazon API Gateway and an EC2 instance for processing lacks the scalability and real-time processing capabilities required for predictive maintenance systems.

QUESTION 41

Answer - A) AWS Lambda for data processing, Amazon Kinesis for real-time data streaming, and Amazon DynamoDB for secure and scalable storage.

A) Correct - AWS Lambda offers fast execution and scalability for algorithmic trading calculations. Amazon Kinesis facilitates real-time data streaming with low latency, essential for market trend analysis. Amazon DynamoDB provides a secure and scalable database solution for storing trading data.

B) Incorrect - While EC2 Auto Scaling and S3 are scalable, they might not offer the real-time processing capability required for high-frequency trading. AWS Shield is primarily for DDoS protection, not comprehensive financial data security.

C) Incorrect - SNS and Step Functions are suitable for workflow management and notifications but may not fulfill real-time data processing and ultra-low latency requirements. RDS Multi-AZ is secure but not optimal for high-speed transactional workloads expected in trading platforms.

D) Incorrect - API Gateway and Lambda are good for managing APIs and backend processing, but Cognito focuses on user authentication, not addressing the primary need for real-time data processing and trade execution.

E) Incorrect - AWS Fargate and SQS provide container management and message queuing, but they do not specifically address the real-time processing and security requirements for financial trading data. AWS KMS offers data encryption, but the scenario demands more comprehensive security and real-time processing capabilities.

QUESTION 42

Answer - [C) Utilize AWS Transit Gateway to simplify network connectivity and routing between your on-premises data center and AWS.]

Option C) AWS Transit Gateway simplifies network connectivity and routing, providing seamless integration between your on-premises environment and AWS. It allows you to centrally manage connectivity and routing policies.

Option A) AWS Direct Connect offers a dedicated network connection but may not provide the same level of flexibility and ease of management as Transit Gateway.

Option B) AWS VPN offers encrypted connectivity but may not be as scalable or efficient as Transit Gateway for large-scale hybrid environments.

Option D) AWS Site-to-Site VPN tunnels over the internet, similar to AWS VPN, but Transit Gateway offers centralized management and scalability advantages.

Option E) AWS Global Accelerator is primarily used for improving global application availability and performance, not specifically for hybrid cloud connectivity.

QUESTION 43

Answer - A) Utilize Amazon CloudFront with AWS Shield for content delivery and DDoS protection, Amazon S3 for storing static content, AWS Lambda@Edge for dynamic content processing, and Amazon Route 53 for DNS management.

Option A - Correct. This solution covers all aspects of the scenario, offering a global reach with CloudFront and Shield for content delivery and security, S3 for static content, Lambda@Edge for dynamic content at edge locations, and Route 53 for DNS management, ensuring high availability and low latency.

Option B - Incorrect. While this setup provides a robust infrastructure with EC2, RDS, and CloudFront, it lacks the edge location processing and direct DDoS protection capabilities that are crucial for global application deployment and security.

Option C - Incorrect. Global Accelerator and ELB improve performance, but EFS is not ideal for global deployments due to its region-specific nature, and this option does not address static and dynamic content delivery optimization.

Option D - Incorrect. CloudFront, Fargate, and DynamoDB address many requirements, but Outposts for local processing, while useful, might not be the most cost-effective or scalable option for global expansion in this scenario.

Option E - Incorrect. Direct Connect, VPN, S3, Glacier, AppSync, and GuardDuty provide a secure and synchronized environment but fail to offer a comprehensive solution for dynamic content delivery and real-time processing at the edge.

QUESTION 44

Answer - [B] Implement Amazon SageMaker for distributed training and inference, utilizing Amazon EFS for shared model storage and Amazon CloudWatch for monitoring.

Option A lacks distributed training for high-performance models and shared storage capability.
Option C's use of AWS Lambda may introduce latency for real-time inference.

Option D's batch inference may not meet the requirement for low-latency predictions.
Option E does not leverage shared storage, which is crucial for distributed training.

Option B allows for both distributed training and shared storage, meeting the requirement for high-performance and low-latency predictions.

QUESTION 45

Answer - B) Implement server-side encryption with AWS Key Management Service (SSE-KMS) and utilize AWS CloudTrail for monitoring

B) Implementing server-side encryption with AWS Key Management Service (SSE-KMS) allows the technology startup to manage encryption keys programmatically via an API and integrate key usage with existing logging and monitoring systems.

A) Server-side encryption with Amazon S3 managed keys (SSE-S3) encrypts the data at rest but may not provide the desired level of control and programmability for key management.

C) Client-side encryption with customer-provided keys (SSE-C) shifts the responsibility of encryption to the client and may not align with the startup's requirement for centralized key management.

D) Implementing server-side encryption with customer-provided keys (SSE-C) and developing custom logging and monitoring solutions introduces complexity and may not offer the same level of integration as AWS KMS and CloudTrail.

E) Enabling AWS CloudTrail provides auditing capabilities but does not directly address the encryption and key management requirements for data at rest in Amazon S3.

QUESTION 46

Answer - [D] Deploy the web application on AWS Fargate for serverless compute, store dynamic data in Amazon DynamoDB, cache frequently accessed data in Amazon ElastiCache, configure Amazon CloudFront for content delivery, and leverage Amazon Route 53 for global DNS routing.

Option A is incorrect because deploying the application on EC2 instances requires managing infrastructure, which may not be as scalable and resilient as a serverless approach like AWS Fargate.

Option B is incorrect because while serverless compute with AWS Lambda is scalable, DynamoDB is better suited for dynamic data storage in this scenario, and ECS is not as fully managed as AWS Fargate.

Option C is incorrect because although Amazon ECS is a container orchestration service, AWS Fargate provides a more serverless and scalable approach for running containers. RDS may introduce management overhead compared to using DynamoDB for dynamic data storage.

Option E is incorrect because although Amazon Aurora is a highly scalable and resilient database, it may not be the best choice for this scenario compared to DynamoDB, especially when combined with serverless compute using AWS Fargate.

QUESTION 47

Answer - [B] Implement serverless functions with AWS Lambda for handling user requests, Amazon DynamoDB for storing user data, and Amazon S3 for static content storage.

Option B is the correct choice because serverless functions with AWS Lambda enable automatic scaling based on demand, while DynamoDB offers automatic scaling and high availability. Storing static content in Amazon S3 ensures high availability and performance. Options A, C, D, and E either lack the same level of scalability, high availability, or suitable services for the specified requirements.

QUESTION 48

Answer - A) Utilize Amazon Inspector to monitor any malicious activity on data stored in Amazon S3. Use security assessments provided by Amazon GuardDuty to check for vulnerabilities on Amazon EC2 instances.

Option A - This choice provides a comprehensive security solution by leveraging Amazon Inspector for monitoring S3 data and Amazon GuardDuty for checking EC2 instances, ensuring robust protection against malicious activities and vulnerabilities.

Option B - While Amazon Inspector is suitable for monitoring, using it for Amazon RDS may not provide the same level of effectiveness in detecting vulnerabilities as when it is used with Amazon S3.

Option C - Although Amazon GuardDuty is effective for monitoring S3, using it for RDS instances may not yield accurate results as it's designed primarily for EC2 instances.

Option D - While Amazon GuardDuty is effective for monitoring S3, using Amazon Inspector for EC2 instances may not provide comprehensive coverage for detecting malicious activities on S3.

Option E - Although AWS Security Hub provides monitoring capabilities, it's not specifically tailored for monitoring S3 data and may not integrate seamlessly with Amazon GuardDuty for EC2 instance vulnerability assessments.

QUESTION 49

Answer - A) {
"Action": [
"s3:GetObject",
"s3:PutObject",
"s3:DeleteObject"
],
"Resource": "arn:aws:s3:::example-bucket/specific-folder/",
"Effect": "Allow"
}

A) This option grants the vendor permissions to read, write, and delete objects within the specific folder, adhering to the requirement of restricting access to only that folder.

B) Allowing the vendor to modify the bucket policy violates the requirement, as they should not have permissions to alter bucket-level settings.

C) Granting the vendor permissions to list the entire bucket may expose other objects within the bucket, which is not aligned with the requirement.

D) This option grants the vendor excessive permissions by allowing them to modify the bucket policy, which is beyond the scope of the requirement.

E) Similar to option D, allowing the vendor to modify the bucket policy is unnecessary and violates the requirement of restricting access to only the specific folder.

QUESTION 50

Answer - D) Utilize Amazon DynamoDB global tables to replicate product inventory data across AWS regions, enabling multi-master replication for real-time updates and ensuring low-latency access for customers worldwide.

Option A introduces unnecessary complexity with AWS DataSync for a straightforward data replication task.

Option B involves manual processing with Lambda, which might introduce latency and scalability issues. Option C focuses on database replication but may not offer real-time synchronization required by the e-commerce company.

Option E, while utilizing DMS, lacks the real-time replication capability provided by DynamoDB global tables, making it less suitable for immediate data availability across regions.

QUESTION 51

Answer - B) Configure Amazon CloudFront with geolocation routing and integrate AWS WAF for security, using Lambda@Edge for content personalization.

A) - Incorrect because default cache settings may not provide the optimal performance for dynamic content.

B) - Correct as it leverages CloudFront for content delivery optimization and Lambda@Edge for content personalization, with AWS WAF integration enhancing security.

C) - Incorrect because it doesn't leverage the full capabilities of CloudFront and misses out on edge location benefits.

D) - Incorrect because, while it suggests optimized cache settings and Lambda@Edge, it lacks the integrated security aspect provided by AWS WAF.

E) - Incorrect as it does not utilize the edge locations for performance improvement.

QUESTION 52

Answer - A) Read-Only Policy.

A) This policy allows only the s3:GetObject action, which permits reading objects from the specified bucket, ensuring that the third-party application can only read objects without the ability to modify them.

B) This policy denies the s3:PutObject action, preventing the application from uploading or modifying objects in the bucket, but it does not address the requirement for read-only access.

C) This policy allows both s3:GetObject and s3:PutObject actions, which would grant the application unnecessary write permissions, violating the requirement for read-only access.

D) This policy allows both s3:ListBucket and s3:GetObject actions, providing unnecessary list permissions and allowing the application to delete objects, which is not required.

E) This policy allows both s3:GetObject and s3:DeleteObject actions, which would grant the application the ability to delete objects from the bucket, violating the requirement for read-only access.

QUESTION 53

Answer - [B] Implement auto-scaling with Amazon EC2.

Option A - Reserved Instances are not suitable for fluctuating traffic patterns as they provide capacity reservation for a fixed term, regardless of usage.

Option B - Correct. Implementing auto-scaling with Amazon EC2 allows resources to automatically adjust based on demand, ensuring cost-effectiveness.

Option C - While Amazon Aurora is a robust database service, it does not directly address the compute resource scaling requirements.

Option D - Migrating to AWS Lambda would entail re-architecting the application and might not be feasible depending on the existing workload.

Option E - While Amazon DynamoDB is a managed NoSQL database, it does not address the compute resource scaling requirements.

QUESTION 54

Answer - [A] Utilize Amazon CloudFront with AWS Global Accelerator for low-latency access.

Option A - Correct. Amazon CloudFront with AWS Global Accelerator provides low-latency access by caching content at edge locations and optimizing global routing, reducing data transfer costs.

Option B - Direct Connect with Route 53 improves routing but may not offer the same cost-effective low-latency access as CloudFront with Global Accelerator.

Option C - S3 Transfer Acceleration improves data upload speed but may not address low-latency access requirements.

Option D - While VPC Endpoint for S3 reduces data transfer costs, it does not directly address the need for low-latency access.

Option E - Transit Gateway facilitates routing between VPCs but may not offer the same low-latency access as CloudFront with Global Accelerator.

QUESTION 55

Answer - [C] Implement IAM policies to restrict access to the S3 bucket based on the role of each user.

A) Incorrect - Making the S3 bucket publicly accessible violates security best practices and exposes sensitive patient data to unauthorized access.

B) Incorrect - Enabling server-side encryption for the S3 bucket addresses data confidentiality but does not enforce access control, leaving patient data vulnerable to unauthorized access.

C) Correct - Implementing IAM policies to restrict access based on the role of each user ensures secure access control, allowing only authorized personnel to access sensitive patient data stored in the S3 bucket.

D) Incorrect - Creating a VPN connection adds unnecessary complexity and does not provide granular access control to restrict access to specific users or roles.

E) Incorrect - Configuring S3 bucket policies based on specific IP addresses is not scalable and may not effectively restrict access to authorized personnel who may access data from different locations or devices.

QUESTION 56

Answer - [A] Utilize Amazon EC2 Auto Scaling with a target tracking scaling policy.

Option A - Correct. Amazon EC2 Auto Scaling with a target tracking scaling policy automatically adjusts the number of Amazon EC2 instances to maintain steady, predictable performance at the lowest possible cost.

Option B - AWS Batch is suitable for batch computing, not for dynamically scaling web applications based on variable traffic.

Option C - While AWS Lambda can efficiently handle peak traffic, it may not be the most cost-effective solution for highly variable traffic throughout the day.

Option D - Amazon ECS with capacity providers can automatically scale containerized workloads, but it may not be the most cost-effective solution compared to Amazon EC2 Auto Scaling for this scenario.

Option E - AWS Outposts is designed for on-premises deployments and may not offer the same cost optimization benefits as Amazon EC2 Auto Scaling for cloud-based workloads.

QUESTION 57

Answer - [D] Configure Amazon RDS Performance Insights to analyze database performance metrics and identify cost-saving opportunities.

Option A - Implementing Amazon RDS Multi-AZ deployment enhances fault tolerance but does not directly address the optimization of database costs.

Option B - While utilizing Amazon RDS Reserved Instances can reduce costs, it may not optimize resource allocation for the specific performance requirements of the database tier.

Option C - Integrating Amazon RDS with Amazon ElastiCache improves performance through caching but may not directly optimize database costs.

Option E - Using Amazon RDS Automated Backups streamlines backup processes but does not focus on optimizing database costs through performance analysis.

Option D - Correct. Configuring Amazon RDS Performance Insights allows for the analysis of database performance metrics, helping identify areas where cost-saving optimizations can be made without compromising performance.

QUESTION 58

Answer - [A] Utilize AWS EC2 Reserved Instances for baseline capacity and supplement with AWS Spot Instances for additional capacity during traffic spikes.

Option A - Correct. Utilizing AWS EC2 Reserved Instances for baseline capacity ensures cost optimization for predictable workloads, while supplementing with AWS Spot Instances allows for additional capacity during traffic spikes at lower costs.

Option B - Implementing AWS Savings Plans provides consistent discounts but may not dynamically scale based on demand fluctuations.

Option C - Combining AWS EC2 On-Demand Instances with AWS Lambda for serverless processing does not directly address the need for dynamic scaling based on demand.

Option D - Deploying a mix of AWS EC2 On-Demand Instances and AWS Spot Instances is a viable option, but it does not specifically emphasize the use of Reserved Instances for baseline capacity.

Option E - Leveraging AWS EC2 Dedicated Hosts guarantees isolated hardware resources but does not offer the flexibility required for dynamic scaling based on demand.

QUESTION 59

Answer - [C] Use a combination of Amazon EC2 On-Demand Instances and Spot Instances with Auto Scaling.

Option C - Correct. Using a combination of On-Demand Instances and Spot Instances with Auto Scaling allows for cost optimization by leveraging Spot Instances during low-demand periods and maintaining performance with On-Demand Instances during high-demand periods.

Option A - Utilizing Amazon EC2 On-Demand Instances may provide consistent performance but may not optimize costs effectively.

Option B - Implementing Amazon EC2 Spot Instances for cost savings during low-demand periods is a good approach, but using them alone may not ensure consistent performance.

Option D - Reserving Amazon EC2 instances provides cost predictability but may not be as flexible or cost-effective as using a combination of On-Demand and Spot Instances.

Option E - Deploying AWS Fargate for serverless container management may be suitable for specific use cases but does not address the cost optimization requirements of the variable traffic scenario.

QUESTION 60

Answer - [C] Configure the Auto Scaling group to use a step scaling policy triggered by sudden increases in the number of requests per minute.

A) Incorrect - Using a scheduled scaling policy triggered at specific times may not accurately align with sudden traffic spikes, potentially resulting in under or over-provisioning of resources.

B) Incorrect - Implementing a target tracking scaling policy based on the number of incoming HTTP requests may not provide the immediate response needed to handle sudden traffic spikes effectively.

C) Correct - Configuring a step scaling policy triggered by sudden increases in the number of requests per minute allows the Auto Scaling group to dynamically adjust the number of instances in response to changing traffic patterns, ensuring optimal performance during traffic spikes.

D) Incorrect - Utilizing a simple scaling policy based on manual adjustments lacks automation and may result in delayed responses to sudden traffic increases, impacting performance.

E) Incorrect - Implementing a predictive scaling policy based on historical traffic patterns may not accurately predict sudden traffic spikes, leading to potential performance issues during peak periods.

QUESTION 61

Answer - [B] Use Amazon CloudFront with Lambda@Edge to cache and deliver multimedia content at edge locations.

Option A - Amazon S3 Transfer Acceleration is suitable for optimizing data transfers but may not offer the same low-latency access as CloudFront with Lambda@Edge for multimedia content delivery.

Option B - Correct. Amazon CloudFront with Lambda@Edge allows for caching and delivering multimedia content at edge locations, ensuring low-latency access and optimizing costs for high traffic volumes.

Option C - Amazon EFS may provide fast access from multiple regions but may not offer the same content delivery and caching capabilities as CloudFront with Lambda@Edge.

Option D - AWS Direct Connect with AWS Transit Gateway provides private connectivity but may not optimize content delivery and reduce latency for multimedia content as effectively as CloudFront with Lambda@Edge.

Option E - Amazon Kinesis Video Streams is suitable for live streaming multimedia content but may not address the requirement for optimizing costs and reducing latency for static product images and videos.

QUESTION 62

Answer - [A] Use AWS CloudFormation to create and manage development and testing environments.

Option A - Correct. AWS CloudFormation enables the creation and management of development and testing environments in a cost-effective and efficient manner, aligning with the requirement for cost optimization and efficient testing environments.

Option B - Deploying Amazon EC2 instances with On-Demand pricing may lead to higher costs compared to utilizing spot instances or other cost-saving measures.

Option C - Amazon RDS with provisioned IOPS may provide optimal performance but may not be the most cost-effective solution for database testing in development environments.

Option D - Amazon S3 Glacier is suitable for long-term storage but may not be ideal for frequent access and testing of data in development environments. Option E - AWS Direct Connect provides dedicated network connectivity but may not directly address the requirement for cost optimization in testing environments.

QUESTION 63

Answer - [A] Utilize Amazon Route 53 latency-based routing and AWS Global Accelerator to distribute traffic efficiently across multiple AWS regions.

Option A - Correct. By using Amazon Route 53 latency-based routing and AWS Global Accelerator, you can efficiently distribute traffic across multiple AWS regions based on latency, optimizing performance while minimizing costs.

Option B - Deploying Amazon CloudFront with AWS Global Accelerator can optimize content delivery, but it may not directly address the cost efficiency of deploying resources across multiple regions.

Option C - Amazon DynamoDB global tables can ensure low-latency access for users but may not directly optimize costs associated with multi-region deployments.

Option D - AWS Direct Connect with AWS Transit Gateway can establish private connectivity between regions but may not directly minimize costs associated with data transfer between regions.

Option E - Amazon S3 cross-region replication ensures data durability and availability but may not directly address the cost efficiency of deploying resources across multiple regions.

QUESTION 64

Answer - [B] Implement AWS Lambda functions with Amazon API Gateway to create a serverless backend that scales automatically.

Option A - Using Amazon EC2 instances with AWS Auto Scaling can provide scalability but may not offer the same level of cost efficiency and automatic scaling as a serverless architecture.

Option B - Correct. Implementing AWS Lambda functions with Amazon API Gateway allows for a serverless backend that scales automatically, optimizing costs and resource utilization.

Option C - Deploying microservices using Amazon ECS Anywhere and on-premises servers may introduce complexity and management overhead, potentially impacting cost efficiency.

Option D - Amazon RDS with Amazon Aurora Serverless provides automatic database scaling but may not directly address cost efficiency for the entire backend architecture.

Option E - While using Amazon S3 for storage and Amazon CloudFront for content delivery can reduce data transfer costs, it does not address the scalability and cost efficiency requirements for backend services.

QUESTION 65

Answer - [D] Utilize AWS Lambda with AWS CloudTrail to automate resource cleanup based on predefined rules.

Option D - Correct. Utilizing AWS Lambda with AWS CloudTrail allows for automation of resource cleanup based on predefined rules, optimizing costs by eliminating unused resources.

Option A - AWS Trusted Advisor analyzes resource utilization but may not provide automated resource cleanup capabilities.

Option B - AWS Compute Optimizer analyzes resource utilization but may not directly automate resource cleanup for cost optimization.

 Option C - AWS Cost Explorer identifies unused resources but may not automate resource cleanup as efficiently as AWS Lambda with AWS CloudTrail.

 Option E - AWS Budgets helps monitor cost limits but may not provide the same level of automation for resource cleanup as AWS Lambda with AWS CloudTrail.

PRACTICE TEST 7 - QUESTIONS ONLY

QUESTION 1

An international organization is looking to implement federated access management to allow their employees to use their existing corporate credentials to access AWS resources. They are considering AWS IAM Identity Center (AWS Single Sign-On) for simplicity. What should be their primary considerations to ensure the solution is secure, scalable, and integrates seamlessly with their existing identity systems?

A) Enable AWS CloudTrail and Amazon GuardDuty for all accounts.

B) Integrate with an external identity provider (IdP) supporting SAML 2.0, configure IAM roles for federated access, and enable AWS Config.

C) Use AWS IAM user accounts for each employee, enforce MFA, and use AWS Organizations for account management.

D) Implement AWS Directory Service as the primary directory, federate with IAM Identity Center, and use AWS Shield for protection.

E) Configure IAM policies to restrict access based on user attributes and implement AWS Lambda for custom authentication flows.

QUESTION 2

An online retail company wants to redesign its application to improve security within its AWS Virtual Private Cloud (VPC). The goal is to ensure that the application's components are isolated in a way that enhances security and minimizes the risk of internal and external attacks. Which strategy would best achieve this objective?

A) Place all application components in a single public subnet and use security groups to control access.
B) Utilize both public and private subnets, placing only externally facing components in the public subnets.
C) Deploy all components in private subnets and use AWS Direct Connect for external access.
D) Create a VPC without subnets and rely on Network Access Control Lists (NACLs) for all security.
E) Use multiple VPCs for each application component to isolate them completely.

QUESTION 3

Your organization is developing a new web application that will handle sensitive customer data. You need to ensure that the application architecture incorporates robust security measures to protect against common web vulnerabilities and unauthorized access.

A) Utilize AWS WAF with custom rules to inspect and filter incoming web traffic for malicious content and protect against common web vulnerabilities

B) Implement AWS Cognito to manage user authentication and authorization for the web application

C) Deploy Amazon Inspector to continuously assess the security posture of the web application and identify vulnerabilities

D) Configure Amazon S3 bucket policies to restrict access to sensitive data and prevent unauthorized access

E) Utilize AWS Secrets Manager to securely store and rotate credentials used by the web application

QUESTION 4

Your organization operates a business-critical application on AWS that requires disaster recovery (DR) capabilities. As the solutions architect, you are tasked with designing a resilient DR solution that ensures minimal data loss and downtime in the event of a disaster. Which architecture should you recommend?

A) Utilize AWS Backup to automate the backup of data to Amazon S3 and Amazon Glacier. Implement Amazon Route 53 latency-based routing to direct traffic to the DR site in a different region.

B) Set up AWS Storage Gateway to replicate data to a DR site in a different region. Implement Amazon CloudFront with AWS Shield for DDoS protection and to improve latency for users accessing the DR site.

C) Configure AWS DataSync to replicate data between the primary and DR environments in real-time. Implement Amazon Route 53 failover routing with health checks to automatically redirect traffic to the DR site when the primary site is unavailable.

D) Deploy AWS Snowball to physically transfer data between the primary and DR environments. Utilize AWS Direct Connect with AWS Transit Gateway to establish secure network connectivity between the environments.

E) Utilize AWS Database Migration Service (DMS) to replicate data between the primary and DR databases in real-time. Implement Amazon CloudFront with AWS WAF for protection against web attacks and to improve content delivery performance.

QUESTION 5

A healthcare provider is migrating its patient appointment scheduling system to AWS and requires a solution that ensures appointment requests are processed in the order they are received while also providing the ability to process multiple requests simultaneously for different medical specialties. Which option should the company choose to implement this requirement?

A) Use Amazon SQS FIFO queue with default settings to process the messages.
B) Use Amazon SQS FIFO queue with a batch mode of 5 messages per operation.
C) Use Amazon SQS FIFO queue with exactly-once processing enabled.
D) Use Amazon SQS standard queue to process the messages.
E) Use Amazon SQS FIFO queue with message deduplication enabled.

QUESTION 6

Your company is migrating its legacy application to AWS and is designing a multi-tier architecture with high availability and security in mind. The architecture includes Amazon EC2 instances for web servers, an RDS MySQL database for data storage, and an Elastic Load Balancer (ELB) for distributing incoming traffic. As the solutions architect, you need to implement a secure IAM strategy to ensure that only authorized users can access the AWS resources. Which approach should you take to achieve this goal?

A) Create IAM users for each team member and provide them with access keys to manage resources.

Implement IAM roles for EC2 instances to access the RDS database securely.

B) Utilize IAM roles for EC2 instances with least privilege permissions to access other AWS services, and configure IAM policies to control access to RDS instances and ELB.

C) Implement IAM groups for different teams within the organization, and assign permissions to groups based on their roles. Use IAM policies to control access to individual EC2 instances, RDS databases, and ELB.

D) Set up IAM roles for each AWS resource in the architecture, and configure cross-account access between resources to ensure secure communication.

E) Deploy IAM policies at the organizational unit level to manage access control for all AWS resources, and use IAM roles for temporary access to resources by EC2 instances.

QUESTION 7

Your organization is migrating its legacy application to AWS. As part of the migration strategy, you need to design a highly secure network architecture within AWS. Which of the following options is a recommended strategy for ensuring secure architecture within public and private subnets?

A) Utilizing AWS Direct Connect for private subnet communication
B) Implementing AWS CloudFront in front of public subnets
C) Configuring network ACLs to restrict traffic between subnets
D) Enabling VPC Flow Logs for monitoring network traffic
E) Utilizing AWS Secrets Manager for managing sensitive data access

QUESTION 8

Your organization is developing a microservices-based application that requires secure communication between services. Each microservice needs to authenticate and authorize requests from other services. Which of the following options provides the most suitable solution for implementing secure API strategies?

A) Utilizing AWS IAM roles and policies for service-to-service authentication
B) Configuring AWS Lambda authorizers in Amazon API Gateway for request validation
C) Implementing OAuth 2.0 authentication with Amazon Cognito for API access control
D) Deploying AWS Certificate Manager (ACM) for SSL/TLS encryption of API endpoints
E) Enabling AWS AppMesh for managing communication between microservices

QUESTION 9

Your organization is designing a secure microservices architecture for a healthcare application. Compliance regulations require strong access controls and encryption for data at rest. Additionally, the architecture must ensure resilience and high availability. Which approach best meets these requirements?

A) Implementing AWS Lambda for serverless microservice deployment, ensuring resilience and high availability, and configuring Amazon RDS with encryption at rest and fine-grained access controls for data storage, meeting compliance regulations

B) Deploying microservices in Amazon ECS with AWS Fargate for serverless container deployment, ensuring resilience and high availability, and utilizing Amazon S3 with server-side encryption for data storage, meeting compliance regulations

C) Leveraging AWS App Mesh for managing microservices traffic, ensuring resilience and high availability, and implementing Amazon DynamoDB with encryption at rest and fine-grained access controls for data storage, meeting compliance regulations

D) Configuring AWS Lambda for serverless microservice deployment, ensuring resilience and high availability, and utilizing Amazon Aurora with encryption at rest and fine-grained access controls for data storage, meeting compliance regulations

E) Deploying microservices in Amazon EKS with AWS Fargate for serverless container deployment, ensuring resilience and high availability, and configuring Amazon Redshift with encryption at rest and fine-grained access controls for data storage, meeting compliance regulations

QUESTION 10

A retail company is migrating its product catalog management system to AWS and requires a solution that ensures low-latency access to product images stored on a file system service. The system must be able to access these images without disruption after migration. Which option is the most suitable solution to meet this requirement?

A) Use Amazon FSx File Gateway to provide low-latency, on-premises access to fully managed file shares in Amazon EFS. The applications deployed on AWS can access this data directly from Amazon EFS.

B) Use Amazon Storage Gateway's File Gateway to provide low-latency, on-premises access to fully managed file shares in Amazon FSx for Windows File Server. The applications deployed on AWS can access this data directly from Amazon FSx in AWS.

C) Use AWS Storage Gateway's File Gateway to provide low-latency, on-premises access to fully managed file shares in Amazon S3. The applications deployed on AWS can access this data directly from Amazon S3.

D) Use Amazon FSx File Gateway to provide low-latency, on-premises access to fully managed file shares in Amazon FSx for Windows File Server. The applications deployed on AWS can access this data directly from Amazon FSx in AWS.

QUESTION 11

An international law firm requires a highly available and durable storage solution for their legal documents that must be retained for a minimum of seven years for compliance. The solution must also ensure cost-effectiveness by automatically transitioning documents to a less expensive storage class after a year of no access and eventually to the most cost-efficient storage class after five years.

A) Implement Amazon S3 with a lifecycle policy to transition to S3 Standard-Infrequent Access after one year and S3 Glacier after five years.

B) Use Amazon EBS with snapshots scheduled to Amazon S3 and lifecycle rules to transition to S3 Glacier Deep Archive for long-term storage.

C) Configure Amazon EFS with lifecycle management to move data to EFS Infrequent Access and then archive to AWS Backup for long-term compliance.

D) Deploy Amazon FSx with automated backup to AWS Backup, utilizing lifecycle policies to move backups to S3 Glacier Deep Archive.

E) Utilize Amazon S3 with Intelligent-Tiering to automatically move data to the most cost-effective access tier based on usage patterns and set deletion policies for data older than seven years.

QUESTION 12

For a financial services company deploying a highly sensitive workload to AWS, ensuring the highest level of security during the deployment process and runtime is paramount. The company needs a strategy that includes immutable deployments to prevent unauthorized changes and drifts, integration with their existing CI/CD pipeline for automated deployments, and stringent access controls.

A) Adopt AWS CodePipeline and AWS CodeBuild for the CI/CD pipeline, utilize Amazon EC2 Auto Scaling groups for immutable deployments, and enforce strict IAM policies for access control.

B) Utilize AWS Lambda for serverless deployment, AWS WAF for securing the application layer, and Amazon S3 with versioning enabled for storing application code securely.

C) Implement AWS CloudFormation for infrastructure as code, Amazon EC2 instances with AWS Systems Manager for patch management, and AWS IAM roles for role-based access control.

D) Configure AWS Fargate for container-based immutable deployments, integrate AWS CodeCommit with AWS CodePipeline for CI/CD, and use AWS Secrets Manager for managing secrets.

E) Leverage Amazon ECS with Amazon ECR for container management and deployment, AWS CloudTrail for logging all deployment activities, and AWS KMS for encryption of deployment artifacts.

QUESTION 13

An e-commerce company experiences a significant increase in traffic during holiday seasons. They require a scalable solution to monitor and respond to potential security incidents automatically, ensuring the integrity and availability of their AWS resources without manual intervention.

A) Implement AWS Auto Scaling to manage traffic spikes, Amazon CloudWatch Alarms for incident detection, and AWS Lambda for executing remediation scripts.

B) Use Amazon CloudFront for content delivery, AWS WAF for filtering malicious web traffic, and Amazon GuardDuty for detecting suspicious activities.

C) Configure AWS Elastic Beanstalk for application deployment, Amazon S3 and Amazon RDS for data storage with encryption, and AWS CloudTrail for monitoring API calls.

D) Deploy AWS Fargate for running containerized applications, utilize AWS Secrets Manager for managing secrets, and Amazon Inspector for automated security assessments.

E) Leverage Amazon EC2 instances with Elastic Load Balancing, AWS Shield for DDoS protection, and AWS Config rules for ensuring compliance and security posture.

QUESTION 14

A global company wants to ensure that their API for international shipment tracking is highly available and secure. They also want to analyze the usage patterns to optimize for cost and performance. What architecture should be recommended to achieve these goals?

A) Utilize Amazon API Gateway for managing the API, Amazon CloudFront for global distribution, AWS Lambda for backend processing, and Amazon QuickSight for usage analysis.

B) Employ AWS Global Accelerator to route traffic, Amazon ECS for containerized shipment tracking, AWS WAF for security, and AWS Cost Explorer for cost analysis.

C) Implement Amazon API Gateway with regional endpoints, use AWS Fargate for scalable backend services, AWS Shield for security, and Amazon Athena for usage pattern analysis.

D) Use Amazon API Gateway with private endpoints, Amazon VPC for network isolation, AWS Direct Connect for dedicated connectivity, and Amazon Redshift for usage analysis.

E) Deploy Amazon API Gateway with a multi-region setup, use Amazon S3 for storing shipment data, AWS CloudTrail for security logging, and AWS Lambda with Amazon Kinesis for real-time usage pattern analysis.

QUESTION 15

A technology startup is facing challenges in performing maintenance tasks on specific Amazon EC2 instances within an Auto Scaling group. Each time maintenance patches are applied, the instances briefly show as out of service, triggering Auto Scaling to provision replacements. What strategies would you recommend as a solutions architect to mitigate this issue effectively?

A) Suspend the HealthCheck process type for the Auto Scaling group and apply the maintenance patch to the instance. Once the instance is ready, manually set the instance's health status back to healthy and activate the HealthCheck process type again.

B) Suspend the ReplaceUnhealthy process type for the Auto Scaling group and apply the maintenance patch to the instance. Once the instance is ready, manually set the instance's health status back to healthy and activate the ReplaceUnhealthy process type again.

C) Put the instance into the Detached state and then update the instance by applying the maintenance patch. Once the instance is ready, exit the Detached state and then return the instance to service.

D) Temporarily suspend the AddToLoadBalancer process type for the Auto Scaling group and apply the maintenance patch to the instance. Once the instance is ready, manually set the instance's health status back to healthy and activate the AddToLoadBalancer process type again.

E) Take a snapshot of the instance, create a new Amazon Machine Image (AMI), and then launch a new instance using this AMI. Apply the maintenance patch to this new instance and then add it back to the Auto Scaling Group by using the manual scaling policy. Terminate the earlier instance that had the maintenance issue.

QUESTION 16

A financial technology startup is expanding its operations globally and requires a robust solution to connect their on-premises data centers across different regions to AWS. They prioritize high availability, low latency, and secure data transfer. The solution must also support dynamic routing to automatically adjust to network changes.

A) Implement AWS Direct Connect along with AWS Transit Gateway, utilizing dynamic routing.
B) Use AWS Site-to-Site VPN connections combined with Amazon Route 53 for health checks and latency-based routing.
C) Deploy a combination of AWS Direct Connect and AWS Site-to-Site VPN, with VPN as a backup.
D) Establish AWS Direct Connect with AWS Global Accelerator to improve performance and availability.
E) Leverage AWS Site-to-Site VPN with AWS CloudMap for service discovery and dynamic routing.

QUESTION 17

A financial institution is planning to migrate its customer data processing system to AWS to improve scalability and security. The system processes highly sensitive financial transactions, requiring compliance with strict regulatory standards. The migration strategy needs to minimize downtime and ensure data integrity and security.

A) Utilize AWS DMS for database migration with encryption in transit, implement AWS Fargate for serverless container management, and AWS KMS for key management.

B) Employ AWS Snowball for secure data transfer, Amazon RDS with Multi-AZ for high availability, and Amazon CloudWatch for monitoring.

C) Configure AWS DataSync for efficient data transfer, AWS Lambda for serverless processing, and Amazon Inspector for security assessments.

D) Leverage AWS Application Discovery Service for migration planning, AWS Snowball Edge for data transfer with on-device encryption, and Amazon GuardDuty for threat detection.

E) Apply AWS S3 Transfer Acceleration for fast data upload, Amazon EC2 Auto Scaling for compute resources, and AWS Shield for DDoS protection.

QUESTION 18

A multinational financial institution is looking to enhance the security of its AWS infrastructure by implementing best practices for managing secrets and configurations. The institution wants to ensure secure storage and access to API keys, database credentials, and other sensitive information while seamlessly integrating with AWS services. Which of the following strategies align with the institution's requirements?

A) Utilize AWS Secrets Manager to securely store and rotate database credentials. Integrate AWS Lambda with Secrets Manager for automated rotation and retrieval of secrets.

B) Store API keys and configuration parameters in plaintext files within an Amazon S3 bucket. Use IAM roles with least privilege access for applications to retrieve secrets directly from S3.

C) Implement AWS Systems Manager Parameter Store to centrally manage application configurations and secrets. Leverage AWS CodeDeploy for deploying configuration changes securely across multiple environments.

D) Maintain a spreadsheet containing sensitive information and share it among authorized team members through an encrypted Amazon S3 bucket. Use AWS Lambda to parse and retrieve secrets from the spreadsheet as needed.

E) Deploy an on-premises secrets management solution and establish VPN connections to securely access secrets stored in an AWS-hosted database.

QUESTION 19

A financial institution is migrating its legacy applications to AWS ECS for containerized deployment. They need to ensure that sensitive information, such as database credentials, is securely managed within their ECS tasks. Which of the following strategies would best address the institution's requirements?

A) Store database credentials directly in Dockerfiles as environment variables. Use IAM roles with strict access policies for ECS tasks to access the environment variables.

B) Implement AWS Secrets Manager to securely store database credentials. Integrate ECS tasks with Secrets Manager for automated retrieval of credentials at runtime.

C) Maintain plaintext configuration files containing database credentials within Docker images. Implement IAM policies to control access to the Docker images in the Amazon ECR repository.

D) Utilize AWS Systems Manager Parameter Store to centrally manage database credentials. Develop custom logic within ECS tasks to retrieve credentials from Parameter Store.

E) Store database credentials in plaintext files within an encrypted Amazon EFS file system. Implement IAM policies to control access to the EFS file system for ECS tasks.

QUESTION 20

A logistics company encountered a spike in unauthorized AWS API queries during non-operational hours, with no discernible impact on system performance. The management seeks an automated solution to promptly alert relevant teams during such occurrences. Which approach would be most effective in this scenario?

A) Implement AWS Config Rules to monitor API activity and define rules to detect unauthorized API calls. Configure AWS Config to trigger an AWS Lambda function upon rule evaluation to notify relevant stakeholders.

B) Create an Amazon CloudWatch metric filter to process AWS CloudTrail logs containing API call details. Establish an alarm based on this metric's rate to send an Amazon SNS notification to the required team.

C) Leverage AWS Trusted Advisor to publish metrics about check results to Amazon CloudWatch. Set up an alarm to track status changes for checks in the Service Limits category for the APIs, triggering notifications when service quotas are exceeded.

D) Use Amazon Athena SQL queries against AWS CloudTrail log files stored in Amazon S3 buckets. Generate reports using Amazon QuickSight for managerial dashboards.

E) Configure AWS CloudTrail to stream event data to Amazon Kinesis. Utilize Amazon Kinesis stream-level metrics in Amazon CloudWatch to trigger an AWS Lambda function that will initiate an error workflow.

QUESTION 21

A company is building a real-time analytics platform to process streaming data from various sources. They want to ensure high availability and scalability. Which architecture should they choose for this scenario?

A) Utilize Amazon Kinesis Data Streams for data ingestion and processing.
B) Use AWS Lambda with Amazon Kinesis Data Firehose to process and load data into Amazon Redshift.
C) Implement Amazon S3 as a data lake for storing and analyzing the streaming data.
D) Employ Amazon SQS to buffer messages between different components.
E) Use Amazon EMR for real-time analytics processing.

QUESTION 22

Your organization is migrating its on-premises applications to AWS and requires a disaster recovery solution with minimal downtime. The applications use a mix of relational and NoSQL databases. Which combination of AWS services should you recommend to achieve this requirement?

A) Amazon RDS Multi-AZ deployment for relational databases with automated failover
B) Amazon DynamoDB Global Tables for multi-region replication of NoSQL databases
C) AWS Backup for centralized backup and restore with cross-region replication
D) AWS CloudFormation for infrastructure as code with automated recovery
E) AWS Direct Connect for dedicated network connectivity with redundant links

QUESTION 23

A media streaming company is planning its disaster recovery (DR) strategy for its video-on-demand platform hosted on AWS. The company requires a solution that ensures high availability and minimal data loss in the event of a disaster, while also optimizing costs. Which AWS service should the company consider for implementing an active-active failover architecture as part of its DR strategy?

A) Utilize Amazon S3 with cross-region replication enabled for storing video assets and metadata, ensuring data durability and low RPO

B) Implement Amazon CloudFront with origin failover and AWS Shield for DDoS protection, ensuring high availability and minimal downtime

C) Deploy Amazon EC2 instances in multiple AWS Regions with Route 53 latency-based routing for active-active failover, minimizing response times and maximizing availability

D) Utilize Amazon Redshift with cross-region snapshots for data replication and disaster recovery, ensuring minimal data loss and efficient query performance

E) Implement AWS Lambda with Amazon DynamoDB Streams for real-time data replication and failover, achieving near-zero RPO and RTO at scale

QUESTION 24

A technology startup is developing a real-time collaboration platform that requires low-latency communication between users located in different regions. The company wants to select the most cost-efficient solution to improve application performance while minimizing expenses. Which option would be most suitable for this scenario?

A) Deploy Amazon EC2 instances in multiple regions and use Amazon RDS cross-region replication to ensure data consistency for real-time collaboration.

B) Utilize Amazon CloudFront with Lambda@Edge to cache frequently accessed content and reduce latency for users across different regions.

C) Implement AWS Global Accelerator to improve application performance by optimizing the network path between users and the collaboration platform.

D) Set up Amazon API Gateway with AWS Lambda to build serverless APIs for real-time data exchange between users in different regions.

E) Configure Amazon ElastiCache with Redis to cache session data and facilitate low-latency communication between users in different regions.

QUESTION 25

A global eCommerce platform utilizes Amazon Aurora to handle transactions and customer data. They've implemented a strategy to use Aurora replicas across multiple regions to improve read performance and ensure disaster recovery. Given the setup with varied instance sizes and failover tiers, which replica is designed to take over in the event the primary database fails?

A) Tier-4 (16 terabytes)
B) Tier-4 (8 terabytes)
C) Tier-10 (32 terabytes)
D) Tier-12 (16 terabytes)
E) Tier-12 (8 terabytes)

QUESTION 26

A software company is planning to migrate its monolithic application to AWS and adopt microservices architecture to improve scalability and resilience. The company aims to implement immutable infrastructure to enhance deployment and management processes. Which approach should the solutions architect recommend to achieve immutable infrastructure on AWS?

A) Utilize AWS AppConfig to manage application configurations and settings dynamically, enabling on-the-fly updates without modifying the underlying infrastructure.

B) Implement AWS OpsWorks to automate infrastructure provisioning and configuration management using Chef, enabling repeatable deployments and ensuring consistency across environments.

C) Use AWS CloudFormation to define infrastructure as code and automate the deployment of AWS resources in a consistent and repeatable manner, promoting immutable infrastructure.

D) Leverage AWS Elastic Beanstalk to deploy and manage applications with ease, allowing automatic scaling and load balancing without worrying about infrastructure provisioning.

E) Configure Amazon ECS Anywhere to run containerized microservices on-premises, ensuring consistency between on-premises and cloud environments.

QUESTION 27

A logistics company is deploying microservices on Amazon ECS to handle package tracking and delivery. The company wants to ensure seamless API updates without affecting existing clients. Which option represents a best practice for API versioning and deployment stages with Amazon API Gateway?

A) Implement API Gateway stage variables and manage multiple stages for versioning
B) Utilize API Gateway resource policies to manage version-specific endpoints for clients
C) Deploy new APIs with different endpoint paths and gradually migrate clients to the updated endpoints
D) Use API Gateway usage plans and API keys to enforce versioning and manage access to different versions of APIs
E) Configure Lambda aliases and versions to handle API updates transparently for existing clients

QUESTION 28

A software development company is designing a serverless architecture for its new application, which will process large amounts of image data. They want to ensure efficient handling of asynchronous tasks in the architecture. Which option provides the best solution for managing asynchronous task execution in a serverless environment using AWS services?

A) Implement AWS Step Functions to coordinate and execute asynchronous tasks across multiple AWS services, ensuring reliable and scalable execution

B) Use Amazon SQS to decouple application components and enable reliable message-based communication between serverless functions

C) Configure Amazon S3 event notifications to trigger AWS Lambda functions for processing image data asynchronously, ensuring scalable and cost-effective execution

D) Deploy AWS Glue to orchestrate ETL jobs for processing image data and transform it into a suitable format for analysis

E) Utilize AWS Fargate with AWS Batch to run containerized tasks in response to image data uploads, providing flexibility and scalability for asynchronous processing

QUESTION 29

A global financial institution needs to ensure high availability and low-latency access to its trading platform across multiple regions. Which AWS service or feature should they use to achieve this goal?

A) Amazon Route 53 with latency-based routing
B) Amazon SQS for message queuing and delivery
C) Amazon RDS Multi-AZ deployment for database redundancy
D) AWS Direct Connect for dedicated network connectivity
E) Amazon S3 cross-region replication for data backup and synchronization

QUESTION 30

An entertainment company aims to analyze viewer preferences in real-time during live streaming events to personalize content recommendations and enhance viewer engagement. They require a solution capable of processing streaming viewer interaction data efficiently and adapting content dynamically. Which AWS service combination should they use to achieve this while ensuring flexibility and scalability?

A) Utilize a Spark Streaming cluster on Amazon EMR to process viewer interaction data before storing it in Amazon RDS

B) Implement Amazon Kinesis Data Analytics to analyze streaming viewer interaction data and store it in Amazon Redshift for further analysis

C) Employ Amazon Kinesis Data Firehose to ingest data and use AWS Lambda to filter and transform before storing it in Amazon DynamoDB

D) Utilize Amazon Kinesis Data Streams with AWS Lambda for real-time data processing and store it in Amazon S3

E) Ingest data directly into Amazon S3 using Amazon Kinesis Data Firehose without intermediate processing

QUESTION 31

An e-commerce platform is scaling rapidly and requires an automated solution to ensure that all newly launched EC2 instances comply with security best practices, including the application of necessary patches and restrictions on administrative access. Which AWS services can provide automation to meet these security requirements?

A) AWS Systems Manager for automated management of EC2 instances, AWS Config to track compliance with company policies, Amazon Inspector for security assessments, and AWS IAM for managing access.

B) Amazon GuardDuty for continuous security monitoring and threat detection, AWS Lambda for executing custom scripts to apply patches, AWS CloudFormation for infrastructure as code, and Amazon EC2 Auto Scaling for managing instance scaling.

C) AWS WAF to apply web application firewall rules, AWS Shield for DDoS protection, AWS Direct Connect for a dedicated network connection, and Amazon RDS for database security.

D) Amazon EMR for data processing and analytics, Amazon Kinesis for real-time data processing, AWS Glue for data cataloging, and Amazon QuickSight for security dashboards.

E) AWS Fargate for running containers without managing servers, AWS Batch for batch computing workloads, Amazon S3 for data storage with encryption, and AWS Step Functions for serverless workflow orchestration.

QUESTION 32

A leading e-commerce company is preparing for a multi-region disaster recovery (DR) setup for its critical application databases. The solution must ensure low recovery point objectives (RPOs) and recovery time objectives (RTOs) while minimizing costs. Which combination of AWS services and features should the company implement to achieve these objectives?

A) Utilize Amazon Aurora with global databases for multi-master replication and fast failover, coupled with Amazon S3 cross-Region replication for backups.

B) Implement Amazon RDS with cross-Region read replicas and use AWS Backup for automated backups and cross-Region replication of backups.

C) Deploy Amazon DynamoDB with global tables for multi-Region replication and use AWS Direct Connect for low-latency connectivity between Regions.

D) Migrate to Amazon Redshift for analytics and scalability and configure cross-Region snapshots for disaster recovery with Amazon S3 replication.

E) Implement Amazon DocumentDB with point-in-time recovery enabled and utilize AWS Snowball for cross-Region data transfer and offline backup.

QUESTION 33

Your organization operates a highly sensitive healthcare application on AWS that requires strict management of sensitive data and configurations. What solution would best meet the security and compliance requirements for managing secrets and sensitive information?

A) Utilize AWS CloudFormation for managing secrets.
B) Implement AWS Secrets Manager to securely manage sensitive data.
C) Store plaintext passwords in S3 buckets with restricted access policies.
D) Implement AWS IAM policies to restrict access to sensitive data.
E) Use plaintext HTTP for API communication.

QUESTION 34

Your company's analytics platform relies on processing large volumes of data in real-time. The platform requires the ability to scale horizontally to handle increasing data loads and must remain resilient to ensure uninterrupted data processing. You are tasked with selecting the most cost-effective solution for this scenario. Which option should you choose?

A) Implement Amazon EMR clusters with Spot Instances
B) Utilize Amazon Kinesis Data Firehose with AWS Glue for data transformation
C) Use AWS Lambda functions triggered by Amazon CloudWatch Events
D) Deploy Apache Kafka clusters on Amazon EC2 instances
E) Utilize Amazon Athena for ad-hoc query analysis

QUESTION 35

A financial institution wants to develop a mobile application for stock trading, requiring real-time market data updates and secure transaction processing. They need a solution that ensures low-latency data streaming and high-level security for user transactions. Which setup should they configure using Amazon API Gateway to meet these requirements effectively?

A) Utilize RESTful APIs on Amazon API Gateway with Amazon Kinesis for real-time market data updates and AWS Lambda for secure transaction processing

B) Implement WebSocket APIs on Amazon API Gateway with Amazon RDS for real-time market data storage and Amazon Cognito for secure transaction processing

C) Create HTTP APIs on Amazon API Gateway and integrate with Amazon Aurora for real-time market data storage and Amazon Secrets Manager for secure transaction processing

D) Deploy GraphQL APIs on Amazon API Gateway with Amazon DynamoDB for real-time market data updates and Amazon KMS for secure transaction processing

E) Configure RESTful APIs on Amazon API Gateway with Amazon Redshift for real-time market data storage and Amazon CloudHSM for secure transaction processing

QUESTION 36

Your organization, a healthcare provider, is planning to migrate its patient records system to AWS for enhanced scalability and reliability. The system deals with sensitive patient data that must be securely encrypted at all times to meet HIPAA compliance. As the solution architect, how would you design the encryption strategy to ensure the highest level of data security while maintaining compliance? Select TWO.

A) Utilize AWS Key Management Service (KMS) to manage encryption keys for Amazon RDS and leverage AWS CloudHSM for hardware security module (HSM) key storage.

B) Deploy Amazon S3 server-side encryption with AWS KMS-managed keys for data at rest and enforce SSL/TLS for encrypting data in transit.

C) Implement Amazon Redshift with encryption at rest enabled and configure AWS Certificate Manager (ACM) for SSL certificate management.

D) Utilize Amazon DynamoDB with client-side encryption enabled and leverage AWS Secrets Manager for key management policies.

E) Configure Amazon Aurora with encryption at rest enabled and utilize AWS KMS for managing encryption keys securely.

QUESTION 37

A financial analytics firm needs to process large datasets using a combination of batch and real-time analysis. They require a scalable storage solution that allows for quick access to data for processing and analysis. Which AWS storage service best fits their needs?

A) Amazon S3 for its scalability and data availability, utilizing S3 Select for efficient data retrieval.
B) Amazon EFS for a fully managed file system that can scale on demand.
C) Amazon DynamoDB for its fast and flexible NoSQL database capabilities.
D) Amazon Redshift for complex queries across large datasets, using Redshift Spectrum.
E) AWS Snowball for large-scale data transfer into and out of AWS.

QUESTION 38

Your company is migrating its legacy database to AWS to improve performance and scalability. The existing database architecture lacks automated scaling capabilities and experiences downtime during maintenance activities. Which combination of AWS services would you recommend to address these challenges and ensure high availability and scalability for the new database solution? Select TWO.

A) Migrate the database to Amazon RDS with Multi-AZ deployment for high availability and automated backups.

B) Utilize Amazon Aurora Serverless for on-demand, auto-scaling database capacity without managing underlying infrastructure.

C) Implement Amazon RDS Read Replicas to offload read traffic and improve database performance.

D) Configure Amazon DynamoDB with on-demand capacity mode to handle unpredictable workloads and scale automatically.

E) Deploy Amazon ElastiCache for Redis to cache frequently accessed data and reduce database load.

QUESTION 39

A healthcare organization is looking to enhance its data processing capabilities by building a scalable architecture for ingesting and transforming patient records from various sources. Security and compliance are top priorities for handling sensitive medical data. Which solution should the organization consider?

A) Deploy Amazon ECS Anywhere for containerized data processing, and use AWS Glue for data transformation.

B) Utilize Amazon Kinesis Data Firehose to ingest data from different sources, and leverage AWS Lambda for serverless data processing.

C) Implement Amazon S3 Glacier for storing patient records, and configure Amazon QuickSight for real-time analytics.

D) Utilize Amazon Redshift for data warehousing, and leverage Amazon Comprehend Medical for extracting medical insights from patient records.

E) Deploy AWS Data Exchange for secure data sharing, and use AWS Transfer Family for ingesting patient records.

QUESTION 40

A logistics company intends to develop a real-time package tracking system to monitor the movement of parcels and provide updates to customers instantly. They require a solution that can process tracking data continuously and generate updates without delays or manual intervention. Which setup should they configure using AWS serverless components to meet these requirements effectively?

A) Utilize AWS Lambda with Amazon S3 for processing tracking data and Amazon RDS for storing update logs

B) Implement Amazon Kinesis Data Firehose with AWS Lambda for processing tracking data and Amazon ElastiCache for storing update logs

C) Ingest tracking data into Amazon Kinesis Data Streams, which triggers an AWS Lambda function for processing and stores update logs in Amazon DynamoDB

D) Ingest tracking data into Amazon SQS, which triggers an AWS Lambda function for processing and stores update logs in Amazon Redshift

E) Use Amazon API Gateway to ingest tracking data, which is processed by an application running on an Amazon EC2 instance, and store update logs in Amazon Elasticsearch Service

QUESTION 41

An online media company plans to launch a global campaign, expecting millions of views on their promotional content hosted on their platform. They need a serverless architecture capable of dynamically scaling to accommodate the high volume of requests and efficiently distributing content with minimal latency to users worldwide, while also analyzing user engagement metrics in real-time. What is the best AWS solution?

A) Amazon CloudFront for content delivery, AWS Lambda for real-time analytics, and Amazon S3 for storing promotional content.

B) Amazon ECS with Fargate for container management, Amazon RDS for user metrics storage, and AWS Global Accelerator for improving application performance.

C) AWS Direct Connect for dedicated network connection, Amazon EC2 Auto Scaling for handling traffic, and Amazon Kinesis for data analytics.

D) Amazon API Gateway for managing API calls, Amazon SQS for decoupling incoming requests, and AWS Step Functions for orchestrating microservices.

E) Amazon SNS for broadcasting notifications to subscribers, Amazon DynamoDB for user metrics storage, and AWS Lambda for backend processing.

QUESTION 42

Your organization requires a hybrid cloud solution that allows seamless data synchronization and replication between on-premises storage systems and AWS S3. You aim to optimize costs while ensuring high availability and low latency for data access. Which approach should you recommend to meet these requirements?

A) Deploy AWS DataSync to transfer data between on-premises storage systems and Amazon S3 over the internet.

B) Utilize AWS Storage Gateway with caching mode to store frequently accessed data on-premises and asynchronously upload data to Amazon S3.

C) Implement AWS Snowball to physically transfer large volumes of data from on-premises storage to Amazon S3.

D) Configure AWS Direct Connect to establish a dedicated network connection between on-premises storage systems and Amazon S3 for low-latency data transfer.

E) Leverage AWS Transfer Family to enable seamless and secure file transfers between on-premises storage systems and Amazon S3.

QUESTION 43

A global news outlet is deploying a mobile application to deliver personalized news content to users worldwide. The application must provide real-time news updates with minimal latency, scale based on user demand, and cache content efficiently to reduce load times. The solution must also integrate a recommendation engine to personalize content delivery based on user preferences and behavior. Considering AWS services and best practices, how should the application be architected to meet these requirements while ensuring cost-effectiveness?

A) Use Amazon Kinesis for real-time data processing, AWS Lambda for executing business logic, Amazon Personalize for content recommendation, and Amazon CloudFront for content delivery.

B) Implement Elastic Load Balancing with Amazon EC2 Auto Scaling, Amazon RDS for user data storage, Amazon ElastiCache for caching, and AWS Glue for data integration and preparation.

C) Deploy Amazon SNS for notifications, Amazon SQS for message queuing, Amazon DynamoDB for user preferences storage, and AWS AppSync for data synchronization across devices.

D) Utilize AWS Fargate for running containerized microservices, Amazon Aurora for database operations, AWS CloudMap for service discovery, and Amazon QuickSight for analytics and personalization insights.

E) Implement Amazon API Gateway for handling API requests, AWS Lambda with Amazon DynamoDB for backend processing and storing user data, Amazon CloudFront with Amazon S3 for caching static content, and use AWS Step Functions to orchestrate serverless workflows.

QUESTION 44

Your company is tasked with designing a cost-efficient solution for training machine learning models on large datasets using Amazon SageMaker. The solution should ensure scalability and high performance during training. Which architecture would be most suitable for this scenario?

A) Utilize Amazon SageMaker for training with Amazon S3 for data storage, leveraging Amazon EBS for model training storage and Amazon CloudWatch for monitoring.

B) Implement Amazon SageMaker for distributed training and inference, utilizing Amazon EFS for shared model storage and Amazon CloudWatch for monitoring.

C) Deploy Amazon SageMaker for training, integrating Amazon RDS for model metadata storage and Amazon CloudWatch for performance monitoring.

D) Utilize Amazon SageMaker for training with Amazon DynamoDB for model metadata storage and Amazon CloudWatch for monitoring and optimization.

E) Implement Amazon SageMaker for distributed training with Amazon S3 for data storage and Amazon CloudWatch for monitoring and optimization.

QUESTION 45

A financial institution is migrating sensitive data to Amazon S3 and requires encryption of the data at rest to comply with industry regulations. The institution also needs to ensure that encryption keys are stored securely and can be rotated periodically. Which option would be the most suitable choice for this scenario?

A) Utilize server-side encryption with Amazon S3 managed keys (SSE-S3) to encrypt the data on Amazon S3

B) Implement server-side encryption with AWS Key Management Service (SSE-KMS) and enable automatic key rotation

C) Use client-side encryption with customer-provided keys (SSE-C) and upload the encrypted data to Amazon S3

D) Implement server-side encryption with customer-provided keys (SSE-C) and manually rotate encryption keys

E) Enable AWS CloudTrail to monitor S3 bucket activities for auditing purposes

QUESTION 46

You are designing a data processing pipeline for a social media platform that processes large volumes of user-generated content, including text, images, and videos. The pipeline must be highly scalable, cost-effective, and capable of processing data in real-time. Which architecture would best meet these requirements?

A) Utilize Amazon Kinesis Data Streams for ingesting real-time data, process data using Amazon EMR, store processed data in Amazon Redshift, and use AWS Lambda to trigger processing tasks.

B) Implement an event-driven architecture using Amazon EventBridge to ingest data, process data using AWS Glue, store processed data in Amazon Aurora, and use AWS Lambda for real-time data processing.

C) Deploy containers on Amazon ECS for data ingestion, process data using Amazon EMR, store processed data in Amazon S3, and use AWS Lambda for real-time data processing.

D) Utilize Amazon Kinesis Data Firehose for ingesting real-time data, process data using AWS Glue, store processed data in Amazon DynamoDB, and use AWS Lambda to trigger processing tasks.

E) Implement a serverless architecture using Amazon S3 for data ingestion, process data using AWS Glue, store processed data in Amazon Redshift, and use AWS Lambda for real-time data processing.

QUESTION 47

You are tasked with designing a highly available architecture for a financial application that processes sensitive customer data. The application must handle sudden increases in transaction volume without compromising data integrity or availability. Which architecture would best meet these requirements?

A) Implement a multi-tier architecture with Amazon EC2 instances deployed in multiple Availability Zones (AZs), Amazon RDS for database storage, and Amazon CloudFront for content delivery.

B) Utilize Amazon Aurora Multi-Master for database redundancy, Amazon S3 for storing transaction logs, and Amazon CloudWatch for monitoring and alerting.

C) Deploy the application on AWS Outposts for data residency requirements, leverage AWS Backup for data protection, and use AWS Shield for DDoS protection.

D) Implement a serverless architecture using AWS Lambda for compute, Amazon DynamoDB for database needs, and AWS KMS for encryption.

E) Utilize Amazon ECS for container orchestration, Amazon ElastiCache for caching frequently accessed data, and Amazon GuardDuty for threat detection.

QUESTION 48

An e-commerce company operates a website that experiences predictable traffic patterns with peak activity during specific hours of the day. The company wants to minimize infrastructure costs while ensuring consistent performance during peak hours. Which pricing option for Amazon EC2 instances would be the most appropriate choice for this scenario?

A) Use reserved instances (RI) for the entire duration of operation
B) Implement on-demand instances for the entire duration of operation
C) Utilize spot instances for the entire duration of operation
D) Employ a combination of reserved instances (RI) and spot instances
E) Implement a mix of reserved instances (RI) and on-demand instances

QUESTION 49

Your company is planning to launch a new mobile application that requires real-time data updates and synchronization across devices. The application must handle concurrent user interactions efficiently while maintaining high performance. Which architecture would best suit these requirements?

A) Utilize Amazon EC2 instances with AWS Auto Scaling for dynamic scaling, Amazon DynamoDB Global Tables for multi-region replication, and Amazon API Gateway for mobile backend services.

B) Deploy AWS Lambda for serverless computing, Amazon DynamoDB Global Tables for multi-region replication, and Amazon API Gateway for mobile backend services.

C) Leverage Amazon ECS for containerized workload management, Amazon Aurora for real-time data storage, and Amazon API Gateway for mobile backend services.

D) Use Amazon EC2 instances with AWS Auto Scaling for dynamic scaling, Amazon RDS Multi-AZ for real-time data storage, and Amazon API Gateway for mobile backend services.

E) Implement AWS Fargate for containerized workload management, Amazon RDS Multi-AZ for real-time data storage, and Amazon API Gateway for mobile backend services.

QUESTION 50

Your company operates a media streaming platform that delivers content to users globally. The platform needs to ensure high availability and low latency for content delivery while optimizing costs. Which solution would best meet the company's requirements?

A) Utilize Amazon CloudFront with custom SSL certificates to distribute media content globally, leveraging AWS Shield and AWS WAF to protect against DDoS attacks and mitigate security threats.

B) Deploy Amazon Elastic Transcoder to encode media files into various formats, and then use Amazon S3 for storage. Configure cross-region replication in S3 for disaster recovery and data redundancy.

C) Implement Amazon Kinesis Video Streams to ingest and process live video streams, leveraging AWS Elemental MediaStore for low-latency delivery and Amazon CloudWatch for monitoring stream performance.

D) Utilize Amazon S3 Transfer Acceleration to optimize data transfer speeds for uploading and downloading media files, and then implement Amazon CloudFront as a CDN to cache and distribute content globally.

E) Deploy Amazon ElastiCache for Redis to cache frequently accessed media files, reducing latency for users. Use Amazon Route 53 with latency-based routing to direct users to the nearest edge location for content delivery.

QUESTION 51

An online video streaming service is experiencing increased load times during peak hours. They wish to use Amazon CloudFront to cache their content effectively. What strategy should they employ to minimize latency and maintain content freshness?

A) Enable automatic cache invalidation on Amazon CloudFront every hour.
B) Utilize Amazon CloudFront with custom cache behaviors for different content types and Lambda@Edge for request manipulation.
C) Configure Amazon S3 as the origin and disable caching on CloudFront.
D) Use AWS Lambda@Edge to compress content dynamically before delivery.
E) Implement AWS WAF on CloudFront distributions to manage cache behavior based on request type.

QUESTION 52

A software development team requires granular access control for different folders within an S3 bucket. Some team members should have read-only access to specific folders, while others need read-write access. Which S3 feature should be utilized to implement this requirement?

A) "Action": ["s3:GetObject"], "Resource": ["arn:aws:s3:::example-bucket/"], "Effect": "Allow" (Read-Only Policy)

B) "Action": ["s3:PutObject"], "Resource": ["arn:aws:s3:::example-bucket/"], "Effect": "Deny" (Deny Modification)

C) "Action": ["s3:GetObject"], "s3:PutObject"], "Resource": ["arn:aws:s3:::example-bucket/"], "Effect": "Allow" (Read and Write Access)

D) "Action": ["s3:ListBucket"], "s3:GetObject"], "Resource": ["arn:aws:s3:::example-bucket/"], "Effect": "Allow" (List and Read Access)

E) "Action": ["s3:GetObject"], "s3:DeleteObject"], "Resource": ["arn:aws:s3:::example-bucket/*"], "Effect": "Allow" (Read and Delete Access)

QUESTION 53

Your organization is migrating its legacy application to a microservices architecture on AWS to improve scalability and reduce operational overhead. As part of this transformation, you need to optimize container management and ensure cost-effectiveness. Which solution aligns best with these objectives using AWS services?

A) Utilize AWS Lambda for container orchestration

B) Implement Amazon ECS Fargate for serverless container management

C) Deploy containers directly on EC2 instances without orchestration

D) Utilize AWS Batch for batch processing

E) Leverage Amazon EKS for Kubernetes-based orchestration

QUESTION 54

Your organization is migrating its on-premises data center to AWS and aims to optimize costs while ensuring high availability and fault tolerance. You need to design a network architecture that minimizes costs while maintaining resilience. What would be the most suitable approach?

A) Implement AWS Transit Gateway with Direct Connect for centralized connectivity

B) Deploy Amazon VPC with NAT Gateways for outbound internet traffic

C) Utilize AWS VPN with AWS Global Accelerator for secure and efficient network connectivity

D) Opt for Amazon CloudFront with Route 53 for low-latency DNS resolution

E) Leverage AWS PrivateLink for private connectivity to AWS services

QUESTION 55

A financial institution wants to implement multi-factor authentication (MFA) for enhanced security when accessing AWS Management Console. Which approach should the solutions architect recommend to enforce MFA for all IAM users?

A) Enable MFA for the root account and encourage IAM users to enable MFA individually.

B) Utilize IAM policies to enforce MFA for all IAM users within the account.

C) Enable MFA for IAM groups and assign IAM users to these groups with MFA enforcement.

D) Require users to authenticate using their corporate LDAP credentials before accessing AWS Management Console.

E) Enable AWS SSO and enforce MFA at the organization level for all users accessing AWS resources.

QUESTION 56

Your company runs a data processing application that requires periodic bursts of compute resources to handle incoming data spikes. However, the application has long periods of inactivity between these bursts. How can you design a cost-optimized compute scaling solution to address this pattern?

A) Utilize Amazon EC2 Spot Instances for cost-effective compute during bursts, supplemented with Amazon EC2 Reserved Instances for baseline capacity

B) Implement AWS Lambda with event-driven triggers to dynamically scale compute resources based on incoming data

C) Configure Amazon EC2 instances with hibernation enabled to save costs during periods of inactivity

D) Deploy AWS Fargate with auto-scaling enabled to automatically adjust containerized compute resources based on demand

E) Utilize AWS Batch with spot fleet integration for efficient management of batch computing jobs

QUESTION 57

Your organization is managing a high-traffic mobile application that relies on Amazon DynamoDB for its NoSQL database needs. However, recent billing reports indicate unexpectedly high costs associated with DynamoDB provisioned throughput and storage. As a solutions architect, you need to implement cost-effective strategies to optimize DynamoDB costs while maintaining optimal performance for the application. What would be the most suitable approach to achieve this objective?

A) Implement Amazon DynamoDB Accelerator (DAX) to improve database read performance and reduce read capacity costs

B) Enable Amazon DynamoDB On-Demand Capacity Mode to automatically scale read and write capacity based on application demand

C) Configure Amazon DynamoDB Auto Scaling to dynamically adjust provisioned capacity based on application traffic patterns

D) Utilize Amazon DynamoDB Global Tables to replicate data across multiple regions and reduce data transfer costs

E) Integrate Amazon DynamoDB with Amazon S3 for data archiving and leverage lifecycle policies to manage storage costs

QUESTION 58

Your organization is deploying a new microservices-based application on AWS to handle variable workloads efficiently. As the solutions architect, you need to recommend an instance purchasing strategy that optimizes costs while ensuring high availability and performance for each microservice. Which of the following strategies would best align with these requirements?

A) Utilize AWS EC2 On-Demand Instances for all microservices to ensure consistent performance and availability

B) Implement AWS Savings Plans with a commitment to a specific instance family to receive discounts on instance usage

C) Deploy AWS EC2 Reserved Instances for microservices with predictable traffic patterns and supplement with AWS Spot Instances for microservices with variable workloads

D) Leverage AWS EC2 Dedicated Hosts to host multiple microservices on isolated hardware for improved security and performance

E) Combine AWS EC2 Spot Instances with AWS Fargate for serverless container orchestration to dynamically scale microservices based on demand

QUESTION 59

Your organization needs to optimize costs for a batch processing workload that is tolerant of interruptions. Which solution would you recommend?

A) Utilize Amazon EC2 Reserved Instances for consistent performance

B) Implement Amazon EC2 On-Demand Instances with manual intervention during interruptions

C) Leverage Amazon EC2 Spot Instances with graceful termination handling

D) Deploy AWS Lambda for serverless batch processing

E) Utilize Amazon ECS Anywhere for hybrid batch processing

QUESTION 60

A retail company is deploying a new e-commerce application and wants to ensure that the application can handle increased traffic during holiday seasons without manual intervention. What Auto Scaling configuration should the solutions architect recommend?

A) Configure the Auto Scaling group to use a target tracking scaling policy based on the number of concurrent database connections.

B) Implement an Auto Scaling group with a scheduled scaling policy triggered at specific times of holiday seasons.

C) Configure the Auto Scaling group to use a step scaling policy triggered by sudden increases in the number of transactions per minute.

D) Utilize an Auto Scaling group with a simple scaling policy based on manual adjustments to instance counts.

E) Implement an Auto Scaling group with a predictive scaling policy based on historical holiday season traffic patterns.

QUESTION 61

Your organization operates a distributed team across multiple geographic locations, and you need to ensure efficient collaboration and data sharing while minimizing costs. Employees frequently access large files stored in Amazon S3 buckets for their work. Which solution should you recommend to optimize data transfer costs for this scenario?

A) Utilize Amazon S3 Transfer Acceleration to optimize data transfers and reduce latency for accessing large files

B) Implement AWS Direct Connect to establish dedicated network connections between on-premises data centers and AWS regions

C) Configure Amazon S3 Cross-Region Replication to replicate frequently accessed data to regions closer to users

D) Use AWS DataSync to transfer data between on-premises storage systems and Amazon S3 buckets

E) Deploy Amazon S3 Glacier for long-term storage of large files and retrieve data as needed

QUESTION 62

Your organization is developing a new microservices-based application that requires efficient testing and development environments. Cost optimization is a key consideration, and you need to design a solution that minimizes expenses while providing scalability and flexibility. Which approach should you recommend?

A) Utilize Amazon EC2 Spot Instances and AWS Fargate Spot for cost-effective testing and development

B) Implement Amazon RDS Multi-AZ deployment for high availability and reliability of database testing

C) Leverage AWS CloudTrail to track API activity and monitor costs associated with development and testing

D) Deploy Amazon S3 Intelligent-Tiering for storage of test data to optimize costs based on access patterns

E) Use AWS Organizations to centrally manage and govern costs across multiple AWS accounts

QUESTION 63

Your organization operates a global e-commerce platform and is experiencing significant fluctuations in demand across different regions. To ensure a seamless user experience and optimize costs, the company wants to implement a solution that dynamically scales resources based on demand while minimizing expenses. As a solutions architect, you are tasked with designing a cost-efficient multi-region architecture that meets these requirements. What approach should you recommend?

A) Utilize Amazon CloudFront with AWS Global Accelerator to cache content at edge locations and distribute traffic efficiently across regions

B) Implement Amazon EC2 Auto Scaling with AWS Auto Scaling groups to automatically adjust the number of EC2 instances based on demand patterns

C) Leverage AWS Lambda with Amazon API Gateway to build serverless applications that scale automatically based on incoming requests

D) Deploy Amazon Aurora Global Database to replicate data across regions and ensure low-latency access for read-heavy workloads

E) Utilize Amazon S3 Transfer Acceleration to optimize data transfer speeds and reduce costs associated with cross-region replication

QUESTION 64

Your organization is migrating its on-premises data center to AWS to improve scalability and reduce infrastructure costs. As part of the migration, you need to design a cost-efficient storage solution for storing large volumes of data.

A) Utilize Amazon S3 Glacier for archival storage and Amazon S3 Intelligent-Tiering for frequently accessed data

B) Implement Amazon EFS for file storage and Amazon EBS for block storage to optimize performance and cost

C) Deploy Amazon FSx for Windows File Server with Amazon CloudWatch to monitor storage usage and optimize costs

D) Utilize Amazon S3 for object storage and Amazon EBS Snapshots for data backups to reduce storage costs

E) Leverage Amazon S3 for object storage and Amazon S3 Lifecycle Policies to transition data to cheaper storage classes over time

QUESTION 65

Your organization is seeking to implement strategies to reduce AWS costs while maintaining performance and availability. As a solutions architect, you need to recommend a solution that optimizes costs without compromising performance.

A) Utilize AWS Auto Scaling to dynamically adjust resources based on traffic patterns and optimize cost

B) Implement Amazon CloudFront to cache content closer to end users and reduce data transfer costs

C) Leverage AWS Compute Optimizer to analyze resource utilization and right-size EC2 instances for cost savings

D) Utilize Amazon EBS Provisioned IOPS SSD volumes to improve performance and cost efficiency for database workloads

E) Implement AWS Lambda with provisioned concurrency to reduce cold starts and optimize costs for serverless workloads

PRACTICE TEST 7 - ANSWERS ONLY

QUESTION 1

Answer - B) Integrate with an external identity provider (IdP) supporting SAML 2.0, configure IAM roles for federated access, and enable AWS Config.

A) - Incorrect because simply enabling AWS CloudTrail and Amazon GuardDuty, while important for monitoring and security, does not address the integration with existing identity systems or the scalability of the federated access solution.

B) - Correct because integrating with an external IdP supporting SAML 2.0, configuring IAM roles for federated access, and enabling AWS Config are fundamental steps in setting up a secure, scalable federated access management system that integrates with existing corporate credentials. This approach leverages the existing identity infrastructure, supports secure access management, and provides configuration recording and assessment for compliance.

C) - Incorrect because using individual IAM user accounts does not leverage federated access and fails to utilize the organization's existing identity infrastructure.

D) - Incorrect because, while AWS Directory Service and IAM Identity Center can work together, this option does not specifically address the need for integration with external identity providers or the scalability of federated access management.

E) - Incorrect because, although restricting access based on user attributes and custom authentication flows can enhance security, this choice does not adequately address the primary goal of integrating with existing corporate credentials for federated access management.

QUESTION 2

Answer - B) Utilize both public and private subnets, placing only externally facing components in the public subnets.

A) Incorrect - Placing all application components in a single public subnet does not provide the necessary isolation and increases the attack surface.

B) Correct - This approach follows the best practice of using public subnets for components that need to be accessible from the internet (e.g., web servers) and private subnets for backend components (e.g., databases), which enhances security by reducing exposure.

C) Incorrect - While using private subnets adds a layer of security, relying solely on AWS Direct Connect for external access is not practical for an online retail application that needs to be accessible over the internet.

D) Incorrect - Creating a VPC without subnets negates the benefits of using a VPC and subnets for network segmentation and security.

E) Incorrect - Using multiple VPCs for each component might unnecessarily complicate the architecture and increase management overhead without providing proportional security benefits. Isolation within a single VPC using subnets is generally sufficient.

QUESTION 3

Answer - [A] Utilize AWS WAF with custom rules to inspect and filter incoming web traffic for malicious content and protect against common web vulnerabilities.

Option A - Correct. Utilizing AWS WAF with custom rules provides protection against common web vulnerabilities by inspecting and filtering incoming web traffic.

Option B - AWS Cognito manages user authentication and authorization but may not directly mitigate common web vulnerabilities like AWS WAF.

Option C - Amazon Inspector assesses security posture but may not focus specifically on protecting against common web vulnerabilities like AWS WAF.

Option D - Amazon S3 bucket policies restrict access to data but may not directly address common web vulnerabilities in the application layer.

Option E - AWS Secrets Manager securely stores credentials but may not directly protect against common web vulnerabilities like AWS WAF.

QUESTION 4

Answer - [C] Configure AWS DataSync to replicate data between the primary and DR environments in real-time. Implement Amazon Route 53 failover routing with health checks to automatically redirect traffic to the DR site when the primary site is unavailable.

Option C - Correct. AWS DataSync enables real-time data replication between the primary and DR environments, while Amazon Route 53 failover routing with health checks automatically redirects traffic to the DR site when needed.

Option A - While AWS Backup and Route 53 latency-based routing offer some resilience, they may not provide real-time data replication or automatic failover.

Option B - AWS Storage Gateway replication and CloudFront with AWS Shield offer some resilience but may not provide real-time data replication or automatic failover.

Option D - AWS Snowball and AWS Direct Connect with Transit Gateway provide data transfer and network connectivity options but may not offer real-time replication or automatic failover.

Option E - AWS DMS and CloudFront with AWS WAF offer some resilience but may not provide real-time replication or automatic failover.

QUESTION 5

Answer - B) Use Amazon SQS FIFO queue with a batch mode of 5 messages per operation.

B) Use Amazon SQS FIFO queue with a batch mode of 5 messages per operation - This option processes appointment requests in the order they are received while allowing for simultaneous processing of multiple requests for different medical specialties through batch mode. It ensures order accuracy and scalability, meeting the company's requirements for sequential requests and parallel processing.

A) Use Amazon SQS FIFO queue with default settings - Default settings may not ensure order accuracy and efficient parallel processing for different medical specialties.

C) Use Amazon SQS FIFO queue with exactly-once processing enabled - While ensuring order accuracy, it may not efficiently handle simultaneous requests due to sequential processing.

D) Use Amazon SQS standard queue to process the messages - Standard queues lack message ordering, which is crucial for maintaining appointment order, and may not efficiently handle simultaneous requests.

E) Use Amazon SQS FIFO queue with message deduplication enabled - While avoiding duplicate messages, it doesn't guarantee order processing, and may not efficiently handle simultaneous requests.

QUESTION 6

Answer - [B] Utilize IAM roles for EC2 instances with least privilege permissions to access other AWS services, and configure IAM policies to control access to RDS instances and ELB.

Option B - Correct. Utilizing IAM roles for EC2 instances with least privilege permissions and configuring IAM policies for RDS instances and ELB ensures secure access control to the AWS resources in the multi-tier architecture.

Option A - Creating IAM users with access keys may not provide the necessary level of security and granularity required for managing access to resources securely.

Option C - While IAM groups can help organize permissions, configuring IAM policies at the individual resource level provides finer control over access.

Option D - Setting up IAM roles for each AWS resource and configuring cross-account access may introduce unnecessary complexity and does not align with best practices for IAM security.

Option E - Deploying IAM policies at the organizational unit level may not provide granular control over access to individual resources within the architecture.

QUESTION 7

Answer - [C] Configuring network ACLs to restrict traffic between subnets.

A) Incorrect - AWS Direct Connect provides a dedicated network connection between on-premises infrastructure and AWS, but it's not specifically for communication within subnets.

B) Incorrect - AWS CloudFront is a content delivery network service and is not used for secure communication between subnets.

C) Correct - Configuring network ACLs allows you to control traffic flow at the subnet level, providing an additional layer of security within the VPC.

D) Incorrect - VPC Flow Logs are used for monitoring network traffic but do not directly contribute to securing communication between subnets.

E) Incorrect - AWS Secrets Manager is used for managing credentials and secrets, not for securing communication between subnets.

QUESTION 8

Answer - [B] Configuring AWS Lambda authorizers in Amazon API Gateway for request validation.

A) Incorrect - While AWS IAM can be used for service authentication, it may not directly integrate with API Gateway for secure API strategies.

B) Correct - AWS Lambda authorizers in Amazon API Gateway allow for custom authorization logic to be executed before a request reaches the backend service, providing a robust solution for secure API strategies and request validation between microservices.

C) Incorrect - OAuth 2.0 authentication with Amazon Cognito is more suitable for user authentication and may not directly address service-to-service communication security.

D) Incorrect - ACM provides SSL/TLS certificates for securing communication but is not specifically designed for API Gateway authentication.

E) Incorrect - AWS AppMesh is a service mesh that helps manage communication between microservices but does not directly provide secure API strategies for authentication and authorization.

QUESTION 9

Answer - [B] Deploying microservices in Amazon ECS with AWS Fargate for serverless container deployment, ensuring resilience and high availability, and utilizing Amazon S3 with server-side encryption for data storage, meeting compliance regulations.

A) While AWS Lambda offers serverless deployment, it may not provide direct control over data storage encryption or compliance with access controls for healthcare data.

B) Deploying microservices in Amazon ECS with AWS Fargate ensures resilience and high availability, while Amazon S3 with server-side encryption meets compliance requirements for data at rest encryption and access controls.

C) AWS App Mesh manages microservices traffic but may not directly address data storage encryption or access controls required for compliance with healthcare regulations.

D) AWS Lambda offers serverless deployment, but Amazon Aurora may not be the most suitable option for data storage encryption and access controls for healthcare data compliance.

E) While deploying microservices in Amazon EKS with AWS Fargate offers resilience and high availability, Amazon Redshift may not be the best choice for data storage encryption and access controls for healthcare data compliance.

QUESTION 10

Answer - A) Use Amazon FSx File Gateway to provide low-latency, on-premises access to fully managed file shares in Amazon EFS. The applications deployed on AWS can access this data directly from Amazon EFS.

A) Use Amazon FSx File Gateway to provide low-latency, on-premises access to fully managed file shares in Amazon EFS. The applications deployed on AWS can access this data directly from Amazon EFS - This option aligns with the requirement by suggesting the use of Amazon FSx File Gateway with Amazon EFS, ensuring low-latency access to product images during and after migration.

B) Use Amazon Storage Gateway's File Gateway to provide low-latency, on-premises access to fully managed file shares in Amazon FSx for Windows File Server. The applications deployed on AWS can access this data directly from Amazon FSx in AWS - This option does not align with the requirement as it suggests using FSx for Windows File Server instead of Amazon EFS, which may not meet the low-latency access requirement.

C) Use AWS Storage Gateway's File Gateway to provide low-latency, on-premises access to fully managed file shares in Amazon S3. The applications deployed on AWS can access this data directly from Amazon S3 - This option does not align with the requirement as it suggests using Amazon S3 instead of Amazon EFS, which may not meet the low-latency access requirement.

D) Use Amazon FSx File Gateway to provide low-latency, on-premises access to fully managed file shares in Amazon FSx for Windows File Server. The applications deployed on AWS can access this data directly from Amazon FSx in AWS - This option does not align with the requirement as it suggests using FSx for Windows File Server instead of Amazon EFS, which may not meet the low-latency access requirement.

QUESTION 11

Answer - A) Implement Amazon S3 with a lifecycle policy to transition to S3 Standard-Infrequent Access after one year and S3 Glacier after five years.

A) Implement Amazon S3 with a lifecycle policy to transition to S3 Standard-Infrequent Access after one year and S3 Glacier after five years. - Correct because S3 provides the required durability and availability, and the lifecycle policy aligns perfectly with the firm's compliance and cost-efficiency requirements.

B) Use Amazon EBS with snapshots scheduled to Amazon S3 and lifecycle rules to transition to S3 Glacier Deep Archive for long-term storage. - Incorrect because EBS is primarily for block storage, not for long-term document storage, and does not directly support the specified lifecycle transitions without additional manual processes.

C) Configure Amazon EFS with lifecycle management to move data to EFS Infrequent Access and then archive to AWS Backup for long-term compliance. - Incorrect as EFS is optimized for file-based storage and does not natively support archiving to Glacier or compliance retention directly.

D) Deploy Amazon FSx with automated backup to AWS Backup, utilizing lifecycle policies to move backups to S3 Glacier Deep Archive. - Incorrect because FSx is focused on specific use cases like Windows File Server and Lustre, not on general document storage and compliance archiving.

E) Utilize Amazon S3 with Intelligent-Tiering to automatically move data to the most cost-effective access tier based on usage patterns and set deletion policies for data older than seven years. - Incorrect as it doesn't specify the transition to Glacier after five years, making it less aligned with the scenario's requirements despite its cost-efficiency.

QUESTION 12

Answer - D) Configure AWS Fargate for container-based immutable deployments, integrate AWS CodeCommit with AWS CodePipeline for CI/CD, and use AWS Secrets Manager for managing secrets.

A) Adopt AWS CodePipeline and AWS CodeBuild for the CI/CD pipeline, utilize Amazon EC2 Auto Scaling groups for immutable deployments, and enforce strict IAM policies for access control. - Incorrect because while it supports CI/CD and access control, using EC2 Auto Scaling for immutable deployments doesn't fully leverage the benefits of containerization for immutability.

B) Utilize AWS Lambda for serverless deployment, AWS WAF for securing the application layer, and Amazon S3 with versioning enabled for storing application code securely. - Incorrect as it focuses on serverless execution and application layer security, but does not address the company's need for immutable deployments in a containerized environment.

C) Implement AWS CloudFormation for infrastructure as code, Amazon EC2 instances with AWS Systems Manager for patch management, and AWS IAM roles for role-based access control. - Incorrect because, although it includes infrastructure as code and access control, it lacks the container-based approach for true immutability in deployments.

D) Configure AWS Fargate for container-based immutable deployments, integrate AWS CodeCommit with AWS CodePipeline for CI/CD, and use AWS Secrets Manager for managing secrets. - Correct as it offers a comprehensive solution that covers container-based immutable deployments, integrates seamlessly with CI/CD pipelines, and securely manages secrets, aligning with the security and compliance needs of financial services.

E) Leverage Amazon ECS with Amazon ECR for container management and deployment, AWS CloudTrail for logging all deployment activities, and AWS KMS for encryption of deployment artifacts. - Incorrect because, while it provides a container management solution and ensures logging and encryption, it doesn't integrate as directly with CI/CD processes or secret management as the correct option does.

QUESTION 13

Answer - B) Use Amazon CloudFront for content delivery, AWS WAF for filtering malicious web traffic, and Amazon GuardDuty for detecting suspicious activities.

A) Implement AWS Auto Scaling to manage traffic spikes, Amazon CloudWatch Alarms for incident detection, and AWS Lambda for executing remediation scripts. - Incorrect because this setup primarily focuses on scaling and basic incident detection without comprehensive traffic analysis and threat detection capabilities.

B) Use Amazon CloudFront for content delivery, AWS WAF for filtering malicious web traffic, and Amazon GuardDuty for detecting suspicious activities. - Correct as it provides a holistic approach to security, combining content delivery optimization, web traffic filtering, and advanced threat detection, suitable for handling high traffic volumes and potential security incidents efficiently.

C) Configure AWS Elastic Beanstalk for application deployment, Amazon S3 and Amazon RDS for data storage with encryption, and AWS CloudTrail for monitoring API calls. - Incorrect because, while ensuring application deployment and data encryption, it lacks the proactive incident detection and response mechanisms provided by CloudFront, WAF, and GuardDuty.

D) Deploy AWS Fargate for running containerized applications, utilize AWS Secrets Manager for managing secrets, and Amazon Inspector for automated security assessments. - Incorrect as it focuses on container management and security assessments, not directly addressing incident response and web traffic filtering needs during peak traffic times.

E) Leverage Amazon EC2 instances with Elastic Load Balancing, AWS Shield for DDoS protection, and AWS Config rules for ensuring compliance and security posture. - Incorrect because, although it offers load balancing and DDoS protection, it doesn't integrate specific mechanisms for real-time threat detection and automated incident response like GuardDuty.

QUESTION 14

Answer - A) Utilize Amazon API Gateway for managing the API, Amazon CloudFront for global distribution, AWS Lambda for backend processing, and Amazon QuickSight for usage analysis.

A) Utilize Amazon API Gateway for managing the API, Amazon CloudFront for global distribution, AWS Lambda for backend processing, and Amazon QuickSight for usage analysis - Correct. This architecture ensures high availability, global reach, secure processing, and effective usage analysis.

B) Employ AWS Global Accelerator to route traffic, Amazon ECS for containerized shipment tracking, AWS WAF for security, and AWS Cost Explorer for cost analysis - Incorrect because Global Accelerator and ECS are not specifically needed for API management and the scenario's requirements. Also, Cost Explorer provides cost management insights rather than usage pattern analysis for optimization.

C) Implement Amazon API Gateway with regional endpoints, use AWS Fargate for scalable backend services, AWS Shield for security, and Amazon Athena for usage pattern analysis - Incorrect because while this setup could provide scalability and security, it lacks the global distribution component that CloudFront offers.

D) Use Amazon API Gateway with private endpoints, Amazon VPC for network isolation, AWS Direct Connect for dedicated connectivity, and Amazon Redshift for usage analysis - Incorrect as it focuses too much on isolation and connectivity, missing the global distribution aspect necessary for an international shipment tracking API.

E) Deploy Amazon API Gateway with a multi-region setup, use Amazon S3 for storing shipment data, AWS CloudTrail for security logging, and AWS Lambda with Amazon Kinesis for real-time usage pattern analysis - Incorrect because, although this offers a good approach to logging and real-time analysis, it complicates the architecture unnecessarily for the given scenario. CloudFront provides a simpler solution for global distribution.

QUESTION 15

Answer - B) Suspend the ReplaceUnhealthy process type for the Auto Scaling group and apply the maintenance patch to the instance. Once the instance is ready, manually set the instance's health status back to healthy and activate the ReplaceUnhealthy process type again.

B) Suspend the ReplaceUnhealthy process type for the Auto Scaling group and apply the maintenance patch to the instance - This option effectively addresses the maintenance challenge by suspending the process responsible for replacing unhealthy instances, allowing the maintenance to proceed without triggering Auto Scaling actions.

A) Suspend the HealthCheck process type for the Auto Scaling group and apply the maintenance patch to the instance - Suspending health checks may not prevent instance replacement and may not efficiently address the maintenance challenge.

C) Put the instance into the Detached state and then update the instance by applying the maintenance patch - Detaching instances may disrupt application availability and may not align with the requirement for uninterrupted maintenance.

D) Temporarily suspend the AddToLoadBalancer process type for the Auto Scaling group and apply the maintenance patch to the instance - Suspending processes related to load balancer integration may not efficiently address the maintenance challenge and may not prevent instance replacement during maintenance.

E) Take a snapshot of the instance, create a new Amazon Machine Image (AMI), and then launch a new instance using this AMI - Creating a new instance from a snapshot introduces complexity and may not efficiently address the maintenance challenge, especially in scenarios where immediate fixes are required.

QUESTION 16

Answer - A) Implement AWS Direct Connect along with AWS Transit Gateway, utilizing dynamic routing.

A) Implement AWS Direct Connect along with AWS Transit Gateway, utilizing dynamic routing - Correct because Direct Connect offers low latency and high throughput, while Transit Gateway provides a hub to connect multiple VPCs and on-premises sites with dynamic routing capabilities.

B) Use AWS Site-to-Site VPN connections combined with Amazon Route 53 for health checks and latency-based routing - Incorrect because Site-to-Site VPN does not offer the same level of performance as Direct Connect, and Route 53's main role is DNS management, not dynamic routing for VPN connections.

C) Deploy a combination of AWS Direct Connect and AWS Site-to-Site VPN, with VPN as a backup - Incorrect as it does not specifically mention the use of dynamic routing, which is crucial for adjusting to network changes.

D) Establish AWS Direct Connect with AWS Global Accelerator to improve performance and availability - Incorrect because Global Accelerator primarily improves internet-facing applications with global users and is not focused on inter-region connectivity.

E) Leverage AWS Site-to-Site VPN with AWS CloudMap for service discovery and dynamic routing - Incorrect because CloudMap is for service discovery within your cloud environment, not for dynamic routing between on-premises and AWS.

QUESTION 17

Answer - D) Leverage AWS Application Discovery Service for migration planning, AWS Snowball Edge for data transfer with on-device encryption, and Amazon GuardDuty for threat detection.

A) Incorrect because AWS DMS and Fargate address different aspects of migration and container management respectively, but do not specifically cater to the high security and compliance needs of financial transactions.

B) Incorrect as AWS Snowball and RDS with Multi-AZ deployment focus on data transfer and database high availability but do not provide comprehensive planning or threat detection capabilities essential for sensitive financial data.

C) Incorrect because while AWS DataSync and Lambda facilitate efficient data transfer and processing, Amazon Inspector's security assessments are not tailored for the migration phase or financial transaction compliance.

D) Correct as AWS Application Discovery Service aids in detailed migration planning, Snowball Edge offers secure data transfer with encryption, and GuardDuty provides continuous monitoring and threat detection, aligning with the security and compliance requirements for financial data migration.

E) Incorrect as S3 Transfer Acceleration and EC2 Auto Scaling enhance data upload speeds and compute scalability, AWS Shield offers DDoS protection which, while important, do not address the secure migration planning and execution needed for financial data.

QUESTION 18

Answer - [A] Utilize AWS Secrets Manager to securely store and rotate database credentials. Integrate AWS Lambda with Secrets Manager for automated rotation and retrieval of secrets.

Option B - Storing secrets in plaintext files within an S3 bucket is not secure and violates best practices for secret management.

Option C - While Parameter Store is suitable for managing configurations and secrets, CodeDeploy is used for deploying applications, not configuration changes.

Option D - Managing secrets in a spreadsheet and sharing them through S3 is insecure and lacks automation for rotation and retrieval.

Option E - Deploying an on-premises solution contradicts the objective of enhancing security on AWS and introduces unnecessary complexity.

QUESTION 19

Answer - [B] Implement AWS Secrets Manager to securely store database credentials. Integrate ECS tasks with Secrets Manager for automated retrieval of credentials at runtime.

Option A - Storing database credentials directly in Dockerfiles as environment variables is not recommended for security reasons and lacks centralized management and rotation capabilities.

Option C - Maintaining plaintext credentials within Docker images poses security risks and lacks automation for rotation and retrieval.

Option D - While Parameter Store can centrally manage configurations, Secrets Manager is specifically designed for securely storing and rotating secrets like database credentials.

Option E - Storing credentials in plaintext files within EFS lacks encryption and may expose data to unauthorized access.

Explanation for Choice B: Utilizing AWS Secrets Manager provides secure storage and rotation of database credentials. Integrating with ECS tasks allows for automated retrieval at runtime, enhancing security and compliance.

QUESTION 20

Answer - B) Create an Amazon CloudWatch metric filter to process AWS CloudTrail logs containing API call details. Establish an alarm based on this metric's rate to send an Amazon SNS notification to the required team.

B) Create an Amazon CloudWatch metric filter to process AWS CloudTrail logs containing API call details. Establish an alarm based on this metric's rate to send an Amazon SNS notification to the required team. -

This option directly addresses the scenario by analyzing CloudTrail logs for unauthorized API queries and triggering real-time alerts using CloudWatch alarms and Amazon SNS notifications.

A) Implement AWS Config Rules to monitor API activity and define rules to detect unauthorized API calls. Configure AWS Config to trigger an AWS Lambda function upon rule evaluation to notify relevant stakeholders. - While AWS Config can monitor API activity, it may not provide real-time alerting capabilities for immediate incident response as required in this scenario.

C) Leverage AWS Trusted Advisor to publish metrics about check results to Amazon CloudWatch. Set up an alarm to track status changes for checks in the Service Limits category for the APIs, triggering notifications when service quotas are exceeded. - While Trusted Advisor offers valuable insights, it may not directly address the need for real-time detection of unauthorized API queries.

D) Use Amazon Athena SQL queries against AWS CloudTrail log files stored in Amazon S3 buckets. Generate reports using Amazon QuickSight for managerial dashboards. - While this option provides insights, it may not offer real-time alerting capabilities as required in this scenario.

E) Configure AWS CloudTrail to stream event data to Amazon Kinesis. Utilize Amazon Kinesis stream-level metrics in Amazon CloudWatch to trigger an AWS Lambda function that will initiate an error workflow. - While this option utilizes streaming data, it may introduce complexity and latency compared to directly analyzing CloudTrail logs for real-time alerts.

QUESTION 21

Answer - [A) Utilize Amazon Kinesis Data Streams for data ingestion and processing.]

A) Kinesis Data Streams is specifically designed for handling real-time data streams with high throughput and low latency, making it suitable for processing streaming data in real-time analytics platforms.

B) Using Lambda with Kinesis Data Firehose and Redshift is not ideal for real-time processing as it introduces additional latency due to batch processing.

C) While S3 is suitable for storing streaming data, it does not provide real-time processing capabilities.

D) SQS is a message queuing service, not ideal for real-time data processing.
E) EMR is not designed for real-time analytics.

QUESTION 22

Answer - [A) Amazon RDS Multi-AZ deployment and B) Amazon DynamoDB Global Tables]

Option A involves Amazon RDS Multi-AZ deployment for relational databases with automated failover, ensuring minimal downtime for disaster recovery.

Option B involves Amazon DynamoDB Global Tables for multi-region replication of NoSQL databases, ensuring continuous availability and disaster recovery.

Option C involves AWS Backup for centralized backup and restore, but it does not directly address automated failover for databases.

Option D involves AWS CloudFormation for infrastructure as code, but it does not directly provide automated recovery for databases.

Option E involves AWS Direct Connect for dedicated network connectivity, but it does not directly provide automated failover for databases.

QUESTION 23

Answer - [C) Deploy Amazon EC2 instances in multiple AWS Regions with Route 53 latency-based routing for active-active failover, minimizing response times and maximizing availability.]

Option C) is correct as it involves deploying EC2 instances in multiple AWS Regions with latency-based routing, enabling active-active failover with minimal response times and maximum availability.

Option A) involves S3 replication but may not provide the same level of application failover capabilities. Option B) involves CDN failover but may not address application-level failover requirements.

Option D) involves Redshift for data analytics but may not achieve the same level of application failover as EC2 instances.

Option E) involves real-time replication but may not achieve the required RPO and RTO objectives for the video-on-demand platform.

QUESTION 24

Answer - C) Implement AWS Global Accelerator to improve application performance by optimizing the network path between users and the collaboration platform.

Option C is correct because AWS Global Accelerator improves application performance by optimizing the network path, making it suitable for low-latency communication between users in different regions while also being cost-efficient. This aligns with the scenario of selecting the most cost-efficient solution to improve application performance.

Option A is incorrect because while deploying Amazon EC2 instances in multiple regions ensures data consistency, it may not provide the same level of network optimization as AWS Global Accelerator.

Option B is incorrect because while Amazon CloudFront with Lambda@Edge caches content and reduces latency, it may not optimize the network path as effectively as AWS Global Accelerator.

Option D is incorrect because while Amazon API Gateway with AWS Lambda can build serverless APIs, it may not provide the same level of network optimization as AWS Global Accelerator.

Option E is incorrect because while Amazon ElastiCache with Redis caches session data, it may not provide the same level of network optimization as AWS Global Accelerator.

QUESTION 25

Answer - A) Tier-4 (16 terabytes)

A) Tier-4 (16 terabytes) - Correct. For failover purposes, Aurora promotes the replica with the highest priority, indicated by the lowest tier number. Between replicas of the same tier, instance size does not dictate priority.

B) Tier-4 (8 terabytes) - Incorrect. While it shares the same tier as the correct answer, instance size is not the primary determinant for failover within the same tier, necessitating a review for clarity on Aurora's failover criteria which primarily consider tier.

C) Tier-10 (32 terabytes) - Incorrect. This option offers a larger size but is not the highest priority for failover due to its tier ranking.

D) Tier-12 (16 terabytes) - Incorrect. It is not prioritized for failover due to its lower tier ranking.

E) Tier-12 (8 terabytes) - Incorrect. It has the lowest priority based on its tier, and the size is not a determining factor for failover.

QUESTION 26

Answer - C) Use AWS CloudFormation to define infrastructure as code and automate the deployment of AWS resources in a consistent and repeatable manner, promoting immutable infrastructure.

Option A is incorrect because while AWS AppConfig manages application configurations dynamically, it does not inherently support the principles of immutable infrastructure where the infrastructure is immutable and replaced rather than updated.

Option B is incorrect because while AWS OpsWorks automates infrastructure provisioning and configuration management, it may not directly align with the goal of achieving immutable infrastructure on AWS.

Option C is correct because AWS CloudFormation allows defining infrastructure as code, enabling the creation of immutable infrastructure and automating the deployment of AWS resources in a consistent and repeatable manner, aligning with the goal of achieving immutable infrastructure on AWS.

Option D is incorrect because while AWS Elastic Beanstalk automates application deployment, it may not inherently support the principles of immutable infrastructure.

Option E is incorrect because while Amazon ECS Anywhere allows running containerized microservices on-premises, it does not directly address the goal of achieving immutable infrastructure on AWS.

QUESTION 27

Answer - A) Implement API Gateway stage variables and manage multiple stages for versioning

Option A - Implementing API Gateway stage variables allows for easy management of multiple deployment stages, enabling seamless API versioning without disrupting existing clients.

Option B - API Gateway resource policies can restrict access but are not primarily designed for versioning and may lead to endpoint proliferation.

Option C - Deploying new APIs with different paths may confuse clients and does not provide a clear versioning strategy.

Option D - API Gateway usage plans and API keys are more focused on access control than versioning and may not provide the desired granularity for API updates.

Option E - Lambda aliases and versions are not directly related to API Gateway versioning and may not offer the flexibility needed for seamless updates while maintaining backward compatibility.

QUESTION 28

Answer - B) Use Amazon SQS to decouple application components and enable reliable message-based communication between serverless functions.

Option B - Amazon SQS provides reliable and scalable message queuing for decoupling application components and managing asynchronous task execution in a serverless environment.

Option A - While AWS Step Functions can orchestrate tasks, Amazon SQS may be a more suitable option for managing asynchronous task execution directly.

Option C - While S3 event notifications can trigger Lambda functions, Amazon SQS offers more control and flexibility for managing message-based communication between serverless functions.

Option D - AWS Glue is primarily used for data integration and ETL tasks, which may not be the best fit for managing asynchronous task execution in a serverless architecture.

Option E - AWS Fargate with AWS Batch is more suitable for batch processing tasks and may not be the optimal choice for managing asynchronous task execution in real-time serverless applications.

QUESTION 29

Answer - A) Amazon Route 53 with latency-based routing.

A) Route 53 with latency-based routing directs users to the region with the lowest latency, optimizing performance.

B) SQS is for messaging, not latency optimization.

C) RDS Multi-AZ provides redundancy within a region, not across regions.

D) Direct Connect offers dedicated connectivity but does not optimize latency across regions.

E) S3 cross-region replication is for data synchronization, not latency optimization.

QUESTION 30

Answer - D) Utilize Amazon Kinesis Data Streams with AWS Lambda for real-time data processing and store it in Amazon S3

D) Amazon Kinesis Data Streams combined with AWS Lambda offers real-time data processing capabilities suitable for analyzing viewer interaction data during live streaming events, personalizing content recommendations, enhancing viewer engagement, ensuring flexibility, and scalability with real-time processing.

A, B) These options involve storing data in relational databases or data warehouses, which may not be suitable for real-time processing and scalability required for analyzing viewer preferences during live streaming events.

C, E) While these options involve using AWS Lambda and Amazon DynamoDB or S3, they may not provide the real-time processing capabilities required for adapting content dynamically and enhancing viewer engagement.

QUESTION 31

Answer - A) AWS Systems Manager for automated management of EC2 instances, AWS Config to track compliance with company policies, Amazon Inspector for security assessments, and AWS IAM for managing access.

A) Correct, because AWS Systems Manager automates the application of patches and management of instances, AWS Config ensures compliance with security policies, Amazon Inspector provides security assessments to identify vulnerabilities, and IAM manages access control effectively.

B) Incorrect, while these services provide important security and infrastructure management capabilities, they do not offer the same level of compliance monitoring, instance management, and access control as the combination in A.

C) Incorrect as WAF, Shield, and Direct Connect focus on network and application layer protection without directly addressing instance compliance and patch management.

D) Incorrect, these services are focused on data processing and analytics, not directly on security compliance and instance management.

E) Incorrect, these services are more oriented towards computing and storage solutions, lacking direct mechanisms for compliance tracking and automated security responses specific to EC2 instances.

QUESTION 32

Answer - [B] Implement Amazon RDS with cross-Region read replicas and use AWS Backup for automated backups and cross-Region replication of backups.]

Option B - Correct because Amazon RDS with cross-Region read replicas and AWS Backup ensures low RPOs and RTOs by providing automated backups and cross-Region replication, meeting the e-commerce company's requirements for disaster recovery.

Option A - Incorrect because while Aurora with global databases offers multi-master replication, it lacks integration with AWS Backup for automated backups essential for disaster recovery.

Option C - Incorrect because DynamoDB with global tables may not offer the same level of cross-Region backup and replication features as Amazon RDS with cross-Region read replicas and AWS Backup.

Option D - Incorrect because Redshift is optimized for analytics and may not offer the same level of disaster recovery features as Amazon RDS with cross-Region read replicas and AWS Backup.

Option E - Incorrect because DocumentDB may not offer the same level of cross-Region backup and replication features as Amazon RDS with cross-Region read replicas and AWS Backup.

QUESTION 33

Answer - [B] Implement AWS Secrets Manager to securely manage sensitive data.

Option A is incorrect as AWS CloudFormation is not specifically designed for managing secrets.
Option C is incorrect as storing plaintext passwords in S3 buckets is a security risk, regardless of access policies.

Option D is correct because implementing AWS IAM policies to restrict access to sensitive data is a recommended practice for security.

Option E is incorrect as plaintext HTTP should not be used for API communication due to security concerns.

Option B is correct because using AWS Secrets Manager to securely manage sensitive data helps protect information according to best practices and compliance requirements.

QUESTION 34

Answer - [A) Implement Amazon EMR clusters with Spot Instances.]

Option A is the most cost-effective solution as it utilizes Amazon EMR clusters with Spot Instances, which can significantly reduce costs for processing large volumes of data. Spot Instances allow you to take advantage of unused EC2 capacity at discounted rates.

Option B introduces unnecessary complexity with data transformation and may not be the most cost-efficient.

Option C, while serverless, may not be suitable for real-time processing at scale.
Option D requires managing and scaling Apache Kafka clusters manually, which may not be cost-effective.

Option E, Amazon Athena, is better suited for ad-hoc queries rather than real-time processing of large volumes of data.

QUESTION 35

Answer - B) Implement WebSocket APIs on Amazon API Gateway with Amazon RDS for real-time market data storage and Amazon Cognito for secure transaction processing

B) Implementing WebSocket APIs on Amazon API Gateway with Amazon RDS ensures low-latency data streaming for real-time market data updates, while leveraging Amazon Cognito provides high-level security for user transactions in the stock trading mobile application.

A, C, D, E) These options either do not provide support for real-time market data updates or involve using services not suitable for secure transaction processing in a financial application.

QUESTION 36

Answer - [A, B]

A) Correct - KMS is suitable for managing encryption keys, and CloudHSM provides secure key storage, aligning with best practices for key management.

B) Correct - S3 server-side encryption with KMS managed keys covers data at rest, and SSL/TLS ensures data in transit encryption, meeting compliance requirements for patient data.

C) Incorrect - Redshift encryption at rest is relevant, but ACM is used for SSL/TLS certificates, not encryption keys.
D) Incorrect - DynamoDB client-side encryption is suitable for data at rest, and Secrets Manager manages secrets but doesn't directly address data encryption.

E) Incorrect - Aurora encryption at rest is relevant, but KMS is typically used for encryption key management, not Secrets Manager.

QUESTION 37

Answer - A) Amazon S3 for its scalability and data availability, utilizing S3 Select for efficient data retrieval.

A) Correct - Amazon S3 provides highly scalable object storage, and S3 Select allows for retrieving only the subset of data needed from within objects, making it ideal for both batch and real-time data processing and analysis.

B) Incorrect - While EFS offers scalable file storage, it's more suited for use cases requiring file system capabilities and persistent storage, not necessarily for large-scale data analytics.

C) Incorrect - DynamoDB offers fast and flexible NoSQL database capabilities suitable for applications requiring consistent, single-digit millisecond latency but may not be the most cost-effective for large-scale data analytics.

D) Incorrect - Amazon Redshift is optimized for data warehousing and analytics but might incur higher costs for storage compared to S3, especially for large datasets requiring frequent access.

E) Incorrect - AWS Snowball is a data transport solution, used for moving large amounts of data into and out of AWS, and does not provide storage or data processing capabilities.

QUESTION 38

Answer - A) Migrate the database to Amazon RDS with Multi-AZ deployment for high availability and automated backups.

B) Utilize Amazon Aurora Serverless for on-demand, auto-scaling database capacity without managing underlying infrastructure.

Option A - Amazon RDS Multi-AZ deployment ensures high availability and automated backups, addressing the downtime concerns of the legacy database.

Option B - Amazon Aurora Serverless provides on-demand, auto-scaling database capacity without the need to manage underlying infrastructure, ensuring scalability and high availability for the new database solution.

Options C, D, and E may provide benefits in specific scenarios but do not fully address the high availability and scalability requirements while minimizing management overhead.

QUESTION 39

Answer - B) Utilize Amazon Kinesis Data Firehose to ingest data from different sources, and leverage AWS Lambda for serverless data processing.

Option A - Amazon ECS Anywhere and AWS Glue are relevant, but AWS Glue alone does not handle real-time processing, making this option less suitable.

Option B - Amazon Kinesis Data Firehose is designed for data ingestion, and AWS Lambda allows for serverless data processing, meeting the scalability, security, and compliance requirements.

Option C - Amazon S3 Glacier is for long-term storage, and Amazon QuickSight is for analytics, but they don't address the real-time processing needs.

Option D - Amazon Redshift is for data warehousing, and Amazon Comprehend Medical is for medical insights, but they don't directly address the ingestion and transformation requirements.

Option E - AWS Data Exchange and AWS Transfer Family focus on data sharing and ingestion, respectively, but do not provide real-time processing capabilities required in the scenario.

QUESTION 40

Answer - C) Ingest tracking data into Amazon Kinesis Data Streams, which triggers an AWS Lambda function for processing and stores update logs in Amazon DynamoD

C) Ingesting tracking data into Amazon Kinesis Data Streams with AWS Lambda allows for real-time processing and instant updates. Storing update logs in Amazon DynamoDB ensures low-latency access and scalability.

A) Processing tracking data with AWS Lambda and Amazon S3 may introduce latency and is not suitable for real-time package tracking systems.

B) Using Amazon Kinesis Data Firehose may not provide the necessary real-time processing capabilities for instant updates.

D) Amazon SQS is not optimized for real-time processing of tracking data, and storing update logs in Amazon Redshift may introduce delays.

E) Using Amazon API Gateway and an EC2 instance for processing lacks the scalability and real-time processing capabilities required for real-time package tracking systems.

QUESTION 41

Answer - A) Amazon CloudFront for content delivery, AWS Lambda for real-time analytics, and Amazon S3 for storing promotional content.

A) Correct - Amazon CloudFront ensures global content delivery with minimal latency, essential for a worldwide campaign. AWS Lambda can efficiently handle real-time analytics on user engagement without provisioning servers. Amazon S3 is ideal for durably storing promotional content and easily integrates with CloudFront for distribution.

B) Incorrect - While ECS with Fargate and RDS are scalable, they may not provide the latency optimization for global content delivery that CloudFront does. Global Accelerator improves performance but doesn't address the serverless, event-driven analytics requirement.

C) Incorrect - Direct Connect is used for a dedicated network connection to AWS, which doesn't directly contribute to the dynamic scalability or global distribution needs of the campaign. EC2 Auto Scaling and Kinesis could be part of a solution but aren't as optimized for serverless architectures as Lambda.

D) Incorrect - API Gateway, SQS, and Step Functions could architect a serverless application but don't specifically address the global content delivery and real-time analytics requirements.

E) Incorrect - SNS, DynamoDB, and Lambda address aspects of the scenario but don't provide a comprehensive solution for global content distribution and real-time analytics as effectively as CloudFront, Lambda, and S3.

QUESTION 42

Answer - [B) Utilize AWS Storage Gateway with caching mode to store frequently accessed data on-premises and asynchronously upload data to Amazon S3.]

Option B) AWS Storage Gateway with caching mode allows you to store frequently accessed data locally on-premises while asynchronously uploading data to Amazon S3, optimizing costs and ensuring high availability.

Option A) AWS DataSync transfers data over the internet, which may not be as efficient for large-scale data synchronization as Storage Gateway with caching mode.

Option C) AWS Snowball is used for physical data transfer, which may not provide the seamless synchronization required for hybrid cloud environments.

Option D) AWS Direct Connect offers dedicated network connectivity but may not directly address the data synchronization and replication requirements.

Option E) AWS Transfer Family is more suitable for secure file transfers, but it may not provide the same level of data synchronization capabilities as Storage Gateway with caching mode.

QUESTION 43

Answer - A) Use Amazon Kinesis for real-time data processing, AWS Lambda for executing business logic, Amazon Personalize for content recommendation, and Amazon CloudFront for content delivery.

A) Correct - Amazon Kinesis and AWS Lambda support real-time processing and dynamic content delivery. Amazon Personalize enables content recommendation, and CloudFront ensures global content delivery with low latency.

B) Incorrect - While this setup provides scalability and caching, it lacks the direct integration of a content recommendation engine like Amazon Personalize and doesn't leverage a global CDN like CloudFront for minimizing latency.

C) Incorrect - SNS, SQS, DynamoDB, and AppSync offer robust backend capabilities, but this approach doesn't specifically address real-time news updates or personalized content delivery on a global scale as effectively as option A.

D) Incorrect - Fargate, Aurora, CloudMap, and QuickSight focus more on backend processing and analytics, missing out on real-time processing and global content delivery optimization provided by Kinesis and CloudFront.

E) Incorrect - API Gateway, Lambda, DynamoDB, CloudFront, and S3 form a solid serverless architecture but don't explicitly include a recommendation engine like Amazon Personalize for optimizing content delivery based on user behavior.

QUESTION 44

Answer - [B] Implement Amazon SageMaker for distributed training and inference, utilizing Amazon EFS for shared model storage and Amazon CloudWatch for monitoring.

Option A's use of EBS may not be cost-efficient for large datasets and lacks scalability.
Option C and D's use of relational databases like RDS and DynamoDB may not be suitable for storing large model metadata.

Option E lacks shared storage for distributed training.

Option B allows for both distributed training and shared storage, meeting the requirement for cost-efficiency, scalability, and high performance during training.

QUESTION 45

Answer - B) Implement server-side encryption with AWS Key Management Service (SSE-KMS) and enable automatic key rotation

B) Implementing server-side encryption with AWS Key Management Service (SSE-KMS) allows the financial institution to ensure encryption keys are stored securely and can be rotated automatically, meeting regulatory requirements.

A) Server-side encryption with Amazon S3 managed keys (SSE-S3) encrypts the data at rest but may not provide the desired control over key rotation and management.

C) Client-side encryption with customer-provided keys (SSE-C) shifts the responsibility of encryption to the client and may not align with the institution's requirement for centralized key management.
D) Implementing server-side encryption with customer-provided keys (SSE-C) and manually rotating encryption keys introduces operational overhead and potential security risks.

E) Enabling AWS CloudTrail provides auditing capabilities but does not directly address the encryption and key rotation requirements for sensitive data at rest in Amazon S3.

QUESTION 46

Answer - [D] Utilize Amazon Kinesis Data Firehose for ingesting real-time data, process data using AWS Glue, store processed data in Amazon DynamoDB, and use AWS Lambda to trigger processing tasks.

Option A is incorrect because although Amazon EMR can process large volumes of data, it may introduce higher operational overhead compared to AWS Glue for data processing. Additionally, Amazon Redshift may not be the most cost-effective solution for storing processed data in this scenario.

Option B is incorrect because while Amazon EventBridge is suitable for event-driven architectures, Amazon Aurora may not be the best choice for storing processed data compared to Amazon DynamoDB, especially in a real-time processing scenario.

Option C is incorrect because deploying containers on Amazon ECS for data ingestion may introduce management overhead compared to using managed services like Amazon Kinesis Data Firehose. Additionally, Amazon S3 may not be the optimal choice for storing processed data compared to Amazon DynamoDB in this scenario.

Option E is incorrect because although Amazon S3 is highly scalable, it may not provide the real-time processing capabilities required for this scenario, and Amazon Redshift may not be the most suitable choice for storing processed data in real-time.

QUESTION 47

Answer - [D] Implement a serverless architecture using AWS Lambda for compute, Amazon DynamoDB for database needs, and AWS KMS for encryption.

Option D is the correct choice because a serverless architecture with AWS Lambda automatically scales to handle sudden increases in transaction volume without compromising data integrity or availability. DynamoDB provides scalability and high availability, while AWS KMS ensures encryption of sensitive data.

Options A, B, C, and E either lack the same level of scalability, data integrity, or suitable services for the specified requirements.

QUESTION 48

Answer - D) Employ a combination of reserved instances (RI) and spot instances

D) Employing a combination of reserved instances (RI) and spot instances allows the e-commerce company to benefit from cost savings with RIs for predictable workloads while leveraging the scalability and cost-effectiveness of spot instances during peak traffic periods.

A) Using reserved instances (RI) for the entire duration may result in underutilization of resources during non-peak hours, leading to higher costs.

B) Implementing on-demand instances for the entire duration may result in higher costs, especially during peak traffic times.

C) Utilizing spot instances for the entire duration may be risky as spot instances can be terminated with short notice, potentially affecting website availability during peak hours.

E) Implementing a mix of reserved instances (RI) and on-demand instances may not fully optimize costs during predictable traffic patterns and may lead to underutilization of reserved capacity.

QUESTION 49

Answer - B) Deploy AWS Lambda for serverless computing, Amazon DynamoDB Global Tables for multi-region replication, and Amazon API Gateway for mobile backend services.

Option B - This approach leverages serverless computing with AWS Lambda for efficient handling of concurrent user interactions, Amazon DynamoDB Global Tables for real-time data storage with multi-region replication, and Amazon API Gateway for mobile backend services, ensuring high performance and real-time data updates across devices.

Option A - While Amazon EC2 instances with AWS Auto Scaling and Amazon DynamoDB offer scalability and real-time data storage, respectively, they may not provide the same level of efficiency and cost-effectiveness as serverless computing with AWS Lambda for this use case. Additionally, Amazon API Gateway may not offer the same level of integration with serverless architectures.

Option C - Although Amazon ECS and Amazon Aurora offer containerized workload management and real-time data storage, respectively, they may not provide the same level of efficiency and scalability as serverless computing with AWS Lambda for handling concurrent user interactions. Additionally, Amazon API Gateway may not offer the same level of integration with containerized architectures.

Option D - While Amazon EC2 instances with AWS Auto Scaling and Amazon RDS Multi-AZ offer scalability and real-time data storage, respectively, they may not provide the same level of efficiency and cost-effectiveness as serverless computing with AWS Lambda for this use case. Additionally, Amazon API Gateway may not offer the same level of integration with EC2 instances.

Option E - Although AWS Fargate and Amazon RDS Multi-AZ offer containerized workload management and real-time data storage, respectively, they may not provide the same level of efficiency and cost-effectiveness as serverless computing with AWS Lambda for handling concurrent user interactions. Additionally, Amazon API Gateway may not offer the same level of integration with containerized architectures.

QUESTION 50

Answer - A) Utilize Amazon CloudFront with custom SSL certificates to distribute media content globally, leveraging AWS Shield and AWS WAF to protect against DDoS attacks and mitigate security threats.

Option B focuses on media file encoding and storage but does not address content delivery optimization or security requirements adequately.

Option C is tailored for live video streams and may not be suitable for static media content delivery. Option D addresses data transfer optimization but lacks comprehensive content delivery and security features provided by CloudFront.

Option E introduces caching but does not leverage a CDN for global content distribution or address security concerns.

QUESTION 51

Answer - B) Utilize Amazon CloudFront with custom cache behaviors for different content types and Lambda@Edge for request manipulation.

A) - Incorrect because frequent invalidation can lead to increased load times and costs.

B) - Correct as it employs custom cache behaviors for efficient content delivery and Lambda@Edge for fine-tuned request handling.

C) - Incorrect because disabling caching would negate the benefits of using CloudFront.
D) - Incorrect, as compression alone does not address cache behavior optimization.
E) - Incorrect because AWS WAF is primarily for security, not for managing cache behavior.

QUESTION 52

Answer - A) Read-Only Policy.

A) This policy allows only the s3:GetObject action, which permits reading objects from the specified bucket, ensuring that the third-party application can only read objects without the ability to modify them.

B) This policy denies the s3:PutObject action, preventing the application from uploading or modifying objects in the bucket, but it does not address the requirement for read-only access.

C) This policy allows both s3:GetObject and s3:PutObject actions, which would grant the application unnecessary write permissions, violating the requirement for read-only access.

D) This policy allows both s3:ListBucket and s3:GetObject actions, providing unnecessary list permissions and allowing the application to delete objects, which is not required.

E) This policy allows both s3:GetObject and s3:DeleteObject actions, which would grant the application the ability to delete objects from the bucket, violating the requirement for read-only access.

QUESTION 53

Answer - [B] Implement Amazon ECS Fargate for serverless container management.

Option A - AWS Lambda is not designed for container orchestration but rather for serverless compute tasks.

Option B - Correct. Implementing Amazon ECS Fargate allows for serverless container management, reducing operational overhead and optimizing costs.

Option C - Deploying containers directly on EC2 instances without orchestration would increase management complexity and hinder cost optimization.

Option D - AWS Batch is for batch processing, not container orchestration.

Option E - Amazon EKS is a Kubernetes-based container orchestration service, which may introduce additional complexity and overhead compared to ECS Fargate.

QUESTION 54

Answer - [A] Implement AWS Transit Gateway with Direct Connect for centralized connectivity.

Option A - Correct. AWS Transit Gateway with Direct Connect provides centralized and cost-effective connectivity, enabling high availability and fault tolerance across multiple VPCs.

Option B - VPC with NAT Gateways addresses outbound internet traffic but may not provide the centralized connectivity required for large-scale migrations.

Option C - AWS VPN with Global Accelerator offers secure connectivity but may not be the most cost-effective solution for centralized connectivity.

Option D - CloudFront with Route 53 improves DNS resolution but may not address the requirements for network architecture optimization.

Option E - PrivateLink facilitates private connectivity to AWS services but may not provide the centralized connectivity needed for data center migration.

QUESTION 55

Answer - [B] Utilize IAM policies to enforce MFA for all IAM users within the account.

A) Incorrect - Enabling MFA for the root account does not enforce MFA for IAM users and relies on individual users to enable MFA, which may lead to inconsistent security practices.

B) Correct - Utilizing IAM policies to enforce MFA for all IAM users within the account ensures consistent application of MFA and enhances security for accessing AWS Management Console.

C) Incorrect - Enabling MFA for IAM groups does not directly enforce MFA for individual IAM users within the groups, and it may be challenging to manage MFA settings at the group level.

D) Incorrect - Requiring users to authenticate using corporate LDAP credentials does not directly enforce MFA for AWS Management Console access and adds complexity to the authentication process.

E) Incorrect - Enabling AWS SSO and enforcing MFA at the organization level may not align with the organization's existing IAM setup and may require additional configuration and management overhead.

QUESTION 56

Answer - [A] Utilize Amazon EC2 Spot Instances for cost-effective compute during bursts, supplemented with Amazon EC2 Reserved Instances for baseline capacity.

Option A - Correct. Utilizing Amazon EC2 Spot Instances for bursts and Amazon EC2 Reserved Instances for baseline capacity offers a cost-effective solution for handling periodic spikes in compute demand.

Option B - While AWS Lambda can handle event-driven scaling, it may not be the most suitable solution for bursty workloads with long periods of inactivity.

Option C - Enabling hibernation on Amazon EC2 instances helps save costs during inactivity but does not address the bursty nature of the workload efficiently.

Option D - AWS Fargate with auto-scaling may provide flexibility but may not be the most cost-effective solution compared to utilizing Amazon EC2 Spot Instances.

Option E - AWS Batch is suitable for batch computing but may not be the most efficient solution for bursty workloads with long periods of inactivity.

QUESTION 57

Answer - [C] Configure Amazon DynamoDB Auto Scaling to dynamically adjust provisioned capacity based on application traffic patterns.

Option A - Implementing Amazon DynamoDB Accelerator (DAX) improves read performance but may not directly address cost optimization concerns.

Option B - Enabling Amazon DynamoDB On-Demand Capacity Mode allows for automatic scaling but may not be the most cost-effective solution for high-traffic applications with fluctuating demand.

Option C - Correct. Configuring Amazon DynamoDB Auto Scaling dynamically adjusts provisioned capacity, ensuring optimal performance while minimizing costs by scaling based on application traffic patterns.

Option D - While Amazon DynamoDB Global Tables provide data replication, they may not directly optimize costs associated with provisioned throughput and storage.

Option E - Integrating Amazon DynamoDB with Amazon S3 for data archiving focuses on storage management but does not directly address provisioned capacity costs.

QUESTION 58

Answer - [C] Deploy AWS EC2 Reserved Instances for microservices with predictable traffic patterns and supplement with AWS Spot Instances for microservices with variable workloads.

Option C - Correct. Deploying AWS EC2 Reserved Instances for microservices with predictable traffic patterns ensures cost optimization, while supplementing with AWS Spot Instances for microservices with variable workloads maximizes cost efficiency and scalability.

Option A - Utilizing AWS EC2 On-Demand Instances for all microservices may result in higher costs and may not dynamically scale based on demand.

Option B - Implementing AWS Savings Plans with a commitment to a specific instance family may provide discounts but does not specifically address the dynamic nature of microservice workloads.

Option D - Leveraging AWS EC2 Dedicated Hosts may offer improved security and performance but does not provide the flexibility required for dynamic scaling.

Option E - Combining AWS EC2 Spot Instances with AWS Fargate for serverless container orchestration introduces complexity and may not be the most cost-effective solution for microservices with predictable traffic patterns.

QUESTION 59

Answer - [C] Leverage Amazon EC2 Spot Instances with graceful termination handling.

Option C - Correct. Leveraging Amazon EC2 Spot Instances with graceful termination handling allows for cost optimization in batch processing workloads that are tolerant of interruptions.

Option A - Utilizing Amazon EC2 Reserved Instances provides cost predictability but may not be suitable for interruptible workloads.

Option B - Implementing Amazon EC2 On-Demand Instances with manual intervention during interruptions may not be as cost-effective or automated as using Spot Instances with graceful termination handling.

Option D - Deploying AWS Lambda for serverless batch processing may be suitable for specific use cases but may not provide the same level of control or customization as EC2 instances.

Option E - Utilizing Amazon ECS Anywhere for hybrid batch processing introduces complexity and may not be as cost-effective as Spot Instances for interruptible workloads.

QUESTION 60

Answer - [C] Configure the Auto Scaling group to use a step scaling policy triggered by sudden increases in the number of transactions per minute.

A) Incorrect - Using a target tracking scaling policy based on the number of concurrent database connections may not accurately reflect the application's overall performance and scalability requirements during holiday seasons.

B) Incorrect - Implementing a scheduled scaling policy triggered at specific times of holiday seasons may not dynamically respond to sudden traffic increases, potentially resulting in under or over-provisioning of resources.

C) Correct - Configuring a step scaling policy triggered by sudden increases in the number of transactions per minute allows the Auto Scaling group to dynamically adjust the number of instances in response to changing traffic patterns during holiday seasons, ensuring optimal performance without manual intervention.

D) Incorrect - Utilizing a simple scaling policy based on manual adjustments lacks automation and may result in delayed responses to sudden traffic increases, impacting performance during holiday seasons.

E) Incorrect - Implementing a predictive scaling policy based on historical holiday season traffic patterns may not accurately predict sudden traffic spikes, leading to potential performance issues during peak holiday periods.

QUESTION 61

Answer - [C] Configure Amazon S3 Cross-Region Replication to replicate frequently accessed data to regions closer to users.

Option A - Amazon S3 Transfer Acceleration optimizes data transfers but may not be the most cost-effective solution for frequent access to large files across multiple geographic locations.

Option B - AWS Direct Connect provides dedicated network connections but may not optimize data transfer costs as effectively as cross-region replication for frequently accessed data.

Option C - Correct. Amazon S3 Cross-Region Replication replicates frequently accessed data to regions closer to users, optimizing data transfer costs and improving access speed.

Option D - AWS DataSync transfers data between on-premises storage systems and Amazon S3 but may not address the requirement for efficient data access across multiple geographic locations.

Option E - Amazon S3 Glacier is suitable for long-term storage but may not provide the same level of accessibility and cost optimization as cross-region replication for frequently accessed data.

QUESTION 62

Answer - [A] Utilize Amazon EC2 Spot Instances and AWS Fargate Spot for cost-effective testing and development.

Option A - Correct. Utilizing Amazon EC2 Spot Instances and AWS Fargate Spot offers cost-effective testing and development environments while providing scalability and flexibility for microservices-based applications.

Option B - Amazon RDS Multi-AZ deployment enhances availability but may not directly address the requirement for cost optimization in testing environments.

Option C - AWS CloudTrail tracks activity but may not directly contribute to cost optimization for testing and development environments.

Option D - Amazon S3 Intelligent-Tiering optimizes storage costs but may not be the most cost-effective solution for testing and development environments with fluctuating access patterns.

Option E - AWS Organizations helps manage costs but may not directly provide cost optimization features for testing and development environments.

QUESTION 63

Answer - [B] Implement Amazon EC2 Auto Scaling with AWS Auto Scaling groups to automatically adjust the number of EC2 instances based on demand patterns.

Option A - Amazon CloudFront with AWS Global Accelerator optimizes content delivery but may not directly address dynamic scaling requirements for application resources.

Option B - Correct. Implementing Amazon EC2 Auto Scaling with AWS Auto Scaling groups allows for automatic adjustment of the number of EC2 instances based on demand patterns, optimizing costs while ensuring scalability.

Option C - AWS Lambda with Amazon API Gateway enables serverless scalability but may not be suitable for all types of workloads, especially those requiring EC2 instances.

Option D - Amazon Aurora Global Database ensures data replication across regions but may not directly address dynamic scaling requirements for application resources.

Option E - Amazon S3 Transfer Acceleration improves transfer speeds but may not directly address the need for dynamic scaling of application resources based on demand.

QUESTION 64

Answer - [A] Utilize Amazon S3 Glacier for archival storage and Amazon S3 Intelligent-Tiering for frequently accessed data.

Option A - Correct. Utilizing Amazon S3 Glacier for archival storage and Amazon S3 Intelligent-Tiering for frequently accessed data optimizes costs based on access patterns.

Option B - Amazon EFS and Amazon EBS may provide performance benefits but may not offer the same cost efficiency as Amazon S3 Glacier and Intelligent-Tiering for large volumes of data.

Option C - While Amazon FSx for Windows File Server and Amazon CloudWatch can monitor storage usage, they may not provide the most cost-efficient solution for storing large volumes of data.

Option D - Using Amazon EBS Snapshots for data backups may be suitable for disaster recovery but may not directly address cost efficiency for primary storage.

Option E - While utilizing Amazon S3 and Lifecycle Policies can transition data to cheaper storage classes, it may not provide the optimal solution for storing large volumes of data with varying access patterns.

QUESTION 65

Answer - [A] Utilize AWS Auto Scaling to dynamically adjust resources based on traffic patterns and optimize cost.

Option A - Correct. Utilizing AWS Auto Scaling allows for dynamic resource adjustment based on traffic patterns, optimizing costs without compromising performance.

Option B - Amazon CloudFront improves content delivery but may not directly optimize costs for compute resources.

Option C - AWS Compute Optimizer analyzes resource utilization but may not provide the same level of dynamic cost optimization as AWS Auto Scaling.

Option D - Amazon EBS Provisioned IOPS SSD volumes improve performance but may not directly optimize costs for compute resources.

Option E - AWS Lambda with provisioned concurrency reduces cold starts but may not address cost optimization for other types of workloads.

PRACTICE TEST 8 - QUESTIONS ONLY

QUESTION 1

For a software development firm using AWS, managing access to development and production environments separately is crucial. They want to implement federated access for their users across these environments using AWS IAM Identity Center. What best practice should they follow to ensure security and compliance?

A) Use the same IAM roles for both development and production environments to simplify management.
B) Enforce a strict separation of duties by creating distinct IAM roles for development and production environments.
C) Allow unrestricted cross-account access to ensure seamless development workflows.
D) Use Amazon S3 to store IAM credentials for development and production access.
E) Implement direct connect for federated access between on-premise and AWS environments.

QUESTION 2

A media company is developing a highly available video processing application on AWS. The application must automatically scale and remain resilient against DDoS attacks. In addition to Elastic Load Balancing (ELB) and Auto Scaling, which AWS services should the company integrate to enhance the security of its application?

A) AWS Shield Standard and Amazon CloudFront
B) Amazon S3 and Amazon RDS
C) AWS WAF and Amazon SQS
D) AWS Shield Advanced and AWS WAF
E) Amazon Route 53 and AWS Direct Connect

QUESTION 3

Your company is deploying a serverless application on AWS Lambda to handle asynchronous tasks. You need to ensure that the application architecture incorporates security best practices to protect against external threats and unauthorized access.

A) Implement AWS IAM roles with least privilege access for Lambda functions to restrict access to AWS resources

 B) Configure AWS Lambda with VPC access to isolate the functions within a private network and control network traffic

 C) Enable AWS CloudTrail logging for Lambda function invocations to track and monitor API activity

 D) Utilize AWS Secrets Manager to securely manage sensitive information such as API keys and database credentials

 E) Implement AWS Lambda layers to share code dependencies across multiple Lambda functions and reduce security risks

QUESTION 4

Your company operates a globally distributed application on AWS that requires low latency and high availability for users worldwide. As the solutions architect, you need to design a resilient architecture that can withstand failures at both the regional and edge locations. Which solution should you recommend?

A) Deploy Amazon EC2 instances in multiple regions and use Amazon Route 53 latency-based routing to direct users to the nearest region. Implement Amazon CloudFront with AWS Shield for DDoS protection and edge location redundancy.

B) Utilize Amazon CloudFront with AWS Global Accelerator to optimize global traffic routing and improve application performance. Implement Amazon Route 53 failover routing to redirect traffic to alternative regions in case of failures.

C) Set up Amazon EC2 instances in an Auto Scaling group across multiple Availability Zones within a region. Implement Amazon Route 53 failover routing to redirect traffic to healthy instances in other AZs during failures.

D) Configure Amazon CloudFront with AWS WAF to protect against web attacks and improve content delivery performance. Use Amazon Route 53 latency-based routing to direct users to the nearest edge location.

E) Deploy Amazon EC2 instances in multiple regions and use Amazon CloudFront with Lambda@Edge to optimize content delivery and application performance. Implement Amazon Route 53 health checks to monitor the availability of edge locations and redirect traffic when necessary.

QUESTION 5

An online gaming company is migrating its multiplayer gaming platform to AWS and requires a solution that ensures player actions are processed promptly and accurately while also providing the ability to handle sudden spikes in player activity during game events. Which option should the company choose to implement this requirement?

A) Use Amazon SQS FIFO queue with exactly-once processing enabled.
B) Use Amazon SQS FIFO queue with a batch mode of 10 messages per operation.
C) Use Amazon SQS FIFO queue with default settings to process the messages.
D) Use Amazon SQS standard queue to process the messages.
E) Use Amazon SQS FIFO queue with message deduplication enabled.

QUESTION 6

Your company is developing a serverless application that requires access to multiple AWS services, including Amazon S3, DynamoDB, and AWS Lambda. Security is a top priority, and you need to ensure that only authenticated users can invoke the Lambda functions and access the associated resources. Which approach should you take to implement secure authentication and authorization for the serverless application?

A) Configure AWS Lambda functions to use API Gateway with IAM authorization for access control. Implement IAM policies to control access to S3 buckets and DynamoDB tables.

B) Utilize Amazon Cognito for user authentication and authorization, and integrate it with AWS Lambda functions using custom authorizers. Implement IAM policies to control access to S3 buckets and DynamoDB tables.

C) Implement AWS Identity and Access Management (IAM) roles for AWS Lambda functions with fine-grained permissions. Configure Amazon S3 bucket policies and DynamoDB IAM policies to control access at the resource level.

D) Deploy AWS Lambda functions within a VPC and use IAM roles for secure access to other AWS services. Implement VPC endpoint policies to control access to S3 and DynamoDB within the VPC.

E) Set up AWS Lambda functions with OAuth 2.0 authorization using Amazon API Gateway. Implement IAM policies to control access to S3 buckets and DynamoDB tables based on user roles.

QUESTION 7

You are designing a microservices architecture for a highly regulated industry that requires strict access control and segregation of network resources. Which of the following options is the most suitable approach for implementing network segmentation and access control?

A) Using AWS Transit Gateway to connect microservices across multiple VPCs
B) Implementing AWS Security Groups to control traffic between microservices
C) Configuring VPC peering to enable communication between microservices
D) Utilizing AWS PrivateLink for private communication between microservices
E) Deploying AWS Network Firewall for filtering traffic between microservices

QUESTION 8

You are tasked with designing a highly available and scalable architecture for a real-time messaging application. Security is a top priority, and the architecture must protect against unauthorized access and data breaches. Which of the following strategies best addresses these security requirements?

A) Utilizing AWS Secrets Manager for managing API keys and credentials
B) Implementing end-to-end encryption using AWS Key Management Service (KMS)
C) Configuring Amazon GuardDuty for continuous threat detection and monitoring
D) Enabling Amazon Cognito for user authentication and access control
E) Deploying AWS Network Firewall to filter traffic and prevent unauthorized access

QUESTION 9

Your company is building a microservices architecture for a financial application. Security and compliance are critical, requiring encryption for data in transit and at rest. Additionally, the architecture must ensure scalable and efficient communication between services. Which option best fulfills these requirements?

A) Deploying microservices in Amazon EKS with AWS Fargate for serverless container deployment, ensuring scalability and efficient communication, and configuring Amazon RDS with encryption at rest and in-transit for data storage, meeting security and compliance requirements

B) Implementing mutual TLS authentication between microservices in Amazon ECS, ensuring secure communication and encryption, and utilizing Amazon DynamoDB with encryption at rest for data storage, meeting security and compliance requirements

C) Utilizing AWS App Mesh for managing microservices traffic, ensuring scalability and efficient communication, and configuring Amazon S3 with server-side encryption for data storage, meeting security and compliance requirements

D) Configuring AWS Lambda for serverless microservice deployment, ensuring scalability and efficient communication, and deploying Amazon Redshift with encryption at rest for data storage, meeting security and compliance requirements

E) Leveraging AWS PrivateLink for private communication between microservices, ensuring scalability and efficient communication, and utilizing Amazon Aurora with encryption at rest and in-transit for data storage, meeting security and compliance requirements

QUESTION 10

A multinational corporation is deploying a new global application that requires frequent uploads of large datasets to Amazon S3 from multiple locations worldwide. The application data is critical for real-time analytics and performance is a top priority. The corporation seeks to minimize upload times and ensure data consistency across their global teams. Which of the following options would effectively meet these requirements?

A) Implement Amazon S3 Transfer Acceleration for faster uploads globally.
B) Establish AWS Direct Connect connections at major sites to improve upload speeds.
C) Configure Amazon S3 cross-region replication for each office location.
D) Enable AWS Global Accelerator to optimize the path to Amazon S3.
E) Use multipart uploads with AWS Snowball Edge for initial large dataset transfers.

QUESTION 11

A media company is looking for a solution to securely share large video files between their global offices. The solution must support fast, reliable access to files and allow for precise access control to ensure that only authorized personnel can view or download the content.

A) Configure Amazon S3 with Cross-Region Replication, S3 bucket policies for precise access control, and enable S3 Transfer Acceleration for fast access.

B) Deploy Amazon EFS with a multi-AZ configuration for high availability, and use IAM roles to manage access permissions.

C) Use Amazon FSx for Lustre with Direct Connect for fast, reliable access and network ACLs for access control.

D) Implement AWS Storage Gateway with a File Gateway configuration to store and share files across offices, using AWS KMS for encryption.

E) Set up an AWS DataSync task to synchronize files across Amazon S3 buckets in different regions, utilizing VPC endpoints for secure file access.

QUESTION 12

A healthcare organization is preparing to deploy a new patient management system on AWS. The deployment must adhere to HIPAA compliance, ensuring that PHI (Protected Health Information) is securely handled at all stages. The organization seeks a deployment method that not only supports rolling updates for minimal downtime but also enforces encryption for data in transit and at rest, alongside detailed auditing capabilities.

A) Deploy the system using AWS Elastic Beanstalk with rolling updates enabled, Amazon RDS with encryption for data storage, and AWS CloudTrail for auditing.

B) Use AWS CodeDeploy for zero-downtime deployment, AWS Lambda for backend processing with environment variables encrypted using AWS KMS, and Amazon CloudWatch Logs for auditing.

C) Implement an AWS CloudFormation template for deployment, Amazon S3 with default encryption for storing PHI, and AWS Config for configuration and compliance auditing.

D) Configure Amazon ECS for deploying containerized applications with AWS Fargate for serverless compute, enable AWS CloudHSM for data encryption, and utilize AWS IAM Access Analyzer for auditing access policies.

E) Leverage AWS CodePipeline for continuous delivery, Amazon EBS with encrypted volumes for data storage, and AWS X-Ray for tracing and auditing application transactions.

QUESTION 13

Following a security breach, a media company wants to enhance their incident response strategy on AWS. They seek to automate the detection of unusual access patterns to their Amazon S3 buckets and to initiate immediate actions to revoke access permissions if unauthorized access is suspected.

A) Use Amazon GuardDuty for monitoring S3 access patterns, AWS Lambda for automatic revocation of permissions, and AWS CloudTrail for auditing access logs.

B) Configure AWS Config to monitor S3 bucket policies, implement AWS CloudTrail for tracking API activity, and use Amazon Macie for detecting sensitive data exposure.

C) Leverage Amazon Inspector to assess S3 bucket security, AWS IAM for managing access policies, and Amazon CloudWatch Events for triggering remediation actions.

D) Implement AWS Step Functions to orchestrate response workflows, Amazon S3 event notifications to detect unusual access, and AWS KMS for managing encryption keys.

E) Deploy Amazon Cognito for user authentication, AWS WAF to block suspicious requests, and AWS Shield Advanced for protection against DDoS attacks on S3 buckets.

QUESTION 14

A software development company is looking to optimize costs while ensuring high availability and scalability for their web applications hosted on AWS. As a solutions architect, which solution would you recommend to achieve cost efficiency without compromising performance? Select TWO.

A) Utilize AWS Lambda with API Gateway for serverless backend to handle variable traffic and reduce operational costs.

B) Implement Amazon ECS with Fargate for containerized microservices to achieve high availability and scalability.

C) Set up Amazon Aurora Serverless for the relational database backend to automatically scale based on demand and optimize costs.

D) Deploy Amazon RDS Multi-AZ with reserved instances for database storage to ensure high availability and cost savings.

E) Utilize Amazon S3 with CloudFront for content delivery and storage to ensure low latency and high availability.

QUESTION 15

A media streaming company is encountering challenges in managing maintenance tasks on specific Amazon EC2 instances within an Auto Scaling group. Whenever maintenance patches are applied, the instances briefly show as out of service, leading to Auto Scaling provisioning replacements. What recommendations would you provide as a solutions architect to efficiently handle this issue?

A) Suspend the DetachInstances process type for the Auto Scaling group and apply the maintenance patch to the instance. Once the instance is ready, manually set the instance's health status back to healthy and activate the DetachInstances process type again.

B) Suspend the ReplaceUnhealthy process type for the Auto Scaling group and apply the maintenance patch to the instance. Once the instance is ready, manually set the instance's health status back to healthy and activate the ReplaceUnhealthy process type again.

C) Put the instance into the Standby state and then update the instance by applying the maintenance patch. Once the instance is ready, exit the Standby state and then return the instance to service.

D) Temporarily suspend the AddToLoadBalancer process type for the Auto Scaling group and apply the maintenance patch to the instance. Once the instance is ready, manually set the instance's health status back to healthy and activate the AddToLoadBalancer process type again.

E) Take a snapshot of the instance, create a new Amazon Machine Image (AMI), and then launch a new instance using this AMI. Apply the maintenance patch to this new instance and then add it back to the Auto Scaling Group by using the manual scaling policy. Terminate the earlier instance that had the maintenance issue.

QUESTION 16

As part of a cloud migration project, a media company needs to ensure its remote editing teams can securely access video assets stored in AWS from various global locations. The solution must provide individual access, enforce strong authentication measures, and allow for network scalability.

A) Set up AWS Client VPN with multi-factor authentication enabled for secure remote access.
B) Configure AWS Direct Connect and use AWS IAM roles to manage individual access permissions.

C) Deploy Amazon WorkSpaces for each remote editor, utilizing AWS Directory Service for authentication.

D) Implement an Amazon Cognito user pool to manage authentication for AWS Client VPN access.

E) Use Amazon VPC peering with security groups to tightly control access between the editing team's networks and the AWS environment.

QUESTION 17

An e-commerce platform is migrating its legacy shopping cart system to AWS to leverage cloud scalability and introduce new AI-driven recommendation features. The migration must ensure zero data loss, enhance the security posture, and incorporate serverless technologies for cost-efficiency.

A) Deploy AWS Server Migration Service for the shopping cart system, Amazon Cognito for user authentication, and leverage AWS Lambda for the recommendation engine.

B) Use AWS Snowball for initial data migration, Amazon DynamoDB for scalable NoSQL storage, and AWS Step Functions to orchestrate serverless workflows.

C) Implement AWS DataSync for online data transfer, AWS Fargate for container management without server provisioning, and Amazon S3 for data storage.

D) Configure AWS Elastic Beanstalk for easy application deployment, Amazon RDS for managed database services, and Amazon CloudFront for content delivery.

E) Apply Amazon S3 Glacier for long-term data archiving, AWS Elastic Load Balancing for traffic distribution, and Amazon Rekognition for AI-driven feature enhancement.

QUESTION 18

A technology startup is designing a serverless application on AWS and needs to implement secure management of API keys and configuration settings. The startup aims to adhere to best practices for secrets management while optimizing costs. Which of the following approaches align with the startup's requirements?

A) Store API keys and configuration settings directly in environment variables within AWS Lambda functions. Implement strict IAM policies to control access to Lambda functions.

B) Leverage AWS AppConfig to store and manage configuration settings securely. Integrate AWS Lambda with AppConfig for dynamically updating application configurations.

C) Use Amazon RDS Parameter Groups to manage database credentials and configuration settings. Implement AWS Lambda triggers to automatically rotate database credentials based on predefined schedules.

D) Maintain a plaintext configuration file within the application codebase stored in an Amazon EFS file system. Use AWS IAM roles to restrict access to the EFS file system.

E) Implement a custom secrets management solution using Amazon S3 buckets and leverage AWS Lambda to retrieve secrets at runtime. Use AWS Key Management Service (KMS) for encryption and decryption of sensitive data.

QUESTION 19

A software development company is designing a CI/CD pipeline for deploying serverless applications on AWS Lambda. They need to implement secure management of environment-specific configurations and secrets during the deployment process. Which of the following approaches would best meet the company's requirements?

A) Embed configuration settings directly within deployment packages. Utilize AWS CodePipeline with IAM roles to restrict access to deployment artifacts.

B) Implement AWS Systems Manager Parameter Store to centrally manage environment-specific configurations and secrets. Use AWS CodePipeline with Parameter Store integration for retrieving configurations during deployments.

C) Store secrets in plaintext files within version-controlled repositories. Implement AWS CodePipeline with IAM roles to control access to the repositories and retrieve secrets during deployments.

D) Utilize AWS Secrets Manager to store and rotate secrets. Develop custom Lambda functions within the CI/CD pipeline to fetch secrets from Secrets Manager during deployments.

E) Maintain configuration settings within AWS Lambda environment variables. Use AWS CodePipeline with Lambda environment variable integration for retrieving configurations during deployments.

QUESTION 20

An online retail platform has noticed a sudden increase in unauthorized AWS API queries during weekends, with no apparent impact on system performance. The management requires an automated solution to promptly alert relevant teams during such occurrences. Which approach would be most effective in this scenario?

A) Create an Amazon CloudWatch metric filter to process AWS CloudTrail logs containing API call details. Establish an alarm based on this metric's rate to send an Amazon SNS notification to the required team.

B) Implement AWS Config Rules to monitor API activity and define rules to detect unauthorized API calls. Configure AWS Config to trigger an AWS Lambda function upon rule evaluation to notify relevant stakeholders.

C) Leverage AWS Trusted Advisor to publish metrics about check results to Amazon CloudWatch. Set up an alarm to track status changes for checks in the Service Limits category for the APIs, triggering notifications when service quotas are exceeded.

D) Use Amazon Athena SQL queries against AWS CloudTrail log files stored in Amazon S3 buckets. Generate reports using Amazon QuickSight for managerial dashboards.

E) Configure AWS CloudTrail to stream event data to Amazon Kinesis. Utilize Amazon Kinesis stream-level metrics in Amazon CloudWatch to trigger an AWS Lambda function that will initiate an error workflow.

QUESTION 21

A startup is designing an event-driven architecture for processing user-generated content. They want to ensure that the system can scale automatically based on the load and maintain high availability. What is the most suitable solution for this requirement?

A) Utilize Amazon SQS for decoupling components and triggering Lambda functions.
B) Implement Amazon SNS to fan out notifications to multiple Lambda functions.

C) Use AWS Step Functions to orchestrate the processing workflow with Lambda functions.

D) Deploy AWS Fargate containers behind an Application Load Balancer for processing tasks.

E) Utilize Amazon Kinesis Data Streams for real-time data processing.

QUESTION 22

Your team is designing a web application that requires high availability and scalability. The application consists of microservices deployed using containers. Which combination of AWS services should you use to achieve fault tolerance and scalability for the microservices architecture?

A) Amazon ECS for container orchestration with automatic scaling

B) Amazon EKS for managed Kubernetes with cluster autoscaling

C) AWS Fargate for serverless container deployment with auto-scaling

D) AWS Auto Scaling for dynamic scaling of EC2 instances with load balancing

E) Amazon CloudWatch for monitoring and alarms with automatic recovery

QUESTION 23

A healthcare organization is designing its disaster recovery (DR) strategy for a critical patient management system hosted on AWS. The organization needs to ensure regulatory compliance, data integrity, and minimal downtime during DR events. Which AWS service should the organization consider for implementing a backup and restore solution as part of its DR strategy?

A) Utilize Amazon S3 Glacier with lifecycle policies for long-term data archival and retrieval, ensuring compliance with regulatory requirements and cost efficiency

B) Implement AWS Backup with centralized management and AWS Organizations integration for automated backup and restore operations, ensuring data integrity and regulatory compliance

C) Deploy Amazon Aurora with Multi-AZ deployment for automated failover and point-in-time recovery, ensuring high availability and minimal data loss during DR events

D) Utilize AWS Storage Gateway with tape gateway configuration for hybrid storage and offline backup, ensuring data durability and regulatory compliance

E) Implement Amazon FSx for Windows File Server with scheduled snapshots and cross-region replication for file-level backup and recovery, ensuring data availability and integrity during DR scenarios

QUESTION 24

A software development company is designing a highly available architecture for its web application, which serves millions of users worldwide. The company requires a solution that can automatically scale based on traffic demands and withstand failures in individual AWS Availability Zones. Which combination of AWS services should the company use to achieve these requirements?

A) Implement Amazon EC2 Auto Scaling with Elastic Load Balancing for automatic scaling and distribution of traffic across multiple instances.

B) Utilize Amazon Route 53 with AWS Global Accelerator for DNS routing and acceleration of traffic to multiple AWS Regions.

C) Deploy Amazon RDS Multi-AZ deployment with Amazon Aurora for high availability and scalability of the database layer.

D) Utilize Amazon EFS with AWS Backup for automatic file replication and backup across multiple AWS Regions.

E) Implement AWS Lambda with Amazon API Gateway for serverless compute and scalable API endpoints.

QUESTION 25

A global e-commerce platform is launching a flash sale exclusively for customers in certain regions to clear excess inventory. They need to ensure that only users from those regions can access the sale. How can they effectively enforce this restriction?

A) Use Amazon Route 53 based geolocation routing policy to restrict access to only users in the designated regions

B) Implement Amazon Route 53 based weighted routing policy to allocate traffic based on pre-defined weights for each region

C) Utilize Amazon Route 53 based latency-based routing policy to direct traffic to the nearest regional server for optimized performance

D) Employ Amazon Route 53 based failover routing policy to reroute traffic to alternative regions in case of server failures

E) Apply Amazon Route 53 based geoproximity routing policy to direct traffic based on the proximity of users to regional servers

QUESTION 26

A media streaming company is re-architecting its platform on AWS to improve performance and scalability. The company wants to adopt immutable infrastructure to streamline deployment processes and minimize configuration drift. Which service should the solutions architect recommend for implementing immutable infrastructure on AWS?

A) Utilize AWS OpsWorks to automate infrastructure provisioning and configuration management using Chef recipes, ensuring consistency across environments.

B) Implement AWS CloudFormation to define infrastructure as code and automate the deployment of AWS resources in a consistent and repeatable manner, promoting immutable infrastructure.

C) Use AWS Systems Manager to automate administrative tasks across AWS resources, enabling efficient management and maintenance of infrastructure configurations.

D) Leverage Amazon ECS Anywhere to run containerized applications on-premises and in the cloud, ensuring consistency and portability across environments.

E) Configure AWS Lambda to automatically scale and execute code in response to events, reducing the operational overhead of managing infrastructure.

QUESTION 27

A social media platform is experiencing rapid growth and needs to handle increasing API traffic while ensuring performance and reliability. Which option allows for efficient throttling and monitoring of APIs with Amazon API Gateway?

A) Implement Amazon API Gateway caching to reduce the load on backend services and monitor cache hit rates

B) Utilize API Gateway usage plans and API keys to enforce throttling limits and monitor API usage metrics

C) Configure API Gateway resource policies to restrict access based on IP address ranges and monitor access logs

D) Use AWS Lambda authorizers with API Gateway to execute custom authorization logic and monitor invocation metrics

E) Deploy Amazon CloudFront in front of API Gateway to leverage edge caching and monitor traffic patterns with Amazon CloudWatch

QUESTION 28

An online gaming platform is deploying a real-time multiplayer game backend on AWS. They need to ensure low latency, high availability, and efficient communication between microservices. The platform will use containers for easy deployment and scalability. Which AWS services and features should be implemented to optimize for these requirements?

A) Deploy using Amazon ECS with the EC2 launch type, implement Amazon GameLift for game session management, use Amazon ECR for container images, and Elastic Load Balancing for traffic distribution.

B) Use Amazon EKS with AWS Fargate for compute, leverage AWS App Mesh for microservices communication, Amazon ECR for container management, and Amazon CloudFront for low latency content delivery.

C) Opt for Amazon ECS, use AWS Direct Connect for low latency connections, Amazon ECR for container images, and AWS Global Accelerator for improved global application performance.

D) Implement Amazon EKS, utilize Amazon MSK for managing game state in real-time, deploy containers with AWS Lambda for serverless event-driven execution, and use Amazon DynamoDB for scalable game data storage.

E) Choose Amazon ECS with Fargate, integrate Amazon ElastiCache for real-time data caching, use Amazon ECR for image management, and AWS PrivateLink for secure microservices communication.

QUESTION 29

A media streaming company wants to ensure uninterrupted service delivery to users worldwide, even during regional outages. Which AWS service or feature can help achieve this objective?

A) Amazon CloudFront with Origin Shield

B) AWS Transit Gateway for network connectivity

C) Amazon S3 transfer acceleration for faster data transfers

D) Amazon Aurora Multi-Master for database redundancy

E) Amazon VPC peering for private connectivity between VPCs

QUESTION 30

A multinational e-commerce platform is planning to migrate its legacy API infrastructure to Amazon API Gateway to improve scalability and performance. They need to support both synchronous and asynchronous communication between client and server. Which approach should they adopt to meet this requirement effectively?

A) Implement RESTful APIs on Amazon API Gateway for synchronous communication and AWS Lambda functions for asynchronous communication

B) Utilize WebSocket APIs on Amazon API Gateway for synchronous communication and Amazon SQS for asynchronous communication

C) Create RESTful APIs on Amazon API Gateway for both synchronous and asynchronous communication

D) Deploy GraphQL APIs on Amazon API Gateway for synchronous communication and Amazon SNS for asynchronous communication

E) Configure HTTP APIs on Amazon API Gateway for synchronous communication and Amazon S3 for asynchronous communication

QUESTION 31

A multinational company must ensure that its AWS infrastructure complies with both internal governance policies and external regulatory requirements. They need to automate the detection of non-compliant resources and remediate the issues without manual intervention. Which combination of AWS services would best fulfill this requirement?

A) AWS Config rules to evaluate compliance, AWS CloudTrail for audit trails, AWS Lambda for automated remediation actions, and Amazon SNS for notifications.

B) Amazon Inspector for security assessments, AWS Trusted Advisor for best practices, Amazon CloudWatch for monitoring, and AWS Step Functions for orchestration.

C) AWS Shield for DDoS protection, AWS WAF for web application firewall rules, AWS Fargate for container management, and Amazon GuardDuty for threat detection.

D) Amazon RDS for database management, Amazon DynamoDB for NoSQL data storage, AWS Direct Connect for private connectivity, and AWS IAM for access control.

E) Amazon EC2 Auto Scaling for managing compute capacity, Amazon EBS for block storage, AWS CodePipeline for continuous integration, and AWS CodeDeploy for automated deployments.

QUESTION 32

A software as a service (SaaS) provider is designing a disaster recovery (DR) solution for its customer data stored in the cloud. The solution must ensure data integrity, availability, and compliance with regulatory requirements. Which combination of AWS services and features should the provider use to meet these requirements effectively?

A) Deploy Amazon RDS with Multi-AZ deployment and utilize AWS Key Management Service (AWS KMS) for encryption at rest and in transit.

B) Utilize Amazon S3 with versioning enabled and cross-Region replication for data redundancy, coupled with AWS Shield for DDoS protection.

C) Implement Amazon DynamoDB with on-demand scaling and DynamoDB Streams for real-time data replication and failover across Regions.

D) Migrate to Amazon Redshift for analytics and scalability and use Redshift Spectrum for querying external data without loading into Redshift.

E) Deploy Amazon Aurora Serverless with auto-scaling and provisioned Aurora Capacity Units (ACUs) for predictable performance during peak hours.

QUESTION 33

Your company is developing a real-time analytics platform that processes large volumes of data from various sources. Security is critical, and you need to secure API communication between the data processing microservices. Which approach would be the most appropriate for ensuring secure API communication while considering scalability and performance?

A) Utilize AWS API Gateway with AWS WAF integration for API protection.
B) Store API keys in plaintext within Lambda environment variables.
C) Implement OAuth 2.0 authentication with Amazon Cognito.
D) Use plaintext HTTP for API communication.
E) Implement AWS Shield for DDoS protection.

QUESTION 34

Your company is migrating its on-premises database to the cloud to improve scalability and resilience. The database requires high availability and automatic failover capabilities. Additionally, cost optimization is a key consideration for the migration. Which AWS service should you choose to meet these requirements most effectively?

A) Amazon RDS Multi-AZ deployment with Amazon Aurora
B) Deploying self-managed database instances on Amazon EC2 with scheduled backups
C) Utilize Amazon RDS with read replicas across multiple Availability Zones
D) Implement Amazon Neptune for graph database requirements
E) Use Amazon DocumentDB with MongoDB compatibility for the migration

QUESTION 35

A financial institution wants to develop a real-time fraud detection system for its online banking platform. They require a solution that can process a large volume of transactions and detect fraudulent activities promptly without manual intervention. Which configuration should they implement using AWS serverless components to meet these requirements effectively?

A) Utilize AWS Lambda with Amazon SQS for processing transactions and Amazon S3 for storing transaction data

B) Implement Amazon Kinesis Data Streams with AWS Lambda for processing transactions and Amazon DynamoDB for storing transaction data

C) Ingest transactions into an Amazon Simple Queue Service (Amazon SQS) standard queue, which triggers an AWS Lambda function for processing and stores transaction data in Amazon Redshift

D) Ingest transactions into Amazon Kinesis Data Firehose, which directly writes data into an auto-scaled Amazon Aurora database for processing

E) Use Amazon Kinesis Data Streams to ingest transactions, which are processed by an application running on an Amazon EC2 instance, and store transaction data in Amazon Elasticsearch Service

QUESTION 36

Your startup company is developing a real-time collaboration platform hosted on AWS to facilitate remote teamwork. The platform requires secure communication between users' devices and the backend servers to prevent unauthorized access to sensitive project data. How would you design the encryption strategy to ensure data security without compromising performance? Select TWO.

A) Deploy Amazon API Gateway with HTTPS protocol and configure Amazon Cognito for user authentication and authorization.

B) Implement AWS CloudFront with SSL/TLS termination at the edge and configure AWS WAF for web application firewall protection.

C) Utilize Amazon EC2 instances with AWS Certificate Manager (ACM) for SSL/TLS certificates and configure VPC security groups for network traffic control.

D) Deploy AWS Network Load Balancer (NLB) with SSL/TLS termination and configure AWS Shield Advanced for DDoS protection.

E) Configure Amazon CloudFront with AWS WAF for web application firewall protection and utilize AWS Direct Connect for private network connectivity between frontend and backend tiers.

QUESTION 37

A software development firm wants to implement a storage solution for their build artifacts that is highly available, durable, and allows for quick retrieval across multiple development environments. Which AWS service should they use?

A) Amazon Glacier for long-term storage and archiving of build artifacts.
B) Amazon EBS for block storage attached directly to their build servers.
C) Amazon S3 with versioning enabled and cross-region replication.
D) Amazon DynamoDB for storing and quickly retrieving metadata about each build artifact.
E) AWS Elastic Beanstalk for deploying and managing applications and artifacts.

QUESTION 38

Your company operates a real-time analytics platform that processes large volumes of streaming data.

The platform requires low-latency access to data for real-time analysis and decision-making. Which combination of AWS services would you recommend to design a high-performing and scalable architecture for this analytics platform?

A) Deploy Amazon Kinesis Data Streams to ingest streaming data and process it in real-time using AWS Lambda for serverless execution.

B) Utilize Amazon Redshift for data warehousing and perform batch processing of streaming data at regular intervals.

C) Implement Amazon EMR for processing large volumes of streaming data using Apache Spark for real-time analytics.

D) Configure Amazon S3 event notifications to trigger AWS Lambda functions for processing incoming streaming data.

E) Deploy Amazon Elasticsearch Service for real-time indexing and search capabilities on streaming data.

QUESTION 39

A retail company wants to design a data ingestion pipeline to process real-time sales data from its online and offline stores. The solution must ensure high availability, fault tolerance, and low latency processing. What architecture should the company implement?

A) Deploy Amazon EMR for processing sales data in batch mode, and use Amazon SQS for queuing real-time sales events.

B) Utilize AWS AppSync for real-time data synchronization, and leverage Amazon Kinesis Data Streams for processing sales events.

C) Implement AWS Lambda for serverless data processing, and use Amazon S3 for storing processed sales data.

D) Configure Amazon RDS for storing transactional data, and leverage Amazon SNS for sending real-time notifications.

E) Deploy Amazon ECS for containerized processing of sales data, and use Amazon S3 Glacier for archiving historical sales data.

QUESTION 40

A financial institution wants to securely store its transaction records in Amazon S3 while ensuring that the data is encrypted at rest. However, the institution wants to have full control over the encryption keys and access to audit logs. Which option provides the most suitable solution for this scenario?

A) Use server-side encryption with Amazon S3 managed keys (SSE-S3) to encrypt the data on Amazon S3
B) Implement client-side encryption with customer-provided keys (SSE-C) and upload the encrypted data to Amazon S3
C) Utilize server-side encryption with AWS Key Management Service (SSE-KMS) keys to encrypt the data on Amazon S3
D) Use server-side encryption with customer-provided keys (SSE-C) to encrypt the data on Amazon S3
E) Enable AWS CloudTrail to monitor S3 bucket activities for auditing purposes

QUESTION 41

For a healthcare application that processes and stores sensitive patient data, a company is seeking a serverless solution that ensures data is encrypted in transit and at rest, can handle peak loads during health crises, and enables secure access for authenticated users only. Which AWS services combination would be most suitable?

A) AWS Lambda for processing, Amazon DynamoDB with encryption at rest for storage, and Amazon Cognito for user authentication.

B) Amazon API Gateway for secure API access, Amazon S3 with server-side encryption for data storage, and AWS Fargate for container management.

C) AWS Step Functions for workflow management, Amazon RDS with encryption for secure storage, and AWS IAM for access management.

D) Amazon SNS for notifications, Amazon SQS for message queuing with SSE, and Amazon EKS for Kubernetes management.

E) Amazon Kinesis for real-time data processing, AWS Secrets Manager for managing encryption keys, and Amazon CloudFront for secure content delivery.

QUESTION 42

Your company has decided to adopt a hybrid cloud architecture to leverage AWS Outposts for running applications that require low-latency access to on-premises data. However, you need to ensure fault tolerance and high availability for these applications. What solution should you implement to meet these requirements?

A) Deploy AWS Outposts with a dual-region configuration to ensure fault tolerance and high availability across multiple geographic regions.

B) Implement AWS Storage Gateway with a stored volume mode to replicate data between AWS Outposts and an Amazon S3 bucket in a different AWS Region.

C) Utilize AWS Outposts with a multi-AZ configuration to ensure fault tolerance and high availability within the same geographic region.

D) Configure AWS Direct Connect to establish a dedicated network connection between AWS Outposts and on-premises data centers for low-latency access.

E) Deploy AWS VPN with redundant tunnels to establish secure connections between AWS Outposts and on-premises data centers.

QUESTION 43

A multinational corporation is launching an online training platform to offer educational courses to users worldwide. The platform needs to support video streaming, interactive quizzes, and downloadable resources. It must ensure high availability, low latency access to content regardless of user location, and scalable storage solutions for a growing library of digital assets. How should the platform be designed using AWS services to meet these complex requirements?

A) Deploy Amazon Elastic Kubernetes Service (EKS) for managing containerized applications, Amazon RDS for quiz data storage, Amazon S3 for hosting downloadable resources, and Amazon CloudFront for streaming video content.

B) Utilize Amazon S3 for storing videos and resources, AWS Lambda for interactive quizzes logic, Amazon DynamoDB for user data, and AWS Global Accelerator to improve global application performance.

C) Implement Amazon EC2 instances for hosting the platform, Amazon Elastic Transcoder for video processing, Amazon ElastiCache for caching, and Elastic Load Balancing across multiple Availability Zones.

D) Use Amazon CloudFront for video streaming and static resources delivery, Amazon API Gateway and AWS Lambda for serving dynamic content, Amazon S3 for storage, and Amazon Aurora Serverless for scalable database needs.

E) Leverage AWS Amplify for backend services, Amazon S3 and Amazon CloudFront for content delivery, AWS Elemental MediaLive for video streaming, and Amazon QLDB for tracking quiz interactions and scores.

QUESTION 44

Your company is building a real-time recommendation system using Amazon SageMaker for a popular e-commerce platform. The system must handle a massive influx of user data and provide personalized recommendations with minimal latency. Which architecture would be most effective for this scenario?

A) Utilize Amazon SageMaker for real-time inference, integrating Amazon DynamoDB for user data storage and Amazon CloudWatch for monitoring.

B) Implement Amazon SageMaker for batch inference, leveraging Amazon RDS for model storage and Amazon CloudWatch for performance monitoring.

C) Deploy Amazon SageMaker for real-time inference with AWS Lambda, storing model artifacts in Amazon S3 for quick access.

D) Utilize Amazon SageMaker for real-time inference with Amazon Aurora for model storage and Amazon CloudWatch for monitoring and optimization.

E) Implement Amazon SageMaker for distributed training and inference, utilizing Amazon EFS for model storage and Amazon CloudWatch for monitoring.

QUESTION 45

A multinational corporation operates a web application that experiences significant traffic fluctuations throughout the day. The application must scale automatically to handle varying loads efficiently. Which pricing option for Amazon EC2 instances would be the most suitable choice for this scenario?

A) Use on-demand instances for the entire duration of operation
B) Implement a mix of reserved instances (RI) and on-demand instances
C) Utilize spot instances for the entire duration of operation
D) Employ a combination of reserved instances (RI) and spot instances
E) Use reserved instances (RI) for the entire duration of operation

QUESTION 46

You are tasked with designing a cost-efficient solution for a media streaming platform that serves video content to millions of users worldwide. The platform must minimize data transfer costs while ensuring low latency for users accessing content from different regions. Which architecture would you recommend for this scenario?

A) Store video content in Amazon S3, deploy Amazon CloudFront with Lambda@Edge for content delivery, utilize Amazon DynamoDB for user metadata storage, and implement Amazon Route 53 for global DNS routing.

B) Utilize Amazon EC2 instances with Amazon EBS volumes for storing video content, deploy Amazon CloudFront for content delivery, utilize Amazon RDS for user metadata storage, and implement Amazon Route 53 for global DNS routing.

C) Store video content in Amazon S3, deploy Amazon CloudFront for content delivery, utilize Amazon Aurora for user metadata storage, and implement Amazon Route 53 for global DNS routing.

D) Utilize Amazon EC2 instances with Amazon EBS volumes for storing video content, deploy Amazon CloudFront with Lambda@Edge for content delivery, utilize Amazon DynamoDB for user metadata storage, and implement Amazon Route 53 for global DNS routing.

E) Store video content in Amazon S3, deploy Amazon CloudFront with AWS Shield for content delivery, utilize Amazon DynamoDB for user metadata storage, and implement Amazon Route 53 for global DNS routing.

QUESTION 47

You are designing a solution for a gaming company that expects a surge in player activity during a scheduled online event. The architecture must support millions of concurrent users while maintaining low latency and high throughput. Which approach would best meet these requirements?

A) Utilize Amazon EC2 instances with AWS Auto Scaling and Amazon RDS for database storage, leverage Amazon CloudFront for content delivery, and use Amazon SQS for message queuing.

B) Implement a serverless architecture with AWS Lambda for compute, Amazon DynamoDB for database needs, and Amazon ElastiCache for in-memory caching.

C) Deploy the application on AWS Outposts for low-latency processing, use Amazon Aurora Global Database for database replication, and leverage Amazon CloudWatch for monitoring.

D) Utilize Amazon ECS for container orchestration, Amazon Kinesis Data Streams for real-time data processing, and Amazon Route 53 for DNS routing.

E) Implement edge computing using AWS Wavelength for deploying applications close to users, leverage Amazon CloudFront for content delivery, and use Amazon Redshift for real-time analytics.

QUESTION 48

A healthcare organization operates a web application for patient management that requires continuous availability and high performance. The organization wants to optimize infrastructure costs without compromising on reliability. Which pricing option for Amazon EC2 instances would be the most suitable choice for this scenario?

A) Use reserved instances (RI) for the entire duration of operation
B) Implement on-demand instances for the entire duration of operation
C) Utilize spot instances for the entire duration of operation
D) Employ a combination of reserved instances (RI) and spot instances
E) Implement a mix of reserved instances (RI) and on-demand instances

QUESTION 49

Your organization is launching a new online gaming platform that requires low-latency communication between players and real-time updates of game state. The platform must be highly available and scalable to support a growing user base. Which architecture would best fulfill these requirements?

A) Utilize Amazon EC2 instances with AWS Auto Scaling for dynamic scaling, Amazon ElastiCache for low-latency data caching, and Amazon RDS Multi-AZ for game state storage.

B) Deploy AWS Lambda for serverless computing, Amazon DynamoDB for real-time data storage, and Amazon API Gateway for communication between players.

C) Leverage Amazon ECS for containerized workload management, Amazon Aurora for real-time data storage, and Amazon SQS for message queuing between players.

D) Use Amazon EC2 instances with AWS Auto Scaling for dynamic scaling, Amazon RDS Multi-AZ for real-time data storage, and Amazon SNS for notification between players.

E) Implement Amazon EMR for big data processing, Amazon RDS Multi-AZ for real-time data storage, and Amazon API Gateway for communication between players.

QUESTION 50

You are tasked with designing a disaster recovery solution for a critical financial application hosted on Amazon RDS. The application requires minimal downtime and zero data loss in the event of a disaster. Which approach would best meet the application's requirements?

A) Implement cross-region read replicas for the Amazon RDS database, with automated failover configured using Amazon Route 53 health checks. Utilize AWS Backup to create scheduled backups for point-in-time recovery.

B) Utilize AWS Backup to create regular snapshots of the Amazon RDS database, storing them in Amazon S3 with versioning enabled. Implement AWS Lambda functions to trigger the restoration process in the event of a disaster.

C) Deploy Amazon Aurora Multi-Master clusters across multiple AWS regions, enabling read and write operations from any cluster instance. Utilize Amazon Route 53 latency-based routing to direct traffic to the nearest cluster for optimal performance.

D) Utilize Amazon RDS Multi-AZ deployment with synchronous replication between primary and standby instances within the same region. Configure Amazon CloudWatch alarms to monitor RDS health metrics and trigger failover to the standby instance if necessary.

E) Implement AWS Database Migration Service (DMS) to replicate the Amazon RDS database to a standby instance deployed in a different AWS region. Configure Amazon Route 53 failover routing policies to redirect traffic to the standby instance during a disaster scenario.

QUESTION 51

A financial news website aims to use Amazon CloudFront to distribute content globally while ensuring high security and fast content updates. How should they configure CloudFront and associated AWS services?

A) Implement CloudFront with default SSL/TLS certificates and manual cache invalidation for content updates.

B) Use CloudFront with AWS Certificate Manager (ACM) for custom SSL/TLS certificates and Lambda@Edge for automatic content updates.

C) Configure CloudFront with S3 origin, enabling S3 event notifications to trigger Lambda functions for cache invalidation.

D) Utilize CloudFront with AWS Shield Advanced for security and schedule regular cache invalidations through CloudWatch Events.

E) Deploy CloudFront with AWS WAF for security and configure dynamic content handling through Lambda@Edge.

QUESTION 52

A company wants to monitor and analyze access patterns to objects stored in an S3 bucket to optimize costs and performance. Which AWS service should be integrated with S3 to achieve this goal?

A) "Action": ["s3:GetObject"], "Resource": ["arn:aws:s3:::example-bucket/"], "Effect": "Allow" (Read-Only Policy)

B) "Action": ["s3:PutObject"], "Resource": ["arn:aws:s3:::example-bucket/"], "Effect": "Deny" (Deny Modification)

C) "Action": ["s3:GetObject"], "s3:PutObject"], "Resource": ["arn:aws:s3:::example-bucket/"], "Effect": "Allow" (Read and Write Access)

D) "Action": ["s3:ListBucket"], "s3:GetObject"], "Resource": ["arn:aws:s3:::example-bucket/"], "Effect": "Allow" (List and Read Access)

E) "Action": ["s3:GetObject"], "s3:DeleteObject"], "Resource": ["arn:aws:s3:::example-bucket/*"], "Effect": "Allow" (Read and Delete Access)

QUESTION 53

Your company is modernizing its monolithic application by transitioning to a microservices architecture on AWS. As part of this transition, you aim to ensure cost optimization without compromising performance. Which practice would be most effective in achieving this goal while utilizing AWS services?

A) Utilize Amazon EFS for shared storage among microservices
B) Implement Amazon ECS Anywhere for container deployment

C) Utilize Amazon DynamoDB for database needs

D) Optimize container resource allocation using AWS Batch

E) Implement Amazon EKS for Kubernetes-based orchestration

QUESTION 54

Your company is deploying a new microservices-based application on AWS and aims to minimize costs while ensuring fault tolerance and scalability. You need to design a network architecture that optimizes costs without compromising performance. What approach should you recommend?

A) Utilize AWS Global Accelerator with Amazon Route 53 for efficient traffic distribution

B) Implement Amazon VPC with AWS Transit Gateway for scalable and cost-effective connectivity

C) Deploy Amazon CloudFront with AWS Shield for DDoS protection and content caching

D) Opt for AWS VPN with AWS Direct Connect for secure hybrid cloud connectivity

E) Leverage AWS PrivateLink for private connectivity between microservices

QUESTION 55

A media company wants to grant temporary access to freelance content creators to upload files to an Amazon S3 bucket. Which approach should the solutions architect recommend to ensure secure and temporary access management?

A) Create IAM users with long-term access credentials for each freelance content creator.

B) Generate IAM roles with time-limited permissions for the freelance content creators to assume when uploading files.

C) Share the S3 bucket access keys with the freelance content creators for direct access.

D) Implement cross-account IAM roles and delegate access to the freelance content creators' AWS accounts.

E) Enable S3 pre-signed URLs for file uploads and share these URLs with the freelance content creators.

QUESTION 56

Your organization operates a microservices architecture where individual components experience varying levels of traffic throughout the day. You need to design a cost-optimized compute scaling solution that can handle these fluctuations efficiently. What approach should you take?

A) Implement Amazon ECS Anywhere to deploy microservices across on-premises and cloud environments for flexible scaling

B) Utilize Amazon EC2 Auto Scaling with a scheduled scaling policy to adjust capacity based on anticipated traffic patterns

C) Leverage Amazon EKS Anywhere to deploy Kubernetes clusters across multiple environments and enable auto-scaling based on resource usage

D) Use AWS Lambda with provisioned concurrency to ensure consistent performance for microservices with unpredictable traffic

E) Deploy AWS Outposts to extend AWS infrastructure to on-premises environments and maintain consistent scaling policies across environments

QUESTION 57

Your company operates a global video streaming platform that leverages Amazon Aurora for its relational database needs. The platform has experienced significant growth, resulting in escalating Aurora database costs. As a solutions architect, you are tasked with implementing a cost-effective solution to manage Aurora database costs while ensuring scalability and high availability. What would be the most appropriate strategy to achieve this objective?

A) Implement Amazon Aurora Serverless to automatically scale database capacity based on application demand and minimize idle resources

B) Utilize Amazon Aurora Global Database to replicate data across multiple AWS Regions and reduce cross-region data transfer costs

C) Configure Amazon Aurora Multi-Master to distribute write traffic across multiple database instances and improve scalability

D) Integrate Amazon Aurora with Amazon ElastiCache to cache frequently accessed data and reduce database load

E) Implement Amazon Aurora Read Replicas to offload read traffic from the primary database instance and optimize performance

QUESTION 58

Your company operates a data analytics platform on AWS that processes large volumes of data from various sources. As part of a cost optimization initiative, you are tasked with designing an architecture that leverages AWS services efficiently while minimizing expenses. Which of the following instance purchasing options would best optimize costs for this scenario?

A) Utilize AWS EC2 On-Demand Instances with Auto Scaling to dynamically adjust capacity based on demand

B) Implement AWS Savings Plans to receive discounts on instance usage regardless of demand fluctuations

C) Deploy AWS EC2 Reserved Instances for the core analytics workload and supplement with AWS Spot Instances for data processing tasks

D) Leverage AWS EC2 Dedicated Hosts to host the data analytics platform for enhanced security and isolation

E) Combine AWS EC2 Spot Instances with AWS Lambda for serverless processing to eliminate the need for manual scaling

QUESTION 59

Your company operates a data analytics platform that processes large volumes of data at irregular intervals. You need to optimize costs for the platform's compute resources while ensuring timely processing of data. What approach should you recommend?

A) Use Amazon EC2 On-Demand Instances for consistent performance
B) Implement Amazon EC2 Reserved Instances for long-term cost predictability

C) Leverage Amazon EC2 Spot Instances with capacity-optimized allocation strategy

D) Deploy AWS Lambda for serverless data processing

E) Utilize Amazon EMR for managed Hadoop clusters

QUESTION 60

A financial services company is deploying a new online banking application and wants to ensure that the application can handle increased transaction volumes during peak hours while minimizing costs. What Auto Scaling strategy should the solutions architect recommend?

A) Configure the Auto Scaling group to use a target tracking scaling policy based on the number of login attempts per minute.

B) Implement an Auto Scaling group with a scheduled scaling policy triggered at specific times of peak usage.

C) Configure the Auto Scaling group to use a step scaling policy triggered by sudden increases in the number of transactions per minute.

D) Utilize an Auto Scaling group with a simple scaling policy based on manual adjustments to instance counts.

E) Implement an Auto Scaling group with a predictive scaling policy based on historical transaction volumes.

QUESTION 61

Your company operates a media streaming platform that serves users globally. To minimize costs while ensuring high availability and low latency for streaming content, you need to design a cost-effective solution for content delivery. Which approach should you recommend for this scenario?

A) Use Amazon CloudFront with AWS WAF to protect against DDoS attacks and optimize content delivery

B) Implement Amazon Route 53 with latency-based routing to direct users to the nearest AWS edge location

C) Utilize Amazon S3 Transfer Acceleration to optimize data transfers and reduce latency for media uploads

D) Deploy Amazon CloudFront with Lambda@Edge to cache and deliver streaming content at edge locations

E) Use AWS Direct Connect with AWS Transit Gateway to establish private connectivity between on-premises data centers and AWS regions

QUESTION 62

Your team is responsible for managing the development and testing environments for a complex application deployed on AWS. Cost optimization is a critical concern, and you need to implement policies to control costs effectively. Which approach should you recommend?

A) Utilize AWS Auto Scaling to dynamically adjust the capacity of development and testing environments based on demand

B) Implement AWS Service Catalog to manage standardized infrastructure and application resources for development and testing

C) Leverage AWS Budgets to set cost and usage budgets for development and testing environments and receive alerts when thresholds are exceeded

D) Use AWS Lambda to automatically start and stop non-production resources based on predefined schedules

E) Deploy AWS Config to continuously monitor the configuration of development and testing resources and enforce compliance rules

QUESTION 63

Your company operates a video streaming platform with users located worldwide. To ensure high availability and low-latency access to content, you have deployed your application in multiple AWS regions. However, the finance team has raised concerns about escalating costs associated with data transfer between regions. As a solutions architect, you need to design a cost-effective solution that minimizes data transfer costs while maintaining high availability. What approach should you recommend?

A) Implement Amazon S3 Transfer Acceleration to optimize data transfer speeds between regions and reduce costs

B) Utilize AWS Direct Connect with AWS Transit Gateway to establish private connectivity between regions and reduce data transfer costs

C) Deploy Amazon CloudFront with AWS Global Accelerator to cache content at edge locations and minimize data transfer between regions

D) Leverage Amazon S3 cross-region replication to automatically replicate data between regions and ensure data durability

E) Utilize Amazon Route 53 latency-based routing to route traffic to the nearest AWS region and minimize data transfer distances

QUESTION 64

Your company operates a data-intensive application that processes large datasets for analytics purposes. The application requires cost-effective data processing solutions to handle varying workloads efficiently. As a solutions architect, you need to recommend a cost-efficient data processing architecture for the application.

A) Utilize Amazon EMR with Amazon S3 for data storage and Apache Spark for distributed data processing

B) Implement AWS Glue with Amazon Athena for serverless data processing and querying of data stored in Amazon S3

C) Deploy Amazon Redshift Spectrum with Amazon S3 to analyze data directly from S3 storage without loading it into Redshift

D) Utilize Amazon Kinesis Data Analytics for real-time data processing and analysis of streaming data

E) Leverage Amazon QuickSight with Amazon Aurora to visualize data and generate insights in real-time

QUESTION 65

Your company is experiencing challenges in controlling AWS costs across various departments and projects. As a solutions architect, you need to recommend a solution that enables granular cost control and accountability.

A) Utilize AWS Organizations to implement consolidated billing and cost allocation tags for detailed cost tracking

B) Implement AWS Budgets to set and monitor cost limits for specific services and projects

C) Leverage AWS Cost and Usage Report with Amazon Athena for custom cost analysis and reporting

D) Utilize AWS Resource Access Manager (RAM) to share AWS resources across accounts and track usage for cost allocation

E) Implement AWS Service Catalog to standardize and control provisioned resources to minimize cost

PRACTICE TEST 8 - ANSWERS ONLY

QUESTION 1

Answer - B) Enforce a strict separation of duties by creating distinct IAM roles for development and production environments.

A) Incorrect - Using the same IAM roles for both environments does not adhere to best practices for security and can lead to accidental exposure or changes to production resources.

B) Correct - Enforcing a strict separation of duties by creating distinct IAM roles for development and production environments minimizes the risk of unauthorized access or changes to sensitive resources, aligning with security best practices.

C) Incorrect - Allowing unrestricted cross-account access can compromise security and compliance, exposing sensitive environments to potential threats.

D) Incorrect - Storing IAM credentials in Amazon S3 is not secure and contradicts AWS security recommendations.

E) Incorrect - AWS Direct Connect is a network service for establishing a dedicated network connection from on-premise to AWS, not for managing federated access or separating duties between environments.

QUESTION 2

Answer - D) AWS Shield Advanced and AWS WAF

A) Incorrect - AWS Shield Standard provides basic DDoS protection, which might not be sufficient for a high-target application like video processing.

B) Incorrect - Amazon S3 and Amazon RDS are storage and database services, respectively, and do not directly contribute to DDoS protection or application security in this context.

C) Incorrect - While AWS WAF helps protect applications from web exploits, and Amazon SQS can decouple components, they do not offer comprehensive protection against DDoS attacks.

D) Correct - AWS Shield Advanced provides enhanced DDoS protection for applications with higher security needs, and AWS WAF allows for custom rules to block malicious web traffic, making this combination ideal for securing a high-profile application against attacks.

E) Incorrect - Amazon Route 53 and AWS Direct Connect are networking services that, while important, do not directly provide the level of security and DDoS protection required for a video processing application.

QUESTION 3

Answer - [A] Implement AWS IAM roles with least privilege access for Lambda functions to restrict access to AWS resources.

Option A - Correct. Implementing AWS IAM roles with least privilege access ensures that Lambda functions have restricted access to AWS resources, enhancing security.

Option B - Configuring AWS Lambda with VPC access isolates functions but may not directly address security best practices related to IAM roles.

Option C - Enabling AWS CloudTrail logging tracks API activity but may not directly relate to IAM roles and least privilege access.

Option D - AWS Secrets Manager manages sensitive information but may not directly relate to IAM roles and access control for Lambda functions.

Option E - AWS Lambda layers share code dependencies but may not directly relate to IAM roles and access control for Lambda functions.

QUESTION 4

Answer - [B] Utilize Amazon CloudFront with AWS Global Accelerator to optimize global traffic routing and improve application performance. Implement Amazon Route 53 failover routing to redirect traffic to alternative regions in case of failures.

Option B - Correct. Amazon CloudFront with AWS Global Accelerator provides optimized global traffic routing, and Route 53 failover routing redirects traffic during failures for resilience.

Option A - While deploying EC2 instances in multiple regions and using CloudFront with Route 53 latency-based routing offer some resilience, they may not provide the same level of performance and failover capabilities as Global Accelerator and Route 53 failover routing.

Option C - Deploying EC2 instances in an Auto Scaling group across multiple AZs offers resilience within a region but may not provide global failover capabilities.

Option D - CloudFront with WAF offers protection and performance but may not provide the same level of global traffic routing and failover as Global Accelerator and Route 53.

Option E - While deploying EC2 instances in multiple regions and using CloudFront with Lambda@Edge offers optimization, it may not provide the same level of global traffic routing and failover as Global Accelerator and Route 53.

QUESTION 5

Answer - B) Use Amazon SQS FIFO queue with a batch mode of 10 messages per operation.

B) Use Amazon SQS FIFO queue with a batch mode of 10 messages per operation - This option ensures prompt and accurate processing of player actions by processing multiple actions in a batch, meeting the company's requirement for timely processing and scalability during game events. The FIFO guarantees order accuracy, and batch processing enhances efficiency.

A) Use Amazon SQS FIFO queue with exactly-once processing enabled - While ensuring order accuracy, it may not efficiently handle sudden spikes in player activity due to sequential processing.

C) Use Amazon SQS FIFO queue with default settings - Default settings may not ensure prompt and accurate processing of player actions, especially during sudden spikes in activity, and may not efficiently handle batch processing.

D) Use Amazon SQS standard queue to process the messages - Standard queues lack message ordering, which is crucial for maintaining player action order, and may not efficiently handle sudden spikes in activity.

 E) Use Amazon SQS FIFO queue with message deduplication enabled - While avoiding duplicate messages, it doesn't guarantee order processing, and may not efficiently handle sudden spikes in player activity.

QUESTION 6

Answer - [B] Utilize Amazon Cognito for user authentication and authorization, and integrate it with AWS Lambda functions using custom authorizers. Implement IAM policies to control access to S3 buckets and DynamoDB tables.

Option B - Correct. Integrating Amazon Cognito with Lambda functions using custom authorizers provides secure user authentication and authorization, and IAM policies control access to S3 buckets and DynamoDB tables.

 Option A - While using API Gateway with IAM authorization for Lambda functions is valid, it may not provide the same level of user management features as Cognito.

 Option C - While IAM roles for Lambda functions and resource-level policies for S3 and DynamoDB provide security, using Cognito offers additional features specifically designed for user authentication and authorization.

 Option D - Deploying Lambda functions within a VPC and using IAM roles for access control may introduce unnecessary complexity for a serverless application.

 Option E - Using OAuth 2.0 with Lambda functions and API Gateway may not provide the same level of user management features as Cognito, and IAM policies alone may not handle user authentication and authorization effectively.

QUESTION 7

Answer - [A] Using AWS Transit Gateway to connect microservices across multiple VPCs.

A) Correct - AWS Transit Gateway allows you to connect multiple VPCs and on-premises networks, providing a centralized hub for routing traffic and enforcing access control policies.

B) Incorrect - AWS Security Groups control traffic at the instance level, not suitable for microservices communication across multiple VPCs.

C) Incorrect - VPC peering enables communication between VPCs but may not offer the centralized management required for strict access control in a microservices architecture.

D) Incorrect - AWS PrivateLink facilitates private communication between VPCs and AWS services, but it's not specifically designed for microservices communication.

E) Incorrect - AWS Network Firewall filters traffic at the subnet level and may not provide the granularity needed for microservices communication across multiple VPCs.

QUESTION 8

Answer - [D] Enabling Amazon Cognito for user authentication and access control.

A) Incorrect - While AWS Secrets Manager can securely store API keys and credentials, it may not provide user authentication and access control mechanisms required for a real-time messaging application.

B) Incorrect - End-to-end encryption using AWS KMS is important for securing data in transit and at rest but does not directly handle user authentication and access control.

C) Incorrect - Amazon GuardDuty is a threat detection service, which is important for monitoring and alerting but may not directly provide user authentication and access control for a messaging application.

D) Correct - Amazon Cognito is specifically designed for user authentication and access control, providing features such as user sign-up and sign-in, multi-factor authentication (MFA), and user pool management, which are essential for securing a real-time messaging application.

E) Incorrect - AWS Network Firewall can help filter traffic, but it's not specifically designed for user authentication and access control in a messaging application.

QUESTION 9

Answer - [A] Deploying microservices in Amazon EKS with AWS Fargate for serverless container deployment, ensuring scalability and efficient communication, and configuring Amazon RDS with encryption at rest and in-transit for data storage, meeting security and compliance requirements.

A) Deploying microservices in Amazon EKS with AWS Fargate ensures scalability and efficient communication, while configuring Amazon RDS with encryption at rest and in-transit meets security and compliance requirements for data in transit and at rest.

B) Mutual TLS authentication between microservices in Amazon ECS ensures secure communication but may not directly address encryption requirements for data at rest or scalability.

C) AWS App Mesh manages microservices traffic but may not directly enforce encryption for data at rest or address scalability requirements.

D) AWS Lambda offers serverless deployment and efficient communication, but Amazon Redshift may not be the most suitable option for data storage encryption and scalability.

E) AWS PrivateLink provides private communication between services but may not directly address encryption requirements for data at rest or ensure scalability.

QUESTION 10

Answer - A) Implement Amazon S3 Transfer Acceleration for faster uploads globally. and E) Use multipart uploads with AWS Snowball Edge for initial large dataset transfers.

A) Implement Amazon S3 Transfer Acceleration for faster uploads globally. - Correct. This service optimizes the transfer path to Amazon S3, accelerating the upload process from any location worldwide, making it ideal for global operations.

B) Establish AWS Direct Connect connections at major sites to improve upload speeds. - Incorrect for the given scenario as Direct Connect is more suited for steady, high-volume data flows rather than optimizing global uploads to S3.

C) Configure Amazon S3 cross-region replication for each office location. - Incorrect. While useful for data availability and redundancy, this doesn't address the upload speed issue from various global locations.

D) Enable AWS Global Accelerator to optimize the path to Amazon S3. - Incorrect. Global Accelerator improves performance for internet traffic routing to AWS services, but S3 Transfer Acceleration is more specific and efficient for S3 uploads.

E) Use multipart uploads with AWS Snowball Edge for initial large dataset transfers. - Correct. For initial large data transfers, Snowball Edge can significantly reduce upload times by allowing physical shipment of data, complementing online transfers for ongoing operations.

QUESTION 11

Answer - A) Configure Amazon S3 with Cross-Region Replication, S3 bucket policies for precise access control, and enable S3 Transfer Acceleration for fast access.

A) Configure Amazon S3 with Cross-Region Replication, S3 bucket policies for precise access control, and enable S3 Transfer Acceleration for fast access. - Correct because S3 offers scalable storage, Cross-Region Replication supports global access, S3 bucket policies provide precise access control, and Transfer Acceleration ensures fast file transfers.

B) Deploy Amazon EFS with a multi-AZ configuration for high availability, and use IAM roles to manage access permissions. - Incorrect for large video files shared globally as EFS is optimized for certain types of workloads and environments, not necessarily for global file sharing with the need for Transfer Acceleration.

C) Use Amazon FSx for Lustre with Direct Connect for fast, reliable access and network ACLs for access control. - Incorrect because FSx for Lustre is designed for compute-intensive workloads and might not offer the same level of access control or cost-effectiveness for simply sharing video files.

D) Implement AWS Storage Gateway with a File Gateway configuration to store and share files across offices, using AWS KMS for encryption. - Incorrect because it's more suited for hybrid cloud storage rather than fast global file sharing.

E) Set up an AWS DataSync task to synchronize files across Amazon S3 buckets in different regions, utilizing VPC endpoints for secure file access. - Incorrect as it focuses on data synchronization rather than the combination of global access, fast transfers, and precise access control provided by S3.

QUESTION 12

Answer - A) Deploy the system using AWS Elastic Beanstalk with rolling updates enabled, Amazon RDS with encryption for data storage, and AWS CloudTrail for auditing.

A) Deploy the system using AWS Elastic Beanstalk with rolling updates enabled, Amazon RDS with encryption for data storage, and AWS CloudTrail for auditing. - Correct because it combines the ease of deployment and management of AWS Elastic Beanstalk with the secure data storage capabilities of Amazon RDS, including encryption, and AWS CloudTrail for compliance auditing, meeting HIPAA requirements.

B) Use AWS CodeDeploy for zero-downtime deployment, AWS Lambda for backend processing with environment variables encrypted using AWS KMS, and Amazon CloudWatch Logs for auditing. - Incorrect as it focuses on deployment and serverless execution but does not provide a comprehensive solution for data storage and compliance auditing specific to HIPAA.

C) Implement an AWS CloudFormation template for deployment, Amazon S3 with default encryption for storing PHI, and AWS Config for configuration and compliance auditing. - Incorrect because, while it offers an infrastructure as code approach and encrypted storage, it doesn't specifically address rolling updates and the relational database needs that might be implied by a patient management system.

D) Configure Amazon ECS for deploying containerized applications with AWS Fargate for serverless compute, enable AWS CloudHSM for data encryption, and utilize AWS IAM Access Analyzer for auditing access policies. - Incorrect as it provides a robust container management and encryption solution but may not directly address the ease of rolling updates and integrated data management and auditing as Elastic Beanstalk, RDS, and CloudTrail do.

E) Leverage AWS CodePipeline for continuous delivery, Amazon EBS with encrypted volumes for data storage, and AWS X-Ray for tracing and auditing application transactions. - Incorrect because it emphasizes continuous delivery and transaction tracing but lacks the specific deployment management, database solutions, and compliance auditing configuration tailored for HIPAA compliance as provided by the correct option.

QUESTION 13

Answer - A) Use Amazon GuardDuty for monitoring S3 access patterns, AWS Lambda for automatic revocation of permissions, and AWS CloudTrail for auditing access logs.

A) Use Amazon GuardDuty for monitoring S3 access patterns, AWS Lambda for automatic revocation of permissions, and AWS CloudTrail for auditing access logs. - Correct because GuardDuty offers advanced threat detection capabilities including unusual access patterns, Lambda allows for automated execution of remediation actions like revoking permissions, and CloudTrail provides necessary auditing capabilities to review access patterns and permissions changes.

B) Configure AWS Config to monitor S3 bucket policies, implement AWS CloudTrail for tracking API activity, and use Amazon Macie for detecting sensitive data exposure. - Incorrect as it focuses more on configuration compliance and data protection, lacking the direct automation for incident response actions based on access patterns.

C) Leverage Amazon Inspector to assess S3 bucket security, AWS IAM for managing access policies, and Amazon CloudWatch Events for triggering remediation actions. - Incorrect because Inspector is more suited for vulnerability assessments than real-time monitoring and automated response to unusual access patterns.

D) Implement AWS Step Functions to orchestrate response workflows, Amazon S3 event notifications to detect unusual access, and AWS KMS for managing encryption keys. - Incorrect as it outlines a workflow orchestration and encryption management approach, but does not specifically address the automated detection and response to unauthorized access.

E) Deploy Amazon Cognito for user authentication, AWS WAF to block suspicious requests, and AWS Shield Advanced for protection against DDoS attacks on S3 buckets. - Incorrect because, while providing security measures, this option does not offer a targeted solution for detecting unusual S3 access patterns and automating immediate response actions.

QUESTION 14

Answer - [A, C]

A) Using AWS Lambda with API Gateway offers a serverless backend solution, allowing the company to handle variable traffic and reduce operational costs while maintaining high availability and scalability.

C) Setting up Amazon Aurora Serverless for the relational database backend enables automatic scaling based on demand, optimizing costs without compromising performance. Implementing Amazon ECS with Fargate, Amazon RDS Multi-AZ with reserved instances, and Amazon S3 with CloudFront are suitable solutions but may not offer the same level of cost efficiency and scalability as Lambda with API Gateway and Aurora Serverless for the company's web applications. ECS with Fargate provides scalability but may involve additional management overhead, while RDS Multi-AZ with reserved instances and S3 with CloudFront may not offer the same level of cost optimization for database storage and content delivery.

QUESTION 15

Answer - [B, C]

B) Suspend the ReplaceUnhealthy process type for the Auto Scaling group and apply the maintenance patch to the instance - This option effectively addresses the maintenance challenge by suspending the process responsible for replacing unhealthy instances, allowing the maintenance to proceed without triggering Auto Scaling actions.

C) Put the instance into the Standby state and then update the instance by applying the maintenance patch - Placing the instance in the Standby state allows for maintenance without triggering Auto Scaling actions, ensuring the continuity of the maintenance process without disruption to the application's availability.

A) Suspend the DetachInstances process type for the Auto Scaling group and apply the maintenance patch to the instance - Suspending detachment processes may not prevent instance replacement and may not efficiently address the maintenance challenge.

D) Temporarily suspend the AddToLoadBalancer process type for the Auto Scaling group and apply the maintenance patch to the instance - Suspending processes related to load balancer integration may not efficiently address the maintenance challenge and may not prevent instance replacement during maintenance.

E) Take a snapshot of the instance, create a new Amazon Machine Image (AMI), and then launch a new instance using this AMI - Creating a new instance from a snapshot introduces complexity and may not efficiently address the maintenance challenge, especially in scenarios where immediate fixes are required.

QUESTION 16

Answer - A) Set up AWS Client VPN with multi-factor authentication enabled for secure remote access.

A) Set up AWS Client VPN with multi-factor authentication enabled for secure remote access - Correct because it offers secure access to AWS networks from remote locations, with MFA providing an additional layer of security.

B) Configure AWS Direct Connect and use AWS IAM roles to manage individual access permissions -

Incorrect as Direct Connect is designed for dedicated network connections and does not directly manage individual user access or authentication.

C) Deploy Amazon WorkSpaces for each remote editor, utilizing AWS Directory Service for authentication - Incorrect because, while WorkSpaces provides virtual desktops which could be used for remote editing, it's an overly complex and potentially expensive solution for the given requirement.

D) Implement an Amazon Cognito user pool to manage authentication for AWS Client VPN access - Incorrect as Cognito is primarily for web and mobile app user management, not VPN access.

E) Use Amazon VPC peering with security groups to tightly control access between the editing team's networks and the AWS environment - Incorrect because VPC peering is for interconnecting VPCs, not for providing secure individual access from various global locations.

QUESTION 17

Answer - B) Use AWS Snowball for initial data migration, Amazon DynamoDB for scalable NoSQL storage, and AWS Step Functions to orchestrate serverless workflows.

A) Incorrect because AWS Server Migration Service and Lambda cater to migration and serverless execution, but Cognito's user authentication doesn't directly contribute to the migration goals of zero data loss and scalability.

B) Correct as AWS Snowball ensures secure and efficient initial data migration, DynamoDB provides a scalable NoSQL solution for the shopping cart data, and Step Functions allow for cost-effective orchestration of serverless components like the recommendation engine.

C) Incorrect because DataSync and Fargate focus on data transfer and container management, which do not directly address the requirement for zero data loss or the introduction of AI-driven recommendation features.

D) Incorrect as Elastic Beanstalk, RDS, and CloudFront offer application deployment, database management, and content delivery but do not provide the specific serverless architecture or data migration capabilities required for the scenario.

E) Incorrect because Glacier is for data archiving which is not relevant to the migration's immediate goals, Elastic Load Balancing distributes traffic which, while important, doesn't address the serverless or AI-enhancement needs, and Rekognition offers AI capabilities but isn't directly related to the shopping cart system migration.

QUESTION 18

Answer - [B] Leverage AWS AppConfig to store and manage configuration settings securely. Integrate AWS Lambda with AppConfig for dynamically updating application configurations.

Option A - Storing secrets directly in environment variables is not recommended for security reasons and lacks centralized management.

Option C - While Parameter Groups manage database configurations, they do not provide dynamic configuration updates like AppConfig.

Option D - Storing plaintext configurations in EFS and managing access with IAM roles is not secure and lacks centralized management for secrets.

Option E - Implementing a custom solution using S3 and Lambda introduces complexity and may not adhere to best practices for secrets management.

QUESTION 19

Answer - [B] Implement AWS Systems Manager Parameter Store to centrally manage environment-specific configurations and secrets. Use AWS CodePipeline with Parameter Store integration for retrieving configurations during deployments.

Option A - Embedding configuration settings within deployment packages lacks flexibility and may expose sensitive information.

Option C - Storing secrets in plaintext files within version-controlled repositories poses security risks and lacks centralized management and rotation capabilities.

Option D - While Secrets Manager can securely store and rotate secrets, using custom Lambda functions within the CI/CD pipeline introduces complexity and may not align with best practices for deployment automation.

Option E - Storing configuration settings within Lambda environment variables lacks centralized management and may lead to inconsistency across environments. Explanation for Choice B: Implementing Parameter Store allows for centralized management of configurations and secrets. Integrating with CodePipeline enables secure retrieval during deployments, enhancing automation and compliance.

QUESTION 20

Answer - A) Create an Amazon CloudWatch metric filter to process AWS CloudTrail logs containing API call details. Establish an alarm based on this metric's rate to send an Amazon SNS notification to the required team.

A) Create an Amazon CloudWatch metric filter to process AWS CloudTrail logs containing API call details. Establish an alarm based on this metric's rate to send an Amazon SNS notification to the required team. - This option directly addresses the scenario by analyzing CloudTrail logs for unauthorized API queries and triggering real-time alerts using CloudWatch alarms and Amazon SNS notifications.

B) Implement AWS Config Rules to monitor API activity and define rules to detect unauthorized API calls. Configure AWS Config to trigger an AWS Lambda function upon rule evaluation to notify relevant stakeholders. - While AWS Config can monitor API activity, it may not provide real-time alerting capabilities for immediate incident response as required in this scenario.

C) Leverage AWS Trusted Advisor to publish metrics about check results to Amazon CloudWatch. Set up an alarm to track status changes for checks in the Service Limits category for the APIs, triggering notifications when service quotas are exceeded. - While Trusted Advisor offers valuable insights, it may not directly address the need for real-time detection of unauthorized API queries.

D) Use Amazon Athena SQL queries against AWS CloudTrail log files stored in Amazon S3 buckets. Generate reports using Amazon QuickSight for managerial dashboards. - While this option provides insights, it may not offer real-time alerting capabilities as required in this scenario.

E) Configure AWS CloudTrail to stream event data to Amazon Kinesis. Utilize Amazon Kinesis stream-level metrics in Amazon CloudWatch to trigger an AWS Lambda function that will initiate an error workflow. - While this option utilizes streaming data, it may introduce complexity and latency compared to directly analyzing CloudTrail logs for real-time alerts.

QUESTION 21

Answer - [C) Use AWS Step Functions to orchestrate the processing workflow with Lambda functions.]

C) AWS Step Functions provides orchestration capabilities, allowing you to define a state machine to coordinate multiple Lambda functions and other AWS services. This ensures scalability and fault tolerance in processing workflows.

A) While SQS is used for decoupling, it doesn't offer orchestration capabilities like Step Functions.
B) SNS is for pub/sub messaging, not workflow orchestration.
D) Fargate containers behind ALB may offer scalability but not as easily orchestrated as Step Functions.
E) Kinesis is for real-time data streams, not workflow orchestration.

QUESTION 22

Answer - [A) Amazon ECS and C) AWS Fargate]

Option A involves Amazon ECS for container orchestration with automatic scaling, ensuring fault tolerance and scalability for microservices.

Option C involves AWS Fargate for serverless container deployment with auto-scaling, providing fault tolerance and scalability without managing infrastructure.

Option B involves Amazon EKS for managed Kubernetes with cluster autoscaling, but it does not directly provide serverless container deployment like AWS Fargate.

Option D involves AWS Auto Scaling for dynamic scaling of EC2 instances with load balancing, but it does not directly manage containerized microservices like Amazon ECS or AWS Fargate.

Option E involves Amazon CloudWatch for monitoring and alarms, but it does not directly provide container orchestration or serverless container deployment.

QUESTION 23

Answer - [B) Implement AWS Backup with centralized management and AWS Organizations integration for automated backup and restore operations, ensuring data integrity and regulatory compliance.]

Option B) is correct as it involves implementing AWS Backup, which provides centralized management and integration with AWS Organizations for automated backup and restore operations, ensuring data integrity and regulatory compliance.

Option A) involves Glacier for long-term archival but may not address automated backup requirements effectively.

Option C) involves Aurora Multi-AZ for database redundancy but may not provide the same level of backup automation.

Option D) involves Storage Gateway for hybrid storage but may not provide centralized management for backup.

Option E) involves FSx for file-level backup but may not achieve the same level of regulatory compliance as AWS Backup.

QUESTION 24

Answer - [A) Implement Amazon EC2 Auto Scaling with Elastic Load Balancing for automatic scaling and distribution of traffic across multiple instances.]

Option A) is correct as it involves using Amazon EC2 Auto Scaling to automatically adjust the number of instances based on traffic demand and Elastic Load Balancing to distribute traffic across multiple instances, ensuring high availability and scalability.

Option B) mentions Amazon Route 53 and AWS Global Accelerator, which are not directly related to auto-scaling and high availability of compute resources.

Option C) mentions Amazon RDS Multi-AZ deployment, which is for database high availability and may not meet the requirements for scaling web application instances.

Option D) mentions Amazon EFS and AWS Backup, which are for file storage and backup, not for auto-scaling compute resources.

Option E) mentions AWS Lambda and Amazon API Gateway, which are for serverless compute and API management, not for managing auto-scaling of EC2 instances.

QUESTION 25

Answer - A) Use Amazon Route 53 based geolocation routing policy to restrict access to only users in the designated regions

A) By using Amazon Route 53's geolocation routing policy, the e-commerce platform can ensure that only users from the specified regions can access the flash sale, effectively managing traffic and optimizing user experience.

B, C, D, E) These options do not directly address the requirement of restricting access to users from specific regions for the flash sale. Weighted routing, latency-based routing, failover routing, and geoproximity routing do not provide the necessary geographic control needed for this scenario.

QUESTION 26

Answer - B) Implement AWS CloudFormation to define infrastructure as code and automate the deployment of AWS resources in a consistent and repeatable manner, promoting immutable infrastructure.

Option A is incorrect because while AWS OpsWorks automates infrastructure provisioning and configuration management, it may not directly align with the goal of achieving immutable infrastructure on AWS.

Option B is correct because AWS CloudFormation allows defining infrastructure as code, enabling the creation of immutable infrastructure and automating the deployment of AWS resources in a consistent and repeatable manner, aligning with the goal of achieving immutable infrastructure on AWS.

Option C is incorrect because while AWS Systems Manager automates administrative tasks, it may not inherently support the principles of immutable infrastructure.

Option D is incorrect because while Amazon ECS Anywhere allows running containerized applications, it does not directly address the goal of achieving immutable infrastructure on AWS.

Option E is incorrect because while AWS Lambda scales and executes code, it does not directly address the goal of achieving immutable infrastructure on AWS.

QUESTION 27

Answer - B) Utilize API Gateway usage plans and API keys to enforce throttling limits and monitor API usage metrics

Option B - API Gateway usage plans and API keys provide built-in mechanisms for enforcing throttling limits and monitoring API usage metrics, ensuring efficient traffic management.

Option A - Amazon API Gateway caching can improve performance but may not offer the granular control needed for efficient throttling and monitoring of API traffic.

Option C - API Gateway resource policies focus on access control rather than throttling and may not provide the required monitoring capabilities.

Option D - AWS Lambda authorizers are primarily for authentication and may not offer the same level of traffic management features as API keys and usage plans.

Option E - Deploying Amazon CloudFront introduces additional complexity and may not offer the same level of control and monitoring as API Gateway usage plans and API keys.

QUESTION 28

Answer - B) Use Amazon EKS with AWS Fargate for compute, leverage AWS App Mesh for microservices communication, Amazon ECR for container management, and Amazon CloudFront for low latency content delivery.

A) Incorrect, because while ECS, GameLift, and ECR are relevant, GameLift is specifically for game session management and not for microservices communication or overall container orchestration optimization.

B) Correct, EKS with Fargate provides scalable and serverless compute, App Mesh enables efficient microservices communication, ECR manages container images securely, and CloudFront reduces latency for a global audience, aligning with the platform's needs.

C) Incorrect, Direct Connect is used for dedicated network connections to AWS, which may reduce latency but doesn't directly address the container orchestration or microservices communication. Global Accelerator improves performance but doesn't fully optimize containerized microservices communication.

D) Incorrect, MSK and Lambda are powerful for event-driven architectures and managing state, but not directly relevant to container orchestration or ensuring low latency in game backend scenarios. DynamoDB is suited for data storage but doesn't address communication needs.

E) Incorrect, while ECS with Fargate and ElastiCache address scalability and real-time caching, PrivateLink focuses on secure service connections and doesn't necessarily optimize for low latency or microservices communication in a gaming context.

QUESTION 29

Answer - A) Amazon CloudFront with Origin Shield.

A) CloudFront with Origin Shield reduces the impact of regional outages by caching content and serving it from an alternate region if necessary.

B) Transit Gateway connects multiple VPCs or on-premises networks but does not mitigate regional outages.

C) S3 transfer acceleration improves data transfer speed but does not address service availability during regional outages.

D) Aurora Multi-Master provides database redundancy within a region, not across regions.

E) VPC peering enables connectivity between VPCs but does not provide global redundancy.

QUESTION 30

Answer - B) Utilize WebSocket APIs on Amazon API Gateway for synchronous communication and Amazon SQS for asynchronous communication

B) Utilizing WebSocket APIs on Amazon API Gateway allows for synchronous communication, while leveraging Amazon SQS enables asynchronous communication, ensuring effective support for both modes of communication.

A, C, D, E) These options either do not provide support for both synchronous and asynchronous communication or involve using services not suitable for the specified requirements.

QUESTION 31

Answer - A) AWS Config rules to evaluate compliance, AWS CloudTrail for audit trails, AWS Lambda for automated remediation actions, and Amazon SNS for notifications.

A) Correct, as AWS Config rules provide continuous monitoring of compliance with policies, CloudTrail offers governance through audit trails, Lambda enables automated remediation of detected issues, and SNS notifies stakeholders of compliance status and issues, fulfilling the requirements for automation in compliance and governance.

B) Incorrect, although Inspector, Trusted Advisor, and CloudWatch are valuable for security and monitoring, they do not provide a direct mechanism for automated detection and remediation of compliance issues as effectively as the combination in A.

C) Incorrect, Shield, WAF, Fargate, and GuardDuty are focused on security and threat detection rather than compliance automation and remediation.

D) Incorrect, as RDS, DynamoDB, Direct Connect, and IAM focus on database management, connectivity, and access control without specifically addressing compliance monitoring and automated remediation.

E) Incorrect, this combination is geared towards scaling, storage, and deployment, lacking specific tools for compliance monitoring and automated issue remediation.

QUESTION 32

Answer - [A) Deploy Amazon RDS with Multi-AZ deployment and utilize AWS Key Management Service (AWS KMS) for encryption at rest and in transit.]

Option A - Correct because Amazon RDS with Multi-AZ deployment ensures high availability and data integrity, while AWS KMS provides encryption for data at rest and in transit, meeting the SaaS provider's requirements for disaster recovery and compliance.

Option B - Incorrect because while S3 offers data redundancy, it may not provide the same level of features for disaster recovery and compliance as Amazon RDS Multi-AZ deployment with AWS KMS encryption.

Option C - Incorrect because DynamoDB, while offering scalability and real-time replication, may not provide the same level of features for disaster recovery and compliance as Amazon RDS Multi-AZ deployment with AWS KMS encryption.

Option D - Incorrect because Redshift is optimized for analytics and may not offer the same level of disaster recovery features as Amazon RDS Multi-AZ deployment with AWS KMS encryption.

Option E - Incorrect because Aurora Serverless may not provide the necessary performance and scalability for critical database workloads during a disaster recovery scenario.

QUESTION 33

Answer - [A] Utilize AWS API Gateway with AWS WAF integration for API protection.

Option B is incorrect as storing API keys in plaintext within Lambda environment variables is a security risk.

Option C is incorrect as OAuth 2.0 authentication with Amazon Cognito is more suitable for user authentication, not API communication.

Option D is incorrect as plaintext HTTP should not be used for API communication due to security concerns.

Option E is incorrect as AWS Shield is focused on DDoS protection, not API communication security. Option A is correct because utilizing AWS API Gateway with AWS WAF integration is a recommended approach for securing API communication, ensuring scalability, and maintaining performance by protecting against common web attacks.

QUESTION 34

Answer - [A) Amazon RDS Multi-AZ deployment with Amazon Aurora.]

Option A provides the most cost-effective solution with high availability and automatic failover capabilities by utilizing Amazon RDS Multi-AZ deployment with Amazon Aurora. This setup ensures resilience and eliminates the need for manual failover.

Option B requires managing database instances manually and may not provide the same level of resilience.

Option C introduces complexity with read replicas and may not be as cost-effective.

Option D and E are not suitable for the given requirements.

QUESTION 35

Answer - B) Implement Amazon Kinesis Data Streams with AWS Lambda for processing transactions and Amazon DynamoDB for storing transaction data

B) Implementing Amazon Kinesis Data Streams with AWS Lambda allows for real-time processing of transactions, meeting the requirement for prompt fraud detection without manual intervention. Storing transaction data in Amazon DynamoDB provides scalability and low-latency access.

A) While AWS Lambda can process transactions, Amazon SQS and Amazon S3 are not suitable for real-time processing and may introduce delays.

C) Ingesting transactions into Amazon Redshift involves additional complexity and is not optimized for real-time processing.

D) Amazon Kinesis Data Firehose does not support auto-scaled Amazon Aurora databases, and using it may introduce latency in processing transactions.

E) Ingesting transactions into Amazon Elasticsearch Service may not provide the necessary real-time processing capabilities and low-latency access required for fraud detection.

QUESTION 36

Answer - [A, C]

A) Correct - API Gateway with HTTPS ensures secure communication, and Cognito provides user authentication and authorization, aligning with best practices for secure frontend-backend communication.

B) Incorrect - While CloudFront with SSL/TLS termination and WAF provide security, they don't directly ensure secure communication between frontend and backend tiers.

C) Correct - EC2 instances with ACM for SSL/TLS certificates ensure secure communication, and VPC security groups control network traffic, providing a secure frontend-backend connection.

D) Incorrect - NLB with SSL/TLS termination and Shield Advanced offer DDoS protection but don't directly address secure communication between frontend and backend tiers.

E) Incorrect - CloudFront with WAF and Direct Connect provide security and connectivity options but don't directly ensure secure communication between frontend and backend tiers.

QUESTION 37

Answer - C) Amazon S3 with versioning enabled and cross-region replication.

A) Incorrect - Amazon Glacier is designed for long-term archival storage with retrieval times ranging from minutes to hours, not suitable for quick retrieval needs.

B) Incorrect - EBS provides block storage for EC2 instances but isn't optimized for sharing or distributing files across environments.

C) Correct - Amazon S3 offers high availability, durability, and quick retrieval. Versioning allows for managing multiple versions of artifacts, and cross-region replication enhances availability and access speed.

D) Incorrect - DynamoDB is a NoSQL database service optimized for applications needing consistent, single-digit millisecond latency at any scale but isn't the best fit for storing large build artifacts.

E) Incorrect - AWS Elastic Beanstalk is an application deployment and management service, not specifically designed for storage or quick retrieval of build artifacts.

QUESTION 38

Answer - A) Deploy Amazon Kinesis Data Streams to ingest streaming data and process it in real-time using AWS Lambda for serverless execution.

Option A - Amazon Kinesis Data Streams allows ingestion and processing of streaming data in real-time, coupled with AWS Lambda for serverless execution, ensuring low-latency access to data for real-time analytics.

Option B - Amazon Redshift is optimized for data warehousing and batch processing, which may not meet the low-latency requirements of the real-time analytics platform.

Option C - Amazon EMR is suitable for processing large volumes of data but may introduce latency compared to real-time processing with Amazon Kinesis.

Option D - Configuring Amazon S3 event notifications with AWS Lambda functions may introduce latency and may not provide real-time processing capabilities.

Option E - Amazon Elasticsearch Service is more suitable for search and indexing rather than real-time analytics on streaming data.

QUESTION 39

Answer - B) Utilize AWS AppSync for real-time data synchronization, and leverage Amazon Kinesis Data Streams for processing sales events.

Option A - Amazon EMR is for batch processing, and Amazon SQS is for queuing, which does not meet the real-time processing requirement.

Option B - AWS AppSync enables real-time synchronization, and Amazon Kinesis Data Streams is designed for real-time data processing, fulfilling the high availability, fault tolerance, and low latency needs.

Option C - While AWS Lambda offers serverless processing, using Amazon S3 for real-time data storage is not efficient for this scenario.

Option D - Amazon RDS and Amazon SNS are not suitable for real-time processing of sales data.
Option E - Amazon ECS and Amazon S3 Glacier are not optimized for real-time data processing, making this option less suitable.

QUESTION 40

Answer - C) Utilize server-side encryption with AWS Key Management Service (SSE-KMS) keys to encrypt the data on Amazon S3

C) Server-side encryption with AWS Key Management Service (SSE-KMS) allows the financial institution to have full control over the encryption keys and access to audit logs.

A) While server-side encryption with Amazon S3 managed keys (SSE-S3) encrypts the data at rest, it does not provide the level of control and auditability required by the financial institution.

B) Client-side encryption with customer-provided keys (SSE-C) shifts the responsibility of encryption to the client, which may not align with the institution's requirement for centralized control.

D) Using server-side encryption with customer-provided keys (SSE-C) also lacks the centralized control and auditing capabilities provided by AWS KMS.

E) Enabling AWS CloudTrail provides auditing capabilities but does not directly address the encryption requirement for data at rest in Amazon S3.

QUESTION 41

Answer - A) AWS Lambda for processing, Amazon DynamoDB with encryption at rest for storage, and Amazon Cognito for user authentication.

A) Correct - AWS Lambda can efficiently process data without managing servers, ideal for varying loads. Amazon DynamoDB offers encryption at rest, securing patient data storage. Amazon Cognito provides user authentication, ensuring secure access.

B) Incorrect - API Gateway, S3 with encryption, and Fargate offer parts of the solution, but Fargate isn't serverless in the context of managing compute resources as Lambda is, which is crucial for handling peak loads dynamically.

C) Incorrect - Step Functions, RDS with encryption, and IAM provide workflow management, secure storage, and access management but don't offer the same level of serverless scalability and simplicity as Lambda and DynamoDB for processing needs.

D) Incorrect - SNS, SQS with SSE, and EKS cover notifications, secure message queuing, and container management but don't address serverless processing and database storage with the same effectiveness as Lambda and DynamoDB.

E) Incorrect - Kinesis, Secrets Manager, and CloudFront address real-time processing, encryption key management, and secure content delivery but don't provide a comprehensive serverless architecture for processing, storing, and securely accessing sensitive health data as effectively as the combination of Lambda, DynamoDB, and Cognito.

QUESTION 42

Answer - [C) Utilize AWS Outposts with a multi-AZ configuration to ensure fault tolerance and high availability within the same geographic region.]

Option C) Utilizing AWS Outposts with a multi-AZ configuration ensures fault tolerance and high availability within the same geographic region, meeting the requirements for running applications that require low-latency access to on-premises data.

Option A) Deploying AWS Outposts with a dual-region configuration may introduce additional complexity and latency, which may not be suitable for applications requiring low-latency access to on-premises data.

Option B) AWS Storage Gateway replicates data asynchronously and may not provide the real-time access required for applications running on AWS Outposts.

Option D) AWS Direct Connect offers dedicated network connectivity but may not directly address fault tolerance and high availability within the same region.

Option E) AWS VPN with redundant tunnels may provide secure connections but may not ensure fault tolerance and high availability to the same extent as a multi-AZ configuration for AWS Outposts.

QUESTION 43

Answer - D) Use Amazon CloudFront for video streaming and static resources delivery, Amazon API Gateway and AWS Lambda for serving dynamic content, Amazon S3 for storage, and Amazon Aurora Serverless for scalable database needs.

A) Incorrect - EKS, RDS, S3, and CloudFront provide the necessary components for such a platform, but managing Kubernetes may introduce complexity not suited for all aspects of the requirement, especially for dynamic scaling and content delivery optimization.

B) Incorrect - S3, Lambda, DynamoDB, and Global Accelerator address storage, compute, and global performance, but this setup may not offer the best user experience for video streaming and interactive content compared to the seamless integration of CloudFront and serverless technologies.

C) Incorrect - Using EC2, Elastic Transcoder, ElastiCache, and ELB offers traditional scaling and processing capabilities but lacks the serverless architecture's benefits for cost-efficiency, scalability, and maintenance ease.

D) Correct - CloudFront optimizes video and content delivery globally. API Gateway and Lambda allow for scalable, serverless backend operations. S3 provides durable storage, and Aurora Serverless offers a scalable database solution, matching the platform's requirements perfectly.

E) Incorrect - While AWS Amplify, S3, CloudFront, MediaLive, and QLDB provide a comprehensive set of services, the combination in D more directly addresses the need for scalability, global reach, and dynamic content delivery with serverless architecture advantages.

QUESTION 44

Answer - [A] Utilize Amazon SageMaker for real-time inference, integrating Amazon DynamoDB for user data storage and Amazon CloudWatch for monitoring.

Option B's batch inference may not meet the requirement for real-time recommendations.
Option C's use of AWS Lambda may introduce latency.
Option D's use of Aurora may not be optimized for model storage.
Option E's use of EFS may not provide the low-latency access required for real-time inference.
Option A leverages SageMaker for real-time inference combined with DynamoDB for user data storage, providing minimal latency and efficient access to personalized recommendations.

QUESTION 45

Answer - D) Employ a combination of reserved instances (RI) and spot instances

D) Employing a combination of reserved instances (RI) and spot instances allows the corporation to benefit from cost savings with RIs for predictable workloads while leveraging the scalability and cost-effectiveness of spot instances during peak traffic periods.

A) Using on-demand instances for the entire duration may result in higher costs, especially during peak traffic times.

B) A mix of reserved instances (RI) and on-demand instances may not fully leverage cost savings during predictable workloads and may not scale efficiently during traffic spikes.

C) Utilizing spot instances for the entire duration may be risky as spot instances can be terminated with short notice, potentially affecting application availability.

E) Using reserved instances (RI) for the entire duration may not be cost-effective during periods of low traffic, as the capacity remains fixed regardless of demand fluctuations.

QUESTION 46

Answer - [A] Store video content in Amazon S3, deploy Amazon CloudFront with Lambda@Edge for content delivery, utilize Amazon DynamoDB for user metadata storage, and implement Amazon Route 53 for global DNS routing.

Option B is incorrect because using EC2 instances with EBS volumes for storing video content may result in higher data transfer costs compared to storing content in Amazon S3. Additionally, RDS may introduce additional costs and management overhead compared to using DynamoDB for user metadata storage.

Option C is incorrect because although Amazon Aurora is a highly scalable database, it may introduce higher costs and management complexity compared to using DynamoDB for user metadata storage in this scenario.

Option D is incorrect because using EC2 instances with EBS volumes may not be as scalable and cost-efficient as storing video content directly in Amazon S3. Additionally, using DynamoDB for user metadata storage is preferable over RDS for this scenario.

Option E is incorrect because although using CloudFront with AWS Shield can enhance security, it may not directly address the requirement to minimize data transfer costs, which can be better achieved by leveraging Lambda@Edge to optimize content delivery.

QUESTION 47

Answer - [B] Implement a serverless architecture with AWS Lambda for compute, Amazon DynamoDB for database needs, and Amazon ElastiCache for in-memory caching.

Option B is the correct choice because a serverless architecture with AWS Lambda automatically scales to handle millions of concurrent users, while DynamoDB provides scalability and low-latency access to data. ElastiCache improves performance by caching frequently accessed data.

Options A, C, D, and E either lack the same level of scalability, low latency, or suitable services for the specified requirements.

QUESTION 48

Answer - A) Use reserved instances (RI) for the entire duration of operation

A) Using reserved instances (RI) for the entire duration ensures continuous availability and high performance while optimizing infrastructure costs through upfront commitments and discounted pricing.

B) Implementing on-demand instances for the entire duration may result in higher costs without the benefit of cost savings offered by reserved instances.

C) Utilizing spot instances for the entire duration may introduce reliability concerns as spot instances can be terminated with short notice, potentially affecting application availability.

D) Employing a combination of reserved instances (RI) and spot instances may add complexity without significant cost benefits for a workload requiring continuous availability.

E) Implementing a mix of reserved instances (RI) and on-demand instances may not provide the same level of cost optimization and reliability needed for a critical healthcare application.

QUESTION 49

Answer - B) Deploy AWS Lambda for serverless computing, Amazon DynamoDB for real-time data storage, and Amazon API Gateway for communication between players.

Option B - This approach utilizes AWS Lambda for serverless computing, ensuring low-latency communication between players, Amazon DynamoDB for real-time data storage, providing high availability and scalability, and Amazon API Gateway for communication between players, ensuring efficient and secure interaction.

Option A - While Amazon EC2 instances with AWS Auto Scaling and Amazon RDS Multi-AZ offer scalability and real-time data storage, respectively, they may not provide the same level of efficiency and low latency as serverless computing with AWS Lambda and Amazon DynamoDB for this use case. Additionally, Amazon ElastiCache may introduce additional complexity without significant benefits for the given requirements.

Option C - Although Amazon ECS and Amazon Aurora offer containerized workload management and real-time data storage, respectively, they may not provide the same level of efficiency and simplicity as serverless computing with AWS Lambda and Amazon DynamoDB for low-latency communication between players. Additionally, Amazon SQS may introduce additional latency compared to direct communication via API Gateway.

Option D - While Amazon EC2 instances with AWS Auto Scaling and Amazon RDS Multi-AZ offer scalability and real-time data storage, respectively, they may not provide the same level of efficiency and simplicity as serverless computing with AWS Lambda and Amazon DynamoDB for low-latency communication between players. Additionally, Amazon SNS may introduce additional latency and complexity compared to direct communication via API Gateway.

Option E - Although Amazon EMR and Amazon RDS Multi-AZ offer scalability and real-time data storage, respectively, they may not provide the same level of efficiency and simplicity as serverless computing with AWS Lambda and Amazon DynamoDB for low-latency communication between players. Additionally, Amazon API Gateway may offer more efficient communication compared to EMR for real-time updates of game state.

QUESTION 50

Answer - A) Implement cross-region read replicas for the Amazon RDS database, with automated failover configured using Amazon Route 53 health checks. Utilize AWS Backup to create scheduled backups for point-in-time recovery.

Option B focuses on backup and restoration but does not address real-time replication or automated failover for disaster recovery.
Option C introduces complexity with Multi-Master clusters and may not offer immediate failover capabilities.

Option D, while utilizing Multi-AZ deployment, lacks cross-region replication for disaster recovery.
Option E involves DMS replication but does not provide automated failover or zero data loss guarantees like cross-region read replicas.

QUESTION 51

Answer - E) Deploy CloudFront with AWS WAF for security and configure dynamic content handling through Lambda@Edge.

A) - Incorrect because manual cache invalidation is not efficient for fast content updates.
 B) - Incorrect, custom SSL/TLS certificates improve security but do not address content update efficiency.

 C) - Incorrect, while innovative, this option doesn't fully utilize CloudFront's capabilities for security and content delivery.

 D) - Incorrect, scheduled cache invalidation may not align with actual content update needs.
 E) - Correct, as it combines CloudFront with AWS WAF for enhanced security and Lambda@Edge for efficient, dynamic content handling.

QUESTION 52

Answer - A) Read-Only Policy.

A) This policy allows only the s3:GetObject action, which permits reading objects from the specified bucket, ensuring that the third-party application can only read objects without the ability to modify them.

 B) This policy denies the s3:PutObject action, preventing the application from uploading or modifying objects in the bucket, but it does not address the requirement for read-only access.

 C) This policy allows both s3:GetObject and s3:PutObject actions, which would grant the application unnecessary write permissions, violating the requirement for read-only access.

 D) This policy allows both s3:ListBucket and s3:GetObject actions, providing unnecessary list permissions and allowing the application to delete objects, which is not required.

E) This policy allows both s3:GetObject and s3:DeleteObject actions, which would grant the application the ability to delete objects from the bucket, violating the requirement for read-only access.

QUESTION 53

Answer - [D] Optimize container resource allocation using AWS Batch.

Option A - Amazon EFS is a shared file storage service and may not be the most cost-effective option for microservices architecture.

Option B - Amazon ECS Anywhere extends ECS to on-premises environments and may not directly relate to cost optimization for cloud-based microservices.

Option C - While Amazon DynamoDB is a managed NoSQL database, it may not directly address cost optimization for microservices architecture.

Option D - Correct. AWS Batch can optimize container resource allocation, ensuring efficient resource utilization and cost optimization.

Option E - Amazon EKS is a Kubernetes-based container orchestration service, which may introduce additional complexity compared to using AWS Batch for resource optimization.

QUESTION 54

Answer - [B] Implement Amazon VPC with AWS Transit Gateway for scalable and cost-effective connectivity.

Option A - Global Accelerator with Route 53 improves traffic distribution but may not provide the same cost-effectiveness as VPC with Transit Gateway for microservices architecture.

Option B - Correct. Amazon VPC with AWS Transit Gateway offers scalable and cost-effective connectivity for microservices, ensuring fault tolerance and scalability while minimizing costs.

Option C - CloudFront with Shield focuses on DDoS protection and content caching but may not address the connectivity requirements for microservices.

Option D - VPN with Direct Connect provides secure hybrid cloud connectivity but may not be the most cost-effective solution for microservices architecture.

Option E - PrivateLink facilitates private connectivity between services but may not offer the scalability and cost-effectiveness needed for microservices deployment.

QUESTION 55

Answer - [B] Generate IAM roles with time-limited permissions for the freelance content creators to assume when uploading files.

A) Incorrect - Creating IAM users with long-term access credentials poses security risks and does not align with the requirement for temporary access.

B) Correct - Generating IAM roles with time-limited permissions ensures secure and temporary access management for freelance content creators, limiting their access to specific tasks and timeframes.

C) Incorrect - Sharing S3 bucket access keys directly with freelance content creators increases the risk of unauthorized access and compromises security.

D) Incorrect - Implementing cross-account IAM roles adds unnecessary complexity and may not be suitable for temporary access requirements.

E) Incorrect - While S3 pre-signed URLs can provide temporary access, they are more suitable for granting access to specific objects rather than managing access for multiple content creators.

QUESTION 56

Answer - [B] Utilize Amazon EC2 Auto Scaling with a scheduled scaling policy to adjust capacity based on anticipated traffic patterns.

Option B - Correct. Utilizing Amazon EC2 Auto Scaling with a scheduled scaling policy allows adjusting capacity based on anticipated traffic patterns, ensuring cost optimization for varying levels of traffic.

Option A - Amazon ECS Anywhere offers flexibility but may not be the most efficient solution for cost-optimized scaling of microservices with varying traffic patterns.

Option C - While Amazon EKS Anywhere provides auto-scaling capabilities, it may introduce complexity and may not be the most cost-effective solution for this scenario.

Option D - AWS Lambda with provisioned concurrency ensures consistent performance but may not be the most suitable solution for microservices with varying traffic patterns.

Option E - AWS Outposts extends AWS infrastructure to on-premises environments but may not provide the same level of flexibility and cost optimization for microservices scaling as Amazon EC2 Auto Scaling.

QUESTION 57

Answer - [E] Implement Amazon Aurora Read Replicas to offload read traffic from the primary database instance and optimize performance.

Option A - Implementing Amazon Aurora Serverless allows for automatic scaling but may not be the most cost-effective solution for managing database costs in a high-traffic scenario.

Option B - While Amazon Aurora Global Database provides data replication, it may not directly address cost optimization concerns related to database scalability.

Option C - Configuring Amazon Aurora Multi-Master improves scalability but may not directly optimize costs associated with database resources.

Option D - Integrating Amazon Aurora with Amazon ElastiCache improves performance through caching but may not directly optimize database costs.

Option E - Correct. Implementing Amazon Aurora Read Replicas offloads read traffic from the primary database instance, optimizing performance and reducing costs by distributing workload across multiple instances.

QUESTION 58

Answer - [C] Deploy AWS EC2 Reserved Instances for the core analytics workload and supplement with AWS Spot Instances for data processing tasks.

Option C - Correct. Deploying AWS EC2 Reserved Instances for the core analytics workload ensures cost optimization for predictable usage, while supplementing with AWS Spot Instances for data processing tasks maximizes cost efficiency for variable workloads.

Option A - Utilizing AWS EC2 On-Demand Instances with Auto Scaling may be efficient but may not fully optimize costs compared to Reserved Instances and Spot Instances.

Option B - Implementing AWS Savings Plans provides discounts but does not specifically address the dynamic nature of data processing tasks and may not offer the same level of cost optimization as Reserved Instances and Spot Instances.

Option D - Leveraging AWS EC2 Dedicated Hosts may offer enhanced security and isolation but may not provide the flexibility required for cost optimization based on workload characteristics.

Option E - Combining AWS EC2 Spot Instances with AWS Lambda for serverless processing introduces complexity and may not be the most cost-effective solution for data processing tasks.

QUESTION 59

Answer - [C] Leverage Amazon EC2 Spot Instances with capacity-optimized allocation strategy.

Option C - Correct. Leveraging Amazon EC2 Spot Instances with capacity-optimized allocation strategy allows for cost optimization in data analytics workloads with irregular processing intervals.

Option A - Using Amazon EC2 On-Demand Instances provides consistent performance but may not be as cost-effective as Spot Instances for irregular workloads.

Option B - Implementing Amazon EC2 Reserved Instances offers cost predictability but may not be suitable for workloads with irregular processing intervals.

Option D - Deploying AWS Lambda for serverless data processing may be suitable for specific use cases but may not provide the same level of control or customization as EC2 instances.

Option E - Utilizing Amazon EMR for managed Hadoop clusters may be suitable for data analytics but does not specifically address cost optimization requirements.

QUESTION 60

Answer - [C] Configure the Auto Scaling group to use a step scaling policy triggered by sudden increases in the number of transactions per minute.

A) Incorrect - Using a target tracking scaling policy based on the number of login attempts per minute may not accurately reflect the overall application workload during peak hours.

B) Incorrect - Implementing a scheduled scaling policy triggered at specific times of peak usage may not dynamically respond to sudden traffic increases, potentially resulting in under or over-provisioning of resources.

C) Correct - Configuring a step scaling policy triggered by sudden increases in the number of transactions per minute allows the Auto Scaling group to dynamically adjust the number of instances in response to changing traffic patterns during peak hours, ensuring optimal performance and cost efficiency.

D) Incorrect - Utilizing a simple scaling policy based on manual adjustments lacks automation and may result in delayed responses to sudden traffic increases, impacting performance during peak hours.

E) Incorrect - Implementing a predictive scaling policy based on historical transaction volumes may not accurately predict sudden traffic spikes, leading to potential performance issues during peak hours.

QUESTION 61

Answer - [D] Deploy Amazon CloudFront with Lambda@Edge to cache and deliver streaming content at edge locations.

Option A - Amazon CloudFront with AWS WAF provides security but may not offer the same content delivery and caching capabilities as CloudFront with Lambda@Edge for media streaming.

Option B - Latency-based routing with Route 53 directs users to the nearest edge location but may not optimize content delivery and reduce latency as effectively as CloudFront with Lambda@Edge.

Option C - Amazon S3 Transfer Acceleration optimizes data transfers but may not provide the same low-latency access as CloudFront with Lambda@Edge for streaming content delivery.

Option D - Correct. Amazon CloudFront with Lambda@Edge allows for caching and delivering streaming content at edge locations, ensuring high availability, low latency, and cost optimization for global users.

Option E - AWS Direct Connect with AWS Transit Gateway provides private connectivity but may not optimize content delivery and reduce latency for streaming content as effectively as CloudFront with Lambda@Edge.

QUESTION 62

Answer - [C] Leverage AWS Budgets to set cost and usage budgets for development and testing environments and receive alerts when thresholds are exceeded.

Option A - AWS Auto Scaling adjusts capacity but may not directly address the need for cost optimization in development and testing environments.

Option B - AWS Service Catalog manages resources but may not provide direct cost control features for development and testing environments.

Option C - Correct. AWS Budgets allows for setting cost and usage budgets, enabling effective cost control and alerting when thresholds are exceeded in development and testing environments.

Option D - AWS Lambda can start and stop resources but may require additional configuration and monitoring compared to AWS Budgets for cost control.

Option E - AWS Config monitors configuration but may not provide the same level of cost control and budgeting features as AWS Budgets for development and testing environments.

QUESTION 63

Answer - [D] Leverage Amazon S3 cross-region replication to automatically replicate data between regions and ensure data durability.

Option A - Amazon S3 Transfer Acceleration improves transfer speeds but may not directly reduce data transfer costs between regions.

Option B - AWS Direct Connect with AWS Transit Gateway can establish private connectivity between regions but may not directly minimize data transfer costs.

Option C - Amazon CloudFront with AWS Global Accelerator optimizes content delivery but may not directly address data transfer costs between regions.

Option D - Correct. Leveraging Amazon S3 cross-region replication allows for automatic replication of data between regions, ensuring data durability while minimizing data transfer costs.

Option E - Amazon Route 53 latency-based routing optimizes traffic routing but may not directly reduce data transfer costs between regions.

QUESTION 64

Answer - [A] Utilize Amazon EMR with Amazon S3 for data storage and Apache Spark for distributed data processing.

Option A - Correct. Utilizing Amazon EMR with Amazon S3 and Apache Spark provides a cost-efficient solution for distributed data processing at scale.

Option B - While AWS Glue and Amazon Athena offer serverless data processing and querying capabilities, they may not be as suitable for large-scale analytics workloads compared to Amazon EMR.

Option C - Amazon Redshift Spectrum with Amazon S3 allows for analyzing data directly from S3 storage, but it may not provide the same level of flexibility and cost efficiency as Amazon EMR for varying workloads.

Option D - Amazon Kinesis Data Analytics is suitable for real-time data processing but may not be the most cost-efficient solution for large-scale batch processing of datasets.

Option E - While Amazon QuickSight with Amazon Aurora offers visualization capabilities, it may not directly address the data processing requirements of the application.

QUESTION 65

Answer - [A] Utilize AWS Organizations to implement consolidated billing and cost allocation tags for detailed cost tracking.

Option A - Correct. Utilizing AWS Organizations enables consolidated billing and cost allocation tags, allowing for granular cost control and accountability across departments and projects.

Option B - AWS Budgets helps monitor cost limits but may not provide the same level of granularity and accountability as AWS Organizations.

Option C - AWS Cost and Usage Report with Amazon Athena allows for custom analysis but may not offer the same level of centralized cost control as AWS Organizations.

Option D - AWS Resource Access Manager (RAM) shares resources but may not directly address cost control and accountability requirements.

Option E - AWS Service Catalog standardizes provisioning but may not provide the same level of cost tracking and accountability as AWS Organizations.

PRACTICE TEST 9 - QUESTIONS ONLY

QUESTION 1

An e-commerce platform is exploring federated access to allow their external partners to access specific AWS resources securely. They aim to leverage AWS IAM Identity Center for this purpose. What security implication should they consider to maintain a secure environment?

A) Federated access eliminates the need for IAM policies.
B) External partners' access should be restricted to only the resources necessary for their tasks.
C) IAM roles should be shared among partners to simplify access management.
D) Security audits are unnecessary for environments accessed via federated access.
E) Federated access inherently secures all AWS resources against external threats.

QUESTION 2

A fintech startup is deploying a new application on AWS that requires strict compliance with financial data protection regulations. The application architecture includes microservices deployed on AWS Lambda, user data stored in Amazon DynamoDB, and transaction logs stored in Amazon S3. Which of the following strategies should be employed to secure application configuration and credentials effectively?

A) Store application credentials in environment variables of the AWS Lambda function.
B) Utilize AWS Secrets Manager to manage and rotate credentials automatically.
C) Keep credentials in a plaintext file within the Amazon S3 bucket with restricted access.
D) Use Amazon DynamoDB to store credentials and encrypt the table with AWS KMS.
E) Embed credentials directly into the application code for Lambda functions.

QUESTION 3

For a media company streaming large volumes of video content, ensuring data security and encryption across various AWS services is critical. They need a solution that secures data at rest within their storage solutions and protects video streams in transit to users' devices. Which AWS services and configurations should be utilized to achieve this level of security?

A) Encrypt video content using Amazon S3 and Amazon CloudFront with AWS KMS, ensuring TLS for data in transit.
B) Use AWS Lambda for video processing with environment variables encryption, and AWS IAM for access control.
C) Store videos in Amazon Glacier with vault lock policy for encryption at rest, and utilize AWS Direct Connect for secure data transfer.
D) Configure AWS Elastic Beanstalk for application deployment with Amazon RDS encryption, and Amazon VPC for network security.
E) Deploy Amazon ECS for container management with encrypted task definitions, and Amazon API Gateway for secure API endpoints.

QUESTION 4

Your organization is designing a highly resilient architecture for its data storage solution on AWS. The solution must ensure data integrity, availability, and durability, even in the face of catastrophic failures. Which architecture should you recommend?

A) Utilize Amazon S3 with versioning enabled to store critical data. Implement Amazon S3 cross-region replication to replicate data to a standby bucket in a different region for disaster recovery.

B) Deploy Amazon EBS volumes with RAID configuration for data redundancy within an Availability Zone (AZ). Implement AWS Backup to automate the backup of EBS snapshots to Amazon S3 for long-term retention.

C) Set up Amazon RDS with Multi-AZ deployment for database redundancy and failover within a region. Implement Amazon RDS cross-region replication to replicate data to a standby instance in a different region for disaster recovery.

D) Utilize Amazon EFS with lifecycle policies to automatically move data between storage classes based on access patterns. Implement Amazon Data Lifecycle Manager to automate the creation and retention of EFS backups in Amazon S3.

E) Deploy Amazon Aurora with Aurora Global Database for multi-region replication and automatic failover. Implement Amazon Aurora Backtrack to rewind the database to a previous state in case of errors or failures.

QUESTION 5

A social media company is migrating its notification system to AWS and needs a solution that ensures notifications are delivered in real-time while also providing the ability to process multiple notifications simultaneously for different user preferences. Which option should the company choose to implement this requirement?

A) Use Amazon SQS FIFO queue with exactly-once processing enabled.
B) Use Amazon SQS FIFO queue with message deduplication enabled.
C) Use Amazon SQS FIFO queue with a batch mode of 5 messages per operation.
D) Use Amazon SQS standard queue to process the messages.
E) Use Amazon SQS FIFO queue with default settings to process the messages.

QUESTION 6

Your company is designing a highly available and scalable web application on AWS that requires secure access control for its resources. The architecture includes Amazon EC2 instances, Amazon RDS for MySQL, and Amazon S3 for storage. As the solutions architect, you need to implement a comprehensive IAM strategy to ensure secure access to these resources. Which approach should you take to achieve this goal?

A) Create IAM users with programmatic access for each team member and provide them with access keys to manage resources. Implement IAM roles for EC2 instances to access the RDS database securely.

B) Utilize IAM roles for EC2 instances with least privilege permissions to access other AWS services, and configure IAM policies to control access to RDS instances and S3 buckets.

C) Implement IAM groups for different teams within the organization, and assign permissions to groups based on their roles. Use IAM policies to control access to individual EC2 instances, RDS databases, and S3 buckets.

D) Set up IAM roles for each AWS resource in the architecture, and configure cross-account access between resources to ensure secure communication.

E) Deploy IAM policies at the organizational unit level to manage access control for all AWS resources, and use IAM roles for temporary access to resources by EC2 instances.

QUESTION 7

Your company is planning to deploy a serverless application on AWS for processing real-time data streams. Security is a top priority, and you need to ensure that the application architecture incorporates robust security measures. Which of the following options is a recommended practice for implementing security in a serverless and event-driven design?

A) Encrypting data at rest using AWS KMS
B) Configuring AWS IAM roles with least privilege access
C) Implementing AWS CloudTrail for auditing API calls
D) Utilizing AWS Network Firewall to filter traffic to serverless functions
E) Enabling AWS Shield Advanced for DDoS protection

QUESTION 8

Your company is developing a serverless application that processes sensitive financial data. Compliance regulations mandate strict access control and audit logging for all data transactions. Which of the following options provides the most suitable solution for meeting these compliance requirements?

A) Configuring AWS CloudTrail for logging all API calls and actions taken on AWS resources
B) Utilizing AWS IAM roles with fine-grained permissions for accessing financial data
C) Implementing AWS Key Management Service (KMS) for encrypting sensitive data at rest
D) Enabling AWS Config for tracking changes to AWS resource configurations and compliance monitoring
E) Deploying AWS Security Hub for centralized security posture management and compliance monitoring

QUESTION 9

Your organization is designing a microservices architecture for a media streaming platform. Security is a top concern, and you need to ensure secure communication between microservices. Additionally, compliance regulations mandate encryption for data in transit. Which option best fulfills these requirements?

A) Implementing mutual TLS authentication between microservices in Amazon ECS, ensuring secure communication and compliance with encryption standards

B) Utilizing AWS App Mesh to manage traffic between microservices, ensuring encryption and compliance with industry regulations

C) Configuring AWS Lambda authorizers in Amazon API Gateway for authentication and authorization, ensuring secure communication and compliance with encryption standards

D) Enabling AWS PrivateLink for private communication between microservices, ensuring encryption and compliance with industry standards

E) Deploying AWS WAF in front of microservices to filter and inspect incoming traffic, ensuring secure communication and compliance with encryption standards

QUESTION 10

A healthcare company needs to regularly upload large genomic datasets to Amazon S3. These datasets are used for bioinformatic analysis and are crucial for developing personalized medicine. The company requires a solution that minimizes upload time and costs while ensuring the data is securely transferred. What combination of AWS services and features should be used to meet these requirements?

A) Use AWS Snowmobile for large dataset transfers and Amazon S3 server-side encryption (SSE) for data security.
B) Implement multipart uploads for efficient data transfer and AWS KMS for encryption during upload.
C) Utilize Amazon S3 Transfer Acceleration for fast uploads and Amazon Macie for data security and privacy.
D) Leverage AWS Direct Connect for consistent network performance and Amazon S3 Object Lock for immutability.
E) Opt for Amazon DataSync for automated data transfers and AWS Shield for protection against DDoS attacks.

QUESTION 11

An e-commerce company requires a backup solution for their dynamic website hosted on AWS. The solution must ensure data integrity and be capable of quickly restoring the website in case of a disaster. The backup strategy should include daily backups, retention for 30 days, and the ability to restore any version of the website within this period.

A) Utilize AWS Backup with a daily backup schedule, set retention for 30 days, and enable versioning on Amazon S3 buckets used for website assets.

B) Implement Amazon EBS snapshots for the EC2 instances running the website, with an Amazon Data Lifecycle Manager policy for 30-day retention.

C) Configure Amazon RDS to take automated daily snapshots, with a custom Lambda function to manage the retention period and restoration process.

D) Deploy AWS Storage Gateway in a VTL configuration for daily backups, with lifecycle policies to transition backups to S3 Glacier for cost-effective storage.

E) Set up Amazon S3 with lifecycle rules to automatically archive website data to S3 Glacier after 30 days and use S3 Versioning for restoring any version within the retention period.

QUESTION 12

For a SaaS provider expanding their services globally, secure and efficient management of deployment pipelines across multiple AWS regions is critical. They require a deployment strategy that supports blue/green deployments to minimize downtime during updates, automatic rollback capabilities in case of deployment failures, and strict access controls to deployment configurations to prevent unauthorized changes.

A) Integrate AWS CodePipeline and AWS CodeDeploy for blue/green deployments, utilize AWS CloudFormation for infrastructure management across regions, and enforce IAM policies for access control.

B) Configure AWS Elastic Beanstalk for multi-region application deployments, use Elastic Beanstalk versioning for rollback, and Amazon Macie for monitoring and securing deployment configurations.

C) Deploy with Amazon ECS and AWS Fargate for container management, leverage Amazon ECR for storing Docker images, and use AWS Config rules for monitoring configuration changes.

D) Utilize AWS Lambda for deploying serverless functions, Amazon S3 for storing deployment artifacts with versioning enabled, and AWS Shield for additional security against DDoS attacks during deployment.

E) Implement multi-region AWS Step Functions for orchestrating deployment workflows, Amazon DynamoDB global tables for state management, and AWS KMS for encrypting deployment configurations.

QUESTION 13

A healthcare application hosted on AWS needs to comply with HIPAA regulations, requiring strict audit trails for all data access and modifications, along with the capability to automatically respond to potential PHI (Protected Health Information) exposure incidents. They are looking for solutions to enhance their incident response capabilities with minimal manual intervention.

A) Configure AWS CloudTrail and Amazon CloudWatch to monitor and alert on PHI access, use AWS Lambda for automated response to incidents, and AWS WAF for application layer protection.

B) Leverage Amazon GuardDuty for detecting potential data exposure incidents, AWS Security Hub for centralized security monitoring, and AWS Step Functions for automated incident response actions.

C) Utilize AWS Config for tracking configuration changes, Amazon Inspector for security assessments, and AWS IAM Access Analyzer for analyzing permission settings.

D) Implement Amazon Macie for identifying and protecting sensitive data, AWS CloudTrail for logging access to PHI, and AWS Lambda for executing automatic remediation workflows.

E) Deploy AWS Shield Advanced for DDoS protection, Amazon RDS with encryption for data security, and Amazon S3 with event notifications for monitoring data modifications.

QUESTION 14

An e-commerce platform experiences periodic spikes in traffic during sales events, resulting in high costs for AWS services. The company wants to identify the underlying reasons for these high costs and implement cost-saving measures. As an AWS Solutions Architect, which approach would you recommend to analyze and address the high costs effectively? Select TWO.

A) Utilize AWS Cost Explorer to analyze usage patterns and identify areas for cost optimization, such as unused resources or overprovisioned instances.

B) Implement AWS Budgets to set custom cost and usage budgets and receive alerts when expenditures exceed predefined thresholds.

C) Set up AWS Trusted Advisor to provide real-time guidance on cost optimization opportunities and best practices for AWS services.

D) Leverage AWS Cost and Usage Reports to analyze detailed cost and usage data, enabling granular cost tracking and optimization.

E) Utilize AWS Savings Plans to reduce costs by committing to a consistent amount of usage over a one- or three-year period, providing significant discounts compared to pay-as-you-go pricing.

QUESTION 15

An e-learning platform is experiencing difficulties in managing maintenance tasks on specific Amazon EC2 instances within an Auto Scaling group. Each time maintenance patches are applied, the instances briefly show as out of service, triggering Auto Scaling to provision replacements. What actions would you recommend as a solutions architect to mitigate this issue efficiently?

A) Suspend the Terminate process type for the Auto Scaling group and apply the maintenance patch to the instance. Once the instance is ready, manually set the instance's health status back to healthy and activate the Terminate process type again.

B) Suspend the ReplaceUnhealthy process type for the Auto Scaling group and apply the maintenance patch to the instance. Once the instance is ready, manually set the instance's health status back to healthy and activate the ReplaceUnhealthy process type again.

C) Stop the instance, apply the maintenance patch, and then start the instance.

D) Temporarily suspend the AddToLoadBalancer process type for the Auto Scaling group and apply the maintenance patch to the instance. Once the instance is ready, manually set the instance's health status back to healthy and activate the AddToLoadBalancer process type again.

E) Take a snapshot of the instance, create a new Amazon Machine Image (AMI), and then launch a new instance using this AMI. Apply the maintenance patch to this new instance and then add it back to the Auto Scaling Group by using the manual scaling policy. Terminate the earlier instance that had the maintenance issue.

QUESTION 16

A healthcare organization with multiple AWS accounts seeks to streamline secure access to its SaaS offerings hosted in AWS. They need a solution to simplify network administration, reduce exposure to the public internet, and ensure private connectivity from their clients' premises to the SaaS applications, irrespective of the AWS account they reside in.

A) Utilize AWS PrivateLink to expose services across accounts with VPC Endpoint Services.
B) Implement inter-region VPC peering across accounts and encrypt traffic with AWS KMS.
C) Set up AWS Transit Gateway to interconnect VPCs and use IAM policies for cross-account access.
D) Deploy AWS Direct Connect and AWS Transit Gateway for account-to-account private connectivity.
E) Establish AWS VPN CloudHub to manage inter-account connectivity and apply AWS Shield for additional security.

QUESTION 17

A healthcare provider is migrating patient record management systems to AWS to comply with health data protection standards and improve system availability. The migration strategy needs to ensure data is encrypted both in transit and at rest, and that the architecture supports disaster recovery.

A) Implement AWS DMS with SSL for data migration, Amazon RDS with encryption at rest for database services, and Amazon Route 53 for DNS failover.

B) Configure AWS Snowball with client-side encryption for data transfer, AWS Elastic Beanstalk for application deployment, and AWS Backup for disaster recovery.

C) Use AWS DataSync for secure data transfer, Amazon EFS for encrypted file storage, and AWS CloudFormation for deploying disaster recovery stacks.

D) Leverage AWS Application Discovery Service for migration planning, Amazon S3 with server-side encryption for data storage, and Amazon CloudWatch alarms for monitoring.

E) Apply Amazon S3 Transfer Acceleration for fast data migration, Amazon DynamoDB with encryption at rest for storage, and Amazon SNS for real-time alerts.

QUESTION 18

An e-commerce company is building a microservices architecture on AWS and needs to securely manage configurations across multiple services. The company wants to ensure that each microservice can securely access its configuration settings while adhering to least privilege principles. Which of the following strategies would best meet the company's requirements?

A) Use AWS Secrets Manager to store configuration settings for each microservice. Implement IAM roles with granular permissions to allow only authorized microservices to retrieve their respective secrets.

B) Store configuration settings in plaintext files within an Amazon S3 bucket. Use IAM roles attached to each microservice to grant access to the corresponding S3 objects.

C) Implement AWS AppConfig with configuration profiles for each microservice. Use AWS Lambda to fetch configuration updates from AppConfig and securely deliver them to microservices.

D) Utilize AWS Systems Manager Parameter Store to store configurations centrally. Create custom IAM policies to grant microservices access to their respective parameter keys.

E) Maintain configuration settings within environment variables directly in the microservice codebase. Implement AWS IAM policies to control access to the environment variables.

QUESTION 19

A multinational e-commerce company is developing a serverless application on AWS Lambda to process customer orders. They need to securely manage API keys and other sensitive information while ensuring compliance with industry regulations. Which of the following strategies would best meet the company's requirements?

A) Store API keys directly in environment variables within Lambda functions. Implement strict IAM policies to control access to Lambda functions.

B) Utilize AWS Secrets Manager to securely store API keys and sensitive information. Integrate AWS Lambda with Secrets Manager for automated retrieval of secrets at runtime.

C) Maintain a plaintext configuration file within the application codebase stored in an encrypted Amazon S3 bucket. Use IAM roles to restrict access to the S3 bucket.

D) Implement AWS Systems Manager Parameter Store to centrally manage API keys and configurations. Develop custom Lambda functions to retrieve configuration settings from Parameter Store.

E) Store sensitive information in plaintext files within an Amazon EFS file system. Implement IAM policies to control access to the EFS file system.

QUESTION 20

A financial institution detected an unexpected surge in unauthorized AWS API queries during off-hours, with no visible impact on system performance. The management seeks an automated solution to promptly alert relevant teams during such occurrences. Which solution would be most suitable in this scenario?

A) Implement AWS Config Rules to monitor API activity and define rules to detect unauthorized API calls. Configure AWS Config to trigger an AWS Lambda function upon rule evaluation to notify relevant stakeholders.

B) Create an Amazon CloudWatch metric filter to process AWS CloudTrail logs containing API call details. Establish an alarm based on this metric's rate to send an Amazon SNS notification to the required team.

C) Leverage AWS Trusted Advisor to publish metrics about check results to Amazon CloudWatch. Set up an alarm to track status changes for checks in the Service Limits category for the APIs, triggering notifications when service quotas are exceeded.

D) Use Amazon Athena SQL queries against AWS CloudTrail log files stored in Amazon S3 buckets. Generate reports using Amazon QuickSight for managerial dashboards.

E) Configure AWS CloudTrail to stream event data to Amazon Kinesis. Utilize Amazon Kinesis stream-level metrics in Amazon CloudWatch to trigger an AWS Lambda function that will initiate an error workflow.

QUESTION 21

A company wants to design a resilient event-driven architecture for processing orders from an e-commerce website. They want to ensure that orders are processed reliably even during peak traffic and system failures. What approach should they take?

A) Utilize Amazon Kinesis Data Firehose to buffer incoming orders and process them with AWS Lambda.
B) Implement Amazon SQS to queue orders and trigger Lambda functions for processing.
C) Use Amazon SNS to fan out orders to multiple processing systems for redundancy.
D) Employ AWS Step Functions to manage the order processing workflow with built-in error handling.
E) Utilize AWS Glue for ETL processing of order data before sending it to downstream systems.

QUESTION 22

Your organization is deploying a data analytics platform that requires real-time processing of streaming data. The platform needs to handle high throughput and ensure fault tolerance. Which combination of AWS services should you use to build this data analytics platform?

A) Amazon Kinesis for real-time data streaming with enhanced fan-out

B) Amazon EMR for big data processing with fault tolerance

C) AWS Lambda for serverless compute with event-driven architecture

D) Amazon Redshift for data warehousing with automatic backups

E) AWS Glue for ETL (Extract, Transform, Load) with data catalog

QUESTION 23

A global manufacturing company is revamping its disaster recovery (DR) strategy for its ERP system hosted on AWS. The company aims to achieve high availability and fault tolerance while optimizing costs. Which AWS service should the company consider for implementing a data archiving and recovery solution as part of its DR strategy?

A) Utilize Amazon S3 Intelligent-Tiering with lifecycle policies for automatically moving data between storage classes based on access patterns, ensuring cost efficiency and data durability

B) Implement Amazon Glacier with Vault Lock for WORM (Write Once, Read Many) storage, ensuring data immutability and compliance with regulatory requirements

C) Deploy AWS Backup with AWS Organizations integration for centralized management of backup policies and data recovery, ensuring regulatory compliance and minimal downtime

D) Utilize Amazon FSx for Lustre with automatic snapshots and cross-region replication for high-performance file system backup and recovery, ensuring minimal data loss and fast recovery times

E) Implement Amazon S3 One Zone-IA with versioning and cross-region replication for cost-effective data storage and recovery, ensuring data availability and durability during DR scenarios

QUESTION 24

A gaming company is developing a real-time multiplayer game that requires low-latency communication between players located in different regions. The company needs a solution that can facilitate secure and efficient communication while minimizing latency. Which combination of AWS services should the company consider to achieve these objectives?

A) Utilize Amazon DynamoDB with Amazon ElastiCache for in-memory caching of game state and real-time player updates.

B) Implement Amazon S3 with Amazon CloudFront for global distribution of game assets and low-latency content delivery.

C) Deploy Amazon EC2 instances with Amazon VPC peering for private network communication between game servers.

D) Utilize Amazon API Gateway with AWS Lambda for serverless compute and scalable API endpoints for player interactions.

E) Implement Amazon Kinesis with AWS Direct Connect for real-time data streaming and dedicated network connectivity between game servers.

QUESTION 25

A multinational entertainment company wants to stream live concerts to audiences in different countries. However, due to licensing agreements, they need to restrict access to viewers only in certain countries. How can they effectively enforce this restriction?

A) Use Amazon Route 53 based geolocation routing policy to restrict access to viewers located in the authorized countries

B) Implement Amazon Route 53 based weighted routing policy to balance traffic across regions based on predetermined weights

C) Utilize Amazon Route 53 based latency-based routing policy to direct viewers to the closest streaming server for optimal performance

D) Employ Amazon Route 53 based failover routing policy to reroute traffic to backup servers in case of server failures

E) Apply Amazon Route 53 based geoproximity routing policy to direct traffic based on the proximity of viewers to streaming servers

QUESTION 26

A retail company is redesigning its e-commerce platform on AWS to enhance performance and resilience. The company aims to adopt immutable infrastructure to streamline deployment processes and reduce operational overhead. Which approach should the solutions architect recommend for implementing immutable infrastructure on AWS?

A) Utilize AWS AppConfig to manage application configurations dynamically and roll out changes gradually to minimize disruption during deployments.

B) Implement AWS CloudFormation to define infrastructure as code and automate the deployment of AWS resources in a consistent and repeatable manner, promoting immutable infrastructure.

C) Use AWS OpsWorks to automate infrastructure provisioning and configuration management using Chef recipes, ensuring consistency across environments.

D) Leverage Amazon ECS Anywhere to run containerized applications on-premises and in the cloud, ensuring consistency and portability across environments.

E) Configure AWS Lambda to automatically scale and execute code in response to events, reducing the need for manual intervention in managing infrastructure.

QUESTION 27

A healthcare provider is building a system to enable communication between microservices handling patient data. The system must ensure fault tolerance and resiliency. Which option facilitates resilient microservices communication with Amazon API Gateway?

A) Configure API Gateway VPC Link integration to establish private connectivity between microservices running in Amazon VPCs

B) Implement AWS PrivateLink to expose microservices privately and securely and route traffic through API Gateway

C) Use API Gateway WebSocket APIs to enable real-time, bidirectional communication between microservices while leveraging built-in scaling and fault tolerance

D) Deploy API Gateway regional endpoints in multiple AWS regions to achieve high availability and fault tolerance for microservices communication

E) Utilize API Gateway HTTP APIs with mutual TLS (mTLS) authentication to encrypt communication between microservices and ensure data integrity

QUESTION 28

A company is designing a serverless architecture for its e-commerce platform to handle fluctuations in traffic during sales events. They need a solution for managing state across their serverless functions. Which option provides the best approach for managing state in a serverless architecture using AWS services?

A) Utilize Amazon DynamoDB to store session state and leverage AWS Lambda to access and update the data

B) Implement Amazon SQS to buffer requests and responses between serverless functions, ensuring state consistency

C) Configure AWS Step Functions to orchestrate serverless workflows and manage state transitions between steps

D) Use Amazon S3 to store stateful data and leverage AWS Lambda to process and update the data asynchronously

E) Implement AWS AppSync to enable real-time data synchronization between serverless functions and client applications

QUESTION 29

A software as a service (SaaS) provider wants to ensure compliance with data sovereignty regulations while maintaining high availability across multiple regions. Which AWS service or feature can help achieve this objective?

A) AWS Global Accelerator for improved global application performance
B) Amazon Route 53 with geo-routing for traffic distribution
C) AWS Outposts for hybrid cloud deployments in regulated regions
D) Amazon CloudFront with regional edge caches for content delivery
E) Amazon S3 Transfer Acceleration for faster data transfers across regions

QUESTION 30

A media streaming company plans to build a real-time chat feature within its application to enhance user engagement. They need a solution that supports bidirectional communication between clients and servers. Which configuration should they implement using Amazon API Gateway to achieve this objective?

A) Create RESTful APIs on Amazon API Gateway and use AWS Lambda functions for bidirectional communication

B) Utilize WebSocket APIs on Amazon API Gateway for bidirectional communication between clients and servers

C) Deploy HTTP APIs on Amazon API Gateway and integrate with Amazon SNS for bidirectional communication

D) Implement GraphQL APIs on Amazon API Gateway and use Amazon DynamoDB for bidirectional communication

E) Configure RESTful APIs on Amazon API Gateway and utilize Amazon SQS for bidirectional communication

QUESTION 31

As part of their move to AWS, a healthcare organization needs to ensure HIPAA compliance across all their cloud resources. They want to automate the process of identifying and protecting sensitive data, monitoring access patterns, and encrypting data at rest and in transit. Which set of AWS services should they leverage to automate these security and compliance requirements?

A) AWS Macie for identifying sensitive data, Amazon CloudWatch for monitoring access patterns, AWS Key Management Service (KMS) for encryption, and AWS IAM for managing access.

B) Amazon GuardDuty for threat detection, AWS WAF for web application firewall, Amazon Inspector for security assessments, and Amazon VPC for network isolation.

C) AWS Shield for DDoS protection, Amazon Cognito for user identity management, AWS Fargate for running containers, and AWS CloudTrail for governance and compliance.

D) AWS Config for resource compliance monitoring, AWS Lambda for executing custom compliance scripts, AWS Secrets Manager for managing secrets, and Amazon SNS for alert notifications.

E) Amazon RDS for database services, Amazon DynamoDB for NoSQL data storage, AWS Direct Connect for secure, dedicated network connections, and AWS Step Functions for serverless workflow orchestration.

QUESTION 32

A healthcare organization is planning a disaster recovery (DR) setup for its patient records database to ensure continuity of operations in case of a regional outage. The solution must meet stringent compliance requirements and ensure minimal downtime. Which approach should the organization take to achieve these objectives effectively?

A) Implement Amazon RDS with Multi-AZ deployment and utilize AWS Backup for automated backups and cross-Region replication of backups.

B) Utilize Amazon Aurora with global databases for multi-master replication and fast failover, coupled with Amazon S3 cross-Region replication for backups.

C) Deploy Amazon DynamoDB with global tables for multi-Region replication and use AWS Direct Connect for low-latency connectivity between Regions.
D) Migrate to Amazon Redshift for analytics and scalability and configure cross-Region snapshots for disaster recovery with Amazon S3 replication.

E) Implement Amazon DocumentDB with point-in-time recovery enabled and utilize AWS Snowball for cross-Region data transfer and offline backup.

QUESTION 33

Your company operates a global e-commerce platform that experiences high traffic volumes, especially during peak seasons. Availability and data integrity are crucial for customer satisfaction. What approach would best ensure high availability and data integrity for your platform while maintaining security on AWS?

A) Deploy the application in a single AWS region without redundancy.
B) Implement AWS CloudFront for content delivery and edge caching.
C) Store sensitive data in plaintext within Lambda environment variables.
D) Implement AWS Step Functions for orchestrating serverless workflows.
E) Encrypt data in transit using HTTPS for API communication.

QUESTION 34

Your company is designing a microservices architecture for a new cloud-native application. Each microservice must be independently scalable and resilient to ensure high availability. Cost optimization is also a key consideration. Which AWS service should you choose to deploy and manage the microservices architecture most effectively?

A) Amazon ECS with AWS Fargate
 B) Utilize AWS Lambda functions with Amazon API Gateway
 C) Deploy microservices as Docker containers on Amazon EC2 instances
 D) Implement microservices using AWS AppSync
 E) Utilize AWS Step Functions to orchestrate microservice workflows

QUESTION 35

An e-commerce platform is planning to develop a recommendation engine to personalize product suggestions for its customers. They need a solution that can analyze customer behavior in real-time and generate recommendations dynamically. Which setup should they configure using AWS serverless components to meet these requirements effectively?

A) Utilize AWS Lambda with Amazon S3 for processing customer behavior data and Amazon RDS for storing recommendation data

 B) Implement Amazon Kinesis Data Firehose with AWS Lambda for processing customer behavior data and Amazon ElastiCache for storing recommendation data

 C) Ingest customer behavior data into Amazon Kinesis Data Streams, which triggers an AWS Lambda function for processing and stores recommendation data in Amazon DynamoDB

D) Ingest customer behavior data into Amazon SQS, which triggers an AWS Lambda function for processing and stores recommendation data in Amazon Redshift

E) Use Amazon API Gateway to ingest customer behavior data, which is processed by an application running on an Amazon EC2 instance, and store recommendation data in Amazon Elasticsearch Service

QUESTION 36

Your financial services company is developing a new mobile banking application hosted on AWS Lambda. The application must adhere to strict regulatory requirements for data encryption, both at rest and in transit, to safeguard customer information. How would you design the encryption strategy for the mobile banking application to ensure compliance and data security? Select TWO.

A) Utilize AWS Lambda with AWS KMS integration for encrypting data at rest and use AWS CloudHSM for secure key storage.

B) Implement Amazon S3 server-side encryption with AWS KMS-managed keys for data at rest and configure Lambda to use HTTPS for encrypting data in transit.

C) Deploy Amazon RDS with encryption at rest enabled and utilize AWS Certificate Manager (ACM) for TLS certificate management in Lambda.

D) Utilize Amazon DynamoDB with client-side encryption enabled for data at rest and configure Lambda to use IAM roles for secure API access.

E) Implement Amazon Redshift with encryption at rest enabled and utilize AWS Secrets Manager for managing encryption keys securely.

QUESTION 37

For an online content management system that stores and serves a vast amount of digital assets, which AWS storage solution allows for cost-effective scalability while ensuring data is stored durably across multiple facilities?

A) Amazon RDS with Multi-AZ deployment for high durability and availability.
B) Amazon EFS for scalable file storage accessible from multiple instances.
C) Amazon S3 with Intelligent-Tiering to automatically move data to the most cost-effective access tier.
D) AWS Storage Gateway for on-premises access to virtually unlimited cloud storage.
E) Amazon DynamoDB with global tables for distributing digital assets across regions.

QUESTION 38

Your company is designing a globally distributed application that requires low-latency access to a database for read-heavy workloads. The database should provide high availability and durability across multiple AWS regions. Which combination of AWS services would you recommend to meet these requirements for the database layer of the application?

A) Implement Amazon RDS with Multi-Region replication to replicate the database across multiple AWS regions for high availability and durability.

B) Utilize Amazon DynamoDB global tables to replicate data across multiple AWS regions for low-latency access and high availability.

C) Deploy Amazon ElastiCache for Redis in multiple regions to cache frequently accessed data and reduce database load.

D) Configure Amazon Aurora Multi-Master for simultaneous write operations across multiple database instances in different AWS regions.

E) Utilize Amazon Neptune for a globally distributed graph database with low-latency access and high availability.

QUESTION 39

A media streaming company is planning to build a data ingestion pipeline to process streaming logs from its video platform. The solution must handle large volumes of data, ensure fault tolerance, and support real-time analytics. What architecture should the company implement?

A) Utilize Amazon Kinesis Video Streams for ingesting streaming logs, and leverage Amazon Redshift for batch processing of analytics data.

B) Deploy Amazon Elasticsearch Service for indexing streaming logs, and use Amazon QuickSight for real-time analytics dashboards.

C) Implement Amazon Kinesis Data Firehose for ingesting streaming logs, and use Amazon Kinesis Data Analytics for real-time data processing.

D) Configure Amazon CloudFront for content delivery, and use Amazon S3 for storing streaming logs.

E) Utilize AWS Direct Connect for network connectivity, and deploy Amazon S3 Glacier for long-term storage of streaming logs.

QUESTION 40

An e-commerce company needs to securely store customer payment information in Amazon S3 while ensuring compliance with industry regulations. The company requires encryption of the data at rest and wants to use encryption keys that are managed by AWS but offers additional control and auditing capabilities. Which option would be the most suitable choice for this scenario?

A) Implement client-side encryption with customer-provided keys (SSE-C) and upload the encrypted data to Amazon S3

B) Use server-side encryption with AWS Key Management Service (SSE-KMS) keys to encrypt the data on Amazon S3

C) Utilize server-side encryption with Amazon S3 managed keys (SSE-S3) to encrypt the data on Amazon S3

D) Use server-side encryption with customer-provided keys (SSE-C) to encrypt the data on Amazon S3

E) Enable AWS CloudTrail to monitor S3 bucket activities for auditing purposes

QUESTION 41

A logistics company is developing a serverless system to optimize their supply chain by automatically rerouting shipments in response to real-time changes in shipping conditions and customer demands. The system needs to quickly process events from various sources, make decisions based on complex business rules, and communicate changes to relevant stakeholders. Which AWS architecture would best support this requirement?

A) AWS Lambda for event processing, Amazon SQS for message queuing, AWS Step Functions for managing the decision-making workflow.

B) Amazon EC2 Auto Scaling for compute resources, Amazon S3 for event storage, Amazon CloudWatch for monitoring shipment conditions.

C) Amazon DynamoDB for storing shipment data, Amazon SNS for broadcasting changes, Amazon API Gateway for interfacing with external systems.

D) AWS Fargate for running containerized applications, AWS IAM for managing permissions, Amazon Kinesis for processing shipment event streams.

E) Amazon RDS for relational data storage, AWS Elastic Beanstalk for application deployment, AWS CloudTrail for logging system activities.

QUESTION 42

Your organization is planning to implement AWS Outposts to extend its existing infrastructure to the AWS Cloud. However, you need to ensure efficient management of compute resources on AWS Outposts while optimizing costs. Which approach should you recommend to achieve this?

A) Utilize AWS Outposts with Amazon EC2 Auto Scaling to automatically adjust compute capacity based on demand, ensuring efficient resource management.

B) Implement AWS Outposts with Amazon EC2 Reserved Instances to reserve capacity in advance and benefit from discounted pricing, optimizing costs.

C) Deploy AWS Outposts with AWS Batch to efficiently run batch computing workloads and optimize resource utilization.

D) Configure AWS Outposts with AWS Elastic Beanstalk to automatically deploy and manage applications, reducing operational overhead and optimizing costs.

E) Utilize AWS Outposts with Amazon EC2 Spot Instances to take advantage of spare capacity at reduced costs, optimizing resource utilization and costs.

QUESTION 43

An enterprise plans to deploy a global application that requires strict compliance with data sovereignty laws, ensuring data is stored and processed only in specific regions. The application will serve dynamic content based on user interaction and location, requiring integration with third-party services for payment processing and customer support. Which AWS services and architectural features should be emphasized to comply with these legal requirements while maintaining a responsive and scalable user experience?

A) Focus on Amazon CloudFront for content delivery, utilize AWS Lambda@Edge for location-based content customization, Amazon S3 and DynamoDB with region-specific deployments for data storage, and AWS WAF for security.

B) Implement Amazon API Gateway for third-party integrations, use Amazon EC2 with Auto Scaling and Amazon RDS in a multi-region setup for compliance, AWS Shield for DDoS protection, and Amazon Route 53 for DNS routing.

C) Use AWS Global Accelerator to route user traffic to the nearest application endpoint, Amazon Elastic Beanstalk for application deployment, Amazon S3 for storing static content, and multi-region Amazon Aurora for database services.

D) Leverage AWS Direct Connect for dedicated network connections, Amazon ECS for container management across regions, Amazon EBS for block storage, and Amazon Cognito for secure user authentication and data processing compliance.

E) Employ Amazon CloudFront with AWS WAF for global content delivery and security, AWS Step Functions for orchestrating interaction flows, Amazon S3 and Amazon RDS with data residency options for storage, and Amazon API Gateway for backend integration.

QUESTION 44

Your company is designing a solution to manage data pipelines for machine learning workflows using Amazon SageMaker. The solution must ensure scalability, reliability, and cost optimization. Which architecture would be most suitable for this requirement?

A) Utilize Amazon SageMaker for model training, integrating Amazon S3 for data storage and Amazon CloudWatch for monitoring, with AWS Glue for data preprocessing.

B) Implement Amazon SageMaker for distributed training and inference, leveraging Amazon EFS for shared model storage and Amazon CloudWatch for monitoring, with AWS Glue for data preprocessing.

C) Deploy Amazon SageMaker for training and inference with Amazon Aurora for model storage and Amazon CloudWatch for performance monitoring, with AWS Glue for data preprocessing.

D) Utilize Amazon SageMaker for training with Amazon RDS for model metadata storage and Amazon CloudWatch for monitoring and optimization, with AWS Glue for data preprocessing.

E) Implement Amazon SageMaker for distributed training with Amazon S3 for data storage and Amazon CloudWatch for monitoring and optimization, with AWS Glue for data preprocessing.

QUESTION 45

A startup is developing a new application and needs to keep costs low during the initial phase. However, it expects rapid growth in the coming months. Which pricing option for Amazon EC2 instances would be the most appropriate choice for this scenario?

A) Utilize reserved instances (RI) for the entire duration of operation
B) Implement on-demand instances for the entire duration of operation
C) Use a combination of reserved instances (RI) and spot instances
D) Employ spot instances for the entire duration of operation
E) Implement a mix of reserved instances (RI) and on-demand instances

QUESTION 46

You are designing an IoT solution for a smart city project that requires collecting sensor data from various devices deployed across the city, including traffic lights, environmental sensors, and surveillance cameras. The solution must be highly scalable, resilient, and capable of processing data in real-time to support applications such as traffic management and environmental monitoring. Which architecture would best meet these requirements?

A) Utilize AWS IoT Core for data ingestion, process data using AWS Lambda, store processed data in Amazon RDS, and leverage Amazon CloudFront for content delivery.

B) Implement an event-driven architecture using Amazon EventBridge for data ingestion, process data using AWS Glue, store processed data in Amazon DynamoDB, and utilize Amazon CloudFront for content delivery.

C) Deploy containers on Amazon ECS for data ingestion, process data using Amazon EMR, store processed data in Amazon S3, and leverage Amazon CloudFront for content delivery.

D) Utilize Amazon Kinesis Data Streams for ingesting real-time data, process data using AWS Lambda, store processed data in Amazon DynamoDB, and use Amazon CloudFront for content delivery.

E) Implement a serverless architecture using Amazon S3 for data ingestion, process data using AWS Glue, store processed data in Amazon Redshift, and utilize Amazon CloudFront for content delivery.

QUESTION 47

You are designing an architecture for an e-commerce platform that experiences periodic spikes in traffic, especially during sales events. The platform must remain responsive and available, even during peak loads, while ensuring efficient cost management. Which approach would best meet these requirements?

A) Utilize Amazon EC2 instances with reserved capacity, Amazon RDS for database storage, and Amazon CloudFront for content delivery.

B) Implement a serverless architecture with AWS Lambda for compute, Amazon DynamoDB for database needs, and Amazon S3 for static content storage.

C) Deploy the application on AWS Outposts for data residency requirements, leverage Amazon ElastiCache for caching frequently accessed data, and use AWS Direct Connect for secure connectivity.

D) Utilize Amazon ECS for container orchestration, Amazon Aurora Serverless for database scalability, and Amazon CloudWatch for monitoring and autoscaling.

E) Implement edge computing using AWS Wavelength for deploying applications close to users, leverage Amazon API Gateway for RESTful APIs, and use Amazon Redshift for analytics.

QUESTION 48

A media streaming company operates a platform that experiences varying levels of user activity throughout the day, with peak usage during evenings and weekends. The company needs to optimize costs while ensuring seamless streaming experiences for users. Which pricing option for Amazon EC2 instances would be the most suitable choice for this scenario?

A) Utilize reserved instances (RI) for the entire duration of operation

B) Implement on-demand instances for the entire duration of operation

C) Utilize spot instances for the entire duration of operation

D) Employ a combination of reserved instances (RI) and spot instances

E) Implement a mix of reserved instances (RI) and on-demand instances

QUESTION 49

You are tasked with designing a performance testing strategy for a cloud-based e-commerce application. The application experiences seasonal traffic spikes, especially during holiday sales events. The testing approach must ensure that the application can handle the increased load without compromising performance. What would be the most suitable strategy for performance testing in this scenario?

A) Implement AWS CloudFormation to automate the provisioning of infrastructure resources, and use AWS CodePipeline to deploy application changes. Leverage AWS X-Ray for distributed tracing and performance analysis, and simulate load using AWS Load Testing Service.

B) Utilize AWS CloudWatch to monitor application metrics, and AWS CloudTrail for logging and auditing API activity. Deploy AWS Inspector for automated security assessments, and conduct load testing using Apache JMeter on Amazon EC2 instances.

C) Leverage AWS Lambda for serverless computing to simulate user interactions, and use Amazon CloudFront for content delivery optimization. Implement AWS CodeDeploy for automated application deployments, and analyze performance using AWS X-Ray.

D) Implement AWS Elastic Beanstalk for managed application hosting, and use AWS CodeCommit for version control. Utilize Amazon Route 53 for DNS routing, and conduct performance testing using Apache JMeter on Amazon EC2 instances.

E) Deploy Amazon ECS for containerized workload management, and use AWS Fargate for serverless compute. Leverage Amazon CloudWatch Logs for monitoring, and conduct performance testing using Gatling on Amazon EC2 instances.

QUESTION 50

Your organization is migrating its legacy data warehouse to AWS to leverage cloud-based analytics capabilities. The data warehouse contains sensitive customer information and must comply with strict regulatory requirements for data protection. Which solution would best ensure data security and compliance during the migration process?

A) Utilize AWS Database Migration Service (DMS) to migrate data from the on-premises data warehouse to Amazon Redshift, ensuring data encryption in transit and at rest. Implement AWS Key Management Service (KMS) for centralized key management and encryption key rotation.

B) Deploy AWS Snowball Edge devices to physically transfer data from the on-premises data warehouse to Amazon S3, encrypting the data using AWS Key Management Service (KMS) managed keys. Use AWS DataSync to synchronize the encrypted data with Amazon Redshift for analysis.

C) Implement AWS Glue to extract, transform, and load (ETL) data from the on-premises data warehouse to Amazon S3, utilizing AWS Lake Formation for data cataloging and access control. Use AWS Direct Connect to establish a dedicated network connection for secure data transfer.

D) Utilize AWS DataSync to continuously replicate data changes from the on-premises data warehouse to Amazon S3, encrypting the data using server-side encryption with AWS KMS-managed keys. Configure AWS Lambda functions to trigger data ingestion into Amazon Redshift for analytics processing.

E) Deploy AWS Data Pipeline to orchestrate the migration of data from the on-premises data warehouse to Amazon Aurora, enabling data encryption at rest using AWS Key Management Service (KMS) customer master keys. Implement AWS CloudTrail to log API calls and monitor data access activities for compliance auditing.

QUESTION 51

For a mobile application backend hosted on AWS, which configuration ensures low latency data delivery with security and data processing at the edge?

A) Utilize Amazon API Gateway with regional endpoints and AWS Lambda functions for backend processing.

B) Deploy Amazon CloudFront in front of Amazon API Gateway, use AWS WAF for security, and Lambda@Edge for request validation and response transformation.

C) Configure Amazon EC2 instances in multiple Availability Zones, protected by AWS Shield.

D) Implement AWS Direct Connect between mobile clients and the AWS VPC hosting the backend.

E) Use Amazon S3 and Amazon CloudFront for static content delivery, with dynamic content handled by Amazon EC2 instances.

QUESTION 52

A financial services company is planning to deploy a critical web application in AWS, requiring high availability and fault tolerance across multiple regions. The application will use Amazon EC2 instances. Which setup ensures that the application remains available even if one AWS region becomes entirely unavailable?

A) Deploy EC2 instances in multiple Availability Zones within a single region and use an Elastic Load Balancer.

B) Deploy EC2 instances in multiple regions and use Amazon Route 53 health checks to route traffic.

C) Use Auto Scaling groups in a single region and configure EC2 Spot Instances for cost efficiency.

D) Implement EC2 instances with Elastic IP addresses in multiple regions and manually switch in case of failure.

E) Deploy EC2 instances in two regions and use AWS Direct Connect to ensure private connectivity between regions.

QUESTION 53

Your company is developing a data processing application that requires periodic batch processing of large datasets. The processing workload varies, and you need to ensure cost optimization for this operation while leveraging AWS services. Which solution would be most suitable for this scenario?

A) Utilize AWS Lambda functions triggered by Amazon S3 events

B) Implement Amazon EMR clusters with spot instances for batch processing

C) Deploy containers on Amazon ECS with reserved capacity for batch processing

D) Utilize AWS Glue for serverless ETL operations

E) Use Amazon Kinesis Data Firehose for real-time data processing

QUESTION 54

Your organization operates a hybrid architecture with on-premises servers and AWS resources. You need to design a network solution that optimizes costs for data transfer between on-premises and AWS environments while ensuring security and compliance. What approach should you recommend?

A) Deploy AWS Direct Connect with AWS Site-to-Site VPN for secure and cost-effective hybrid connectivity

B) Utilize Amazon VPC Peering for private connectivity between on-premises and AWS VPCs

C) Implement AWS Transit Gateway with AWS VPN for centralized and scalable hybrid connectivity

D) Opt for AWS Global Accelerator with AWS Shield for DDoS protection and low-latency access

E) Leverage AWS PrivateLink for private connectivity to AWS services from on-premises environments

QUESTION 55

A technology company is migrating its on-premises infrastructure to AWS and needs to ensure that IAM users can securely access AWS resources without the need for long-term credentials. What solution should the solutions architect recommend to meet this requirement?

A) Utilize IAM roles with temporary security credentials generated by AWS STS for IAM users.

B) Enable IAM user access keys and rotate them regularly to minimize the risk of unauthorized access.

C) Share the AWS account root credentials with IAM users for direct access to AWS resources.

D) Configure AWS Single Sign-On (SSO) to authenticate IAM users with their corporate credentials.

E) Implement cross-account IAM roles and delegate access to IAM users' personal AWS accounts.

QUESTION 56

Your company operates an e-commerce platform that experiences significant traffic spikes during seasonal sales events. You need to design a cost-optimized compute scaling solution that can efficiently handle these periodic bursts in traffic while minimizing costs during off-peak periods. What approach should you take?

A) Utilize AWS Lambda with provisioned concurrency to ensure consistent performance during traffic spikes

B) Implement Amazon EC2 Auto Scaling with predictive scaling to anticipate traffic patterns and scale proactively

C) Leverage AWS Fargate with spot capacity to take advantage of cost savings during traffic spikes

D) Deploy Amazon EKS with horizontal pod autoscaling to dynamically adjust Kubernetes resources based on demand

E) Utilize Amazon EC2 Reserved Instances for baseline capacity and supplement with Amazon EC2 Spot Instances during traffic spikes

QUESTION 57

Your organization is managing a high-throughput web application that utilizes Amazon ElastiCache for caching frequently accessed data. However, recent cost analysis reveals unexpectedly high ElastiCache costs, primarily attributed to inefficient resource allocation. As a solutions architect, you need to implement cost-effective strategies to optimize ElastiCache costs without compromising application performance. What would be the most effective approach to achieve this goal?

A) Implement Amazon ElastiCache Reserved Nodes to commit to a predefined usage period and receive significant cost savings

B) Utilize Amazon ElastiCache for Redis Multi-AZ with Automatic Failover to enhance fault tolerance and reduce costs

C) Configure Amazon ElastiCache Auto Discovery to automatically detect and connect to ElastiCache nodes, reducing operational overhead

D) Integrate Amazon ElastiCache with Amazon CloudWatch to monitor cache usage and identify opportunities for cost optimization

E) Use Amazon ElastiCache Data Persistence to store cache data on disk, reducing memory usage and lowering costs

QUESTION 58

Your organization is planning to deploy a batch processing system on AWS to process large volumes of data periodically. The system needs to be cost-effective while ensuring timely processing of data. As the solutions architect, you are tasked with selecting the most suitable instance purchasing option for this scenario. Which of the following options would best meet the requirements?

A) Utilize AWS EC2 On-Demand Instances with fixed-size Auto Scaling groups to maintain a consistent processing capacity

B) Implement AWS Savings Plans with a commitment to a specific instance family to receive discounts on instance usage

C) Deploy AWS EC2 Reserved Instances for the batch processing workload with a one-year term commitment

D) Leverage AWS EC2 Spot Instances for batch processing tasks and handle interruptions using Spot Fleet

E) Combine AWS EC2 Spot Instances with AWS Lambda for serverless processing to eliminate the need for manual scaling

QUESTION 59

Your organization is developing a microservices-based application that requires cost-efficient compute resources for each component. You need to recommend an approach that optimizes costs while ensuring scalability and reliability. What should you suggest?

A) Use Amazon EC2 On-Demand Instances for each microservice
B) Implement Amazon ECS with Fargate for serverless container management
C) Leverage Amazon EC2 Spot Instances with containerized workloads
D) Deploy AWS Lambda for serverless microservices
E) Utilize AWS Outposts for on-premises microservice deployment

QUESTION 60

A social media platform experiences highly unpredictable traffic patterns due to viral content and sudden user engagement spikes. The platform wants to ensure optimal performance and cost efficiency while handling these fluctuations. What Auto Scaling strategy should the solutions architect recommend?

A) Configure the Auto Scaling group to use a target tracking scaling policy based on the number of likes per minute.

B) Implement an Auto Scaling group with a scheduled scaling policy triggered at specific times of peak user activity.

C) Configure the Auto Scaling group to use a step scaling policy triggered by sudden increases in the number of comments per minute.

D) Utilize an Auto Scaling group with a simple scaling policy based on manual adjustments to instance counts.

E) Implement an Auto Scaling group with a predictive scaling policy based on historical engagement patterns.

QUESTION 61

Your organization manages a large dataset stored in Amazon S3 across multiple regions. Data is frequently replicated between regions for disaster recovery purposes, leading to high data transfer costs. You need to design a cost-effective solution to minimize data transfer costs while ensuring data integrity and availability. What should you recommend for this scenario?

A) Utilize AWS Snow Family to transfer large amounts of data between regions at a lower cost

B) Implement AWS DataSync to automate and optimize data transfers between Amazon S3 buckets in different regions

C) Configure Amazon S3 Cross-Region Replication to replicate data only for critical datasets between regions

D) Use Amazon S3 Transfer Acceleration to optimize data transfers and reduce latency for cross-region replication

E) Deploy Amazon S3 Glacier for long-term storage of replicated data to reduce data transfer costs

QUESTION 62

Your company is developing a new application that requires extensive testing across multiple environments on AWS. Cost optimization is a priority, and you need to implement a solution to minimize expenses associated with non-production resources. Which approach should you recommend?

A) Utilize Amazon CloudWatch Events to trigger AWS Lambda functions for automated resource management based on utilization metrics

 B) Implement AWS Trusted Advisor to analyze non-production resource usage and recommend cost optimization measures

 C) Leverage Amazon S3 Object Lock to enforce retention policies on test data and prevent accidental deletions

 D) Use AWS Resource Access Manager (RAM) to share non-production resources across multiple AWS accounts and reduce costs

 E) Deploy AWS Trusted Advisor to monitor non-production resource usage and identify opportunities for cost optimization

QUESTION 63

Your organization operates a global social media platform with millions of active users. Due to the critical nature of the platform, you have deployed redundant resources across multiple AWS regions to ensure high availability and disaster recovery. However, the operations team has noticed a significant increase in costs associated with inter-region data transfer. As a solutions architect, you need to design a cost-efficient multi-region architecture that maintains high availability while reducing data transfer costs. What approach should you recommend?

A) Utilize Amazon Route 53 latency-based routing to route traffic to the nearest AWS region and minimize data transfer distances

 B) Implement AWS Global Accelerator with Amazon CloudFront to optimize content delivery and reduce data transfer costs between regions

 C) Deploy AWS Direct Connect with AWS Transit Gateway to establish private connectivity between regions and reduce data transfer costs

 D) Leverage Amazon S3 Transfer Acceleration to optimize data transfer speeds between regions and minimize costs

 E) Utilize Amazon DynamoDB global tables to replicate data across regions and ensure low-latency access for users

QUESTION 64

Your organization operates a serverless architecture on AWS, utilizing AWS Lambda extensively for various backend processes. However, the finance department has raised concerns about escalating costs associated with Lambda function invocations. As a solutions architect, you need to design a cost-efficient solution that maintains the benefits of serverless architecture while reducing expenses.

A) Implement AWS Lambda provisioned concurrency to reduce cold starts and optimize costs associated with function invocations

B) Utilize Amazon API Gateway caching to reduce the number of Lambda function invocations and lower costs

C) Leverage AWS Step Functions to orchestrate Lambda function workflows and optimize costs by minimizing function invocations

D) Deploy AWS Fargate with Amazon ECS to run containerized workloads and reduce costs compared to serverless functions

E) Utilize Amazon SQS to decouple components and process Lambda function invocations asynchronously, reducing costs

QUESTION 65

Your organization is planning to optimize AWS costs by enhancing visibility and accountability across teams. As a solutions architect, you need to recommend a solution that provides comprehensive cost insights and accountability measures.

A) Implement AWS Cost Explorer with custom reporting to analyze cost trends and anomalies
B) Utilize AWS Budgets to set and track cost limits for individual teams and projects
C) Implement AWS IAM policies to restrict access to costly services and features based on user roles
D) Leverage AWS Service Catalog to standardize and control provisioned resources to minimize cost
E) Utilize AWS Trusted Advisor to identify cost optimization opportunities and best practices

PRACTICE TEST 9 - ANSWERS ONLY

QUESTION 1

Answer - B) External partners' access should be restricted to only the resources necessary for their tasks.

A) Incorrect - Federated access does not eliminate the need for IAM policies; they are essential for defining permissions for federated users.

B) Correct - Limiting external partners' access to only the resources needed for their tasks follows the principle of least privilege, enhancing the security of the AWS environment.

C) Incorrect - Sharing IAM roles among partners can compromise security by providing broader access than necessary.

D) Incorrect - Security audits are crucial for identifying and mitigating risks, even in environments accessed via federated access.

E) Incorrect - Federated access focuses on identity management and authentication, not on securing AWS resources against all external threats. Security measures must be applied across all aspects of the AWS environment.

QUESTION 2

Answer - B) Utilize AWS Secrets Manager to manage and rotate credentials automatically.

A) - Incorrect because storing sensitive information in environment variables can expose them to risk if not properly managed.

B) - Correct as AWS Secrets Manager is specifically designed to handle secret management with built-in capabilities for rotation, which aligns with best practices for security and compliance.

C) - Incorrect because storing credentials, even with restricted access, in plaintext on Amazon S3 is not a secure practice.

D) - Incorrect while DynamoDB with AWS KMS encryption offers data at rest security, using it solely for credential storage does not leverage AWS's dedicated tools for secrets management.

E) - Incorrect as embedding credentials in application code is a security risk and goes against the principle of least privilege and secure secret storage.

QUESTION 3

Answer - A) Encrypt video content using Amazon S3 and Amazon CloudFront with AWS KMS, ensuring TLS for data in transit.

A) Correct - Amazon S3 offers secure storage with encryption at rest capabilities when integrated with AWS KMS for key management. Amazon CloudFront, when used in conjunction with AWS KMS, can serve encrypted content securely over TLS, addressing both at-rest and in-transit encryption requirements for video streaming.

B) Incorrect - AWS Lambda and AWS IAM are essential for processing and access control but do not directly address the encryption of video content at rest and in transit as comprehensively as S3 and CloudFront.

C) Incorrect - Amazon Glacier provides long-term storage with encryption at rest, but AWS Direct Connect, while secure, is primarily used for a dedicated network connection and does not focus on encrypting streaming content to users.

D) Incorrect - AWS Elastic Beanstalk and Amazon RDS offer application deployment and database encryption, but this does not specifically cater to the encryption needs of streaming video content at rest and in transit.

E) Incorrect - Amazon ECS and Amazon API Gateway are critical for container management and API security but do not provide a direct solution for encrypting video content stored and streamed to end-users.

QUESTION 4

Answer - [A] Utilize Amazon S3 with versioning enabled to store critical data. Implement Amazon S3 cross-region replication to replicate data to a standby bucket in a different region for disaster recovery.

Option A - Correct. Amazon S3 with versioning and cross-region replication provides resilient data storage with built-in durability and disaster recovery capabilities.

Option B - While EBS volumes with RAID and AWS Backup offer some redundancy and backup capabilities, they may not provide the same level of durability and disaster recovery as S3 cross-region replication.

Option C - Amazon RDS Multi-AZ deployment and cross-region replication offer database redundancy and disaster recovery, but they may not be as cost-effective or scalable as S3 for storing large volumes of data.

Option D - Amazon EFS with lifecycle policies and Data Lifecycle Manager offer data management capabilities but may not provide the same level of durability and disaster recovery as S3 cross-region replication.

Option E - Amazon Aurora with Global Database and Backtrack offers resilience and recovery options for databases but may not be as suitable for general-purpose data storage as S3.

QUESTION 5

Answer - C) Use Amazon SQS FIFO queue with a batch mode of 5 messages per operation.

C) Use Amazon SQS FIFO queue with a batch mode of 5 messages per operation - This option ensures real-time delivery of notifications while allowing for simultaneous processing of multiple notifications for different user preferences through batch mode. It ensures order accuracy and scalability, meeting the company's requirements for real-time delivery and parallel processing.

A) Use Amazon SQS FIFO queue with exactly-once processing enabled - While ensuring order accuracy, it may not efficiently handle simultaneous notifications due to sequential processing.

B) Use Amazon SQS FIFO queue with message deduplication enabled - While avoiding duplicate messages, it doesn't guarantee order processing, and may not efficiently handle simultaneous notifications.

D) Use Amazon SQS standard queue to process the messages - Standard queues lack message ordering, which is crucial for maintaining notification order, and may not efficiently handle simultaneous notifications.

E) Use Amazon SQS FIFO queue with default settings - Default settings may not ensure real-time delivery and order accuracy, especially when processing multiple notifications simultaneously.

QUESTION 6

Answer - [B] Utilize IAM roles for EC2 instances with least privilege permissions to access other AWS services, and configure IAM policies to control access to RDS instances and S3 buckets.

Option B - Correct. Utilizing IAM roles for EC2 instances with least privilege permissions and configuring IAM policies for RDS instances and S3 buckets ensures secure access control to the AWS resources in the architecture.

Option A - Creating IAM users with access keys may not provide the necessary level of security and granularity required for managing access to resources securely.

Option C - While IAM groups can help organize permissions, configuring IAM policies at the individual resource level provides finer control over access.

Option D - Setting up IAM roles for each AWS resource and configuring cross-account access may introduce unnecessary complexity and does not align with best practices for IAM security.

Option E - Deploying IAM policies at the organizational unit level may not provide granular control over access to individual resources within the architecture.

QUESTION 7

Answer - [B] Configuring AWS IAM roles with least privilege access.

A) Incorrect - Encrypting data at rest using AWS KMS is essential for data security but is not directly related to serverless and event-driven design security.

B) Correct - Configuring AWS IAM roles with least privilege access ensures that serverless functions have only the necessary permissions, reducing the attack surface and enhancing security.

C) Incorrect - AWS CloudTrail provides visibility into API calls but is not specific to serverless application security.

D) Incorrect - AWS Network Firewall is not directly applicable to serverless architectures as it primarily operates at the network level.

E) Incorrect - AWS Shield Advanced provides DDoS protection, which is important for overall AWS security but is not specific to serverless application security.

QUESTION 8

Answer - [A] Configuring AWS CloudTrail for logging all API calls and actions taken on AWS resources.

A) Correct - AWS CloudTrail provides comprehensive logging of all API calls and actions taken on AWS resources, enabling auditability and compliance with regulations by tracking data transactions and access.

B) Incorrect - While AWS IAM roles with fine-grained permissions are essential for access control, they do not provide the logging and audit capabilities required for compliance.

C) Incorrect - AWS KMS is used for encrypting data at rest and does not directly address audit logging requirements.

D) Incorrect - AWS Config tracks changes to AWS resources and ensures compliance with configurations but does not provide the same level of detailed logging as AWS CloudTrail.

E) Incorrect - AWS Security Hub helps manage security posture and compliance but does not offer the same level of logging and audit capabilities as AWS CloudTrail.

QUESTION 9

Answer - [A] Implementing mutual TLS authentication between microservices in Amazon ECS, ensuring secure communication and compliance with encryption standards.

A) Implementing mutual TLS authentication between microservices in Amazon ECS ensures secure communication by verifying the identity of each service and encrypting data in transit, meeting compliance requirements for encryption standards.

B) While AWS App Mesh manages traffic between microservices, it may not directly enforce encryption or address compliance with encryption standards for data in transit.

C) AWS Lambda authorizers in Amazon API Gateway handle authentication and authorization for APIs but may not directly address secure communication between microservices or compliance with encryption standards.

D) AWS PrivateLink provides private communication between services but may not explicitly enforce encryption or compliance with encryption standards for data in transit.

E) AWS WAF filters traffic but does not directly handle secure communication between microservices or ensure compliance with encryption standards for data in transit.

QUESTION 10

Answer - B) Implement multipart uploads for efficient data transfer and AWS KMS for encryption during upload.

A) Use AWS Snowmobile for large dataset transfers and Amazon S3 server-side encryption (SSE) for data security. - Incorrect. Snowmobile is designed for exabyte-scale data transfer, likely overkill for the described scenario.

B) Implement multipart uploads for efficient data transfer and AWS KMS for encryption during upload. - Correct. Multipart uploads increase upload efficiency for large files, and AWS KMS provides the needed security for sensitive healthcare data.

C) Utilize Amazon S3 Transfer Acceleration for fast uploads and Amazon Macie for data security and privacy. - Incorrect. While this combination offers speed and security, the specific needs around efficient large file handling and encryption suggest B as a better solution.

D) Leverage AWS Direct Connect for consistent network performance and Amazon S3 Object Lock for immutability. - Incorrect. This solution does not prioritize upload speed or cost efficiency as required.

E) Opt for Amazon DataSync for automated data transfers and AWS Shield for protection against DDoS attacks. - Incorrect. While DataSync and Shield offer valuable benefits, they don't directly address the primary concerns of upload efficiency and secure data transfer in this context.

QUESTION 11

Answer - A) Utilize AWS Backup with a daily backup schedule, set retention for 30 days, and enable versioning on Amazon S3 buckets used for website assets.

A) Utilize AWS Backup with a daily backup schedule, set retention for 30 days, and enable versioning on Amazon S3 buckets used for website assets. - Correct because AWS Backup provides centralized backup across AWS services with scheduling and retention management, and S3 versioning allows for the restoration of any version within the retention period.

B) Implement Amazon EBS snapshots for the EC2 instances running the website, with an Amazon Data Lifecycle Manager policy for 30-day retention. - Incorrect because this focuses solely on the EC2 level without considering the entirety of the website's assets and the simplicity of restoration that AWS Backup offers.

C) Configure Amazon RDS to take automated daily snapshots, with a custom Lambda function to manage the retention period and restoration process. - Incorrect as it only covers the database aspect of the website, not the complete solution for website backup and restoration.

D) Deploy AWS Storage Gateway in a VTL configuration for daily backups, with lifecycle policies to transition backups to S3 Glacier for cost-effective storage. - Incorrect because it's more complex and less suited for the direct requirement of easy restoration and daily backup management.

E) Set up Amazon S3 with lifecycle rules to automatically archive website data to S3 Glacier after 30 days and use S3 Versioning for restoring any version within the retention period. - Incorrect as it doesn't offer the centralized management and direct restoration capabilities of AWS Backup, focusing instead on S3-specific data management.

QUESTION 12

Answer - A) Integrate AWS CodePipeline and AWS CodeDeploy for blue/green deployments, utilize AWS CloudFormation for infrastructure management across regions, and enforce IAM policies for access control.

A) Integrate AWS CodePipeline and AWS CodeDeploy for blue/green deployments, utilize AWS CloudFormation for infrastructure management across regions, and enforce IAM policies for access control. - Correct because it offers a comprehensive solution that includes managing deployments with blue/green strategies for minimal downtime, using CloudFormation for consistent infrastructure setup across regions, and applying IAM policies to secure access to deployment configurations.

B) Configure AWS Elastic Beanstalk for multi-region application deployments, use Elastic Beanstalk versioning for rollback, and Amazon Macie for monitoring and securing deployment configurations. - Incorrect as Elastic Beanstalk provides an environment for easy deployment and scaling, but it does not inherently offer the same level of control over blue/green deployments, nor the cross-region infrastructure management as CodePipeline and CodeDeploy do.

C) Deploy with Amazon ECS and AWS Fargate for container management, leverage Amazon ECR for storing Docker images, and use AWS Config rules for monitoring configuration changes. - Incorrect because, while offering a robust container management solution, it doesn't directly address the blue/green deployment strategy, automatic rollback, and strict IAM access controls in a multi-region context as the correct option.

D) Utilize AWS Lambda for deploying serverless functions, Amazon S3 for storing deployment artifacts with versioning enabled, and AWS Shield for additional security against DDoS attacks during deployment. - Incorrect as it focuses on serverless computing and does not fully cover the deployment strategy requirements, cross-region management, or access control specifics for deployment configurations.

E) Implement multi-region AWS Step Functions for orchestrating deployment workflows, Amazon DynamoDB global tables for state management, and AWS KMS for encrypting deployment configurations. - Incorrect because, while it offers an advanced workflow orchestration and encryption of configurations, it does not provide a direct solution for blue/green deployments and IAM-based access control for deployment configurations as effectively as CodePipeline and CodeDeploy.

QUESTION 13

Answer - D) Implement Amazon Macie for identifying and protecting sensitive data, AWS CloudTrail for logging access to PHI, and AWS Lambda for executing automatic remediation workflows.

A) Configure AWS CloudTrail and Amazon CloudWatch to monitor and alert on PHI access, use AWS Lambda for automated response to incidents, and AWS WAF for application layer protection. - Incorrect because while it offers monitoring and automated response, it doesn't include a specific solution for identifying PHI like Amazon Macie.

B) Leverage Amazon GuardDuty for detecting potential data exposure incidents, AWS Security Hub for centralized security monitoring, and AWS Step Functions for automated incident response actions. - Incorrect as it focuses on general security monitoring and automated responses without the specific PHI identification and protection capabilities that Macie provides.

C) Utilize AWS Config for tracking configuration changes, Amazon Inspector for security assessments, and AWS IAM Access Analyzer for analyzing permission settings. - Incorrect because, although important for compliance and security posture, these services do not offer direct incident response or PHI protection capabilities as Macie does.

D) Implement Amazon Macie for identifying and protecting sensitive data, AWS CloudTrail for logging access to PHI, and AWS Lambda for executing automatic remediation workflows. - Correct because Macie specifically helps in identifying PHI and sensitive data, CloudTrail logs all access and modifications, and Lambda enables automated actions to protect data and comply with HIPAA.

E) Deploy AWS Shield Advanced for DDoS protection, Amazon RDS with encryption for data security, and Amazon S3 with event notifications for monitoring data modifications. - Incorrect as it focuses on data protection and DDoS mitigation, not directly addressing incident response or PHI exposure incidents with the targeted approach that Macie and CloudTrail provide.

QUESTION 14

Answer - [A, C, D]

A) Using AWS Cost Explorer allows the e-commerce platform to analyze usage patterns and identify areas for cost optimization, such as unused resources or overprovisioned instances.

C) Setting up AWS Trusted Advisor provides real-time guidance on cost optimization opportunities and best practices for AWS services, helping the company effectively address high costs.

D) Leveraging AWS Cost and Usage Reports enables detailed analysis of cost and usage data, facilitating granular cost tracking and optimization. Implementing AWS Budgets and utilizing Savings Plans are also effective approaches, but may not provide the same level of detailed analysis and real-time guidance as Cost Explorer and Trusted Advisor for identifying and addressing the underlying reasons for high costs.

QUESTION 15

Answer - B) Suspend the ReplaceUnhealthy process type for the Auto Scaling group and apply the maintenance patch to the instance. Once the instance is ready, manually set the instance's health status back to healthy and activate the ReplaceUnhealthy process type again.

B) Suspend the ReplaceUnhealthy process type for the Auto Scaling group and apply the maintenance patch to the instance - This option effectively addresses the maintenance challenge by suspending the process responsible for replacing unhealthy instances, allowing the maintenance to proceed without triggering Auto Scaling actions.

A) Suspend the Terminate process type for the Auto Scaling group and apply the maintenance patch to the instance - Suspending termination processes may not prevent instance replacement and may not efficiently address the maintenance challenge.

C) Stop the instance, apply the maintenance patch, and then start the instance - Stopping the instance may disrupt application availability, and manually starting it again may not align with the requirement for uninterrupted maintenance.

D) Temporarily suspend the AddToLoadBalancer process type for the Auto Scaling group and apply the maintenance patch to the instance - Suspending processes related to load balancer integration may not efficiently address the maintenance challenge and may not prevent instance replacement during maintenance.

E) Take a snapshot of the instance, create a new Amazon Machine Image (AMI), and then launch a new instance using this AMI - Creating a new instance from a snapshot introduces complexity and may not efficiently address the maintenance challenge, especially in scenarios where immediate fixes are required.

QUESTION 16

Answer - A) Utilize AWS PrivateLink to expose services across accounts with VPC Endpoint Services.

A) Utilize AWS PrivateLink to expose services across accounts with VPC Endpoint Services - Correct because PrivateLink securely exposes your services to other accounts via VPC Endpoints, avoiding public internet exposure and simplifying network administration.

B) Implement inter-region VPC peering across accounts and encrypt traffic with AWS KMS - Incorrect because VPC peering does not inherently simplify network administration for SaaS offerings and requires additional configuration for cross-account connectivity.

C) Set up AWS Transit Gateway to interconnect VPCs and use IAM policies for cross-account access - Incorrect as it focuses on interconnecting VPCs rather than providing a streamlined solution for SaaS access.

D) Deploy AWS Direct Connect and AWS Transit Gateway for account-to-account private connectivity - Incorrect because, while it provides a robust connectivity solution, it's more complex and not specifically tailored for SaaS application access like PrivateLink.

E) Establish AWS VPN CloudHub to manage inter-account connectivity and apply AWS Shield for additional security - Incorrect because VPN CloudHub is designed for connecting multiple sites, not for the specific scenario of accessing SaaS applications across AWS accounts.

QUESTION 17

Answer - C) Use AWS DataSync for secure data transfer, Amazon EFS for encrypted file storage, and AWS CloudFormation for deploying disaster recovery stacks.

A) Incorrect because DMS and RDS address database migration and storage with encryption, but Route 53's DNS failover alone doesn't fully support a comprehensive disaster recovery plan for healthcare data.
B) Incorrect as Snowball and Elastic Beanstalk cater to data transfer and application deployment, but AWS Backup, while providing disaster recovery, doesn't ensure the encryption requirement during transit.

C) Correct as AWS DataSync secures data during transfer, EFS offers encrypted file storage solutions, and CloudFormation allows for the systematic deployment of infrastructure that meets disaster recovery and compliance needs, aligning with healthcare standards.

D) Incorrect because while Application Discovery Service, S3 encryption, and CloudWatch alarms are valuable for planning, storage, and monitoring, they do not constitute a complete solution for the specific requirements of encrypted data migration and disaster recovery planning.

E) Incorrect as S3 Transfer Acceleration and DynamoDB provide fast data migration and encrypted storage, but SNS alerts, focusing on notification, do not address the comprehensive needs of secure migration and disaster recovery for patient records.

QUESTION 18

Answer - [A] Use AWS Secrets Manager to store configuration settings for each microservice. Implement IAM roles with granular permissions to allow only authorized microservices to retrieve their respective secrets.

Option B - Storing configurations in plaintext files in S3 is not secure and lacks centralized management and rotation capabilities.

Option C - While AppConfig is suitable for managing configurations, it does not directly address secure access to secrets and may introduce unnecessary complexity.

Option D - While Parameter Store provides centralized configuration management, it may not offer

granular access control for microservices.
Option E - Storing configurations in environment variables directly within code may lead to security vulnerabilities and lacks centralized management.

QUESTION 19

Answer - [B] Utilize AWS Secrets Manager to securely store API keys and sensitive information. Integrate AWS Lambda with Secrets Manager for automated retrieval of secrets at runtime.

Option A - Storing API keys directly in environment variables within Lambda functions is not recommended for security reasons and lacks centralized management and rotation capabilities.
Option C - Storing plaintext configurations in an S3 bucket introduces security risks and lacks automation for retrieval and rotation.

Option D - While Parameter Store can centrally manage configurations, Secrets Manager is specifically designed for securely storing and rotating secrets like API keys.

Option E - Storing sensitive information in plaintext files within EFS lacks encryption and may expose data to unauthorized access. Explanation for Choice B: Utilizing AWS Secrets Manager provides secure storage and rotation of secrets like API keys. Integrating with Lambda allows for automated retrieval at runtime, enhancing security and compliance.

QUESTION 20

Answer - B) Create an Amazon CloudWatch metric filter to process AWS CloudTrail logs containing API call details. Establish an alarm based on this metric's rate to send an Amazon SNS notification to the required team.

B) Create an Amazon CloudWatch metric filter to process AWS CloudTrail logs containing API call details. Establish an alarm based on this metric's rate to send an Amazon SNS notification to the required team. - This option directly addresses the scenario by analyzing CloudTrail logs for unauthorized API queries and triggering real-time alerts using CloudWatch alarms and Amazon SNS notifications.

 A) Implement AWS Config Rules to monitor API activity and define rules to detect unauthorized API calls. Configure AWS Config to trigger an AWS Lambda function upon rule evaluation to notify relevant stakeholders. - While AWS Config can monitor API activity, it may not provide real-time alerting capabilities for immediate incident response as required in this scenario.

 C) Leverage AWS Trusted Advisor to publish metrics about check results to Amazon CloudWatch. Set up an alarm to track status changes for checks in the Service Limits category for the APIs, triggering notifications when service quotas are exceeded. - While Trusted Advisor offers valuable insights, it may not directly address the need for real-time detection of unauthorized API queries.

 D) Use Amazon Athena SQL queries against AWS CloudTrail log files stored in Amazon S3 buckets. Generate reports using Amazon QuickSight for managerial dashboards. - While this option provides insights, it may not offer real-time alerting capabilities as required in this scenario.

 E) Configure AWS CloudTrail to stream event data to Amazon Kinesis. Utilize Amazon Kinesis stream-level metrics in Amazon CloudWatch to trigger an AWS Lambda function that will initiate an error workflow. - While this option utilizes streaming data, it may introduce complexity and latency compared to directly analyzing CloudTrail logs for real-time alerts.

QUESTION 21

Answer - [D) Employ AWS Step Functions to manage the order processing workflow with built-in error handling.]

D) AWS Step Functions provides built-in error handling and retries, ensuring resilient workflow management.
 A) Kinesis Data Firehose is primarily for data loading, not orchestration.
 B) While SQS is for queuing, it lacks built-in workflow management capabilities.
 C) SNS is for pub/sub messaging, not workflow orchestration.
 E) AWS Glue is for ETL processing, not workflow orchestration.

QUESTION 22

Answer - [A) Amazon Kinesis and C) AWS Lambda]

Option A involves Amazon Kinesis for real-time data streaming with enhanced fan-out, ensuring high throughput and fault tolerance.

 Option C involves AWS Lambda for serverless compute with event-driven architecture, providing fault tolerance and scalability for real-time data processing.

 Option B involves Amazon EMR for big data processing, but it does not directly handle real-time streaming data like Amazon Kinesis or AWS Lambda.

 Option D involves Amazon Redshift for data warehousing, but it is not designed for real-time data processing.

 Option E involves AWS Glue for ETL processes, but it does not directly handle real-time streaming data processing.

QUESTION 23

Answer - [A) Utilize Amazon S3 Intelligent-Tiering with lifecycle policies for automatically moving data between storage classes based on access patterns, ensuring cost efficiency and data durability.]

Option A) is correct as it involves utilizing Amazon S3 Intelligent-Tiering with lifecycle policies, which automatically moves data between storage classes based on access patterns, ensuring cost efficiency and data durability.

Option B) involves Glacier for WORM storage but may not provide the same level of automation for data movement.

Option C) involves AWS Backup for centralized management but may not focus specifically on data archiving.

Option D) involves FSx for Lustre but may not achieve the same level of cost efficiency as S3 Intelligent-Tiering.

Option E) involves S3 One Zone-IA but may not provide the same level of data durability as Intelligent-Tiering.

QUESTION 24

Answer - [E) Implement Amazon Kinesis with AWS Direct Connect for real-time data streaming and dedicated network connectivity between game servers.]

Option E) is correct as it involves using Amazon Kinesis for real-time data streaming and AWS Direct Connect for dedicated network connectivity between game servers, ensuring low-latency communication.

Option A) mentions Amazon DynamoDB and Amazon ElastiCache, which are for data storage and caching, not for real-time communication between game servers.

Option B) mentions Amazon S3 and Amazon CloudFront, which are for content storage and delivery, not for real-time communication.

Option C) mentions Amazon EC2 instances and VPC peering, which may not provide the low-latency communication required for real-time multiplayer gaming.

Option D) mentions Amazon API Gateway and AWS Lambda, which are for API management and serverless compute, not for real-time communication between game servers.

QUESTION 25

Answer - A) Use Amazon Route 53 based geolocation routing policy to restrict access to viewers located in the authorized countries

A) By utilizing Amazon Route 53's geolocation routing policy, the entertainment company can restrict access to the live concerts to viewers only in the authorized countries, ensuring compliance with licensing agreements.

B, C, D, E) These options do not directly address the requirement of restricting access to viewers from specific countries for the live concerts. Weighted routing, latency-based routing, failover routing, and geoproximity routing do not provide the necessary geographic control needed for this scenario.

QUESTION 26

Answer - B) Implement AWS CloudFormation to define infrastructure as code and automate the deployment of AWS resources in a consistent and repeatable manner, promoting immutable infrastructure.

Option A is incorrect because while AWS AppConfig manages application configurations dynamically, it may not inherently support the principles of immutable infrastructure where the infrastructure is immutable and replaced rather than updated.

Option B is correct because AWS CloudFormation allows defining infrastructure as code, enabling the creation of immutable infrastructure and automating the deployment of AWS resources in a consistent and repeatable manner, aligning with the goal of achieving immutable infrastructure on AWS.

Option C is incorrect because while AWS OpsWorks automates infrastructure provisioning and configuration management, it may not directly align with the goal of achieving immutable infrastructure on AWS.

Option D is incorrect because while Amazon ECS Anywhere allows running containerized applications, it does not directly address the goal of achieving immutable infrastructure on AWS.

Option E is incorrect because while AWS Lambda scales and executes code, it does not directly address the goal of achieving immutable infrastructure on AWS.

QUESTION 27

Answer - B) Implement AWS PrivateLink to expose microservices privately and securely and route traffic through API Gateway

Option B - Implementing AWS PrivateLink allows for private and secure communication between microservices, while routing traffic through API Gateway provides additional control and monitoring capabilities.

Option A - API Gateway VPC Link integration offers private connectivity but may not provide the same level of control and scalability as AWS PrivateLink.

Option C - API Gateway WebSocket APIs enable real-time communication but may not be the best fit for traditional microservices communication scenarios.

Option D - Deploying API Gateway regional endpoints in multiple regions improves availability but may introduce additional complexity and latency in microservices communication.

Option E - API Gateway HTTP APIs with mTLS authentication offer security but may not provide the same level of flexibility and control as AWS PrivateLink for microservices communication.

QUESTION 28

Answer - A) Utilize Amazon DynamoDB to store session state and leverage AWS Lambda to access and update the data.

Option A - Amazon DynamoDB is a fully managed NoSQL database that provides low-latency access to data, making it ideal for managing state in serverless architectures. AWS Lambda can easily interact with DynamoDB to store and retrieve session state.

Option B - While Amazon SQS can help with message buffering, it's not specifically designed for managing state across serverless functions.

Option C - AWS Step Functions are used for orchestrating workflows but may not be the best fit for managing state across serverless functions directly.

Option D - Amazon S3 is an object storage service and may not offer the same level of performance and scalability required for managing state in real-time serverless applications.

Option E - AWS AppSync is primarily used for building GraphQL APIs and may not be the optimal choice for managing state between serverless functions.

QUESTION 29

Answer - B) Amazon Route 53 with geo-routing for traffic distribution.

A) Global Accelerator improves performance but does not address data sovereignty. B) Route 53 with geo-routing ensures compliance by directing users to specific regions based on their geographic location.

C) Outposts extends AWS infrastructure to on-premises locations but may not address data sovereignty concerns.

D) CloudFront with regional edge caches improves content delivery but does not manage traffic based on data sovereignty.

E) S3 Transfer Acceleration improves data transfer speed but does not address data sovereignty.

QUESTION 30

Answer - B) Utilize WebSocket APIs on Amazon API Gateway for bidirectional communication between clients and servers

B) Leveraging WebSocket APIs on Amazon API Gateway facilitates bidirectional communication between clients and servers, meeting the requirement for building a real-time chat feature within the application.
A, C, D, E) These options either do not provide bidirectional communication capabilities or involve using services not suitable for real-time chat functionality.

QUESTION 31

Answer - A) AWS Macie for identifying sensitive data, Amazon CloudWatch for monitoring access patterns, AWS Key Management Service (KMS) for encryption, and AWS IAM for managing access.

A) Correct, as Macie automatically identifies sensitive data, CloudWatch monitors access patterns to detect potential unauthorized access, KMS provides encryption at rest and in transit, and IAM ensures that only authorized users can access specific AWS resources, aligning with HIPAA compliance requirements.

B) Incorrect, while these services enhance overall security, they do not specifically address the HIPAA requirement for sensitive data identification, encryption, and access monitoring as comprehensively as the services in A.

C) Incorrect, Shield and Cognito focus on DDoS protection and user identity but do not cover sensitive data identification, encryption, and access monitoring required for HIPAA compliance.

D) Incorrect, Config, Lambda, Secrets Manager, and SNS provide a strong foundation for compliance and secrets management but do not offer the same level of data protection and encryption as the combination in A.

E) Incorrect, RDS, DynamoDB, Direct Connect, and Step Functions focus on database management, connectivity, and workflow orchestration, lacking specific capabilities for data protection and compliance monitoring essential for HIPAA.

QUESTION 32

Answer - [A) Implement Amazon RDS with Multi-AZ deployment and utilize AWS Backup for automated backups and cross-Region replication of backups.]

Option A - Correct because Amazon RDS with Multi-AZ deployment ensures high availability and minimal downtime, while AWS Backup provides automated backups and cross-Region replication, meeting the healthcare organization's requirements for disaster recovery and compliance.

Option B - Incorrect because while Aurora with global databases offers multi-master replication, it may not meet the stringent compliance requirements and downtime objectives of the healthcare organization as effectively as Amazon RDS Multi-AZ deployment with AWS Backup.

Option C - Incorrect because DynamoDB with global tables may not offer the same level of cross-Region backup and replication features as Amazon RDS Multi-AZ deployment with AWS Backup.

Option D - Incorrect because Redshift is optimized for analytics and may not offer the same level of disaster recovery features as Amazon RDS Multi-AZ deployment with AWS Backup.

Option E - Incorrect because DocumentDB may not offer the same level of disaster recovery capabilities as Amazon RDS Multi-AZ deployment with AWS Backup.

QUESTION 33

Answer - [E] Encrypt data in transit using HTTPS for API communication.

Option A is incorrect as deploying the application in a single AWS region without redundancy increases the risk of downtime.

Option B is incorrect as while AWS CloudFront can improve performance, it's not directly related to ensuring data integrity or minimizing downtime.

Option C is incorrect as storing sensitive data in plaintext within Lambda environment variables is a security risk.

Option D is incorrect as AWS Step Functions are for orchestrating workflows, not for ensuring data integrity or security.

Option E is correct because encrypting data in transit using HTTPS for API communication is a best practice for securing data transmission and maintaining data integrity, especially for an e-commerce platform handling sensitive customer information.

QUESTION 34

Answer - [A) Amazon ECS with AWS Fargate.]

Option A provides the most cost-effective solution for deploying and managing microservices with scalability and resilience. Amazon ECS with AWS Fargate allows you to run containers without managing the underlying infrastructure, reducing operational overhead and costs.

Option B, while serverless, may not be the most cost-effective for microservices with variable traffic. Option C requires managing EC2 instances manually and may not provide the same level of scalability. Option D and E are not suitable for deploying microservices in a cost-effective manner.

QUESTION 35

Answer - C) Ingest customer behavior data into Amazon Kinesis Data Streams, which triggers an AWS Lambda function for processing and stores recommendation data in Amazon DynamoDB

C) Ingesting customer behavior data into Amazon Kinesis Data Streams with AWS Lambda allows for real-time analysis and dynamic generation of recommendations. Storing recommendation data in Amazon

DynamoDB ensures low-latency access and scalability.

A) Processing customer behavior data with AWS Lambda and Amazon S3 may introduce latency and is not suitable for real-time analysis.

B) Using Amazon Kinesis Data Firehose may not provide the necessary real-time processing capabilities for dynamic recommendation generation.

D) Amazon SQS is not optimized for real-time processing of customer behavior data, and storing recommendation data in Amazon Redshift may introduce delays.

E) Using Amazon API Gateway and an EC2 instance for processing lacks the scalability and real-time processing capabilities required for dynamic recommendation generation.

QUESTION 36

Answer - [B, D]

A) Incorrect - While Lambda integration with KMS is relevant for encryption, CloudHSM is not typically used for Lambda encryption key storage.

B) Correct - S3 server-side encryption with KMS keys covers data at rest, and HTTPS ensures data in transit encryption, meeting regulatory requirements for data encryption.

C) Incorrect - RDS encryption at rest is relevant, but ACM is used for SSL/TLS certificates, not encryption keys in Lambda.

D) Correct - DynamoDB client-side encryption covers data at rest, and IAM roles provide secure API access for data in transit, ensuring compliance with regulatory requirements.

E) Incorrect - Redshift encryption at rest is relevant, but Secrets Manager is typically used for managing secrets, not encryption keys for Lambda.

QUESTION 37

Answer - C) Amazon S3 with Intelligent-Tiering to automatically move data to the most cost-effective access tier.

A) Incorrect - RDS is a relational database service for structured data, not optimized for storing or serving vast amounts of digital assets.

B) Incorrect - EFS provides scalable file storage but might not be the most cost-effective for storing a vast amount of digital assets due to its price point compared to object storage options.

C) Correct - Amazon S3 with Intelligent-Tiering is ideal for storing a vast amount of data, offering durability across multiple facilities and cost-effectiveness by automatically moving data to the most cost-effective access tier based on usage patterns.

D) Incorrect - AWS Storage Gateway integrates on-premises IT environments with cloud storage but isn't the best choice for online content management systems focused on serving digital assets.

E) Incorrect - DynamoDB is a NoSQL database service for structured data, not suited for storing large volumes of digital assets like an online content management system would require.

QUESTION 38

Answer - B) Utilize Amazon DynamoDB global tables to replicate data across multiple AWS regions for low-latency access and high availability.

Option B - Amazon DynamoDB global tables replicate data across multiple AWS regions, providing low-latency access and high availability for read-heavy workloads.

Option A - Amazon RDS with Multi-Region replication may introduce higher latency compared to Amazon DynamoDB global tables for read-heavy workloads.

Option C - Amazon ElastiCache for Redis caches frequently accessed data but may not provide the same level of durability and availability as Amazon DynamoDB global tables.

Option D - Amazon Aurora Multi-Master allows simultaneous write operations but may not be the best choice for read-heavy workloads across multiple regions.

Option E - Amazon Neptune is a graph database suitable for specific use cases but may not offer the same low-latency access and high availability as Amazon DynamoDB global tables for read-heavy workloads.

QUESTION 39

Answer - C) Implement Amazon Kinesis Data Firehose for ingesting streaming logs, and use Amazon Kinesis Data Analytics for real-time data processing.

Option A - Amazon Kinesis Video Streams is not designed for processing logs, and Amazon Redshift is for data warehousing, not real-time analytics.

Option B - Amazon Elasticsearch Service is for indexing, and Amazon QuickSight is for analytics, but they don't handle real-time processing as efficiently as the services in option C.

Option C - Amazon Kinesis Data Firehose ingests streaming logs, and Amazon Kinesis Data Analytics provides real-time processing, meeting the requirements for fault tolerance and real-time analytics.

Option D - Amazon CloudFront and Amazon S3 are not specifically designed for ingesting and processing streaming logs in real-time.

Option E - AWS Direct Connect and Amazon S3 Glacier are not optimized for real-time data processing and analytics, making this option less suitable.

QUESTION 40

Answer - B) Use server-side encryption with AWS Key Management Service (SSE-KMS) keys to encrypt the data on Amazon S3

B) Server-side encryption with AWS Key Management Service (SSE-KMS) provides the required encryption of data at rest while offering additional control and auditing capabilities through AWS KMS.

A) Client-side encryption with customer-provided keys (SSE-C) shifts the responsibility of encryption to the client and may not offer the desired control and auditing features.

C) Server-side encryption with Amazon S3 managed keys (SSE-S3) encrypts the data at rest but may not provide the additional control and auditing capabilities required by the e-commerce company.

D) Using server-side encryption with customer-provided keys (SSE-C) also lacks the centralized control and auditing capabilities provided by AWS KMS.

E) Enabling AWS CloudTrail provides auditing capabilities but does not directly address the encryption requirement for data at rest in Amazon S3.

QUESTION 41

Answer - A) AWS Lambda for event processing, Amazon SQS for message queuing, AWS Step Functions for managing the decision-making workflow.

A) Correct - AWS Lambda allows for rapid processing of events. Amazon SQS queues messages from various sources, decoupling components for greater resilience. AWS Step Functions orchestrates the workflow, making complex routing decisions based on business rules.

B) Incorrect - EC2 Auto Scaling, S3, and CloudWatch provide scalability, storage, and monitoring but lack the serverless event-driven architecture and workflow management capabilities that Lambda, SQS, and Step Functions offer.

C) Incorrect - DynamoDB, SNS, and API Gateway support data storage, notification, and external communication but don't provide the cohesive event processing and decision workflow management found in the A option.

D) Incorrect - Fargate, IAM, and Kinesis cater to container management, security, and event stream processing but don't offer the simplicity and direct workflow orchestration capabilities of Step Functions combined with Lambda and SQS.

E) Incorrect - RDS, Elastic Beanstalk, and CloudTrail focus on data storage, application deployment, and activity logging. They do not provide the serverless, event-driven approach needed for real-time shipment rerouting.

QUESTION 42

Answer - [A) Utilize AWS Outposts with Amazon EC2 Auto Scaling to automatically adjust compute capacity based on demand, ensuring efficient resource management.]

Option A) Utilizing AWS Outposts with Amazon EC2 Auto Scaling allows for automatic adjustment of compute capacity based on demand, ensuring efficient resource management and cost optimization.

Option B) Amazon EC2 Reserved Instances may provide cost savings but may not offer the same level of flexibility and efficiency as Auto Scaling for dynamic workload management.

Option C) AWS Batch is designed for batch computing workloads and may not provide the same level of flexibility for managing compute resources on AWS Outposts.

Option D) AWS Elastic Beanstalk is a platform-as-a-service offering and may not offer the same level of control and optimization for compute resources on AWS Outposts as Auto Scaling.
Option E) Amazon EC2 Spot Instances may provide cost savings but may not be suitable for applications requiring consistent performance on AWS Outposts.

QUESTION 43

Answer - A) Focus on Amazon CloudFront for content delivery, utilize AWS Lambda@Edge for location-based content customization, Amazon S3 and DynamoDB with region-specific deployments for data storage, and AWS WAF for security.

A) Correct - CloudFront ensures fast global content delivery. Lambda@Edge allows for dynamic content customization based on user location, meeting data sovereignty by processing data at edge locations. S3 and DynamoDB support region-specific deployments for compliance. WAF enhances security.

B) Incorrect - API Gateway, EC2 with Auto Scaling, RDS, and Shield provide scalability and security but may not efficiently handle dynamic content customization and strict data residency as Lambda@Edge and region-specific S3/DynamoDB deployments.

C) Incorrect - Global Accelerator, Elastic Beanstalk, S3, and multi-region Aurora provide a robust infrastructure but lack the edge computing aspect for location-based content customization and might not meet specific data sovereignty requirements as directly as option A.

D) Incorrect - Direct Connect, ECS, EBS, and Cognito offer dedicated connectivity, container management, and authentication but don't directly address the compliance and dynamic content delivery requirements at the edge.

E) Incorrect - While this setup includes CloudFront and WAF for delivery and security, the specific combination in A more effectively addresses dynamic content customization at the edge and compliance with data sovereignty laws through region-specific storage and processing.

QUESTION 44

Answer - [E] Implement Amazon SageMaker for distributed training with Amazon S3 for data storage and Amazon CloudWatch for monitoring and optimization, with AWS Glue for data preprocessing.

Option A's use of S3 for training may not support distributed training effectively.
Option B's use of EFS for shared storage may introduce performance bottlenecks.
Option C's use of Aurora may not be optimized for model storage.
Option D's use of RDS may not be suitable for storing large model metadata.
Option E leverages S3 for scalable and cost-efficient data storage, combined with CloudWatch for monitoring and optimization, and AWS Glue for data preprocessing, making it the most suitable choice for managing data pipelines for machine learning workflows with scalability, reliability, and cost optimization.

QUESTION 45

Answer - B) Implement on-demand instances for the entire duration of operation

B) Implementing on-demand instances for the entire duration allows the startup to keep costs low during the initial phase without upfront commitments, while still accommodating rapid growth without the need for capacity planning.

A) Utilizing reserved instances (RI) may not be suitable for a startup during the initial phase due to upfront costs and uncertainty about future workload patterns.

C) Using a combination of reserved instances (RI) and spot instances may introduce complexity and may not align with the startup's goal of keeping costs low initially.

 D) Employing spot instances for the entire duration may be risky as spot instance availability and pricing are subject to fluctuations.

 E) Implementing a mix of reserved instances (RI) and on-demand instances may not provide the flexibility needed for rapid growth and cost optimization during the initial phase.

QUESTION 46

Answer - [D] Utilize Amazon Kinesis Data Streams for ingesting real-time data, process data using AWS Lambda, store processed data in Amazon DynamoDB, and use Amazon CloudFront for content delivery.

Option A is incorrect because using AWS IoT Core for data ingestion may be more suitable for IoT scenarios compared to directly using AWS Lambda. Additionally, storing processed data in Amazon RDS may introduce higher costs and management overhead compared to DynamoDB.

Option B is incorrect because while Amazon EventBridge is suitable for event-driven architectures, AWS Glue may not be the best choice for real-time data processing compared to AWS Lambda.

Option C is incorrect because deploying containers on Amazon ECS for data ingestion may introduce management overhead compared to using managed services like Amazon Kinesis Data Streams for ingesting real-time data. Additionally, Amazon S3 may not be the optimal choice for storing processed data compared to Amazon DynamoDB in this scenario.

Option E is incorrect because although Amazon S3 is highly scalable, it may not provide the real-time processing capabilities required for this scenario, and Amazon Redshift may not be the most suitable choice for storing processed data in real-time.

QUESTION 47

Answer - [B] Implement a serverless architecture with AWS Lambda for compute, Amazon DynamoDB for database needs, and Amazon S3 for static content storage.

Option B is the correct choice because a serverless architecture with AWS Lambda automatically scales to handle periodic spikes in traffic without incurring costs during idle periods.

DynamoDB provides scalability and high availability, while S3 ensures efficient storage and delivery of static content. Options A, C, D, and E either lack the same level of cost efficiency, scalability, or suitable services for the specified requirements.

QUESTION 48

Answer - D) Employ a combination of reserved instances (RI) and spot instances

D) Employing a combination of reserved instances (RI) and spot instances allows the media streaming company to benefit from cost savings with RIs during predictable usage periods while leveraging the scalability and cost-effectiveness of spot instances during peak usage times.

 A) Using reserved instances (RI) for the entire duration may result in underutilization of resources during non-peak hours, leading to higher costs.

B) Implementing on-demand instances for the entire duration may result in higher costs, especially during peak usage times.

C) Utilizing spot instances for the entire duration may be risky as spot instances can be terminated with short notice, potentially affecting streaming availability during peak hours.

E) Implementing a mix of reserved instances (RI) and on-demand instances may not fully optimize costs during varying user activity levels and may lead to underutilization of reserved capacity.

QUESTION 49

Answer - A) Implement AWS CloudFormation to automate the provisioning of infrastructure resources, and use AWS CodePipeline to deploy application changes. Leverage AWS X-Ray for distributed tracing and performance analysis, and simulate load using AWS Load Testing Service.

Option A - This strategy covers automation of infrastructure provisioning and deployment, comprehensive performance analysis using AWS X-Ray, and load simulation using AWS Load Testing Service, which is well-suited for handling seasonal traffic spikes.

Option B - While AWS CloudWatch and AWS CloudTrail offer monitoring and logging capabilities, and Apache JMeter is suitable for load testing, AWS Inspector may not be the most efficient choice for performance testing in this scenario. Additionally, manual provisioning of EC2 instances for load testing may not be as scalable or cost-effective as using a dedicated load testing service like AWS Load Testing Service.

Option C - Although AWS Lambda can simulate user interactions and AWS CodeDeploy facilitates automated deployments, the lack of dedicated load testing tools and reliance on manual analysis with AWS X-Ray may not provide the level of performance testing required for seasonal traffic spikes. Additionally, Amazon CloudFront and AWS CodeDeploy may not directly address load testing needs.

Option D - While AWS Elastic Beanstalk provides managed hosting and Amazon Route 53 offers DNS routing, Apache JMeter may not be the most efficient choice for load testing, especially during seasonal traffic spikes. Additionally, manual provisioning of EC2 instances for load testing may not be as scalable or cost-effective as using a dedicated load testing service like AWS Load Testing Service.

Option E - Although Amazon ECS and AWS Fargate offer containerized workload management and serverless compute, respectively, and Amazon CloudWatch Logs provide monitoring capabilities, conducting performance testing with Gatling on EC2 instances may not be as efficient or scalable as using a dedicated load testing service like AWS Load Testing Service. Additionally, Gatling may not provide the same level of integration with AWS services as other load testing tools.

QUESTION 50

Answer - A) Utilize AWS Database Migration Service (DMS) to migrate data from the on-premises data warehouse to Amazon Redshift, ensuring data encryption in transit and at rest. Implement AWS Key Management Service (KMS) for centralized key management and encryption key rotation.

Option B involves physical data transfer, which may not be suitable for sensitive customer information and introduces additional complexity.

Option C focuses on ETL processes but does not provide real-time data replication or encryption features for compliance.

Option D, while utilizing DataSync, lacks direct migration to Redshift and may require additional processing steps.

Option E involves Aurora, which may not be the ideal choice for a data warehouse migration and introduces unnecessary complexity with CloudTrail for compliance monitoring.

QUESTION 51

Answer - B) Deploy Amazon CloudFront in front of Amazon API Gateway, use AWS WAF for security, and Lambda@Edge for request validation and response transformation.

A) - Incorrect because it does not leverage edge locations for performance improvement.
B) - Correct, as CloudFront and Lambda@Edge provide low latency and security, while AWS WAF ensures data protection.
C) - Incorrect, as it does not optimize for edge location benefits.
D) - Incorrect, Direct Connect is not feasible for mobile client connections.
E) - Incorrect, as it does not include security and data processing enhancements at the edge.

QUESTION 52

Answer - B) Deploy EC2 instances in multiple regions and use Amazon Route 53 health checks to route traffic.

A) Deploying in multiple AZs enhances availability but doesn't protect against regional outages.
B) Correct, as deploying in multiple regions with Route 53 health checks allows for automatic traffic routing to healthy regions.

C) Auto Scaling and Spot Instances improve scalability and cost but don't address inter-region fault tolerance.
D) Elastic IPs and manual switching can be cumbersome and slow in a disaster scenario.
E) Direct Connect enhances connectivity but doesn't automatically handle failover between regions.

QUESTION 53

Answer - [B] Implement Amazon EMR clusters with spot instances for batch processing.

Option A - AWS Lambda may not be suitable for batch processing of large datasets due to its execution time limitations.

Option B - Correct. Amazon EMR clusters with spot instances provide a cost-effective solution for batch processing with the ability to handle large datasets.

Option C - While Amazon ECS can be used for batch processing, utilizing reserved capacity may not offer the same level of cost optimization as spot instances.

Option D - AWS Glue is more suitable for ETL operations, not batch processing of large datasets.
Option E - Amazon Kinesis Data Firehose is used for real-time data streaming, not batch processing.

QUESTION 54

Answer - [A] Deploy AWS Direct Connect with AWS Site-to-Site VPN for secure and cost-effective hybrid connectivity.

Option A - Correct. AWS Direct Connect with Site-to-Site VPN provides secure and cost-effective hybrid connectivity, optimizing data transfer costs between on-premises and AWS environments.

Option B - VPC Peering offers private connectivity but may not provide the same cost-effectiveness and security compliance requirements for hybrid environments.

Option C - Transit Gateway with VPN offers centralized connectivity but may not be as cost-effective as Direct Connect with Site-to-Site VPN for data transfer between on-premises and AWS.

Option D - Global Accelerator with Shield focuses on DDoS protection and low-latency access but may not address the specific cost optimization requirements for data transfer.

Option E - PrivateLink facilitates private connectivity to AWS services but may not be the most suitable solution for optimizing data transfer costs between on-premises and AWS environments.

QUESTION 55

Answer - [A] Utilize IAM roles with temporary security credentials generated by AWS STS for IAM users.

A) Correct - Utilizing IAM roles with temporary security credentials generated by AWS STS ensures secure access to AWS resources without the need for long-term credentials, enhancing security and compliance.

B) Incorrect - Enabling IAM user access keys and rotating them regularly does not eliminate the need for long-term credentials and increases the risk of unauthorized access if not managed properly.

C) Incorrect - Sharing the AWS account root credentials with IAM users is highly discouraged due to security risks and violates AWS best practices for access management.

D) Incorrect - Configuring AWS Single Sign-On (SSO) authenticates IAM users with corporate credentials but may not eliminate the need for long-term credentials and may introduce additional complexity.

E) Incorrect - Implementing cross-account IAM roles and delegating access to IAM users' personal AWS accounts adds unnecessary complexity and may not align with the organization's access control requirements.

QUESTION 56

Answer - [B] Implement Amazon EC2 Auto Scaling with predictive scaling to anticipate traffic patterns and scale proactively.

Option B - Correct. Implementing Amazon EC2 Auto Scaling with predictive scaling allows the system to anticipate traffic patterns and scale proactively, ensuring efficient handling of periodic traffic spikes while minimizing costs during off-peak periods.

Option A - While AWS Lambda with provisioned concurrency ensures consistent performance, it may not be the most efficient solution for handling significant traffic spikes during seasonal events.

Option C - AWS Fargate with spot capacity offers cost savings but may not provide the same level of predictability and proactive scaling as Amazon EC2 Auto Scaling with predictive scaling.

Option D - Amazon EKS with horizontal pod autoscaling may provide flexibility but may introduce complexity and may not be the most cost-effective solution for this scenario.

Option E - While utilizing a combination of Reserved Instances and Spot Instances may provide cost optimization, it may not offer the proactive scaling capabilities needed to efficiently handle periodic traffic spikes.

QUESTION 57

Answer - [D] Integrate Amazon ElastiCache with Amazon CloudWatch to monitor cache usage and identify opportunities for cost optimization.

Option A - Implementing Amazon ElastiCache Reserved Nodes can provide cost savings but may not address inefficiencies in resource allocation.

Option B - While utilizing Amazon ElastiCache Multi-AZ with Automatic Failover enhances fault tolerance, it may not directly optimize costs associated with resource allocation.

Option C - Configuring Amazon ElastiCache Auto Discovery reduces operational overhead but does not focus on optimizing costs.

Option D - Correct. Integrating Amazon ElastiCache with Amazon CloudWatch allows for monitoring cache usage and identifying opportunities for cost optimization based on actual usage patterns.

Option E - Using Amazon ElastiCache Data Persistence reduces memory usage but may not directly optimize costs associated with resource allocation.

QUESTION 58

Answer - [D] Leverage AWS EC2 Spot Instances for batch processing tasks and handle interruptions using Spot Fleet.

Option D - Correct. Leveraging AWS EC2 Spot Instances for batch processing tasks provides significant cost savings, and handling interruptions using Spot Fleet ensures timely processing of data.

Option A - Utilizing AWS EC2 On-Demand Instances with fixed-size Auto Scaling groups may result in higher costs compared to Spot Instances for batch processing workloads.

Option B - Implementing AWS Savings Plans may provide discounts but may not fully optimize costs for batch processing tasks with variable workloads.

Option C - Deploying AWS EC2 Reserved Instances with a one-year term commitment may offer cost savings but may not provide the flexibility required for batch processing tasks with fluctuating demands.

Option E - Combining AWS EC2 Spot Instances with AWS Lambda for serverless processing introduces complexity and may not be the most suitable solution for batch processing tasks.

QUESTION 59

Answer - [B] Implement Amazon ECS with Fargate for serverless container management.

Option B - Correct. Implementing Amazon ECS with Fargate allows for cost-efficient serverless container management, ensuring scalability and reliability for microservices-based applications.

Option A - Using Amazon EC2 On-Demand Instances for each microservice may provide consistent performance but may not be as cost-efficient or scalable as serverless container management.

Option C - Leveraging Amazon EC2 Spot Instances with containerized workloads may optimize costs but may introduce complexity and reliability concerns for microservices.

Option D - Deploying AWS Lambda for serverless microservices may be suitable for specific use cases but may not provide the same level of control or customization as container-based solutions.

Option E - Utilizing AWS Outposts for on-premises microservice deployment is suitable for hybrid architectures but may not provide the same cost efficiency as serverless container management.

QUESTION 60

Answer - [C] Configure the Auto Scaling group to use a step scaling policy triggered by sudden increases in the number of comments per minute.

A) Incorrect - Using a target tracking scaling policy based on the number of likes per minute may not accurately reflect the overall workload of the platform during viral content spikes.

B) Incorrect - Implementing a scheduled scaling policy triggered at specific times of peak user activity may not dynamically respond to sudden traffic increases, potentially resulting in under or over-provisioning of resources.

C) Correct - Configuring a step scaling policy triggered by sudden increases in the number of comments per minute allows the Auto Scaling group to dynamically adjust the number of instances in response to changing traffic patterns during viral content spikes, ensuring optimal performance and cost efficiency.

D) Incorrect - Utilizing a simple scaling policy based on manual adjustments lacks automation and may result in delayed responses to sudden traffic increases, impacting performance during unpredictable traffic patterns.

E) Incorrect - Implementing a predictive scaling policy based on historical engagement patterns may not accurately predict sudden traffic spikes, leading to potential performance issues during viral content outbreaks.

QUESTION 61

Answer - [C] Configure Amazon S3 Cross-Region Replication to replicate data only for critical datasets between regions.

Option A - AWS Snow Family is suitable for transferring large amounts of data but may not provide continuous replication and real-time data transfer optimization between regions.

Option B - AWS DataSync automates data transfers but may not offer the same cost optimization for continuous replication between regions as cross-region replication.

Option C - Correct. Amazon S3 Cross-Region Replication allows for replicating data only for critical datasets between regions, minimizing data transfer costs while ensuring data integrity and availability.

Option D - Amazon S3 Transfer Acceleration optimizes data transfers but may not address the specific requirement for minimizing data transfer costs between regions for disaster recovery purposes.

Option E - Amazon S3 Glacier is suitable for long-term storage but may not provide real-time data replication and low-latency access required for disaster recovery scenarios.

QUESTION 62

Answer - [A] Utilize Amazon CloudWatch Events to trigger AWS Lambda functions for automated resource management based on utilization metrics.

Option A - Correct. Using Amazon CloudWatch Events with AWS Lambda allows for automated resource management based on utilization metrics, effectively minimizing expenses associated with non-production resources.

Option B - AWS Trusted Advisor provides recommendations but may not directly offer automated resource management for cost optimization.

Option C - Amazon S3 Object Lock enforces retention policies but may not directly address the need for cost optimization in non-production environments.

Option D - AWS Resource Access Manager (RAM) shares resources but may not provide the same level of automated cost optimization as Amazon CloudWatch Events with AWS Lambda.

Option E - AWS Trusted Advisor monitors usage but may not offer the same level of automated resource management for cost optimization as Amazon CloudWatch Events with AWS Lambda.

QUESTION 63

Answer - [B] Implement AWS Global Accelerator with Amazon CloudFront to optimize content delivery and reduce data transfer costs between regions.

Option A - Amazon Route 53 latency-based routing optimizes traffic routing but may not directly reduce data transfer costs between regions.

Option B - Correct. Implementing AWS Global Accelerator with Amazon CloudFront can optimize content delivery and reduce data transfer costs between regions, ensuring cost-efficient multi-region architecture while maintaining high availability.

Option C - AWS Direct Connect with AWS Transit Gateway can establish private connectivity between regions but may not directly minimize data transfer costs.

Option D - Amazon S3 Transfer Acceleration improves transfer speeds but may not directly reduce data transfer costs between regions.

Option E - Amazon DynamoDB global tables ensure data replication across regions but may not directly address the issue of reducing data transfer costs between regions.

QUESTION 64

Answer - [A] Implement AWS Lambda provisioned concurrency to reduce cold starts and optimize costs associated with function invocations.

Option A - Correct. Implementing AWS Lambda provisioned concurrency reduces cold starts and optimizes costs associated with function invocations.

Option B - Amazon API Gateway caching may reduce function invocations but may not directly address cost efficiency related to Lambda function invocations.

Option C - AWS Step Functions orchestrate workflows but may not directly optimize costs associated with Lambda function invocations.

Option D - AWS Fargate with Amazon ECS runs containerized workloads but may not directly provide the benefits of serverless architecture.

Option E - Utilizing Amazon SQS for asynchronous processing may reduce costs but does not directly address the cost efficiency of Lambda function invocations.

QUESTION 65

Answer - [A] Implement AWS Cost Explorer with custom reporting to analyze cost trends and anomalies.

Option A - Correct. Implementing AWS Cost Explorer with custom reporting provides comprehensive cost insights and allows for analysis of cost trends and anomalies, enhancing visibility and accountability.

Option B - AWS Budgets helps track cost limits but may not provide the same level of comprehensive cost insights and analysis as AWS Cost Explorer with custom reporting.

Option C - While AWS IAM policies can restrict access to services, they primarily focus on security rather than providing cost insights and accountability.

Option D - AWS Service Catalog helps standardize resource provisioning but may not directly address cost insights and accountability across teams.

Option E - AWS Trusted Advisor identifies cost optimization opportunities but may not offer the same level of detailed cost analysis and reporting as AWS Cost Explorer.

PRACTICE TEST 10 - QUESTIONS ONLY

QUESTION 1

In the context of using AWS for a large educational institution, the IT department needs to manage federated access for students, faculty, and staff, utilizing AWS IAM Identity Center and integrating with their existing identity provider. Which best practice should they follow to optimize the security and efficiency of their federated access implementation?

A) Consolidate all users into a single IAM role to reduce the complexity of role management.
B) Use AWS Lambda to automatically assign IAM roles based on user activity.
C) Utilize attribute-based access control (ABAC) to dynamically assign permissions based on the user's attributes.
D) Rely solely on the external identity provider's security for access control.
E) Use a single sign-on mechanism for access to non-AWS applications only.

QUESTION 2

An e-commerce platform is experiencing rapid growth and needs to ensure its AWS infrastructure can securely handle increasing traffic volumes, especially during peak shopping periods. The platform requires a solution to protect against web-based attacks and manage sudden surges in traffic. Which AWS services should be integrated to secure the platform's workload and applications while maintaining high performance?

A) Amazon S3 and Amazon Glacier for data storage and archiving
B) AWS Auto Scaling and Amazon CloudWatch for traffic management
C) Amazon CloudFront and AWS Shield Standard for DDoS protection
D) AWS WAF and Amazon Route 53 for web security and DNS management
E) AWS Fargate and AWS Lambda for serverless application scaling

QUESTION 3

A multinational corporation with strict data residency and compliance requirements needs to securely manage and encrypt personally identifiable information (PII) stored in their global AWS infrastructure. The solution must include centralized key management and the ability to enforce data encryption policies across multiple AWS regions. Which set of AWS services should the corporation implement to meet these requirements?

A) Centralize key management with AWS KMS and enforce encryption policies using AWS Organizations service control policies (SCPs).

B) Implement AWS CloudHSM for hardware-based key management and use Amazon Macie for data classification and encryption.

C) Use Amazon RDS with multi-region encryption and AWS IAM for encryption policy enforcement.
D) Deploy AWS Secrets Manager for storing sensitive information and Amazon Inspector for security assessments.

E) Utilize AWS WAF for web application firewall protection and AWS Shield for data encryption.

QUESTION 4

Your company is developing a microservices-based application on AWS that requires high availability and fault tolerance. Each microservice will be deployed as a separate container using Amazon ECS. As the solutions architect, you need to design a resilient architecture that ensures continuous availability of the application despite failures at the container or host level. Which solution should you recommend?

A) Deploy Amazon ECS tasks across multiple Availability Zones within a region. Implement Amazon ECS Service Auto Scaling to automatically adjust the number of tasks based on load and health checks.

B) Utilize Amazon EKS to manage the Kubernetes environment for deploying and scaling microservices. Implement AWS Fargate to run containers without managing the underlying infrastructure.

C) Set up Amazon ECS tasks with ECS Capacity Providers to automatically provision and scale infrastructure resources based on workload demand. Implement Amazon ECS rolling updates to maintain high availability during deployments.

D) Deploy microservices as AWS Lambda functions instead of containers to leverage serverless architecture for automatic scaling and high availability.

E) Configure Amazon ECS tasks with Amazon EC2 Spot Instances to reduce costs while maintaining availability. Implement Amazon ECS rolling deployments to minimize downtime during updates.

QUESTION 5

A financial institution is migrating its transaction processing system to AWS and requires a solution that ensures transactions are processed accurately and efficiently while also providing the ability to handle high transaction volumes during peak hours. Which option should the company choose to implement this requirement?

A) Use Amazon SQS FIFO queue with a batch mode of 10 messages per operation.
B) Use Amazon SQS FIFO queue with exactly-once processing enabled.
C) Use Amazon SQS FIFO queue with default settings to process the messages.
D) Use Amazon SQS standard queue to process the messages.
E) Use Amazon SQS FIFO queue with message deduplication enabled.

QUESTION 6

Your company is developing a microservices-based application on AWS that requires secure authentication and authorization mechanisms. The architecture includes Amazon ECS for container orchestration, Amazon API Gateway for RESTful APIs, and AWS Lambda for serverless compute. As the solutions architect, you need to implement a robust IAM strategy to ensure only authorized users can access the application services. Which approach should you take to achieve this goal?

A) Configure IAM roles for ECS tasks with granular permissions to access other AWS services securely. Implement API Gateway with IAM authorization for access control to Lambda functions.

B) Utilize AWS Identity and Access Management (IAM) policies attached to ECS task definitions to control access to AWS resources. Configure API Gateway with Amazon Cognito user pools for user authentication and authorization.

C) Implement IAM roles for ECS services to securely access other AWS services. Use Lambda authorizers with API Gateway for OAuth 2.0 authorization to authenticate users and control access to APIs.

D) Set up IAM policies at the AWS account level to manage access control for all AWS resources. Configure API Gateway with AWS Lambda authorizers to authenticate users and authorize access to Lambda functions.

E) Deploy AWS Fargate tasks within a VPC and use IAM roles for secure access to other AWS services. Implement API Gateway with Amazon Cognito user pools for user authentication and authorization.

QUESTION 7

Your organization is designing a disaster recovery (DR) solution for its critical applications hosted on AWS. As part of the DR strategy, you need to ensure seamless data replication between primary and secondary regions while maintaining data integrity and security. Which of the following options provides the most suitable solution for ensuring secure data replication across regions?

A) Configuring cross-region replication for Amazon S3 buckets
B) Using AWS DataSync for transferring data between regions
C) Implementing AWS Direct Connect for dedicated inter-region communication
D) Enabling AWS Artifact for compliance documentation of replication processes
E) Deploying AWS VPN connections between primary and secondary regions

QUESTION 8

You are designing a web application that requires user authentication and authorization. The application must support social identity providers such as Google and Facebook for user sign-in. Additionally, the application needs to ensure secure access to AWS resources for authenticated users. Which of the following options is the most suitable solution for implementing secure application access and user management?

A) Using AWS Secrets Manager for storing social identity provider credentials
B) Configuring AWS Cognito user pools with social identity federation for user authentication
C) Implementing AWS IAM roles and policies for controlling access to AWS resources
D) Enabling AWS Single Sign-On (SSO) for centralized user management and access control
E) Deploying Amazon API Gateway with OAuth 2.0 authorization for API access

QUESTION 9

Your company is developing a microservices architecture for a real-time analytics application. Security is paramount, and compliance regulations require encryption for data at rest. Additionally, the architecture must ensure efficient communication between services. Which approach best meets these requirements?

A) Deploying microservices in Amazon EKS with AWS Fargate for serverless container deployment, ensuring efficient communication and scalability, and configuring Amazon RDS with encryption at rest and fine-grained access controls for data storage, meeting security and compliance requirements

B) Implementing mutual TLS authentication between microservices in Amazon ECS, ensuring secure communication and encryption, and utilizing Amazon DynamoDB with encryption at rest for data storage, meeting security and compliance requirements

C) Leveraging AWS App Mesh for managing microservices traffic, ensuring efficient communication and scalability, and implementing Amazon S3 with server-side encryption for data storage, meeting security and compliance requirements

D) Configuring AWS Lambda for serverless microservice deployment, ensuring efficient communication and scalability, and deploying Amazon Redshift with encryption at rest for data storage, meeting security and compliance requirements

E) Utilizing AWS PrivateLink for private communication between microservices, ensuring efficient communication and scalability, and utilizing Amazon Aurora with encryption at rest and in-transit for data storage, meeting security and compliance requirements

QUESTION 10

An international news agency is looking to improve the efficiency of video file uploads from field reporters to Amazon S3 for quick news turn-around. Reporters often work in areas with variable internet connectivity. Which AWS solutions should the agency implement to ensure fast and reliable uploads regardless of the reporters' location?

A) Configure AWS Snowball devices for physical data transport from field locations.
B) Enable Amazon S3 Transfer Acceleration to speed up file uploads.
C) Set up AWS Direct Connect links at main offices for enhanced connectivity.
D) Use AWS DataSync for automated and accelerated file transfer.
E) Implement multipart uploads alongside Amazon S3 Transfer Acceleration.

QUESTION 11

A research institution needs to store large datasets resulting from their studies securely. The storage solution must offer both high durability and security, including at-rest encryption and controlled access for multiple research teams, each with different access rights. Furthermore, the institution requires the ability to analyze this data periodically without moving it from its secure location.

A) Configure Amazon S3 with S3 bucket policies for fine-grained access control, enable server-side encryption with AWS KMS for at-rest encryption, and use Amazon Athena for in-place querying.

B) Deploy Amazon EFS with encryption at rest, use network file system (NFS) permissions for access control, and integrate with Amazon Redshift for data analysis.

C) Implement Amazon FSx for Lustre, use POSIX-compliant file permissions for access control, and utilize AWS Glue for data cataloging and ETL processes.

D) Utilize Amazon DynamoDB with encryption at rest enabled, IAM policies for access management, and Amazon EMR for data analysis.

E) Set up AWS Storage Gateway in a file gateway configuration for on-premises access to S3, enable encryption with AWS KMS, and use Amazon SageMaker for data analysis.

QUESTION 12

An online gaming company is launching a new game that requires frequent updates and hotfixes to enhance player experience and maintain security. They need a secure deployment process that allows for quick updates with minimal player disruption. The process must include mechanisms for automatic scaling based on player demand, instant rollback in case of issues with new releases, and rigorous security checks before deployment to production environments.

A) Use AWS CodeDeploy for automated deployments, Amazon CloudWatch alarms for rollback triggers, and AWS Auto Scaling to adjust resources based on load.

B) Implement AWS Elastic Beanstalk for application deployment, enabling Elastic Load Balancing for traffic distribution, and AWS WAF for pre-deployment security checks.

C) Configure AWS CodePipeline for continuous integration and delivery, integrate AWS Lambda for custom deployment scripts, and Amazon S3 for storing secure artifacts.

D) Leverage Amazon ECS with AWS Fargate for deploying containerized game updates, set up AWS CodeStar for project management, and Amazon Inspector for security assessments.

E) Deploy with Amazon EC2 instances managed through AWS Systems Manager for patching and updates, utilize Amazon RDS with Multi-AZ deployments for database scaling, and AWS Shield for advanced DDoS protection.

QUESTION 13

An online gaming platform is looking to enhance their security posture by implementing a comprehensive logging and monitoring solution that can detect and automatically respond to security incidents, such as unauthorized access attempts or abnormal user behavior. They also want the ability to perform forensic analysis in case of a security breach.

A) Use AWS CloudTrail for logging API calls, Amazon GuardDuty for detecting suspicious activities, and Amazon CloudWatch for monitoring and alerts.

B) Implement AWS Lambda for automated incident response, AWS WAF for filtering malicious traffic, and Amazon S3 for storing log files securely.

C) Deploy Amazon Inspector for automated security assessments, Amazon CloudWatch Logs Insights for log analysis, and AWS Step Functions for orchestrating incident response workflows.

D) Configure Amazon GuardDuty for threat detection, AWS Security Hub for centralized security monitoring, and AWS Lambda functions for executing remediation actions based on alerts.

E) Leverage AWS Config for continuous configuration audit and recording, AWS Shield for DDoS protection, and Amazon S3 Glacier for long-term log storage and forensic analysis.

QUESTION 14

A healthcare organization needs to securely store and manage patient data in compliance with HIPAA regulations while ensuring high availability and performance. As an AWS Solutions Architect, which solution architecture would you recommend to meet these requirements effectively? Select TWO.

A) Deploy Amazon RDS Multi-AZ with encryption for database storage to ensure high availability and data security compliance with HIPAA regulations.

B) Utilize Amazon S3 with server-side encryption and versioning enabled for secure and compliant storage of patient data.

C) Implement AWS Direct Connect to establish private connectivity between on-premises systems and AWS for secure data transfer and compliance with HIPAA regulations.

D) Set up Amazon CloudFront with AWS WAF to protect against common web exploits and ensure secure content delivery for healthcare applications.

E) Utilize Amazon API Gateway with AWS Lambda for serverless backend to handle variable traffic and reduce operational costs while maintaining compliance with HIPAA regulations.

QUESTION 15

A gaming company is encountering challenges in managing maintenance tasks on specific Amazon EC2 instances within an Auto Scaling group. Whenever maintenance patches are applied, the instances briefly show as out of service, leading to Auto Scaling provisioning replacements. What strategies would you recommend as a solutions architect to efficiently handle this issue?

A) Suspend the ReplaceUnhealthy process type for the Auto Scaling group and apply the maintenance patch to the instance. Once the instance is ready, manually set the instance's health status back to healthy and activate the ReplaceUnhealthy process type again.

B) Suspend the HealthCheck process type for the Auto Scaling group and apply the maintenance patch to the instance. Once the instance is ready, manually set the instance's health status back to healthy and activate the HealthCheck process type again.

C) Put the instance into the Detached state and the update the instance by applying the maintenance patch. Once the instance is ready, exit the Detached state and then return the instance to service.

D) Temporarily suspend the AddToLoadBalancer process type for the Auto Scaling group and apply the maintenance patch to the instance. Once the instance is ready, manually set the instance's health status back to healthy and activate the AddToLoadBalancer process type again.

E) Take a snapshot of the instance, create a new Amazon Machine Image (AMI), and then launch a new instance using this AMI. Apply the maintenance patch to this new instance and then add it back to the Auto Scaling Group by using the manual scaling policy. Terminate the earlier instance that had the maintenance issue.

QUESTION 16

An e-commerce company operating globally requires a low-latency network architecture to connect its distributed AWS environments. The architecture must support rapid scaling, high resilience, and secure communication across AWS regions and their on-premises data centers.

A) Architect a global network using AWS Global Accelerator and AWS Transit Gateway for optimized path selection.

B) Deploy multiple AWS Site-to-Site VPN connections with Amazon Route 53 for latency-based routing.

C) Use AWS Direct Connect and AWS Transit Gateway, with Direct Connect Gateways for multi-region connectivity.

D) Implement a meshed network topology with inter-region VPC peering and Amazon CloudFront for content delivery.

E) Configure AWS Transit Gateway with AWS Shield Advanced for secure, scalable multi-region connectivity.

QUESTION 17

A software development company is moving its DevOps pipeline to AWS to take advantage of cloud flexibility and enhance security. The migration must optimize for continuous integration/continuous deployment (CI/CD) workflows, support scalable compute resources, and ensure code and artifacts are securely managed and stored.

A) Use AWS CodePipeline for CI/CD workflows, AWS CodeBuild for secure code compilation, and Amazon ECR for storing container images.

B) Implement Amazon WorkSpaces for development environments, AWS Lambda for scalable compute resources, and AWS CodeCommit for secure code storage.

C) Configure AWS Snowball Edge for codebase transfer, Amazon EC2 Auto Scaling for compute scalability, and AWS Key Management Service (KMS) for encryption key management.

D) Leverage AWS DataSync for transferring application code, Amazon ECS for container management, and Amazon CodeGuru for security analysis of code.

E) Apply AWS Direct Connect for connecting to AWS, AWS Fargate for serverless container execution, and Amazon S3 with versioning for artifact storage.

QUESTION 18

A healthcare organization is migrating its legacy applications to AWS and needs to securely manage database credentials and other secrets. The organization wants to automate the rotation of secrets to enhance security and compliance. Which of the following solutions would best address the organization's requirements?

A) Implement AWS Secrets Manager to store database credentials and other secrets. Configure rotation policies within Secrets Manager to automatically rotate credentials according to predefined schedules.

 B) Store secrets in plaintext format within an encrypted Amazon RDS instance. Implement custom scripts on EC2 instances to manually rotate secrets when necessary.

 C) Utilize AWS Systems Manager Parameter Store to centrally manage secrets and configurations. Develop AWS Lambda functions to trigger secret rotation based on predefined events or schedules.

 D) Maintain secrets in a spreadsheet stored in an encrypted Amazon S3 bucket. Use AWS CloudWatch Events to trigger AWS Lambda functions for secret rotation based on predefined conditions.

 E) Implement a custom secrets management solution using AWS Lambda and DynamoDB. Store secrets in DynamoDB tables encrypted with AWS KMS and schedule Lambda functions to rotate secrets periodically.

QUESTION 19

A technology startup is building a microservices architecture on AWS using AWS Fargate for container orchestration. They need to implement secure management of secrets and sensitive data within their containerized applications. Which of the following approaches would best suit the startup's requirements?

A) Embed secrets directly within Docker containers as environment variables. Utilize IAM roles with least privilege access for containers to retrieve secrets at runtime.

B) Implement AWS Secrets Manager to securely store and rotate secrets. Integrate applications running on Fargate with Secrets Manager for secure retrieval of secrets.

C) Store secrets in plaintext files within Docker volumes attached to containers. Implement IAM policies to control access to the Docker volumes.

D) Utilize AWS Systems Manager Parameter Store to manage secrets centrally. Develop custom scripts within containers to fetch secrets from Parameter Store.

E) Maintain a spreadsheet containing sensitive information stored in an encrypted Amazon S3 bucket. Use IAM policies to control access to the S3 bucket and retrieve secrets at runtime.

QUESTION 20

A technology company encountered a sudden surge in unauthorized AWS API queries during non-business hours, with no discernible impact on system performance. The management requires an automated solution to promptly alert relevant teams during such occurrences. Which approach would be most effective in this scenario?

A) Create an Amazon CloudWatch metric filter to process AWS CloudTrail logs containing API call details. Establish an alarm based on this metric's rate to send an Amazon SNS notification to the required team.

B) Implement AWS Config Rules to monitor API activity and define rules to detect unauthorized API calls. Configure AWS Config to trigger an AWS Lambda function upon rule evaluation to notify relevant stakeholders.

C) Leverage AWS Trusted Advisor to publish metrics about check results to Amazon CloudWatch. Set up an alarm to track status changes for checks in the Service Limits category for the APIs, triggering notifications when service quotas are exceeded.

D) Use Amazon Athena SQL queries against AWS CloudTrail log files stored in Amazon S3 buckets. Generate reports using Amazon QuickSight for managerial dashboards.

E) Configure AWS CloudTrail to stream event data to Amazon Kinesis. Utilize Amazon Kinesis stream-level metrics in Amazon CloudWatch to trigger an AWS Lambda function that will initiate an error workflow.

QUESTION 21

A media streaming company is designing an architecture to process incoming video files uploaded by users. They want to ensure that the system can handle sudden spikes in upload traffic without losing data. What solution should they implement?

A) Utilize Amazon Kinesis Data Streams for real-time processing of video uploads.
B) Implement Amazon SQS to queue video upload requests and trigger processing tasks with AWS Lambda.

C) Use Amazon S3 as the storage backend and trigger AWS Batch jobs for processing uploaded videos.

D) Employ Amazon SNS to fan out video upload notifications to multiple processing services.

E) Utilize AWS Direct Connect for high-speed, dedicated network connectivity to handle upload spikes.

QUESTION 22

Your team is designing a serverless application that requires event-driven architecture and high availability. The application needs to process user requests in real-time with minimal latency. Which combination of AWS services should you use to build this serverless application?

A) AWS Lambda for serverless compute with event-driven triggers

B) Amazon API Gateway for HTTP endpoints with built-in caching

C) Amazon DynamoDB for NoSQL database with auto-scaling

D) Amazon S3 for object storage with server-side encryption

E) Amazon SQS for message queuing with dead-letter queues

QUESTION 23

A multinational e-commerce company is redesigning its data storage architecture to ensure scalability and security for its expanding customer base. The company requires a solution that can efficiently handle large volumes of customer data while maintaining high levels of data security. Which AWS service should the company consider to meet these requirements?

A) Utilize Amazon S3 with versioning enabled and cross-region replication for data durability and availability.

B) Implement Amazon EFS with automatic lifecycle policies and encryption at rest for scalable and secure file storage.

C) Deploy Amazon RDS with Multi-AZ deployment and encryption at rest for scalable and secure relational database storage.

D) Utilize Amazon EBS with Provisioned IOPS SSD volumes and snapshots for scalable and secure block storage.

E) Implement AWS Backup with centralized management and Amazon S3 integration for automated backup and recovery operations.

QUESTION 24

A multinational corporation is looking to optimize its cloud infrastructure costs while ensuring high availability and performance for its global workforce. The company's current AWS bill is significantly higher than anticipated, and they need to identify the underlying reasons for the high costs. Which solution would best address this scenario?

A) Utilize AWS Cost Explorer to analyze cost trends and identify areas of overspending.

B) Implement AWS Trusted Advisor to receive recommendations for cost optimization based on best practices.

C) Configure AWS Budgets to set cost thresholds and receive alerts when expenditures exceed predefined limits.

D) Deploy AWS Compute Optimizer to analyze resource utilization and identify opportunities for rightsizing instances.

E) Set up AWS Savings Plans to automatically apply discounts to usage patterns and reduce overall costs.

QUESTION 25

A regional news network is launching a live news streaming service catering to viewers in specific states within a country. They need to ensure that only viewers from those states can access the live streams. How can they effectively enforce this restriction?

A) Use Amazon Route 53 based geolocation routing policy to restrict access to viewers located in the designated states

B) Implement Amazon Route 53 based weighted routing policy to distribute traffic evenly across the designated states

C) Utilize Amazon Route 53 based latency-based routing policy to direct viewers to the nearest regional streaming server for improved performance

D) Employ Amazon Route 53 based failover routing policy to redirect traffic to alternative servers in case of server failures

E) Apply Amazon Route 53 based geoproximity routing policy to direct traffic based on the proximity of viewers to regional streaming servers

QUESTION 26

A healthcare organization is migrating its legacy applications to AWS to modernize its infrastructure and improve security and compliance. The organization aims to implement immutable infrastructure to enhance deployment reliability and minimize configuration errors. Which service should the solutions architect recommend for implementing immutable infrastructure on AWS?

A) Utilize AWS AppConfig to manage application configurations dynamically and perform A/B testing to validate changes before deploying them to production environments.

B) Implement AWS CloudFormation to define infrastructure as code and automate the deployment of AWS resources in a consistent and repeatable manner, promoting immutable infrastructure.

C) Use AWS Systems Manager to automate administrative tasks across AWS resources, enabling efficient management and maintenance of infrastructure configurations.

D) Leverage Amazon EKS Anywhere to deploy Kubernetes clusters on-premises and ensure consistent infrastructure management across hybrid environments.

E) Configure Amazon ECS Anywhere to run containerized applications on-premises and in the cloud, ensuring consistency and portability across environments.

QUESTION 27

An online gaming company is designing a microservices architecture to support its multiplayer gaming platform. The company needs a solution for discovering and communicating with microservices across different environments. Which option enables effective microservices discovery and direct communication with Amazon API Gateway?

A) Implement AWS Lambda functions to act as service registries and use Amazon SNS for asynchronous communication between microservices

B) Utilize AWS App Mesh to manage microservices communication and implement Amazon API Gateway for external API access

C) Deploy microservices as Docker containers on Amazon ECS and use AWS App Runner for service discovery and routing based on HTTP paths

D) Utilize Amazon ECS Service Discovery with Route 53 for DNS-based service discovery and implement API Gateway REST APIs for client communication

E) Configure AWS Direct Connect to establish private connectivity between microservices running in different VPCs and use API Gateway for API management and access control

QUESTION 28

A logistics company is designing a real-time tracking system for its fleet using AWS. The system will use containerized microservices for scalability and rapid deployment. The company needs to ensure robust monitoring, logging, and quick scalability to handle varying loads, especially during peak shipping periods. Which AWS services and strategies should be incorporated to fulfill these operational requirements effectively?

A) Implement Amazon ECS with Auto Scaling, integrate with Amazon CloudWatch for monitoring and logging, use Amazon ECR for secure image storage, and AWS CloudFormation for infrastructure as code.

B) Deploy Amazon EKS with AWS Fargate for serverless compute, use Amazon MSK for handling fleet messages, integrate Amazon CloudWatch for monitoring, and leverage AWS Lambda for event-driven scalability.

C) Use Amazon ECS with EC2 launch type, leverage Amazon SNS for notification services, integrate AWS X-Ray for tracing, and use Amazon RDS for data storage.

D) Opt for Amazon EKS, implement Kubernetes Horizontal Pod Autoscaler for scalability, use Amazon CloudWatch Logs Insights for in-depth log analysis, and Amazon ECR for container image management.

E) Choose Amazon ECS with Fargate, integrate AWS Step Functions for orchestrating microservices, use AWS Elastic Beanstalk for application deployment, and leverage Amazon CloudWatch for monitoring and logging.

QUESTION 29

A gaming company wants to deploy its multiplayer game globally while ensuring low latency and high availability. Which AWS service or feature should they use to route users to the nearest game server?

A) Amazon Route 53 with latency-based routing
B) AWS Global Accelerator for improved global application performance
C) Amazon CloudFront with geo-routing for traffic distribution

D) Amazon VPC peering for private connectivity between game servers

E) Amazon API Gateway for managing API requests from game clients

QUESTION 30

A social media platform wants to enable third-party developers to build applications that interact with its platform through APIs. They need to ensure security and scalability while providing access to various functionalities. Which approach should they adopt using Amazon API Gateway to fulfill this requirement?

A) Utilize RESTful APIs on Amazon API Gateway with OAuth 2.0 authentication and authorization for third-party access

B) Implement WebSocket APIs on Amazon API Gateway with API keys for third-party developers

C) Create HTTP APIs on Amazon API Gateway with AWS IAM authentication for third-party application access

D) Deploy GraphQL APIs on Amazon API Gateway with AWS Cognito user pools for third-party authentication

E) Configure RESTful APIs on Amazon API Gateway with custom authorizers using AWS Lambda for third-party access control

QUESTION 31

A global retail company is deploying a new application on AWS that must comply with international data protection regulations, including the GDPR. They need to continuously monitor their AWS environment to ensure compliance and quickly remediate any non-compliant resources. Which combination of AWS services would best enable automated compliance monitoring and remediation for their international operations?

A) AWS Config for monitoring resource compliance, AWS CloudTrail for tracking user activity, AWS Lambda for automated remediation tasks, and Amazon GuardDuty for threat detection.

B) Amazon QuickSight for compliance dashboards, AWS WAF for application security, Amazon Cognito for user authentication, and Amazon RDS for secure data storage.

C) AWS KMS for encryption key management, AWS Secrets Manager for handling secrets, Amazon VPC for network security, and AWS IAM for access control.

D) Amazon Inspector for security vulnerability assessments, AWS Trusted Advisor for best practice checks, AWS Fargate for container security, and Amazon S3 for encrypted data storage.

E) Amazon EC2 for compute resources, Amazon EBS for block storage with encryption, AWS CodeBuild for secure code deployment, and AWS Step Functions for workflow automation.

QUESTION 32

A technology startup is designing a disaster recovery (DR) strategy for its cloud-native application. The solution must ensure rapid recovery and scalability while minimizing costs. Which combination of AWS services and features should the startup use to achieve these objectives effectively?

A) Deploy Amazon Aurora Serverless with auto-scaling and provisioned Aurora Capacity Units (ACUs) for predictable performance during peak hours.

B) Utilize Amazon DynamoDB with on-demand scaling and DynamoDB Streams for real-time data replication and failover across Regions.

C) Implement Amazon RDS with Multi-AZ deployment and utilize read replicas for scaling read operations during peak hours.

D) Migrate to Amazon Redshift for analytics and scalability and use Redshift Concurrency Scaling for handling concurrent queries during peak hours.

E) Implement Amazon DocumentDB with MongoDB compatibility and use DocumentDB global clusters for cross-Region replication and failover.

QUESTION 33

Your organization is looking to optimize costs while ensuring the reliability and performance of its AWS infrastructure. What approach would best achieve this balance for your architecture?

A) Utilize AWS Auto Scaling to automatically adjust resources based on demand.
B) Store sensitive data in plaintext within DynamoDB tables.
C) Implement AWS Lambda functions for serverless computing.
D) Deploy microservices in a single AWS region without redundancy.
E) Use Amazon S3 for long-term storage of sensitive data without encryption.

QUESTION 34

Your company is planning to implement a data lake solution on AWS to store and analyze large volumes of structured and unstructured data. Cost optimization is a critical factor in the design, and you need to select the most cost-effective storage solution for long-term retention of infrequently accessed data. Which AWS service should you choose for this scenario?

A) Amazon S3 Glacier
B) Utilize Amazon EBS volumes for block storage
C) Deploy Amazon RDS with data archiving enabled
D) Implement Amazon Elastic File System (Amazon EFS) for shared file storage
E) Utilize Amazon Aurora Serverless for on-demand database capacity

QUESTION 35

A media streaming platform wants to develop a content recommendation system to enhance user engagement. They require a solution that can analyze user interactions with different media content and suggest relevant content in real-time. Which configuration should they implement using AWS serverless components to meet these requirements effectively?

A) Utilize AWS Lambda with Amazon S3 for processing user interactions and Amazon RDS for storing recommendation data

B) Implement Amazon Kinesis Data Firehose with AWS Lambda for processing user interactions and Amazon ElastiCache for storing recommendation data

C) Ingest user interactions into Amazon Kinesis Data Streams, which triggers an AWS Lambda function for processing and stores recommendation data in Amazon DynamoDB

D) Ingest user interactions into Amazon SQS, which triggers an AWS Lambda function for processing and stores recommendation data in Amazon Redshift

E) Use Amazon API Gateway to ingest user interactions, which are processed by an application running on an Amazon EC2 instance, and store recommendation data in Amazon Elasticsearch Service

QUESTION 36

Your company is planning to migrate its legacy database infrastructure to AWS to improve scalability and reduce operational overhead. The database contains sensitive financial data that must be encrypted to comply with industry regulations. As the solution architect, how would you design the encryption strategy for the AWS-hosted database to ensure compliance and data security while minimizing performance impact? Select TWO.

A) Deploy Amazon Aurora with encryption at rest enabled and utilize AWS KMS for managing encryption keys securely. Implement AWS Direct Connect for dedicated network connectivity to the database.

B) Utilize Amazon RDS with encryption at rest enabled and configure AWS Certificate Manager (ACM) for SSL/TLS certificates in the application layer.

C) Implement Amazon DynamoDB with client-side encryption enabled and use AWS CloudHSM for secure key storage and management.

D) Deploy Amazon Redshift with encryption at rest enabled and leverage AWS Secrets Manager for managing encryption keys securely. Configure Amazon CloudFront with SSL/TLS termination at the edge for secure database access.

E) Utilize Amazon DocumentDB with encryption at rest enabled and leverage AWS Certificate Manager (ACM) for SSL/TLS certificates to encrypt data in transit.

QUESTION 37

A multinational corporation requires a secure, scalable, and highly available storage solution for storing confidential documents that must be accessible across various global offices. Which configuration ensures data security and compliance with minimal latency?

A) Use AWS Snowball for secure, large-scale data transfers into Amazon S3, then enable Amazon S3 Transfer Acceleration.
B) Deploy Amazon EFS with encryption at rest and in transit, accessible over AWS Direct Connect.
C) Implement Amazon S3 with default encryption, cross-region replication, and Amazon CloudFront for distribution.
D) Configure Amazon RDS with encryption at rest and Multi-AZ deployment for storing documents.
E) Leverage Amazon S3 Glacier with Vault Lock for secure and compliant archival storage.

QUESTION 38

Your company is building a new social media platform that requires real-time data analytics on user interactions, such as likes, comments, and shares. The platform needs to handle unpredictable spikes in traffic while ensuring low-latency access to analytics data. Which combination of AWS services would you recommend to design a high-performing and scalable analytics architecture for this social media platform?

A) Utilize Amazon Kinesis Data Firehose to capture streaming data and load it into Amazon Redshift for analytics processing.

B) Deploy Amazon DynamoDB for storing user interaction data and perform real-time analytics using Amazon Kinesis Data Analytics.

C) Implement Amazon Redshift Spectrum to query data directly from the data lake stored in Amazon S3 for real-time analytics.

D) Configure Amazon RDS with Multi-AZ deployment and read replicas to handle unpredictable spikes in traffic and ensure low-latency access to analytics data.

E) Utilize Amazon Managed Streaming for Apache Kafka (Amazon MSK) to ingest streaming data and process it in real-time using Apache Flink on Amazon EMR.

QUESTION 39

A manufacturing company is looking to build a scalable data ingestion pipeline for processing sensor data from IoT devices deployed across its factories globally. The solution must ensure high availability, reliability, and real-time processing of sensor data. What architecture should the company implement?

A) Deploy AWS IoT Core for ingesting sensor data, and use AWS Lambda for real-time data processing.
B) Utilize Amazon Redshift for data warehousing, and leverage Amazon S3 for storing sensor data.
C) Implement Amazon Kinesis Data Streams for ingesting sensor data, and use Amazon EMR for batch processing of analytics data.
D) Configure Amazon S3 Glacier for long-term storage of sensor data, and use Amazon DynamoDB for real-time analytics.
E) Utilize AWS IoT Greengrass for edge processing of sensor data, and deploy Amazon RDS for storing processed sensor data.

QUESTION 40

A media company is storing sensitive video content in Amazon S3 and requires encryption of the data at rest. However, the company wants to manage the encryption keys on-premises and securely upload the encrypted data to Amazon S3. Which option would be the most appropriate solution for this requirement?

A) Utilize server-side encryption with Amazon S3 managed keys (SSE-S3) to encrypt the data on Amazon S3

B) Implement client-side encryption with customer-provided keys (SSE-C) and upload the encrypted data to Amazon S3

C) Use server-side encryption with AWS Key Management Service (SSE-KMS) keys to encrypt the data on Amazon S3

D) Use server-side encryption with customer-provided keys (SSE-C) to encrypt the data on Amazon S3
E) Enable AWS CloudTrail to monitor S3 bucket activities for auditing purposes

QUESTION 41

An entertainment company wishes to create a serverless backend for their new mobile game that can scale to accommodate millions of users, collect gameplay data, and analyze player behavior to offer personalized experiences. The architecture must ensure low latency, high availability, and real-time data processing capabilities. What AWS services would form the backbone of this backend?

A) Amazon Kinesis for data ingestion, AWS Lambda for data processing, Amazon DynamoDB for user data storage.

B) AWS Global Accelerator for performance optimization, Amazon RDS for gameplay data storage, Amazon SNS for user notifications.

C) Amazon API Gateway for handling API requests, Amazon SQS for queuing messages, AWS Fargate for running backend services.

D) Amazon CloudFront for content delivery, AWS Step Functions for orchestrating user interactions, Amazon S3 for storing static assets.

E) AWS AppSync for real-time data synchronization, Amazon Elasticache for low-latency data access, Amazon EKS for Kubernetes cluster management.

QUESTION 42

Your company is designing a hybrid cloud architecture to support real-time data analytics applications that require low-latency access to on-premises data sources. You need to ensure high performance and resilience for these applications while minimizing costs. Which combination of AWS services would best meet these requirements?

A) Implement AWS Direct Connect for secure connectivity between on-premises data sources and Amazon Kinesis for real-time data ingestion. Utilize Amazon Redshift for data warehousing and analysis.

B) Deploy AWS Storage Gateway with caching mode for data synchronization between on-premises storage systems and Amazon S3. Utilize Amazon Athena for querying data in Amazon S3.

C) Utilize AWS AppSync for real-time data synchronization between on-premises databases and Amazon DynamoDB for low-latency access. Utilize Amazon QuickSight for data visualization and analysis.

D) Configure AWS DataSync for efficient data transfer between on-premises storage systems and Amazon S3. Utilize Amazon EMR for real-time data processing and analysis.

E) Implement AWS VPN for secure connectivity between on-premises data sources and Amazon RDS for data storage. Utilize AWS Lambda for real-time data processing and analysis.

QUESTION 43

A software development company is creating a collaborative code editing platform accessible globally. The platform must support real-time code collaboration, version control, and integration with multiple development tools. It requires a scalable architecture that minimizes latency for users distributed around the world and ensures secure access and storage of code. What AWS services and configurations should the company implement to build this platform efficiently?

A) Integrate AWS CodeCommit for version control, Amazon WorkSpaces for a cloud desktop environment, AWS Lambda for real-time collaboration logic, and Amazon CloudFront for global content delivery.

B) Utilize Amazon EC2 instances for hosting the platform, AWS Direct Connect for reduced latency, Amazon EFS for shared file storage, and AWS CodePipeline for continuous integration/continuous deployment (CI/CD).

C) Deploy Amazon Chime SDK for real-time collaboration, Amazon DynamoDB for storing user data and code snippets, Amazon S3 for versioned code storage, and AWS Global Accelerator to optimize application performance.

D) Use Amazon API Gateway for RESTful API management, Amazon DynamoDB and Amazon S3 with cross-region replication for data storage, AWS AppSync for real-time data synchronization, and Amazon CloudFront for distributing static assets.

E) Implement AWS Amplify for full-stack app development, AWS Fargate for running containers without managing servers, Amazon RDS with Multi-AZ deployment for relational data storage, and Amazon SQS for message queuing between services.

QUESTION 44

Your company is tasked with improving the speed and efficiency of machine learning model inference using Amazon SageMaker endpoints. The solution must ensure low latency and high throughput for serving predictions to users. Which architecture would be most appropriate for achieving this goal?

A) Utilize Amazon SageMaker for real-time inference, integrating Amazon DynamoDB for model storage and Amazon CloudWatch for monitoring.

B) Implement Amazon SageMaker for batch inference, leveraging Amazon RDS for model storage and Amazon CloudWatch for performance monitoring.

C) Deploy Amazon SageMaker for real-time inference with AWS Lambda for serverless, event-driven processing, storing model artifacts in Amazon S3 for quick access.

D) Utilize Amazon SageMaker for real-time inference, integrating Amazon Aurora for model storage and Amazon CloudWatch for monitoring.

E) Implement Amazon SageMaker for real-time inference with Amazon Elastic File System (Amazon EFS) for shared model storage, utilizing Amazon CloudWatch for monitoring and optimization.

QUESTION 45

A gaming company operates a multiplayer online game with variable player activity throughout the day. The company needs a cost-effective solution that can handle sudden spikes in player traffic without incurring high infrastructure costs. Which pricing option for Amazon EC2 instances would be the most suitable choice for this scenario?

A) Use reserved instances (RI) for the entire duration of operation
B) Implement on-demand instances for the entire duration of operation
C) Utilize spot instances for the entire duration of operation
D) Employ a combination of reserved instances (RI) and spot instances
E) Implement a mix of reserved instances (RI) and on-demand instances

QUESTION 46

You are tasked with designing a solution for a financial services company to securely process and analyze large volumes of transaction data in real-time. The solution must comply with industry regulations for data security and privacy. Which architecture would you recommend for this scenario?

A) Utilize Amazon Kinesis Data Streams for ingesting real-time data, process data using AWS Lambda, store processed data in Amazon RDS with encryption, and use Amazon CloudFront for content delivery.

B) Implement an event-driven architecture using Amazon EventBridge for data ingestion, process data using AWS Glue, store processed data in Amazon Redshift with encryption, and utilize Amazon CloudFront for content delivery.

C) Deploy containers on Amazon ECS for data ingestion, process data using Amazon EMR, store processed data in Amazon S3 with encryption, and leverage Amazon CloudFront for content delivery.

D) Utilize Amazon Kinesis Data Firehose for ingesting real-time data, process data using AWS Glue, store processed data in Amazon DynamoDB with encryption, and use Amazon CloudFront for content delivery.

E) Implement a serverless architecture using Amazon S3 for data ingestion, process data using AWS Glue, store processed data in Amazon Redshift with encryption, and utilize Amazon CloudFront for content delivery.

QUESTION 47

You are tasked with designing a solution for a media streaming platform that needs to deliver high-quality video content to a global audience. The architecture must provide low-latency streaming, high availability, and cost efficiency. Which approach would best meet these requirements?

A) Utilize Amazon EC2 instances with AWS Auto Scaling and Amazon RDS for database storage, leverage Amazon CloudFront for content delivery, and use Amazon ElastiCache for caching frequently accessed data.

B) Implement a serverless architecture with AWS Lambda@Edge for compute, Amazon DynamoDB for database needs, and Amazon S3 for storing video files.

C) Deploy the application on AWS Outposts for data residency requirements, use Amazon Redshift for real-time analytics, and leverage Amazon CloudWatch for monitoring.

D) Utilize Amazon ECS for container orchestration, Amazon Kinesis Video Streams for real-time video processing, and Amazon Route 53 for DNS routing.

E) Implement edge computing using AWS Wavelength for deploying applications close to users, leverage Amazon CloudFront for content delivery, and use Amazon Aurora for high-performance database needs.

QUESTION 48

A financial institution operates a trading platform that requires low-latency access and high availability. The platform experiences predictable usage patterns during trading hours and occasional spikes during market volatility. The institution aims to optimize infrastructure costs while ensuring reliable performance. Which pricing option for Amazon EC2 instances would be the most appropriate choice for this scenario?

A) Use reserved instances (RI) for the entire duration of operation

B) Implement on-demand instances for the entire duration of operation

C) Utilize spot instances for the entire duration of operation

D) Employ a combination of reserved instances (RI) and spot instances

E) Implement a mix of reserved instances (RI) and on-demand instances

QUESTION 49

You are tasked with optimizing the performance of a serverless application hosted on AWS Lambda. The application performs image processing tasks triggered by events from Amazon S3. However, the current configuration experiences latency issues during peak usage periods. What would be the most effective approach to improve the performance of the application?

A) Increase the memory allocation for AWS Lambda functions to improve processing speed, and utilize Amazon CloudFront for caching frequently accessed images. Implement Amazon API Gateway caching to reduce latency for repeated requests, and leverage Amazon CloudWatch for performance monitoring.

B) Optimize the code logic within AWS Lambda functions to reduce execution time, and enable concurrent executions to process multiple events simultaneously. Implement Amazon DynamoDB Accelerator (DAX) to cache image metadata for faster retrieval, and use Amazon CloudWatch for performance monitoring.

C) Deploy AWS Lambda functions in multiple AWS regions to distribute processing load geographically, and use Amazon S3 Transfer Acceleration for faster data uploads. Implement Amazon CloudFront with Lambda@Edge for image resizing and optimization, and utilize Amazon CloudWatch for performance monitoring.

D) Implement Amazon SQS as a buffer between Amazon S3 events and AWS Lambda functions to handle bursts of incoming events more efficiently. Configure AWS Lambda provisioned concurrency to maintain a pool of warm instances, and leverage AWS X-Ray for performance monitoring and tracing.

E) Increase the timeout configuration for AWS Lambda functions to allow longer processing times, and implement Amazon S3 Event Notifications with AWS Step Functions to parallelize image processing tasks. Utilize Amazon CloudWatch Logs Insights for real-time performance analysis, and leverage Amazon CloudFront for content delivery optimization.

QUESTION 50

Your company operates a web application that experiences significant fluctuations in traffic throughout the day. During peak hours, the application needs to scale dynamically to accommodate increased user demand while maintaining cost efficiency. Which approach would be most suitable for optimizing performance and cost during peak traffic periods?

A) Utilize Amazon EC2 Spot Instances to handle peak traffic periods, leveraging the cost savings of Spot Instances for temporary compute capacity. Implement Amazon CloudWatch alarms to trigger scaling actions based on CPU utilization, ensuring optimal resource allocation.

B) Deploy Amazon RDS Multi-AZ deployment for a managed relational database service, ensuring high availability and durability during peak traffic periods. Utilize Amazon ElastiCache for caching frequently accessed data, reducing database load and improving application performance.

C) Implement Amazon DynamoDB with provisioned capacity to handle peak traffic periods, ensuring consistent performance and scalability. Configure auto-scaling for DynamoDB read and write capacity, dynamically adjusting resources based on workload demands.

D) Utilize AWS Lambda functions to handle incoming requests during peak traffic periods, reducing the need for constantly running EC2 instances. Store application data in Amazon Aurora Serverless for on-demand scalability, optimizing resource utilization and cost efficiency.

E) Leverage Amazon SQS as a message queue to decouple application components and handle bursts of incoming requests. Use Amazon ECS with Fargate to deploy containerized application components, ensuring efficient resource utilization and automatic scaling based on workload demand.

QUESTION 51

A global content provider wants to optimize their live streaming service for high performance and cost efficiency. They plan to use Amazon CloudFront, Amazon S3, and AWS Lambda@Edge. Which approach ensures efficient delivery and cost control?

A) Configure CloudFront with price class set to use all edge locations and Lambda@Edge for content manipulation.

B) Set up CloudFront with a limited set of edge locations closest to the user base, and use Amazon S3 transfer acceleration for content delivery.

C) Use CloudFront with an optimized cache policy and S3 origin, employing Lambda@Edge for content compression and customization.

D) Implement a multi-CDN strategy using CloudFront and another CDN provider, with S3 as the origin.

E) Deploy CloudFront with AWS WAF and AWS Shield for security, disregarding edge location selection for cost control.

QUESTION 52

An online gaming company wants to dynamically scale its fleet of Amazon EC2 instances based on demand to maintain game server performance. Which configuration optimally adjusts the number of instances in response to player traffic?

A) Configure a static number of instances to match peak expected traffic.
B) Utilize an EC2 Auto Scaling group with scheduled scaling actions.
C) Implement an EC2 Auto Scaling group with dynamic scaling policies based on CPU utilization.
D) Deploy EC2 instances within an Elastic Beanstalk environment for automatic scaling.
E) Use AWS Lambda functions instead of EC2 instances for dynamic scaling.

QUESTION 53

Your organization hosts a web application on Amazon EC2 instances, experiencing daily traffic spikes during certain hours, leading to increased compute costs. To optimize costs without compromising performance, which approach would be most appropriate utilizing AWS services?

A) Use Amazon RDS for database hosting
B) Implement Amazon CloudFront for content delivery

C) Utilize Amazon EC2 Spot Instances for compute resources
D) Deploy containers with Amazon EKS for microservices architecture
E) Use Amazon S3 for static content storage

QUESTION 54

Your company is developing a global web application that requires low-latency access and high availability. However, you need to optimize costs for data transfer between regions. What solution would you recommend to achieve these objectives?

A) Implement AWS Global Accelerator with Amazon Route 53 for optimized global routing
B) Deploy Amazon CloudFront with AWS WAF for content delivery and web application firewall
C) Utilize AWS Direct Connect with AWS Transit Gateway for centralized and cost-effective connectivity
D) Opt for Amazon S3 Transfer Acceleration for faster data uploads to S3
E) Leverage Amazon VPC with AWS VPN for secure and scalable connectivity between regions

QUESTION 55

A retail company wants to restrict access to sensitive customer data stored in an Amazon RDS database to specific departments within the organization. What solution should the solutions architect recommend to enforce granular access control?

A) Implement IAM policies to restrict access based on the IP addresses of specific departments' office networks.

B) Configure Amazon RDS security groups to allow access only from the IP addresses of specific departments.

C) Utilize IAM roles with federated access to enforce department-based access control for the RDS database.

D) Share the RDS master user credentials with each department and rely on department heads to manage access.

E) Create separate RDS instances for each department and grant access based on database instance ownership.

QUESTION 56

Your organization runs a media streaming service that experiences a significant increase in demand during live events, such as sports matches or concerts. You need to design a cost-optimized compute scaling solution that can handle these short-lived traffic spikes efficiently. What approach should you take?

A) Utilize AWS Lambda with provisioned concurrency to ensure consistent performance during traffic spikes

B) Implement Amazon EC2 Auto Scaling with target tracking scaling policies to adjust capacity based on predefined metrics

C) Leverage Amazon ECS with service auto scaling to automatically adjust the number of running tasks based on demand

D) Use AWS Fargate with spot capacity to take advantage of cost savings during traffic spikes

E) Deploy Amazon EKS with managed node groups and horizontal pod autoscaling to dynamically adjust Kubernetes resources based on demand

QUESTION 57

Your company operates a global e-commerce platform that experiences seasonal spikes in traffic, particularly during holiday sales events. The platform utilizes Amazon Redshift for its data warehousing needs. However, during peak traffic periods, Redshift costs have become a significant concern due to the need for additional compute resources to handle increased query loads. As a solutions architect, you are tasked with implementing a cost-effective solution to manage Amazon Redshift costs during peak traffic periods while ensuring query performance. What would be the most suitable strategy in this scenario?

A) Utilize Amazon Redshift Spectrum to offload query processing to Amazon S3 and reduce compute costs during peak traffic periods

B) Implement Amazon Redshift Concurrency Scaling to automatically add and remove query processing capacity based on demand

C) Configure Amazon Redshift Enhanced VPC Routing to optimize network traffic and reduce data transfer costs

D) Enable Amazon Redshift Query Queues to prioritize and manage query workload during peak traffic periods

E) Integrate Amazon Redshift with Amazon RDS to offload read-intensive queries and reduce compute costs

QUESTION 58

Your company operates a web application that experiences spikes in traffic during promotional events and holidays. As part of a cost optimization initiative, you are tasked with designing an architecture that can handle these traffic spikes efficiently while minimizing expenses. Which of the following instance purchasing options would best optimize costs for this scenario?

A) Utilize AWS EC2 Reserved Instances with a one-year term commitment for baseline capacity and supplement with AWS EC2 On-Demand Instances during traffic spikes

B) Implement AWS Savings Plans with a commitment to a specific instance family to receive discounts on instance usage regardless of demand fluctuations

C) Deploy AWS EC2 Spot Instances for all instances to take advantage of cost savings during traffic spikes
D) Leverage AWS EC2 Auto Scaling with On-Demand Instances to dynamically adjust capacity based on demand

E) Combine AWS EC2 Reserved Instances with AWS Lambda for serverless processing to eliminate the need for manual scaling

QUESTION 59

Your company runs a web application that experiences predictable spikes in traffic during certain periods of the day. You need to optimize costs for the application's compute resources while maintaining performance. What approach should you recommend?

A) Utilize Amazon EC2 On-Demand Instances with Auto Scaling based on a fixed schedule
B) Implement Amazon EC2 Reserved Instances for long-term cost predictability
C) Leverage Amazon EC2 Spot Instances with scheduled scaling policies
D) Deploy AWS Lambda for serverless web application hosting
E) Utilize AWS Wavelength for ultra-low latency application hosting

QUESTION 60

An online gaming platform wants to ensure that its multiplayer games can handle increasing player loads during peak gaming hours. What Auto Scaling configuration should the solutions architect recommend to achieve this?

A) Configure the Auto Scaling group to use a target tracking scaling policy based on the number of login attempts per minute.

B) Implement an Auto Scaling group with a scheduled scaling policy triggered at specific times of peak gaming hours.

C) Configure the Auto Scaling group to use a step scaling policy triggered by sudden increases in the number of active game sessions per minute.

D) Utilize an Auto Scaling group with a simple scaling policy based on manual adjustments to instance counts.

E) Implement an Auto Scaling group with a predictive scaling policy based on historical player activity patterns.

QUESTION 61

Your company operates a global e-commerce platform that serves customers across different continents. You need to design a solution to minimize data transfer costs while ensuring low-latency access to product images and videos stored in Amazon S3. Which approach should you recommend for this scenario?

A) Use Amazon S3 Transfer Acceleration to optimize data transfers and reduce latency for accessing multimedia content globally

B) Implement Amazon CloudFront with Lambda@Edge to cache and deliver multimedia content at edge locations

C) Deploy Amazon Elastic File System (Amazon EFS) to store multimedia files and enable fast access from multiple regions

D) Utilize Amazon S3 Glacier for long-term storage of multimedia content and retrieve data as needed

E) Use AWS Direct Connect with AWS Transit Gateway to establish private connectivity between on-premises data centers and AWS regions

QUESTION 62

Your organization is developing a new mobile application backend that requires efficient testing and development environments on AWS. Cost optimization is crucial, and you need to design a solution that minimizes expenses while ensuring scalability and flexibility. Which approach should you recommend?

A) Deploy Amazon DynamoDB Accelerator (DAX) for caching to improve the performance of database testing

B) Utilize AWS Direct Connect for dedicated network connectivity between mobile devices and development environments

C) Implement Amazon EBS Snapshots for backup and recovery of test data in development environments

D) Use AWS Lambda for serverless compute in testing environments to eliminate the cost of idle resources

E) Leverage Amazon EC2 Spot Instances for cost-effective testing and development environments

QUESTION 63

Your company operates a global e-commerce platform with customers in various regions. To ensure high availability and disaster recovery, you have deployed your application in multiple AWS regions. However, the finance department has identified a significant portion of the budget being spent on data transfer costs between regions. As a solutions architect, you need to design a cost-optimized multi-region architecture that maintains high availability while reducing expenses. What approach should you recommend?

A) Implement Amazon CloudFront with AWS Global Accelerator to cache content at edge locations and minimize data transfer between regions

B) Utilize Amazon S3 Transfer Acceleration to optimize data transfer speeds between regions and reduce costs

C) Deploy Amazon DynamoDB global tables to replicate data across regions and ensure low-latency access for users

D) Leverage AWS Direct Connect with AWS Transit Gateway to establish private connectivity between regions and reduce data transfer costs

E) Utilize Amazon Route 53 latency-based routing to route traffic to the nearest AWS region and minimize data transfer distances

QUESTION 64

Your company operates a web application with a global user base, and you need to design a cost-efficient solution for managing user authentication and authorization. The solution should provide secure access to resources while minimizing costs.

A) Implement Amazon Cognito for user authentication and authorization, with fine-grained access control policies to manage resource access

B) Utilize AWS IAM Identity Federation to federate user identities with existing corporate directory services and enforce access policies

C) Deploy AWS Directory Service with Active Directory for centralized user management and seamless integration with on-premises resources

D) Leverage Amazon S3 bucket policies and IAM roles to control access to resources directly through AWS services

E) Utilize AWS Single Sign-On (SSO) to manage user access to multiple AWS accounts and applications through a centralized portal

QUESTION 65

Your company is seeking to implement cost-effective data transfer solutions between on-premises data centers and AWS cloud resources. As a solutions architect, you need to recommend a solution that minimizes data transfer costs while ensuring reliable connectivity.

A) Utilize AWS Direct Connect to establish dedicated network connections between on-premises data centers and AWS regions

B) Implement AWS DataSync to automate data transfers between on-premises storage and Amazon S3

C) Leverage AWS Transfer Family to enable secure FTP, FTPS, and SFTP transfers to and from Amazon S3

D) Utilize Amazon S3 Transfer Acceleration to optimize data transfer speeds for large-scale uploads to Amazon S3

E) Implement AWS VPN CloudHub to establish VPN connections between multiple on-premises data centers and AWS regions

PRACTICE TEST 10 - ANSWERS ONLY

QUESTION 1

Answer - C) Utilize attribute-based access control (ABAC) to dynamically assign permissions based on the user's attributes.

A) Incorrect - Consolidating all users into a single IAM role does not follow the principle of least privilege and increases security risks.

B) Incorrect - While AWS Lambda can automate tasks, it's not a best practice for automatically assigning IAM roles based on user activity without considering security implications.

C) Correct - ABAC allows for fine-grained access control that adjusts permissions dynamically based on the user's attributes, enhancing both security and efficiency.

D) Incorrect - Relying solely on the external identity provider's security measures does not ensure comprehensive access control within AWS.

E) Incorrect - Single sign-on should be used for simplifying access both to AWS and non-AWS applications, improving user experience and security.

QUESTION 2

Answer - C) Amazon CloudFront and AWS Shield Standard for DDoS protection

A) Incorrect - Amazon S3 and Amazon Glacier provide storage solutions but do not directly address security against web-based attacks or traffic management.

B) Incorrect - AWS Auto Scaling and Amazon CloudWatch help manage application scalability and monitoring, but they do not provide direct protection against web-based attacks.

C) Correct - Amazon CloudFront distributes traffic globally to improve application performance, while AWS Shield Standard offers DDoS protection, which together enhance the security and performance of the e-commerce platform during high traffic volumes.

D) Incorrect - AWS WAF provides protection against web exploits, and Amazon Route 53 manages DNS, but without the global distribution and initial DDoS protection, this combination is less effective for the scenario described.

E) Incorrect - AWS Fargate and AWS Lambda facilitate serverless application scaling, which can help manage traffic surges but do not directly address the security aspect of web-based attacks.

QUESTION 3

Answer - A) Centralize key management with AWS KMS and enforce encryption policies using AWS Organizations service control policies (SCPs).

A) Correct - AWS KMS allows for centralized key management suitable for multinational corporations, supporting encryption across services and regions. AWS Organizations with service control policies enables the enforcement of encryption policies across the corporation's AWS accounts and regions, ensuring compliance with data residency requirements.

B) Incorrect - AWS CloudHSM provides dedicated hardware key management, and Amazon Macie classifies and protects sensitive data, but they do not provide the centralized policy enforcement capability across multiple regions as effectively as AWS KMS combined with AWS Organizations.

C) Incorrect - Amazon RDS supports encryption, and AWS IAM manages access control, but this combination lacks the centralized key management and policy enforcement capabilities provided by AWS KMS and AWS Organizations.

D) Incorrect - AWS Secrets Manager is designed for secrets management, and Amazon Inspector for security assessments; neither directly addresses the need for centralized key management and encryption policy enforcement across regions.

E) Incorrect - AWS WAF and AWS Shield focus on web application and DDoS protection, respectively, and do not address the specific requirements for data encryption and centralized policy management across a global AWS infrastructure.

QUESTION 4

Answer - [A] Deploy Amazon ECS tasks across multiple Availability Zones within a region. Implement Amazon ECS Service Auto Scaling to automatically adjust the number of tasks based on load and health checks.

Option A - Correct. Deploying ECS tasks across multiple AZs and using ECS Service Auto Scaling ensures high availability and fault tolerance at the container level.

Option B - While EKS and Fargate offer managed Kubernetes environments and serverless container execution, they may not provide the same level of control over availability and scaling as ECS tasks with Service Auto Scaling.

Option C - ECS Capacity Providers and rolling updates offer scalability and reliability but may not provide the same level of automated scaling and fault tolerance as ECS Service Auto Scaling.

Option D - While Lambda functions offer automatic scaling and high availability, they may not be suitable for all microservices architectures, especially those requiring persistent state or long-running tasks.

Option E - Using EC2 Spot Instances and rolling deployments can reduce costs and downtime, but they may not provide the same level of fault tolerance as ECS tasks across multiple AZs with Service Auto Scaling.

QUESTION 5

Answer - A) Use Amazon SQS FIFO queue with a batch mode of 10 messages per operation

A) Use Amazon SQS FIFO queue with a batch mode of 10 messages per operation - This option ensures accurate and efficient processing of transactions by processing multiple transactions in a batch, meeting the company's requirement for timely processing and scalability during peak hours. The FIFO guarantees order accuracy, and batch processing enhances efficiency.

B) Use Amazon SQS FIFO queue with exactly-once processing enabled - While ensuring order accuracy, it may not efficiently handle high transaction volumes during peak hours due to sequential processing.

C) Use Amazon SQS FIFO queue with default settings - Default settings may not ensure transaction accuracy and efficient processing, especially during peak hours, and may not efficiently handle batch processing.

D) Use Amazon SQS standard queue to process the messages - Standard queues lack message ordering, which is crucial for maintaining transaction order, and may not efficiently handle high transaction volumes.

E) Use Amazon SQS FIFO queue with message deduplication enabled - While avoiding duplicate messages, it doesn't guarantee order processing, and may not efficiently handle high transaction volumes during peak hours.

QUESTION 6

Answer - [C] Implement IAM roles for ECS services to securely access other AWS services. Use Lambda authorizers with API Gateway for OAuth 2.0 authorization to authenticate users and control access to APIs.

Option C - Correct. Implementing IAM roles for ECS services and using Lambda authorizers with API Gateway for OAuth 2.0 authorization provides secure access control mechanisms for the microservices-based application.

Option A - While configuring IAM roles for ECS tasks is valid, using API Gateway with IAM authorization may not provide the same level of user management features as OAuth 2.0 with Lambda authorizers.

Option B - Although IAM policies attached to ECS task definitions can control access to AWS resources, using Amazon Cognito with API Gateway does not offer the same level of flexibility and control as Lambda authorizers for OAuth 2.0 authentication.

Option D - Setting up IAM policies at the AWS account level may not provide granular control over access to individual resources within the microservices architecture, and Lambda authorizers offer more advanced authentication and authorization features compared to AWS account-level policies.

Option E - Deploying Fargate tasks within a VPC may introduce unnecessary complexity, and using Amazon Cognito with API Gateway may not provide the same level of control over user authentication and authorization as Lambda authorizers.

QUESTION 7

Answer - [A] Configuring cross-region replication for Amazon S3 buckets.

A) Correct - Configuring cross-region replication for Amazon S3 buckets ensures that data is automatically copied to a secondary region, providing both data redundancy and security.

B) Incorrect - AWS DataSync is used for transferring data between on-premises storage and AWS, not specifically between regions for disaster recovery.

C) Incorrect - AWS Direct Connect provides a dedicated network connection to AWS but is not directly related to data replication between regions.

D) Incorrect - AWS Artifact provides compliance documentation but is not involved in the actual data replication process.

E) Incorrect - AWS VPN connections provide secure communication but are not specifically designed for data replication between regions.

QUESTION 8

Answer - [B] Configuring AWS Cognito user pools with social identity federation for user authentication.

A) Incorrect - AWS Secrets Manager is used for storing and rotating secrets, such as database credentials, but it's not specifically designed for social identity provider credentials or user authentication.

B) Correct - AWS Cognito user pools allow for user authentication and authorization, including integration with social identity providers like Google and Facebook for user sign-in, making it a suitable solution for secure application access and user management.

C) Incorrect - While AWS IAM roles and policies control access to AWS resources, they do not handle user authentication or social identity provider integration for web applications.

D) Incorrect - AWS Single Sign-On (SSO) provides centralized user management and access control but may not integrate directly with social identity providers for web application sign-in.

E) Incorrect - Amazon API Gateway with OAuth 2.0 authorization is primarily used for controlling access to APIs and may not address user authentication and authorization for web applications.

QUESTION 9

Answer - [C] Leveraging AWS App Mesh for managing microservices traffic, ensuring efficient communication and scalability, and implementing Amazon S3 with server-side encryption for data storage, meeting security and compliance requirements.

A) Deploying microservices in Amazon EKS with AWS Fargate ensures efficient communication and scalability, but configuring Amazon RDS with encryption at rest may not be the most suitable option for data storage encryption and access controls.

B) Mutual TLS authentication between microservices in Amazon ECS ensures secure communication but may not directly address encryption requirements for data at rest or efficient communication.

C) AWS App Mesh manages microservices traffic, ensuring efficient communication and scalability, while Amazon S3 with server-side encryption meets security and compliance requirements for data at rest encryption.

D) AWS Lambda offers serverless deployment and scalability, but Amazon Redshift may not be the best choice for data storage encryption and access controls.

E) AWS PrivateLink provides private communication between services and ensures scalability, but Amazon Aurora may not directly address encryption requirements for data at rest or in-transit.

QUESTION 10

Answer - B) Enable Amazon S3 Transfer Acceleration to speed up file uploads. and E) Implement multipart uploads alongside Amazon S3 Transfer Acceleration.

A) Configure AWS Snowball devices for physical data transport from field locations. - Incorrect. Snowball is impractical for the dynamic and immediate needs of field reporters.

B) Enable Amazon S3 Transfer Acceleration to speed up file uploads. - Correct. This service optimizes data transfer to S3 globally, ideal for reporters uploading files from various locations.

C) Set up AWS Direct Connect links at main offices for enhanced connectivity. - Incorrect. Direct Connect improves connectivity for fixed locations, not suitable for field reporters in varying locations.

D) Use AWS DataSync for automated and accelerated file transfer. - Incorrect. While DataSync is efficient for data transfer, it requires a more stable connection than might be available to field reporters.

E) Implement multipart uploads alongside Amazon S3 Transfer Acceleration. - Correct. Multipart uploads increase upload efficiency, especially for large files, and complement S3 Transfer Acceleration for reporters in the field.

QUESTION 11

Answer - A) Configure Amazon S3 with S3 bucket policies for fine-grained access control, enable server-side encryption with AWS KMS for at-rest encryption, and use Amazon Athena for in-place querying.

A) Configure Amazon S3 with S3 bucket policies for fine-grained access control, enable server-side encryption with AWS KMS for at-rest encryption, and use Amazon Athena for in-place querying. - Correct because S3 provides high durability and security, bucket policies and KMS offer the required access control and encryption, and Athena allows for analysis without moving the data.

B) Deploy Amazon EFS with encryption at rest, use network file system (NFS) permissions for access control, and integrate with Amazon Redshift for data analysis. - Incorrect because EFS is optimized for certain use cases and does not support in-place querying of data like Athena does with S3.

C) Implement Amazon FSx for Lustre, use POSIX-compliant file permissions for access control, and utilize AWS Glue for data cataloging and ETL processes. - Incorrect for large datasets needing periodic analysis without movement, as FSx for Lustre is optimized for high-performance computing rather than secure storage and in-place analysis.

D) Utilize Amazon DynamoDB with encryption at rest enabled, IAM policies for access management, and Amazon EMR for data analysis. - Incorrect because it focuses on NoSQL database storage, not the secure, scalable file storage and in-place querying provided by S3 and Athena.

E) Set up AWS Storage Gateway in a file gateway configuration for on-premises access to S3, enable encryption with AWS KMS, and use Amazon SageMaker for data analysis. - Incorrect as it adds unnecessary complexity for the scenario, which is better served by the direct use of S3, Athena, and KMS for storage, security, and analysis.

QUESTION 12

Answer - C) Configure AWS CodePipeline for continuous integration and delivery, integrate AWS Lambda for custom deployment scripts, and Amazon S3 for storing secure artifacts.

A) Use AWS CodeDeploy for automated deployments, Amazon CloudWatch alarms for rollback triggers, and AWS Auto Scaling to adjust resources based on load. - Incorrect because, while it supports automated deployments and scaling, it lacks the integrated CI/CD pipeline and pre-deployment security check mechanism provided in other options.

B) Implement AWS Elastic Beanstalk for application deployment, enabling Elastic Load Balancing for traffic distribution, and AWS WAF for pre-deployment security checks. - Incorrect as Elastic Beanstalk simplifies deployment and management but does not offer the same level of control and integration with CI/CD processes for quick updates and hotfixes as the correct option.

C) Configure AWS CodePipeline for continuous integration and delivery, integrate AWS Lambda for custom deployment scripts, and Amazon S3 for storing secure artifacts. - Correct because CodePipeline facilitates continuous integration and delivery, Lambda allows for flexible deployment automation, and S3 ensures secure artifact storage, meeting the requirements for quick updates, scalability, instant rollback, and security.

D) Leverage Amazon ECS with AWS Fargate for deploying containerized game updates, set up AWS CodeStar for project management, and Amazon Inspector for security assessments. - Incorrect as it provides a strong container management and security assessment framework but doesn't explicitly address the CI/CD integration for frequent game updates as comprehensively as the correct option.

E) Deploy with Amazon EC2 instances managed through AWS Systems Manager for patching and updates, utilize Amazon RDS with Multi-AZ deployments for database scaling, and AWS Shield for advanced DDoS protection. - Incorrect because it focuses on infrastructure management and protection rather than the agile deployment process required for frequent game updates and hotfixes.

QUESTION 13

Answer - D) Configure Amazon GuardDuty for threat detection, AWS Security Hub for centralized security monitoring, and AWS Lambda functions for executing remediation actions based on alerts.

A) Use AWS CloudTrail for logging API calls, Amazon GuardDuty for detecting suspicious activities, and Amazon CloudWatch for monitoring and alerts. - Incorrect because, while this option provides comprehensive logging and detection capabilities, it lacks the integration of a centralized security monitoring solution with automated remediation actions as Security Hub and Lambda provide.

B) Implement AWS Lambda for automated incident response, AWS WAF for filtering malicious traffic, and Amazon S3 for storing log files securely. - Incorrect as it focuses on response and traffic filtering but does not offer the breadth of detection, centralized monitoring, and integrated response provided by GuardDuty, Security Hub, and Lambda.

C) Deploy Amazon Inspector for automated security assessments, Amazon CloudWatch Logs Insights for log analysis, and AWS Step Functions for orchestrating incident response workflows. - Incorrect because it emphasizes assessments and log analysis but does not directly address real-time threat detection and automated incident response.

D) Configure Amazon GuardDuty for threat detection, AWS Security Hub for centralized security monitoring, and AWS Lambda functions for executing remediation actions based on alerts. - Correct as it offers a holistic approach to security incident detection, centralized monitoring, and automated response, aligning with the platform's requirements for security posture enhancement and forensic readiness.

E) Leverage AWS Config for continuous configuration audit and recording, AWS Shield for DDoS protection, and Amazon S3 Glacier for long-term log storage and forensic analysis. - Incorrect because it concentrates on configuration audit, DDoS protection, and log storage, missing the integrated detection and automated response system that is crucial for addressing the platform's needs.

QUESTION 14

Answer - [A, B]

A) Deploying Amazon RDS Multi-AZ with encryption ensures high availability and data security compliance with HIPAA regulations for database storage.

B) Utilizing Amazon S3 with server-side encryption and versioning enabled offers secure and compliant storage of patient data, meeting HIPAA regulatory requirements effectively. Implementing AWS Direct Connect, CloudFront with WAF, and API Gateway with Lambda are suitable solutions but may not offer the same level of compliance with HIPAA regulations and data security for healthcare applications as RDS Multi-AZ and S3 with encryption and versioning. Direct Connect focuses on network connectivity, CloudFront with WAF on web application security, and API Gateway with Lambda on serverless backend processing, which may not fully meet the healthcare organization's requirements for compliance and data security.

QUESTION 15

Answer - [B, D]

B) Suspend the HealthCheck process type for the Auto Scaling group and apply the maintenance patch to the instance - Suspending health checks may not prevent instance replacement and may not efficiently address the maintenance challenge.

 D) Temporarily suspend the AddToLoadBalancer process type for the Auto Scaling group and apply the maintenance patch to the instance - Suspending processes related to load balancer integration may not efficiently address the maintenance challenge and may not prevent instance replacement during maintenance.

 A) Suspend the ReplaceUnhealthy process type for the Auto Scaling group and apply the maintenance patch to the instance - Suspending the process responsible for replacing unhealthy instances may effectively address the maintenance challenge by preventing unnecessary instance replacements.

 C) Put the instance into the Detached state and then update the instance by applying the maintenance patch - Detaching instances may disrupt application availability and may not align with the requirement for uninterrupted maintenance.

 E) Take a snapshot of the instance, create a new Amazon Machine Image (AMI), and then launch a new instance using this AMI - Creating a new instance from a snapshot introduces complexity and may not efficiently address the maintenance challenge, especially in scenarios where immediate fixes are required.

QUESTION 16

Answer - C) Use AWS Direct Connect and AWS Transit Gateway, with Direct Connect Gateways for multi-region connectivity.

A) Architect a global network using AWS Global Accelerator and AWS Transit Gateway for optimized path selection - Incorrect because Global Accelerator primarily improves internet-facing service performance, not intra-company connectivity.

B) Deploy multiple AWS Site-to-Site VPN connections with Amazon Route 53 for latency-based routing - Incorrect as Site-to-Site VPN may not meet the low-latency requirements for global operations compared to Direct Connect.

C) Use AWS Direct Connect and AWS Transit Gateway, with Direct Connect Gateways for multi-region connectivity - Correct because it combines low-latency, high-bandwidth connectivity with scalable, secure inter-region connectivity.

D) Implement a meshed network topology with inter-region VPC peering and Amazon CloudFront for content delivery - Incorrect because, while it addresses global distribution, it doesn't provide a comprehensive solution for connecting on-premises data centers.

E) Configure AWS Transit Gateway with AWS Shield Advanced for secure, scalable multi-region connectivity - Incorrect because it focuses on DDoS protection (Shield Advanced) rather than addressing the core requirement of low-latency and scalable network architecture.

QUESTION 17

Answer - A) Use AWS CodePipeline for CI/CD workflows, AWS CodeBuild for secure code compilation, and Amazon ECR for storing container images.

A) Correct as CodePipeline and CodeBuild provide a secure, integrated CI/CD pipeline suitable for DevOps, while ECR offers a secure repository for container images, aligning with the need for secure management and storage of code and artifacts.

B) Incorrect because WorkSpaces and Lambda address development environments and compute resources but do not offer a comprehensive CI/CD solution. CodeCommit secures code storage but doesn't cover the CI/CD and container management aspects.

C) Incorrect as Snowball Edge and EC2 Auto Scaling address data transfer and compute scalability, but KMS alone does not fulfill the CI/CD workflow optimization requirement.

D) Incorrect because DataSync and ECS cater to data transfer and container management, but CodeGuru focuses on code review, not the overall CI/CD pipeline security and scalability.

E) Incorrect as Direct Connect provides dedicated connectivity, Fargate offers container execution without provisioning servers, and S3 versioning supports artifact storage, but this combination doesn't offer an integrated approach to CI/CD workflows or secure code compilation.

QUESTION 18

Answer - [A] Implement AWS Secrets Manager to store database credentials and other secrets. Configure rotation policies within Secrets Manager to automatically rotate credentials according to predefined schedules.

Option B - Storing secrets in plaintext within an encrypted RDS instance is not recommended for security reasons, and manual rotation introduces operational overhead and potential errors.
Option C - While Parameter Store can manage secrets, it may not offer built-in rotation capabilities like Secrets Manager.

Option D - Storing secrets in a spreadsheet and using CloudWatch Events for rotation lacks automation and may not meet security best practices.

Option E - Implementing a custom solution using Lambda and DynamoDB adds unnecessary complexity and may not offer the same level of security and compliance as Secrets Manager.

QUESTION 19

Answer - [B] Implement AWS Secrets Manager to securely store and rotate secrets. Integrate applications running on Fargate with Secrets Manager for secure retrieval of secrets.

Option A - Embedding secrets directly within Docker containers is not recommended for security reasons and lacks centralized management and rotation capabilities.

Option C - Storing secrets in plaintext files within Docker volumes poses security risks and lacks automation for rotation and retrieval.

Option D - While Parameter Store can centrally manage configurations, Secrets Manager is specifically designed for securely storing and rotating secrets.

Option E - Managing sensitive information in a spreadsheet within an S3 bucket lacks automation for rotation and retrieval and introduces unnecessary complexity.

Explanation for Choice B: Implementing Secrets Manager provides secure storage and rotation of secrets within containerized applications. Integrating with Fargate allows for automated retrieval at runtime, enhancing security and compliance.

QUESTION 20

Answer - A) Create an Amazon CloudWatch metric filter to process AWS CloudTrail logs containing API call details. Establish an alarm based on this metric's rate to send an Amazon SNS notification to the required team.

A) Create an Amazon CloudWatch metric filter to process AWS CloudTrail logs containing API call details. Establish an alarm based on this metric's rate to send an Amazon SNS notification to the required team. - This option directly addresses the scenario by analyzing CloudTrail logs for unauthorized API queries and triggering real-time alerts using CloudWatch alarms and Amazon SNS notifications.

B) Implement AWS Config Rules to monitor API activity and define rules to detect unauthorized API calls. Configure AWS Config to trigger an AWS Lambda function upon rule evaluation to notify relevant stakeholders. - While AWS Config can monitor API activity, it may not provide real-time alerting capabilities for immediate incident response as required in this scenario.

C) Leverage AWS Trusted Advisor to publish metrics about check results to Amazon CloudWatch. Set up an alarm to track status changes for checks in the Service Limits category for the APIs, triggering notifications when service quotas are exceeded. - While Trusted Advisor offers valuable insights, it may not directly address the need for real-time detection of unauthorized API queries.

D) Use Amazon Athena SQL queries against AWS CloudTrail log files stored in Amazon S3 buckets. Generate reports using Amazon QuickSight for managerial dashboards. - While this option provides insights, it may not offer real-time alerting capabilities as required in this scenario.

E) Configure AWS CloudTrail to stream event data to Amazon Kinesis. Utilize Amazon Kinesis stream-level metrics in Amazon CloudWatch to trigger an AWS Lambda function that will initiate an error workflow. - While this option utilizes streaming data, it may introduce complexity and latency compared to directly analyzing CloudTrail logs for real-time alerts.

QUESTION 21

Answer - [B) Implement Amazon SQS to queue video upload requests and trigger processing tasks with AWS Lambda.]

B) SQS provides queuing capability, ensuring that upload requests are processed in an orderly manner, while Lambda allows for scalable, event-driven processing of these requests.

A) Kinesis Data Streams is more suitable for continuous data streaming, not batch processing of uploaded videos.

C) S3 is appropriate for storage but does not handle processing tasks directly.
D) SNS is for pub/sub messaging, not for queueing and processing.
E) Direct Connect enhances network connectivity but doesn't directly address processing scalability.

QUESTION 22

Answer - [A) AWS Lambda and B) Amazon API Gateway]

Option A involves AWS Lambda for serverless compute with event-driven triggers, ensuring high availability and minimal latency for processing user requests in real-time.

Option B involves Amazon API Gateway for HTTP endpoints with built-in caching, providing low-latency access to serverless functions.

Option C involves Amazon DynamoDB for a NoSQL database with auto-scaling, but it does not directly provide event-driven architecture or serverless compute.

Option D involves Amazon S3 for object storage, but it does not directly handle event-driven architecture or real-time processing.

Option E involves Amazon SQS for message queuing, but it does not directly integrate with AWS Lambda for serverless compute.

QUESTION 23

Answer - [A) Utilize Amazon S3 with versioning enabled and cross-region replication for data durability and availability.]

Option A) is correct as Amazon S3 provides scalable object storage with versioning and cross-region replication, ensuring data durability and availability.

Option B) refers to Amazon EFS, which is a file storage service and may not be suitable for object storage needs.

Option C) mentions Amazon RDS, which is for relational databases and may not meet the requirements for storing large volumes of customer data.

Option D) mentions Amazon EBS, which is block storage and may not provide the scalability needed for large volumes of data.

Option E) mentions AWS Backup, which is used for backup and recovery, but does not address the primary requirement of scalable data storage.

QUESTION 24

Answer - A) Utilize AWS Cost Explorer to analyze cost trends and identify areas of overspending.

Option A is correct because AWS Cost Explorer provides detailed insights into cost trends and allows analysis of spending patterns to identify areas of overspending. This solution aligns with the scenario of optimizing cloud infrastructure costs and identifying reasons for high costs.

Option B is incorrect because while AWS Trusted Advisor offers recommendations for cost optimization, it does not provide detailed cost analysis to identify specific areas of overspending.

Option C is incorrect because while AWS Budgets helps set cost thresholds and receive alerts, it does not offer detailed analysis to identify underlying reasons for high costs.

Option D is incorrect because while AWS Compute Optimizer analyzes resource utilization, it focuses on rightsizing instances rather than identifying overall cost trends.

Option E is incorrect because while AWS Savings Plans offer discounts, they do not provide detailed analysis of cost trends or identify specific areas of overspending.

QUESTION 25

Answer - A) Use Amazon Route 53 based geolocation routing policy to restrict access to viewers located in the designated states

A) By using Amazon Route 53's geolocation routing policy, the news network can ensure that only viewers from the specified states can access the live news streams, effectively managing traffic and complying with regional restrictions.

B, C, D, E) These options do not directly address the requirement of restricting access to viewers from specific states for the live news streaming service. Weighted routing, latency-based routing, failover routing, and geoproximity routing do not provide the necessary geographic control needed for this scenario.

QUESTION 26

Answer - B) Implement AWS CloudFormation to define infrastructure as code and automate the deployment of AWS resources in a consistent and repeatable manner, promoting immutable infrastructure.

Option A is incorrect because while AWS AppConfig manages application configurations dynamically, it may not inherently support the principles of immutable infrastructure where the infrastructure is immutable and replaced rather than updated.

Option B is correct because AWS CloudFormation allows defining infrastructure as code, enabling the creation of immutable infrastructure and automating the deployment of AWS resources in a consistent and repeatable manner, aligning with the goal of achieving immutable infrastructure on AWS.

Option C is incorrect because while AWS Systems Manager automates administrative tasks, it may not directly support the goal of achieving immutable infrastructure.

Option D is incorrect because while Amazon EKS Anywhere facilitates Kubernetes deployment, it does not directly address the goal of achieving immutable infrastructure on AWS.

Option E is incorrect because while Amazon ECS Anywhere allows running containerized applications, it does not directly address the goal of achieving immutable infrastructure on AWS.

QUESTION 27

Answer - D) Utilize Amazon ECS Service Discovery with Route 53 for DNS-based service discovery and implement API Gateway REST APIs for client communication

Option D - Amazon ECS Service Discovery with Route 53 provides DNS-based service discovery, while API Gateway REST APIs offer a scalable and flexible way to manage client communication with microservices. Option A - Using Lambda functions as service registries may introduce complexity and scalability challenges, while SNS is more suited for messaging than service discovery.

Option B - AWS App Mesh manages service-to-service communication but may not be the most straightforward solution for microservices discovery and client communication.

Option C - AWS App Runner is primarily for running containerized applications and may not provide the same level of service discovery functionality as ECS Service Discovery.

Option E - AWS Direct Connect offers private connectivity but is not directly related to microservices discovery and may not provide the same level of flexibility as DNS-based service discovery with Route 53.

QUESTION 28

Answer - D) Opt for Amazon EKS, implement Kubernetes Horizontal Pod Autoscaler for scalability, use Amazon CloudWatch Logs Insights for in-depth log analysis, and Amazon ECR for container image management.

A) Incorrect, ECS with Auto Scaling and CloudWatch addresses scalability and monitoring, but lacks the Kubernetes-specific advantages for container orchestration and scalability provided by EKS and the Horizontal Pod Autoscaler.

B) Partially correct, EKS with Fargate and CloudWatch covers serverless compute and monitoring, but MSK for fleet messages is over-specific and Lambda doesn't directly relate to containerized microservices scalability in this context.

C) Incorrect, ECS with EC2, SNS, and X-Ray provides monitoring and notification services, but doesn't leverage the full scalability and deployment speed that Kubernetes on EKS offers for containerized applications.

D) Correct, EKS with the Horizontal Pod Autoscaler offers precise scalability for containerized services, CloudWatch Logs Insights allows for advanced log analysis, and ECR provides secure container image management, meeting the needs for robust monitoring and rapid scalability.

E) Incorrect, while ECS with Fargate and CloudWatch offers scalable and monitored container deployment, Step Functions and Elastic Beanstalk are not as closely aligned with container orchestration and rapid scaling needs as Kubernetes features on EKS.

QUESTION 29

Answer - A) Amazon Route 53 with latency-based routing.

A) Route 53 with latency-based routing directs users to the nearest game server based on latency, ensuring low latency.

B) Global Accelerator improves performance but may not route users to the nearest server.

C) CloudFront with geo-routing distributes traffic based on geographic location but may not optimize latency.

D) VPC peering enables private connectivity between servers but does not manage user traffic.

E) API Gateway manages API requests but does not route users to game servers based on latency.

QUESTION 30

Answer - A) Utilize RESTful APIs on Amazon API Gateway with OAuth 2.0 authentication and authorization for third-party access

A) Utilizing RESTful APIs on Amazon API Gateway with OAuth 2.0 authentication and authorization ensures secure and scalable access for third-party developers while providing fine-grained control over access to various functionalities.

B, C, D, E) These options either do not provide adequate security measures or are not suitable for enabling third-party access to the platform's functionalities.

QUESTION 31

Answer - A) AWS Config for monitoring resource compliance, AWS CloudTrail for tracking user activity, AWS Lambda for automated remediation tasks, and Amazon GuardDuty for threat detection.

A) Correct, as AWS Config provides a detailed view of resource compliance against regulations like GDPR, CloudTrail offers visibility into user activities affecting compliance, Lambda enables automated remediation to quickly address non-compliance, and GuardDuty enhances security posture through threat detection, making this combination ideal for meeting GDPR requirements and ensuring continuous compliance.

B) Incorrect, while QuickSight, WAF, Cognito, and RDS offer valuable services for analytics, security, and data storage, they do not provide the comprehensive compliance monitoring, user activity tracking, and automated remediation capabilities as efficiently as the services in A.

C) Incorrect, KMS, Secrets Manager, VPC, and IAM are crucial for encryption, secrets handling, and access control but lack the automated compliance monitoring and remediation framework provided by Config and Lambda.

D) Incorrect, Inspector, Trusted Advisor, Fargate, and S3 focus on security assessments, best practices, container security, and data storage but do not offer the comprehensive automated compliance monitoring and remediation capabilities needed for GDPR compliance as A does.

E) Incorrect, EC2, EBS, CodeBuild, and Step Functions provide infrastructure, storage, code deployment, and automation but do not directly address the requirements for continuous compliance monitoring and automated remediation as the combination in A does.

QUESTION 32

Answer - [C] Implement Amazon RDS with Multi-AZ deployment and utilize read replicas for scaling read operations during peak hours.]

Option C - Correct because Amazon RDS with Multi-AZ deployment ensures high availability and scalability, while read replicas help scale read operations, meeting the startup's requirements for rapid recovery and scalability at a lower cost.

Option A - Incorrect because Aurora Serverless may not provide the necessary performance and scalability for critical database workloads during a disaster recovery scenario.
Option B - Incorrect because DynamoDB, while offering scalability and real-time replication, may not provide the same level of features for disaster recovery and scalability as Amazon RDS Multi-AZ deployment with read replicas.

Option D - Incorrect because Redshift is optimized for analytics and may not offer the same level of disaster recovery features as Amazon RDS Multi-AZ deployment with read replicas.
Option E - Incorrect because DocumentDB may not offer the same level of disaster recovery capabilities as Amazon RDS Multi-AZ deployment with read replicas.

QUESTION 33

Answer - [A] Utilize AWS Auto Scaling to automatically adjust resources based on demand.

Option B is incorrect as storing sensitive data in plaintext within DynamoDB tables is a security risk.
Option C is incorrect as while AWS Lambda functions offer scalability, they do not directly address high availability concerns.
Option D is incorrect as deploying microservices in a single AWS region without redundancy increases the risk of downtime.

Option E is incorrect as sensitive data stored in Amazon S3 should be encrypted.
Option A is correct because utilizing AWS Auto Scaling to automatically adjust resources based on demand helps optimize costs while maintaining reliability and performance, ensuring that the infrastructure scales efficiently to meet varying workloads.

QUESTION 34

Answer - [A] Amazon S3 Glacier.]

Option A is the most cost-effective solution for long-term retention of infrequently accessed data in a data lake scenario. Amazon S3 Glacier provides durable, secure, and low-cost storage for archived data, making it ideal for this use case.

Option B, C, and D are not suitable for long-term data retention due to their characteristics or cost considerations.
Option E, Amazon Aurora Serverless, is designed for databases and not suitable for storage of large

volumes of data.

QUESTION 35

Answer - C) Ingest user interactions into Amazon Kinesis Data Streams, which triggers an AWS Lambda function for processing and stores recommendation data in Amazon DynamoDB

C) Ingesting user interactions into Amazon Kinesis Data Streams with AWS Lambda allows for real-time analysis and dynamic generation of content recommendations. Storing recommendation data in Amazon DynamoDB ensures low-latency access and scalability.

A) Processing user interactions with AWS Lambda and Amazon S3 may introduce latency and is not suitable for real-time analysis.

B) Using Amazon Kinesis Data Firehose may not provide the necessary real-time processing capabilities for dynamic content recommendation systems.

D) Amazon SQS is not optimized for real-time processing of user interactions, and storing recommendation data in Amazon Redshift may introduce delays.
E) Using Amazon API Gateway and an EC2 instance for processing lacks the scalability and real-time processing capabilities required for dynamic content recommendation systems.

QUESTION 36

Answer - [A, B]

A) Correct - Aurora with encryption at rest and KMS for key management ensures compliance with industry regulations, and Direct Connect provides dedicated and secure network connectivity, minimizing performance impact.

B) Incorrect - While RDS encryption at rest is relevant, ACM is used for SSL/TLS certificates, not encryption keys in the application layer, which might impact compliance with data security regulations.
C) Incorrect - DynamoDB client-side encryption is suitable for data at rest, but CloudHSM is not typically used for DynamoDB encryption key storage and management.

D) Incorrect - Redshift encryption at rest is relevant, but Secrets Manager is typically used for managing secrets, not encryption keys for Redshift. CloudFront with SSL/TLS termination doesn't directly address database encryption.

E) Incorrect - DocumentDB encryption at rest is relevant, but ACM is used for SSL/TLS certificates, not encryption keys in transit. CloudFront with SSL/TLS termination doesn't directly address database encryption.

QUESTION 37

Answer - C) Implement Amazon S3 with default encryption, cross-region replication, and Amazon CloudFront for distribution.

A) Incorrect - AWS Snowball is used for large-scale data transfers and does not directly address the requirement for minimal latency in global access.

B) Incorrect - While EFS offers scalable file storage, using it across global offices might introduce latency, and AWS Direct Connect, while reducing latency, might not be feasible for all office locations.

C) Correct - Amazon S3 provides secure and scalable storage with default encryption for security. Cross-region replication ensures data availability across global offices, and CloudFront distribution reduces latency for global access.

D) Incorrect - RDS is a managed database service for structured data, less suited for document storage compared to object storage solutions.

E) Incorrect - S3 Glacier is optimized for long-term archival storage with retrieval times that may not meet the need for quick, global access to confidential documents.

QUESTION 38

Answer - B) Deploy Amazon DynamoDB for storing user interaction data and perform real-time analytics using Amazon Kinesis Data Analytics.

Option B - Amazon DynamoDB is suitable for storing user interaction data and provides low-latency access, while Amazon Kinesis Data Analytics enables real-time analytics on streaming data, ensuring high performance and scalability for the social media platform.

Option A - Amazon Kinesis Data Firehose and Amazon Redshift may introduce latency compared to the real-time processing capabilities of Amazon DynamoDB and Amazon Kinesis Data Analytics.
Option C - Amazon Redshift Spectrum queries data from the data lake, which may not provide real-time analytics capabilities required by the social media platform.

Option D - Amazon RDS with Multi-AZ deployment and read replicas may not offer the same level of scalability and real-time analytics capabilities as Amazon DynamoDB and Amazon Kinesis Data Analytics.
Option E - Amazon MSK and Apache Flink on Amazon EMR may provide real-time processing but may introduce complexity and management overhead compared to the fully managed solution with Amazon DynamoDB and Amazon Kinesis Data Analytics.

QUESTION 39

Answer - A) Deploy AWS IoT Core for ingesting sensor data, and use AWS Lambda for real-time data processing.

Option A - AWS IoT Core handles ingestion of sensor data from IoT devices, and AWS Lambda enables real-time data processing, ensuring high availability, reliability, and real-time processing.

Option B - Amazon Redshift and Amazon S3 are not optimized for real-time processing of sensor data.
Option C - While Amazon Kinesis Data Streams can ingest data in real-time, Amazon EMR is for batch processing, not real-time analytics.

Option D - Amazon S3 Glacier is for long-term storage, and Amazon DynamoDB is for real-time analytics, but they don't handle real-time processing efficiently.
Option E - AWS IoT Greengrass is for edge processing, but it doesn't provide the scalability and global availability needed for processing sensor data from factories globally.

QUESTION 40

Answer - B) Implement client-side encryption with customer-provided keys (SSE-C) and upload the encrypted data to Amazon S3

B) Client-side encryption with customer-provided keys (SSE-C) allows the media company to manage the encryption keys on-premises and securely upload the encrypted data to Amazon S3.
 A) Server-side encryption with Amazon S3 managed keys (SSE-S3) encrypts the data at rest but does not allow for on-premises management of encryption keys.
 C) Server-side encryption with AWS Key Management Service (SSE-KMS) requires using AWS KMS to manage the encryption keys, which may not align with the company's requirement for on-premises key management.

 D) Using server-side encryption with customer-provided keys (SSE-C) may not provide the desired control over encryption keys managed on-premises.
 E) Enabling AWS CloudTrail provides auditing capabilities but does not directly address the encryption requirement for data at rest in Amazon S3.

QUESTION 41

Answer - A) Amazon Kinesis for data ingestion, AWS Lambda for data processing, Amazon DynamoDB for user data storage.

A) Correct - Amazon Kinesis efficiently ingests real-time gameplay data. AWS Lambda processes this data, enabling scalability for millions of users. Amazon DynamoDB offers fast, scalable storage for player data, supporting personalized experiences.

B) Incorrect - Global Accelerator and RDS provide performance optimization and relational data storage but may not offer the real-time processing and scalability for gameplay data like Kinesis and Lambda. SNS is suitable for notifications but doesn't address the real-time data processing need.

C) Incorrect - API Gateway, SQS, and Fargate can handle API requests, message queuing, and backend services but lack the direct real-time data processing and analysis capabilities of Kinesis and Lambda for a gaming backend.

D) Incorrect - CloudFront, Step Functions, and S3 are great for content delivery, workflow orchestration, and asset storage but don't specifically address real-time gameplay data processing and storage needs.
E) Incorrect - AppSync, Elasticache, and EKS offer real-time data synchronization, caching, and container management but aren't as directly suited for the scalable, serverless, real-time data processing and storage architecture required by the mobile game as Kinesis, Lambda, and DynamoDB.

QUESTION 42

Answer - [A) Implement AWS Direct Connect for secure connectivity between on-premises data sources and Amazon Kinesis for real-time data ingestion. Utilize Amazon Redshift for data warehousing and analysis.]

Option A) AWS Direct Connect ensures secure and low-latency connectivity between on-premises data sources and Amazon Kinesis for real-time data ingestion, while Amazon Redshift provides high-performance data warehousing and analytics capabilities.

 Option B) AWS Storage Gateway with caching mode and Amazon Athena are more suitable for data synchronization and querying, but may not provide the real-time processing and analytics capabilities required.

Option C) AWS AppSync and Amazon DynamoDB offer real-time data synchronization and low-latency access, but may not provide the analytics capabilities of Amazon Redshift.

Option D) AWS DataSync and Amazon EMR are suitable for data transfer and processing, but may not offer the same level of real-time analytics as Amazon Redshift.

Option E) AWS VPN and Amazon RDS may provide secure connectivity and data storage, but may not offer the real-time data ingestion and analytics capabilities required for the scenario.

QUESTION 43

Answer - D) Use Amazon API Gateway for RESTful API management, Amazon DynamoDB and Amazon S3 with cross-region replication for data storage, AWS AppSync for real-time data synchronization, and Amazon CloudFront for distributing static assets.

A) Incorrect - CodeCommit, WorkSpaces, Lambda, and CloudFront provide a strong foundation for version control and global delivery, but this combination lacks the real-time collaboration and integration capabilities with development tools as directly as option D.
B) Incorrect - EC2, Direct Connect, EFS, and CodePipeline focus on hosting, connectivity, storage, and CI/CD but do not offer an optimized solution for real-time collaboration and global scalability as efficiently as option D.
C) Incorrect - Chime SDK, DynamoDB, S3, and Global Accelerator address real-time collaboration and data storage but lack the comprehensive development integration and serverless scalability provided in D.
D) Correct - API Gateway, DynamoDB, S3 with cross-region replication, AppSync, and CloudFront offer a scalable, secure, and efficient architecture for real-time collaboration, version control, and global access with minimal latency.

E) Incorrect - Amplify, Fargate, RDS, and SQS provide robust development and deployment tools but fall short in offering the real-time, global collaboration experience and tool integration as seamlessly as the services in D.

QUESTION 44

Answer - [C] Deploy Amazon SageMaker for real-time inference with AWS Lambda for serverless, event-driven processing, storing model artifacts in Amazon S3 for quick access.

Options A and B are not suitable for achieving low latency and high throughput as they involve either real-time or batch inference methods.
Option D's use of Aurora may introduce latency.
Option E's use of EFS for shared storage may not optimize for high throughput.
Option C leverages AWS Lambda for real-time inference, allowing for serverless, event-driven architecture, ensuring low latency and high throughput for serving predictions to users, making it the most appropriate choice for achieving the goal.

QUESTION 45

Answer - D) Employ a combination of reserved instances (RI) and spot instances

D) Employing a combination of reserved instances (RI) and spot instances allows the gaming company to benefit from cost savings with RIs for predictable workloads while leveraging the scalability and cost-effectiveness of spot instances during sudden traffic spikes.

A) Using reserved instances (RI) for the entire duration may not accommodate sudden spikes in player traffic efficiently and could lead to over-provisioning.
B) Implementing on-demand instances for the entire duration may result in higher costs during peak player activity periods.

C) Utilizing spot instances for the entire duration may be risky as spot instances can be terminated with short notice, potentially affecting game server availability.
E) Implementing a mix of reserved instances (RI) and on-demand instances may not provide the scalability and cost optimization needed for sudden traffic spikes in the game environment.

QUESTION 46

Answer - [D] Utilize Amazon Kinesis Data Firehose for ingesting real-time data, process data using AWS Glue, store processed data in Amazon DynamoDB with encryption, and use Amazon CloudFront for content delivery.

Option A is incorrect because using Amazon RDS may introduce higher costs and management overhead compared to DynamoDB for storing real-time transaction data. Additionally, CloudFront is typically used for content delivery and may not be directly related to processing and analyzing transaction data.

Option B is incorrect because while Amazon EventBridge is suitable for event-driven architectures, storing processed data in Amazon Redshift may not be the best choice compared to DynamoDB for real-time transaction processing.

Option C is incorrect because deploying containers on Amazon ECS may introduce management overhead compared to using managed services like Amazon Kinesis Data Firehose for ingesting real-time data. Additionally, Amazon S3 may not be the optimal choice for storing real-time transaction data compared to DynamoDB.

Option E is incorrect because although Amazon S3 is highly scalable, it may not provide the real-time processing capabilities required for transaction data, and Amazon Redshift may not be the most suitable choice for storing processed data in real-time.

QUESTION 47

Answer - [B] Implement a serverless architecture with AWS Lambda@Edge for compute, Amazon DynamoDB for database needs, and Amazon S3 for storing video files.

Option B is the correct choice because a serverless architecture with Lambda@Edge allows for low-latency content delivery to a global audience. DynamoDB provides scalability and high availability for storing metadata, while S3 offers cost-effective storage for video files. Options A, C, D, and E either lack the same level of low latency, scalability, or suitable services for the specified requirements.

QUESTION 48

Answer - D) Employ a combination of reserved instances (RI) and spot instances

D) Employing a combination of reserved instances (RI) and spot instances allows the financial institution to benefit from cost savings with RIs for predictable usage periods while leveraging the scalability and cost-effectiveness of spot instances during market volatility spikes.

A) Using reserved instances (RI) for the entire duration may not accommodate sudden spikes in trading activity efficiently and could lead to over-provisioning.

B) Implementing on-demand instances for the entire duration may result in higher costs, especially during peak trading hours.

C) Utilizing spot instances for the entire duration may be risky as spot instances can be terminated with short notice, potentially affecting platform availability during market volatility.

E) Implementing a mix of reserved instances (RI) and on-demand instances may not provide the same level of cost optimization and reliability needed for a critical trading platform.

QUESTION 49

Answer - D) Implement Amazon SQS as a buffer between Amazon S3 events and AWS Lambda functions to handle bursts of incoming events more efficiently. Configure AWS Lambda provisioned concurrency to maintain a pool of warm instances, and leverage AWS X-Ray for performance monitoring and tracing.

Option D - This approach introduces Amazon SQS as a buffer to handle bursts of incoming events efficiently, leveraging AWS Lambda provisioned concurrency to maintain a pool of warm instances for faster processing. Additionally, AWS X-Ray provides comprehensive performance monitoring and tracing capabilities for identifying and addressing latency issues.

Option A - While increasing memory allocation for AWS Lambda functions and utilizing Amazon CloudFront for caching can improve performance, they may not directly address the latency issues during peak usage periods. Implementing Amazon API Gateway caching and leveraging Amazon CloudWatch for monitoring are beneficial but may not provide the same level of efficiency as using SQS as a buffer and AWS X-Ray for tracing.

Option B - Although optimizing code logic and enabling concurrent executions can improve performance, they may not fully address the latency issues during peak usage periods. Implementing DynamoDB Accelerator (DAX) for caching and using Amazon CloudWatch for monitoring are useful, but they may not provide the same level of efficiency as using SQS as a buffer and AWS X-Ray for tracing.

Option C - Deploying AWS Lambda functions in multiple regions and utilizing S3 Transfer Acceleration may improve performance but may introduce additional complexity and cost. While leveraging CloudFront with Lambda@Edge and using CloudWatch for monitoring are beneficial, they may not provide the same level of efficiency as using SQS as a buffer and AWS X-Ray for tracing.

Option E - Although increasing the timeout configuration and parallelizing tasks can improve performance, they may not fully address the latency issues during peak usage periods. Implementing S3 Event Notifications with Step Functions and utilizing CloudWatch Logs Insights are beneficial, but they may not provide the same level of efficiency as using SQS as a buffer and AWS X-Ray for tracing.

QUESTION 50

Answer - A) Utilize Amazon EC2 Spot Instances to handle peak traffic periods, leveraging the cost savings of Spot Instances for temporary compute capacity. Implement Amazon CloudWatch alarms to trigger scaling actions based on CPU utilization, ensuring optimal resource allocation.

Option B focuses on database deployment and caching but does not address compute capacity optimization.

Option C relies on DynamDB, which may not be the most cost-effective solution for variable traffic. Option D, while utilizing Lambda and Aurora Serverless, may not provide the required performance and scalability during peak traffic periods.

Option E involves SQS and ECS but does not directly address the need for compute capacity scaling during peak traffic.

QUESTION 51

Answer - C) Use CloudFront with an optimized cache policy and S3 origin, employing Lambda@Edge for content compression and customization.

A) - Incorrect, as using all edge locations without considering geographical data could lead to higher costs.
 B) - Incorrect, transfer acceleration is beneficial but does not address all aspects of performance and cost optimization.
 C) - Correct, because it optimizes cache policy and uses Lambda@Edge for performance, addressing both efficiency and cost.
 D) - Incorrect, a multi-CDN strategy may increase complexity and costs without guaranteed performance benefits.
 E) - Incorrect, as security services are vital but the question focuses on performance and cost efficiency.

QUESTION 52

Answer - C) Implement an EC2 Auto Scaling group with dynamic scaling policies based on CPU utilization.

A) A static setup can lead to overprovisioning or underprovisioning.
B) Scheduled scaling lacks flexibility for unexpected demand spikes.
C) Correct, as it dynamically adjusts capacity based on actual usage, offering cost-efficiency and performance.
D) Elastic Beanstalk provides an easier deployment option but less control over scaling metrics.
E) Lambda offers serverless but may not suit all game server requirements or architectures.

QUESTION 53

Answer - [C] Utilize Amazon EC2 Spot Instances for compute resources.

Option A - While Amazon RDS can optimize database management, it does not directly address the compute cost optimization requirements.
 Option B - Amazon CloudFront improves content delivery but does not impact compute costs directly.
 Option C - Correct. Utilizing Amazon EC2 Spot Instances can significantly reduce compute costs, especially during traffic spikes, without compromising performance.

Option D - Amazon EKS is a container orchestration service and may not directly address compute cost optimization for EC2 instances.

Option E - Amazon S3 is for storage and does not directly optimize compute costs.

QUESTION 54

Answer - [A] Implement AWS Global Accelerator with Amazon Route 53 for optimized global routing.

Option A - Correct. AWS Global Accelerator with Route 53 optimizes global routing for low-latency access while minimizing data transfer costs between regions.

Option B - CloudFront with WAF focuses on content delivery and web application security but may not address the specific cost optimization requirements for data transfer between regions.

Option C - Direct Connect with Transit Gateway offers centralized connectivity but may not provide the same level of optimization for data transfer costs between regions.

Option D - S3 Transfer Acceleration improves data upload speed but may not directly address the cost optimization requirements for data transfer between regions.

Option E - VPC with VPN offers secure connectivity between regions but may not offer the same level of cost optimization for data transfer as Global Accelerator with Route 53.

QUESTION 55

Answer - [C] Utilize IAM roles with federated access to enforce department-based access control for the RDS database.

A) Incorrect - Implementing IAM policies based on IP addresses may not provide granular access control and may be challenging to manage as departments' office networks change.

B) Incorrect - Configuring Amazon RDS security groups based on IP addresses is limited in granularity and does not provide fine-grained access control at the IAM level.

C) Correct - Utilizing IAM roles with federated access allows for department-based access control to the RDS database, ensuring granular and centralized management of permissions.

D) Incorrect - Sharing RDS master user credentials with departments increases the risk of unauthorized access and violates security best practices for access management.

E) Incorrect - Creating separate RDS instances for each department adds unnecessary complexity and resource overhead, making it challenging to manage and maintain.

QUESTION 56

Answer - [C] Leverage Amazon ECS with service auto scaling to automatically adjust the number of running tasks based on demand.

Option C - Correct. Leveraging Amazon ECS with service auto scaling allows for automatic adjustment of the number of running tasks based on demand, efficiently handling short-lived traffic spikes while optimizing costs.

Option A - While AWS Lambda with provisioned concurrency ensures consistent performance, it may not be the most efficient solution for handling significant traffic spikes in a media streaming service scenario.

Option B - Amazon EC2 Auto Scaling with target tracking scaling policies adjusts capacity based on predefined metrics but may not offer the same level of flexibility and efficiency as Amazon ECS with service auto scaling for short-lived traffic spikes.

Option D - AWS Fargate with spot capacity offers cost savings but may not provide the same level of flexibility and efficiency as Amazon ECS with service auto scaling for handling traffic spikes in a media streaming service scenario.

Option E - Amazon EKS with managed node groups and horizontal pod autoscaling may provide flexibility but may introduce complexity and may not be the most cost-effective solution for this scenario.

QUESTION 57

Answer - [B] Implement Amazon Redshift Concurrency Scaling to automatically add and remove query processing capacity based on demand.

Option A - Utilizing Amazon Redshift Spectrum offloads query processing to Amazon S3 but may not directly address cost optimization concerns during peak traffic periods.

Option B - Correct. Implementing Amazon Redshift Concurrency Scaling automatically adjusts query processing capacity based on demand, optimizing costs while ensuring query performance during peak traffic periods.

Option C - Configuring Amazon Redshift Enhanced VPC Routing optimizes network traffic but may not directly address compute cost concerns.

Option D - Enabling Amazon Redshift Query Queues prioritizes query workload but does not automatically adjust query processing capacity based on demand.

Option E - Integrating Amazon Redshift with Amazon RDS offloads read-intensive queries but may not directly optimize compute costs during peak traffic periods.

QUESTION 58

Answer - [D] Leverage AWS EC2 Auto Scaling with On-Demand Instances to dynamically adjust capacity based on demand.

Option D - Correct. Leveraging AWS EC2 Auto Scaling with On-Demand Instances allows for dynamic adjustments in capacity based on demand, ensuring efficient handling of traffic spikes while minimizing expenses.

Option A - Utilizing AWS EC2 Reserved Instances with a one-year term commitment may offer cost savings but may not provide the flexibility required for handling unpredictable traffic spikes.

Option B - Implementing AWS Savings Plans may provide discounts but does not specifically address the need for dynamic scaling based on demand fluctuations.

Option C - Deploying AWS EC2 Spot Instances for all instances may introduce reliability concerns during traffic spikes due to potential interruptions.

Option E - Combining AWS EC2 Reserved Instances with AWS Lambda for serverless processing introduces complexity and may not be the most suitable solution for handling traffic spikes.

QUESTION 59

Answer - [C] Leverage Amazon EC2 Spot Instances with scheduled scaling policies.

Option C - Correct. Leveraging Amazon EC2 Spot Instances with scheduled scaling policies allows for cost optimization during predictable spikes in traffic, ensuring performance while minimizing costs.

Option A - Using Amazon EC2 On-Demand Instances with Auto Scaling based on a fixed schedule may provide performance but may not be as cost-effective as Spot Instances for predictable traffic spikes.

Option B - Implementing Amazon EC2 Reserved Instances offers cost predictability but may not be suitable for dynamic traffic patterns.

Option D - Deploying AWS Lambda for serverless web application hosting may be suitable for specific use cases but may not provide the same level of control or customization as EC2 instances.

Option E - Utilizing AWS Wavelength for ultra-low latency application hosting is suitable for edge computing but may not specifically address cost optimization requirements for predictable traffic spikes.

QUESTION 60

Answer - [C] Configure the Auto Scaling group to use a step scaling policy triggered by sudden increases in the number of active game sessions per minute.

A) Incorrect - Using a target tracking scaling policy based on the number of login attempts per minute may not accurately reflect the overall workload of the gaming platform during peak gaming hours.

B) Incorrect - Implementing a scheduled scaling policy triggered at specific times of peak gaming hours may not dynamically respond to sudden traffic increases, potentially resulting in under or over-provisioning of resources.

C) Correct - Configuring a step scaling policy triggered by sudden increases in the number of active game sessions per minute allows the Auto Scaling group to dynamically adjust the number of instances in response to changing traffic patterns during peak gaming hours, ensuring optimal performance and player experience.

D) Incorrect - Utilizing a simple scaling policy based on manual adjustments lacks automation and may result in delayed responses to sudden traffic increases, impacting player experience during peak gaming hours.

E) Incorrect - Implementing a predictive scaling policy based on historical player activity patterns may not accurately predict sudden traffic spikes, leading to potential performance issues during peak gaming hours.

QUESTION 61

Answer - [B] Implement Amazon CloudFront with Lambda@Edge to cache and deliver multimedia content at edge locations.

Option A - Amazon S3 Transfer Acceleration optimizes data transfers but may not provide the same low-latency access as CloudFront with Lambda@Edge for multimedia content delivery.

Option B - Correct. Amazon CloudFront with Lambda@Edge allows for caching and delivering multimedia content at edge locations, ensuring low-latency access and optimizing costs for global e-commerce platforms.

Option C - Amazon EFS may provide fast access from multiple regions but may not offer the same content delivery and caching capabilities as CloudFront with Lambda@Edge.

Option D - Amazon S3 Glacier is suitable for long-term storage but may not provide the low-latency access required for serving multimedia content in real-time.

Option E - AWS Direct Connect with AWS Transit Gateway provides private connectivity but may not optimize content delivery and reduce latency for multimedia content as effectively as CloudFront with Lambda@Edge.

QUESTION 62

Answer - [E] Leverage Amazon EC2 Spot Instances for cost-effective testing and development environments.

Option A - Amazon DynamoDB Accelerator (DAX) improves performance but may not directly address the need for cost optimization in testing and development environments.

Option B - AWS Direct Connect provides dedicated network connectivity but may not directly contribute to cost optimization for testing and development environments.

Option C - Amazon EBS Snapshots facilitate backup but may not be the most cost-effective solution for testing and development environments.

Option D - AWS Lambda offers serverless compute but may not eliminate all costs associated with testing environments, especially for long-running tasks.

Option E - Correct. Leveraging Amazon EC2 Spot Instances provides cost-effective testing and development environments while ensuring scalability and flexibility.

QUESTION 63

Answer - [A] Implement Amazon CloudFront with AWS Global Accelerator to cache content at edge locations and minimize data transfer between regions.

Option A - Correct. Implementing Amazon CloudFront with AWS Global Accelerator allows for caching content at edge locations, reducing data transfer between regions while ensuring high availability.

Option B - Amazon S3 Transfer Acceleration improves transfer speeds but may not directly reduce data transfer costs between regions.

Option C - Amazon DynamoDB global tables ensure data replication across regions but may not directly address the issue of reducing data transfer costs between regions.

Option D - AWS Direct Connect with AWS Transit Gateway can establish private connectivity between regions but may not directly minimize data transfer costs.

Option E - Amazon Route 53 latency-based routing optimizes traffic routing but may not directly reduce data transfer costs between regions.

QUESTION 64

Answer - [A] Implement Amazon Cognito for user authentication and authorization, with fine-grained access control policies to manage resource access.

Option A - Correct. Implementing Amazon Cognito provides a cost-efficient solution for user authentication and authorization with fine-grained access control policies.

Option B - While AWS IAM Identity Federation allows for federating user identities, it may not provide the same level of cost efficiency and granularity in access control as Amazon Cognito.

Option C - Deploying AWS Directory Service with Active Directory may offer centralized user management but may introduce additional costs and complexity compared to Amazon Cognito.

Option D - Utilizing Amazon S3 bucket policies and IAM roles may control access to resources but may not offer the same level of user management and authentication features as Amazon Cognito.

Option E - AWS Single Sign-On (SSO) manages user access to multiple accounts and applications but may not directly provide user authentication and authorization features required for the web application.

QUESTION 65

Answer - [B] Implement AWS DataSync to automate data transfers between on-premises storage and Amazon S3.

Option B - Correct. Implementing AWS DataSync automates data transfers between on-premises storage and Amazon S3, minimizing data transfer costs and ensuring reliable connectivity.

Option A - AWS Direct Connect provides dedicated connections but may not offer the same level of automation and cost-effectiveness for data transfers as AWS DataSync.

Option C - AWS Transfer Family enables secure transfers but may not be the most cost-effective solution for large-scale data transfers.

Option D - Amazon S3 Transfer Acceleration optimizes speed but may not minimize data transfer costs for on-premises data centers.

Option E - AWS VPN CloudHub establishes VPN connections but may not be the most cost-effective solution for data transfer between on-premises data centers and AWS.

ABOUT THE AUTHOR

Step into the world of Anand, and you're in for a journey beyond just tech and algorithms. While his accolades in the tech realm are numerous, including penning various tech-centric and personal improvement ebooks, there's so much more to this multi-faceted author.

At the heart of Anand lies an AI enthusiast and investor, always on the hunt for the next big thing in artificial intelligence. But turn the page, and you might find him engrossed in a gripping cricket match or passionately cheering for his favorite football team. His weekends? They might be spent experimenting with a new recipe in the kitchen, penning down his latest musings, or crafting a unique design that blends creativity with functionality.

While his professional journey as a Solution Architect and AI Consultant, boasting over a decade of AI/ML expertise, is impressive, it's the fusion of this expertise with his diverse hobbies that makes Anand's writings truly distinctive.

So, as you navigate through his works, expect more than just information. Prepare for stories interwoven with passion, experiences peppered with life's many spices, and wisdom that transcends beyond the tech realm. Dive in and discover Anand, the author, the enthusiast, the chef, the sports lover, and above all, the storyteller.

Printed in France by Amazon
Brétigny-sur-Orge, FR